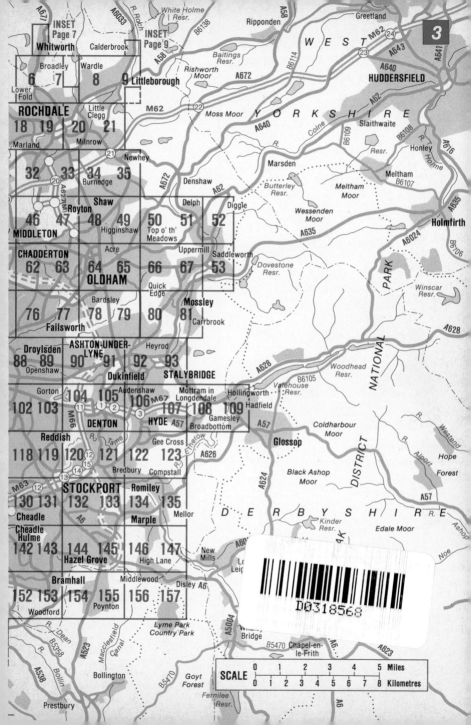

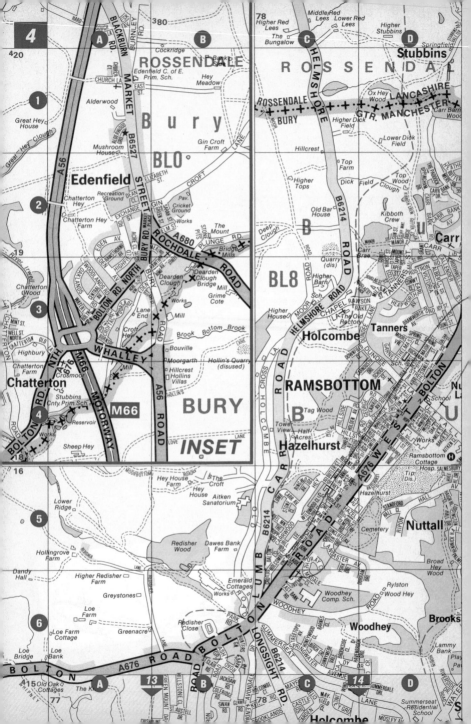

A-Z MANCHESTER Street Atlas

CONTENTS

REFERENCE

Motorway	**M66**	County Boundary	+ · + · + · +
A Road	A57	District Boundary	— · — · — · —
Under Construction	(Est. Comp. 1993)	Posttown Boundary By arrangement with the Post Office	———
Proposed	(Proposed)		
B Road	B5228	Postcode Boundary (Within Post Towns)	— — — —
Dual Carriageway		Ambulance Station	✚
One Way Street Traffic flow on 'A' Roads is indicated by a heavy line on the drivers left.	→	Car Park Selected	P
Restricted Access		Church or Chapel	†
		Fire Station	■
B.R. Railway	Level Crossing / ECCLES	Hospital	H
	RAMSBOTTOM	House Numbers 'A' and 'B' Roads only	2 23
Private Railway			
Metrolink (LRT) The boarding of Metrolink trains at stations may be limited to a single direction, indicated by the arrow.	G. Mex	Information Centre	𝚒
		National Grid Reference	³85
		Police Station	▲
Map Continuation 10	Large Scale City Centre 160	Post Office	★
		Toilet	▽

SCALE

Map Pages 4-159
1:18103 (3½ inches to 1 mile)

Miles 0 — ¼ — ½
Metres 0 — 250 — 500 — 750

Central Area 160-167
1:9051 (7 inches to 1 mile)

Miles 0 — ⅛ — ¼
Metres 0 — 100 — 200 — 300

Geographers' A-Z Map Co. Ltd.

Head Office:
Fairfield Road, Borough Green,
Sevenoaks, Kent. TN15 8PP
Telephone 0732-781000

Showrooms:
44 Gray's Inn Road, London. WC1X 8LR
Telephone 071-242-9246

Edition 8

KEY TO MAP PAGES

2

LANCASHIRE

Wheelton

Ewood Bridge
INSET Page 4
Edenfield

Stubbins

RAMSBOTTOM **4** **5** Bank Lane

Rooley Moor

Belmont Resr.

Edgworth

B6391

Greenmount

Wood Road

Wolstenholme

Egerton **10** **11** **12** Tottington **13** **14** Burrs **15** **16** **17**
Eagley

Sharples

Walshaw **BURY**

Heywood

22 **23** Heaton **24** **25** **26** Ainsworth **27** **28** **29** Gigg **30** **31**

Deane **BOLTON** Little Lever Heywood

36 **37** **38** **39** **40** **41** **42** **43** **44** **45** Langley
Lever Edge Radcliffe Whitefield Rhodes

Farnworth

Over Hulton **54** **55** Kearsley **56** **57** **58** **59** **60** **61**
Walkden Prestwich

LARGE SCALE CITY CENTRE
160 161 162 163
164 165 166 167

Tyldesley **68** **69** **70** **71** **72** **73** **74** **75**
Astley Worsley Swinton Pendlebury Crumpsall

Boothstown
Moss Brook **ECCLES** **SALFORD**

82 **83** **84** **85** **86** **87**

MANCHESTER

94 **95** **96** **97** **98** **99** **100** **101**
Irlam URMSTON STRETFORD Moss Side

Carrington

110 **111** **112** **113** **114** **115** **116** **117**
Partington **SALE** Didsbury

Woodhouses Brooklands

124 **125** **126** **127** **128** **129**
Gatley

ALTRINCHAM **136** **137** **138** **139** **140** **141**
Hale Peel Hall Heald Green

MANCHESTER AIRPORT

148 **149** **150** **151**
Handforth

WILMSLOW

158 **159**

Alderley Edge

INSET Page 159

CHESHIRE

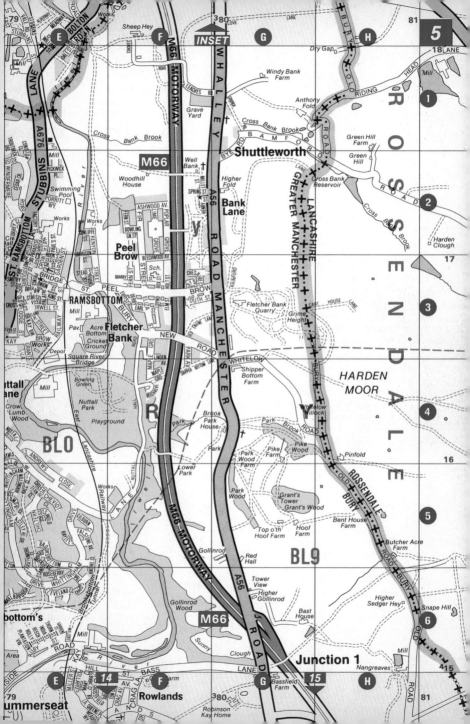

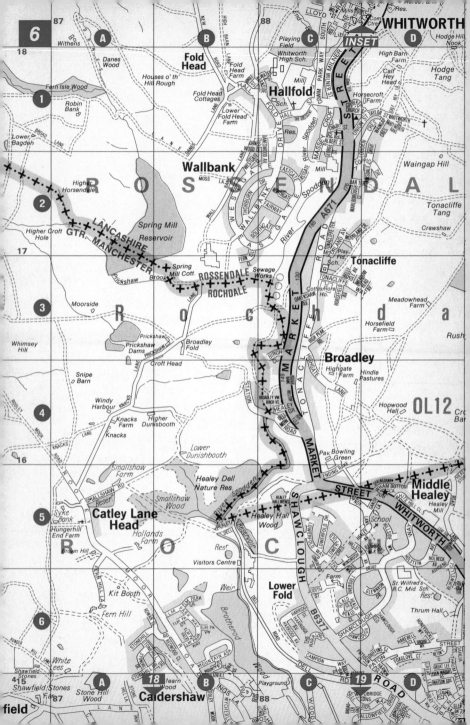

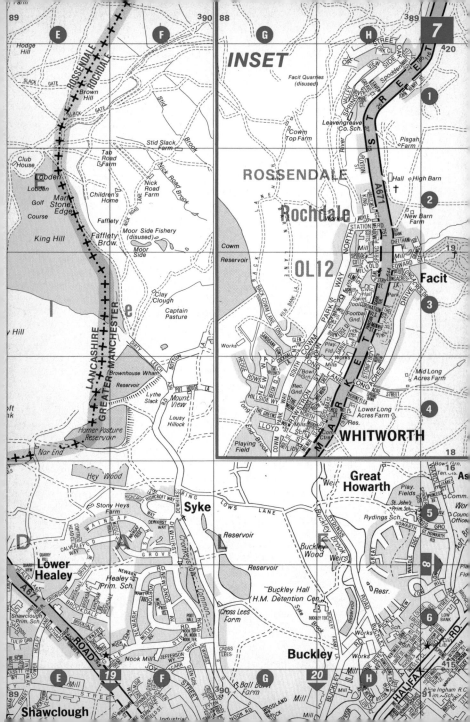

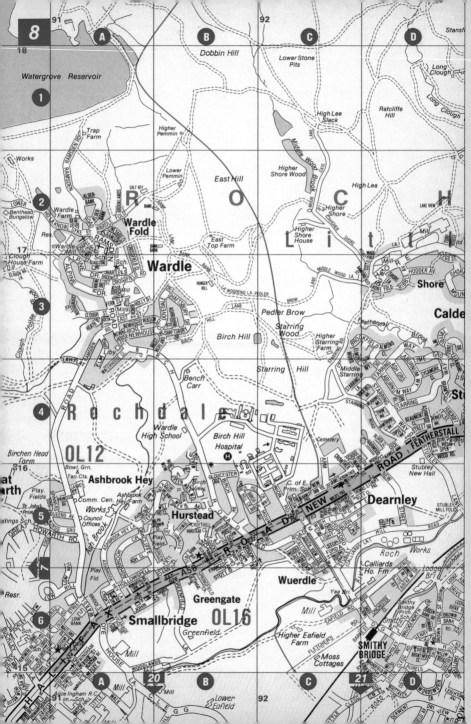

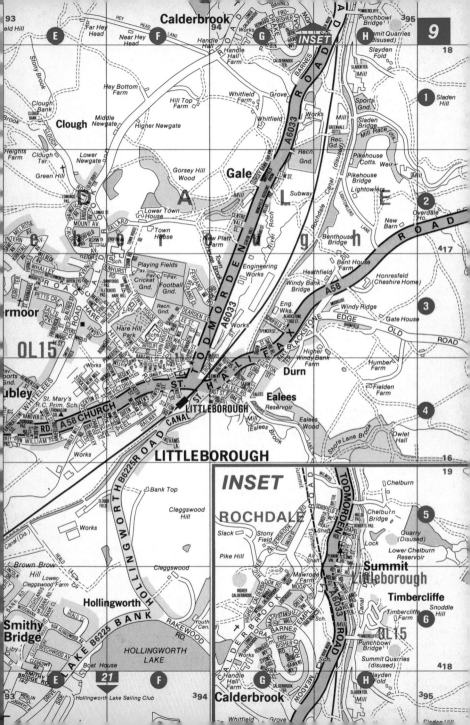

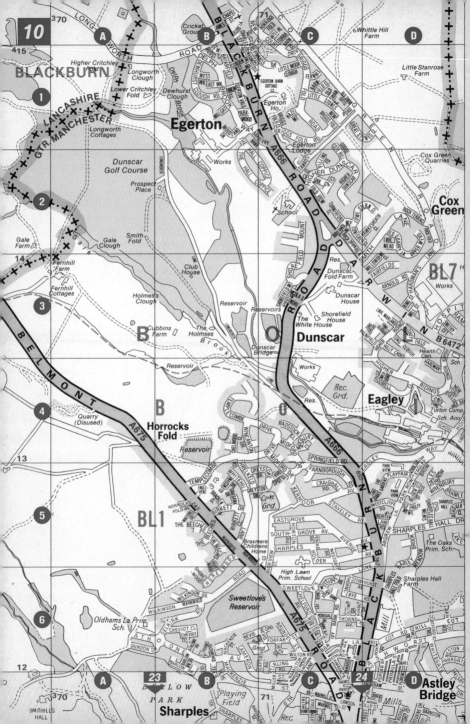

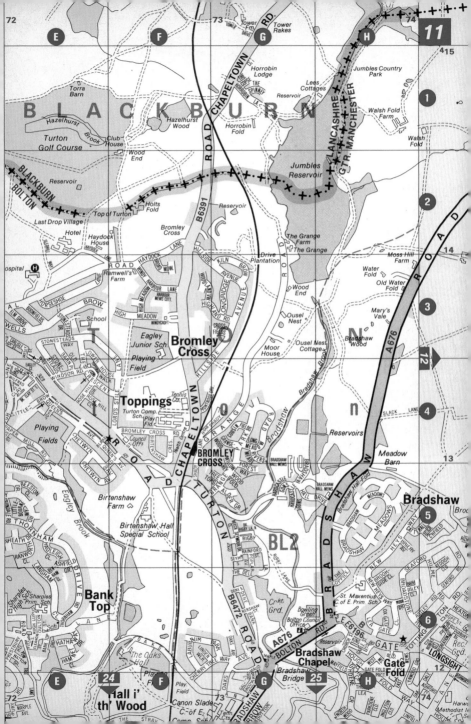

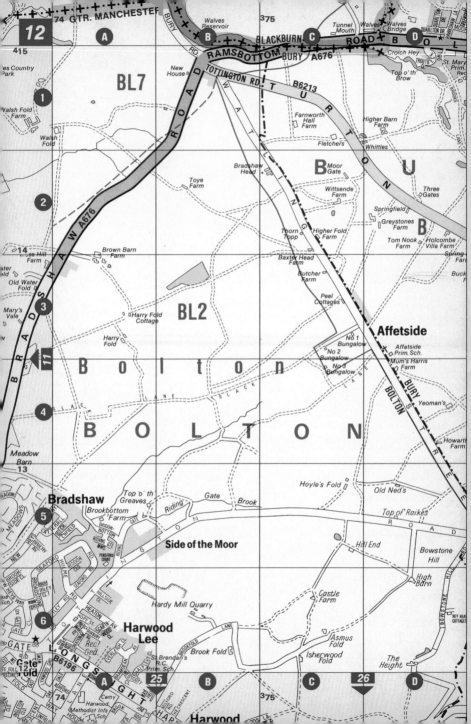

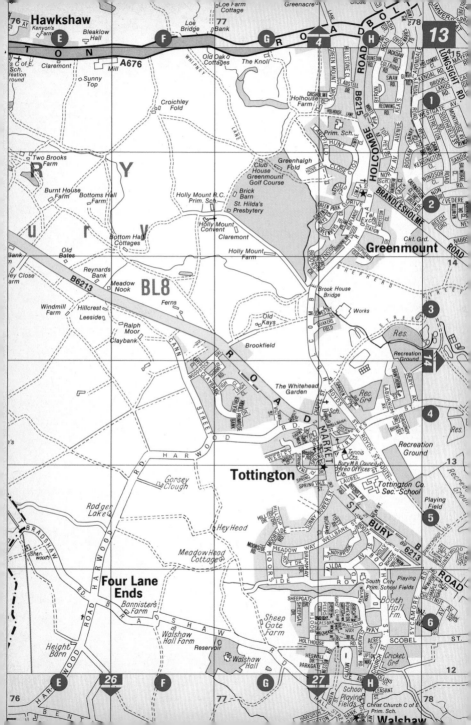

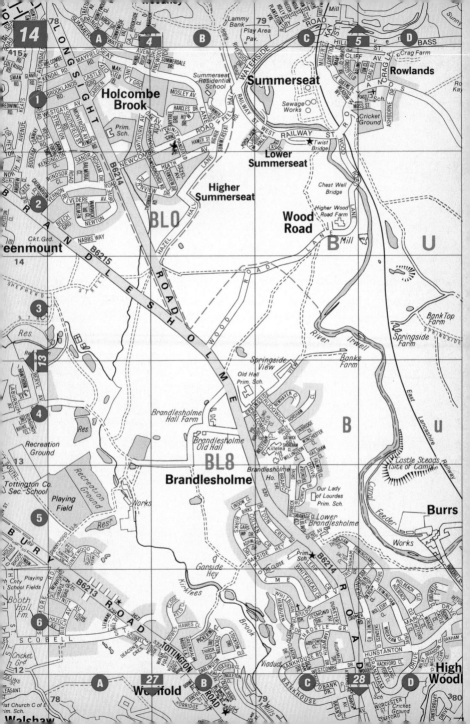

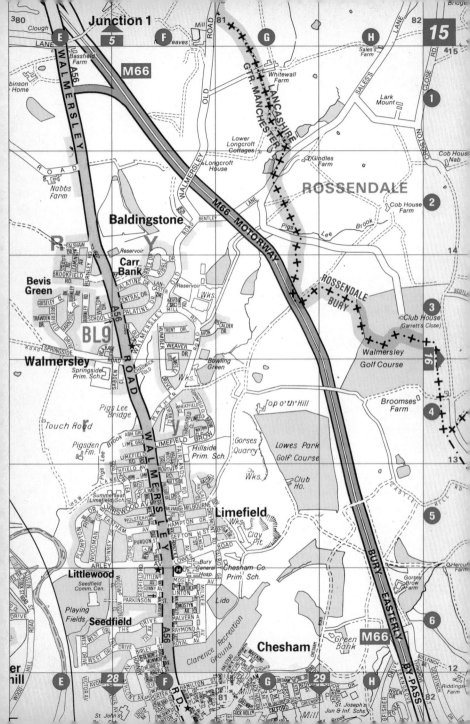

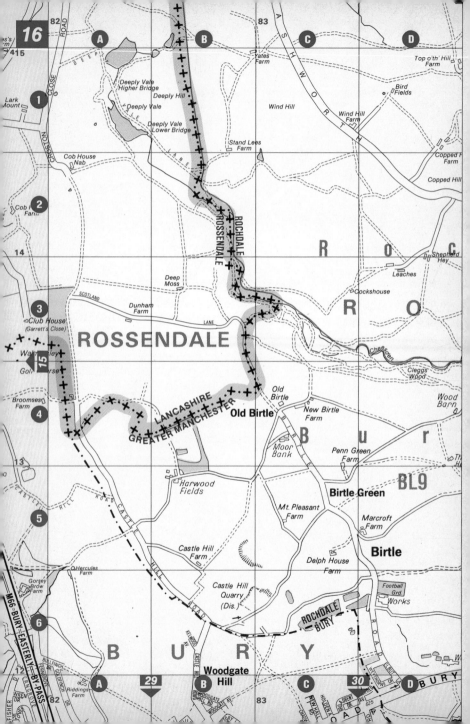

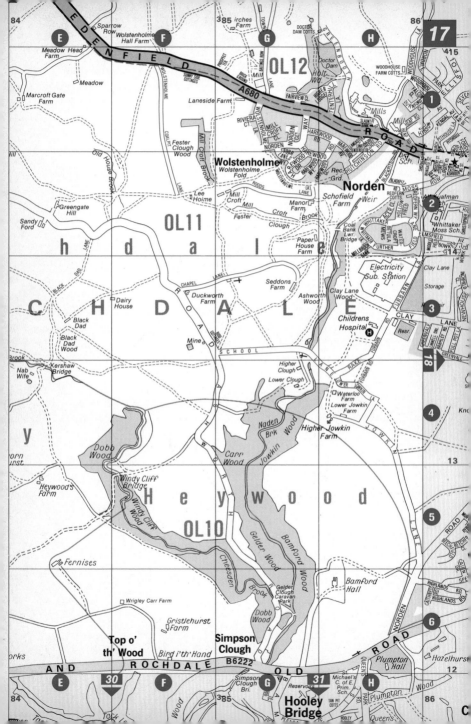

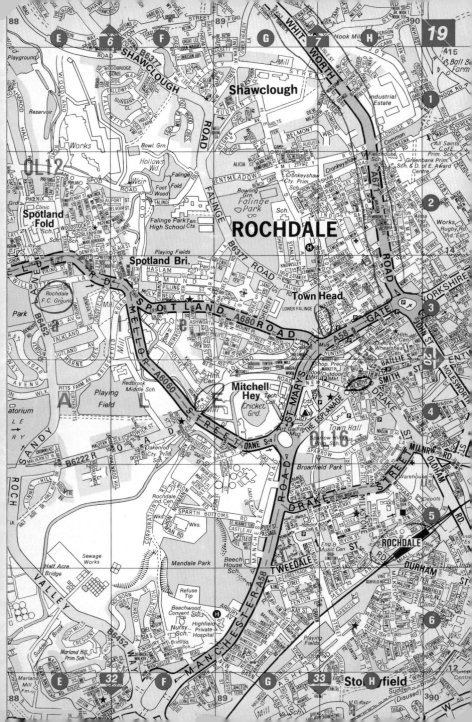

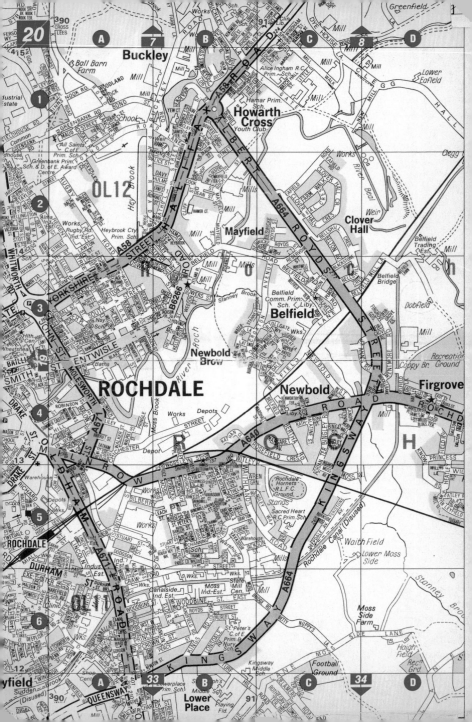

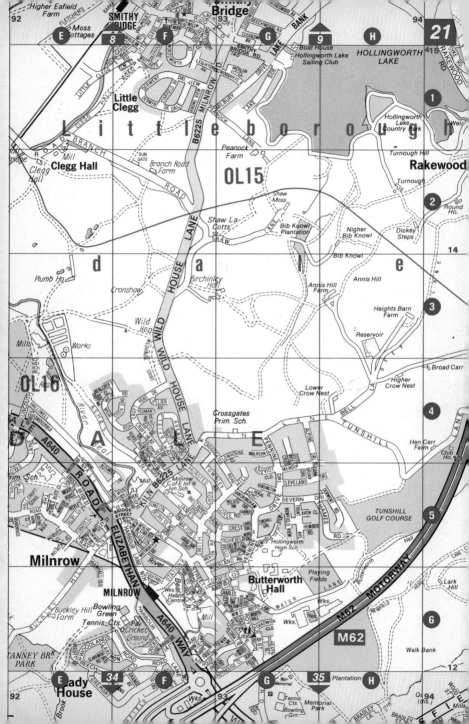

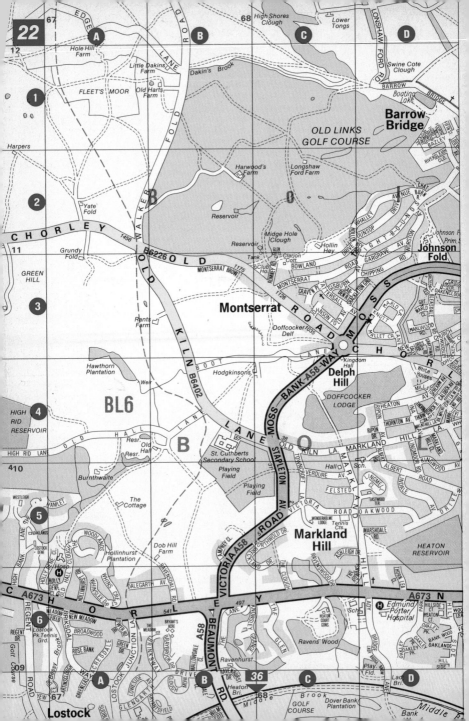

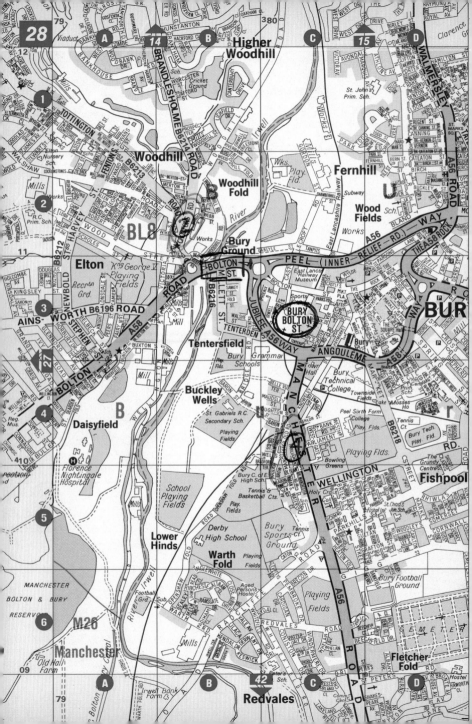

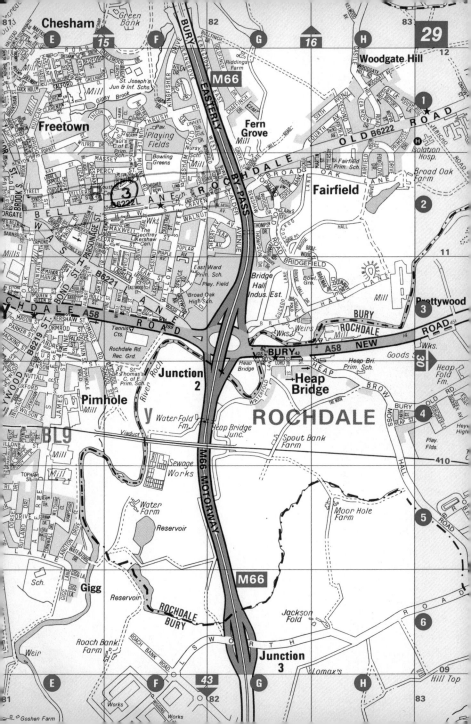

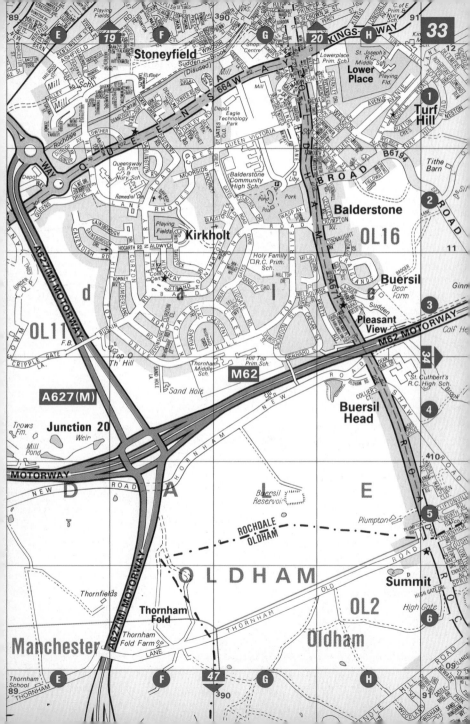

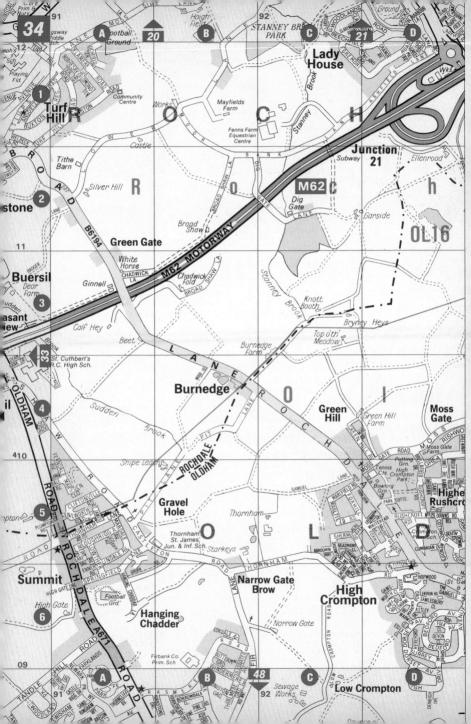

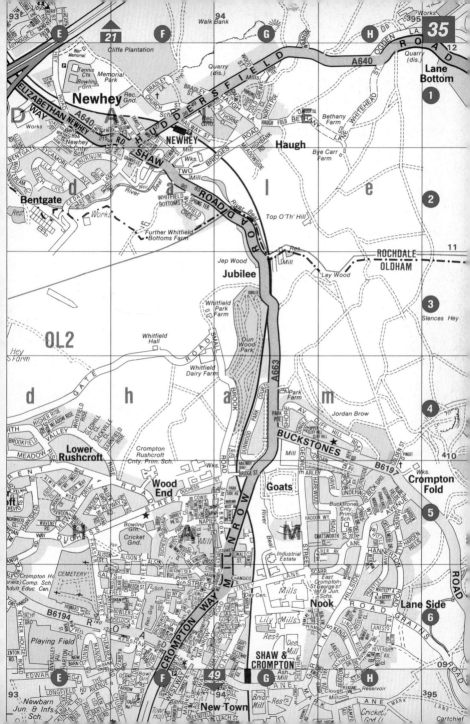

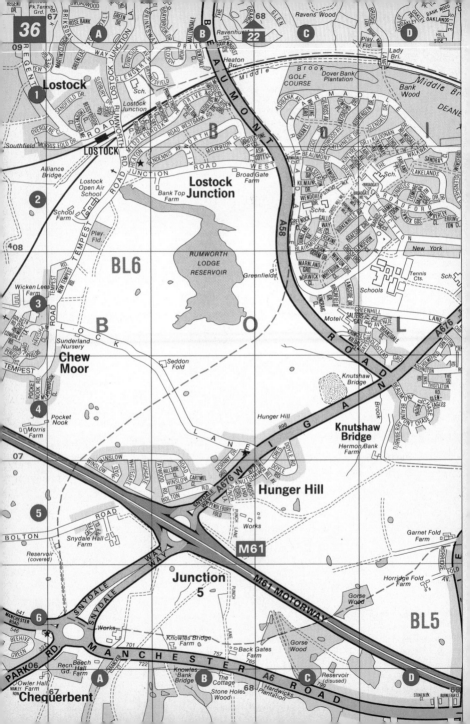

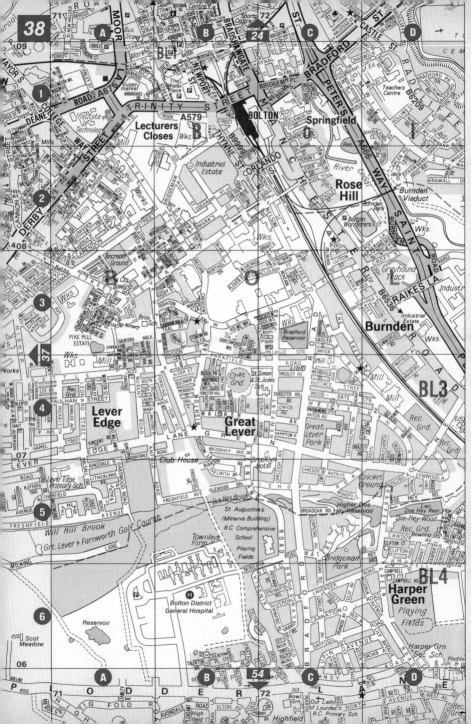

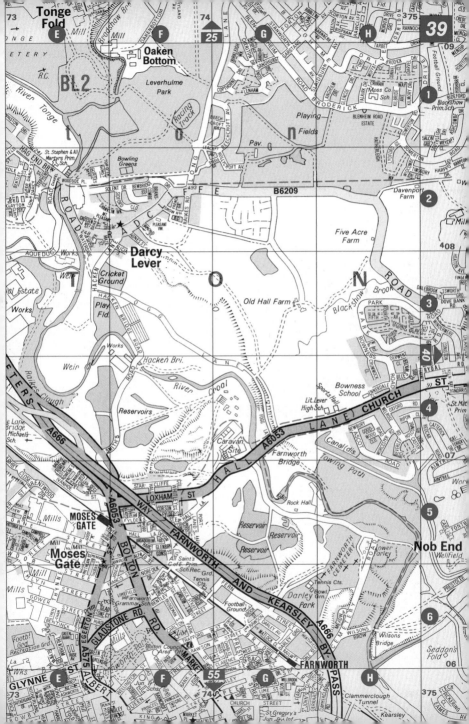

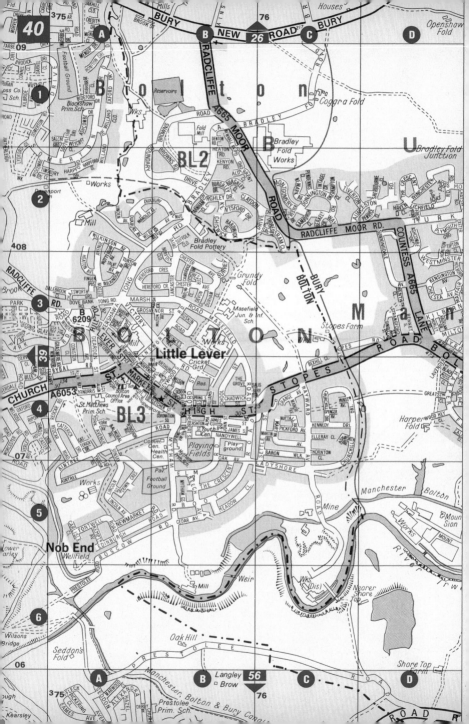

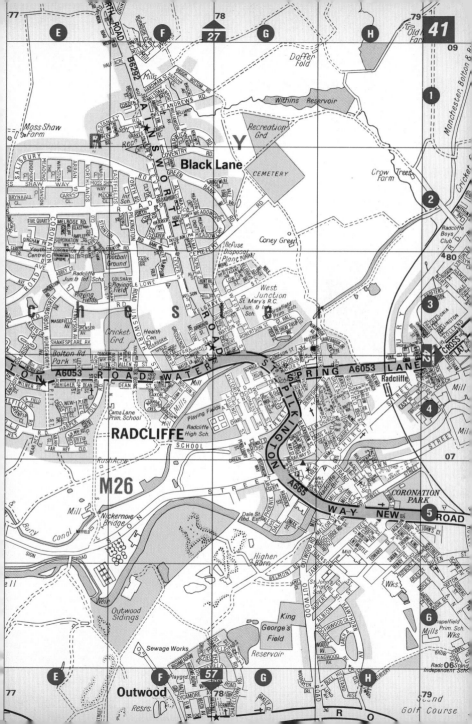

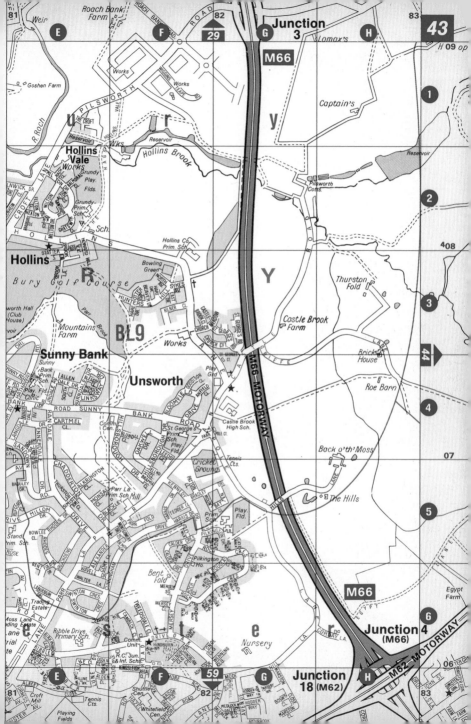

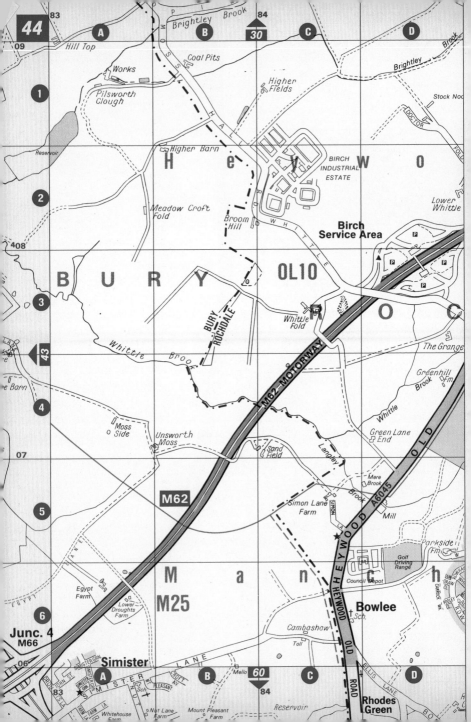

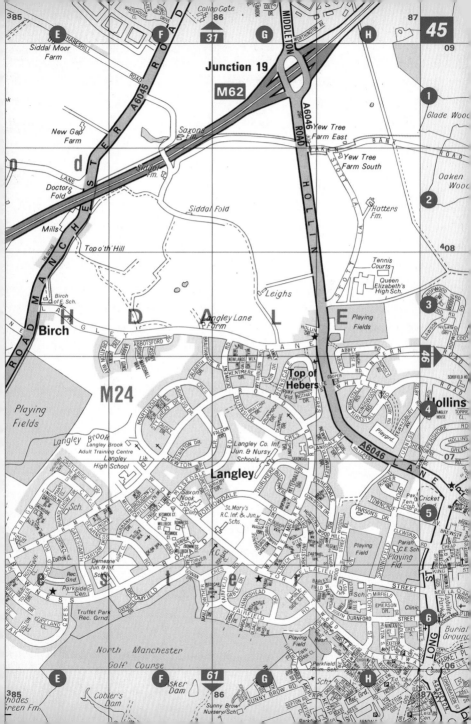

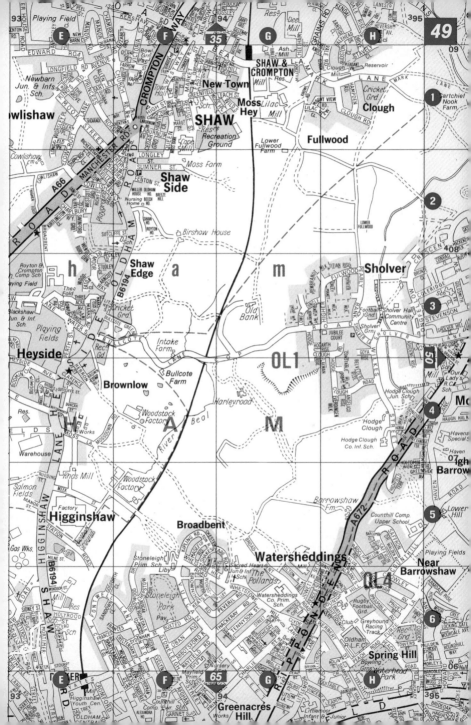

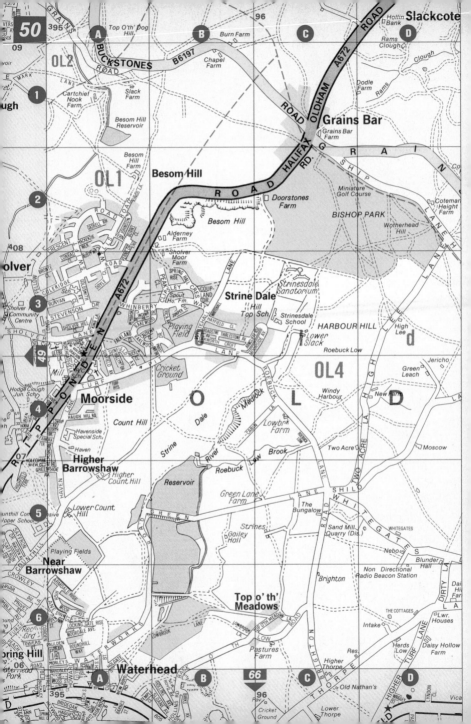

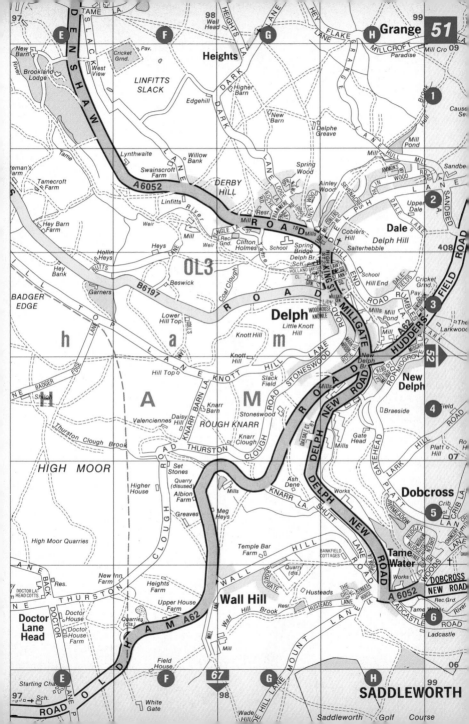

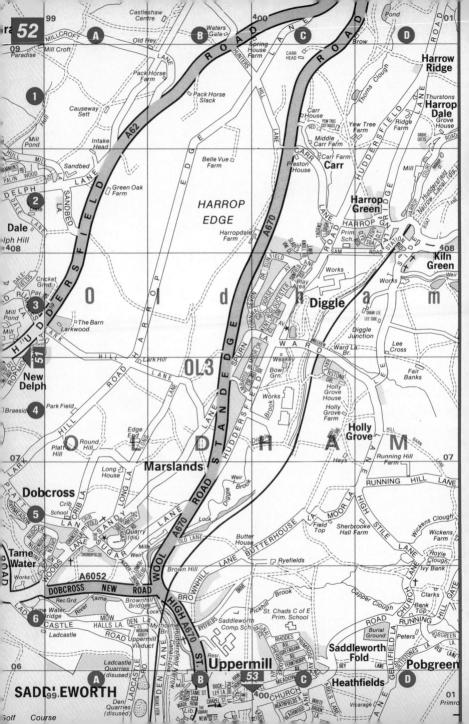

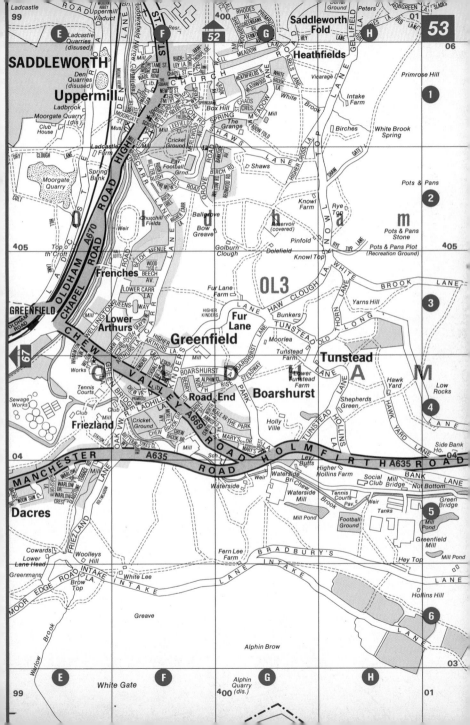

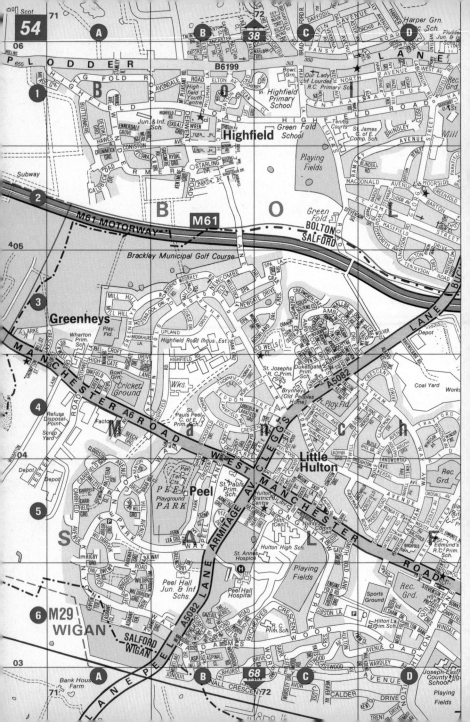

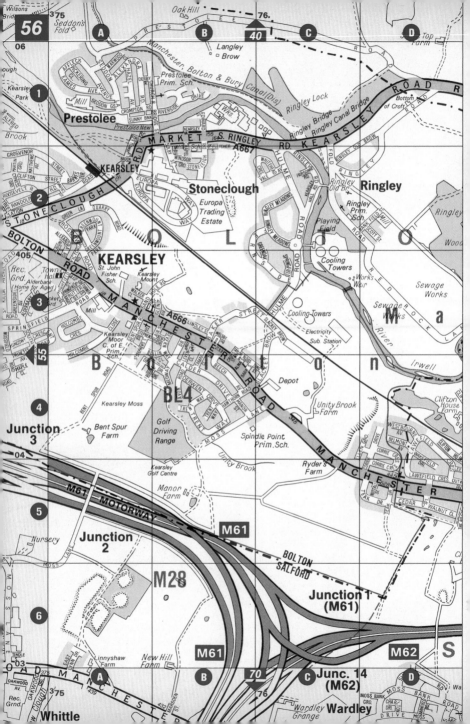

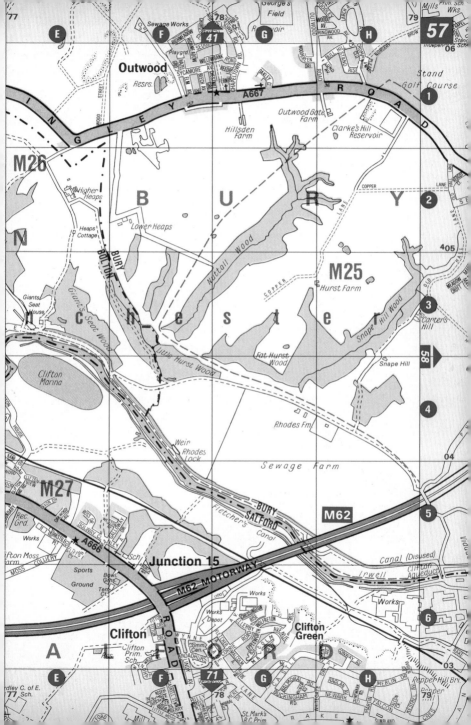

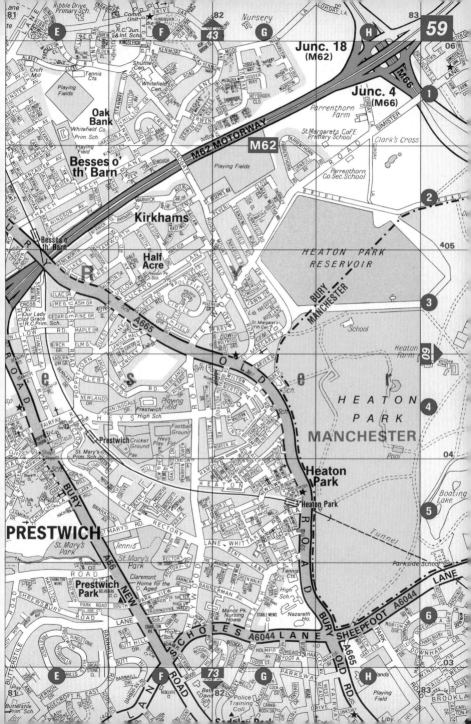

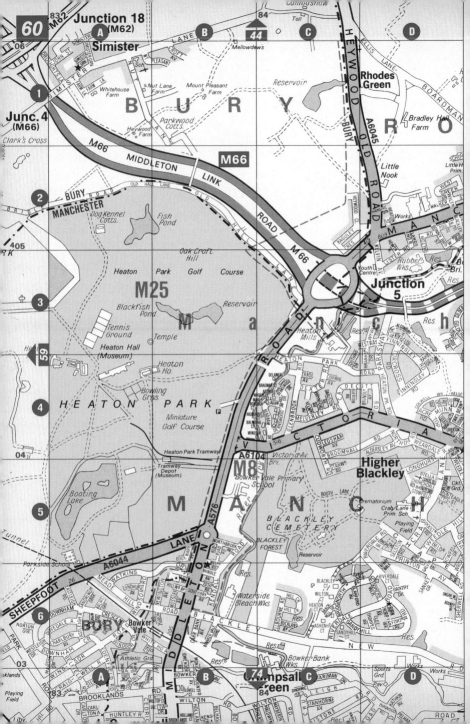

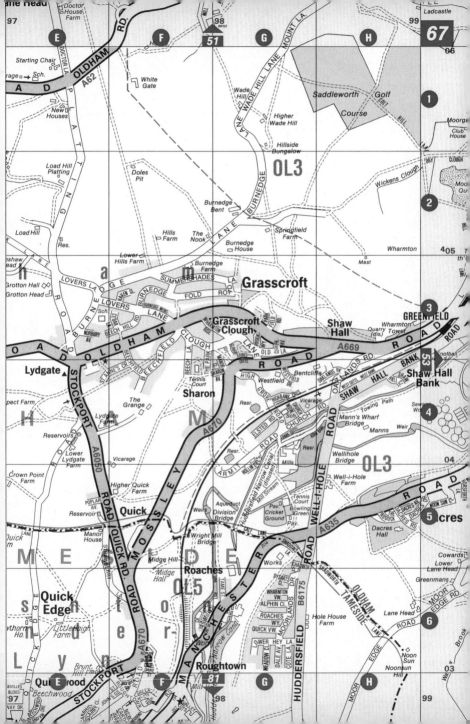

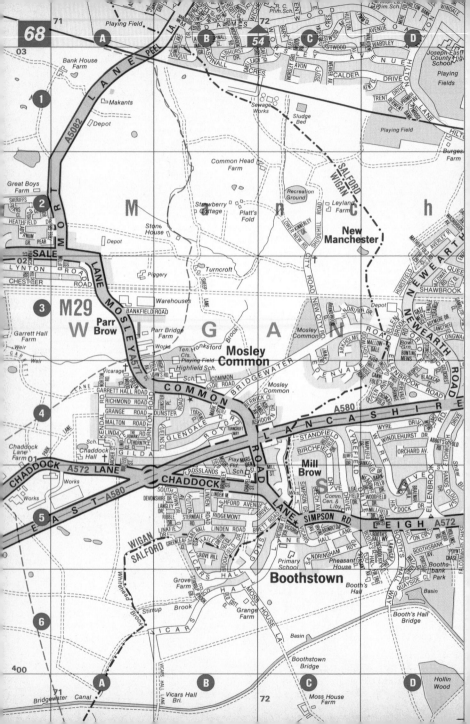

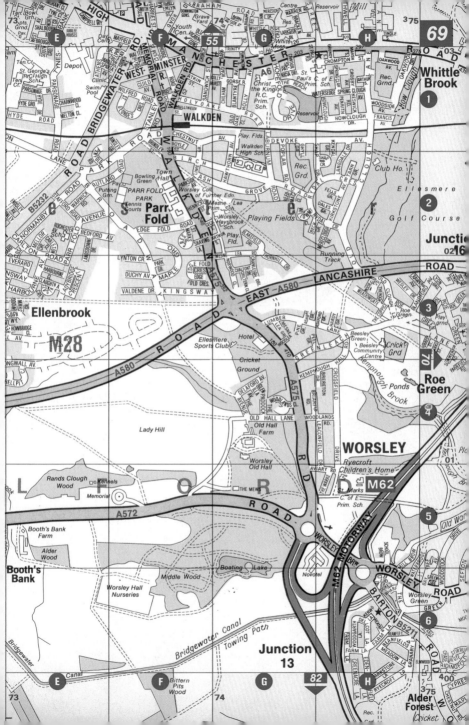

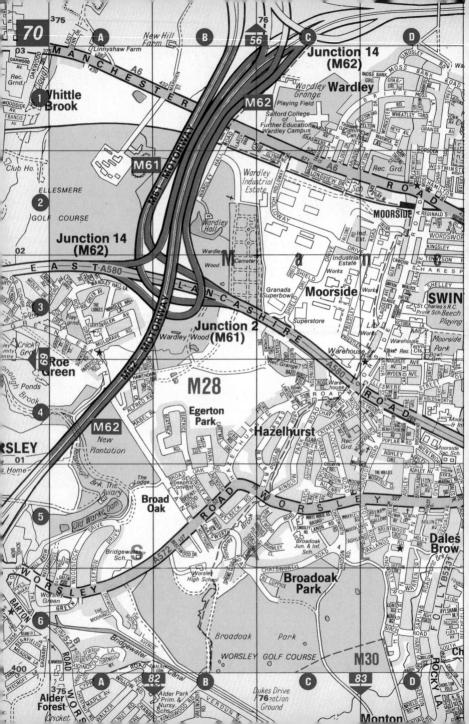

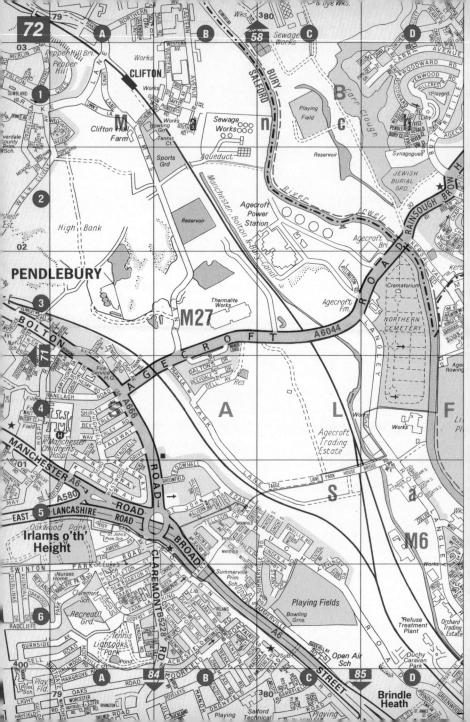

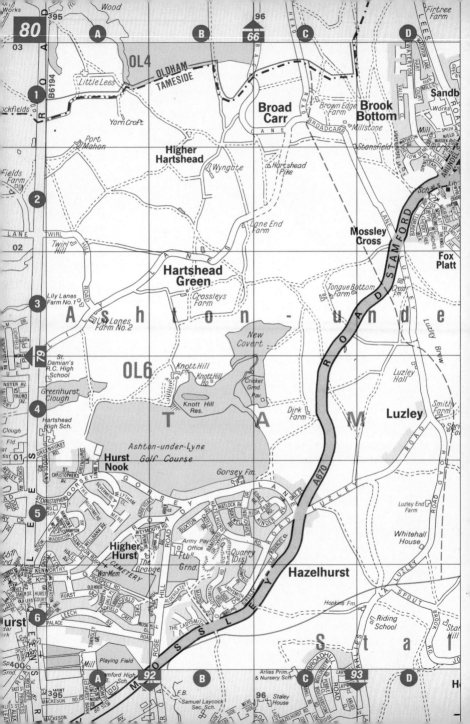

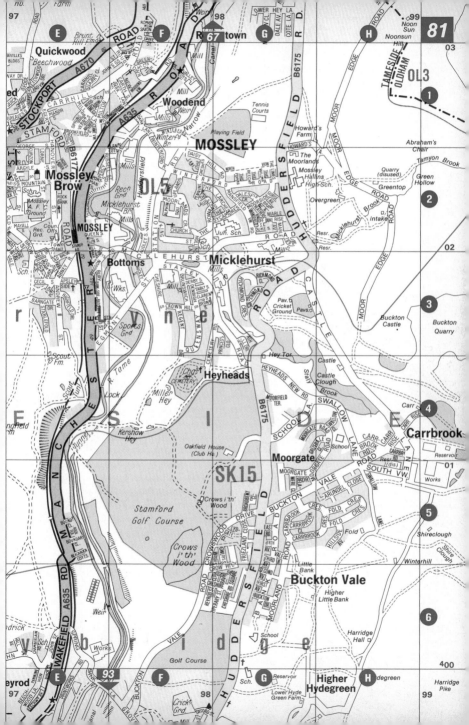

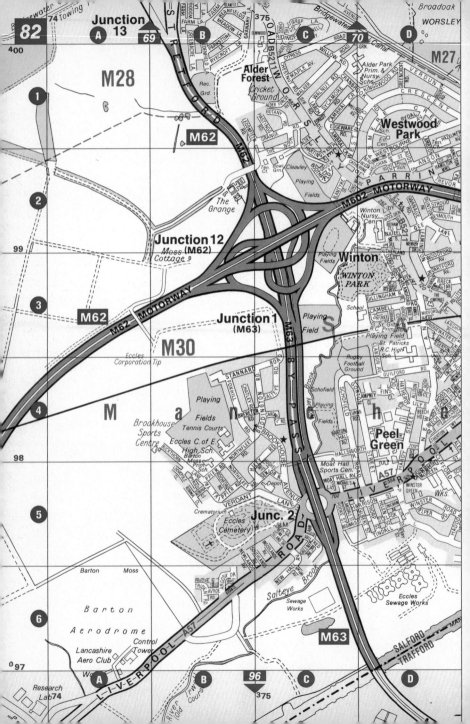

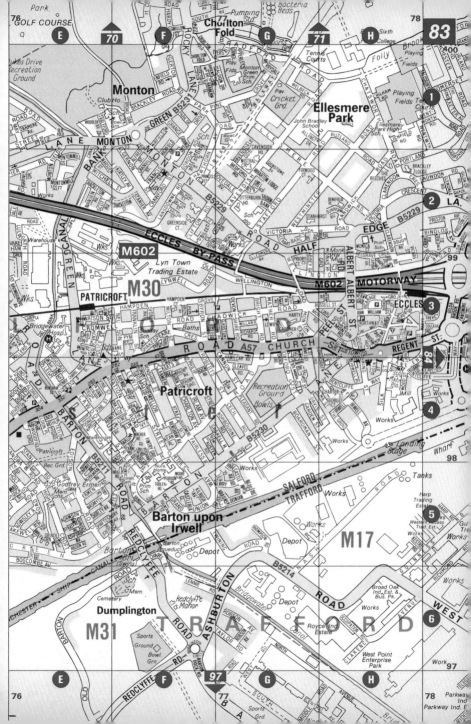

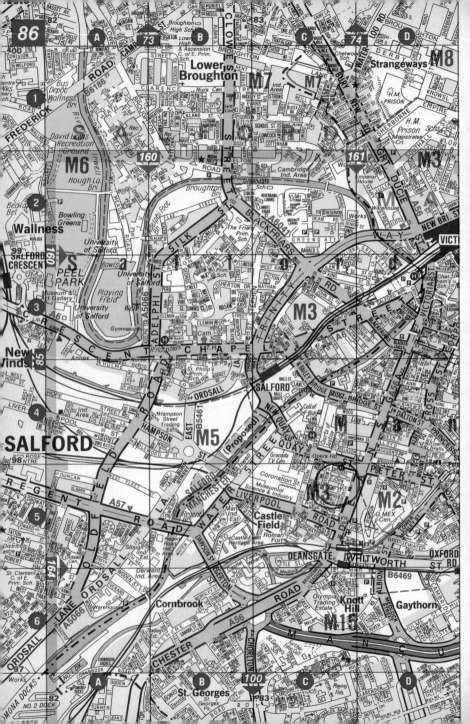

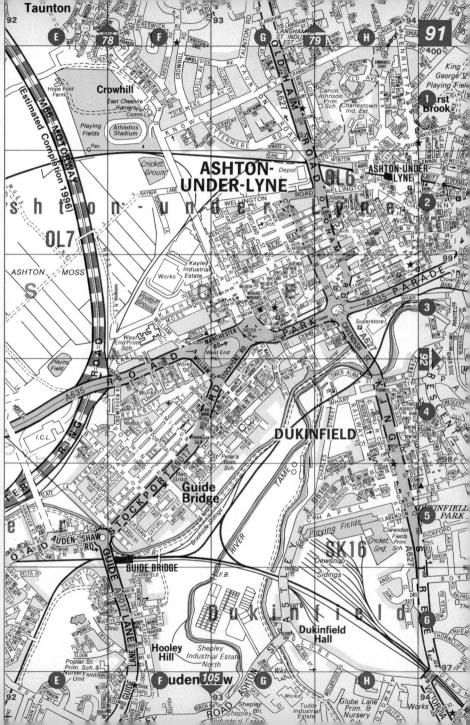

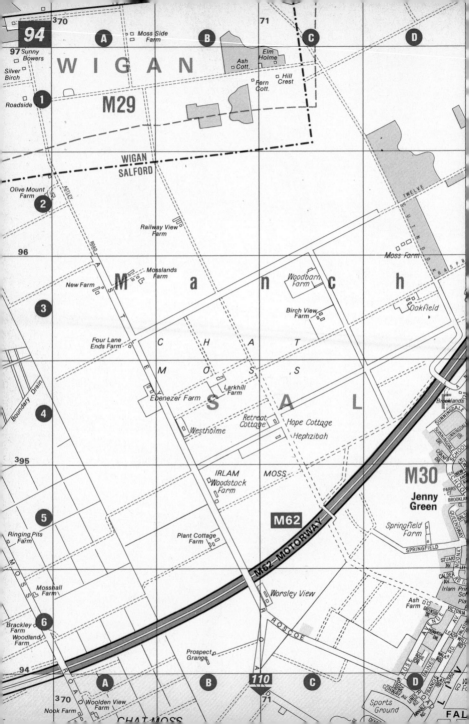

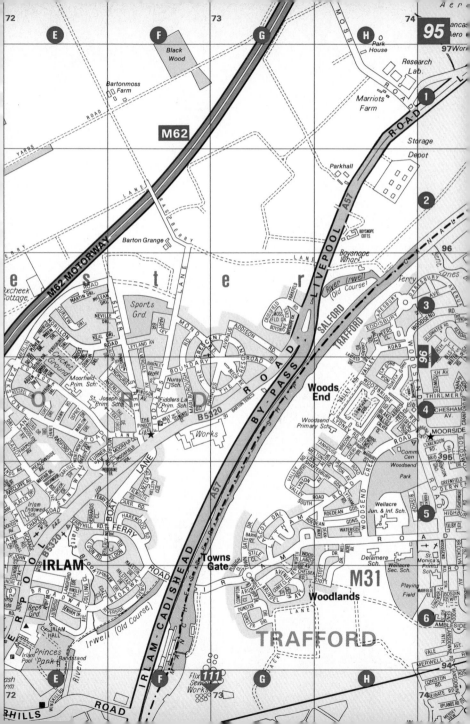

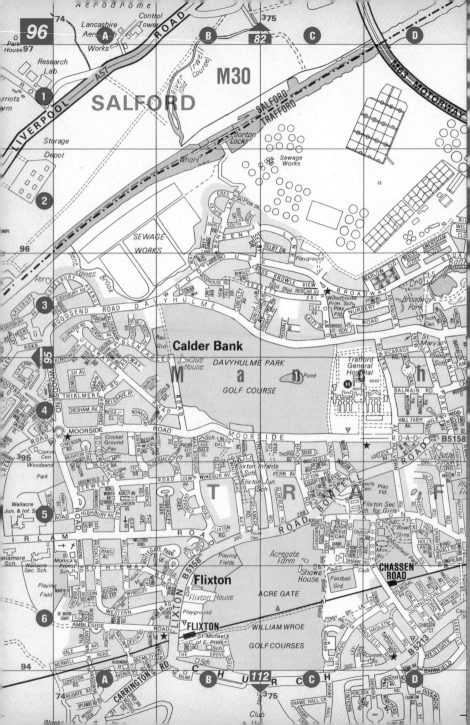

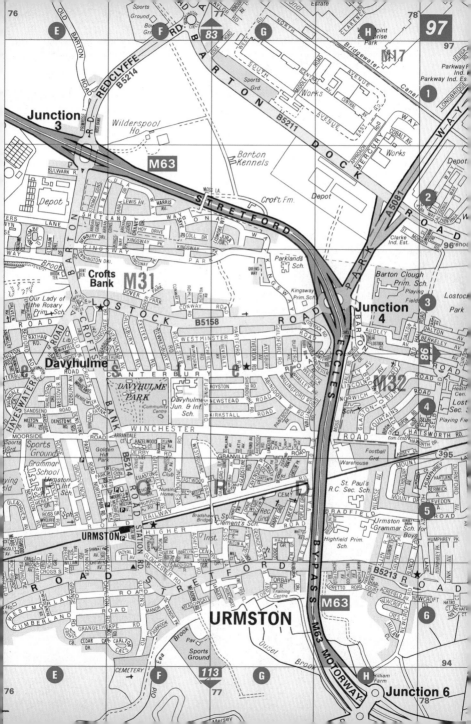

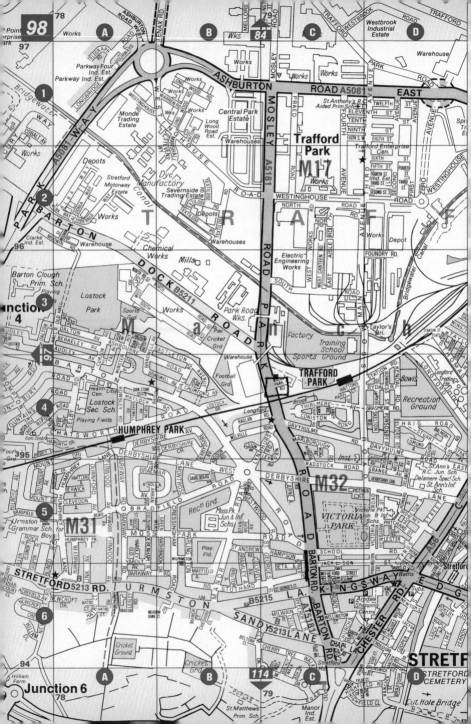

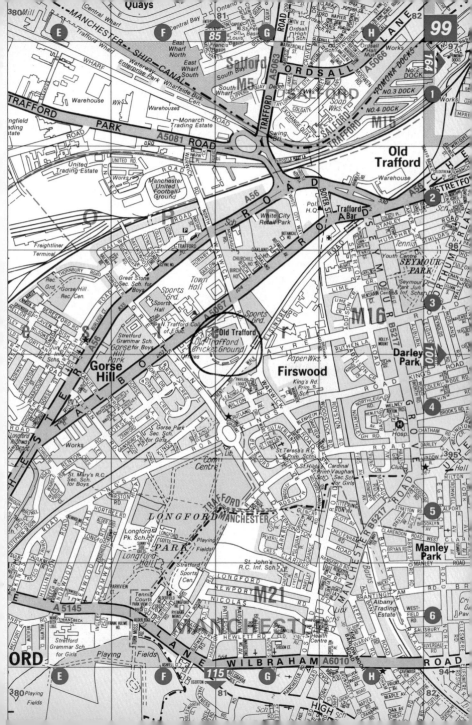

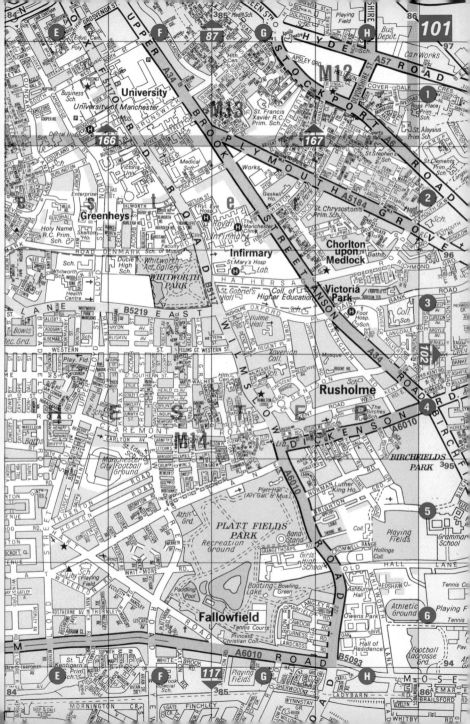

105

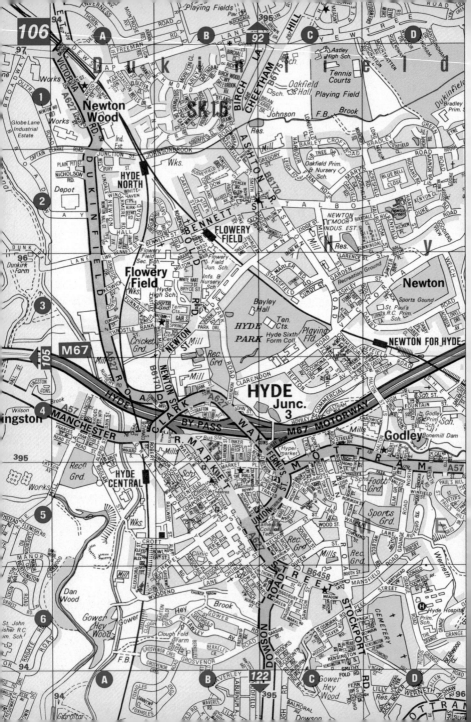

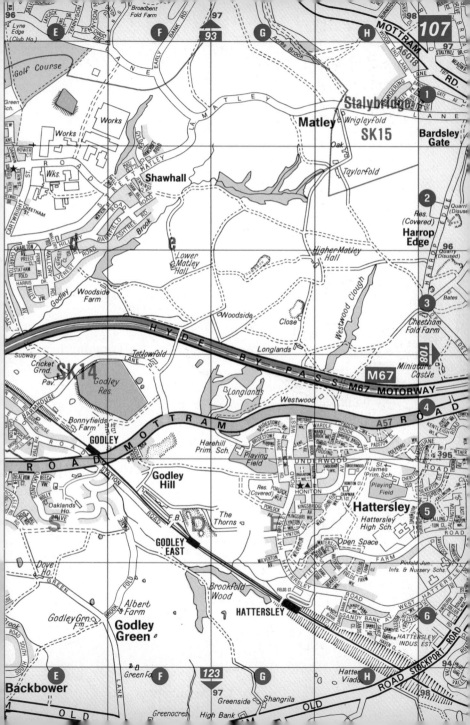

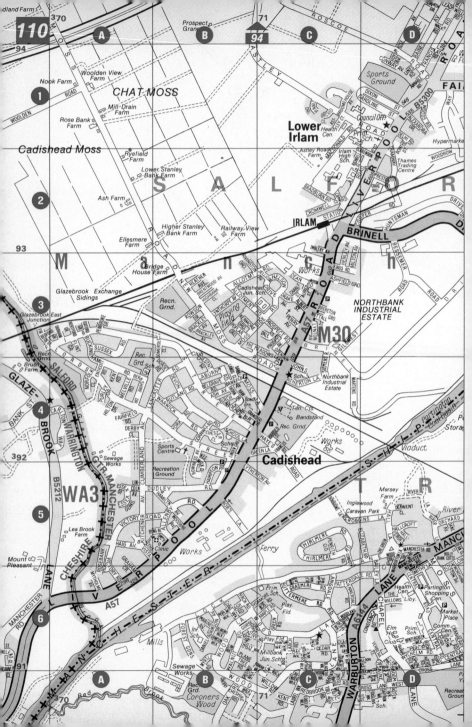

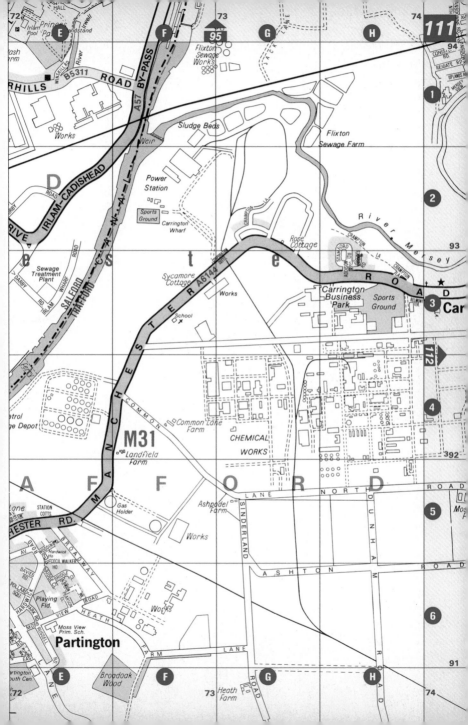

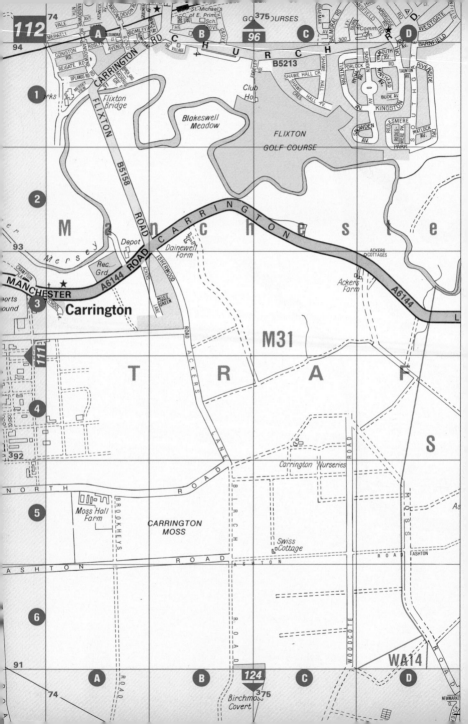

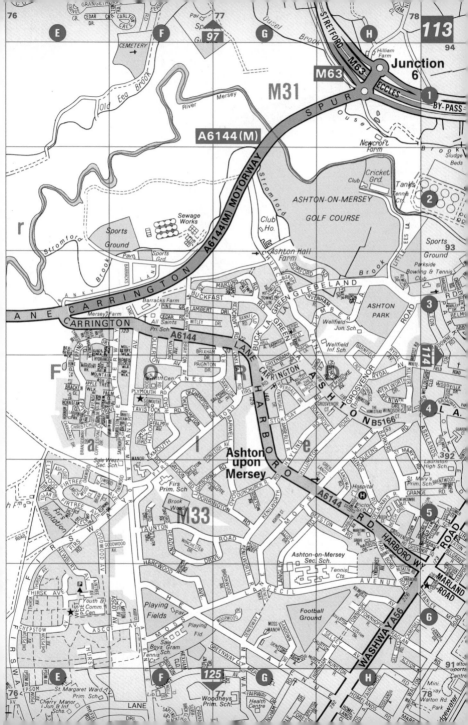

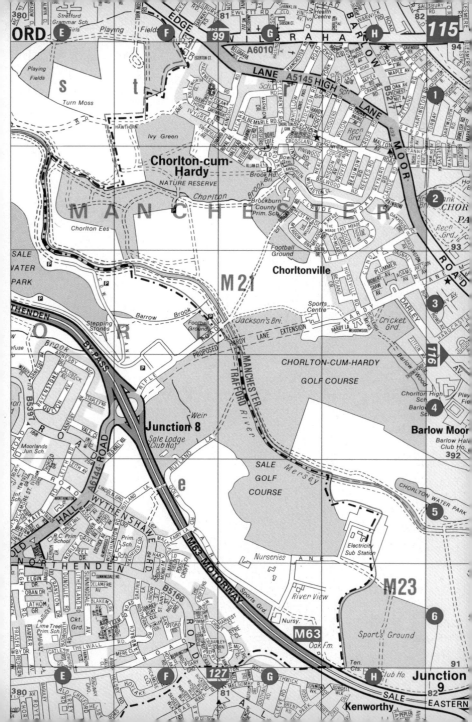

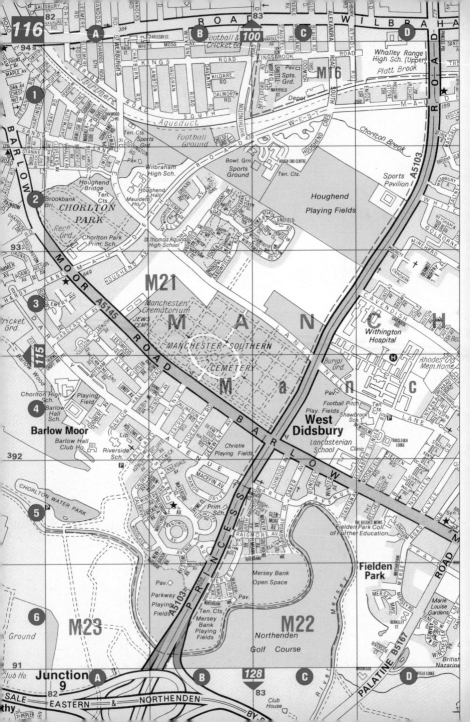

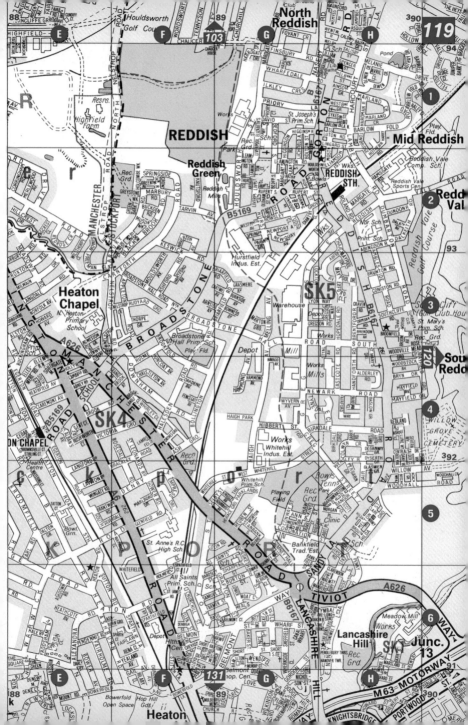

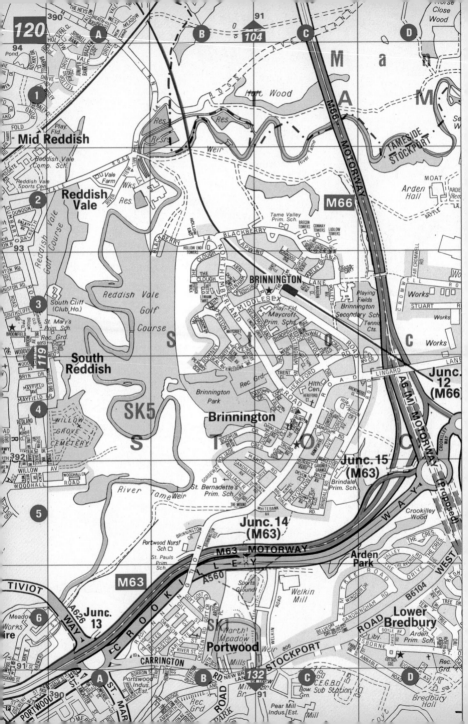

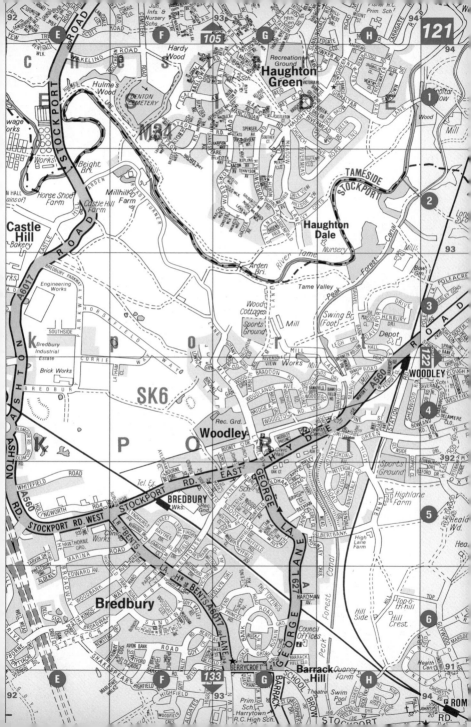

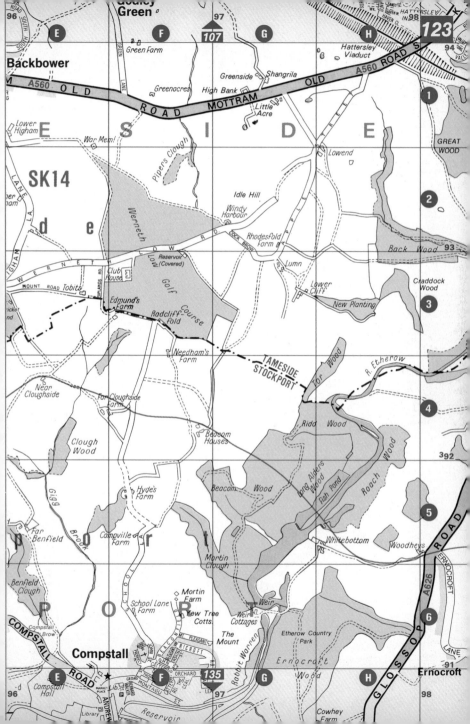

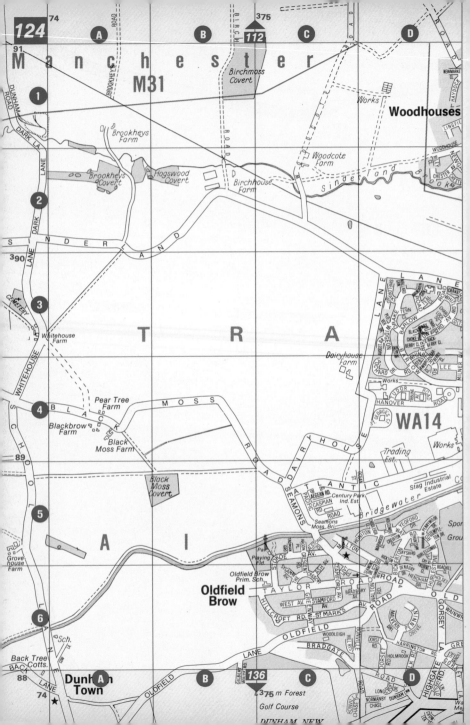

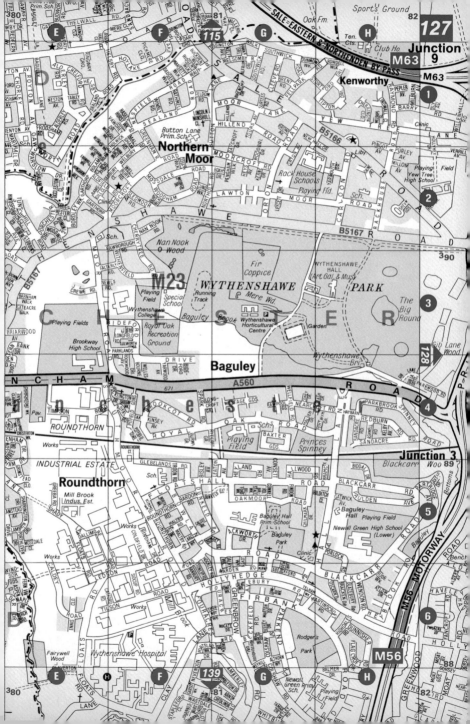

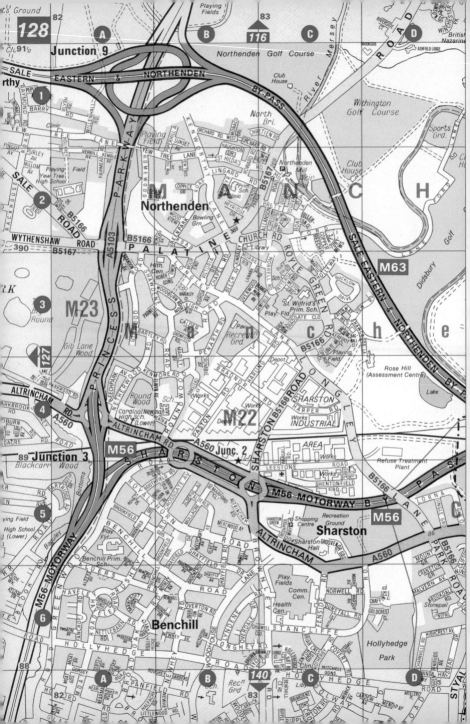

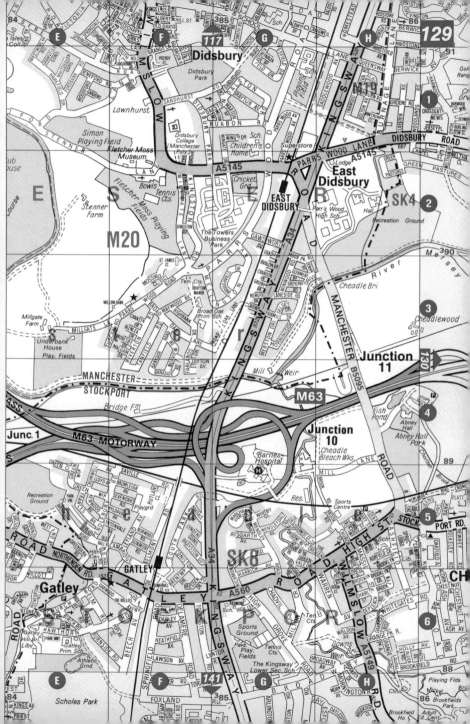

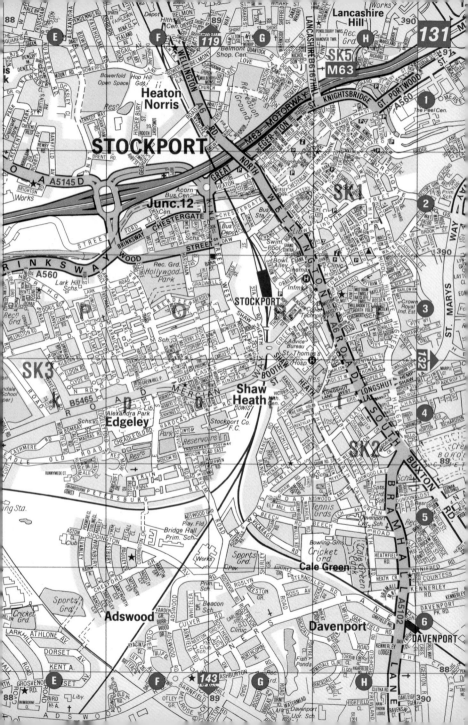

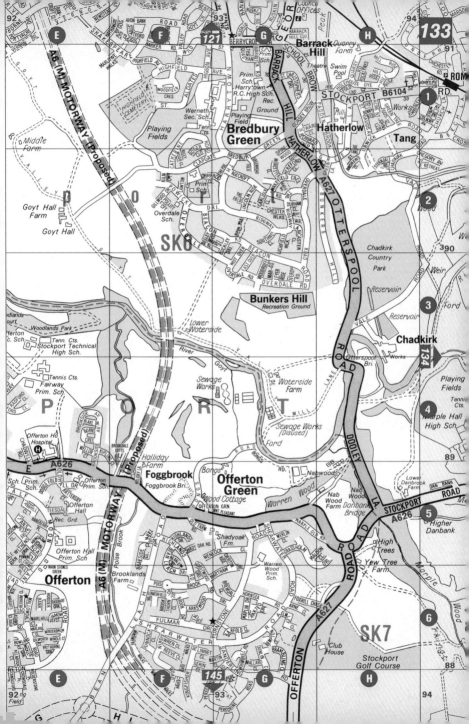

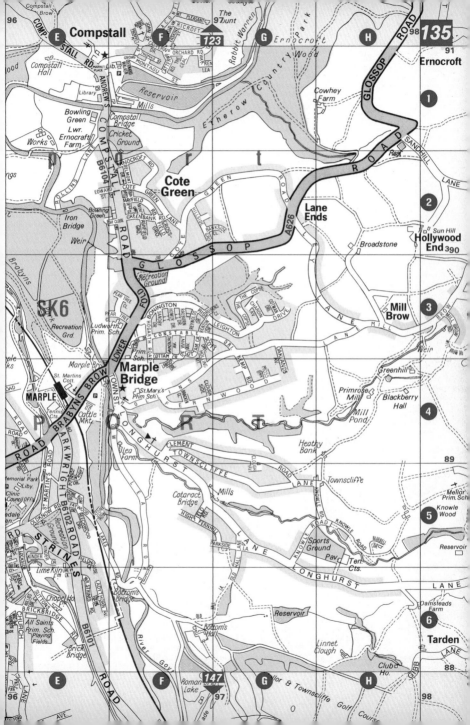

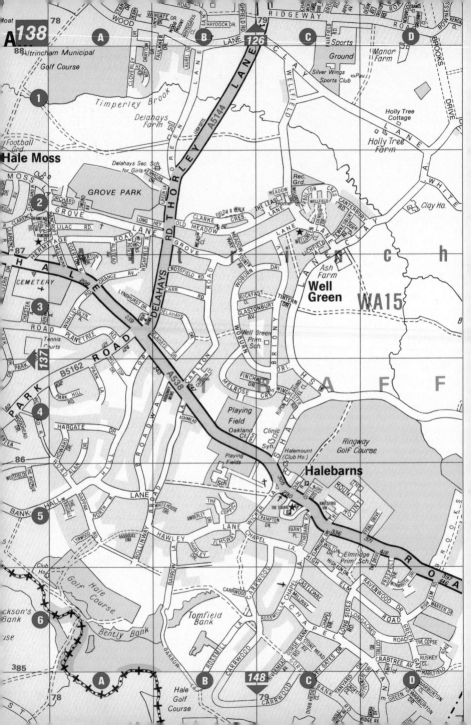

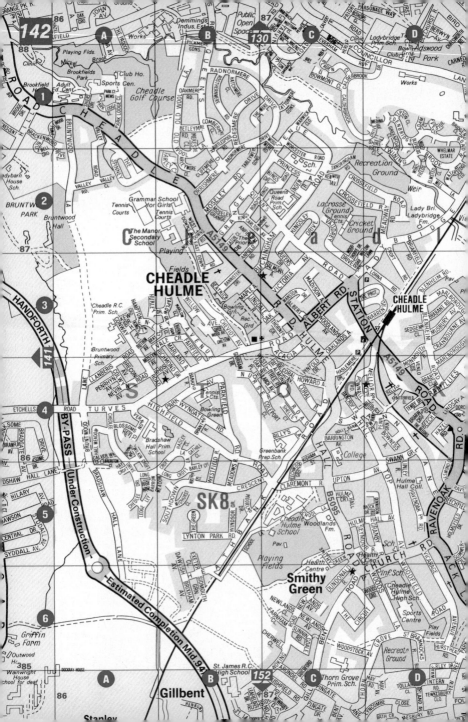

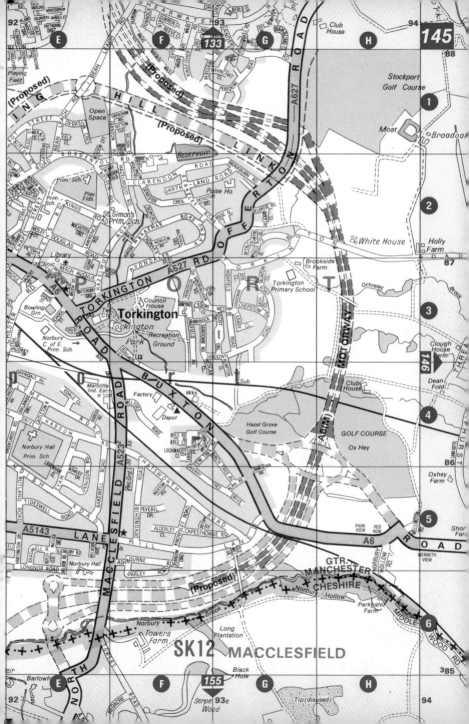

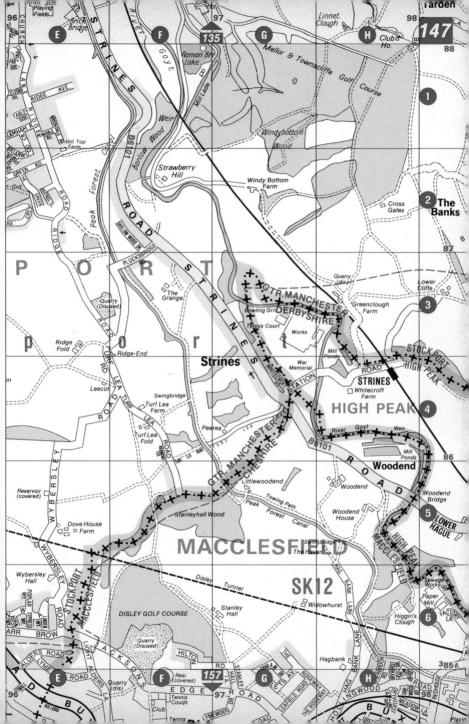

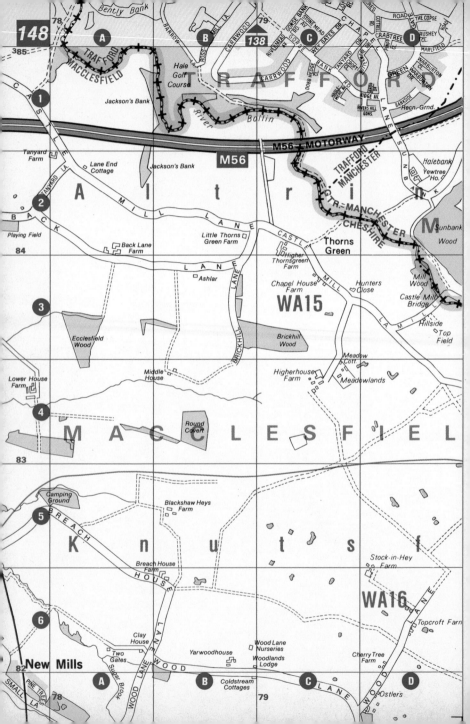

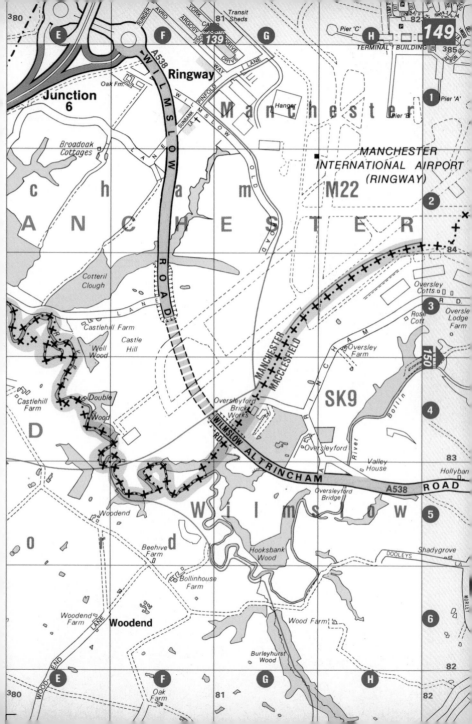

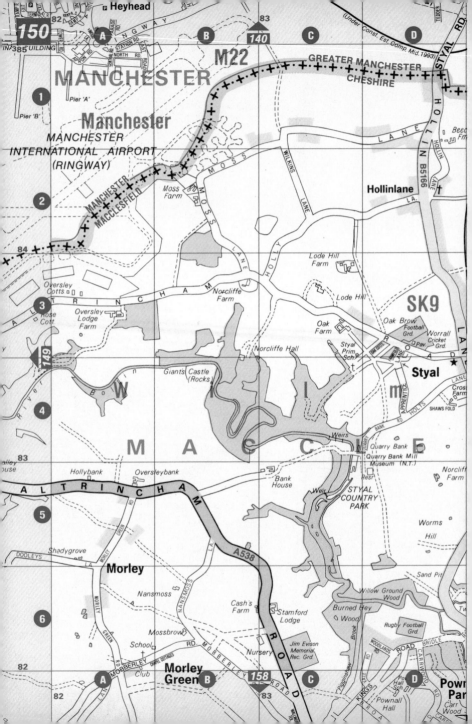

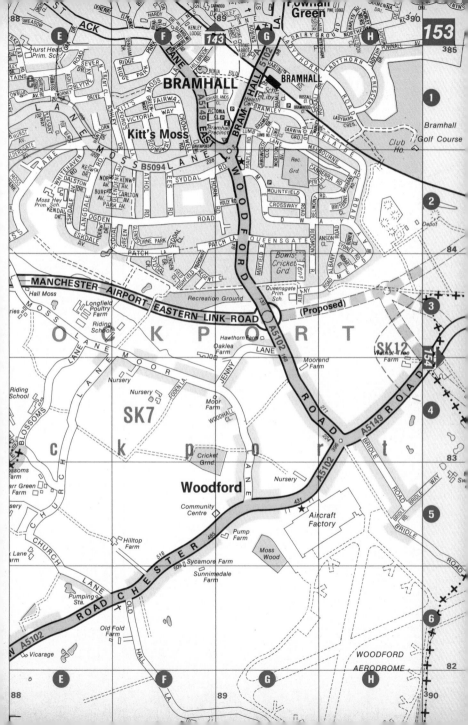

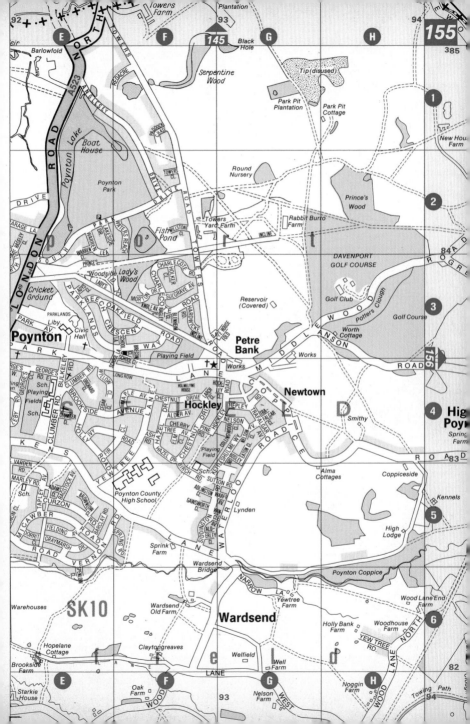

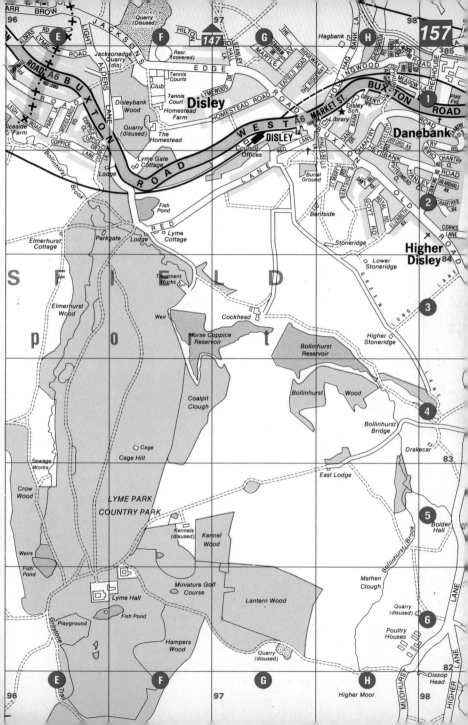

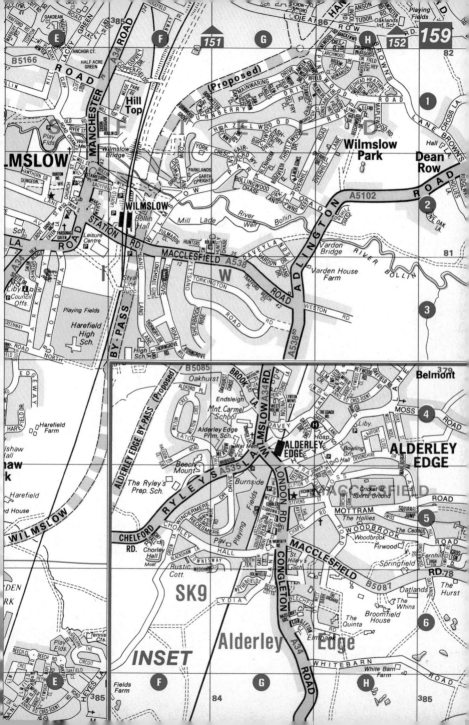

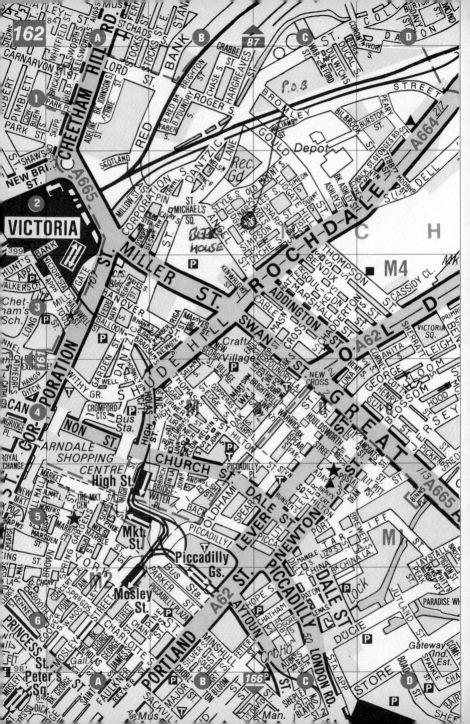

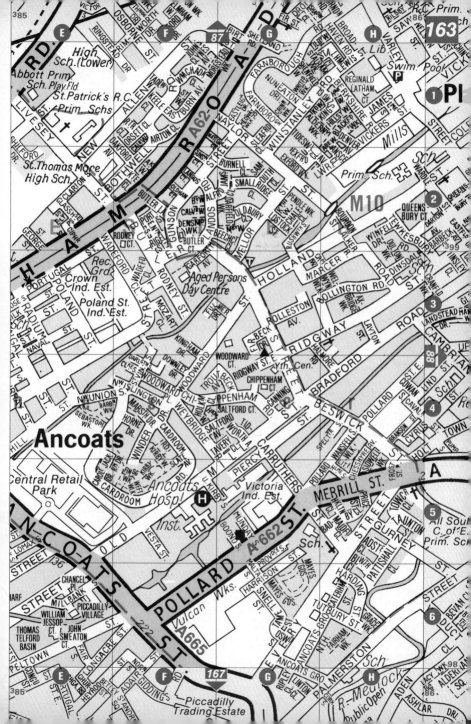

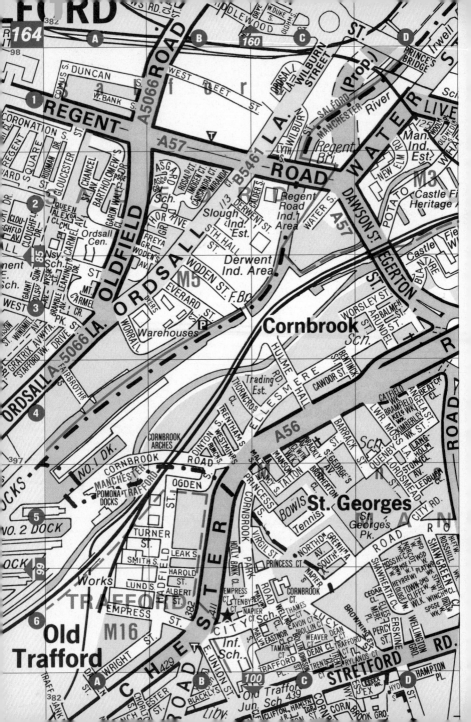

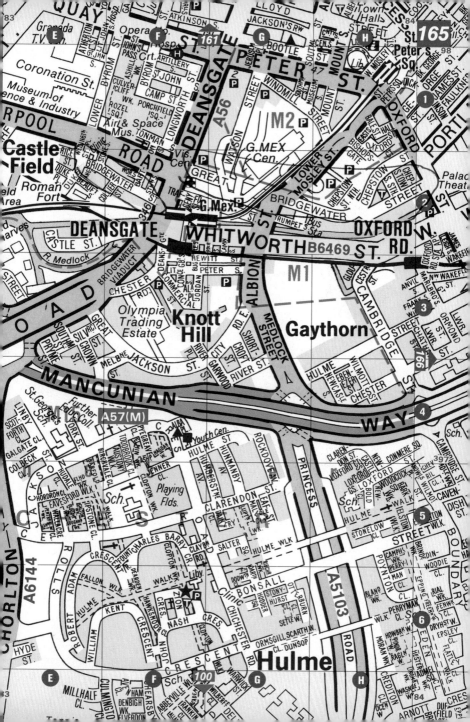

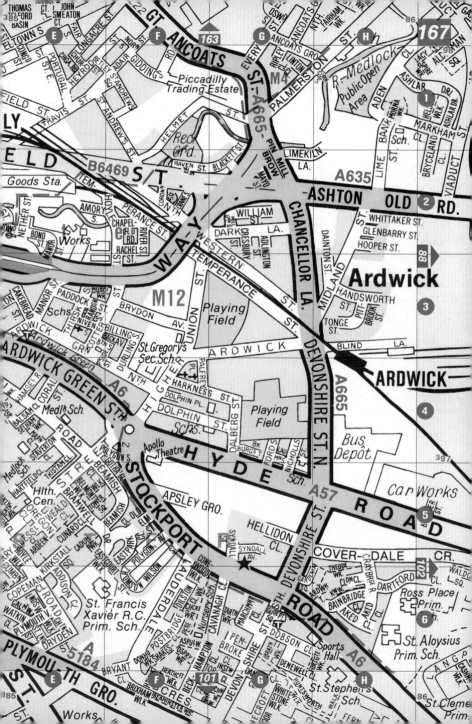

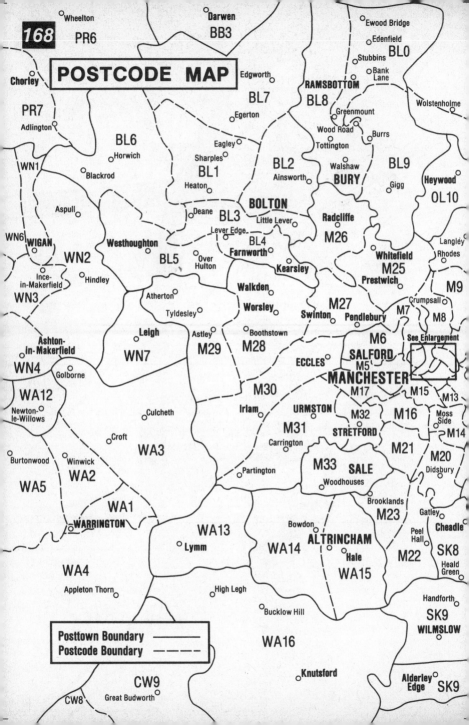

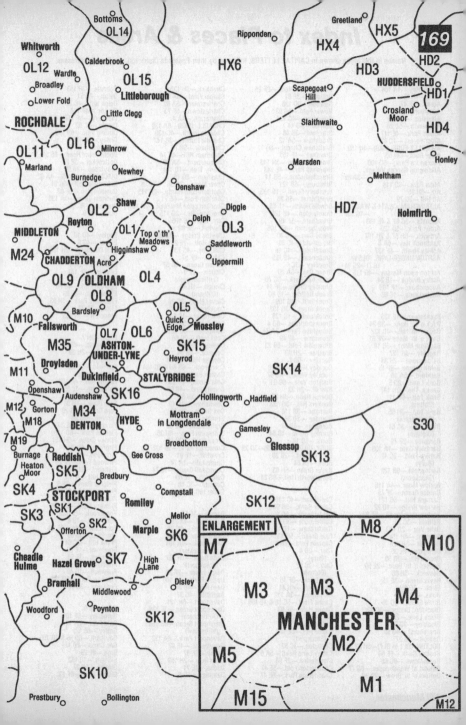

Index to Places & Areas

Names in this index shown in CAPITAL LETTERS, followed by their Postcode District(s), are Postal addresses.

Glodwick.—4F 65
Glodwick Brook —5E 65
Goats.—5G 35
Godley.—4D 106
Godley Green.—6F 107
Godley Hill.—5F 107
Gorse Hill.—4E 99
Gorton.—3F 103
Grains Bar.—1C 50
Grange.—1H 51
Grasscroft.—3G 67
Grasscroft Clough.—3G 67
Gravel Hole.—5B 34
Great Horrocks.—1F 87
Great Howarth.—5H 7
Great Lever.—4B 38
Greave.—3D 18
Greavefold.—5B 122
Greenacre Hill.—1G 65
Greenacres.—2H 65
Greenacres Moor.—1G 65
Green End.—4B 118
Greenfield.—3F 53
Green Gate.—2A 34
    (Balderstone)
Greengate.—6B 8
    (Smallbridge)
Greenheys.—2E 101
    (Manchester)
Greenheys.—3A 54
    (Walkden)
Green Hill.—2D 62
    (Manchester)
Green Hill.—4C 34
    (Oldham)
Greenmount.—2H 13
Greenside.—2G 89
Grotton.—4D 66
Guide Bridge.—5F 91

Hadfield.—2H 109
Haggate.—4A 48
Hague, The.—5E 109
Hale.—3H 137
Halebarns.—5C 138
Hale Moss.—2H 137
Half Acre.—3F 59
Hallfold.—1C 6
Hall i' th' Wood.—1D 24
Halliwell.—2A 24
Handforth.—3A 152
Hanging Chadder.—6A 34
Harden Park.—6D 158
Harper Green.—6D 38
Harpurhey.—4G 75
Harrop Dale.—1D 52
Harrop Edge.—2A 108
Harrop Green.—2C 52
Harrop Ridge.—1D 52
Hartshead Green.—3B 80
Harwood.—1H 25
Harwood Lee.—6A 12
Hatherlow.—1H 133
Hathershaw.—6D 64
Hattersley.—5H 107
Haugh.—1G 35
Haughton Dale.—2H 121
Hawk Green.—2D 146
Hawkshaw.—1E 13
Hazel Grove.—3D 144
Hazelhurst.—6C 80
    (Ashton-under-Lyne)
Hazelhurst.—4C 4
    (Bury)
Hazelhurst.—4C 70
    (Manchester)
Heady Hill.—3B 30
Heald Green.—5F 141
Healds Green.—4F 47
Heap Bridge.—4G 29
Heathfields.—1G 53
Heaton.—5E 23
Heaton Chapel.—3E 119
Heaton Mersey.—6A 118
Heaton Moor.—5C 118
Heaton Norris.—1F 131
Heaton Park.—5H 59
Heaviley –5A 132

Heights.—1F 51
Heyhead.—6A 140
Heyrod.—1G 93
Heyside.—3E 49
HEYWOOD. (OL10)—3G 31
Higginshaw.—5E 49
High Crompton.—6C 34
Higher Barrowshaw.—5A 50
Higher Blackley.—5D 60
Higher Boarshaw.—5D 46
Higher Broughton.—4G 73
Higher Crumpsall.—2D 74
Higher Disley.—2H 157
Higher Hartshead.—2B 80
Higher Hurst.—5A 80
Higher Hydegreen.—6H 81
Higher Openshaw.—6H 89
Higher Poynton.—4A 156
Higher Rushcroft.—5D 34
Higher Stake Hill.—3F 47
Higher Summerseat.—2B 14
Higher Woodhill.—6D 14
Highfield.—1B 54
High Lane.—6C 146
Hightown.—5A 74
Hill Top.—5F 55
    (Manchester)
Hill Top.—1F 159
    (Wilmslow)
Hilton Park.—1F 73
Hockley.—4F 155
Holcombe.—3C 4
Holcombe Brook.—1A 14
Holden Fold.—5A 48
Hollingworth.—2F 109
    (Hyde)
Hollingworth.—6E 9
    (Littleborough)
Holliniane.—2D 150
Hollins.—3E 43
    (Bury)
Hollins.—4A 46
    (Manchester)
Hollins.—1A 78
    (Oldham)
Hollins Green.—1C 78
Hollins Vale.—2E 43
Hollinwood.—2A 78
Holly Grove.—4D 52
Hollywood End.—2H 135
Holt Lane End.—4H 77
Holts.—5A 66
Holt Town.—3A 88
Hooley Bridge.—1E 31
Hooley Brow.—2F 31
Hooley Hill.—6F 91
Hope Green.—6D 154
Hopwood.—4G 31
Horrocks Fold.—4B 10
Houghton Green.—1G 121
Howarth Cross.—1B 20
Hulme.—1D 100 & 6G 165
Hunger Hill.—5C 36
Hurst.—6H 79
Hurst Brook.—1A 92
Hurstead.—5B 8
Hurst Knoll.—6G 79
Hurst Nook.—4A 80
HYDE. (SK14)—4B 106
Hydes —4D 92

Infirmary.—3G 101
Irlam.—5E 95
Irlams o' th' Height.—5H 7*

Jenny Green.—5D 94
Jericho.—1A 30
John Lee Fold.—6B 46
Johnson Fold.—2D 22
Jubilee.—3G 35

Kearsley.—3A 56
Kenworthy.—1H 127
Kenyon Fold.—6A 18
Kersal.—3E 73
Kersal Dale –3G 73

Kiln Green.—3D 52
Kingston.—4H 105
Kirkhams.—2F 59
Kirkholt.—2F 33
Kitt's Moss.—1F 153
Knott Hill.—6C 86 & 3F 165
Knott Lanes.—4D 78
Knowls Lane.—4C 66
Knutshaw Bridge.—4D 36

Lacey Green.—5F 151
Ladybarn.—2A 118
Lady House.—1C 34
Lancashire Hill.—6H 119
Landslow Green.—1D 108
Lane Bottom.—1H 35
Lane End.—6H 31
Lane Ends.—2G 135
    (Marple Bridge)
Lane Ends.—5B 122
    (Romiley)
Lane Side.—6H 35
Langley.—5G 45
Lark Hill.—1A 62
Lecturers Closes —1A 38
Lees.—4A 66
Leesbrook.—3H 65
Leesfield.—4H 65
Levenshulme.—5D 102
Lever Edge.—4A 38
Ley Hey Park.—4C 134
Lily Hill.—5C 42
Limefield.—5G 15
    (Bury)
Lime Field.—1G 61
    (Manchester)
Lime Gate.—2A 78
Limehurst.—5D 78
Lime Side.—2B 78
Lindow Moss.—2A 158
Linnyshaw.—6H 55
Little Bolton.—4A 84
LITTLEBOROUGH. (OL15)—4F 9
Little Clegg.—1F 21
Little Green.—6C 46
Little Hulton.—4C 54
Little Lever.—3B 40
Littlemoss.—1D 90
Little Park.—1A 62
Littlewood.—6E 15
Longsight.—3B 102
    (Manchester)
Long Sight.—5C 48
    (Oldham)
Lostock.—1A 36
Lostock Junction.—2B 36
Low Crompton.—1C 48
Lower Arthurs.—3F 53
Lower Bredbury.—6D 120
Lower Broughton.—1B 86
Lower Crumpsall.—3E 75
Lower Fold.—6C 6
Lower Healey.—5E 7
Lower Hinds.—5B 28
Lower Irlam.—1C 110
Lower Kersal.—4E 73
Lower Moor.—1E 65
Lower Place.—1H 33
Lower Pools.—3E 23
Lower Roe Cross.—2B 108
Lower Rushcroft.—4E 35
Lower Summerseat.—1C 14
Low Side.—5G 65
Luzley.—4D 80
Luzley Brook.—2D 48
Lydgate.—4E 67

MANCHESTER. (M1 to M4, M7 to
    M32 & M34 to M35)—1E 87
Manley Park.—5A 100
Markland Hill.—5C 22
Marland.—6D 18
Marple.—5C 134
Marple Bridge.—4F 135
Marple Dale.—3B 134
Marslands.—5B 52
Matley - 1H 107

Mayfield.—2B 20
Medlock Vale.—1A 90
Micklehurst.—3G 81
Middle Healey.—5D 6
Middleton.—1B 62
Middleton Junction.—3D 62
Middlewood.—2A 156
Mid Reddish.—1H 119
Midway.—5D 154
Mile End.—5B 132
Miles Platting.—2A 88
Millbrook.—1H 93
Mill Brow.—4C 68
    (Manchester)
Mill Brow.—3H 135
    (Stockport)
Mill Hill.—5D 24
Mills Hill.—1E 63
Milnrow.—5E 21
Mitchell Hey.—4G 19
Monton.—1F 83
Montserrat.—3B 22
Moorclose.—1C 62
Moorgate.—4G 81
Moorhey.—2F 65
Moorside.—3C 70
    (Manchester)
Moorside.—4A 50
    (Oldham)
Morley.—6A 150
Morley Green.—6B 150
Morris Green.—5G 37
Moses Gate.—5E 39
Mosley Common.—3B 68
Moss Gate.—4D 34
Moss Grove.—1B 78
Moss Hey.—1G 49
Mossley.—1G 81
Mossley Brow.—2E 81
Mossley Cross.—2D 80
Moss Nook.—6D 140
Moss Side.—3C 100
Moston.—3A 76
Mottram in Longdendale.
                          —3C 108
Mudd.—5C 108
Mumps.—2E 65

Narrow Gate Brow —6B 34
Near Barrowshaw
                          —6H 49
Nether Lees.—4H 65
Newall Green.—1G 139
Newbold.—4C 20
Newbold Brow.—3B 20
New Bury.—2C 55
New Delph.—4H 51
New Earth.—4G 65
Newhey.—1E 35
New Manchester.—2C 68
New Mills.—6A 148
New Moston.—2E 77
Newton.—3D 106
Newton Heath.—6B 76
Newton Wood.—1A 106
Newtown.—1F 87
    (Manchester)
New Town.—1F 49
    (Oldham)
Newtown.—4G 155
    (Stockport)
Newtown.—1E 71
    (Swinton)
New Windsor –3H 85
                          & 5A 160
Nimble Nook.—4G 63
Nob End.—5A 40
Nook.—6H 35
Norbury Moor.—5D 144
Norden.—2H 17
Norris Bank.—1D 130
Norris Hill.—1D 130
Northenden.—2B 128
Northern Moor.—2F 127
North Moor.—2B 64
North Reddish.—6G 103
Nutsford Vale –3D 102
Nuttall –5D 4

INDEX TO STREETS

HOW TO USE THIS INDEX

1. Each street name is followed by its Postal District and then by its map page reference; e.g. Abberley Dri. M10—1D 76 is in the Manchester 10 Postal District and it is to be found in square 1D on page 76. However, with the now general usage of Postal Coding, it is not recommended that this index should be used as a means of addressing mail.

2. A strict alphabetical order is followed in which Av., Rd., St. etc. (even though abbreviated) are read in full and as part of the street name; e.g. Abbots Clo. appears after Abbotsbury Clo. but before Abbots Ct.

3. Streets & Subsidiary names not shown on the Maps, appear in the Index in Italics with the thoroughfare to which it is connected shown in brackets.

4. The Postcode for any Town or locality used in Postal addresses can be found in the Index to Places on pages 170, 171 & 172 or the Postcode Map on pages 168 & 169.

GENERAL ABBREVIATIONS

All : Alley	Clo : Close	Junct : Junction	Pl : Place
App : Approach	Comn : Common	La : Lane	Rd : Road
Arc : Arcade	Cotts : Cottages	Lit : Little	S : South
Av : Avenue	Ct : Court	Lwr : Lower	Sq : Square
Bk : Back	Cres : Crescent	M : Manchester	Sta : Station
BL : Bolton	Dri : Drive	Mnr : Manor	SK : Stockport
Boulevd : Boulevard	E : East	Mans : Mansions	St : Street
Bri : Bridge	Embkmt : Embankment	Mkt : Market	Ter : Terrace
B'way : Broadway	Est : Estate	M : Mews	Up : Upper
Bldgs : Buildings	Gdns : Gardens	Mt : Mount	Vs : Villas
Bus : Business	Ga : Gate	N : North	Wlk : Walk
Cen : Centre	Gt : Great	OL : Oldham	WA : Warrington
Chu : Church	Grn : Green	Pal : Palace	W : West
Chyd : Churchyard	Gro : Grove	Pde : Parade	Yd : Yard
Circ : Circle	Ho : House	Pk : Park	
Cir : Circus	Ind : Industrial	Pas : Passage	

Abberley Dri. M10—1D 76
Abberton Rd. M20—3E 117
Abbey Clo. M26—2E 41
Abbey Clo. M32—4H 97
Abbey Clo. WA14—4C 136
Abbey Ct. M18—1G 103
Abbey Ct. M26—3E 41
Abbey Ct. SK1—3B 132
Abbey Cres. OL10—1D 30
Abbeydale. OL12-3G 19
(off Spotland Rd.)
Abbeydale Clo. OL6—5A 80
Abbeydale Gdns. M28—6E 55
Abbey Dri. BL8—4G 27
Abbey Dri. M27—2E 71
Abbey Dri. OL15—6D 8
Abbeyfield Sq. M11-5D 88
(off Herne St.)
Abbey Gdns. SK14—4B 108
Abbey Gro. M30—3G 83
Abbey Gro. OL9—4G 63
Abbey Gro. SK1—3B 132
Abbey Gro. SK14—4B 108
Abbey Hey La. M11—6G 89
Abbey Hey La. M18—2G 103
Abbey Hills Rd. OL8 & OL4—4F 65
Abbey Rd. M24—3H 45
Abbey Rd. M33—3A 114
Abbey Rd. M35—2H 89
(Droylsden)
Abbey Rd. M35—3H 77
(Failsworth)
Abbey Rd. OL3—2G 51
Abbey Rd. SK8—6C 130
Abbeyville Wlk. M15—2C 100
Abbeywood Av. M18—3G 103
(in two parts)
Abbotsbury Clo. M12—1C 102
Abbotsbury Clo. SK12—2D 154
Abbots Clo. M33—4D 114
Abbots Ct. M33—4D 114
Abbotsfield Clo. M31—4H 95
Abbot's Fold Rd. M28—4D 68
Abbotsford Dri. M24—3F 45
Abbotsford Gro WA14—3G 125

Abbotsford Rd. BL1—4E 23
Abbotsford Rd. M21—5H 99
Abbotsford Rd. OL1—6F 49
Abbotsford Rd. OL9—1E 63
Abbotside Clo. M16—4B 100
Abbotsleigh Dri. SK7—3H 143
Abbot St. BL3—2A 38
Abbott St. OL9—3C 64
Abbott St. OL11—2B 32
Abden St. M26—4G 41
Abels La. OL3—1G 53
Aber Av. SK2—1C 144
Abercarn Clo. M8—4B 74
Abercorn Rd. BL1—1F 23
Abercorn St. OL4—3H 65
Aberdare Wlk. M9-4G 61
(off Brockford Dri.)
Aberdaron Wlk. M13—6F 87 & 4D 166
Aberdeen. M30-3G 83
(off St Andrews Ct.)
Aberdeen Cres. SK3—3F 131
Aberdeen Gro. SK3—3F 131
Aberdeen Ho. M15—2F 101
Aberdeen St. M15—2F 101
Aberford Rd. M23—6G 127
Abergale St. SK2—6A 132
Abergele Rd. M14—1A 118
Abergele St. SK2—6A 132
Abernant Clo. M11—4B 88
Aber Rd. SK8—5C 130
Abersoch Av. M14—1A 118
Abingdon Av. M25—5D 42
Abingdon Clo. M25—5D 42
Abingdon Clo. OL9—5H 63
Abingdon Clo. OL11—6G 19
Abingdon Rd. BL2—5E 25
Abingdon Rd. M31—4G 97
Abingdon Rd. SK5—2H 119
Abingdon Rd. SK7—3G 143
Abingdon St. M1—5E 87 & 1A 166
Abingdon St. OL6—3B 92
Abinger Wlk. M10—1F 89
Abington Rd. M33—6B 114
Abney Rd. OL5—3E 81
Abney Rd. SK4—4E 119

Aboukir St. OL16—3B 20
Abraham St. OL4—6G 49
Abram Clo. M14—6E 101
Abram St. M6—5D 72
Absalom Dri. M8—3B 74
Abson St. OL1—6A 48
Acacia Av. M27—5E 71
Acacia Av. M34—4G 105
Acacia Av. SK8—3C 142
Acacia Av. SK9—4C 158
Acacia Av. WA15—2H 137
Acacia Dri. M6—2B 84
Acacia Dri. WA15—2H 137
Acacia Gro. SK5—5H 119
Acacia Rd. OL8—2B 78
Academy Wlk. M15—2C 100
Acer Clo. OL11—2H 17
Acer Gro. M7—4H 73
Aches St. M18—2F 103
Ackers La. M31—3A 112
(in two parts)
Ackersley Ct. SK8—5D 142
Ackers St. M13—2F 101
Acker St. OL16—3H 19
Ack La. E. SK7—6E 143
Ack La. W. SK8—5D 142
Ackroyd Av. M18—1H 103
Ackroyd St. M11—6G 89
(in two parts)
Ackworth Dri. M23—5G 127
Ackworth Rd. M27—2E 71
Acme Dri. M27—3H 71
Acomb St. M14—4F 101
Acomb St. M15—2F 101
Acorn Av. SK8—6A 130
Acorn Av. SK14—1C 122
Acorn Bus. Cen. SK4—2F 131
Acorn Clo. M19—1B 118
Acorn St. OL4—3A 66
Acorn Way. OL1—2C 64
Acre Barn. OL2—5C 34
Acre Clo. BL0—2A 4
Acre Field. BL2—1F 25
Acre Field. M33—6A 114
Acrefield Av M31—6H 97

Acrefield Av. SK4—5C 118
Acregate. M31—5C 96
Acre La. OL1—6E 49
Acre La. SK8—2D 152
Acresbrook Av. BL8—6H 13
Acresbrook Wlk. BL8—6H 13
Acresdale. BL6—6A 22
Acresfield Av. M34—4C 90
Acresfield Clo. M27—5G 71
Acresfield Mall. BL1-6B 24
(off Arndale Cen.)
Acresfield Rd. M6—6B 72
Acresfield Rd. M24—4B 46
Acresfield Rd. M28—5D 54
Acresfield Rd. SK14—2D 106
Acresfield Rd. WA15—3A 126
Acres La. SK15—4F 93
Acres Pass. M21—1G 115
Acres Rd. M21—1G 115
Acres Rd. SK8—6E 129
Acres St. BL8—6H 13
Acre St. M26—4E 41
Acre St. M34—4E 105
Acre St. OL12—4H 7
Acre St. SK6—1H 133
Acre Top Rd. M9—4D 60
Acre View. BL0—3A 4
Acton Av. M10—1D 88
Acton Sq. M5—3H 85
Acton St. OL12—2A 20
Adair St. M1—5G 87 & 1F 167
Adair St. OL11—3B 32
Adam Clo. SK8—1D 142
Adams Av. M21—3H 115
Adams Clo. SK12—5E 155
Adamson Gdns. M20—6D 116
Adamson Rd. M30—5E 83
Adamson St. SK16—1A 106
Adamson Wlk. M14—4F 101
Adam St. BL3—2B 38
Adam St. OL6—2A 92
Adam St. OL8—1D 78
Ada St. BL0—4D 4
Ada St. M9—2F 75
Ada St. OL4—3E 65

Alderley Dri. SK6—6E 121
Alderley Lodge. SK9—4D 158
Alderley Rd. M31—5C 96
Alderley Rd. M33—1E 127
Alderley Rd. SK5—4H 119
Alderley Rd. SK9—4D 158
Alderley St. OL6—6H 79
Alderman Sq. M12—5A 88
Aldermary Rd. M21—4B 116
Aldermaston Gro. M9—3D 60
Aldermere Cres. M31—5A 96
Alderminster Av. M28—4C 54
Alderney Wlk. M10—2H 87 & 1G 163
Alder Rd. M24—5C 46
Alder Rd. M35—6F 77
Alder Rd. OL11—3D 32
Alder Rd. SK8—6H 129
Alders Av. M22—6A 128
Alders Ct. OL8—3E 79
Aldersgate Rd. SK2—5B 132
Aldersgate Rd. SK8—2E 153
Aldersgreen Av. SK6—6D 146
Aldershot Wlk. M11—4B 88
Alderside Rd. M9—3F 75
Aldersley Av. M9—4D 60
Alderson St. M6—1G 85
Alderson St. OL9—2C 64
Alders Rd. M22—6A 128
Alders Rd. SK12—6E 147
Alders Rd. SK15—2H 93
Alder St. BL3—4B 38
Alder St. M6—3F 85
Alder St. M30—1C 82
Aldersyde St. BL3—4H 37
Alderue Av. M22—5B 128
Alderway. BL0—1E 5
Alderwood Av. SK4—2C 130
Alderwood Gro. BL0—1A 4
Alderwood Wlk. M8—5B 74
Aldfield Rd. M23—2E 127
Aldford Clo. M20—6G 117
Aldford Gro. BL2—2B 40
Aldford Pl. SK9—4F 159
Aldham Av. M10—1E 89
Aldington Rd. SK9—3G 159
Aldred Clo. M8—5D 74
Aldred St. BL3—4F 37
Aldred St. M5—3H 85
Aldred St. M30—4E 83
Aldred St. M35—4E 77
Aldridge Wlk. M11—5B 88
Aldsworth Dri. BL3—3A 38
Aldsworth Dri. M10—5G 75
Aldwick Av. M20—6E 117
Aldwinians Clo. M34—2E 105
Aldwych. OL11—2F 33
Aldwych Av. M14—4F 101
Aldwyn Clg. M34—2F 105
Aldwyn Cres. SK7—3C 144
Aldwyn Pk. Rd. M34—5C 90
Alexander Av. M35—3G 77
Alexander Dri. BL9—5E 43
Alexander Dri. OL16—5E 21
Alexander Dri. WA15—5A 126
Alexander Gdns. M7—1B 86
Alexander Rd. BL2—4E 25
Alexander St. M6—3E 83
Alexander St. OL11—3B 32
Alexandra Av. M14—5D 100
Alexandra Av. M25—1E 59
Alexandra Av. SK14—5A 106
Alexandra Cen. Retail Pk. OL4
—3D 64
Alexandra Clo. SK3—5E 131
Alexandra Cres. OL1—6F 49
Alexandra Dri. M19—2B 118
Alexandra Gro. M30—1D 110
Alexandra Ho. OL1—1F 65
Alexandra M. OL8—4E 65
Alexandra Rd. BL4—2A 56
Alexandra Rd. M16—4C 100
Alexandra Rd. M26—1A 56
Alexandra Rd. M28—4E 55
Alexandra Rd. M30—4D 82
Alexandra Rd. M33—5C 114
Alexandra Rd. M34—3G 105
Alexandra Rd. OL6—2H 91

Alexandra Rd. OL8—5E 65
Alexandra Rd. SK4—6E 119
Alexandra Rd. S. M16—4C 100
Alexandra St. BL4—2F 55
Alexandra St. M7—2B 86
Alexandra St. OL6—1B 92
Alexandra St. OL8—4E 65
Alexandra St. OL10—5G 31
Alexandra St. SK14—6A 106
Alexandra Ter. M19—6C 102
Alexandra Ter. M33—3A 114
Alexandra Ter. OL4—4H 49
Alford Av. M20—1E 117
Alford Gro. BL2—1H 39
Alford Rd. SK4—3D 118
Alford St. OL9—1H 77
Alfred Av. M28—4A 70
Alfred James Clo. M10—2G 87 & 2F 163
Alfred St. BL0—4D 4
Alfred St. BL3—3D 38
Alfred St. BL4—5F 39
(Farnworth)
Alfred St. BL4—1H 55
(Farnworth)
Alfred St. BL7—1B 10
Alfred St. BL9—5E 29
Alfred St. M9—3F 75
Alfred St. M28—6F 55
Alfred St. M30—3C 110
(Cadishead)
Alfred St. M30—2F 83
(Eccles)
Alfred St. M35—3F 77
Alfred St. OL2—6E 33
Alfred St. OL6—1B 92
Alfred St. OL9—3A 64
(Oldham, in two parts)
Alfred St. OL9—6G 63
(White Gate)
Alfred St. OL12—3H 7
Alfred St. OL15—3E 9
Alfred St. SK14—4A 106
Alfreton Av. M34—1G 121
Alfreton Rd. SK2—5D 132
Alfreton Wlk. M10—5A 76
(off Thorpebrook Rd.)
Alfriston Dri. M23—1G 127
Algernon Rd. M28—5E 55
Algernon St. BL4—5F 39
Algernon St. M27—3D 70
Algernon St. M30—2F 83
Algernon St. OL6—3B 92
Alger St. OL6—1B 92
Algreave Rd. SK3—3C 130
Alice Ingram Ct. OL12—2D 18
Alice St. BL3—2G 37
Alice St. M27—3H 71
Alice St. M33—5D 114
Alice St. M35—5A 90
Alice St. OL12—2B 20
Alice St. SK14—2C 122
Alicia Ct. OL12—2G 19
Alicia Dri. OL12—2G 19
Alicia St. BL3—2F 39
Alison St. M14—4D 100
Alison St. OL2—5B 48
Alixandra Ct. M31—6A 96
Alker Rd. M10—2H 87 & 2H 163
Alkrington Clo. BL9—5E 43
Alkrington Ct. M24—4B 62
Alkrington Grn. M24—3H 61
Alkrington Hall Rd. N. M24—2H 61
Alkrington Hall Rd. S. M24—3G 61
Alkrington Pk. Rd. M24—1G 61
Allams St. M11—3A 88
Allanbrooke Wlk. M15—2C 100
Allan Ct. M21—2G 115
Allandale Ct. M7—2A 74
Allandale Rd. M19—6B 102
Allan Roberts Clo. M9—2F 75
Allanson Rd. M22—2C 128
Alldis St. SK2—6B 132
Allen Av. SK14—1D 122
Allenby Rd. M27—5C 70
Allenby Rd. M30—5B 110
Allenby St. OL2—6E 35
Allenby Wlk. M10—6E 75
Allen Clo. OL2—1E 49

Allendale Dri. BL9—4E 43
Allendale Gdns. BL1—3A 24
Allendale Wlk. M13—1F 101 & 6D 166
Allen Rd. M31—5H 97
Allen St. BL3—4A 40
Allen St. BL8—2A 28
Allen St. M26—4E 41
(in two parts)
Allen St. OL8—3B 64
Allen St. OL16—5A 20
Allerdean Wlk. SK4—6A 118
Allerford Clo. M16—3C 100
Allerton Ho. BL1—5A 24
(off Duke St. N.)
Allerton Wlk. M13—1F 101 & 6D 166
Alley St. OL4—4G 65
Allgreave Clo. M33—1E 127
Allingham St. M13—3A 102
Allington. OL11—5G 19
Allington Dri. M30—1G 83
Alliott Wlk. M15—2C 100
Allison Gro. M30—4D 82
Allison St. M8—6B 74
Allonby Wlk. M24—5E 45
Allotment Rd. M30—3B 110
Alloway Wlk. M10—5B 76
All Saint's Clo. OL2—2B 48
All Saints' Rd. SK4—5G 119
All Saints Rd. BL1—5B 24
All Saints St. M10—4C 88
All Saints Ter. OL16—1B 20
Allwood St. M5—4B 86 & 5C 160
Alma Ind. Est. OL12—2H 19
Alma La. SK9—3D 158
Alma Rd. M19—1C 118
Alma Rd. M33—1G 125
Alma Rd. SK4—4D 118
Alma Rd. SK7—5G 145
Alma St. BL3—3G 37
(Bolton)
Alma St. BL3—4B 40
(Little Lever)
Alma St. BL4—4B 56
Alma St. M26—2F 41
Alma St. M30—4D 82
Alma St. OL12—2H 19
Alma St. SK14—4A 106
Alma St. SK15—3F 93
Alminstone Clo. M10—1F 89
Almond Av. BL9—2G 29
Almond Clo. M6—2G 85
Almond Clo. M35—5F 77
Almond Clo. OL15—3D 8
Almond Clo. SK3—3E 131
Almond Ct. SK16—4A 92
Almond Dri. M33—3H 113
Almond Gro. BL1—2B 24
Almond Gro. M16—2H 99
Almond Rd. OL4—6H 49
Almond St. BL1—1B 24
Almond St. BL4—1E 55
Almond St. M10—1F 87
Almond Tree Rd. SK8—4C 142
Almond Wlk. M31—6B 110
Alms Hill Rd. M8—5C 74
Almshouses. M33—5E 115
Alness Rd. M16—4C 100
Alnwick Dri. BL9—2E 43
Alnwick Rd. M9—4F 61
Alperton Wlk. M10—1F 89
Alpha Ct. M34—4C 104
Alpha Pl. M15—6C 86 & 3F 165
Alpha Rd. M32—5C 98
Alpha St. M6—2F 85
Alpha St. M11—6G 89
Alpha St. M26—3F 41
Alpha St. W. M6—2E 85
Alphin Clo. OL3—4F 53
Alphin Clo. OL5—6G 67
Alphin Sq. OL5—2F 81
Alphonsus St. M16—3A 100
Alpine Dri. OL2—4A 48
Alpine Dri. OL12—3A 8
Alpine Dri. OL16—4G 21
Alpine Rd. SK1—1A 132
Alpine St. M11—2D 88
Alpine Ter. BL4—1G 55
Alpington Wlk. M10—1C 76

Alport Av. M16—5A 100
Alport Gro. SK13—5G 109
(off Melandra Castle Rd.)
Alport Lea. SK13—5G 109
(off Hathersage Cres.)
Alport Way. SK13—5G 109
(off Melandra Castle Rd.)
Alresford Rd. M6—6B 72
Alresford Rd. M24—4H 61
Alric Wlk. M22—5C 140
Alsham Wlk. M8—5C 74
Alstead Av. WA15—2A 138
Alston Av. M32—4B 98
Alston Av. M33—6H 113
Alston Dri. OL2—5F 35
Alston Clo. SK7—4A 144
Alstone Dri. WA14—5C 124
Alstone Gdns. M19—4B 118
Alston Rd. M18—2G 103
Alston St. BL3—4A 38
Alston St. BL8—1A 28
Alston Wlk. M24—5E 45
Altair Av. M22—4B 140
Altair Pl. M7—1A 86
Altcar Gro. SK5—5G 103
(in two parts)
Alt Fold Dri. OL8—6H 65
Alt Gro. OL6—5F 79
Altham Clo. BL9—6B 28
Altham Wlk. M10—5A 76
(off Craiglands Av.)
Alt Hill La. OL6—3G 79
Alt Hill Rd. OL6—2G 79
Althorn Wlk. M23—6G 127
Althorpe Wlk. M10—1F 89
Alt La. OL8—1G 79
Alton Av. M31—4H 95
Alton Clo. BL9—2E 43
Alton Clo. OL6—4G 79
Alton Rd. SK9—1C 158
Alton Sq. M11—6G 89
Alton St. M9—5F 75
Alton St. OL8—6D 64
Altrincham Rd. M23, M22 & SK8
—4D 126
(in four parts)
Altrincham Rd. SK9—4G 149
Altrincham St. M1—5F 87 & 2C 166
(in two parts)
Altrincham St. OL9—1B 64
Alt Rd. OL6—5F 79
Alt. Wlk. M25—5G 43
Alum Cres. BL9—4E 43
Alvanley Clo. M33—2B 126
Alvanley Cres. SK3—5E 131
Alvanley St. SK6—5G 121
Alvan Sq. M11—6G 89
Alva Rd. OL4—5H 49
Alvaston Av. SK4—6D 118
Alvaston Rd. M18—3G 103
Alveley Av. M20—4G 117
Alverstone Rd. M20—3G 117
Alvington Gro. SK7—4A 144
Alvon Ct. SK14—5E 107
Alwin Rd. OL2—5E 35
Alwinton Av. SK4—6A 118
Alworth Rd. M9—5E 61
Alwyn Dri. M13—3A 102
Ambassador Pl. WA15—6G 125
Ambergate St. M11—3B 88
Amberidge Wlk. M15—2E 101
(off Duxbury Sq.)
Amberley Clo. BL3—2D 36
Amberley Dri. M23—1G 139
Amberley Dri. M30—6E 95
Amberley Dri. WA15—5B 138
Amberley Rd. M33—4G 113
Amberley Wlk. OL9—2A 64
Amber St. M4—3E 87 & 3B 162
Amberwood. OL9—1E 63
Amberwood Dri. M23—5D 126
Amblecote Dri. E. M28—3C 54
Amblecote Dri. W. M28—3C 54
Ambleside. SK15—2E 93

Ambleside Av. OL7—1F 91
Ambleside Av. WA15—6C 126
Ambleside Clo. BL2—1H 25
Ambleside Clo. M24—6G 45
Ambleside Rd. M31—5A 54
Ambleside Rd. SK5—2H 119
Ambleside Way. M9—1A 76
Ambrose Cres. OL3—4B 52
Ambrose Dri. M20—5B 116
Ambrose Gdns. M20—5B 116
Ambrose St. M12—6C 88
Ambrose St. OL11—6H 19
Ambrose St. SK14—2C 122
Ambush St. M11—6H 89
Amelia St. SK14—5C 106
Amelia St. W. M34—3F 105
Amersham Clo. M31—2D 96
Amersham Pl. M19—3C 118
Amersham St. M5—4F 85
Amesbury Gro. SK5—4H 119
Amesbury Rd. M9—5G 61
Amherst Rd. M20 & M14—2G 117
Amlwch Av. SK2—5D 132
Ammon's Way. OL3—2H 51
Ammon Wrigley Clo. OL1—2D 64
Amory St. M12—5G 87 & 2E 167
Amos Av. M10—1E 89
Amos St. M6—3E 85
Amos St. M9—4G 75
Ampleforth Gdns. M26—2E 41
Ampney Clo. M30—4D 82
Amport Wlk. M10—1C 76
Amwell St. M8—4D 74
Amy St. M24—6B 46
Amy St. OL12—2D 18
Ancaster Wlk. M10—1C 76
Anchorage Quay. M5—5G 85
Anchorage Rd. M31—6A 98
Anchorage Wlk. M18—1E 103
Anchor Clo. M19—6E 103
Anchor Ct. M8—2B 74
Anchor Ct. SK9—1E 159
Anchor La. BL4 & M28—1B 54
Anchor St. OL1—1D 64
Ancoats Gro. M4—4H 87 & 6G 163
Ancoats Gro. N. M4—4H 87 & 6G 163
Ancoats St. OL4—3A 66
Ancroft Gdns. BL3—4G 37
Anderton Clo. BL8—4F 27
Anderton Dri. OL6—6A 80
Anderton Pl. M7—6H 73
Anderton Way. SK9—4H 151
Andoc Av. M30—3A 84
Andover St. M30—4E 83
Andover Wlk. M8—2C 74
Andre St. M11—3E 89
Andrew Clo. BL8—2H 13
Andrew Clo. M26—6A 42
Andrew Ct. M20—3F 117
Andrew Gro. SK16—5B 92
Andrew La. BL1—5D 10
Andrew La. SK6—4C 146
Andrew Rd. M9—1F 75
Andrews Av. M31—4A 96
Andrew's Brow. M10—1F 89
Andrews Clo. M34—1H 121
Andrews La. M4—4E 87 & 5B 162
Andrew St. BL9—3E 29
Andrew St. M9—5F 75
Andrew St. M24—2C 62
Andrew St. M35—1C 90
  (Droylsden)
Andrew St. M35—3E 77
  (Failsworth)
Andrew St. OL5—3E 81
Andrew St. OL6—6H 79
Andrew St. OL9—1H 63
Andrew St. SK4—1F 131
Andrew St. SK6—1E 135
Andrew St. SK14—4D 106
Andy Nicholson Wlk. M9
　　　　　　　—3H 75
Anerley Rd. M20—5F 117
Anfield Clo. BL9—4F 43
Anfield M. SK8—2B 142
Anfield Rd. BL3—4A 38
Anfield Rd. M10—2D 76
Anfield Rd. M33—4C 114

Anfield Rd. SK8—2B 142
Angela Av. OL2—5C 48
Angela St. M15—6B 86 & 4D 164
Angel Clo. SK16—6H 91
Angelico Rise. OL1—4H 49
Angelo St. BL1—2H 23
  (in two parts)
Angel St. M4—2E 87 & 2B 162
Angel St. M34—3G 105
Angel St. SK7—2D 144
Angier Gro. M34—4F 105
Anglesea Av. M7—3F 75
Anglesea Av. SK2—5H 131
Anglesey Clo. OL7—5E 79
Anglesey Dri. SK12—1E 155
Anglesey Gro. SK8—5B 130
Anglesey Rd. OL7—5D 78
Angleside Av. M19—5A 118
Angle St. BL2—4D 24
Anglia Gro. BL3—3G 37
Angouleme Way. BL9—3C 28
Angus Av. OL10—4C 30
Angus St. M3—5C 86 & 2E 165
Aniline St. M11—4D 88
Anita St. M4—3F 87 & 3D 162
Annable Rd. M18—1G 103
Annable Rd. M30—1D 110
Annable Rd. M34—8A 90
Annable Rd. SK6—6D 120
Annald Sq. M35—5A 90
Annan St. M34—3F 105
Annecy Clo. BL8—1H 27
Annersley Av. OL2—1E 49
Annesley Gdns. M18—1F 103
Annesley Rd. M10—2E 77
Anne St. SK16—5B 92
Annie Darby Ct. M9—4F 75
Annie St. BL0—5C 4
Annie St. M5—3E 85
Annis Clo. SK9—4H 159
Annisdale Clo. M30—3D 82
Annisfield Av. OL3—4F 53
Annis Rd. BL3—3F 37
Annis Rd. SK9—4H 159
Ann Sq. OL4—1H 65
Ann's Rd. M25—6D 58
Ann St. BL4—2G 55
Ann St. M34—4E 105
Ann St. OL7—5F 91
Ann St. OL10—2F 31
Ann St. OL12—6B 8
Ann St. OL16 & OL12—5H 19
Ann St. SK5—5G 119
Ann St. SK14—4A 106
Anscombe Clo. M10—2H 87 & 1H 163
Anscombe Wlk. M10—2H 87 & 1H 163
Ansdell Av. M21—1A 116
Ansdell Dri. M35—3G 89
Ansdell Rd. OL16—1H 33
Ansdell St. M8—4C 74
Ansell Clo. M18—1F 103
Ansford Wlk. M9—4E 75
  (off Westmere Dri.)
Ansleigh Av. M8—2C 74
Ansley Gro. SK4—6D 118
Anslow Clo. M10—6F 75
Anson Av. M27—5E 71
Anson Clo. SK7—2H 153
Anson Rd. M14—3H 101
Anson Rd. M27—5E 71
Anson Rd. M34—5A 104
Anson Rd. SK9—6A 152
Anson Rd. SK12—3H 155
Anson St. BL1—2B 24
Anson St. M30—2D 82
Anson View. M14—4H 101
Answell Av. M8—1C 74
Antares Av. M7—2B 86
　　　　　　　& 1C 160
Anthistle Ct. M5—5D 84
Anthony St. BL3—4B 38
Anthony St. OL5—2D 80
Anton Wlk. M9—4F 75
Antrim Clo. M19—2H 129
Anvil St. BL4—2F 55
Anvil St. M1—6D 86 & 3H 165
Anvil Way. OL1—2C 64
Apethorn La. SK14—2A 122
Apfel La. OL9—2H 63

Apollo Av. BL9—4D 42
Apollo Wlk. M12—1C 102
Apperley Grange. M30—1G 83
Appian Way. M7 & M8—5A 74
Appleby Av. M12—4C 102
Appleby Av. SK14—2A 106
Appleby Av. WA15—6C 126
Appleby Gdns. BL2—4C 24
Appleby Lodge. M14—5H 101
Appleby Rd. SK8—1F 141
Appleby Wlk. OL2—3C 48
Apple Clo. BL8—6G 65
Applecross Wlk. M11—5E 89
Appledore Dri. BL2—2H 25
Appledore Dri. M23—4D 126
Appledore Wlk. OL9—3H 63
Appleford Dri. M8—5D 74
Apple St. SK14—2G 123
Apple Ter. BL1—3H 23
Appleton Clo. M33—5B 114
Appleton Gro. M33—1G 125
Appleton Rd. SK4—3F 119
Appleton Rd. WA15—4G 137
Appleton Wlk. SK9—6A 152
Apple Tree Ct. M5—3G 85
Apple Tree Wlk. M33—4E 113
Applewood. OL9—2D 62
Apprentice Ct. M9—3G 75
Apprentice La. SK9—4D 150
Approach Rd. M31—2H 97
Apron Rd. M22—1A 150
Apsley Clo. WA14—4D 136
Apsley Gro. M12—1G 101 & 5F 167
Apsley Gro. WA14—4D 136
Apsley Pl. OL3—3G 91
Apsley Rd. M34—3F 105
Apsley Side. SK5—3E 81
Aqueduct Rd. BL3—3E 39
Aragon Dri. OL10—3E 31
Aragon Way. SK6—5C 134
Arbor Av. M19—2B 118
Arbor Clo. M6—2F 85
Arbor Dri. M19—2B 118
Arbor Gro. M28—5A 54
Arbor St. M35—2A 90
Arbory Av. M10—3B 76
Arbour Clo. BL9—5E 15
Arbour Rd. OL4—5A 66
Arbroath St. M11—4F 89
Arbury Av. OL11—6G 19
Arbury Av. SK3—4B 130
Arcade, The. SK5—4C 120
Arcade, The. SK5—5D 92
Arcadia Av. M33—2A 126
Archer Av. BL2—5E 25
Archer Gro. BL2—5E 25
Archer Pk. M24—1G 61
Archer St. M11—3C 88
Archer St. M34—4A 68
Archer St. OL5—1E 81
Archer St. SK2—6C 132
Arch St. BL1—4C 24
Arclid Clo. SK9—6A 152
Arcon Clo. OL16—5E 21
Arcon Dri. M16—4C 100
Arcon Pl. SK1—6B 120
Arcon Pl. WA14—5C 124
Ardale Av. M10—1C 76
Ardcombe Av. M9—4E 61
Ardeen Wlk. M13—1G 101
　　　　　　　& 5E 167
Arden Av. M24—4B 62
Arden Clo. BL9—5C 28
Arden Clo. OL6—5B 80
Arden Clo. SK8—6G 141
Arden Ct. SK7—4F 143
Ardenfield. M34—2G 121
Ardenfield Dri. M22—2C 140
Arden Gro. M10—2C 76
Arden Lodge Rd. M23—4D 126
Arden Rd. SK6—2E 121
Ardens Clo. M27—1D 70
Arden St. OL9—6G 63
Ardent Way. M25—2F 73
Arden Wlk. M33—4E 113
Arderne Rd. WA15—3A 126
Ardern Field St. SK1—4H 131
Ardern Rd. M8—1B 74
Ardern Wlk. SK1—2G 131

Ardingley Wlk. M23—3D 126
Ardmore Wlk. M22—3C 140
Ardwick Grn. N. M12—6G 87 & 3E 167
Ardwick Grn. S. M13—6G 87 & 3E 167
Ardwick Ter. M12—1H 101 & 6H 167
Argo St. BL3—3H 37
Argosy Dri. M30—6B 82
Argosy Dri. WA15—6F 139
Argus St. OL8—2A 78
Argyle Av. M14—3A 102
Argyle Av. M25—1E 59
Argyle Av. M28—4E 55
Argyle Cres. OL10—4D 30
Argyle Pde. OL10—4C 30
Argyle St. BL9—6F 15
Argyle St. M18—1F 103
Argyle St. M27—4E 71
Argyle St. M35—4A 90
Argyle St. OL1—1F 65
Argyle St. OL5—2E 81
Argyle St. OL10—4B 30
Argyle St. OL16—1G 33
Argyle St. SK7—3E 145
Argyll Av. M32—5B 98
Argyll Clo. M35—4H 77
Argyll Pk. Rd. M35—4H 77
Argyll Rd. OL9—6F 63
Argyll Rd. SK8—6B 130
Argyll St. OL6—2C 92
Arkholme. M28—3C 68
Arkholme Wlk. M10—4B 76
Arkley Wlk. M13—1F 101 & 5D 166
Ark St. M19—5C 102
Arkwright Dri. SK6—5E 135
Arkwright Rd. SK6—4E 135
Arkwright St. OL6—3A 64
Arkwright Way. M4—3E 87
  (off Arndale Cen.)
Arkwright Way. OL11—3G 33
Arlen Ct. BL2—2D 38
Arlen Rd. BL2—2D 38
Arlen Way. OL10—4D 30
Arley Av. BL9—5E 15
Arley Av. M20—4D 116
Arley Clo. WA14—3F 125
Arley Dri. M33—1A 126
Arley Dri. OL2—5G 35
Arley Gro. SK3—1F 143
Arley Ho. M7—4H 73
Arleymere Clo. SK8—2B 142
Arley Moss Wlk. M13—6F 87 & 4D 166
Arley St. M26—6H 41
Arley St. SK14—4A 106
Arley Way. M34—6G 105
Arlies Clo. SK15—1E 93
Arlies La. SK15—1E 93
Arlies St. OL6—1B 92
Arlington Av. M25—1G 73
Arlington Av. M27—5D 70
Arlington Av. M34—5G 105
Arlington Clo. BL9—1B 14
Arlington Cres. SK9—4B 158
Arlington Dri. SK2—2A 144
Arlington Dri. SK12—4D 154
Arlington Rd. M32—5B 98
Arlington Rd. SK8—1G 141
Arlington St. BL3—4B 38
Arlington St. M3—2B 86 & 2D 160
Arlington St. M8—3B 74
Arlington St. OL6—2A 92
Arlington Way. SK9—4B 158
Arliss Av. M19—1C 118
Armadale Av. M9—5A 62
Armadale Clo. SK3—6H 131
Armadale Ct. BL3—2C 36
Armadale Ct. OL10—4B 30
Armadale Rd. BL3—1C 36
Armadale Rd. SK6—5C 84
Armadale Rise. OL4—6A 50
Armentieres Sq. SK15—4E 93
Armhope Ter. SK3—3G 131
Armitage Av. M28—5B 54
Armitage Clo. M24—2F 61
Armitage Clo. OL16—1C 122
Armitage Gro. M28—5B 54
Armitage Ho. M6—2C 84
Armitage Owen Wlk. M10—4A 76
Armitage Pl. WA14—2F 137
Armitage Rd. WA14—2F 137

Armitage St. M30—4E 83
Armit Rd. OL3—5G 67
Armour Pl. M9—1E 75
Arm Rd. OL15—5C 8
Armstrong Hurst Clo. OL12—6H '
Arncliffe Clo. BL4—6F 39
Arncliffe Dri. M23—2G 139
Arncliffe Rise. OL4—3B 50
Arncot Rd. BL1—6D 10
Arncott Clo. OL2—3E 49
Arndale Cen. M24—1H 61
Arndale Shopping Cen. M4 & M2
        —3E 87 & 4A 162
Arndale Shopping Cen. M32—6C 98
Arne Clo. SK2—6G 133
Arnesby Av. M33—4E 115
Arnesby Gro. BL2—5D 24
Arne St. OL9—4G 63
Arnfield Dri. M28—5D 68
Arnfield Rd. M20—3F 117
Arnfield Rd. M34—6F 91
Arnfield Rd. SK3—6F 13'
Arnold Av OL10—6G 31
Arnold Av. SK14—2D 122
Arnold Clo. SK16—6E 93
Arnold Dri. M24—4C 46
Arnold Dri. M35—4A 90
Arnold Rd. BL7—3D 10
Arnold Rd. M16—6C 100
Arnold Rd. SK14—2D 122
Arnold St. BL1—3G 23
Arnold St. OL1—1E 65
Arnold St SK3—4G 131
Arnold Wlk. M34—2G 121
Arnott Cres. M15—2D 100
Arnside Av. OL9—3G 63
Arnside Av. SK4—3F 119
Arnside Av. SK7—3C 144
Arnside Clo. OL2—6H 35
Arnside Clo SK6—5C 146
Arnside Clo SK8—1F 14'
Arnside Dri. M6—2B 84
Arnside Dri. OL11—6A 18
Arnside Dri. SK14—3A 106
Arnside Gro. BL2—5G 25
Arnside Gro. M33—3B 114
Arnside St. M14—4F 10'
Arran Av. M32—5A 98
Arran Av. M33—6C 114
Arran Av. OL8—6D 64
Arran Clo. BL3—1C 36
Arrandale Ct. M31—4F 97
Arran Gdns. M31—2E 97
    (in three parts)
Arran Gro. M26—2E 41
Arran Rd. SK16—6A 92
Arran St. M7—5H 73
Arran St. M10—3H 75
Arran Wlk. OL10—4C 30
Arras Gro. M34—4H 103
Arreton Sq. M14—4H 101
Arrowfield Rd. M21—3B 116
Arrowhill Rd. M26—5F 27
Arrowscroft Way. SK14—2F 109
Arrowsmith Wlk. M11—4B 88
    (off Redfield Clo.)
Arrow St. BL1—5A 24
Arrow St. M7—6H 73
Arrow Trading Est. M34—2D 104
Arthington St OL16—3B 20
Arthog Dri. WA15—5H 137
Arthog Rd. M20—6G 117
Arthog Rd. WA15—5H 137
Arthur Av. M28—4E 55
Arthur La. BL2—2A 26
Arthur Pits. OL11—4B 18
Arthur Rd. M16—1D 100
Arthurs & Alice Kenyon Ind Est. OL4
        —3H 65
Arthurs La. OL3—3F 53
Arthur St. BL1—5A 24
Arthur St. BL3—4B 40
Arthur St. BL4—1F 55
Arthur St. BL8—3A 28
Arthur St. M27—4D 70
    'in two parts'

Arthur St. M28—1H 69
    (Walkden)
Arthur St. M28—2G 69
    (Worsley)
Arthur St. M30—4E 83
Arthur St. OL2—6E 35
Arthur St. OL10—3F 31
Arthur St. OL12—3F 19
Arthur St. SK5—2G 119
Arthur Ter. SK5—2G 119
Artillery Pl. M22—1D 140
Artillery St. BL3—2B 38
Artillery St. M3—5C 86 & 1F 165
Arundale Av. M16—6C 100
Arundale Clo. SK14—4B 108
Arundale Gro. SK14—4B 108
Arundel Av. M25—2F 59
Arundel Av. M31—6G 95
Arundel Av. OL11—1E 33
Arundel Av. SK7—5D 144
Arundel Clo. BL8—5C 14
Arundel Clo. SK15—5H 81
Arundel Clo. WA15—4C 138
Arundel Ct. M46—2D 40
Arundel Gro. SK2—1B 144
Arundel Rd. SK8—6C 142
Arundel St. BL1—6C 10
Arundel St. M15—6B 86 & 3D 164
Arundel St. M27—2C 70
Arundel St. OL4—2G 65
Arundel St. OL5—2D 80
Arundel St. OL6—3C 92
Arundel St. OL11—1E 33
Arundel Wlk. OL9—3G 63
Asby Clo. M24—5F 45
Ascension Rd. M7—1B 86
Ascot Av. M32—4F 99
Ascot Av. M33—6E 113
Ascot Clo. OL9—2A 64
Ascot Clo. OL11—3A 18
Ascot Ct. M33—6F 113
Ascot Dri. M31—5G 95
Ascot Dri. SK7—3G 145
Ascot Gro. SK2—4B 132
Ascot M. M7—5H 73
Ascot Pde. M19—3B 118
Ascot Rd. BL3—4H 39
Ascot Rd. M10—1D 88
Ascot Wlk. M6—6E 73
Ascroft Ct. OL1—3D 64
Ascroft St. OL1—3D 64
Asgard Dri. M5—5A 86 & 2B 164
Asgard Gro. M5—5A 86 & 2B 164
Ash Av. M30—4B 110
Ash Av. SK8—6A 130
Ash Av. WA14—6C 124
Ashawe Clo. M28—6A 54
Ashawe Gro. M28—6A 54
Ashawe Ter. M28—6A 54
Ashbank Av. BL3—1C 36
Ashbee St. BL1—2A 24
Ashberry Clo. SK9—1G 159
Ashborne Dri. BL9—1D 14
Ashbourne Av. BL2—1D 38
Ashbourne Av. M24—4C 46
Ashbourne Av. M31—5A 96
Ashbourne Av. SK8—5B 130
Ashbourne Clo. OL12—3B 8
Ashbourne Cres. M33—1D 126
Ashbourne Dri. OL6—5B 80
Ashbourne Dri. SK6—1C 156
Ashbourne Gro. M7—4A 74
Ashbourne Gro. M25—6B 42
Ashbourne Gro. M28—3G 69
Ashbourne Rd. M6—6A 72
Ashbourne Rd. M30—4G 83
Ashbourne Rd. M32—3A 98
Ashbourne Rd. M34—5F 105
Ashbourne Rd. SK7—5F 145
Ashbourne Sq. OL8—4C 64
Ashbourne St. OL11—2A 18
Ashbridge. M35—5H 77
Ashbrook Av. M34—4B 104
Ashbrook Clo. M25—1F 59
Ashbrook Clo. M34—4B 104
Ashbrook Clo. SK8—4F 141
Ashbrook Cres OL12 - 6A 8

Ashbrook Farm Clo. SK5—5H 103
Ashbrook Hey La. OL12—5A 8
Ashbrook La. SK5—5H 103
Ashbrook St. M11—6A 94
Ashburner St. BL1—1A 38
Ashburn Av. M19—4B 118
Ashburn Flats. OL10—3E 31
    (off School St.)
Ashburn Gro. SK4—6E 119
Ashburn Rd. SK4—6E 119
Ashburton Clo. SK14—5A 108
Ashburton Rd. SK3—1G 143
Ashburton Rd. E. M17—1B 98
Ashburton Rd. W. M31 & M17
        —6F 83
Ashbury Clo. BL3—2A 38
Ashbury Pl. M10—1A 88
Ashby Av. M19—5A 118
Ashby Clo. BL3—4E 39
Ashby Gro. M25—2F 59
Ash Clo. OL6—6H 79
Ash Clo. SK14—3C 108
Ashcombe Dri. BL2—1A 40
Ashcombe Dri. M26—2D 40
Ashcombe Wlk. M11—4B 88
    (off Aldershot Wlk.)
Ashcott Av. M22—1B 140
Ashcott Clo. BL6—2C 36
Ash Ct. SK6—4G 121
Ashcroft. OL12—5B 8
Ashcroft Av. M6—1E 85
Ashcroft Clo. SK9—4C 158
Ashcroft St. OL9—4G 63
Ashdale Dri. BL3—2C 36
Ashdale Clo. SK5—4H 119
Ashdale Cres. M35—4H 89
Ashdale Dri. M20—4H 117
Ashdale Dri. SK8—3F 141
Ashdene. OL6—3B 92
Ashdene. OL12—5D 6
Ashdene Clo. OL1—6A 48
Ashdene Cres. BL2—6H 11
Ashdene Rise. OL1—3H 49
Ashdene Rd. M20—3H 117
Ashdene Rd. SK4—1H 129
Ashdene Rd. SK9—4C 158
Ashdown Av. M9—5F 61
Ashdown Av. SK6—4A 122
Ashdown Dri. BL2—2E 25
Ashdown Dri. M27—5G 51
Ashdown Dri. M28—4C 68
Ashdown Gro. M9—5F 61
Ashdown Rd. SK4—6E 119
Ashdown Ter. M9—5F 61
Ashdown Way. M2—5C 34
Ash Dri. M27—2C 70
Ashenhurst Clo. M9—6C 60
Asher St. BL3—5G 37
Ashes Clo. SK15—5G 93
Ashes Dri. BL2—5H 25
Ashes La. OL4—3B 66
Ashes La. OL16—4E 21
Ashes La. SK15—5G 93
Ashfell Ct. M21—6F 99
Ash Field. M34—2G 105
Ashfield Av. OL11—6H 19
Ashfield Clo. M26—2E 85
Ashfield Cres. OL4—2B 66
Ashfield Cres. SK8—5H 129
Ashfield Dri. M10—1F 89
Ashfield Gro. BL1—5E 11
Ashfield Gro. M18—3H 103
Ashfield Gro. M30—3C 110
Ashfield Gro. SK3—1H 143
Ashfield Gro. SK6—2F 135
Ashfield Ho. OL11—6H 19
Ashfield La. OL16—1D 34
Ashfield Lodge. M20—1D 128
Ashfield Rd. M13—4A 102
Ashfield Rd. M31—5F 97
Ashfield Rd. M33—4B 114
Ashfield Rd. OL11—1E 33
Ashfield Rd. SK3—1H 143
Ashfield Rd. SK14—4H 109
Ashfield Rd. WA15—2G 137
Ashfield Sq. M35 - 3H 89

Ashfield St. M11—3B 88
Ashfield St. OL8—6A 64
Ashford. M33—5E 113
Ashford Av. M27—5C 70
Ashford Av. M28—5B 68
Ashford Av. M30—5E 83
Ashford Av. SK5—5H 103
Ashford Clo. BL2—1G 25
Ashford Clo. BL8—4H 27
Ashford Clo. SK9—3G 151
Ashford Grn. SK13-6G 109
    (off Ashford M.)
Ashford Gro. M28—3H 69
Ashford M. SK13—6G 109
Ashford Rd. M20—2E 117
Ashford Rd. SK4—3F 119
Ashford Rd. SK9—5D 158
Ashford St. OL10—3B 30
Ashford Wlk. BL1—4A 24
Ashford Wlk. OL9—3H 63
Ashgate Av. M22—1C 140
Ashgill Wlk. M9-4G 75
    (off Fernclough Rd.)
Ash Gro. BL0—6B 4
Ash Gro. BL1—5F 23
Ash Gro. BL2—2H 25
Ash Gro. BL8—6A 14
Ash Gro. BL9—4F 15
Ash Gro. M14—3A 102
Ash Gro. M25—3E 59
Ash Gro. M27—6D 70
Ash Gro. M28—2F 69
Ash Gro. M32—1C 114
Ash Gro. M35—5A 90
Ash Gro. OL2—1B 48
Ash Gro. OL4—2C 66
    (in two parts)
Ash Gro. OL15—0D 8
Ash Gro OL16—2E 35
    (Milnrow)
Ash Gro. OL16—4H 33
    (Rochdale)
Ash Gro. SK4—4F 119
Ash Gro. SK6—6C 134
Ash Gro. SK8—5F 141
Ash Gro. SK9—4G 151
Ash Gro. SK15—2D 92
Ash Gro. WA14—4E 137
Ash Gro. WA15—4H 125
Ash Hill Dri. OL5—3G 81
Ashill Wlk. M3—5C 86 & 1F 165
Ashington Clo. BL1—2F 23
Ashington Dri. BL8—4F 27
Ashkirk St. M18—2F 103
Ashlands. M33—4A 114
Ashlands Av. M10—2C 76
Ashlands Av. M27—5C 70
Ashlands Av. M28—4C 68
Ashlands Dri. M34—1E 105
Ashlands Rd. WA15—2A 126
Ash La. WA15—4C 138
Ashlar Dri. M12—5H 87 & 1H 167
Ashlea Dri. OL4—3D 66
Ashleigh Clo. OL2—5C 48
Ashleigh Dri. BL1—5C 22
Ashleigh Rd. WA15—3B 126
Ashley Av. BL2—5F 25
Ashley Av. M16—3B 100
Ashley Av. M27—5D 70
Ashley Av. M31—5A 96
Ashley Clo. OL11—1C 32
Ashley Ct. M27—1F 71
Ashley Ct. OL12—3H 7
Ashley Ct. WA15—4G 137
Ashley Ct. Dri. M10—2F 77
Ashley Cres. M27—4D 70
Ashley Dri. M33—1G 125
Ashley Dri. SK7—1E 153
Ashley Gdns. SK6—5B 146
Ashley Gro. BL4—1H 55
Ashley La. M9—3H 75
Ashley Mill La. N. WA14—5F 137
Ashley Rd. M35—3G 89
Ashley Rd. SK2—3C 132
Ashley Rd. SK9—6F 151
Ashley Rd WA14 & WA15—2F 137

Ashley St. M4—2F 87 & 2C 162
Ashley St. M6—3E 85
Ashley St. OL9—1A 64
Ashley Wlk. WA15—3G 137
Ash Lodge. SK12—3D 154
Ashlor St. BL9—4C 28
Ashlyn Gro. M14—1H 117
Ashmead. WA15—4B 138
Ashmill Wlk. M9—5E 75
Ashmond Rd. OL4—3B 66
Ashmont St. 13—1D 86
Ashmoor Rd. M22—4C 140
Ashmoor Wlk. M22—4C 140
Ashmore Av. SK3—4B 130
Ashmount Dri. OL12—1H 19
Ashness Dri. BL2—4G 25
Ashness Dri. M24—4F 45
Ashness Dri. SK7—5G 143
Ashness Gro. BL2—4G 25
Ashness Pl. BL2—4G 25
Ashop Wlk. M15—6C 86 & 4F 165
Ashover Clo. BL1—5D 10
Ashover Clo. M12—1B 102
Ashover St. M32—4E 99
Ashridge Clo. BL6—1A 36
Ashridge Dri. M30—5E 83
Ash Rd. BL4—4H 55
Ash Rd. M31—6B 110
Ash Rd. M34—4H 103
Ash Rd. M35—3H 89
Ash Rd. SK12—4F 155
Ash Sq. OL4—1H 65
Ashstead Rd. M33—2C 126
Ash St. BL2—1C 38
Ash St. BL9—3E 29
Ash St. M6—3F 85
Ash St. M9—4F 75
Ash St. M24—6C 46
Ash St. M34—6D 90
Ash St. M35—3E 77
Ash St. OL4—3F 65
Ash St. OL10—2D 30
Ash St. OL11—3C 32
Ash St. SK3—3D 130
Ash St. SK7—2D 144
Ashton Av. M14—5G 125
Ashton Ct. M33—5G 113
Ashton Ct. M34—1F 105
Ashton Cres. OL9—6G 63
Ashton Field Dri. M28—5E 55
Ashton Gdns. OL11—6G 19
Ashton Hill La. M35—5A 90
Ashton Ho. OL6—2H 91
Ashton La. M24—1B 62
Ashton La. M33—4G 113
Ashton New Rd. M11—4A 88
Ashton Old Rd. M12 & M11—5A 88
Ashton Rd. M9—4F 61
Ashton Rd. M31 & M33—6G 111
Ashton Rd. M34—2E 105
Ashton Rd. M35—4A 90
(Droylsden)
Ashton Rd. M35—5A 78
(Failsworth)
Ashton Rd. OL8—4C 64
Ashton Rd. SK6—4E 121
Ashton Rd. SK14—1B 106
Ashton Rd. E. M35—3F 77
Ashton Rd. W. M35—4E 77
Ashton's Pl. SK15—4D 92
Ashton St. BL3—3F 37
(Bolton)
Ashton St. BL3—4B 40
(Little Lever)
Ashton St. OL9—6G 63
Ashton St. OL10—3E 31
Ashton St. OL11—6G 19
Ashton St. SK6—3A 122
Ashton St. SK15—4D 92
Ashton St. SK16—1G 105
Ash Tree Av. M34—3H 89
Ash Tree Dri. SK16—6D 92
Ash Tree Gro. M34—2H 89
Ash Tree Rd. M8—2C 74
Ashtree Rd. SK14—2F 107
Ashurst Av. M11—3D 88
Ashurst Clo. BL2—2H 25

Ashurst Dri. SK3—6D 130
Ashurst Gdns. OL6—6F 79
Ashurst Rd. M22—1D 140
Ashville Ter. M10—2H 75
Ash Wlk. M24—3H 61
Ash Wlk. M33—4F 113
Ash Wlk. OL9—1H 63
Ash Wlk. WA14—3A 136
Ashwater Wlk. M9—4G 61
(off Brockford Dri.)
Ashway Clough N. SK2—6D 132
Ashway Clough S. SK2—6E 133
Ashwell Rd. M23—4H 127
Ashwell St. BL2—2D 24
Ashwin Wlk. M8—5B 74
Ashwood. OL9—2E 63
Ashwood. WA14—4D 136
Ashwood Av. BL0—2F 5
Ashwood Av. M20—5C 116
Ashwood Av. M28—4E 55
Ashwood Av. M33—6G 113
Ashwood Av. M34—4A 104
Ashwood Cres. SK6—4D 134
Ashwood Dri. BL8—5B 14
Ashwood Dri. OL2—2A 48
Ashwood Dri. OL15—4D 8
Ashwood Dri. SK12—1H 157
Ashworth Av. BL3—4C 40
Ashworth Av. M31—5A 96
Ashworth Av. M34—6E 91
Ashworth Clo. OL2—1F 49
Ashworth Clo. OL9—5H 63
Ashworth Clo. OL15—2E 9
Ashworth Clo. WA14—4D 136
Ashworth La. BL1—6D 10
Ashworth La. SK14—5B 108
Ashworth Rd. OL11—1C 16
Ashworth Rd. OL11 & OL10—4G 17
Ashworth St. BL4—1E 55
Ashworth St. BL8—2A 28
(in two parts)
Ashworth St. M34—3E 105
Ashworth St. M35—5D 76
Ashworth St. OL1—3D 64
Ashworth St. OL10—5F 31
Ashworth St. OL12—3F 19
Ashworth Ter. BL2—1G 25
Ashworth View. M5—6H 85
(off Ordsall Dri.)
Ashwy Clough S. SK2—6E 133
Asia St. BL4—3C 38
Askern Av. M22—2B 140
Askill Dri. M24—6F 45
Askrigg Wlk. M13—3B 102
Aspen Clo. SK4—2C 130
Aspen Clo. WA15—6E 127
Aspen Grn. M34—5G 105
Aspen Way. SK6—6E 147
Aspenwood Clo. SK6—4C 134
Aspenwood Dri. M33—5E 113
Aspenwood Dri. OL9—2E 63
Aspinall Clo. M28—6B 54
Aspinall Cres. M28—6B 54
Aspinall Gro. M28—6B 54
Aspinall St. M14—2C 62
Aspinall St. OL10—3G 31
Aspinal St. M14—4G 101
Aspin La. M4—2E 87 & 2A 162
Aspland Rd. SK14—1D 122
Aspley St. SK1—2H 131
Aspull Wlk. M13—6F 167
Asquith Rd. M19—3B 118
Asquith St. SK5—6H 103
Assheton Av. M34—4C 90
Assheton Clo. OL6—2H 91
Assheton Cres. M10—1F 89
Assheton Rd. M10—1F 89
Assheton Rd. OL2—6D 34
Assheton St. M24—5A 46
Assheton Way. M24—1A 62
Astan Av. M35—2F 89
Astbury Av. M21—5A 116
Astbury Av. M34—4D 90
Astbury Clo. WA15—5G 125
Astbury Cres. SK3—5F 131
Astbury St. M26—6H 41
Astbury Wlk. SK8—6C 130

Aster Av. BL4—6C 38
Aster St. OL1—6C 48
Aster Wlk. M31—6D 110
Astley Clo. OL2—6D 34
Astley Ct. M30—1C 110
Astley Gdns. SK16—5H 91
Astley Gro. SK15—2D 92
Astley La. BL1—2A 24
Astley M. SK16—4H 91
Astley Rd. BL2—6A 12
Astley Rd. M30—2A 94
Astley Rd. SK15—3D 92
Astley St. BL1—3A 24
Astley St. M11—4E 89
Astley St. SK4—2G 131
Astley St. SK14—3A 106
Astley St. SK15—5E 93
Astley St. SK16—6G 91
Astley Ter. SK16—4A 92
Aston Av. M14—5D 100
Aston Clo. SK3—5E 131
Aston Gdns. BL4—6F 39
Aston Way. SK9—2H 151
Astor Rd. M5—4B 84
Astor Rd. M19—2A 118
Astral M. M14—4H 101
Atcham Gro. M9—3D 60
Athens Dri. M28—1E 69
Athens St. SK1—2A 132
Atherfield. BL2—1G 25
Atherfield Clo. M18—1H 103
Atherley Gro. M10 & OL9—1F 77
Atherstone. OL12—3G 19
(off Spotland Rd.)
Atherstone Av. M8—1B 74
Atherstone Clo. BL8—1A 28
Atherton Av. SK14—3C 108
Atherton Gro. M30—4E 83
Atherton Gro. SK14—3C 108
Atherton La. M30—4C 110
Atherton St. M3—4C 86 & 6E 161
Atherton St. M30—4D 82
Atherton St. OL4—4A 66
(Lees)
Atherton St. OL4—3B 66
(Springhead)
Atherton St. SK3—3F 131
Atherton Way. M30—4D 82
Athlone Av. BL1—6A 10
Athlone Av. BL9—1D 28
Athlone Av. SK8—6E 131
Athol Ct. OL8—5D 64
Athole St. M5—4F 85
Atholl Av. M32—5A 98
Atholl Clo. BL3—1D 36
Atholl Dri. OL10—4C 30
Athol Rd. M16—6C 100
Athol Rd. SK7—2F 153
Athol St. M18—4G 103
Athol St. M30—4D 82
Athol St. OL6—2A 92
Athol St. OL12—2B 20
Athol St. SK4—6F 119
Athos Wlk. M10—1C 76
Athur La. BL2—2A 26
Atkinson Av. BL3—4D 38
Atkinson Rd. M31—5F 97
Atkinson Rd. M33—3A 114
Atkinson St. M3—4C 86 & 6F 161
Atkinson St. OL9—1B 64
Atkinson St. OL11—3C 32
Atkinson St. SK1—4A 132
Atkin St. M28—1F 69
Atlantic St. WA14—5C 124
Atlantic Wlk. M11—4B 88
(off Yeoman Wlk.)
Atlas Ho. BL1—5B 24
Atlas St. OL7—6E 79
Atlas St. OL8—3C 64
Atlas St. SK16—5B 92
Atlee Way. M12—4A 88
Atlow Dri. M23—6H 127
Attenburys La. WA14—3G 125
Attenbury's Pk. Est. WA14—3G 125
Attercliffe Rd. M21—2G 115
Attingham Wlk. M34—6E 105
Attleboro Rd. M10—4A 76
Attwood St. M12—4C 102

Atwood Rd. M20—6F 117
Atwood Rd. WA15—6B 126
Atworth Gdns. M7—4F 73
Auberson Rd. BL3—4H 37
Aubrey Rd. M20—2A 118
Aubrey St. M5—5G 85
Aubrey St. OL11—6H 19
Auburn Av. SK6—5F 121
Auburn Av. SK14—6C 106
Auburn Dri. M31—6G 97
Auburn Rd. M16—3H 99
Auburn Rd. M34—5D 104
Auburn St. BL3—3H 37
Auburn St. M1—4F 87 & 6C 162
Auckland Dri. M6—6E 73
Auckland Rd. M19—1B 118
Audax Wlk. M10—1D 88
Auden Clo. M11—4F 89
Audenshaw Hall Gro. M34—6B 90
Audenshaw Rd. M34—6B 90
Audlem Wlk. M10—3H 87
Audlem Wlk. SK8—6C 130
Audley Av. M32—3H 97
Audley Rd. M19—5D 102
Audley St. OL5—2F 81
(in two parts)
Audley St. OL6—3C 92
Audlum Ct. BL9—3E 29
Audrey Av. M18—2G 103
Audrey St. M9—3H 75
Augusta Clo. OL12—1G 19
Augusta St. OL12—1G 19
Augustine Clo. M15—3C 100
Augustus St. BL3—3C 38
Augustus St. M3—1E 87
Augustus Way. M15—3B 100
Austell Rd. M22—5B 140
Austen Av. BL9—1D 42
Austen Rd. M30—4F 83
Austen Wlk. OL1—3A 50
Auster Clo. M14—1E 117
Austin Dri. M20—5G 117
Austin Gro. M19—1B 118
Austin St. BL8—6E 15
Austonley Wlk. M15—6C 86 & 4F 165
Avalon Dri. M20—3G 129
Avebury Clo. M8—5B 74
Avebury Rd. M23—6G 127
Avenham Clo. M15—2C 100
Avening Wlk. M22—3A 140
Avens Rd. M31—6D 110
Avenue St. BL1—5H 23
Avenue St. SK1—1H 131
Avenue, The. BL2—6D 24
Avenue, The. BL9—6F 15
Avenue, The. M7—6G 73
Avenue, The. M30—4F 83
Avenue, The. M31—5A 96
Avenue, The. M33—6F 113
Avenue, The. OL2—1E 49
Avenue, The. SK6—5D 120
Avenue, The. SK8—4E 141
Avenue, The. SK9—5G 159
Avenue, The. SK14—3H 109
Avenue, The. WA15—5H 137
Averhill. M28—3D 68
Averill St. M10—6D 76
Aveson Av. M21—3H 115
Avian Clo. M30—6A 82
Avian Dri. M14—1F 117
Aviary Rd. M28—5H 69
Aviemore Wlk. M14—5E 89
Avis St. OL2—6F 35
Avocet Dri. M20—3E 95
Avocet Dri. WA14—3D 124
Avon Bank. SK6—6F 121
Avonbrook Dri. M10—1F 77
Avoncliffe Clo. BL1—2H 23
Avon Clo. M28—1C 68
Avon Clo. OL16—5G 21
Avon Clo. SK6—5C 134
Avon Ct. M15—1B 100 & 6C 164
Avoncourt Dri. M20—5E 117
Avondale. M27—1G 71
Avondale Av. BL9—1C 28
Avondale Av. SK7—3F 145
Avondale Ct. OL11—6D 32
Avondale Cres. M31—4E 97

Avondale Dri. BL0—1H 13
Avondale Dri. M6—6H 71
Avondale Lodge. M33—6B 114
Avondale Rd. BL4—1B 54
Avondale Rd. M25—6C 42
Avondale Rd. M32—3E 99
Avondale Rd. SK3—4D 130
Avondale Rd. SK7—2F 145
Avondale St. BL1—4G 23
Avondale St. M8—4C 74
Avon Dri. BL9—3F 15
Avon Flats. OL10—3E 31
 (off Kay St.)
Avon Gdns. M19—3C 118
Avonlea Dri. M19—3A 118
Avonlea Rd. M33—2F 125
Avonlea Rd. M35—3G 89
Avonmore Wlk. M9—6E 61
Avon Rd. BL4—4B 56
Avon Rd. M19—3B 118
Avon Rd. OL2—5F 35
Avon Rd. OL9—1F 63
Avon Rd. OL10—3C 30
Avon Rd. SK8—6G 141
Avon Rd. WA15—5G 137
Avon St. BL1—4F 23
Avon St. BL8—5D 64
Avon St. SK3—4G 131
Avril Clo. SK5—1H 119
Avro Clo. M16—6F 101
Avroe Rd. M30—6B 82
Avro Way. WA15—6F 139
Awburn Rd. SK14—6A 108
Axbridge Wlk. M10—3H 87 & 3H 163
Axford Clo. M8—5B 74
Axminster Wlk. SK7—6G 143
Axon Sq. M16—3D 100
Aycliffe Av. M21—4B 116
Aycliffe Gro. M13—4A 102
Aylesbury Av. M31—3G 97
Aylesbury Av. M34—6F 105
Aylesbury Clo. M5—4G 85
Aylesbury Gro. SC—4C 46
Aylesby Av. M18—3D 102
Aylesby Ct. M21—6B 100
Aylesford Rd. M14—4H 101
Aylesford Wlk. BL1—4A 24
Aylestone Rd. M10—4A 76
Aylsham Clo. SK6—4F 121
Aylsham M. M27—6D 70
Aylwin Dri. M33—6C 114
Ayr Av. OL8—6D 64
Ayr Clo. SK7—3G 145
Ayr Gro. OL10—4C 30
Ayrshire Rd. M7—5F 73
Ayr St. BL2—1E 25
Ayrton Gro. M28—3C 54
Aysgarth Av. M18—2G 103
Aysgarth Av. SK6—5B 122
Aysgarth Av. SK8—5G 129
Ayshford Clo. WA14—5D 124
Ayton Gro. M14—3A 102
Aytoun St. M1—4E 87 & 6B 162
Azalea Av. M18—1F 103

Babbacombe Gro. M9—4D 60
Babbacombe Rd. SK2—5C 132
Baber Wlk. BL1—1A 24
Bk. Acton St. M1—5F 87 & 1C 166
Bk. Albany St. OL11—6A 20
Bk. Albion Pl. BL9—1D 28
Bk. All Saints St. BL1-5B 24
 (off Bark St.)
Bk. Apple Ter. BL1—3H 23
Bk. Argyle St. BL9—6F 15
Bk. Ashley St. M4—2F 87 & 2C 162
Bk. Ashworth St. BL8—2A 28
Bk. Astley St. BL1—3A 24
Bk. Avondale St. BL1—4G 23
Bk. Baldwin St. N. BL3—2A 38
Bk. Balloon St. M4—3E 87 & 3A 162
Bk. Bank St. M8—1E 87
Bk. Belfast St. BL3—1A 24
Bk. Bennett's La. BL1—3G 23
Bk. Birch St. BL9—2D 28
 (in two parts)

Bk. Bolton Rd. S. BL8—3A 28
Bk. Bower La. SK14—1D 122
Bk. Bowness Rd. BL3—3H 37
Bk. Bradshaw St. OL16—3A 20
Bk. Bridge St. BL0—3E 5
Bk. Bridge St. M3—4D 86
Bk. Brierley Rd. BL9—5C 28
Bk. Brook St. N. BL9—1E 29
 (in two parts)
Bk. Broom St. BL2—6C 24
Bk. Burgess Ter. M12—6H 87 & 4G 167
Bk. Burnley Rd. BL9—3E 15
Bk. Burton St. M12—6G 87 & 3E 167
Bk. Bury Rd. S. BL2—6G 25
 (in two parts)
Bk. Byrom St. S. BL8—1H 27
Bk. Cambridge St. BL1—4A 24
Bk. Cambridge St. OL7—4F 91
Bk. Camp St. M7—6H 73
Bk. Canning St. BL9—1D 28
Bk. Cateaton St. BL9—1D 28
Bk. Chapel St. BL8—4H 13
Bk. Chapel St. M19—6C 102
Bk. Chapel St. M30—3H 83
Bk. Chapel St. OL12—2A 8
Bk. Chapel St. SK7—2E 145
Bk. Cheapside. BL1—6B 24
Bk. Chesham Rd. N. BL9-6G 15
 (off Chesham Rd.)
Bk. Chesham Rd. S. BL9—1E 29
Bk. China La. M1—4F 87 & 5C 162
Bk. Chorley Old Rd. S. BL1—4E 23
Bk. Church Rd. N. BL1—3F 23
Bk. Clay St. E. BL7—4E 11
Bk. Clifton St. BL9—1D 28
Bk. Cowm La. OL12—3G 7
Bk. Crostons Rd. BL8—2B 28
Bk. Dale St. OL16—6F 21
Bk. Darwen Rd. N. BL7—2C 10
Bk. Dashwood Rd. M25—4E 59
Bk. Deacon's Dri. M6—5B 72
Bk. Deane Chu. La. BL3—3F 37
Bk. Delamere St. S. BL9-6G 15
 (off Delamere St.)
Bk. Demesne St. SK15—3G 93
Bk. Denton St. BL9—1D 28
Bk. Devonshire Rd. BL1—4E 23
Bk. Devon St. N. BL9—5C 28
Bk. Devon St. S. BL9—5D 28
Bk. Deyne Av. M25—5F 59
Bk. Dumers La. M26—2C 42
Bk. Duncan St. M7—4G 73
Bk. East St. BL9—4D 28
Bk. Edenfield Rd. OL12—1G 17
Bk. Eden St. BL1—1A 24
Bk. Eldon St. BL9—1D 28
Bk. Elsworth St. M3—2E 87
Bk. Everton St. N. BL1—3B 24
Bk. Fairhaven Rd. BL1—2B 24
Bk. Fern St. E. BL3—1G 37
Bk. Fletcher St. M26—1B 56
Backford Wlk. M20—2E 117
Bk. Foundry St. M4—2E 87 & 1B 162
Bk. Garden St. M3—3C 86 & 4F 161
Bk. George St. M1—5E 87 & 1A 166
 (in two parts)
Bk. Georgiana St. BL9—3D 28
Bk. Gigg La. BL9—5D 28
Bk. Grafton St. WA14—1F 137
Bk. Grantham Clo. BL1—4A 24
Bk. Grosvenor St. BL9—5D 28
Bk. Hamel St. SK14—2D 106
Bk. Hamilton St. M7—4H 73
Bk. Hanover St. M4—3E 87 & 3A 162
Bk. Hanson St. BL9—1D 28
Bk. Harvey St. BL1—3H 23
Bk. Harvey St. BL8—2A 23
Bk. Haslam St. BL9—1E 29
Bk. Hatfield Rd. BL1—4G 23
Bk. Heywood St. BL9—4E 29
Bk. Higher Swan La. W. BL3—4H 37
Bk. Hilton St. BL9—5D 28
Bk. Hilton St. M7—4H 73
Bk. Holland St. BL1—1B 24
Bk. Hope St. M7—4H 73
Bk. Hope St. OL1—2F 65
Bk. Hornby St. BL9—1D 28
Bk. Horne St. N. BL9—5C 28

Bk. Horne St. S. BL9—5C 28
Bk. Hotel St. BL1—6B 24
Bk. Howe St. M7—4G 73
Bk. Hulme St. M5—4A 86 & 5B 160
Bk. Hulton La. S. BL3—5E 37
Bk. Huntley Mt. Rd. BL9—1F 29
Bk. Ingham St. BL9—4E 29
Bk. Ivanhoe St. BL3—5E 39
Bk. Ivy Bank Rd. BL1—6C 10
Bk. Ivy Rd. BL1—4G 23
Bk. James St. BL3—4B 40
Bk. James St. OL15—4D 8
Bk. Johnson St. M4—2E 87 & 1A 162
Bk. John St. BL3—1A 38
Bk. Kingholm Gdns. BL1—4H 23
Bk. King St. BL1—1C 64
Bk. Knowl St. SK15—3F 93
Bk. La. BL1—5A 24
Back La. M7—6G 73
Back La. OL4 & OL6—6C 66
 (Oldham)
Back La. OL4—6E 51
 (Scouthead)
Back La. OL7—1D 90
 (in two parts)
Back La. OL12—1A 18
 (Rochdale)
Back La. OL12—3G 7
 (Whitworth)
Back La. SK14—4C 108
Back La. WA14—6A 124
Back La. WA15—2A 148
Bk. Lathom St. BL9-1E 29
 (off Lathom St.)
Bk. Lee St. OL3—1F 53
Bk. Lever St. BL3—3A 38
Bk. Lightburne Av. BL1—6F 23
Bk. Linton Av. BL9—6F 15
Bk. Louise St. OL12—6H 7
Bk. Lucas St. BL9—2E 29
Bk. Lydia St. BL2—6C 24
Bk. Manchester Old Rd. BL9—4C 28
Bk. Manchester Rd. E. BL9-5C 28
 (off Parkhills Rd.)
Bk. Manchester Rd. W. BL9—2D 42
 (Blackford Bridge)
Bk. Manchester Rd. W. BL9—5C 28
 (Bury)
Bk. Manor St. BL9—3E 29
Bk. Market St. M26—1B 56
Bk. Markland Hill La. BL1—4D 22
Bk. Markland Hill La. W. BL1—4D 22
Bk. Maskill St. N. BL9—1D 28
Bk. Massie St. SK8—5H 129
Bk. Mawdsley St. BL1—6B 24
Bk. Maxwell St. BL1—1A 24
Bk. Melbourne St. SK15—3E 93
Bk. Mere Gdns. BL1—5A 24
Bk. Merton St. BL8—2B 28
Bk. Milner Av. BL9—6F 15
Bk. Mirey La. BL6—3A 36
Bk. Monmouth St. BL9—6F 15
Bk. Nelson St. N. BL9—5D 28
Bk. Nelson St. S. BL9—5D 28
Bk. New George St. BL8—2A 28
Bk. New St. M35—5A 90
Bk. Newton St. BL1—3A 24
Bk. Nook Ter. OL12—6F 7
Bk. Oldham Rd. OL16—5A 20
Bk. Olga St. BL1—3H 23
Bk. Olive Bank. BL8—1H 27
Back o' th' Low Rd. OL4—6B 50
Back o' th' Moss La. OL10—2E 31
 (in two parts)
Bk. Parkfield View. OL16—3H 33
Bk. Parkhills Rd. BL9—4E 29
Bk. Parkhills Rd. N. BL9—5D 28
Bk. Parkhills Rd. S. BL9—5C 28
Bk. Patience St. OL12—2G 7
Bk. Piccadilly. M4 & M1—4E 87 &
 5B 162
Bk. Pine St. OL16-2F 35
 (off Pine St.)
Bk. Platting La. OL12—1G 33
Bk. Pool Fold. M2—4D 86 & 5H 161
Bk. Porter St. BL9—1D 28
Bk. Portland St. OL6—3G 91
Bk. Prestbury Clo. BL9—4E 29

Bk. Quay St. M3—4C 86
Bk. Queen St. BL9—3E 29
Bk. Quickwood. OL5—1F 81
Bk. Rake St. BL9—1D 28
Bk. Ramsden Rd. OL12—2A 8
Bk. Red Bank. M4—2E 87 & 1B 162
Bk. Rigby La. N. BL2—5G 11
Bk. Roman Rd. M7—5A 74
Bk. Rooley Moor Rd. OL12—2E 19
Bk. Rossini St. BL1—2H 23
Bk. Rowena St. BL3—5E 39
Bk. Royds St. OL16—6A 20
Bk. St Anne's St. BL9—1D 28
Bk. St George's Rd. BL1—5A 24
Bk. St George's Rd. M4—2F 87 & 2D 162
Bk. St James St. OL1—2F 65
Bk. Salford St. BL9—1F 29
Bk. Sapling Rd. S. BL3—5F 37
Bk. School St. BL9—4F 29
Bk. Scott St. OL8—4D 64
Bk. Settle St. N. BL3—4H 37
Bk. Shepard St. BL9—3E 29
Bk. Shipton St. BL1—1F 23
Bk. Somerset Rd. W. BL1—5F 23
Bk. South Pde. M3—4C 86
Bk. Spear St. M1—3F 87 & 4C 162
Bk. Spring Gdns. BL1—1B 38
Bk. Spring St. W. BL9—4D 28
Bk. Square St. BL0—3E 5
Bk. Stanley St. BL0—4D 4
Back St. M25—4D 58
Bk. Thomasson Clo. BL1—4A 24
Bk. Thomas St. M4—3E 87 & 4B 162
Bk. Thorns Rd. BL1—2A 24
Bk. Tonge Moor Rd. E. BL2—2D 24
Bk. Tootal Rd. M5—3D 84
Bk. Tottington Rd. BL8-1H 27
 (off Sawyer St.)
Bk. Tottington Rd. BL8—1A 28
Bk. Tottington Rd. N. BL8—1A 28
Bk. Turner St. M4—3E 87 & 4B 162
Bk. Union Rd. OL12—5C 8
Bk. Vernon St. BL1—5A 24
Bk. Vernon St. BL9—1D 28
Bk. Walmersley Rd. E. BL9—5F 15
 (in three parts)
Bk. Walmersley Rd. W. BL9—4F 15
 (in five parts)
Bk. Walshaw Rd. N. BL8—2A 28
Bk. Walshaw Rd. S. BL8—2A 28
Bk. Wellington Rd. S. BL9-5C 28
 (off Wellington Rd.)
Backwell Wlk. M4-3G 87
 (off Marsworth Dri.)
Bk. Whitegate. OL15—5C 8
Bk. Wigan Rd. N. BL3—3E 37
 (in two parts)
Bk. Willows La. BL3—3G 37
Bk. Woking Gdns. BL1—4A 24
Bk. Young St. BL4—2G 55
Bacon Av. M34—2G 121
Bacup St. M10—3A 76
Badby Clo. M4—4H 87 & 5H 163
Baddeley Clo. SK3—6F 131
Badder St. BL1—5B 24
Baden St. M11—5A 88
Bader Dri. OL10—6F 31
Badger Edge La. OL4—4E 51
Badger La. OL16—3H 33
 (in three parts)
Badgers Wlk. M22—4C 140
Badminton Rd. M21—6A 100
Bagnall Clo. OL3—6C 52
Bagnall Clo. OL12—1B 18
Bagnall Ct. M22—2C 128
Bagnall Wlk. M22—2C 128
Bagot St. BL4—3A 56
Bagot St. M11—3E 89
Bagot St. M27—2C 70
Bagshaw St. SK14—2C 106
Bagslate Moor La. OL11—3B 18
Bagslate Moor Rd. OL11—4B 18
Bagstock Av. SK12—5E 155
Baguley Cres. M24—2C 60
Baguley Cres. SK3—5F 131
Baguley Dri. BL9—5E 43

Baguley La M33— 1E 127
(in three parts)
Baguley Rd. M33—5E 115
Baguley St. M35—4B 90
Baildon Rd. OL12—2D 18
Baildon St. M10—2A 76
Bailey La. BL2—4G 25
(in two parts)
Bailey La. M22—4H 139
Bailey La. M31—6D 110
Bailey Rd. M17—6A 84
Bailey St. M11—4F 89
Bailey St. M25—4G 59
Bailey St. OL1—2E 65
Bailey Wlk. WA14—4E 137
Baillie St. OL16—4H 19
(in four parts)
Baillie St. E. OL16—3A 20
Bainbridge Clo. M12—1H 101 & 6H 167
Baines Av. M30—1D 110
Baines St. BL1—5F 23
Bain St. M27—4F 71
Bainton Wlk. M9—4E 61
Baird St. M1—5F 87 & 1D 166
Baitings Row. OL12—1G 17
Baker Ho. OL2—3C 48
(off Royton Hall Wlk.)
Baker St. BL0—4D 4
Baker St. BL4—3B 56
Baker St. M24—6B 46
Baker St. OL7—5E 79
Baker St. OL10—5G 31
Baker St. SK4—6G 119
Baker St. SK15—4F 93
Baker St. WA15—4C 126
Baker Ter. M34—3B 104
Bakewell Av. M34—1G 121
Bakewell Av. OL6—5B 80
Bakewell Bank. SK13—6F 109
(off Bakewell Gdns.)
Bakewell Clo. SK13—6F 109
(off Bakewell M.)
Bakewell Fold. SK13—6F 109
(off Bakewell M.)
Bakewell Gdns. SK13—6F 109
(off Bakewell Gdns.)
Bakewell Grn. SK13—6F 109
(off Bakewell Gdns.)
Bakewell Gro. SK13—6F 109
(off Bakewell M.)
Bakewell Lea. SK13—6F 109
(off Bakewell M.)
Bakewell M. SK13—6F 109
Bakewell Rd. M30—5E 83
Bakewell Rd. M32—4A 98
Bakewell Rd. M35—3G 89
Bakewell Rd. SK7—5E 145
Bakewell St. M18—3E 103
Bakewell St. SK3—3F 131
Bakewell Wlk. SK13—6F 109
(off Bakewell M.)
Balcary Gro. BL1—5F 23
Balcombe Clo. BL8—4C 14
Balderstone Rd. OL11—3F 33
Baldock Rd. M20—6H 117
Baldwin Rd. M19—3B 118
Baldwin St. BL3—2H 37
Bale St. M2—5D 86 & 1H 165
Balfour Gro. SK5—6H 103
Balfour Rd. M31—4D 96
Balfour Rd. OL12—2E 19
Balfour Rd. WA14—4F 125
Balfour St. BL3—1H 37
Balfour St. M6—5E 73
Balfour St. M8—3C 74
Balfour St. OL2—6F 35
Balfour St. OL4—2G 65
Balham Wlk. M12—1B 102
Ballantine St. M10—1E 89
Ballard Clo. OL15—2F 9
Ballater Av. M31—6C 96
Ballater Clo. OL10—4D 30
Ballater Wlk. M8—4B 74
Ballbrook Av. M20—4E 117
Ballbrook Ct. M20—5F 117
Balleratt St. M19—6C 102
Balliol Clo. SK6—5A 122
Balliol St. M8—3C 74
Balliol St. M27—3E 71
Balloon St. M4— 3E 87 & 3A 162

Ball St. OL16—3A 20
Ballygreen. OL11—2C 32
Baimain Av. M18—4E 103
Balmain Rd. M31—4D 96
Balmer Dri. M23—1H 139
Balmfield St. M8—5C 74
Balmforth St. M15—6B 86 & 3D 164
Balmoral Av. BL3—4A 40
Balmoral Av. M25—2E 59
Balmoral Av. M31—6D 96
Balmoral Av. M32—4D 98
Balmoral Av. M34—6D 90
Balmoral Av. OL2—3D 48
Balmoral Av. OL11—3D 18
Balmoral Av. SK8—3C 142
Balmoral Av. SK14—1C 122
Balmoral Clo. BL8—2A 14
Balmoral Clo. BL9—2E 43
Balmoral Clo. OL16—5G 21
Balmoral Ct. M9—4B 60
Balmoral Dri. M34—3A 104
Balmoral Dri. OL10—4C 30
Balmoral Dri. SK6—6C 146
Balmoral Dri. SK12—4D 154
Balmoral Dri. SK15—2E 93
Balmoral Dri. WA14—3H 125
Balmoral Grange. M25—6A 60
Balmoral Gro. SK7—2F 145
Balmoral Ho. M30—3E 83
(off Police St.)
Balmoral Rd. BL4—2E 55
Balmoral Rd. M14—1H 117
Balmoral Rd. M27—1G 71
Balmoral Rd. M31—6C 96
Balmoral Rd. SK4—6C 118
Balmoral Rd. WA15—1G 137
Balmoral Rd. M18—3E 103
Balmoral Way. SK9—3D 158
Balmore Ct. OL10—4A 30
Balm St. BL0—5C 4
(in two parts)
Balsam Clo. M13—6G 87 & 4E 167
Balshaw Av. M30—5D 94
Balshaw Clo. BL3—2G 37
Balshaw Ct. M30—5E 95
Baltic St. M5—3E 85
Baltimore St. M10—6H 75
Bamber Av. M33—6E 115
Bamburgh Clo. M26—2C 40
Bamburgh Dri. OL7—6C 78
Bambury St. BL9—2D 28
Bamford Av. M24—5A 46
Bamford Av. M34—1F 121
Bamford Clo. BL9—1A 30
Bamford Clo. SK8—5H 141
Bamford Ct. OL11—5D 18
(off Half Acre M.)
Bamford Fold. SK13—6G 109
(off Castleton Cres.)
Bamford Gdns. WA15—5D 126
Bamford Grn. SK13—6G 109
(off Castleton Cres.)
Bamford Gro. M20—6E 117
Bamford Gro. OL6—5B 80
Bamford La. SK13—6G 109
Bamford M. SK13—6G 109
Bamford Pl. OL12—2G 19
Bamford Rd. BL0—1G 5
Bamford Rd. M9—4F 61
Bamford Rd. M20—6E 117
Bamford Rd. OL10—1E 31
Bamfords Pas. OL15—3E 9
Bamford St. M11—3D 88
Bamford St. OL2—3C 48
Bamford St. OL9—1A 64
Bamford St. OL15—3D 8
(Caldermoor)
Bamford St. OL15—4D 8
(Stubley)
Bamford St. SK1—3H 131
Bamford Way. OL11—5B 18
Bampton Clo. SK2—4B 132
Bampton Rd. M22—4B 140
Bampton Wlk. M24—5G 45
Banbury Dri. WA14—3G 125
Banbury M. M27—2D 70
Banbury Rd. M23—6F 127
Banbury Rd M24—4H 61

Banbury St. BL2—4E 25
Banbury St. SK1—2H 131
Bancroft Av. SK8—4C 142
Bancroft Clo. SK6—6E 121
Bancroft Ct. WA15—2H 137
Bancroft Fold. SK14—2F 107
Bancroft Rd. M27—2E 71
Bancroft Rd. WA15—2A 138
Banff Gro. OL10—4C 30
Bangor Ho. BL1—4A 2
Bangor Rd. SK8—5B 130
Bangor St. BL1—5A 24
Bangor St. BL6—3C 92
Bangor St. OL16—5B 20
Bangor St. SK5—5H 119
Banham St. M9—2F 75
Bank. OL12—2A 8
Bank Barn La. OL12—2B 8
Bankbottom. SK14—2H 109
Bank Bri. M11—2D 88
Bank Clo. OL15—6E 9
Banker St. BL3—2E 39
Bankfield Av. M13—4A 102
Bankfield Av. M30—4B 110
Bankfield Av. M35—3A 90
Bankfield Av. SK4—1E 131
Bankfield Clo. BL2—4C 26
Bankfield Cotts. OL3—5H 51
Bankfield Cotts. SK14—4G 123
Bankfield Dri. M28—4D 68
Bankfield Dri. OL8—1F 79
Bankfield Ho. SK6—4H 121
Bankfield La. OL11—3A 18
Bankfield M. BL9—6D 28
Bankfield Rd. M29—3A 68
Bankfield Rd. SK6—4H 121
Bankfield Rd. SK8—4B 142
Bankfield St. BL3—2G 37
(in two parts)
Bankfield St. M9—2F 75
Bank Field St. M26—2D 56
Bank Field St. SK5—5G 119
Bankfield Trading Est. SK5
                        —5G 119
Bank Gro. M28—3B 54
Bankhall La. WA15—5G 137
Bankhall Rd. SK4—6C 118
Bankhall Wlk. M9—4G 75
(off Broadwell Dri.)
Bank Hill St. OL4—2G 65
Bankhouse Rd. BL8—6C 14
Bank Ho. Rd. M9—5D 60
Banklands Clo. M30—4G 93
Bank La. M6 & M27—6B 72
Bank La. M28—3B 54
Bank La. OL3—5H 53
Bank La. OL12—2B 8
Bankley St. M19—6C 102
Bankmill Clo. M13—6F 87 & 4D 166
Bank Pl. BL8—2A 28
Bank Rd. M8—1C 74
Bank Rd. SK6—6G 121
Bank St. SK15—6G 81
Banks St. WA15—6D 126
Bank Side. OL5—3A 80
Bankside. SK14—6H 107
Bankside. WA15—1D 148
Bankside Av. M26—3B 42
Bankside Av. OL3—2G 53
Bankside Clo. SK6—2F 135
Bankside Clo. SK9—6H 151
Bankside Ct. SK4—1C 130
Bankside Rd. M20—4F 129
Bankside Wlk. SK14—5H 107
Banks La. SK1—3B 132
Bank Sq. SK9—2E 159
Bank St. BL1—6B 24
Bank St. BL4—1F 55
Bank St. BL8—1F 27
Bank St. BL9—3C 28
Bank St. M3—3B 86 & 4C 160
Bank St. M8—3B 74
Bank St. M11—3D 88
(in two parts)

Bank St. M25—6C 42
Bank St. M26—5H 41
Bank St. M33—4C 114
Bank St. M34—1F 105
(Audenshaw)
Bank St. M34—1G 121
(Denton)
Bank St. M35—5H 89
Bank St. OL2—6E 35
Bank St. OL4—3H 85
Bank St. OL5—3E 81
Bank St. OL7—3H 91
Bank St. OL10—3D 30
(in two parts)
Bank St. SK6—4H 121
Bank St. SK8—5A 130
Bank St. SK14—6C 108
(Broadbottom)
Bank St. SK14—2H 109
(Hadfield)
Bank St. SK14—4B 106
(Hyde)
Bank St. WA3—4A 110
Bankswood Clo. SK14—3H 109
Bank Ter. OL10—1C 6
Bank Ter. SK14—2H 109
Bank, The. OL16—4H 19
Bank Top. BL9—2F 15
Bank Top. OL6—3A 92
Bank Top Gro. BL1—6E 11
Bank Top Pk. OL4—3H 65
Bank Top St. OL10—2D 30
Bank View. BL2—2G 55
Bankwell Clo. M15—2C 100
Bank Wood. BL1—6D 22
Banky La. M33—3E 113
Bannatyne Clo. M10—2E 77
Bannerdale Clo. M13—2B 102
Bannerman Av. M25—6F 59
Bannerman Rd. M35—6B 90
Bannerman Sq. M16—3D 100
Bannerman St. M7—4A 74
Banner Wlk. M11—4B 88
Bannister Dri. SK8—3B 142
Bannister St. BL2—5C 26
Bannister St. SK1—4H 131
Bann St. SK3—3G 131
Banstead Av. M22—4B 128
Bantock St. M4—4G 101
Bantry Dri. M9—6D 60
Bantry St. BL3—2A 38
Bantry St. OL12—1A 20
Baptist St. M4—2F 87 & 2C 162
Barathea Clo. OL11—2A 32
Barbara Rd. BL3—5E 37
Barbara St. BL3—3H 37
Barbeck Clo. M10—2A 88
Barberry Clo. WA14—4D 124
Barberry Wlk. M31—6D 110
Barbican St. M20—2F 117
Barbirolli Mall. M4—3E 87
(off Arndale Cen.)
Barbirolli Sq. M4—3E 87
(off Arndale Cen.)
Barbon Wlk. M4—3G 87 & 4E 163
Barchester Av. BL2—4G 25
Barcheston Rd. SK8—1G 141
Barcicroft Rd. M19 & SK4—5A 118
Barcicroft Wlk. M19—5A 118
Barclay Dri. M30—2G 83
Barclay Rd. SK12—5E 155
Barclays Av. M6—5B 72
Barcliffe Av. M10—1C 76
Barclyde St. OL11—6G 19
Barcombe Clo. OL4—5H 49
Barcombe Wlk. M9—4F 75
(in two parts)
Barcroft Rd. BL1—3F 23
Barcroft St. BL9—2D 28
Bardell Cres. SK12—5D 154
Bardon Clo. BL1—4H 23
Bardon Rd. M23—5F 127
Bardsea Av. M22—4B 140
Bardsley Av. M35—4F 77
Bardsley Clo. BL2—6H 11
Bardsley Clo. SK14—5A 108
Bardsley Ga. Av. SK15— 1A 108

Bardsley St. M10—6D 76
Bardsley St. M24—6A 46
Bardsley St. OL4—4A 66 (Lees)
Bardsley St. OL4—6A 50 (Oldham)
Bardsley St. OL9—6F 63
Bardsley St. SK4—6F 119
Bardsley Vale Av. OL8—3E 79
Barehill St. OL15—3F 9
Bare St. BL1—6A 24
Barff Rd. M5—3C 84
Barfold Clo. SK2—6G 133
Barfold Wlk. M15—1C 100 & 5E 165
Barford Wlk. M23—1H 139
Bar Gap Rd. OL1—1D 64
Baric Clo. M30—4H 83
Baring St. M1—5F 87 & 2D 166
Barker Rd. SK6—6F 121
Barkers La. M33—4H 113
Barker St. BL4—2C 28
Barker St. M3—1D 86 & 1G 161
Barker St. OL4—4D 30
Barke St. OL15—6C 8
Barking St. M10—2A 88
Bark St. BL1—6A 24 (in two parts)
Bark Wlk. M15—1D 100 & 5H 165
Barkway Rd. M32—5A 98
Barkwell La. OL5—2D 80
Barkworth Wlk. M10—5B 76
Bar La. BL1—6C 10
Barlby Wlk. M10—5B 76
Barlea Av. M10—2D 76
Barley Brook Meadow. BL1—5D 10
Barleycorn Clo. M33—6F 115
Barley Ct. SK14—3H 109
Barley Croft. SK8—5B 142
Barleycroft Clo. M16—3D 100
Barley Croft Rd. SK14—1C 106
Barley Dri. SK7—6G 143
Barleyfield Wlk. M24—6H 45
Barley Hall St. OL10—2G 31
Barleywood Wlk. SK15—6H 93
Barlow Cres. SK6—6D 134
Barlow Fold. BL9—2D 42
Barlow Fold. SK5—1H 119
Barlow Fold. SK6—6B 122
Barlow Fold Clo. BL9—2D 42
Barlow Fold Rd. SK5—1H 119
Barlow Fold Rd. SK6—6B 122
Barlow Hall Rd. M21—4A 116
Barlow Ho. OL8—4D 64
Barlow La. M30—3E 83
Barlow La. N. SK5—1H 119
Barlow Moor Clo. OL12—1A 18
Barlow Moor Ct. M20—5D 116
Barlow Moor Rd. M21—5H 99
Barlow Moor Rd. M21 & M20 —1H 115
Barlow Pk. Av. BL1—6B 10
Barlow Rd. M19—6C 102
Barlow Rd. M32—3F 99
Barlow Rd. SK9—6F 151
Barlow Rd. SK16—5B 92
Barlow Rd. WA14—3D 124
Barlow's Croft. M3—3C 86 & 4F 161
Barlow's La. S. SK7—2C 144
Barlows Rd. M5—4A 86 & 6A 160
Barlow St. BL1—6C 24
Barlow St. BL9—2D 28
Barlow St. M26—4H 41
Barlow St. M28—5F 55
Barlow St. M30—4F 83
Barlow St. OL4—3E 65
Barlow St. OL10—5G 31
Barlow St. OL16—4A 20
Barlow Ter. M21—4B 116
Barlow Wlk. SK5—1H 119
Barlow Wood Dri. SK6—2F 147
Barmeadow. OL3—5H 51
Barmhouse Clo. SK14—4E 107
Barmouth St. M11—5B 88
Barmouth Wlk. OL8—1H 77
Barnaby Rd. SK12—5D 154
Barnacre Av. BL2—6H 25
Barnacre Av. M23—2F 139
Barnard Av. M25—2F 59

Barnard Av. SK4—1D 130
Barnard Clo. OL7—6D 78
Barnard Rd. M18—4D 102
Barnard St. BL2—5E 25
Barnbrook St. M28—2E 29
Barnby St. M12—4C 102
Barn Clo. M31—5G 95
Barnclose Rd. M22—4B 140
Barncroft Clo. SK6—6E 121
Barncroft Gdns. M22—6A 128
Barncroft Rd. BL4—1F 55
Barndale Clo. BL2—5C 26
Barnes Av. SK4—1C 130
Barnes Clo. BL0—6C 4
Barnes Clo. BL4—1G 55
Barnes Meadow. OL15—6G 9
Barnes St. BL4—6D 38
Barnes St. OL4—1A 66
Barnet Rd. BL1—3G 23
Barnett Av. M20—3F 117
Barnett Ct. OL10—3E 31
Barnett Dri. M3—3B 86 & 3D 160
Barnfield. M31—6D 96
Barnfield. OL15—3H 9
Barnfield Av. SK6—6B 122
Barnfield Clo. BL7—1C 10
Barnfield Clo. M5—4F 85
Barnfield Cres. M33—3H 113
Barnfield Dri. M28—5D 68
Barnfield Rise. OL2—4E 35
Barnfield Rd. M19—5A 118
Barnfield Rd. M27—1D 70
Barnfield Rd. SK14—2E 107
Barnfield Rd. E. SK3—1F 143
Barnfield Rd. W. SK3—1F 143
Barnfield St. M34—3D 104
Barnfield St. OL10—3G 31
Barnfield St. OL12—1H 19
Barnfield Wlk. WA15—6C 126 (in two parts)
Barn Fold. OL4—4A 66
Barngate Dri. OL5—3E 81
Barngate Rd. SK8—5E 129
Barn Gro. M34—6E 91
Barnham Wlk. M23—3E 127
Barnhill Av. M25—1F 73
Barnhill Dri. M25—1F 73
Barnhill Rd. M25—6E 59
Barnhill St. M14—3D 100
Barnley Clo. M30—4F 95
Barnsdale Dri. M8—5C 74
Barnsfold Av. M14—1G 117
Barnsfold Rd. SK6—2D 146
Barnside. OL12—1C 6
Barnside Av. M28—1G 69
Barnside Clo. BL9—3E 15
Barnside Way. M35—4A 78
Barnsley St. SK1—3A 132
Barns Pl. WA15—5C 138
Barnstaple Dri. M10—5E 75
Barnstead Av. M20—4H 117
Barnston Av. M14—5F 101
Barnston Clo. BL1—1B 24
Barn St. BL1—6A 24
Barn St. M25—2D 58
Barn St. OL1—3C 64
Barn St. SK1—6H 119
Barnswell St. M10—6C 76
Barn Wlk. M11—6G 89
Barnway Wlk. M10—1C 76
Barnwell Clo. M34—2E 105
Barnwood Clo. BL1—4A 24 (off Barnwood Dri.)
Barnwood Dri. BL1—4A 24
Barnwood Rd. M23—2G 139
Barnwood Ter. BL1—4A 24 (off Barnwood Dri.)
Baroness Gro. M7—1A 86
Baron Fold. M28—4C 54
Baron Fold Cres. M28—4B 54
Baron Fold Gro. M28—4B 54
Baron Fold Rd. M28—4B 54
Baron Grn. SK8—6H 141
Barons Ct. M35—5D 76
Baron St. BL9—4B 28 (in two parts)

Baron St. OL4—4F 65
Baron St. OL16—4H 19
Baron St. SK14—2D 122
Baron Wlk. BL3—4C 40
Barrack Hill. SK6—1G 133
Barrack Hill Clo. SK6—6G 121
Barracks La. M33—3F 113
Barrack St. BL3—1A 38
Barrack St. M15—6B 86 & 4C 164
Barra Dri. M17—2F 97
Barrass St. M11—6F 89
Barratt Gdns. M24—3F 45
Barrett Av. BL4—2H 55
Barrett St. BL9—3E 29
Barrett St. OL4—4F 65
Barrfield Rd. M6—1E 85
Barr Hill Av. M6—6C 72
Barrie Way. BL1—1D 24
Barrington Av. M35—4H 89
Barrington Av. SK8—4C 142
Barrington Clo. WA14—5F 125
Barrington Rd. WA14—5F 125
Barrington St. M11—3E 89
Barrisdale Clo. BL3—2D 36
Barrow Bri. Rd. BL1—1D 22
Barrow Brook. M33—3F 115
Barrowfield Rd. M22—3G 139
Barrowfields. M24—5A 46
Barrow Hill Rd. M8—6B 74
Barrow La. WA15—6B 138
Barrow Meadow. SK8—5A 142
Barrows Ct. BL1—1B 38
Barrow St. M3—4B 86 & 5C 160
Barr St. BL4—4B 56
Barrule Av. SK7—4E 145
Barry Ct. M20—3F 117
Barry Cres. M28—6C 54
Barrygate Clo. M15—2E 101
Barry Lawson Clo. M8—4B 74
Barry Rise. WA14—3C 136
Barry Rd. M23—1H 127
Barry Rd. SK5—4H 119
Barry St. OL1—1F 65
Barsham Dri. BL3—2H 37
Bar Ter. OL12—2C 6
Bartlam Pl. OL1—2D 64
Bartlemore St. OL1—6E 49
Bartlett Rd. OL2—1E 49
Bartlett St. M11—6D 88
Bartley Rd. M22—3A 128
Barton Arc. M3—3D 86 (off Deansgate)
Barton Av. M31—5D 96
Barton Clo. SK9—5H 151
Barton Dock Rd. M31 & M32—1G 97
Barton Fold. SK14—6B 106
Barton Hall Av. M30—4C 82
Barton La. M30—5F 83
Barton Moss Rd. M30—1H 95
Barton Rd. BL4—2D 54
Barton Rd. M24—1H 61
Barton Rd. M27—5G 71
Barton Rd. M28—6H 69
Barton Rd. M30—4E 83
Barton Rd. M31—3E 97
Barton Rd. M32—3H 97
Barton Rd. SK4—2A 130
Barton Sq. M2—4D 86 & 5G 161
Barton St. BL4—2G 55
Barton St. M3—5C 86 & 2F 165 (in two parts)
Barton St. M27—1F 71
Barton St. OL1—1B 64
Barton Ter. M30—4G 95
Barton Wlk. BL4—2D 54
Barwell Clo. SK5—1H 119
Barwell Rd. M33—4G 113
Barwell Sq. BL4—5D 38
Barwick Pl. M33—5A 114
Basford Rd. M16—4H 99
Bashall St. BL1—5G 23
Basil Ct. OL16—5B 20
Basildon Clo. M13—2H 101
Basil St. BL3—2A 38
Basil St. M14—4G 101
Basil St. OL16—5B 20

Basil St. SK4—6F 119
Basle Clo. SK7—1G 143
Baslow Av. M19—5D 102
Baslow Clo. SK13—6G 109 (off Baslow M.)
Baslow Dri. SK7—5F 145
Baslow Dri. SK8—6G 141
Baslow Fold. SK13—6G 109 (off Castleton M.)
Baslow Grn. SK13—6G 109 (off Castleton Cres.)
Baslow Gro. SK5—4H 119
Baslow M. SK13—6G 109
Baslow Rd. M32—4A 98
Baslow Rd. M34—1F 121
Baslow Rd. M35—2G 89
Baslow St. M11—4A 88
Baslow Way. SK13—6G 109 (off Castleton Cres.)
Basset Av. M6—6G 73
Bassett Clo. OL12—6E 7
Bassett Gdns. OL12—6E 7
Bassett Way. OL12—1G 19
Bassey Wlk. M16—3C 100
Bass La. BL9—6F 5
Bass St. BL2—6E 25
Bass St. SK16—5H 91
Basten Dri. M7—5A 74
Batchelor Clo. M21—2C 116
Bates Clo. OL11—4D 32
Bateson Dri. OL4—3B 66
Bateson St. SK1—1A 132
Bateson Way. OL8—4D 64
Bates St. M13—3B 102
Bates St. SK16—5A 92
Bath Clo. SK7—3G 145
Bath Cres. M16—2A 100
Bath Cres. SK8—1D 152
Bath Pl. WA14—3F 137
Bath St. BL1—5B 24
Bath St. OL9—2H 63 (Chadderton)
Bath St. OL9—4A 64 (Oldham)
Bath St. OL12—2A 20
Bath St. WA14—2F 137
Batley St. OL5—2D 80
Battenberg Rd. BL1—5G 23
Battersbay Gro. SK7—3E 145
Battersby St. SK2—5E 133
Battersby St. BL9—2H 29
Battersby St. M11—6G 89
Battersby St. OL11—5D 18
Battersea Rd. SK4—2A 130
Battle La. SK5—2D 120
Batty St. M8—6E 75
Baum, The. OL16—3H 19
Baxendale St. BL1—1A 24
Baxter Gdns. M23—4G 127
Baxter Rd. M33—5B 114
Baybutt St. M26—4A 42
Baycliffe Wlk. M8—5B 74
Baycroft Gro. M23—2G 127
Baydon Av. M8—5B 74
Bayfield Gro. M10—2A 76
Bayford St. M10—4B 76
Bayley Ind. Est. SK15—4D 92
Bayley St. BL1—5H 23
Bayley St. SK15—3C 92
Baynard Wlk. M9—5D 60
Baynham Av. M20—6F 117
Baysdale Av. BL3—3D 36
Baysdale Dri. OL2—2A 48
Baysdale Wlk. M11—4B 88
Bayston Wlk. M12—1B 102 (off Gortonvilla Wlk.)
Bay St. OL9—2B 64
Bay St. OL10—2D 30
Bay St. OL12—2A 20
Bay St. SK1—3H 131
Bayswater Av. M10—1D 88
Bayswater St. BL3—5G 37
Baythorpe St. BL1—2B 24
Bay Tree Av. M28—6A 70
Baytree Av. OL9—1E 63
Baytree Dri. SK6—5F 121
Baytree Gro. BL0—1B 14
Baytree La. M24—6D 46

Baywood St. M9—3F 75
Bazaar St. M6—1G 85
Bazley Rd. M22—2B 128
Bazley St. BL1—1D 22
Beacon Dri. M23—3G 139
Beaconsfield. SK6—6E 123
Beaconfield Av. SK14—5C 106
Beacon Rd. SK6—2F 133
Beaconsfield. M14—2G 117
Beaconsfield Rd. WA14—4F 125
Beaconsfield St. BL3—1H 37
Beaconsfield Ter. OL5—2D 80
Beadham Dri. M9—4C 60
Beaford Dri. M22—5C 140
Beagle Wlk. M22—5C 140
Beal Clo. SK4—6H 117
Beal Cres. OL16—2C 20
Bealcroft Clo. OL16—4E 21
Bealcroft Wlk. OL16—4E 21
Beale Gro. M21—1H 115
Bealey Av. M26—2C 42
Bealey Clo. M18—1D 102
Bealey Clo. M26—3B 42
Bealey Dri. BL9—6B 28
Beal La. OL12—1G 49
Beal Ter. OL16—5F 21
Beal View. OL2—5H 31
Beal Wlk. M25—1G 59
Beaminster Av. SK4—6C 118
Beaminster Clo. SK4—6C 118
*Beaminster Ct. SK4—6C 118
(off Beaminster Clo.)
Beaminster Rd. SK4—6B 118
Beaminster Wlk. M13—2G 101
Beamish Clo. M13—1G 101 & 5F 167
Beamsley Rd. M22—3H 139
Beanfields. M28—6H 69
Beanfield Ter. M28—6H 69
Bean Leach Av. SK2—5F 133
Bean Leach Dri. SK2—5F 133
Bean Leach Rd. SK7 & SK2—1E 145
Beard Rd. M18—3E 103
Beard St. M35—4H 89
Beard St. OL2—4C 48
Beardwood Rd. M9—5F 61
Bearwood Clo. SK14—6D 106
Beathwaite Dri. SK7—4E 143
Beatrice Av. M18—3H 103
Beatrice Av. SK8—3B 142
Beatrice Rd. BL1—5G 23
Beatrice Rd. M28—4B 70
Beatrice St. BL4—1D 54
Beatrice St. M27—2D 70
Beatrice St. M34—4E 105
Beatrice St. OL11—4F 19
Beatrice Wignall St. M35—5A 90
*Beatson Wlk. M4—3G 87
(off Caroline Dri.)
Beattock Clo. M15—6B 86 &
4D 164
Beauchamp St. OL6—1A 92
Beaufont Dri. OL4—4G 65
Beaufort Av. M20—4E 117
Beaufort Av. M27—4D 70
Beaufort Av. M33—6C 114
Beaufort Chase. SK9—6B 152
Beaufort Clo. SK9—4H 159
Beaufort Clo. SK14—6A 108
Beaufort Rd. M33—6C 114
Beaufort Rd. OL6—2B 92
Beaufort Rd. SK2—1D 54
Beaufort Rd. SK14—5A 108
Beaufort St. M3—5C 86 & 2E 165
Beaufort St. M25—5G 59
Beaufort St. M30—2D 82
Beaufort St. OL12—2E 19
Beaulieu. WA15—3H 137
Beaumaris Clo. M12—1B 102
Beaumaris Cres. SK7—5C 144
Beaumonds Way. OL11—5C 18
Beaumont Chase. BL3—4D 36
Beaumont Clo. OL15—4D 8
Beaumont Ct. SK9—2G 151
Beaumont Dri. BL3—2C 36
Beaumont Rd BL1, BL6 & BL3
—6B 22
Beaumont Rd. M21—2H 115
Beaumont St. OL6—2A 92

Beauvale Av. SK2—4C 132
Beaver Dri. BL9—3F 43
Beaver Ho. SK1—3B 132
Beaver Rd. M20—6F 117
Beaver St. M1—5E 87 & 2A 162
Beaver Wlk. SK14—6H 107
Bebbington Clo. M33—6F 115
Bebbington St. M11—4E 89
Beccles Rd. M33—2B 126
Beckenham Clo. BL8—4H 27
Beckenham Rd. M8—4C 74
Becket Av. M7—5A 74
Becket Meadows. OL4—3F 65
*Becket Meadow St. OL4—3F 65
Beckett St. M18—2E 103
Beckett St. OL4—2A 66
Beckfield Rd. M23—6G 127
Beckfoot Dri. M13—4A 102
Beckford St. M10—6G 75
Beck Gro. M28—2G 69
Beck Gro. OL2—5H 35
Beckhampton Clo. M13—2G 101 &
6F 167
Beckley Av. M25—1E 73
Beckley Clo. OL2—2E 49
Beckside. SK5—6A 104
Beck St. M3—3C 86 & 4E 161
Beck St. M11—6G 89
Beckton Gdns. M22—2A 140
Becontree. M23—4E 127
Becontree Av. M34—3G 105
Beddell's La. SK9—3D 158
Bede St. BL1—3B 23
*Bedfont Wlk. M9—2G 75
(off Polworth Rd.)
Bedford Av. M16—5B 100
Bedford Av. M27—4E 71
Bedford Av. M28—2E 69
Bedford Av. M33—1D 126
Bedford Av. SK14—4C 106
Bedford Ct. M7—2H 73
Bedford Ct. WA15—5C 126
Bedford Dri. WA15—4C 126
Bedford Gro. M30—3A 110
Bedford Rd. M16—4G 99
Bedford Rd. M30—2G 83
Bedford Rd. M31—3E 97
Bedford St. BL1—5H 23
Bedford St. BL7—1B 10
Bedford St. BL9—1E 29
Bedford St. M25—4G 59
Bedford St. OL6—3A 92
Bedford St. OL10—3G 31
Bedford St. SK5—1G 119
Bedford St. SK15—4D 92
Bedford Wlk. M34—6F 105
Bedlam Grn. BL9—3D 28
Bedlington Clo. M23—
5D 126
Bednal Av. M10—1A 88
Bedwell Clo. M16—4D 100
Bedworth Clo. BL2—2D 38
Beechacre. BL0—4F 5
Beech Av. BL3—5B 40
Beech Av. BL4—1C 54
(Farnworth)
Beech Av. BL4—4B 56
(Kearsley)
Beech Av. M6—1E 85
Beech Av. M22—3B 128
Beech Av. M25—2D 58
Beech Av. M26—1F 57
Beech Av. M28—5C 68
Beech Av. M30—4G 95
Beech Av. M31—6E 97
Beech Av. M32—6E 99
Beech Av. M34—3D 104
Beech Av. M35—4H 89
Beech Av. OL1—5G 47
Beech Av. OL3—3F 53
Beech Av. OL4—1H 65
Beech Av. SK3—5H 131
Beech Av. SK6—5B 134
Beech Av. SK7—3E 145
Beech Av. SK8—6F 129
Beech Av. SK13—6H 109
Beech Av. WA15—3B 126
Beech Clo BL2—5G 11

Beech Clo. M25—6G 59
Beech Clo. M31—6D 110
Beech Clo. OL12—4G 7
Beech Clo. SK9—6E 159
Beech Cotts. SK9—6G 159
Beech Ct. M6—2G 85
Beech Ct. M8—2B 74
Beech Ct. M14—1G 117
Beech Ct. M21—6F 99
Beech Ct. M33—5H 113
Beech Ct. SK9—3G 159
Beech Cres. SK12—3E 155
Beechcroft. M25—6G 59
Beechcroft Av. BL2—1G 39
Beechcroft Clo. M10—2H 87 &
2G 163
Beechcroft Gro. BL2—1G 39
*Beecher Wlk. M9—5F 75
(off Kelvington Dri.)
Beeches, The. BL1—5B 10
Beeches, The. M20—5D 116
Beeches, The. M30—2H 83
Beeches, The. OL5—2B 81
Beeches, The. OL10—3E 31
Beeches, The. OL12—4G 7
Beeches, The. SK8—4D 142
Beechey Sq. OL1—1E 65
Beechfield. M33—1H 125
Beechfield. OL4—3F 67
Beechfield. OL11—5A 18
Beechfield. WA14—2E 137
Beechfield Av. M26—6A 42
Beechfield Av. M28—4C 54
Beechfield Av. M31—4C 96
Beechfield Av. SK9—4B 158
Beechfield Clo. OL11—5A 18
Beechfield Dri. BL9—6C 28
Beechfield Rd. BL1—3F 23
Beechfield Rd. M27—6D 70
Beechfield Rd. OL16—4E 21
Beechfield Rd. SK3—1H 143
Beechfield Rd. SK8—5D 142
Beechfield Rd. SK9—6G 159
Beechfield Rd. SK14—4G 109
Beechfield St. M8—5C 74
Beech Gro. BL2—2A 14
Beech Gro. M6—1E 85
Beech Gro. M14—2H 117
Beech Gro. M28—4A 54
Beech Gro. M33—5H 113
Beech Gro. OL7—4F 91
Beech Gro. SK9—3D 158
Beech Gro. SK15—5D 92
Beech Gro. Clo. BL9—1F 29
Beech Hill Rd. OL4—3F 67
Beech Holme Gro. SK2—3C 132
Beech Ho. M30—4D 82
Beech Ho. OL2—2F 49
Beech Hurst Clo. M16—5B 100
Beech La. OL4—4F 67
Beech La. SK6—1A 134
Beech La. SK9—3D 158
Beech Lawn. WA14—1E 137
Beech M. M21—1G 115
Beech M. SK2—6A 132
Beech M., The. M20—6D 116
Beech Mt. M9—3F 75
Beech Mt. OL7—5E 79
Beechpark Av. M22—4A 128
Beech Range. M19—6C 102
Beech Rd. M21—1G 115
Beech Rd. M33—5D 114
Beech Rd. SK3 & SK1—5H 131
Beech Rd. SK6—6D 146
Beech Rd. SK8—4D 142
Beech Rd. SK9—6E 159
Beech Rd. WA15—2G 137
Beech St. BL1—3B 24
Beech St. BL9—3F 29
(Bury)
Beech St. BL9—6E 5
(Summerseat)
Beech St. M24—1H 61
Beech St. M26—6A 42
Beech St. M27—4F 71
Beech St. M30—4D 82
Beech St. M35—3E 77
Beech St. OL1—2E 65

Beech St. OL2—6F 35
Beech St. OL9—6H 63
Beech St. OL11—5F 19
Beech St. OL16—1E 35
Beech St. SK14—4B 106
Beech Tree Bank. M25—5E 59
Beechurst Rd. SK8—6D 130
Beech View. SK14—5E 107
Beech Vs. M33—5D 114
Beech Wlk. M24—3H 61
Beech Wlk. M32—6C 98
Beechway. SK6—6D 146
Beechway. SK9—4D 158
Beechwood. OL6—5H 35
Beechwood. WA14—4D 136
Beechwood Av. BL0—3F 5
Beechwood Av. M21—1A 116
Beechwood Av. M31—4A 96
Beechwood Av. OL15—6E 9
Beechwood Av. SK5—5H 119
Beechwood Av. SK6—1A 134
Beechwood Av. SK15—1G 93
Beechwood Dri. M28—5B 70
Beechwood Dri. M33—5E 113
Beechwood Dri. OL2—1A 48
Beechwood Dri. OL5—1E 81
Beechwood Dri. SK6—5E 135
Beechwood Dri. SK9—1H 159
Beechwood Gro. M9—4G 75
Beechwood Gro. SK8—5C 142
Beechwood La. SK15—1G 93
Beechwood Rd. M25—6H 59
Beechwood Rd. OL8—1D 78
Beechwood St. BL3—4B 38
Beede St. M11—5D 88
Beedon Av. BL3—3A 40
Beehive Grn. BL5—6A 36
Beehive St. OL8—6D 64
Beeley St. M6—6F 73
Beeley St. SK14—5C 106
Beeston Av. M7—5F 73
Beeston Av. WA15—5H 125
Beeston Clo. BL1—5E 11
Beeston Gro. M25—2F 59
Beeston Gro. SK3—6G 131
Beeston Rd. M33—5G 113
Beeston St. M9—3G 75
Beeth St. M11—6F 89
Beeton Gro. M13—3A 102
Beever St. M14—2A 100
Beever St. OL1—2E 65
Begley Clo. SK6—2F 133
Begonia Av. BL4—6D 38
Begonia Wlk. M12—1B 102
Beightons Wlk. OL12—5D 6
Belbeck St. BL8—3A 28
Belcroft Dri. M28—3A 54
Belcroft Gro. M28—4A 54
Belding Av. M10—2F 77
Beldon Rd. M9—5D 60
Belfield Clo. M16—3C 20
Belfield Mill La. OL16—3C 20
Belfield Old Rd. OL16—3C 20
Belfield Rd. M20—5F 117
Belfield Rd. M25—6A 60
Belfield Rd. OL16—3B 20
Belfield Rd. SK5—4H 103
Belfield Trading Est. OL16—3D 20
Belford Av. M34—4A 104
Belford Dri. BL3—3A 38
Belford Rd. M32—4D 98
Belford Wlk. M23—5G 127
Belfort Dri. M5—5H 85
Belfry Clo. SK9—1G 159
Belgate Clo. M12—3C 102
Belgian Ter. OL2—3D 48
Belgium St. OL11—4A 18
Belgrave Av. M14—4A 102
Belgrave Av. M31—4A 96
Belgrave Av. M35—3H 77
Belgrave Av. OL8—5E 65
Belgrave Av. SK6—4D 134
Belgrave Clo. M26—3G 41

Belgrave Ct. M34—3D 104
Belgrave Ct. OL8—4D 64
Belgrave Cres. M30—2H 83
Belgrave Cres. SK2—1B 144
Belgrave Dri. M26—3G 41
Belgrave Dri. M26—3G 41
Belgrave Gdns. BL1—3A 24
Belgrave Rd. M10—2E 77
Belgrave Rd. M30—4B 110
Belgrave Rd. M33—5A 114
Belgrave Rd. OL8—5D 64
Belgrave WA14—2E 137
Belgrave St. BL1—4A 24
(in two parts)
Belgrave St. M26—3F 41
Belgrave St. M34—3D 104
Belgrave St. OL10—4E 31
(in two parts)
Belgrave St. OL12—2F 19
Belgrave St. S. BL1—4A 24
Belgravia M21—1G 115
Belgravia M. OL2—6G 35
Belhaven Rd. M8—1B 74
Bellairs St. BL3—4G 37
Bellamy Ct. M18—2G 103
Bella St. BL3—3G 37
Bell Clough Rd. M35—2B 90
Bell Cres. M11—5A 88
Belldale Clo. SK4—1C 130
Belle Isle Av. OL12—3C 6
Bellerby Clo. M25—1C 58
Belleville Av. M22—5C 140
Belle Vue Av. M12—2B 102
Belle Vue St. M12—1C 102
Belle Vue Ter. BL9—4C 28
Bellew St. M11—5A 88
Bellfield Av. OL8—1D 78
Bellfield Av. SK8—4D 142
Bellingham Clo. BL8—3F 27
Bellingham St. M8—6C 74
Bellis Clo. M12—4A 88
Bell La. BL9—2E 29
Bell Meadow Dri. OL11—6B 18
Bellott St. M8—5C 74
Bellot Wlk. OL1—1C 64
Bellpit Clo. M28—4E 69
Bellscroft Av. M10—4B 76
Bellshill Cres. OL16—3C 20
Bell St. M35—3B 90
Bell St. OL1—2E 65
Bell St. OL16—3H 19
Bell Ter. M30—5E 83
Belmont Av. M24—2A 84
Belmont Av. M27—4D 56
Belmont Av. M34—3D 104
Belmont Av. OL4—2B 66
Belmont Clo. SK4—6G 119
Belmont Dri. BL8—4G 27
Belmont Dri. SK6—1F 135
Belmont Rd. M26—6G 41
Belmont Rd. M33—5A 114
Belmont Rd. SK7—2G 153
Belmont Rd. SK8—5F 129
Belmont Rd. WA15—3G 137
Belmont Shopping Cen. SK4
—1G 131
Belmont St. M5—4D 84
Belmont St. M16—2B 100
Belmont St. M30—2F 83
Belmont St. OL1—1C 64
Belmont St. OL4—4A 66
Belmont St. SK4—6F 119
Belmont Ter. M31—3H 111
Belmont View. BL2—1H 25
Belmont Wlk. M13—1G 101 & 5E 167
Belmont Way. OL9—1A 64
Belmont Way. OL12—1G 19
Belmont Way. SK4—1F 131
Belmore Av. M8—2F 74
Belper Rd. M30—5D 82
Belper Rd. SK4—2B 130
Belper St. BL3—2E 39
Belper St. OL6—1H 91
Belper Wlk. M18—1E 103
Belper Way. M34—1G 121
(in two parts)
Belsay Dri. M23—1G 139

Belstone Av. M23—2G 139
Belstone Clo. SK7—3H 143
Belsyde Wlk. M9—4G 75
(off Norbet Wlk.)
Belthorne Av. M9—1A 76
Belton Av. OL16—2C 20
Beltone Clo. M32—6B 98
Belton Wlk. M8—5C 74
Belton Wlk. OL9—3B 64
Belvedere Av. BL8—2A 14
Belvedere Av. SK5—5H 103
Belvedere St. M25—6E 59
Belvedere Dri. SK6—6C 120
Belvedere Dri. SK16—4C 92
Belvedere Rise. OL1—4H 49
Belvedere Rd. M6—2G 85
Belvedere Rd. M14—1A 118
Belvedere St. M6—2H 85
Belvoir Av. M19—5C 102
Belvoir Av. SK7—5E 145
Belvoir St. BL2—6E 25
Belvoir St. OL12—2E 19
Belvor Av. M34—6E 91
Belwood Rd. M21—2G 115
Bembridge Clo. M14—4G 101
Bembridge Dri. BL3—2F 39
Bembridge Rd. M34—1H 121
Bempton Clo. SK2—6G 133
Bemrose Av. WA14—5E 125
Benbecula Way. M31—2E 97
Benbow Av. M12—2B 102
Benbow St. M33—4B 114
Ben Brierley Way. OL1—2D 64
Benbrook Gro. SK9—5A 152
Bench Carr. OL12—2G 19
Benchill Av. M22—6B 128
Benchill Ct. Rd. M22—1C 140
Benchill Cres. M22—6A 128
Benchill Dri. M22—6A 128
Benchill Rd. M22—5A 128
Bendall St. M11—5G 89
Ben Davies Ct. SK6—6A 122
Bendemeer. M31—4E 97
Bendix St. M4—2F 87 & 2C 162
Benfield Av. M10—1C 76
Benfield St. OL10—3F 31
Benfield Wlk. M24—4F 45
Benfleet Clo. M12—1C 102
Bengal La. OL6—1A 92
Bengal Sq. OL6—1A 92
Bengal St. M4—3F 87 & 3D 162
Bengal St. SK3—3G 131
Benhale Wlk. M8—5C 74
(off Tamerton Dri.)
Benham Clo. BL4—6F 39
Benham Clo. M20—6G 117
Benin Wlk. M10—6C 76
Benja Fold. SK7—1F 153
Benjamin Wilson Ct. M7—1B 86
(off Fitzwilliam St.)
Benmore Clo. OL10—3C 30
Benmore Rd. M9—5H 61
Bennet St. M26—3D 40
Bennett Clo. SK3—3E 131
Bennett Dri. M7—5A 74
Bennett Rd. M8—2B 74
Bennett's La. BL1—2G 23
Bennett St. M12—1A 102
Bennett St. M32—6C 98
Bennett St. OL7—4F 91
Bennett St. OL11—6A 20
Bennett St. SK3—3E 131
Bennett St. SK14—2A 106
Bennett St. SK15—4E 93
Benny La. M35—2C 90
Benson Clo. M7—6A 74
Benson St. BL9—4E 29
Benson Wlk. SK9—5H 151
Ben St. M11—3D 88
Bentcliffe Way. M30—4H 83
Bentfield Cres. OL16—1E 35
Bentfold Dri. BL9—5E 43
Bentgate Clo. OL16—1E 35
Bentgate St. OL16—2E 35
Benthall Wlk. M34—1E 121
Bentham Clo. BL8—2E 27
Bent Hill S. BL3—3E 37
Bentinck Ho. OL6—3G 91

Bentinck Rd. WA14—1E 137
Bentinck St. BL1—4F 23
Bentinck St. BL4—6E 39
Bentinck St. M15—6B 86 & 3C 164
Bentinck St. OL6 & OL7—2G 91
(in two parts)
Bentinck St. OL8—5D 64
Bentinck St. OL12—2E 19
Bentinck Ter. OL6—3G 91
Bent La. M8—4B 74
Bent La. M25—5G 59
Bent Lanes. M31—2B 96
(in four parts)
Bentley Av. M24—2D 46
Bentley Clo. M26—3B 42
Bentley Ct. M7—3A 74
Bentley Hall Rd. BL8—1C 26
Bentley Rd. M7—3A 74
Bentley Rd. M21—6G 99
Bentley Rd. M34—4F 105
Bentleys, The. SK5—6H 119
Bentley St. BL2—2E 39
Bentley St. BL4—6F 39
Bentley St. OL1—1F 65
Bentley St. OL9—2H 63
Bentley St. OL12—1F 19
Bentmeadows. OL12—2G 19
Benton Dri. SK6—3F 135
Benton St. M9—4H 75
Bents Av. M31—6B 96
Bents Av. SK6—6F 121
Bentside Rd. SK12—2H 157
Bents La. SK6—6F 121
Bent Spur Rd. BL4—4A 56
Bent St. BL4—2G 55
Bent St. M8—1E 87
Bent Ter. M30—3E 97
Bentworth Wlk. M9—4G 75
Benville Wlk. M10—5B 76
(off Troydale Dri.)
Benwick Ter. BL1—3A 24
Benyon St. OL4—3A 66
Berberis Wlk. M33—3E 113
Beresford Av. BL3—2G 37
Beresford Cres. OL4—1H 65
Beresford Cres. SK5—4G 103
Beresford Rd. M13—4B 102
Beresford Rd. M32—3E 99
Beresford St. M14—4D 100
Beresford St. M35—4E 77
Beresford St. OL4—1H 65
Beresford St. OL16—1F 35
Berger St. M10—6D 76
Bergman Wlk. M10—5B 76
(off Harmer Clo.)
Berigan Clo. M12—2A 102
Berisford Clo. WA15—4G 125
Berkeley Av. M14—3A 102
Berkeley Av. M32—3A 98
Berkeley Av. OL9—6F 63
Berkeley Clo. SK2—3C 132
Berkeley Clo. SK14—6B 106
Berkeley Ct. M8—2A 74
Berkeley Ct. M20—6D 116
Berkeley Cres. M26—2C 40
Berkeley Cres. SK14—6B 106
Berkeley Dri. OL2—5B 48
Berkeley Rd. BL1—1A 24
Berkeley Rd. SK7—2F 145
Berkeley St. OL2—2B 48
Berkley Av. M19—6C 102
Berkley Dri. OL16—1H 33
Berkley St. OL6—2G 91
Berkley Wlk. OL15—4D 8
Berkshire Clo. OL9—4H 63
Berkshire Rd. M10—2H 87 & 1H 163
Berkshire Pl. OL9—4A 64
Berlin Rd. SK3—5F 131
Berlin St. BL3—1G 37
Bernard Gro. BL1—3G 23
Bernard St. M9—3F 75
Bernard St. OL12—6E 7
Bernard Walker Ct. SK6—1F 135
Berne Clo. OL9—3A 64
Berne Clo. SK7—1G 143

Bernice Av. OL9—3H 63
Bernice St. BL1—3G 23
Bernington Wlk. BL2—4C 24
Berrie Gro. M19—1D 118
Berry Brow. M10—1F 89
Berrycroft La. SK6—6G 121
Berry St. M1—5F 87 & 2D 166
Berry St. M27—1F 71
Berry St. M30—5D 82
Berry St. OL3—4F 53
Berry St. SK15—5G 93
Bertha Rd. OL16—4C 20
Bertha St. BL1—3H 23
Bertha St. M11—5D 88
Bertha St. OL2—2F 49
Bertie St. OL11—1D 32
Bertram St. M12—1C 102
Bertram St. M33—5E 115
Bertrand Rd. BL1—6G 23
Bert St. BL3—4F 37
Berwick Av. M25—2E 59
Berwick Av. M31—5A 98
Berwick Av. SK4—6H 117
Berwick Clo. M28—4B 68
Berwick Clo. OL10—4C 30
Berwick St. OL16—5B 20
Berwyn Av. M9—4D 60
Berwyn Av. M24—1C 62
Berwyn Av. SK8—6D 130
Beryl Av. BL8—4H 13
Beryl St. BL1—2B 24
Besom La. SK15—2H 93
Bessemer Rd. M30—2D 110
Bessemer St. M11—6E 89
Bessemer Way. OL1—2C 64
Bessybrook Clo. BL6—1A 36
Beswick Dri. M35—5G 77
Beswick Royds St. OL16—2B 20
Beswicke St. OL12—3G 19
Beswicke St. OL15—4G 9
Beswick Row. M4—2E 87 & 2A 162
Beswicks La. SK9—6A 158
Beswick St. M4—3H 87 & 4H 163
Beswick St. M35—4B 90
Beswick St. OL2—5C 48
Beta Av. M32—6C 98
Beta St. BL1—5A 24
Bethany La. OL16—1G 35
Bethel Av. M35—4E 77
Bethel St. M11—4D 88
Bethel St. OL10—3E 31
Bethesda Ho. M8—3A 74
Bethesda St. OL8—5D 64
Bethnall Dri. M14—6E 101
Betjeman Pl. OL2—5H 35
Betleymere Rd. SK8—1B 142
Betley Rd. SK5—6H 103
Betley St. M1—5G 87 & 1E 167
Betley St. M26—3A 42
Betley St. OL10—4E 31
Betnor Av. SK1—2B 132
Betony Clo. OL12—6D 6
Bettwood Dri. M8—1A 74
Betty Nuppy's La. OL16—6C 20
Betula Gro. M7—5H 73
Betula M. OL11—2H 17
Beulah St. M11—6E 89
Bevan Clo. M12—4A 88
Bevendon Sq. M7—5A 74
Beverdale Clo. M11—5C 88
Bevereley Clo. OL6—5F 79
Beveridge St. M14—4E 101
Beverley Av. M31—3G 97
Beverley Av. M34—5G 105
Beverley Flats. OL10—3E 31
(off Wilton St.)
Beverley Pl. OL16—3A 20
Beverley Rd. BL1—5F 23
Beverley Rd. BL3—4H 39
Beverley Rd. M27—4A 72
Beverley Rd. SK2—3C 132
Beverley St. M9—2G 75
Beverley Wlk. OL8—4C 64
Beverley Wlk. SK6—6G 133
Beverly Rd. M14—2H 117
Beverston Dri. M7—5A 74

Bevill Sq. M3—3C 86 & 3E 161
Bevis Grn. BL9—3F 15
Bewick St. BL2—2D 24
Bewley St. OL8—1B 78
Bewley Wlk. M10—5A 76
Bexhill Av. WA15—5H 125
Bexhill Clo. BL3—4C 40
Bexhill Dri. M13—4A 102
Bexhill Rd. SK3—1G 143
Bexhill Wlk. OL9—3H 63
Bexington Wlk. M16—4C 100
Bexley Clo. M31—3D 96
Bexley Dri. BL8—4H 27
Bexley Dri. M28—5E 55
Bexley Sq. M3—3B 86 & 4D 160
Bexley St. OL9—4A 64
Bexley Wlk. M10—5B 76
 (off John Foran Clo.)
Beyer Clo. M18—2E 103
Bibby La. M19—3B 118
Bibby St. BL9—2D 42
Bibby St. SK14—2B 106
Bickerdike Av. M12—4C 102
Bickerstaffe Clo. OL2—1E 49
Bickerton Ct. OL9—6A 64
Bickerton Dri. SK7—4A 144
Bickerton Rd. WA14—6D 124
Bickley Wlk. M16—3D 100
Bidbury Av. M22—2H 139
Biddall Dri. M23—5H 127
Biddisham Wlk. M10—6F 75
Biddulph Av. SK2—6C 132
Bideford Dri. BL2—1A 40
Bideford Dri. M23—3F 127
Bideford Rd. OL11—2B 32
Bideford Rd. SK2—2C 132
Bidston Av. M14—5F 101
Bidston Clo. OL2—1H 49
Bidston Dri. SK9—4A 152
Bidworth La. SK13—6F 109
Bigginwood Wlk. M10—4A 76
 (off Halliford Rd.)
Bignor St. M8—5C 74
Bilbao St. BL1—5G 23
Bilberry St. OL16—5A 20
Bilbrook Dri. M4—2F 87 & 1C 162
Billing Av. M12—6G 87 & 3F 167
Billinge Clo. BL1—5B 24
Billington Rd. M27—3C 72
Bill La. M25—1D 58
Bill Williams Clo. M11—5E 89
Billy La. M27—1F 71
Billy Meredith Clo. M14—4E 101
Billy's La. SK8—4C 142
Billy Whelan Wlk. M10—6B 76
Bilsand Wlk. M10—6C 76
Bilson Dri. SK3—4D 130
Bilson Sq. OL16—6G 21
Bilton Wlk. M8—3F 75
Binbrook Wlk. BL3—3B 38
Bincombe Wlk. M13—2G 101
Bindloss Av. M30—2A 84
Bindon Wlk. M9—4F 75
 (off Carisbrook St.)
Bingham Dri. M23—5F 127
Bingham St. M27—3F 71
Bingley Clo. M11—5B 88
Bingley Dri. M31—3B 96
Bingley Rd. OL16—4C 20
Bingley Sq. OL16—4C 20
Bingley Ter. OL16—4C 20
Bingley Wlk. M27—3D 72
Binns Nook Rd. OL12—1A 20
Binns Pl. M4—4F 87 & 5D 162
Binns St. SK15—4C 92
Binn's Ter. OL15—3F 9
 (off Barehill St.)
Binsley Clo. M30—6E 95
Binstead Clo. M14—4A 102
Birchacre Gro. M14—2H 117
Birchall Grn. SK6—4F 121
Birch Av. BL8—6A 14
Birch Av. M6—6C 72
Birch Av. M16—3G 99
Birch Av. M24—2A 62
Birch Av. M25—3D 58
Birch Av. M30—4B 110
Birch Av. M33—6B 114

Birch Av. M35—5F 77
Birch Av. OL1—5G 47
Birch Av. OL8—1B 78
Birch Av. OL12—5B 8
Birch Av. SK4—5D 118
Birch Av. SK6—1B 134
Birch Av. SK9—3D 158
Birch Clo. OL12—3C 6
Birch Ct. M13—4A 102
Birch Ct. SK16—5B 92
Birch Cres. OL16—2E 35
Birchdale. WA14—3E 137
Birchdale Av. SK8—3F 141
Birch Dri. M27—3H 71
Birch Dri. OL4—4B 66
Birch Dri. SK7—3C 144
Birchenall St. M10—3H 75
Birchen Bower Dri. BL8—6H 13
Birchen Bower Wlk. BL8—6H 13
Birchenlea St. OL9—6G 63
Birches, The. M33—4G 113
Birches, The. OL5—2D 80
Birchfield. BL2—5A 12
Birchfield Av. BL9—4A 30
Birchfield Dri. M28—4C 68
Birchfield Dri. OL11—6E 19
Birchfield Gro. BL3—3C 36
Birchfield Rd. SK3—4C 130
Birchfields. WA15—4H 137
Birchfields Av. M13—4A 102
Birchfields Rd. M13 & M14—4A 102
Birchfold. M28—5D 54
Birchfold Clo. M28—5D 54
Birchgate Wlk. BL3—3A 38
Birch Gro. BL0—6C 4
Birch Gro. M14—4H 101
Birch Gro. M25—3E 59
Birch Gro. M31—1A 112
Birch Gro. M34—1F 105
 (Audenshaw)
Birch Gro. M34—4E 105
 (Denton)
Birch Gro. WA15—6E 127
Birch Hall La. M13—5A 102
Birch Hey Clo. SK6—3G 121
Birch Hill Cres. OL12—5B 8
Birch Hill La. OL12—3B 8
Birch Hill Wlk. OL15—4D 8
Birch Ho. M16—3G 99
Birch Ind. Est. OL10—2C 44
Birchington Rd. M14—1E 117
Birchin La. M4—4E 87 & 5B 162
Birchinlee Av. OL2—4H 47
Birch La. M13—4A 102
Birch La. SK16—5B 92
 (in two parts)
Birch Lea Clo. BL9—6D 28
Birchleaf Gro. M5—3C 84
Birch Mt. OL12—5B 8
Birch Polygon. M14—4H 101
Birch Rd. BL4—3H 55
Birch Rd. M8—2D 74
Birch Rd. M24—5C 46
Birch Rd. M27—6D 70
Birch Rd. M28—2F 69
Birch Rd. M31—5B 112
 (Carrington)
Birch Rd. M31—6B 110
 (Partington)
Birch Rd. OL3—2G 53
Birch Rd. OL12—3A 8
Birch Rd. SK8—6E 129
Birch Rd. SK12—5F 155
Birch St. BL2—1C 38
Birch St. BL9—1D 28
Birch St. M12—1C 102
Birch St. M26—2C 42
Birch St. M35—4B 90
Birch St. OL7—4E 91
Birch St. OL10—4F 31
Birch St. OL12—3A 8
Birch St. SK15—1G 93
Birch Tree Av. SK7—4G 145
Birch Tree Clo. WA14—4E 137
Birch Tree Ct. M22—2B 140
Birch Tree Dri. M22—2B 140
Birchvale Clo. M15—6C 86 & 4E 165
Birchvale Dri. SK6—6B 122

Birch Vs. OL12—4C 6
Birchway. SK6—6D 146
Birchway. SK7—6F 143
Birchwood. OL9—2E 63
Birchwood Clo. SK4—2C 130
Birchwood Dri. SK9—1G 159
Birchwood Rd. M24—5C 46
Birchwood Way. SK16—1B 106
Bird Hall Av. SK8—1E 143
Birdhall Gro. M19—1C 118
Bird Hall La. SK3—4D 130
Bird Hall Rd. SK8—6D 130
Birdlip Dri. M23—2G 139
Birkbeck St. SK15—4G 92
Birkby Dri. M24—5G 45
Birkdale Av. OL2—5C 48
Birkdale Clo. OL10—5F 31
Birkdale Clo. SK7—6H 143
Birkdale Clo. SK14—2C 106
Birkdale Dri. BL8—3H 27
Birkdale Gdns. BL3—2H 37
Birkdale Gro. M30—3H 83
Birkdale Gro. SK5—4H 119
Birkdale Rd. OL16—1A 34
Birkdale Rd. SK5—4G 119
Birkdale St. M8—4C 74
Birkenhills Dri. BL3—2C 36
Birket St. M11—4C 88
Birkett Clo. BL1—5B 10
Birkett Dri. BL1—5B 10
Birkinbrook Clo. M25—6E 43
Birkleigh Wlk. BL2—1G 39
Birks Av. OL4—1B 66
Birks Dri. BL8—5B 14
Birkworth Ct. SK2—5D 132
Birley Wlk. WA15—4H 125
Birley Ct. M5—3G 85
Birley Pk. M20—6D 116
Birley St. BL1—1A 24
Birley St. BL9—6F 15
Birley St. OL12—2A 20
Birling Dri. M23—1H 139
Birnham Gro. OL10—4C 30
Birstall Wlk. M23—5G 127
Birtenshaw Cres. BL7—4F 11
Birtle Rd. BL9—4C 16
Birtles Av. SK5—4H 103
Birtles Clo. SK8—6C 130
Birtlespool Rd. SK8—4C 142
Birtles, The. M22—2B 140
Birtles Way. SK9—1H 151
Birtley Wlk. M10—2G 87 & 2F 163
Birt St. M10—1H 87
Birwood Rd. M8—1D 74
Biscay Clo. M11—4B 88
Bishop Clo. M16—3C 100
Bishop Clo. OL7—6E 79
Bishop Marshall Clo. M10—6F 75
Bishop Marshall Way. M24—3F 45
Bishop Rd. M6—1B 84
Bishop Rd. M31—5H 95
Bishopsbridge Clo. BL3—3B 38
Bishop's Clo. BL3—5C 38
Bishops Clo. SK8—6C 130
Bishops Clo. WA14—4D 136
Bishopscourt. M7—3G 73
Bishopsgate. M2—5D 86 & 1H 165
Bishops Ga. St. OL9—3G 63
Bishops M. M33—3G 113
Bishop's Rd. BL3—5C 38
Bishops Rd. M25—6G 59
Bishops St. SK1—2A 132
Bishop St. M24—2D 62
Bishop St. OL16—2B 20
Bishopton M19—6E 103
Bishop Wlk. OL7—4G 91
Bisley Av. M23—5F 127
Bisley St. OL8—3B 64
Bismark St. OL4—4E 65
Bispham Av. BL2—6H 25
Bispham Av. SK5—5H 103
Bispham Clo. BL8—4F 27
Bispham Gro. M7—4A 74
Bispham St. BL2—5E 25
Bittern Clo. OL11—4B 18
Bittern Clo. SK12—3A 154

Bittern Dri. M35—2C 90
Blackbank St. BL1—3B 24
Blackberry Clo. WA14—3D 124
Blackberry La. SK5—2B 120
Black Brook Rd. SK4—2F 119
Blackburn Gdns. M20—5E 117
Blackburn Pl. M3—2B 86 & 2C 160
Blackburn Pl. M5—4A 86 & 6A 160
Blackburn Rd. BL0—1A 4
Blackburn Rd. BL1 & BL7—1A 24
Blackburn St. M3—2B 86 & 2C 160
Blackburn St. M16—2A 100
Blackburn St. M25—5G 59
Blackburn St. M26—4G 41
Blackcap Clo. M28—4D 68
Blackcarr Rd. M23—6F 127
Black Dad La. OL11—3E 17
Blackden Wlk. SK9—6H 151
Blackett St. M12—5H 87 & 2G 167
Blackfield La. M7—3G 73
Blackfields. M7—3G 73
Blackford Av. BL9—3D 42
Blackford Rd. M20—2D 118
Blackford Wlk. M10—2H 87 & 1H 163
Blackfriars Rd. M3—3D 86 & 2E 160
Blackfriars St. M3—3D 86 & 4G 161
Blackhill Clo. M13—6F 87 & 4D 166
Black Horse St. BL1—6A 24
Black Horse St. BL4—2G 55
Black Leach. OL4—2C 66
Blackleach Dri. M28—4F 55
Blackledge St. BL3—3G 37
Blackley Clo. BL9—5E 43
Blackley Ct. M9—6C 60
Blackley New Rd. M9—6B 60
Blackley Pk. Rd. M9—2F 75
Blackley St. M16—2A 100
Blackley St. M24—2D 60
Blacklock St. M8—1D 86
Blackmoor. SK14—3C 108
Black Moss Clo. M26—4D 40
Blackpits Rd. OL11—2H 17
Blackpool St. M11—3E 89
 (in two parts)
Blackrock Cotts. OL5—5E 81
Blackrock St. M11—4B 88
Blackrod Dri. BL8—4F 27
Black Sail Wlk. OL1—6E 49
Blackshaw Ho. BL3—1G 37
Blackshaw La. BL3—1G 37
Blackshaw La. OL2—3D 48
Blackshaw La. SK9—5F 159
Blackshaw Row. BL3—2G 37
Blackshaw St. SK3—3G 131
Blacksmith La. OL11—1B 32
Blackstock St. M13—3G 101
Blackstone Av. OL16—3C 20
Blackstone Edge Ct. OL15—3G 9
Blackstone Edge Old Rd. OL15
 —3G 9
Blackstone Rd. SK2—6D 132
Blackstone Wlk. M9—5F 75
Blackthorn Av. M19—2C 118
Blackthorn Clo. OL12—1G 19
Blackthorne Clo. BL1—4E 23
Blackthorne Dri. M33—1F 125
Blackthorne Rd. SK14—3C 122
Blackwin St. M12—1C 102
Blackwood Dri. M23—3D 126
Blackwood St. BL3—3C 38
Bladen Clo. SK8—1C 142
Blair Av. M28—5D 54
Blair Av. M31—5A 96
Blair Clo. M33—2E 125
Blair Clo. OL2—6F 35
Blair Clo. SK7—5C 144
Blairhall Av. M10—4A 76
Blair La. BL2—4F 25
Blairmore Dri. BL3—2C 36
Blair M16—6C 100
Blair St. BL4—3B 56
Blair St. BL7—3D 10
Blair St. M16—2B 100
Blair St. OL12—2F 19
Blakedown Wlk. M12—2A 102
 (off Cochrane Av.)
Blake Dri. SK2—4E 133
Blakefield Dri. M28—2G 69

Blake Gdns. BL1—3H 23
Blakelock St. OL2—6E 35
Blakemere Av. M33—6E 115
Blakemore Wik. M12—4A 88
Blake St. BL1—3H 23
Blake St. BL7—4E 11
Blake St. OL16—3A 20
Blakeswell Clo. M31—4H 95
Blakey Clo. BL3—3D 36
Blakey St. M12—3C 102
Blanche St. OL12—1A 20
Blanche Wik. OL1—1E 65
Bland Clo. M35—4E 77
Blandford Av. M28—3H 69
Blandford Clo. BL8—6D 14
Blandford Ct. SK13—8E 93
Blandford Dri. M10—1D 76
Blandford Rd. M30—3D 82
Blandford Rd. SK4—1D 130
Blandford St. M6—1H 85
Blandford St. OL6—2G 91
Blandford St. SK15—3E 93
Bland Rd. M25—1F 73
Bland St. BL9—2D 28
Bland Wik. M16—3C 100
Blanefield Clo. M21—2C 116
Blanshard Wik. M15—1D 100 & 6H 165
Blantyre Av. M28—1G 69
Blantyre Rd. M27—5H 71
Blantyre St. M15—6B 86 & 3D 164
Blantyre St. M27—3D 70
Blantyre St. M30—2C 82
Blanwood Dri. M8—4D 74
Blaven Clo. SK3—6H 131
Blaydon St. M1—5F 87 & 1C 166
Blazemoss Bank. SK2—6D 132
Bleackley St. BL8—1A 28
Bleak Hey Rd. M22—3D 140
Bleakley St. M25—6C 42
Bleaklow Fold. SK13—6G 109
  (off Castleton Cres.)
Bleaklow Gdns. SK13—6G 109
  (off Castleton Cres.)
Bleaklow La. SK13—6G 109
Bleaklow Wik. SK13—6G 109
  (off Castleton Cres.)
Bleak St. BL2—3D 24
Bleasby St. OL4—2G 65
Bleasdale Clo. BL9—4E 43
Bleasdale Rd. M22—3G 139
Bleasdale St. OL2—2B 48
Bleasedale Rd. BL1—3D 22
Bleatarn Rd. SK1—4B 132
Bledlow Clo. M30—2G 83
Blencarn Wik. M9—4F 75
Blendworth Clo. M8—4B 74
Blenheim Av. M16—5B 100
Blenheim Av. OL1—4H 49
Blenheim Clo. BL9—2D 42
Blenheim Clo. OL10—3G 31
Blenheim Clo. SK9—2G 159
Blenheim Clo. SK12—3F 155
Blenheim Clo. WA14—3F 137
Blenheim Ct. M9—4C 60
  (off Deanswood Dri.)
Blenheim Rd. BL2—6F 25
Blenheim Rd. M16—4G 99
Blenheim Rd. SK8—3D 142
Blenheim Rd. Est. BL2—1H 39
Blenheim St. OL12—2E 19
Blenmar Clo. M26—2A 42
Blériot St. BL3—4H 37
Bletchley Clo. M13—2H 101
Bletchley Rd. SK4—2A 130
Blethyn Clo. BL3—5F 37
Blinco Rd. M31—6H 97
Blind La. M12—6H 87 & 3H 167
Blindsill Rd. BL4—2D 54
Blisworth Av. M30—5G 83
Blisworth Clo. M4—4H 87
  & 5H 163
Blithfield Wik. M34—5E 105
Block La. OL9—5H 63
Blocksage St. SK16—6B 92
Blodwell St. M6—3F 85
Blofield Ct. BL4—2F 55
Blomley St. OL11—3C 32
Bloomfield Dri. BL9—4F 43
Bloomfield Dri. M28—4C 68

Bloomfield Rd. BL4—3F 55
Bloomfield St. BL1—2A 24
Bloomsbury Gro. WA15—5A 126
Bloomsbury La. WA15—5A 126
Bloom St. BL0—5C 4
Bloom St. M1—5E 87 & 1A 166
  (in two parts)
Bloom St. M3—3C 86 & 4E 161
Bloom St. SK3—3E 131
Blossom Pl. OL16—3H 19
Blossoms Hey. SK8—4A 142
Blossoms Hey Wik. SK8—4A 142
Blossoms La. SK7—5C 152
Blossom St. M3—3C 86 & 3F 161
Blossom St. M4—3F 87 & 4D 162
Bloxham Wik. M9—5H 61
Blucher St. M5—4A 86 & 5A 160
Blucher St. M12—1A 102
Blucher St. OL7—5E 79
Blue Bell Av. M10—2A 76
Blue Bell Clo. SK14—2D 106
Bluebell Dri. OL11—2B 32
Bluebell Dri. SK6—5H 135
Bluebell Gro. SK8—1H 141
Blueberry Dri. OL2—6H 35
Blueberry Rd. WA14—3C 136
Bluefields. OL2—5H 35
Bluestone Dri. SK4—6A 118
Bluestone Rd. M10—3A 76
Bluestone Rd. M34—5A 104
Bluestone Ter. M34—5A 104
Blundell Clo. BL9—4F 43
Blundell St. BL1—6A 24
Blundering La. SK15—1H 107
Blunn St. OL8—5D 64
Blyth Av. M23—1A 128
Blyth Av. OL15—6D 8
Blyth Clo. WA15—5C 126
Blythe Av. SK7—1E 153
Blyton St. M15—2F 101
Blyton Way. M34—1F 121
Boad St. M1—5F 87 & 1D 166
Boardale Dri. M24—6G 45
Boardman Clo. BL1—3A 24
Boardman Clo. SK5—5H 119
Boardman Fold Clo. M24
  —4A 62
Boardman Fold Rd. M24—4H 61
Boardman La. M24—1D 60
Boardman Rd. M8—1B 74
Boardman St. BL1—3A 24
Boardman St. M30—4G 83
Boardman St. SK14—5B 106
Board St. BL3—1H 37
Board St. OL6—1B 92
Boar Grn. Clo. M10—4C 76
Boarshaw Clough. M24—5B 46
Boarshaw Cres. M24—5C 46
Boarshaw La. M24—4D 46
Boarshaw Rd. M24—6A 46
Boarshurst La. OL3—4F 53
Boat La. M22—2C 128
Boat La. M30—5F 95
Boat La. OL3—2D 52
Bobbin Wik. M4—4G 87
  (off Cardroom Rd.)
Bobbin Wik. OL4—3E 65
Bob Massey Clo. M11—4E 89
Bob's La. M30—5B 110
Boddens Hill Rd. SK4—2C 130
Boddington Rd. M30—4C 82
Bodiam Rd. BL8—2H 13
Bodley St. M11—3E 89
Bodmin Clo. OL2—4E 49
Bodmin Cres. SK5—4B 120
Bodmin Dri. SK7—6G 143
Bodmin Rd. M33—4F 113
Bodmin Wik. M23—6G 127
Bodney Way. M9—6D 60
Bognor Rd. SK3—1G 143
Bolam Clo. M23—2E 127
Boland Dri. M14—1G 117
Bolderrod Pl. OL1—1E 65
Bolderstone Pl. SK2—1E 145
Bold Row. M27—4F 71
Bold St. BL1—6B 24
Bold St. BL9—2E 29
Bold St. M15—2C 100
Bold St. M16—3C 100

Bold St. M27—1F 71
Bold St. WA14—2F 137
Bolesworth Clo. M21—1F 115
Boleyn Ct. OL10—4E 31
Boleywood Ct. SK9—6F 151
Bolholt Ter. BL8—1H 27
Bolivia St. M5—3C 84
Bollin Av. WA14—5D 136
Bollin Clo. BL4—3A 56
Bollin Clo. M15—1B 100
Bollin Clo. SK9—1F 159
Bollin Ct. M15—1B 100 & 6C 164
Bollin Ct. SK9—2F 159
Bollin Ct. WA14—4D 136
Bollin Dri. M33—1B 126
Bollin Dri. WA14—3G 125
Bollings Yd. BL1—1B 38
Bollington Clo. OL7—4G 91
Bollington Rd. M10—3H 87 & 3H 163
Bollington Rd. SK4—4F 119
Bollington St. OL7—4G 91
Bollingwood Chase. SK9—2G 159
Bollin Hill. SK9—1D 158
Bollin Sq. WA14—4D 136
Bollin Wik. SK5—4H 119
Bollin Wik. SK9—2E 159
Bollin Way. M25—5G 43
Bollinway. WA15—5A 138
Bolney Wik. M10—1H 87
Bolshaw Farm La. SK8—1G 151
Bolshaw Rd. SK8—1F 151
Boltmeadow. SK3—5E 53
Bolton Av. M19—1H 129
Bolton Clo. M25—1D 72
Bolton Clo. SK12—3D 154
Bolton Rd. BL2—6G 11
Bolton Rd. BL4—5F 39
  (Farnworth)
Bolton Rd. BL4—2G 55
  (Kearsley)
Bolton Rd. BL5 & BL3—5A 36
Bolton Rd. BL7—1H 11
Bolton Rd. BL8—5G 27
  (Bury)
Bolton Rd. BL8—6A 4
  (Hawkshaw)
Bolton Rd. M6—5B 72
Bolton Rd. M26—3D 40
Bolton Rd. M27—1F 71
Bolton Rd. M28—5F 55
Bolton Rd. OL11—1A 32
Bolton Rd. N. BL0—3A 4
  (Edenfield)
Bolton Rd. N. BL0—1E 5
  (Ramsbottom)
Bolton Rd. W. BL0—6B 4
Bolton St. BL0—4D 4
Bolton St. BL1—3B 24
Bolton St. BL9—3B 28
Bolton St. M3—3C 86 & 4E 161
Bolton St. M26—4F 41
Bolton St. OL4—2F 65
  (in two parts)
Bolton St. SK5—2G 119
Bolton Yd. OL3—1F 53
Bombay Rd. SK3—4E 131
Bombay Sq. M1—5E 87
  (off Whitworth St.)
Bombay St. M1—5E 87
  & 2B 166
Bombay St. OL6—1B 92
Bonar Clo. SK3—3E 131
Bonar Rd. SK3—3E 131
Boncarn Dri. M23—1G 139
Bonchurch Wik. M18—1D 102
Bondmark Rd. M18—1E 103
Bond Sq. M7—5A 74
Bond St. BL0—3B 4
Bond St. BL9—3E 29
Bond St. M12—6H 87 & 2E 167
Bond St. M34—4F 105
Bond St. OL12—1A 20
Bond St. SK15—2E 93
Bongs Rd. SK2—5F 133
  (in two parts)
Bonhill Wik. M11—3D 88
Bonington Rise. SK6—3F 135

Bonis Cres. SK2—1C 144
Bonny Brow St. M24—2D 60
Bonnyfields. SK6—1H 133
Bonsall Bank. SK13—5G 109
  (off Melandra Castle Rd.)
Bonsall Clo. SK13—5G 109
  (off Melandra Castle Rd.)
Bonsall Fold. SK13—5G 109
  (off Melandra Castle Rd.)
Bonsall St. M15—1D 100 & 6G 165
Bonscale Cres. M24—4G 45
Bonthe St. M30—1D 110
Bonville Chase. WA14—1C 136
Bonville Rd. WA14—6C 124
Boodle St. OL8—2H 91
Bookham Wik. M9—3G 75
Boond St. M3—3C 86 & 3F 161
Boond St. M4—4H 87 & 5G 163
Boonfields. BL7—3E 11
Booth Av. M14—2H 117
Boothby Ct. M27—2D 70
Boothby Rd. M27—2E 71
Boothby St. SK2—1C 144
Booth Clo. SK15—4D 92
Boothcote. M34—1D 104
Booth Ct. BL4—1F 55
Booth Dri. M31—2B 96
Boothfield. BL8—2A 28
Boothfield Av. M22—5B 128
Boothfield Dri. M22—5B 128
Boothfield Rd. M22—5A 128
Booth Hall Rd. M9—6A 62
Booth Hill. OL1—6C 48
Booth La. M9—5C 60
Booth Rd. BL3—5B 40
Booth Rd. M16—4A 100
Booth Rd. M33—3B 114
Booth Rd. M34—6A 90
Booth Rd. SK9—6E 151
Booth Rd. WA14—1E 137
Boothroyden Clo. M24—2D 60
  (in two parts)
Boothroyden Rd. M24 & M9—2E 61
  (in two parts)
Boothroyden Ter. M9—3E 61
Boothsbank Av. M28—5D 68
Booth's Hall Gro. M28—5D 68
Booth's Hall Rd. M28—5D 68
Booth's Hall Way. M28—5D 68
Booth St. BL1—2G 23
Booth St. BL8—5H 13
Booth St. M2—4D 86 & 6H 161
Booth St. M3—3D 86 & 4G 161
Booth St. M24—3D 62
Booth St. M34—2F 105
Booth St. M35—4E 77
Booth St. OL4—3A 66
Booth St. OL6—3H 91
Booth St. OL9—3C 64
Booth St. SK3—4G 131
Booth St. SK14—2E 109
  (Hollingworth)
Booth St. SK14—6C 106
  (Hyde)
Booth St. SK15—5C 92
Booth St. E. M13—1F 101 & 5C 166
Booth St. W. M15—1E 101 & 6A 166
Booth Way. BL8—6G 13
Boothway. M30—3H 83
Boot La. BL1—4B 22
Bootle St. M2—4D 86 & 6G 161
Bordale Av. M9—4H 75
Bordan St. M11—5B 88
Bordesley Av. M28—3C 54
Bordley Wik. M23—2E 127
Bordon Rd. SK3—4D 130
Boringdon Clo. M10—5B 76
Borland Av. M10—2D 76
Borough Arc. SK14—4B 106
Borough Av. M26—2B 42
Borough Av. M27—2G 71
Borough Rd. M5—4D 84
Borough Rd. WA15—1G 137
Borough St. SK15—4E 93
Borron St. SK1—1A 132
Borrowdale Av. BL1—5E 23
Borrowdale Av. SK8—1F 141

Borrowdale Clo. OL2—1B 48
Borrowdale Cres. M20—5C 116
Borrowdale Cres. OL7—6D 78
Borrowdale Dri. BL9—4E 43
Borrowdale Dri. OL11—1B 32
Borrowdale Rd. M24—5F 45
Borrowdale Rd. SK2—4B 132
Borrowdale Ter. SK15—1E 93
Borsden St. M27—1D 70
Borth Av. SK2—4B 132
Borth Wlk. M23—5F 127
Borwell St. M18—1F 103
Boscobel Rd. BL3—5D 38
Boscombe Av. M30—5E 83
Boscombe Dri. SK7—3C 144
Boscombe St. M14—5F 101
Boscombe St. SK5—5H 103
Boscow Rd. BL3—5A 40
Bosden Av. SK7—2E 145
Bosden Clo. SK1—3H 131
(off Bosden Fold)
Bosden Clo. SK9—2H 151
Bosden Fold. SK1—3H 131
Bosdenfold Rd. SK7—2E 145
Bosden Hall Rd. SK7—2E 145
Bosdin Rd. E. M31—6A 96
Bosdin Rd. W. M31—6A 96
Bosley Av. M20—1E 117
Bosley Clo. SK9—5H 151
Bosley Dri. SK12—4G 155
Bosley St. SK3—3C 130
Bossall Av. M9—5G 61
Bossington Clo. SK2—3C 132
Bostock Wlk. M13—6F 87 & 4D 166
Boston Clo. SK7—6D 143
Boston Clo. SK7—6F 143
Boston Ct. M5—5E 85
Boston St. BL1—3A 24
Boston St. OL8—5D 64
Boston St. SK14—4C 106
Boston Wlk. M34—6G 105
Boswell Av. M34—3E 47
Boswell Way. M24—3E 47
Bosworth Clo. M25—1G 59
Bosworth Sq. OL11—1D 32
Bosworth St. M11—5C 88
Bosworth St. OL11—1D 32
Botanical Av. M16—2G 99
Botanical Ho. M16—2G 99
Botany Clo. OL10—2D 30
Botany La. OL6—1A 92
Botany Rd. M30—1C 82
Botany Rd. SK6—3G 121
Botha Clo. M11—6F 89
Botham Clo. M15—2E 101
Botham St. M30—2D 82
Bothwell Rd. M10—2G 87 & 2F 163
Bottesford Av. M20—4D 116
Bottomley Side. M9—1E 75
Bottom o' th' Moor. BL2—3F 25
Bottom o' th' Moor. OL1—2F 65
Bottom St. SK14—4D 106
Boulder Dri. M23—3G 139
Boulderstone Rd. SK15—1E 93
Bouldon Dri. BL8—6C 14
Boulevard, The. SK7—3E 145
Boulevard, The. SK14—3F 109
Bouley Wlk. M12—1B 102
Boulton St. M3—3C 86
Boundary Clo. OL5—5E 81
(in two parts)
Boundary Clo. SK6—4A 122
Boundary Dri. BL2—2A 40
Boundary Gdns. BL1—3H 23
Boundary Gdns. OL1—6C 48
Boundary Grn. M34—2E 105
Boundary Gro. M33—6F 115
Boundary La. M15—1E 101 & 5A 166
Boundary Pk. Rd. OL1—6A 48
Boundary Rd. M27—2F 71
Boundary Rd. M30—4F 95
Boundary Rd. SK8—5B 130
Boundary St. BL1—3H 23
Boundary St. BL9—2D 28
Boundary St. M12—2C 102
Boundary St. OL11—5G 19
Boundary St. OL15—3E 5
Boundary St. E. M13—6E 87 & 4B 166

Boundary St. W. M15—1E 101 & 5A 166
Boundary, The. M27—5E 57
Boundary Wlk. OL11—6G 19
Bourdon St. M10—2H 87 & 2H 163
Bourget St. M8—3B 74
Bournbrook Av. M28—3C 54
Bourne Av. M27—4F 71
Bourne Dri. M10—2B 76
Bourne Ho. M5—3F 85
Bournelea Av. M19—3B 118
Bourne Rd. SK9—3G 158
Bourne St. SK4—5G 119
Bourne St. SK9—3C 158
Bourne Wlk. BL1—4B 24
Bournville Av. SK4—5G 119
Bournville Gro. M19—6D 102
Bourton Clo. BL8—2H 27
Bourton Dri. M18—3D 102
Bowden Clo. OL11—5D 32
Bowden La. SK6—4C 134
Bowden Rd. M27—4G 71
Bowden St. BL1—4F 23
Bowden St. BL3—1H 37
Bowden St. M34—4E 105
Bowden St. SK7—2E 145
Bowden St. SK14—2B 106
Bowden View. M31—5D 96
Bowder Clo. SK14—6A 108
Bowdon Av. M14—6D 100
Bowdon Rise. WA14—3F 137
Bowdon Rd. WA14—2E 137
Bowdon St. SK3—3F 131
(in two parts)
Bowen Clo. SK7—2H 153
Bowen St. BL1—4F 23
Bower Av. OL12—5B 8
Bower Av. SK4—6E 119
Bower Av. SK7—4D 144
Bower Ct. SK14—2E 107
Bowerfield Av. SK7—5D 144
Bowerfield Cres. SK7—5D 144
Bowerfold La. SK4—1E 131
Bower Gro. SK15—3G 93
Bower La. OL9—1G 77
Bower Rd. WA15—4G 137
Bowers Av. M31—3D 96
Bowers St. M14—2A 118
Bower St. BL9—2G 29
Bower St. M8—4A 74
Bower St. M10—6H 75
Bower St. OL1—2E 65
Bower St. SK5—5H 103
Bower Ter. M35—2C 90
Bowery Av. SK8—1B 152
Bowes Clo. BL8—6B 14
Bowes St. M14—4D 100
Bowfell Circ. M31—4D 96
Bowfell Dri. SK6—5C 146
Bowfell Gro. M9—5D 60
Bowfell Rd. M31—5C 96
Bowfield Wlk. M40—6C 76
Bowgreave Av. BL2—6H 25
Bow Grn. M. WA14—3D 136
Bow Grn. Rd. WA14—4B 136
Bowgreen Wlk. M15—1B 100 & 5D 164
Bowker Av. M31—4B 96
Bowker Av. M34—1H 121
Bowker Bank Av. M8—1B 74
Bowker Clo. OL11—2A 18
Bowker Ct. M7—5H 73
Bowkers Row. BL1—6B 24
Bowker St. M7—5H 73
Bowker St. M26—4G 41
Bowker St. M28—6D 54
Bowker St. SK14—4C 106
Bowker Vale Gdns. M9—6B 60
Bowlacre Rd. SK14—3B 122
Bowland Av. M18—3A 104
Bowland Clo. BL8—2E 27
Bowland Clo. OL2—5C 34
Bowland Clo. OL6—4G 79
Bowland Clo. SK2—6E 133
Bowland Ct. M33—5B 114
Bowland Dri. BL1—3C 22
Bowland Gro. OL16—1D 34
Bowland Rd. M23—5F 127
Bowland Rd. M34—4B 104

Bowland Rd. SK6—4H 121
Bowland Rd. SK13—6H 109
Bow La. M2—4D 86 & 6H 161
Bow La. OL10—3F 31
Bow La. WA14—5C 136
Bowlee Clo. BL9—5E 43
Bowler St. M19—1D 118
Bowler St. OL2—6F 35
Bowlers Wlk. OL12—1H 19
Bowley Av. M22—3G 139
Bowling Grn. St. BL0—2F 5
(in two parts)
Bowling Grn. St. OL10—3F 31
Bowling Grn. St. SK14—5B 106
Bowling Grn. Way. OL11—4B 18
Bowling Rd. M18—4G 103
Bowling St. OL9—1H 77
Bowman Cres. OL6—2B 92
Bowmeadow Grange. M12—3B 102
Bowmead Wlk. M8—5B 74
Bowmont Clo. SK8—1C 142
Bowness Av. M30—5B 110
Bowness Av. OL12—2E 19
Bowness Av. SK4—3G 119
Bowness Av. SK8—4D 142
Bowness Ct. M24—5F 45
Bowness Dri. M33—4H 113
Bowness Rd. BL3—3H 37
(Bolton)
Bowness Rd. BL3—3H 39
(Little Lever)
Bowness Rd. M24—5E 45
Bowness Rd. OL7—1F 91
Bowness Rd. WA15—6D 126
Bowness St. M11—6H 89
Bowness St. M32—4D 98
Bowscale Clo. M13—3B 102
Bowstone Hill Rd. BL2—6D 12
Bow St. BL1—6B 24
Bow St. M2—4D 86 & 5G 161
Bow St. OL1—2D 64
Bow St. OL6—3A 92
(off Nelson St.)
Bow St. OL6—2H 91
(off Warrington St.)
Bow St. OL11—2D 32
Bow St. SK3—3E 131
Bow Vs. WA14—3D 136
Boxgrove Rd. M33—4G 113
Boxgrove Wlk. M8—5B 74
Boxhill Dri. M23—2G 127
Box St. BL0—3F 5
Box St. OL15—4E 9
Boxtree Av. M18—3F 103
Box Wlk. M31—6C 110
Boyd St. M12—6C 88
Boyd's Wlk. SK16—6A 92
Boyer St. M16—2H 99
Boyle St. BL1—4E 23
Boyle St. M8—5D 74
Boysnope Cotts. M30—2H 95
Boysnope Cres. M30—3G 95
Brabant Clo. SK8—4D 142
Brabant Rd. SK8—3D 142
Brabham Clo. M21—1H 115
Brabyns Av. SK6—6B 122
Brabyns Brow. SK6—4E 135
Brabyns Rd. SK14—2C 122
Bracadale Dri. SK3—1G 143
Bracdale Dri. SK3—6G 131
Bracewell Clo. M12—2C 102
Bracken Av. M28—6G 55
Brackenbury Wlk. M15—2E 101
Bracken Clo. BL1—5B 10
Bracken Clo. M33—4E 113
Bracken Clo. M35—3C 90
Bracken Clo. OL4—3B 66
Bracken Clo. OL10—5F 31
Bracken Clo. SK6—4F 135
Bracken Clo. SK14—1F 109
Bracken Dri. M23—6H 137
Brackenfield Wlk. WA15—5D 126
Brackenhall Clo. OL10—3C 30
Brackenhurst Av. OL5—2G 81
Brackenside. SK5—1A 120
Brackenwood Dri. SK8—1H 141
Brackenwood M. SK9—1H 159
Brackley Av. M15—6B 86 & 4C 164

Brackley Av. M30—3B 110
Brackley Ct. M22—3B 128
Brackley Lodge. M30—2H 83
Brackley Rd. BL3—6E 37
Brackley Rd. M30—1F 83
Brackley Rd. SK4—5E 119
Brackley Sq. OL1—1E 65
Brackley St. BL4—1F 55
(in two parts)
Brackley St. M28—5E 55
Brackley St. OL1—1E 65
Bracknell Dri. M9—6C 60
Bracondale Av. BL1—3F 23
Bradbourne Clo. BL3—2A 38
Bradburn Av. M30—4F 83
Bradburn Clo. M30—3F 83
Bradburn Gro. M30—4F 83
Bradburn Rd. M30—2C 110
Bradburn St. M30—4F 83
Bradburn Wlk. M8—5D 74
(off Moordown Clo.)
Bradbury Av. WA14—6C 124
Bradbury's La. OL3—5G 53
Bradbury St. BL9—2E 43
Bradbury St. OL7—1G 91
Bradbury St. SK14—6C 106
Bradbury Wlk. OL2—3C 48
(off Shaw St.)
Bradda Mt. SK7—3A 144
Braddan Av. M33—6C 114
Bradden Clo. M5—4G 85
Braddocks Clo. OL12—5B 8
Braddon Av. M31—5F 97
Braddon Rd. SK6—4G 121
Braddon St. M11—4E 89
Bradfield Av. M6—3C 84
Bradfield Clo. SK5—5G 103
Bradfield Rd. M31 & M32—5H 97
Bradford Av. BL3—4D 38
Bradford Clo. M10—2C 76
Bradford Cres. BL3—3C 38
Bradford Pk. Dri. BL2—1D 38
Bradford Rd. BL4 & BL3—1C 54
Bradford Rd. M10—3H 87 & 4H 163
Bradford Rd. M30—6E 71
Bradford St. BL2—1C 38
Bradford St. BL4—2F 55
Bradford St. OL1—1C 64
Bradford Ter. BL9—4B 28
Bradgate St. BL8—4H 141
Bradgate Clo. M22—3C 128
Bradgate Rd. M33—1B 126
Bradgate Rd. WA14—6C 124
Bradgate St. OL7—4G 91
Brading Wlk. M22—5C 140
Bradley Av. M7—4F 73
Bradley Clo. M34—6E 91
Bradley Clo. WA15—4G 125
Bradley Dri. BL9—5F 43
Bradley Fold. SK15—3F 93
Bradley Fold Rd. BL2—1B 40
Bradley Grn. Rd. SK14—1D 106
Bradley Ho. OL8—4D 64
Bradley La. BL2—2B 40
Bradley La. M32—2B 114
Bradley La. OL16—1F 35
Bradley's Clo. M1—4F 87 & 5C 162
Bradley St. M1—3F 87 & 4C 162
Bradley St. OL16—1F 35
Bradley St. SK16—6G 91
Bradnor Rd. M22—4B 128
Bradshaw Av. M20—2F 117
Bradshaw Av. M25—5C 42
Bradshaw Av. M35—6E 77
Bradshaw Brow. BL2—1E 25
Bradshaw Cres. SK6—4E 135
Bradshaw Fold Av. M10—6D 62
Bradshawgate. BL2—6B 24
Bradshaw Hall Dri. BL2—5G 11
Bradshaw Hall La. SK8—5H 141
(in two parts)
Bradshaw Hall M. BL2—4G 11
Bradshaw La. M32—6D 98
Bradshaw Meadows. BL2—5H 11
Bradshaw Rd. BL2—6H 11
Bradshaw Rd. BL8—5E 13
Bradshaw Rd. SK6—4D 134
Bradshaw St. BL2- 1B 38 & 3A 162

Bradshaw St. M4—3E 87 & 3A 162
Bradshaw St. M7—5A 74
Bradshaw St. M24—2C 62
Bradshaw St. M26—4F 41
Bradshaw St. OL1—2D 64
Bradshaw St. OL10—3G 31
(in two parts)
Bradshaw St. OL16—3A 20
Bradshaw St. N. M7—4H 73
Bradshaw Trading Est. M24—3C 62
Bradstock Clo. M16—4C 100
Bradstone Rd. M8—6B 74
Bradwell Av. M20—3D 116
Bradwell Av. M32—4A 98
Bradwell Dri. SK8—6G 141
Bradwell Fold. SK13—6G 109
(off Buxton M.)
Bradwell Lea. SK13—5G 109
(off Buxton M.)
Bradwell Pl. BL2—4D 24
Bradwell Rd. SK7—5E 145
Bradwell Ter. SK13—6G 109
(off Buxton M.)
Bradwell Wlk. M31—4H 95
Bradwen Av. M8—2C 74
Bradwen Clo. M34—6G 105
Brady St. SK1—1A 132
Braemar Av. M35—6C 96
Braemar Av. M32—5A 98
Braemar Ct. M9—4C 60
Braemar Dri. BL9—3H 29
Braemar Dri. M33—1E 125
Braemar Gro. OL10—4C 30
Braemar La. M28—5D 68
Braemar Rd. M14—1A 118
Braemar Rd. SK7—2F 145
Braemar Wlk. BL3—2C 36
Braemore Clo. OL2—5C 34
Braemore Dri. SK14—6B 108
Braeside. M32—6A 98
Brae Side. OL8—1C 78
Braeside Clo. SK2—5F 133
Braeside Gro. BL3—2C 36
Braewood Clo. BL9—2G 29
Bragadale Ct. OL10—4B 30
Brageham St. M18—2E 103
Brailsford Av. SK13—5G 109
Brailsford Clo. SK13—5G 109
(off Hathersage Cres.)
Brailsford Gdns. SK13—5G 109
(off Hathersage Cres.)
Brailsford Grn. SK13—5G 109
(off Melandra Castle Rd.)
Brailsford M. SK13—5G 109
Brailsford Rd. BL2—2E 25
Brailsford Rd. M14—1A 118
Braintree Rd. M22—5C 140
Braithwaite Rd. M24—3F 45
Brakehouse Clo. OL16—5E 21
Brakesmere Gro. M28—5B 54
Braley St. M12—6F 87 & 3D 166
Bramall Clo. SK7—5F 43
Bramall Ct. M3—2B 86
Bramall Cres. M28—2B 86 & 2D 160
Bramall Mt. SK2—6H 131
Bramber Way. OL9—1E 63
Bramble Av. M5—6A 86 & 3A 164
Bramble Av. OL4—6H 49
Bramble Clo. OL15—4D 8
Bramble Meadow. M5—6H 85
(off W. Park St.)
Bramble Wlk. M22—3A 140
Bramble Wlk. M33—4E 113
Bramblewood. OL9—1E 63
Brambling Clo. M34—3C 90
Brambling Clo. SK2—6G 133
Bramcote Av. BL2—2D 38
Bramcote Av. M23—5H 127
Bramdean Av. BL2—6A 12
Bramfield Wlk. M15—6B 86 & 4D 164
Bramhall Av. BL2—1A 26
Bramhall Clo. M33—6E 115
Bramhall Clo. OL16—5E 21
Bramhall Clo. WA15—5D 126
Bramhall La. SK2 & SK3—5H 131
Bramhall La. SK7—3G 143
Bramhall La. S. SK7—1G 153
Bramhall Moor La. SK7—4A 144

Bramhall Pk. Rd. SK7—4F 143
Bramhall Rd. SK7—4E 143
Bramhall St. BL3—4D 38
Bramhall St. M18—2G 103
Bramhall St. SK14—3B 106
Bramhall Wlk. M34—5E 105
Bramham Rd. SK6—1E 147
Bramhope Wlk. M9—4F 75
Bramley Av. M19—1C 118
Bramley Av. M32—5B 98
Bramley Clo. M27—5C 70
Bramley Clo. SK7—1G 153
Bramley Cres. SK4—2D 130
Bramley Dri. BL8—5C 14
Bramley Dri. SK7—1G 153
Bramley Meade. M7—4H 73
Bramley Rd. BL1—5D 10
Bramley Rd. OL11—3A 18
Bramley Rd. SK7—1G 153
Bramley St. M7—1C 86
Brammall La. SK3—2H 143
Brammay Dri. BL8—5G 13
Brampton Rd. BL3—4E 37
Brampton Rd. SK7—3H 143
Brampton Wlk. M10—5B 76
Bramway. SK6—6D 146
Bramway. SK6—6E 143
Bramwell Dri. M13—1G 101 & 5E 167
Bramwell St. SK1—3B 132
Bramwood Ct. SK7—1G 153
Bramworth Av. BL0—3D 4
Brancaster Rd. M1—6E 87 & 3B 166
Branch Rd. OL15—1E 21
Brancker St. BL5—6A 36
Brandish Clo. M13—2H 101
Brandle Av. BL8—1A 28
Brandlehow Dri. M24—5E 45
Brandlesholme Rd. BL8—3A 14
Brandon Av. M22—3A 128
Brandon Av. M30—6G 71
Brandon Av. M34—4H 103
Brandon Av. SK8—4F 141
Brandon Brow. OL1—1C 64
Brandon Clo. BL8—6D 14
Brandon Cres. OL2—5E 35
Brandon Rd. M6—6H 71
Brandon St. OL16—5E 21
(off Nall St.)
Brandram Rd. M25—5G 59
Brandsby Gdns. M5—5G 85
Brandwood. OL1—6E 47
Brandwood Av. M21—5B 116
Brandwood Clo. M28—3C 68
Brandwood St. BL3—3G 37
Branfield Av. SK8—4H 141
Brankgate Ct. M20—4E 117
Branksome Av. M25—5E 59
Branksome Dri. M6—6G 71
Branksome Dri. M9—4D 60
Branksome Dri. SK8—4H 141
Branksome Rd. SK4—2D 130
Bransby Av. M9—5G 61
Branscombe Dri. M33—4E 113
Branscombe Gdns. BL3—2F 39
Bransdale Av. OL2—3A 48
Bransdale Clo. BL3—3D 36
Bransford Rd. M31—3E 97
Branson St. M10—3H 87 & 4H 163
Branson Wlk. WA15—5D 126
Branston Rd. M10—1D 76
Brantfell Gro. BL2—5H 25
Brantingham Rd. M21 & M16
—6H 99
Brantwood Clo. OL2—2A 48
Brantwood Ct. M7—3H 73
Brantwood Dri. BL2—5H 25
Brantwood Rd. M7—3H 73
Brantwood Rd. SK4—5E 119
Brantwood Rd. SK8—4B 142
Brantwood Ter. M9—4H 75
Brassey St. M24—6A 46
Brassey St. OL6—1H 91
Brassington Av. M5—5H 85
Brassington Av. M21—2H 115
Brassington Cres. SK13—5F 109
Brassington Gdns. M5—5H 85
Brassington Rd. SK4—5A 118
Brathay Clo. BL2—3H 25

Bratton Wlk. M13—1H 101 & 6G 167
Brattray Dri. M24—4G 45
Braunston Clo. M30—5G 83
Braxton Wlk. M9—3G 75
Bray Av. M30—2D 82
Braybrook Dri. BL1—6B 22
Bray Clo. SK8—3A 142
Brayford St. M22—4B 140
Brayshaw Clo. OL10—4E 31
Brayside Rd. M20 & M19—5H 117
Brayston Gdns. SK8—5F 129
Brayton Av. M20—1G 129
Brayton Av. M33—3F 113
Brazenose St. M2—4D 86 & 6G 161
Brazil St. M1—5E 87 & 1B 166
Brazley Av. BL3—4C 38
Breach Ho. La. WA5a 148
Bread St. M18—1G 103
Breamore Cres. M7—4F 73
Brean Wlk. M22—4A 140
Brechin Wlk. M11—4E 89
Brechin Way. OL10—4C 30
Breckland Dri. BL1—5B 22
Breckles Pl. BL3—2H 37
(off Kershaw St.)
Breck Rd. M30—3D 82
Brecon Av. M19—2B 118
Brecon Av. M31—4H 95
Brecon Av. M34—6F 105
Brecon Av. SK8—4A 142
Brecon Clo. OL2—1A 48
Brecon Clo. SK12—3F 155
Brecon Cres. OL6—5F 79
Brecon Dri. BL9—6C 28
Brecon Towers. SK5—2C 120
Brecon Wlk. OL8—1H 77
Bredbury Dri. BL4—1G 55
Bredbury Grn. SK6—2G 133
Bredbury Parkway. SK6—3E 121
Bredbury Rd. M14—5F 101
Bredbury St. OL9—3H 63
Bredbury St. SK14—2B 106
Brede Wlk. M23—2D 126
Breeze Hill. OL2—2F 49
Breeze Hill. OL4—4H 65
Breeze Mt. M25—1F 73
Breightmet Dri. BL2—6G 25
Breightmet Fold La. BL2—5H 25
Breightmet St. BL2—1B 38
Brellafield Dri. OL2—4D 34
Brenbar Cres. OL12—4H 7
Brenchley Dri. M23—1G 127
Brencon Av. M23—2C 126
Brendall Clo. SK2—6G 133
Brendon Av. M10—4A 76
Brendon Av. SK5—3H 119
Brendon Dri. M34—4D 90
Brendon Hills. OL2—4B 48
Brenley Wlk. M9—3F 75
(off Alderside Rd.)
Brennan Clo. M15—2E 101
Brennan Ct. OL8—1A 78
Brennock Clo. M11—5B 88
Brentbridge Rd. M14—1F 117
Brent Clo. BL2—2B 40
Brent Clo. SK12—3B 154
Brentfield Av. M8—5B 74
Brentford Av. BL1—3F 23
Brentford St. SK5—3H 119
Brentford St. M9—4G 75
Brent Moor Rd. SK7—2A 144
Brentnall St. SK1—3H 131
Brentnor Rd. M10—1C 76
Brenton Av. M33—5A 114
Brent Rd. M23—1G 127
Brent Rd. SK4—2E 131
Brentwood. M6—1E 85
Brentwood. M31—6B 96
Brentwood. M33—5A 114
Brentwood Av. M28—5B 70
Brentwood Av. M30—3B 110
Brentwood Av. M31—5F 97
Brentwood Av. WA14—4G 125
Brentwood Clo. M16—4D 100
Brentwood Clo. OL15—3G 93
Brentwood Clo. SK5—4C 120
Brentwood Clo. SK15—3G 93
Brentwood Ct. M25—6D 58

Brentwood Cres. WA14—5G 125
Brentwood Dri. BL3—5E 39
Brentwood Dri. M30—1F 83
Brentwood Dri. SK8—6F 129
Brentwood Rd. M27—5D 70
Brereton Clo. WA14—4E 137
Brereton Ct. SK8—4A 142
Brereton Gro. M30—3C 110
Brereton Rd. M28—4H 69
Brereton Rd. M30—4B 82
Brereton Rd. SK9—4A 158
Breslyn St. M3—2D 86
Brethren's St. M35—5A 90
Bretland Gdns. SK14—6A 108
Bretland Wlk. M22—2D 140
Brettargh St. M6—1G 85
Bretton Wlk. M22—5B 140
Brett Rd. SK6—5C 68
Brett St. M22—2C 128
Brewers Grn. M20—2D 144
Brewer St. M1—4F 87 & 5C 162
Brewerton Rd. OL4—4G 65
Brewery St. SK1—6H 119
Brewery St. WA14—1F 137
Brewster St. M9—3F 75
Brewster St. M24—5A 46
Brian Av. M35—2C 90
Brian Farrell Dri. SK16—1C 106
Brian Rd. BL4—5C 38
Brian St. OL11—3B 32
Briar Av. OL4—6H 49
Briar Av. SK7—3E 145
Briar Clo. M34—4C 96
Briar Clo. M33—5E 113
Briar Cres. M22—6C 128
Briardene. M34—2G 105
Briardene Gdns. M22—1C 140
Briarfield. BL7—1B 10
Briarfield Rd. BL4—6C 38
Briarfield Rd. M20 & M19—3H 117
Briarfield Rd. M28—4G 69
Briarfield Rd. SK4—3G 119
Briarfield Rd. SK8—2D 142
Briarfield Rd. WA15—6C 126
Briarfields Rd. OL3—5A 52
Briar Gro. OL9—6H 47
Briar Gro. SK6—4G 121
Briar Hill Av. M28—5A 54
Briar Hill Clo. M28—5A 54
Briar Hill Ct. M6—2G 85
(off Briar Hill Way)
Briar Hill Gro. M28—5A 54
Briar Hill Way. M6—2G 85
Briarlands Av. M33—1H 125
Briarlands Clo. SK7—1F 153
Briar Lea Clo. BL3—3A 38
Briarlea Gdns. M19—4A 118
Briarley Gdns. SK6—3A 122
Briarmere Wlk. OL9—2A 64
Briarstead Clo. SK7—6F 143
Briar St. OL11—5F 19
Briarthorn Clo. SK6—2E 147
Briarwood. SK9—2F 159
Briarwood Av. M23—3E 127
Briarwood Av. M35—2G 89
Briarwood Chase. SK8—4D 142
Briarwood Cres. SK6—2E 147
Brice St. SK16—5H 91
Brickbridge Rd. SK6—6E 135
Brickfield St. OL16—1B 20
Brick Ground. OL12—1G 17
Brickhill La. WA15—3B 148
Brickkiln Row. WA14—4E 137
Brickley St. M3—2E 87 & 1A 162
Bricknell Wlk. M22—2D 140
Brick St. BL9—2E 29
Brick St. M4—3E 87 & 4B 162
Bridcam St. M8—6C 74
Briddon St. M3—2D 86 & 1G 161
Brideoak St. M8—4C 74
Brideoak St. OL4—1A 66
Bride St. BL1—3A 24
(in two parts)
Bridge Av. SK6—4G 121
Bridge Bank Rd. OL15—6D 8
Bridge Clo. M31—6E 111
Bridge Dri. SK8—1H 141
Bridge Dri. SK9—4H 151

Bridgefield Av. SK9—6G 151
Bridgefield Clo. SK6—6C 146
Bridgefield Cres. OL4—3B 66
Bridgefield Dri. BL9—3G 29
Bridgefield St. M26—4H 41
Bridgefield St. OL11 —4F 19
Bridgefield St. SK1—1G 131
Bridgefield Wlk. M26—4H 41
Bridgefold Rd. OL11—4E 19
Bridgeford St. M15—1E 101 & 6B 166
Bridge Gro. WA15—4H 125
Bridge Hall Dri. BL9—2G 29
Bridge Hall Fold. BL9—3G 29
Bridge Hall Ind. Est. BL9—3G 29
Bridge Hall La. BL9—3G 29
Bridge La. SK7—4H 143
Bridgelea Rd. M20—3F 117
Bridgeman Pl. BL2—1C 38
Bridgeman St. BL3—3H 37
Bridgeman St. BL4—6F 39
Bridgemere Clo. M26—2F 41
Bridgend Clo. M12—1C 102
Bridgend Clo. SK8—1D 142
Bridgenorth Av. M31—5H 97
Bridgenorth Dri. OL15—6D 8
Bridgenorth Rd. M9—6C 60
Bridge Rd. BL9—4B 28
Bridge Rd. M23—4D 126
Bridges Av. BL9—1D 42
Bridges Ct. BL3—1B 38
(off Soho St.)
Bridge St. BL0—3E 5
Bridge St. BL1—5B 24
Bridge St. BL4—6G 39
Bridge St. BL9—1E 29
Bridge St. M3—4C 86 & 5F 161
Bridge St. M24—1A 62
Bridge St. M26—1B 56
Bridge St. M27—3G 71
Bridge St. M34—6F 91
Bridge St. M35—5G 89
Bridge St. OL1—3E 65
Bridge St. OL2—5G 35
Bridge St. OL3—2F 53
Bridge St. OL4—6B 66
Bridge St. OL10—3E 31
Bridge St. OL11—4C 32
Bridge St. OL12—6A 8
(Rochdale)
Bridge St. OL12—4G 7
(Whitworth)
Bridge St. OL16—5F 21
Bridge St. SK1—1H 131
Bridge St. SK15—4D 92
Bridge St. Brow. SK1—1H 131
Bridge St. W. M3—4C 86 & 5F 161
Bridges Way. M34—2F 121
Bridgewater Clo. SK8—6H 141
& 5B 162
Bridgewater Rd. M27—4H 71
Bridgewater Rd. M28—4B 68
(Mosley Common)
Bridgewater Rd. M28—1E 69
(Worsley)
Bridgewater Rd. WA14—4F 125
Bridgewater St. BL1—1H 37
Bridgewater St. BL4—1F 55
Bridgewater St. M3—5C 86 & 2E 165
(Manchester)
Bridgewater St. M3—2C 86 & *F 16*
(Salford)
Bridgewater St. M28—5D 54
Bridgewater St. M30—3D 82
Bridgewater St. M32—5E 99
Bridgewater St. M33—4B 104
Bridgewater St. OL1—1E 65
Bridgewater Viaduct M15—6C 86
& 3F 165
Bridgeway. SK6—5C 134
Bridgewood Lodge. OL10—3D 30
Bridle Clo. M31—5A 96
Bridle Clo. M35—2C 90
Bridle Rd. M25—2G 59
Bridle Rd. SK7—4H 153
Bridle Rd. SK9—6D 150
Bridle Way. SK7—5H 153
Bridlington Av. M6—2C 84
Bridlington Clo. M10—5C 76

Bridlington Sq. OL11—5H 19
Bridport Av. M10—3D 76
Bridson La. BL2—3F 25
Bridson St. M5—4E 85
Bridson St. OL4—2G 65
Bridstowe Av. SK14—4G 107
Bridstowe Av. SK14—4G 107
Brief St. BL2—4E 25
Brien Av. WA14—4F 125
Briercliffe Clo. M18—1F 103
Briercliffe Rd. BL3—2G 37
Brierfield Dri. BL9—3E 15
Brierholme Av. BL7—2C 10
Brierley Av. M25—5C 42
Brierley Av. M35—4F 77
Brierley Clo. M34—5E 105
Brierley Clo. OL6—5C 80
Brierley Dri. M24—2A 62
Brierley Rd. M27—2E 71
Brierleys Pl. OL15—3E 9
Brierley St. BL2—2C 38
Brierley St. BL9—5H 103
Brierley St. OL8—6D 64
Brierley St. OL9—1A 64
Brierley St. OL10—3F 31
Brierley St. SK15—4F 93
Brierley St. SK16—4B 92
Brierley Wlk. OL9—1A 64
Brierton Dri. M22—4H 139
Briery Av. BL2—5H 11
Brigade St. BL1—6G 23
Briggs Clo. M33—2E 125
Briggs Fold Clo. BL7—1C 10
Briggs Fold Rd. BL7—1C 10
Briggs Rd. M32—3F 99
Briggs St. M3—2B 86 & 2D 160
Brigham St. M11—5E 89
Brightman St. M18—1F 103
Brighton Av. BL1—4E 23
Brighton Av. M7—5A 74
Brighton Av. M19—2B 118
Brighton Av. M31—4A 96
Brighton Av. SK5—5H 103
Brighton Clo. SK8—1E 143
Brighton Gro. M14—5H 101
Brighton Gro. M31—5A 96
Brighton Gro. M33—4A 114
Brighton Gro. SK14—6C 106
Brighton Pl. M13—1F 101 & 6C 166
Brighton Range. M18—3H 103
Brighton Rd. OL4—6C 50
Brighton Rd. SK4—2E 131
Brighton St. BL9—2F 29
Brighton St. M4—2E 87 & 1B 162
Bright Rd. M30—3G 83
Brightstone Wlk. M13—3A 102
Bright St. BL9—2E 29
Bright St. M26—3A 42
Bright St. M34—3E 105
Bright St. M35—4B 90
Bright St. OL6—3B 92
Bright St. OL8—4B 64
Bright St. OL9—5G 63
Bright St. OL16—5A 20
Brightwell Wlk. M4—3F 87
& 4C 162
Brigsteer Wlk. M10—6F 75
(off Thornton St. N.)
Briksdal Way. BL6—6A 22
Brimelow St. SK6—6C 120
Brimfield Wlk. M10—5C 76
Brimpton Wlk. M8—5B 74
(off Kenford Wlk.)
Brimrod La. OL11—6F 19
Brindale Rd. SK5—5C 120
Brindfale Rd. SK5—5C 120
Brindle Av. SK6—6D 134
Brindle Clo. M6—1F 85
Brindle Heath Rd. M6—*1F 85*
Brindle Mt. M6—1F 85
Brindle Rise. M6—1F 85
Brindle Wlk. M15—1E 101 & 5A 166
Brindle Way. OL2—6H 35
Brindley Av. M9—4D 60
Brindley Av. M33—3C 114
Brindley Clo. BL4—1D 54
Brindley Clo. M30—6F 83
Brindley Dri. M28—5C 68
Brindley Gro. SK9—6A 152

Brindley Lodge. M27—5E 7*
Brindley Rd. M16—2H 99
Brindley St. BL1—1B 24
Brindley St. M27—1F 71
Brindley St. M28—5B 68
(Boothstown)
Brindley St. M28—1F 69
(Worsley)
Brindley St. M30—2D 82
Brinell Dri. M30—2C 110
Brinkburn Rd. SK7—2G 145
Brinklow Clo. M11—6G 89
Brinkshaw Av. M22—2C 140
Brinksway. BL1—6A 22
Brinksway. SK3—3D 130
Brinksworth Clo. BL2—5A 26
Brinnington Cres. SK5—5B 120
Brinnington Rise. SK5—5B 120
Brinnington Rd. SK1 & SK5—6A 120
Brinscome Av. M22—3A 140
Brinsop Sq. M12—1D 102
Brinston Wlk. M10—4A 76
Brinsworth Dri. M8—5C 74
Briony Av. WA15—3C 138
Brisbane Clo. SK7—2H 153
Brisbane Rd. SK7—2H 153
Briscoe La. M10—2B 88
Briscoe St. OL1—1D 64
Briscoe Wlk. M24—5E 45
Bristol Av. BL2—4E 25
Bristol Av. M19—1D 118
Bristol Av. OL6—4F 79
Bristol Clo. SK8—6G 14*
Bristol Ct. M7—2A 74
Bristol St. M7—2A 74
Bristowe St. M11—2F 89
Britain St. BL9—1C 42
Britannia Av. OL2—1G 49
Britannia Rd. M33—4B 114
Britannia St. M6—5E 73
Britannia St. M11—6C 80
Britannia St. OL7—5F 91
Britannia St. OL10—3D 30
Britnall Av. M12—2A 102
Briton St. OL2—5C 48
Briton St. OL16—3A 20
Brittannia St. OL1—2E 65
Britton St. OL9—2A 64
Britwell Wlk. M8—3E 75
(off Mawdsley Dri.)
Brixham Av. SK8—6B 142
Brixham Dri. M33—3F 113
Brixham Rd. M16—3H 99
Brixham Wlk. M13—2G 101
Brixham Wlk. SK7—6G 143
Brixton Av. M20—3E 117
Brixworth Wlk. M9—6G 61
(off Greendale Dri.)
Broach St. BL3—3A 38
Broad Acre. OL12—1A 18
Broadacre. SK15—1A 108
Broadacre Rd. M18—4G 103
Broadbent. OL2—2E 49
Broadbent Av. OL6—5G 79
Broadbent Clo. SK14—6A 108
Broadbent Clo. SK15—5G 81
Broadbent Dri. BL9—1A 30
Broadbent Rd. OL1—5G 49
Broadbent St. M27—4D 70
Broadbent St. SK14—3B 106
Broadbottom Rd. SK14—6B 108
Broadcarr La. OL5—1C 80
Broadfield Clo. M34—5G 105
Broadfield Dri. OL15—6D 8
Broadfield Gro. SK5—4G 103
Broadfield Rd. M14—3E 101
Broadfield Rd. SK5—4G 103
Broadfield Stile. OL16—5G 19
Broadfield St. OL10—4D 30
Broadfield St. OL16—5H 19
Broadford Ct. OL10—4B 30
Broadford Rd. BL3—2D 36
Broadgate. BL3—2D 36
Broadgate. OL3—6G 51
Broadgate Ho. BL3—2D 36
Broadgate Meadow M27—4F 71
Broadgate Wlk. M9—3G 75
(off Roundham Wlk.)

Broadgreen Gdns. BL4—5F 39
Broadhalgh Av. OL11—4C 18
Broadhalgh Rd. OL11—5C 18
Broadhaven Rd. M10—1H 87
Broadhead Wlk. M25—6F 43
Broad Hey. SK6—6B 122
Broadhill Clo. SK7—3A 14*
Broadhill Rd. M19—3A 118
Broadhill Rd. SK15—6C 80
Broadhurst. M34—2G 105
Broadhurst Av. M27—6F 57
Broadhurst Av. OL1—6A 48
Broadhurst Ct. BL3—3H 37
Broadhurst Gro. OL6—5G 79
Broadhurst St. BL3—3H 37
Broadhurst St. M26—2F 41
Broadhurst St. SK3—4G 13*
Broad Ing. OL12—2E 19
Broadlands Av. OL10—5A 30
Broadlands Cres. OL10—5A 30
Broadlands Rd. M27—5C 70
Broadlands Wlk. M10—5A 76
Broadlands Way. OL10—5A 30
Broad La. OL12—1A 6
Broad La. OL16—2H 33
Broad La. WA15—5A 138
Broadlea. M31—4E 97
Broadlea Gro. OL12—1E 19
Broadlea Rd. M19—4A 118
Broadley Av. M22—1B 140
Broadley View. OL12—4C 6
Broad Meadow. BL7—2F 1*
Broadmeadow Av M16
—6D 100
Broadmoss Dri. M9—6A 62
Broadoak Av. M22—6A 128
Broad Oak Clo. OL8—1E 79
Broadoak Ct. M8—5D 74
Broadoak Cres. OL6—6F 79
Broadoak Dri. M22—6B 128
Broad Oak Ind. Est & Bus. Pk. M17
—6H 83
Broad Oak La. BL9—2G 29
Broad Oak La. M20—3F 129
Broad Oak Pk. M30—1F 83
Broadoak Rd. BL3—5C 38
Broadoak Rd. M22—1A 140
Broad Oak Rd. M28—5B 70
Broadoak Rd. OL6—6F 79
Broadoak Rd. OL11—5A 18
Broadoak Rd. SK7—3G 143
Broadoaks Rd. M31—6D 96
Broadoaks Rd. M33—5A 114
Broad Oak Ter. BL9—2A 30
Broad o' th' La. BL1—1A 24
Broad Rd. M33—4C 114
Broad Shaw La. OL16—3B 34
(in two parts)
Broadstone Av. OL4—3B 50
Broadstone Clo. M25—6E 59
Broadstone Hall Rd N SK4
—3F 119
Broadstone Hall Rd S. SK4 & SK5
—3F 119
Broadstone Rd. BL2—6H 11
Broadstone Rd. SK4 & SK5—3F 119
Broad St. BL9—3C 28
Broad St. M6—6B 72
(in two parts)
Broad St. M24—2E 61
Broad Wlk. M6—2G 85
Broad Wlk. SK9—1C 158
Broadway. BL4—6C 38
Broadway. M5—5E 85
Broadway. M28—2F 69
Broadway. M30—6E 95
Broadway. M31—5E 11*
(Partington)
Broadway. M31—3C 96
(Urmston)
Broadway. M35—5A 90
(Droylsden)
Broadway M35, M10, OL9, OL1 &
OL2—4D 76
(Failsworth)
Broadway. SK2—4C 132
Broadway. SK7—3G 143
Broadway SK8—1G 14*

Broadway. SK9—3E 159
Broadway. SK16 & SK14—1H 105
Broadway. WA15—4A 138
Broadway Av. SK8—6G 129
Broadway Ind. Area. M35—5H 85
Broadway M. WA15—4B 138
Broadway St. OL8—5D 64
Broadway, The. SK6—5E 121
Broadwell Dri. M9—3G 75
Broadwood. BL6—6A 22
Broadwood Clo. SK12—6D 146
Broady St. M32—6C 98
Broche Clo. OL11—2B 32
Brock Av. BL2—6H 25
Brock Clo. M11—6F 89
Brock Dri. SK8—5D 142
Brockenhurst Dri. BL2—2H 25
Brockford Dri. M9—4G 61
Brocklebank Rd. M14—1G 117
Brocklebank Rd. OL16—4D 20
Brocklehurst Av. BL9—4D 28
Brocklehurst St. M9—3A 76
Brockley Av. M14—5F 101
Brock St. M1—4F 87 & 5G 162
Brockton Wlk. M8—3C 74
Brocton Ct. M7—2H 73
Brodick St. M10—3H 75
Brodie Clo. M30—3D 82
Brogan St. M18—2F 103
Brogden Dri. SK8—6F 129
Brogden Gro. M33—6A 114
Brogden Ter. M33—5A 114
Bromborough Av. M20—1E 117
Bromfield. OL12—3G 19
(off Spotland Rd.)
Broming St. M11—3B 88
Bromleigh Av. SK8—5F 129
Bromley Av. M31—6A 96
Bromley Av. OL2—1A 48
Bromley Cres. OL6—5F 79
Bromley Cross Rd. BL7—4F 1?
Bromley Rd. M33—1C 126
Bromley St. M4—2F 87 & 1C 162
Bromley St. M34—3F 105
Bromlow St. M11—4E 89
Brompton Av. M35—3H 77
Brompton Rd. M14—5F 101
Brompton Rd. M32—4H 97
Brompton Rd. SK4—1C 130
Brompton St. OL4—4E 65
Brompton Ter. SK16—4H 91
(off Astley St.)
Bromsgrove Av. M30—3E 83
Bromshill Dri. M7—5A 74
Bromwich Dri. M9—4F 75
Bromwich St. BL2—1C 38
Bronte Av. M19—1D 42
Bronte Clo. BL1—4H 23
Bronte Clo. OL11—3H 49
Bronville Clo. OL1—6A 48
Brookash Rd. M22—5E 141
Brook Av. M19—5D 102
Brook Av. M27—4F 71
Brook Av. M35—4G 69
Brook Av. OL2—5G 35
Brook Av. OL3—1G 53
Brook Av. SK4—4F 119
Brook Av. WA15—5G 125
Brook Bank. BL2—2E 25
Brookbottom. BL2—5A 12
Brook Bottom Rd. M26—1F 4?
Brookburn Rd. M21—1G 115
Brook Clo. M25—1F 59
Brook Clo. WA15—5G 125
Brookcot Rd. M23—4F 127
Brookcroft Av. M22—5B 128
Brookcroft Rd. M22—6B 128
Brookdale. OL12—6E 7
Brookdale Av. M10—6D 76
Brookdale Av. M34—6D 90
(Audenshaw)
Brookdale Av. M34—5H 105
(Denton)
Brookdale Av. SK6—1E 147
Brookdale Clo. BL1 -3B 24

Brookdale Cotts. SK2—5E 133
Brookdale Rise. SK7—4H 143
Brookdale Rd. SK7—4H 143
Brookdale Rd. SK8—6D 128
Brookdale St. M35—4E 77
Brookdean Clo. BL1—2G 23
Brookdene Rd. BL9—6E 43
Brookdene Rd. M19—3A 118
Brook Dri. M25—1F 59
Brook Dri. SK6—1D 146
Brooke Av. SK9—3H 151
Brooke Dri. SK9—3H 151
Brookes St. M24—5B 46
Brooke Way. SK9—3H 151
Brookfield. M25—5F 59
Brookfield. OL2—4E 35
Brookfield. SK13—4G 109
Brookfield Av. BL2—4C 26
(in two parts)
Brookfield Av. M6—2C 84
Brookfield Av. M21—1A 116
Brookfield Av. M31—5C 96
Brookfield Av. OL2—4B 48
Brookfield Av. SK1—4A 132
Brookfield Av. SK6—5G 121
Brookfield Av. SK12—4C 154
Brookfield Av. WA15—3H 125
Brookfield Clo. SK1—4A 132
Brookfield Clo. M25—5F 59
Brookfield Cres. SK8—1H 141
Brookfield Dri. M27—2E 71
Brookfield Dri. M28—5B 68
Brookfield Dri. OL15—3C 8
Brookfield Dri. WA15—4A 126
Brookfield Gdns. M22—5A 128
Brookfield Gro. OL6—3B 92
Brookfield Ind. Est. SK13—4G 109
Brookfield Rd. BL9—3E 15
Brookfield Rd. M8—2C 74
Brookfield Rd. M30—1D 82
Brookfield Rd. SK8—6H 129
Brookfields. OL5—1E 81
Brookfield St. BL2—6D 24
Brookfield St. M34—6C 90
Brookfield St. OL8—4D 64
Brookfield Ter. SK7—1F 145
Brookfield Ter. SK15—3G 93
Brookfold. M35—3E 77
Brookfold La. BL2—1H 25
Brook Fold La. SK14—6F 107
Brookfold Rd. SK4—3F 119
Brook Gdns. BL2—1G 25
Brook Gdns. OL10—3E 31
Brook Grn. La. M18—4H 103
Brook Gro. M30—5E 95
Brookhay Wlk. M11—5B 88
Brookhead Av. M20—2D 116
Brookhead Dri. SK8—6C 130
Brookhey Av. BL3—4B 38
Brook Hey Clo. OL12—5B 8
Brookheys Rd. M31—5A 112
Brookhill St. M10—2A 88
Brookhouse Av. BL4—3E 55
Brookhouse Av. M30—4C 82
Brook Ho. Clo. BL2—2G 25
Brookhurst La. M28—3A 54
Brookhurst Rd. M18—3F 103
Brookland Av. BL4—2E 55
Brookland Clo. M30—5D 94
Brookland Gro. BL1—4F 23
Brooklands. OL12—2A 8
Brooklands Av. M20—3E 117
Brooklands Av. M34—5D 104
Brooklands Av. OL9—4H 63
Brooklands Clo. M34—3D 104
Brooklands Clo. SK4—4F 119
Brooklands Ct. M8—1B 74
Brooklands Ct. M33—1B 126
Brooklands Ct. OL11—4E 19
Brooklands Cres. M33—6B 114
Brooklands Dri. M35—2C 90
Brooklands Dri. OL4—3D 66
Brooklands Ho. M33—6B 114
Brooklands Pde. OL4—3D 66
Brooklands Rd. BL0—1A 14
Brooklands Rd. M25—1A 74
Brooklands Rd. M27—5D 70

Brooklands Rd. M33 & M23
—1B 126
Brooklands Rd. OL16—2H 33
Brooklands Rd. SK5—5G 103
Brooklands Rd. SK7—4E 145
Brooklands Sta. App. M33—6A 114
Brooklands St. OL2—2B 48
Brooklands, The. OL10—3E 31
Brook La. BL9—2E 43
Brook La. OL3—5H 51
Brook La. OL4—3A 66
Brook La. OL8—5E 65
Brook La. SK9—6B 158
Brook La. WA15—5G 125
Brooklawn Dri. M20—5F 117
Brooklawn Dri. M25—3G 59
Brookleigh Rd. M20—3H 117
Brooklyn Av. M16—5H 99
Brooklyn Av. M31—5A 96
Brooklyn Av. OL15—2E 9
Brooklyn Av. OL16—5B 8
Brooklyn Ct. M20—2G 117
Brooklyn Cres. SK8—5H 129
Brooklyn Pl. SK8—5H 129
Brooklyn Rd. SK2—5C 132
Brooklyn Rd. SK8—6H 129
Brooklyn St. BL1—4A 24
Brooklyn St. OL1—6G 49
Brook M. M14—1H 117
Brook Rd. M14—2G 117
Brook Rd. M31—4E 96
Brook Rd. SK4—4E 119
Brook Rd. SK8—5H 129
Brooks Av. M26—1F 41
Brooks Av. SK7—2D 144
Brooks Av. SK14—6C 106
Brooksbottom Clo. BL0—5E 5
Brooks Dri. M23 & WA15—4D 126
Brooks Dri. M35—5E 77
Brooks Dri. WA15—5D 138
Brooks End. OL11—2A 18
Brookshaw St. BL9—1D 28
(in two parts)
Brookshaw St. M11—4C 88
Brookside. M20—1D 128
Brookside. OL4—3H 65
Brookside. OL5—1D 80
Brookside. SK9—4G 159
Brookside. SK14—4E 107
Brookside Av. BL4—2E 55
Brookside Av. M35—2C 90
Brookside Av. OL4—3D 66
Brookside Av. SK2—4E 133
Brookside Av. SK12—4E 155
Brookside Clo. BL0—6C 4
Brookside Clo. BL2—6H 5
Brookside Clo. SK8—1H 141
Brookside Clo. SK14—3H 109
(Hadfield)
Brookside Clo. SK14—4E 107
(Hyde)
Brookside Cotts. OL11—6H 19
Brookside Cres. M19—5C 102
Brookside Cres. BL8—2G 13
Brookside Cres. M24—3C 62
Brookside Cres. M28—6G 55
Brookside Dri. M7—2H 73
Brookside La. SK6—6C 146
Brookside Rd. BL2—5F 25
Brookside Rd. M10—2A 76
Brookside Rd. M33—1A 126
Brookside Rd. SK8—5E 129
Brookside Ter. OL3—3G 51
(off High St. Delph)
Brookside Ter. SK9—6B 158
Brookside Vs. SK8—5E 129
Brookside Wlk. M26—6F 27
Brooksmouth. BL8—3B 28
Brook's Pl. OL8—5C 64
Brook's Pl. OL12—3G 19
Brook's Rd. M16—4H 99
Brookstone Clo. M21—3B 116
Brook St. BL2—4A 26
Brook St. BL4—6G 39
Brook St. BL9—2E 29
Brook St. M1—6E 87 & 3B 166
(in two parts)
Brook St. M6—1H 85

Brook St. M26—2A 56
(Prestolee)
Brook St. M26—4H 41
(Radcliffe)
Brook St. M27—3D 70
Brook St. M33—4C 114
Brook St. M35—5C 76
Brook St. OL1—2E 65
Brook St. OL2—4B 48
Brook St. OL9—1H 63
Brook St. OL12—3A 8
Brook St. OL15—4G 9
Brook St. OL16—5B 20
Brook St. SK1—4H 131
Brook St. SK7—3E 145
Brook St. SK8—5B 130
Brook St. SK14—4C 106
Brook St. E. OL6—3G 91
Brook St. W. OL6—3G 91
Brook Ter. M12—4B 102
Brook Ter. M31—3E 97
Brook Ter. OL16—1G 35
Brookthorn Clo. SK2—6F 133
Brookthorpe Av. M19—3A 118
Brookthorpe Rd. BL8—2G 27
Brook Vs. M9—4G 75
Brook Way. M34—1F 121
Brookway. OL4—3G 67
(Grasscroft)
Brookway. OL4—4A 66
(Lees)
Brookway. WA15—4H 125
Brookway Clo. M19—5A 118
Brookwood Av. M8—3E 75
Brookwood Av. M33—6G 113
Broom Av. M7—3A 74
Broom Av. M19—1D 118
Broom Cres. M6—2C 84
Broomedge. M7—3H 73
Broome Gro. M35—5F 77
Broomehouse Av. M30—1C 110
Broome St. OL9—3B 64
Broomfield. M6—5B 72
Broomfield. M27—5B 72
Broomfield Av. M9—2F 75
Broomfield Av. SK3—3H 119
Broomfield Clo. BL2—5C 26
Broomfield Clo. SK8—5H 129
Broomfield Clo. SK9—1H 159
Broomfield Ct. M20—5E 117
Broomfield Ct. WA15—2G 137
Broomfield Cres. M24—6F 45
Broomfield Cres. SK2—1A 144
Broomfield Dri. M8—4B 74
Broomfield Dri. SK5—3H 119
Broomfield La. WA15—2G 137
Broomfield Rd. BL3—3G 37
Broomfield Rd. SK4—5E 119
Broomfields. M35—2G 105
Broomfield Sq. OL11—6H 19
Broomfield Ter. OL16—1F 35
Broom Gro. M34—3G 105
Broomhall Rd. M9—4C 60
Broomhall Rd. M27—5B 72
Broomhurst Av. OL8—5B 64
Broom La. M7—3H 73
Broom La. M19—1D 118
Broom Rd. M31—6D 110
Broom Rd. WA15—2G 137
Broomstair Rd. M34—1F 105
Broom St. BL2—6C 24
Broom St. BL8—3B 28
Broom St. M27—4F 71
Broom St. OL16—1F 35
Broomville Av. M33—5B 114
Broomwood Gdns. WA15—6C 126
Broomwood Rd. WA15—6C 126
Broomwood Wlk. M15—1E 101
(off Chevril Clo.)
Broseley Av. M20—6H 117
Broseley Rd. M16—5G 99
Brotherod Hall Rd. OL12—1E 19
Brotherton Clo. M15—1B 100 & 5C 164
Brotherton Dri. M3—3B 86 & 3D 160
Brougham St. M28—6E 55
Brougham St. SK15—4D 92
Brough St. M11—6G 89
Broughton Av. M28—4C 54

Burnell Clo. M10—2H 87 & 2G 163
Burnell Ct. OL10—6F 31
Burnett Av. M5—5H 85
Burnett Clo. M16—6F 75
Burnett Gdns. M5—5H 85
Burnfield Rd. M18—4F 103
Burnfield Rd. SK5—4G 103
Burnham Av. BL1—4E 23
Burnham Av. SK5—6H 103
Burnham Clo. SK8—3B 142
Burnham Dri. M19—1B 118
Burnham Dri. M31—4E 97
Burnham Wlk. BL4—6F 39
Burnleigh Ct. BL5—6D 36
Burnley La. OL9 & OL1—5G 47
Burnley Rd. BL0—1A 4
Burnley Rd. BL9—3E 15
(in two parts)
Burnley St. M35—3G 77
Burnley St. OL9—2H 63
Burnmoor Rd. BL2—5H 25
Burnsall Av. M25—1C 58
Burnsall Gro. OL2—3B 48
Burnsall Wlk. M22—3G 139
Burns Av. BL9—1D 42
Burns Av. M27—2D 70
Burns Av. SK8—5B 130
Burns Clo. M11—4A 88
Burns Clo. OL1—2A 50
Burns Cres. SK2—4E 133
Burns Fold. SK16—6E 93
Burns Gdns. M25—6D 58
Burns Gro. M35—3A 90
Burnside. BL0—3A 4
Burnside. OL2—5H 35
Burnside. SK14—3H 109
Burnside. SK15—6H 93
Burnside Av. M6—6H 71
Burnside Av. SK4—3G 119
Burnside Clo. M26—6F 27
Burnside Clo. OL10—4F 31
Burnside Clo. SK6—6F 121
Burnside Clo. SK15—6H 93
Burnside Cres. M24—4G 45
Burnside Dri. M19—2A 118
Burnside Rd. BL1—3F 23
Burnside Rd. OL16—5C 20
Burnside Rd. SK8—6E 129
Burns Rd. M26—4D 54
Burns Rd. M34—2G 121
Burns St. BL3—1B 38
Burns St. OL10—4F 31
Burnthorpe Av. M9—6D 60
Burnthorpe Clo. OL11—5A 18
Burntwood Wlk. M9—3G 75
(off Naunton Wlk.)
Burran Rd. M22—5B 140
Burrell St. M13—6F 87
(off Hanworth Clo.)
Burrows Av. M21—3H 115
Burrswood Av. BL9—5F 15
Burrwood Dri. SK3—6F 131
Bursiem Av. M20—1E 117
Burstead St. M18—6G 89
Burstock St. M4—2F 87 & 1D 162
Burston St. M18—1E 103
Burtinshaw St. M18—2F 103
Burton Av. BL8—1F 27
Burton Av. M20—3E 117
Burton Av. M32—6B 98
Burton Av. WA15—2A 126
Burton Dri. SK12—3D 154
Burton Gro. M28—3C 70
Burton Ho. SK9—2E 159
Burton Rd. M20—5D 116
Burton St. M10—1F 87
Burton St. M41—1H 61
Burton St. OL4—3A 66
Burton St. SK4—6G 119
Burton St. M3—3B 86 & 3C 160
Burton Wlk. SK4—6G 119
(off Heskith St.)
Burtonwood St. M24—6H 45
Burtree St. M12—1C 102
Burwell Clo. OL12—6D 6
Burwell Gro. M23—4F 127
Bury Av. M16—5A 100
Bury & Bolton Rd. M26—6C 26

Bury Easterly By-Pass. BL9—6H 15
Bury New Rd. BL2—6C 24
(Bolton)
Bury New Rd. BL2—6A 26
(Breightmet)
Bury New Rd. BL9 & OL10—3G 29
Bury New Rd. M25 M7 & M8—1D 58
Bury Old Rd. BL2—4A 26
(Ainsworth)
Bury Old Rd. BL2—6C 24
(Bolton, in two parts)
Bury Old Rd. BL9 & OL10—4A 30
(Heap)
Bury Old Rd. BL9—4H 5
(Walmersley)
Bury Old Rd. M25 & M8—6G 59
Bury Pl. M11—3E 89
Bury Rd. BL0—2A 4
Bury Rd. BL2—6D 24
Bury Rd. BL7—1A 12
Bury Rd. BL8—5H 13
Bury Rd. M26—3H 41
Bury Rd. OL11—6A 18
Bury & Rochdale Old Rd. BL9 &
    OL10—1B 30
Bury St. BL1—6C 24
Bury St. M3—3C 86 & 3F 161
Bury St. M26—3A 42
Bury St. OL5—3E 81
Bury St. OL10—3D 30
Bury St. SK5—6H 119
Bushell St. BL3—3F 37
Bushey Dri. M23—6G 127
Busheyfield Clo. SK14—2B 106
Bushfield Wlk. M23—4E 127
Bushgrove Wlk. M9—4F 61
(off Claygate Dri.)
Bushmoor Wlk. M13—2H 101
Bushnell Wlk. M9—4F 61
(off Eastlands Rd.)
Bush St. M10—6G 75
Bushton Wlk. M10—6E 75
Bushway Wlk. M8—5D 74
(off Geneva Wlk.)
Bushycroft. SK14—3C 108
Busk Rd. OL9—1A 64
Busk Wlk. OL9—1A 64
Butcher La. BL9—3D 28
Butcher La. M23—4D 126
(in two parts)
Butcher St. OL2—2A 48
Bute Av. OL8—6D 64
Bute St. BL1—4F 23
Bute St. M5—4D 84
Bute St. M10—3H 75
Bute St. M30—5D 82
Butler Ct. M10—2G 87 & 2F 163
Butler Grn. OL9—5G 63
Butler La. M4—2G 87 & 2F 163
Butler St. BL0—5C 4
Butler St. M4—2G 87 & 2F 163
Butley St. SK7—1E 145
Butman St. M18—1H 103
Buttercup Av. M28—6B 54
Buttercup Dri. OL11—2B 32
Buttercup Dri. SK3—1F 143
Butterfield Clo. SK8—4D 142
Butterhouse La. OL3—5C 52
Butter La. M3—4D 86
Butterley Clo. SK16—6D 92
Buttermere. OL11—1F 33
Buttermere Av. M27—5F 71
Buttermere Av. OL10—5F 31
Buttermere Clo. BL3—3H 39
Buttermere Dri. BL0—2D 4
Buttermere Dri. M24—5G 45
Buttermere Dri. WA15—1D 148
Buttermere Gro. OL2—6B 34
Buttermere Rd. BL4—1A 54
Buttermere Rd. M31—6C 110
Buttermere Rd. OL4—1H 65
Buttermere Rd. OL7—1G 91
Buttermere Rd. SK8—2F 141
Buttermere Ter. SK15—2E 93
Butterstile La. M25—2D 72
Butterwick Clo. M12—4D 102
Butterworth Hall. OL16—6G 21
Butterworth La. OL9—6E 63

Butterworth Pl. OL15—3E 9
Butterworth St. M11—5C 88
Butterworth St. M24—2C 62
Butterworth St. M26—3H 41
Butterworth St. OL2—4E 49
Butterworth St. OL9—1H 63
Butterworth St. OL15—4E 9
Butterworth Way. OL3—4F 53
Buttery Ho. La. WA15—3E 139
Butt Hill Av. M25—6F 59
Butt Hill Ct. M25—6F 59
Butt Hill Dri. M25—6F 59
Butt Hill Rd. M25—6F 59
Butt La. OL5—5D 66
Button Hole. OL2—6H 35
Button La. M23—1G 127
Buttress St. M18—1E 103
Butts La. OL3—3E 51
Butts, The. OL16—4H 19
Buxted Rd. OL1—6F 49
Buxton Av. M20—3D 116
Buxton Av. OL6—5B 80
Buxton Clo. SK13—5G 109
(off Buxton M.)
Buxton Cres. M33—2D 126
Buxton Cres. OL16—1H 33
Buxton La. M35—4G 89
Buxton La. SK6—6C 134
Buxton M. SK13—5G 109
Buxton Old Rd. SK12—1H 157
Buxton Pl. OL8—4C 64
Buxton Rd. M32—4A 98
Buxton Rd. SK2—5A 132
Buxton Rd. SK7, SK6 & SK12
    —4F 145
Buxton Rd. SK12—1H 157
Buxton Rd. W. SK12—1E 157
Buxton St. BL8—3A 28
Buxton St. M1—5F 87 & 2D 166
Buxton St. OL10—4F 31
Buxton St. OL12—2H 7
Buxton St. SK7—2D 144
Buxton St. SK8—6E 129
Buxton Ter. SK14—1F 109
Buxton Wlk. SK13—6G 109
(off Buxton M.)
Buxton Way. M34—1F 121
Bycroft Wlk. M10—1F 89
Byer Clo. M33—6G 115
Bye Rd. BL0—2G 5
Bye St. M34—6F 91
Byfield Rd. M22—1A 140
Byland Av. OL4—5H 65
Byland Av. SK8—1D 152
Byland Clo. BL1—3A 24
Byland Gdns. M26—3E 41
Bylands Clo. SK12—3D 154
Bylands Fold. SK16—1B 106
Byland Wlk. M22—4B 140
Byng Av. M30—5B 110
Byng St. BL4—1F 55
Byng St. OL10—5G 31
Byng St. E. BL2—1B 38
Byng St. W. BL3—1B 38
Byre Clo. M33—6G 115
Byrom Av. M19—6E 103
Byrom Ct. M30—4H 89
Byrom Pde. M19—6E 103
Byrom St. BL8—1H 27
Byrom St. M3—5C 86 & 1F 165
Byrom St. M5—5G 85
Byrom St. M16—3B 100
Byrom St. SK15—4D 92
Byrom St. WA14—2F 137
Byron Av. M25—6D 58
Byron Av. M26—3D 40
Byron Av. M27—3E 71
Byron Av. M35—3A 90
Byron Dri. SK8—5B 130
Byron Gro. SK5—6G 103
Byron Rd. M24—5B 46
Byron Rd. M32—4E 99
Byron Rd. M34—1F 121
Byron St. M30—3F 83
Byron St. OL2—3C 48
Byron St. OL8—1H 77
Byron Wlk. BL4—2D 54
Byrth Rd. OL8—3D 78

Bywell Wlk. M8—4B 74
(off Levenhurst Rd.)
Bywood Wlk. M7—6A 74

Cabin La. OL4—4B 50
Cablestead Wlk. M11—5B 88
(off Cotteridge Wlk.)
Cable St. BL1—5B 24
Cable St. M3—3C 86 & 3F 161
Cable St. M4—3F 87 & 3C 162
Cabot Pl. SK5—5H 119
Caddington Rd. M21—1A 116
Cadleigh Wlk. M10—4A 76
Cadman St. M12—6H 87 & 4G 167
Cadmium Wlk. M18—3E 103
Cadnam Dri. M22—2D 140
Cadogan Pl. M7—2A 74
Cadogan St. M14—3E 101
Cadum Wlk. M13—1G 101 & 5E 167
Caen Av. M10—3A 76
Caernarvon Clo. BL8—2H 13
Caernarvon St. SK7—4C 144
Caernarvon Way. M34—6F 105
Caesar St. OL11—3G 33
Cairn Dri. M6—6G 73
Cairn Dri. OL11—5A 18
Cairngorm Dri. BL3—2C 36
Cairns Pl. OL6—6H 79
Cairn Wlk. M11—4B 88
Caister Av. M25—2E 59
Caister Clo. M31—6G 95
Caistor St. SK1—6B 120
Caistor Wlk. OL1—2D 64
Caithness Dri. BL3—1C 36
Caithness Rd. OL11—6A 18
Cajetan ho. M24—4H 61
Cakebread St. M12—6G 87 & 3E 167
Calbourne Cres. M12—4D 102
Calcot Wlk. M23—5F 127
Calcutta Rd. SK3—4E 131
Caldbeck Av. BL1—4D 22
Caldbeck Av. M33—4E 115
Caldbeck Dri. BL4—2A 54
Caldbeck Dri. M24—6G 45
Caldecott Rd. M9—4C 60
Calder Av. M22—3B 128
Calder Av. M30—6D 94
Calder Av. OL15—3C 9
Calderbank Av. M31—3A 96
Calderbrook Dri. SK8—1C 142
Calderbrook Rd. OL15—6G 9
(Calderbrook)
Calderbrook Rd. OL15—3E 9
(Littleborough)
Calderbrook Ter. OL15—1G 9
Calderbrook Wlk. M9—4F 75
Calder Clo. SK5—4H 119
Calder Clo. SK12—5D 154
Caldercourt. M31—3A 96
Calder Cres. M25—5F 43
Calder Dri. BL4—4B 56
Calder Dri. BL9—3G 15
Calder Dri. M27—2E 71
Calder Dri. M28—1C 68
Calder Flats. OL10—3E 31
(off Wilton St.)
Calder Gro. OL2—5E 35
Calder Rd. BL3—4A 38
Caldershaw La. OL12—1C 18
Caldershaw Rd. OL12—2C 18
Calder St. M5—5B 86 & 2C 164
Calder St. OL16—1B 20
Caldervale Av. M21—5A 116
Calder Wlk. M25—5E 45
Calder Wlk. M25—5F 43
Calder Way. M25—5F 43
Caldey Rd. M23—6E 127
Caldwell St. SK5—6H 103
Caldy Dri. BL0—6C 4
Caldy Rd. M6—6B 72
Caldy Rd. SK9—4H 151
Caledon Av. M10—3A 76
Caledonia Dri. M30—5G 83
Caledonia St. BL3—2G 37
Caledonia St. M26—3A 42
(in two parts)
Caledonia Way. M32—2A 98

Carlyle Clo. M8—5C 74
Carlyle St. BL9—2C 28
Carlyn Av. M33—5D 114
Carmel Av. M5—5A 86 & 2A 164
Carmel Clo. M5—5A 86 & 2A 164
Carmel Ct. M8—1B 74
Carmenna Dri. SK7—6H 143
Carmichael Clo. M31—6C 110
Carmichael St. SK3—3E 131
Carmona Dri. M25—5E 59
Carmona Gdns. M7—2G 73
Carnaby St. M9—2H 75
Carna Rd. SK5—5G 103
Carnarvon St. M3—1D 86 & 1H 161
Carnarvon St. M7—4A 74
Carnarvon St. OL8—1H 77
Carnarvon St. SK1—2A 132
Carnation Rd. BL4—6C 38
Carnation Rd. OL4—5A 66
Carnation St. M3—2D 86 & 1H 161
Carnegie Av. M19—6D 102
Carnforth Av. OL11—6D 32
Carnforth Dri. BL8—1A 14
Carnforth Rd. M33—6A 114
Carnforth Rd. SK4—3E 119
Carnforth Rd. SK8—1D 142
Carnforth Sq. OL11—6D 32
Carnforth St. M14—4F 101
Carnoustie Clo. M10—4C 76
Carnoustie Clo. SK9—1G 159
Carnoustie Dri. BL0—4D 4
Carnoustie Dri. SK8—4G 141
Carnwood Clo. M10—1F 89
Caroline Dri. M4—4G 87 & 5E 163
Caroline St. BL3—3H 37
Caroline St. M7—1C 86
Caroline St. M30—1D 110
Caroline St. OL6—2A 92
Caroline St. SK3—4F 131
Caroline St. SK15—4E 93
Carpenters La. M4—3E 87 & 4B 162
Carradale Dri. M33—4E 113
Carradale Wlk. M10—5A 76
Carr Av. M25—1D 72
Carr Bank Av. BL0—2D 4
Carr Bank Av. M9—6B 60
Carr Bank Dri. BL0—2D 4
Carr Bank Rd. BL0—2D 4
Carrbrook Clo. SK15—5G 81
Carrbrook Cres. SK15—5G 81
Carrbrook Rd. SK15—4H 81
(in two parts)
Carrbrook Ter. M26—3H 41
Carr Brow. SK6—6E 147
Carr Clo. SK1—3B 132
Carrfield Av. M28—5A 54
Carrfield Av. SK3—1A 144
Carrfield Av. WA15—5D 126
Carrfield Clo. M28—5A 54
Carrfield Gro. M28—5A 54
Carrgate Rd. M34—6H 105
Carrgreen Clo. M19—4B 118
Carr Gro. OL16—5G 21
Carr Head. OL3—1C 52
Carrhill Quarry Clo. OL5—1E 81
Carrhill Rd. OL5—1E 81
Carr Ho. Rd. OL4—2B 66
Carriage Dri., The. SK14—2H 109
Carriage St. M16—2B 100
Carrick Gdns. M22—1B 140
Carrie St. BL1—5F 23
Carrill Gro. M19—6C 102
Carrill Gro. E. M19—6C 102
Carrington Bus. Pk. M31—3H 111
Carrington Dri. BL3—2B 38
Carrington Field St. SK1—4H 131
Carrington La. M31 & M33—
                               2B 112
Carrington Rd. M14—1G 117
Carrington Rd. M31—1A 112
Carrington Rd. SK1—6A 120
Carrington Spur. M33 & M31
                               —3E 113
Carrington St. M27—2H 71
Carrington St. OL9—6H 63
Carr La. OL3—2C 52
(Diggle)
Carr La. OL3—3F 53
(Greenfield)

Carr La. SK9—6A 158
Carrmoor Rd. M13—2G 101
Carrock Wlk. M24—6D 44
Carron Av. M9—2H 75
Carron Gro. BL2—2H 25
Carroway St. M10—6G 75
Carr Rise. SK15—4H 81
Carr Rd. M30—5F 95
Carr Rd. WA15—3B 138
Carrs Av. SK8—5C 130
Carrsfield Rd. M22—5C 128
Carrslea Clo. M26—2E 41
Carrs Rd. SK8—5B 130
Carr St. SK2—3C 132
Carr St. M27—4D 70
Carr St. OL6—4H 79
Carrsvale Av. M31—4D 96
Carrswood Rd. M23—3C 126
Carruthers Clo. OL10—2H 31
Carruthers St. M4—3H 87 & 4G 163
Carrwood. WA15—6B 138
Carr Wood Av. SK7—5G 143
Carrwood Hey. BL0—5C 4
Carr Wood Rd. SK7—4F 143
Carrwood Rd. SK9—6D 150
Carsdale Rd. M22—5C 140
Carslake Av. BL1—5G 23
Carslake Rd. M10—6F 75
Carson Rd. M19—1C 118
Carstairs Av. SK2—1A 144
Carstairs Clo. M8—4B 74
Car St. OL1—2E 65
Carter Clo. M34—5F 105
Carter Pl. SK14—2B 106
Carter St. BL3—3C 38
Carter St. BL4—2G 55
Carter St. M7—6H 73
Carter St. OL5—3E 81
Carter St. SK14—2B 106
Carter St. SK15—3E 93
Carthage St. OL8—5D 64
Carthorpe Arch. M5—4F 85
Cart House La. BL0—3H 5
Cartleach Gro. M28—1C 68
Cartleach La. M28—1B 68
Cartledge St. M1—5F 87 & 2D 166
Cartmel. OL12—3G 19
(off Spotland Rd.)
Cartmel Av. OL16—1D 34
Cartmel Av. SK4—3G 119
Cartmel Clo. BL3—5B 36
Cartmel Clo. BL9—4E 43
Cartmel Clo. OL8—6B 64
Cartmel Clo. SK7—2C 144
Cartmel Clo. SK8—2G 141
Cartmel Cres. BL2—3E 25
Cartmel Cres. OL9—1F 77
Cartmel Dri. WA15—5D 126
Cartmel Gro. M28—4B 70
Cartmell Ct. M9—5A 62
Cartmel Wlk. M9—4F 75
Cartmel Wlk. M24—5G 45
Cartridge Clo. M22—1D 140
Cartridge St. OL10—3E 31
Cartwright Rd. M21—1F 115
Cartwright St. M34—1F 105
Cartwright St. OL4—3F 65
Cartwright St. SK14—2E 107
Carver Av. M25—4G 59
Carver Clo. M16—2H 99
Carver Dri. SK6—6C 134
Carver Rd. SK6—6C 134
Carver Rd. WA15—3G 137
Carver St. M16—2H 99
Carver Wlk. M15—2D 100
(off Arnott Cres.)
Carwood Dell. SK7—6G 143
Cashmere Rd. SK3—4E 131
Cashmore Wlk. M12—1A 102
Caspian Rd. WA14—5C 124
Cassandra Ct. M5—5A 86 &
                               2B 164
Cassidy Clo. M4—3F 87 & 3D 162
Cassidy Ct. M5—5E 85
Cassidy Gdns. M24—3F 45
Casson Ga. OL12—2G 19
Casson St. M35—4F 77
Castle Av. M34—5E 105
Castle Av. OL11—5G 19

Castlebrook Clo. BL9—3F 43
Castle Ct. OL6—4F 79
Castle Croft. BL2—2F 25
Castlecroft Rd. BL9—3C 28
Castledene Av. M6—2E 85
Castle Farm Dri. SK2—6B 132
Castle Farm La. SK2—5B 132
Castlefield Av. M7—3A 74
Castleford Clo. BL1—5H 23
Castleford St. OL1—6A 48
Castleford Wlk. M21—2B 116
Castle Gro. BL0—1A 14
Castle Hall Clo. SK15—4E 93
Castle Hill. OL11—5G 19
Castle Hill. SK6—2E 121
Castle Hill Cres. OL11—5G 19
Castle Hill Rd. BL9—5H 15
Castle Hill Rd. M25—1H 73
Castle Hill St. BL2—2D 24
(in two parts)
Castle La. SK15—3G 81
Castlemere Dri. OL2—5H 35
Castlemere Rd. M9—6E 61
Castlemere St. OL11—5G 19
Castlemere Ter. OL11—5H 19
Castle M. BL4—2F 55
Castle Mill La. WA15—6A 138
Castle Mill St. OL1—2F 65
Castlemoor Av. M7—3F 73
Castlerigg Dri. M24—4E 45
Castlerigg Dri. OL2—1A 48
Castle Rd. BL9—4G 43
Castleshaw Rd. SK2—6D 132
Castle St. BL2—6C 24
Castle St. BL4—2F 55
Castle St. BL9—3C 28
(Bury)
Castle St. BL9—1D 14
(Summerseat)
Castle St. M3—5C 86 & 2E 165
Castle St. M24—2D 62
Castle St. M30—3H 83
Castle St. M35—3B 90
Castle St. SK3—4F 131
Castle St. SK14—3H 109
(Hadfield)
Castle St. SK14—4D 106
(Hyde)
Castle St. SK15—4E 93
Castleton Av. M32—3B 98
Castleton Bank. SK13—6G 109
(off Castleton Cres.)
Castleton Ct. M34—1G 121
Castleton Cres. SK13—6G 109
Castleton Dri. SK6—1D 156
Castleton Grn. SK13—6G 109
(off Castleton Cres.)
Castleton Gro. OL6—5B 80
Castleton Ho. SK13—6G 109
(off Castleton Cres.)
Castleton Rd. M7—2A 74
Castleton Rd. OL2—5A 34
Castleton Rd. SK7—4E 145
Castleton S. OL11—2D 32
Castleton St. BL2—3D 24
Castleton St. OL9—3A 64
Castleton St. WA14—4E 125
Castleton Ter. SK13—6G 109
Castleton Wlk. M11—4B 88
Castleton Way. M34—1G 121
Castle Wlk. OL6—4F 79
Castle Wlk. SK15—4E 93
Castleway. M6—1E 85
Castle Way. M27—1G 71
Castleway. OL11—4B 32
Castleway. WA15—6C 138
Castlewood Gdns. SK2—6C 132
Castlewood Rd. M7—3E 73
Castlewood Sq. BL2—4E 25
Castle Yd. SK1—1H 131
Caston Clo. M16—3C 100
Catchdale Clo. M9—4E 61
Catches Clo. OL11—3D 18
Catches La. OL11—3D 18
Cateaton St. BL9—2D 28
Cateaton St. M3—3D 86 & 4H 161
Caterham St. M4—4H 87 &
                               6H 163
Catesby Rd. M16—4B 100

Catfield Wlk. M15—6B 86 & 4D 164
Catford Rd. M23—6E 127
Cathedral App. M3—3D 86 & 3H 161
Cathedral Clo. SK16—1B 106
Cathedral Gates. M3—3D 86 & 4H 161
Cathedral Rd. OL9—6F 47
Cathedral St. M3—3D 86 & 3H 161
Cathedral Yd. M3—3D 86 & 4H 161
Catherine Rd. M8—2A 74
Catherine Rd. M27—4C 70
Catherine Rd. SK6—2F 133
Catherine Rd. WA14—2E 137
Catherine St. BL3—5F 37
Catherine St. BL9—1C 42
Catherine St. M11—6G 89
Catherine St. M30—2C 82
Catherine St. M34—4D 104
Catherine St. OL4—3A 66
Catherine St. SK7—2E 145
Catherine St. SK14—4B 106
Catherine St. E. M34—4D 104
Catherston Clo. M16—4C 100
Catlow La. M4—3E 87 & 4B 162
Catlow St. M7—1C 86
Caton Clo. BL9—5C 28
Caton St. OL16—5H 19
Cato St. BL0—5C 4
Catterall Cres. BL2—5H 11
Catterick Av. M20—6G 117
Catterick Av. M33—1E 125
Catterick Dri. BL3—4A 40
Catterick Rd. M20—6G 117
Catterwood Dri. SK6—6F 123
Catterwood Rd. SK6—1F 135
Cattlin Way. OL8—1A 78
Causeway, The. WA14—1F 137
Causewood Clo. OL4—3A 50
Causey Dri. M24—4F 45
Cavalier St. M3—3H 87 & 4H 163
Cavalry St. M4—2E 87 & 2B 162
Cavanagh Clo. M13—1H 101 & 6G 167
Cavan Clo. SK3—4B 130
Cavell Way. M5—4G 85
Cavendish Av. M20—3D 116
Cavendish Av. M27—6A 58
Cavendish Ct. M7—2H 73
Cavendish Ct. M9—4C 60
(off Deanswood Dri.)
Cavendish Ct. M31—5G 97
(off Cavendish Rd.)
Cavendish Ct. SK4—1B 130
Cavendish Gdns. M20—3D 116
Cavendish Gro. M30—2G 83
Cavendish Ho. M30—1G 83
Cavendish Pl. M11—3C 88
Cavendish Pl. M27—3G 71
Cavendish Rd. M7—2G 73
Cavendish Rd. M20—3D 116
Cavendish Rd. M28—5B 70
Cavendish Rd. M30—2G 83
Cavendish Rd. M31—5G 97
(in two parts)
Cavendish Rd. M32—3E 99
Cavendish Rd. OL11—2E 33
Cavendish Rd. SK4—1B 130
Cavendish Rd. SK7—4D 144
Cavendish Rd. WA14—2E 137
Cavendish St. M15—1E 101 & 5A 166
(in two parts)
Cavendish St. OL6—2G 91
Cavendish St. OL8—3C 64
Cavendish Ter. M21—1H 115
Cavenham Gro. BL1—5G 23
Cavenham Wlk. M9—4E 75
(off Hendham Vale)
Caversham Dri. M9—3G 75
Cawdor Av. BL4—5D 38
Cawdor Ct. BL4—5E 39
Cawdor Ho. M30—5F 83
(off Enfield Clo.)
Cawdor Pl. WA15—5C 126
Cawdor Rd. M14—6G 101
Cawdor St. M15—6B 86 & 4C 164
Cawdor St. M27—3D 70
Cawdor St. M28—1G 69
Cawdor St. M30—4E 83
Cawdor Wlk. BL4—5E 39
Cawley Av. M25—1D 72

Cawood Sq. SK5—2C 120
Cawston Wlk. M8—5C 74
Cawthorne Ct. M27—2D 70
Caxton Rd. M14—6F 101
Caxton St. OL10—3F 31
Caxton St. OL11—3C 32
Caxton Way. M5—3H 85
Caygill St. M3—3C 86 & 3F 161
Cayley St. OL16—4B 20
Caythorpe St. M14—4E 101
Cayton St. M12—4C 102
Ceal, The. SK6—1F 135
Cecil Av. M33—6G 113
Cecil Ct. SK3—3D 130
Cecil Dri. M31—5A 96
Cecilia Ct. N. BL3—3C 38
Cecilia Ct. S. BL3—3C 38
Cecilia St. BL3—3C 38
Cecil Rd. M9—4F 61
Cecil Rd. M30—4G 83
Cecil Rd. M32—6C 98
Cecil Rd. WA15—3G 137
Cecil St. BL2—6C 24
Cecil St. BL9—4D 28
Cecil St. M15—2F 101
Cecil St. M28—6F 55
(Walkden)
Cecil St. M28—2F 69
(Worsley)
Cecil St. OL2—4A 48
Cecil St. OL5—3E 81
Cecil St. OL7—4G 91
Cecil St. OL8—4C 64
Cecil St. OL11—6H 19
Cecil St. OL15—4D 8
Cecil St. SK3—4G 131
Cecil St. SK15—4F 93
Cecil St. SK16—5H 91
Cecil Wlk. OL7—4F 91
Cecil Walker Ho. M31—5E 111
Cedar Av. BL3—5B 40
Cedar Av. M25—3D 58
Cedar Av. OL6—6H 79
Cedar Av. OL10—2E 31
Cedar Av. SK7—3E 145
Cedar Av. WA14—1E 137
Cedar Clo. BL3—5B 40
Cedar Clo. SK12—4E 155
Cedar Ct. M14—1G 117
Cedar Cres. BL0—2E 5
Cedar Cres. OL9—1H 63
Cedar Dri. M27—5D 56
Cedar Dri. M31—6E 97
Cedar Dri. M35—3C 90
Cedar Gro. BL4—1D 54
Cedar Gro. M14—1H 117
Cedar Gro. M25—3E 59
Cedar Gro. M34—4E 105
Cedar Gro. OL2—1B 48
(Royton)
Cedar Gro. OL2—1F 49
(Shaw)
Cedar Gro. SK4—4E 119
Cedar Gro. SK16—5D 92
Cedar La. OL4—3F 67
Cedar La. OL16—2E 35
Cedar Lawn. SK8—3C 142
Cedar Pl. M7—1A 86
Cedar Rd. M24—1C 62
Cedar Rd. M31—6C 110
Cedar Rd. M33—3F 113
Cedar Rd. M35—5F 77
Cedar Rd. SK2—1B 144
Cedar Rd. SK6—1C 146
Cedar Rd. SK8—6E 129
Cedar Rd. WA15—2G 137
Cedars Rd. M22—2B 140
Cedar St. BL9—2F 29
Cedar St. OL4—2G 65
(in two parts)
Cedar St. OL6—1B 92
Cedar St. OL12—2H 19
Cedar St. SK14—2C 106
Cedarway. SK9—5C 158
Cedarwood Av. SK4—2C 130
Cedric Rd. M8—1A 74
Cedric Rd. OL4—2G 65

Cedric St. M5—3D 84
Celandine Clo. OL15—3D 8
Celia St. M8—3E 75
Cellini Sq. BL1—4H 23
Celtic St. SK1—3A 132
Cemetery La. BL9—5D 28
Cemetery Rd. BL0—5C 4
Cemetery Rd. BL2—6D 24
Cemetery Rd. BL6—4H 39
Cemetery Rd. M5—4E 85
Cemetery Rd. M26—3F 41
Cemetery Rd. M27—2E 71
Cemetery Rd. M34—1F 105
(Audenshaw)
Cemetery Rd. M34—6F 105
(Denton)
Cemetery Rd. M35—4H 89
(Droylsden)
Cemetery Rd. M35—5F 77
(Failsworth)
Cemetery Rd. OL2—2A 48
Cemetery Rd. OL5—4F 81
Cemetery St. M24—6A 46
Cennick Clo. OL4—3H 65
Ceno St. OL1—6E 49
Centaur Clo. M27—1F 71
Centaur Way. M8—4B 74
Central Av. BL0—3A 4
Central Av. BL4—1C 54
Central Av. BL9—6B 28
Central Av. M6—5C 72
Central Av. M19—5C 102
Central Av. M27—1B 72
Central Av. M28—4E 55
Central Av. M31—1G 97
(in two parts)
Central Av. M33—2F 125
Central Av. OL3—4F 53
Central Av. OL15—3F 9
Central Dri. BL9—3F 15
Central Dri. M27—4H 71
Central Dri. M31—5F 97
Central Dri. SK5—4H 119
Central Dri. SK6—6A 122
Central Dri. SK7—3F 143
Central Dri. SK8—5H 141
Central Ind. Est. M24—1H 61
Central Retail Pk. M4—4G 87 & 5E 163
Central Rd. M20—4E 117
Central Rd. M22—1A 150
Central Rd. M31—6D 110
Central St. BL1—6A 24
Central St. M2—4D 86
Central Way. WA14—1F 137
Centre Gdns. BL1—4H 23
Centre Pk. Rd. BL1—4H 23
Centre Vale. OL15—2G 9
Centre Vale Clo. OL15—2G 9
Centurion Gro. M7—5A 74
Century Gdns. OL12—3H 19
Century Pk. Ind. Est. WA14—5C 124
Century St. M33—5C 86 & 2F 165
Cestrian St. BL3—4B 38
Ceylon St. M10—5A 76
Ceylon St. OL4—4H 65
Chadderton Clo. M20—3G 117
Chadderton Dri. BL9—5E 43
Chadderton Hall Rd. OL9 & OL1
—6F 47
Chadderton Heights. OL1—4F 47
Chadderton Ind. Est. M24—4C 62
Chadderton Pk. Rd. OL9—1F 63
Chadderton St. M4—3F 87 & 3C 162
Chadderton Way. OL1 & OL9—5H 47
Chaddesley Wlk. M11—5B 88
Chaddock La. M28—5A 68
Chadkirk Rd. SK6—2H 133
Chadvil Rd. SK8—6G 129
Chadwell Rd. SK2—4E 133
Chadwick Clo. M14—4F 101
Chadwick Clo. OL16—6G 21
Chadwick Fold. BL9—4F 15
Chadwick Hall Rd. OL11—6G 21
Chadwick La. OL10 & OL11—3H 31
Chadwick La. OL16—3A 34
Chadwick Rd. M30—3G 83
Chadwick St. BL2—1C 38

Chadwick St. BL3—4B 40
Chadwick St. BL9—1A 30
Chadwick St. M27—3F 71
Chadwick St. OL6—3C 92
Chadwick St. OL9—2B 64
Chadwick St. OL10—3H 31
Chadwick St. OL11—4F 19
Chadwick St. OL16—4E 21
Chadwick St. SK1—3H 131
Chadwick St. SK6—6D 134
Chadwick St. SK14—4D 106
Chadwick Ter. OL12—5D 6
Chadwick Wlk. M27—3F 71
Chadworth Clo. OL5—5G 67
Chaffinch Clo. M22—6D 128
Chaffinch Clo. M35—2C 90
Chaffinch Dri. BL9—1G 29
Chain Bar La. SK14—5B 108
Chainhurst Wlk. M13—1G 101
(off Ardeen Wlk.)
Chain Rd. M9—5D 60
Chain St. M1—4E 87 & 6A 162
Chain Wlk. M9—4G 61
Chalcombe Grange. M12—2B 102
Chale Clo. M10—2H 87 & 2G 163
Chale Dri. M24—3C 62
Chale Grn. BL2—2G 25
Chalfont Av. M31—5G 97
Chalfont Clo. OL8—5F 65
Chalfont Dri. M8—4C 74
Chalfont Dri. M28—3G 69
Chalfont Ho. M5—3F 85
Chalfont St. BL1—3B 24
(in two parts)
Chalford Rd. M23—2G 139
Challenor Sq. M12—1C 102
Challinor St. BL1—5F 23
Chalter Wlk. M7—5B 74
Chamber Hall Clo. OL8—5B 64
Chamberhall St. BL9—2C 28
Chamber Ho. Dri. OL11—1B 32
Chamberlain Rd. SK15—6E 81
Chamberlain St. BL3—1H 37
Chamber Rd. OL2—6E 35
Chamber Rd. OL8—6A 64
Chambers Ct. SK14—4C 108
Chambersfield Ct. M5—4F 85
Champagnole St. SK16—4H 91
(off Astley St.)
Champneys Wlk. M9—5F 75
Chancel Av. M5—5A 86 & 2A 164
Chancel Clo. SK16—1A 106
Chancel La. SK9—1E 159
Chancellor La. M12—5H 87 & 2G 167
Chancel Pl. M1—4G 87 & 6E 163
Chancel Pl. OL16—4H 19
Chancery La. BL1—6B 24
Chancery La. M2—4D 86 & 6H 161
Chancery La. OL2—6G 35
Chancery La. OL3—5A 52
Chancery Pl. M2—4D 86 & 6H 161
Chancery St. OL4—3G 65
Chancery St. OL9—1A 64
Chancery Wlk. OL9—1A 64
Chandley Ct. SK1—4A 132
(off Ward St.)
Chandley St. SK8—5H 129
Chandos Gro. M5—3D 84
Chandos Rd. M21—6A 100
Chandos Rd. M25—1F 73
Chandos Rd. SK4—3D 118
Chandos Rd. S. M21—1A 116
Chandos St. OL2—6G 35
Channing Cl. OL16—5B 20
Channing Sq. OL16—5B 20
Channing St. OL16—5B 20
Chantlers Av. BL8—4G 27
Chantler's St. BL8—3G 27
Chantry Clo. SK5—2G 119
Chantry Clo. SK12—2H 157
Chantry Fold. SK12—1H 157
Chantry Rd. SK12—1H 157
Chapel All. BL1—6B 24
(off Deansgate)
Chapel Clo. SK16—5A 92
Chapel Cotts. SK16—5B 92
Chapel Ct. M33—3G 113
Chapel Ct. SK6—6D 134

Chapel Ct. SK9—3D 158
Chapel Ct. SK14—6A 106
Chapel Ct. WA14—1F 137
Chapel Croft. OL2—3B 48
Chapel Dri. WA15—6C 138
Chapelfield. M26—6A 42
Chapelfield Clo. SK15—1H 93
Chapelfield Dri. M28—6D 54
Chapelfield Rd. M12—5G 87 & 2F 167
Chapelfield Rd. M34—4F 105
Chapel Fields. SK6—6D 134
Chapelfield St. BL1—2A 24
Chapel Ga. OL16—5F 21
Chapel Grn. M34—4F 105
Chapel Gro. M31—5G 97
Chapel Hill. OL15—3F 9
Chapelhill Dri. M9—6E 61
Chapel Ho. SK6—6E 135
Chapel Ho. SK7—1C 144
Chapel La. BL8—3C 4
Chapel La. M9—5D 60
Chapel La. M31 & WA13—6D 110
Chapel La. M32—6C 98
Chapel La. M33—3G 113
Chapel La. OL2—3B 48
Chapel La. OL11—3F 17
Chapel La. SK9—3C 158
Chapel La. SK14—2H 109
Chapel La. WA15—5B 138
Chapel Meadow. M28—4D 68
Chapel Pl. BL2—2E 39
Chapel Pl. M31—5F 83
Chapel Rd. M22—3B 128
Chapel Rd. M25—2D 72
Chapel Rd. M27—4C 70
Chapel Rd. M30—5E 95
Chapel Rd. M33—4B 114
Chapel Rd. OL3—3E 53
Chapel Rd. OL8—6A 64
Chapel Rd. SK9—5G 159
Chapel St. BL1—5B 24
(in two parts)
Chapel St. BL3—4B 40
Chapel St. BL4—1G 55
Chapel St. BL7—1B 10
Chapel St. BL8—4G 13
Chapel St. BL9—3D 28
Chapel St. M3—3B 86 & 4C 160
Chapel St. M19—6C 102
Chapel St. M24—6H 45
(Middleton, in two parts)
Chapel St. M24—2E 61
(Rhodes)
Chapel St. M25—5E 59
Chapel St. M26—1B 56
Chapel St. M27—2G 71
Chapel St. M28—5B 68
Chapel St. M30—4E 83
Chapel St. M34—1F 105
Chapel St. M35—4B 90
Chapel St. OL2—3B 48
(Royton)
Chapel St. OL2—6F 35
(Shaw)
Chapel St. OL3—1F 53
(in two parts)
Chapel St. OL4—3A 66
Chapel St. OL5—2E 81
Chapel St. OL6—2A 92
Chapel St. OL10—3F 31
(in two parts)
Chapel St. OL11—1G 33
Chapel St. OL12—2A 8
(Wardle)
Chapel St. OL12—1C 6
(Whitworth)
Chapel St. OL15—5H 9
Chapel St. SK4—1H 129
Chapel St. SK6—4H 121
(Woodley)
Chapel St. SK7—2E 145
Chapel St. SK8—6H 129
Chapel St. SK9—5G 159
Chapel St. SK14—5B 106
Chapel St. SK15—3E 93
Chapel St. SK16—5H 91
Chapel Ter. M20—2F 117
Chapeltown Rd. BL7—4F 11

Chapeltown Rd. M26—1G 57
Chapeltown St. M1—5F 87 & 1D 166
Chapel Wlk. M24—2E 61
Chapel Wlk. M25—3E 73
(Prestwich)
Chapel Wlk. M25—6F 43
(Whitefield)
Chapel Wlk. M30—3H 83
Chapel Wlk. SK6—5D 134
Chapel Wlk. SK14—2H 109
Chapel Wlk. SK15—4F 93
Chapel Walks. M2—4D 86 & 5H 161
Chapel Walks. M33—4B 114
Chapel Walks. SK8—1D 152
Chapelway Gdns. OL2—2B 48
Chapman Ct. SK14—5H 107
Chapman M. M18—2F 103
Chapman Rd. SK14—6A 108
Chapman St. BL1—4F 23
Chapman St. M18—1F 103
Chappell Rd. M35—3A 90
Chapter St. M10—1B 88
Charcoal Rd. WA14—1A 136
Charcon Wlk. OL2—3C 48
Chard Dri. M22—4B 140
Chardin Av. SK6—3G 135
Chard St. M26—4G 41
Charfield St. M10—6D 76
Charges St. OL7—4F 91
Chariot St. M11—5F 89
Charlbury Av. M25—6A 60
Charlbury Av. SK5—2H 119
Charlbury Way. OL2—2E 49
Charlecote St. SK12—3F 155
Charles Av. M34—6A 90
Charles Av. SK6—4A 134
Charles Barry Cres. M15—1C 100 & 5F 165
Charles Ct. WA15—5B 126
(in two parts)
Charles Craddock Dri. M7—5B 74
Charles Halle Rd. M15—2E 101
Charles Holden St. BL1—1H 37
Charles Ho. BL1—5B 24
Charles M. OL16—6G 21
Charles Morris Clo. M35—3H 77
Charles Rupert St. BL1—3B 24
Charles St. BL1—5B 24
Charles St. BL4—2G 55
(Farnworth)
Charles St. BL4—6G 39
(Kearsley)
Charles St. BL7—1B 10
Charles St. BL9—2D 28
Charles St. M1—6E 87 & 3A 166
Charles St. M6—1F 85
(in two parts)
Charles St. M25—2D 58
Charles St. M27—2D 70
Charles St. M30—3C 110
Charles St. M34—2F 105
Charles St. M35—4G 89
Charles St. OL2—3B 48
Charles St. OL7—3H 91
Charles St. OL9—3A 64
Charles St. OL10—5G 31
Charles St. OL12—3H 7
Charles St. OL15—4E 9
Charles St. SK1—4H 131
Charles St. SK7—2D 144
Charles St. SK16—5H 91
Charleston Clo. OL8—6D 64
Charleston St. OL8—5D 64
Charlestown Clo. OL6—2H 91
Charlestown Ind. Est. OL6—1H 91
Charlestown Rd. M9—1F 75
Charlestown Rd. E. SK2—2A 144
Charlestown Rd. W. SK3—2H 143
Charles Whittaker St. OL12—2B 18
Charlesworth Av. M34—1F 121
Charlesworth St. M11—5B 88
Charlesworth St. SK1—4H 131
Charley Av. M7—1B 86
Charlock Sq. WA14—3D 124
Charlock Wlk. M31—6D 110
Charlotte St. BL0—4D 4
Charlotte St. BL1—3A 24
Charlotte St. M1—4E 87 & 6A 162

Charlotte St. M1—4E 87 & 6A 162
Charlotte St. OL16—1H 33
Charlotte St. SK1—6B 120
Charlotte St. SK8—6H 129
Charlsworth Av. BL3—4D 38
Charlton Av. M26—5F 59
Charlton Av. M30—4F 83
Charlton Av. SK14—2E 107
Charlton Ct. M25—6F 59
Charlton Dri. M27—1D 70
Charlton Dri. M33—5C 114
Charlton Pl. M12—6F 87 & 3D 166
Charlton Rd. M19—5D 102
Charmouth Wlk. M22—1D 140
Charnley Clo. M10—2A 88
Charnley St. M25—1D 58
Charnock Dri. BL1—4A 24
Charnville Rd. SK8—6D 128
Charnwood Av. M34—4B 104
Charnwood Clo. M28—1E 69
Charnwood Clo. OL2—5C 34
Charnwood Clo. OL6—4G 79
Charnwood Cres. SK7—5D 144
Charnwood Rd. M9—4F 61
Charnwood Rd. SK6—4A 122
Charter. M30—4H 83
Charter Av. M26—5A 42
Charter Rd. WA15—1G 137
Charter St. M3—2D 86 & 1H 161
Charter St. OL1—1E 65
Charter St. OL16—1G 33
Chartwell Clo. M5—3F 85
Chartwell Dri. M23—4D 126
Chaseley Rd. M6—1E 85
Chaseley Rd. OL12—3G 19
Chase St. M4—2E 87 & 1B 162
Chase, The. BL1—6E 23
Chase, The. M28—6A 70
Chasetown Clo. M23—5D 126
Chassen Av. M31—5C 96
Chassen Ct. M31—6D 96
Chassen Rd. BL1—6F 23
Chassen Rd. M31—5D 96
Chataway Rd. M8—3E 75
Chatburn Av. OL11—6D 32
Chatburn Ct. OL2—5E 35
Chatburn Gdns. OL10—3B 30
Chatburn Rd. BL1—2D 22
Chatburn Rd. M21—1A 116
Chatcombe Rd. M22—3G 139
Chatfield Rd. M21—1H 115
Chatford Clo. M7—1C 86
Chatham Ct. M20—3E 117
Chatham Gdns. BL3—2H 37
Chatham Gro. M20—3E 117
Chatham Pl. BL3—2H 37
Chatham Rd. M16—4H 99
Chatham Rd. M18—4G 103
Chatham St. M1—4F 87 & 6C 162
Chatham St. SK3—3E 131
Chatham St. SK14—2C 122
Chatley Rd. M30—4B 82
Chatley St. M3—1D 86
Chatsworth Av. SK2—5H 131
Chatsworth Av. M25—4F 59
Chatsworth Clo. BL9—2E 43
Chatsworth Clo. M31—5G 97
Chatsworth Clo. OL2—5H 35
Chatsworth Clo. WA15—6C 126
Chatsworth Clo. M9—4C 60
(off Deanswood Dri.)
Chatsworth Ct. SK2—6A 132
Chatsworth Cres. M32—4H 97
Chatsworth Gro. BL3—3A 40
Chatsworth Gro. M16—5B 100
Chatsworth Rd. M18—2E 103
Chatsworth Rd. M26—2D 40
Chatsworth Rd. M28 & M27—5B 70
Chatsworth Rd. M30—1H 83
Chatsworth Rd. M32—4A 98
Chatsworth Rd. M35—2G 89
Chatsworth Rd. SK6—1D 156
Chatsworth Rd. SK7—4F 145
Chatsworth Rd. SK8—1D 142
Chatsworth Rd. SK9—5B 158
Chatsworth St. OL4—4G 65
Chatsworth St. OL12—6E 7
Chattock Clo. M16—4C 100

Chatton Clo. BL8—3F 27
Chatwell Ct. OL16—1G 35
Chatwood Rd. M10—1D 76
Chaucer Av. M26—3E 41
Chaucer Av. M34—2G 121
Chaucer Av. M35—4A 90
Chaucer Av. SK5—6F 103
Chaucer Ho. SK5—6F 103
Chaucer M. SK1—2B 132
Chaucer Rise. M34—6B 104
Chaucer Rd. M24—5B 46
Chaucer St. BL1—3H 23
Chaucer St. OL1—3C 64
Chaucer St. OL2—2C 48
Chaucer St. OL11—3C 32
Chaucer Wlk. M13—1G 101 & 6F 167
Chaumont Way. OL6—2H 91
Chauncy Rd. M10—3E 77
Chaytor Av. M10—4A 76
Cheadle Av. M7—4E 73
Cheadle Grn. SK8—5H 129
Cheadle Old Rd. SK3—4D 130
Cheadle Rd. SK8—1A 142
Cheadle St. BL1—6A 24
Cheadle St. M11—5F 89
Cheam Clo. M11—6D 88
Cheam Rd. WA15—3H 125
Cheapside. M2—4D 86 & 5H 161
Cheap Side. M24—5A 46
Cheapside. OL1—2C 64
Cheddar St. M18—1F 103
Chedlee Dri. SK8—4A 142
Ciedlin Dri. M23—1G 139
Chedworth Cres. M28—3C 54
Chedworth Gro. BL3—2A 38
(off Parrot St.)
Cheeryble St. M11 & M35—6H 89
Cheesden Wlk. M25—6G 43
Cheetham Av. M24—6B 46
Cheetham Fold Rd. SK14—1B 122
Cheetham Gdns. SK15—4F 93
Cheetham Hill. OL2—1F 49
Cheetham Hill. OL12—2H 7
Cheetham Hill Rd. M4 & M8—2E 87 & 1A 162
Cheetham Hill Rd. M8—3B 74
Cheetham Hill Rd. SK16 & SK15—1B 106
Cheetham Pde. M8—3B 74
Cheetham Rd. M27—4G 71
Cheethams Cres. OL2—3E 49
Cheetham St. M10—6G 75
Cheetham St. M24—1H 61
Cheetham St. M26—4A 42
Cheetham St. M35—3G 77
(in two parts)
Cheetham St. OL1—2F 65
Cheetham St. OL2—1G 49
Cheetham St. OL16—3H 19
Cheetham St. SK14—2E 107
Cheetham Wlk. SK14—4C 106
Cheetwood Rd. M8—1D 86
Cheetwood St. M8—1C 86
Chelburne Clo. SK2—6D 132
Chelburn View. OL15—6G 9
Cheldon Wlk. M10—4A 76
Chelford Av. BL1—6C 10
Chelford Clo. M13—2H 101
Chelford Clo. M24—5C 46
Chelford Clo. WA15—5G 125
Chelford Ct. SK9—2A 152
Chelford Dri. M27—1E 71
Chelford Gro. SK3—6E 131
Chelford Rd. M16—4A 100
Chelford Rd. M33—1E 127
Chelford Rd. SK9—5F 159
(Alderley Edge)
Chelford Rd. SK9—2H 151
(Handforth)
Chellow Dene. OL5—2D 80
Chelmer Gro. OL10—2C 30
Chelmsford Av. M10—1D 88
Chelmsford Rd. SK3—3E 131
Chelmsford St. OL8—4C 64
Chelmsford Wlk. M34—6G 105
Chelsea Av. M26—3D 40
Chelsea Clo. OL2—6F 35
Chelsea Rd. BL3—4H 37

Chelsea Rd. M10—6B 76
Chelsea Rd. M11—6G 95
Chelsea St. BL9—2D 42
Chelsea St. OL11—1D 76
Chelsfield Gro. M21—1B 116
Chelston Av. M10—1D 76
Chelston Dri. SK8—1G 151
Cheltenham Cres. M7—3A 74
Cheltenham Dri. M33—5C 114
Cheltenham Grn. M24—3A 62
Cheltenham Rd. M21—5H 99
Cheltenham Rd. M24—3A 62
Cheltenham Rd. SK3—4C 130
Cheltenham St. M6—1G 85
Cheltenham St. OL1—6F 49
Cheltenham St. OL11—1D 32
Chelt Wlk. M22—3H 139
Chelwood Clo. BL1—4B 10
Chemist St. BL1—4B 24
Cheney Clo. M11—6F 89
Chepstow Av. M33—6E 113
Chepstow Clo. OL11—3B 18
Chepstow Dri. OL1—6F 49
Chepstow Dri. SK7—3G 145
Chepstow Rd. M21—6G 99
Chepstow Rd. M27—1G 71
Chepstow St. M1—5D 86 & 2H 165
Chepstow St. N. M1—5D 86 & 2H 165
Chepstow St. S. M1—5D 86 & 2H 165
Chequers Rd. M21—1H 115
Cherington Rd. SK8—1G 141
Cheriton Av. M33—4C 114
Cheriton Clo. SK14—5H 107
Cheriton Dri. BL2—1G 39
Cheriton Rise. SK2—5G 133
Cheriton Rd. M31—4H 95
Cherrington Clo. M23—1H 127
Cherrington Dri. OL11—5D 32
Cherry Av. BL9—2G 29
Cherry Av. OL6—5F 79
Cherry Av. OL8—6G 65
Cherry Ct. M33—5A 114
Cherry Croft. SK6—2C 134
(in two parts)
Cherry Dri. M27—3G 71
Cherry Gro. OL2—1A 48
Cherry Gro. OL11—3C 18
Cherry Gro. OL15—5E 93
Cherry Hall Dri. OL2—6C 34
Cherry Holt Av. SK4—5B 118
Cherry La. M33—1E 125
Cherry Orchard Clo. SK7—4F 143
Cherry St. M25—4G 59
Cherryton Wlk. M13—1G 101 & 6E 167
Cherry Tree Av. BL4—1B 54
Cherry Tree Av. SK12—4F 155
Cherry Tree Clo. SK9—6A 152
Cherry Tree Ct. M6—3G 85
Cherry Tree Dri. SK7—5F 145
Cherry Tree Est. SK6—1D 134
Cherry Tree La. SK2—1C 144
Cherry Tree La. SK6—1C 134
Cherrytree Rd. M23—2F 127
Cherry Tree Rd. SK8—4B 142
Cherry Tree Wlk. M32—6C 98
Cherry Tree Wlk. OL5—2D 80
Cherry Tree Way. BL2—1D 24
Cherry Wlk. M31—6B 110
Cherry Wlk. SK8—5E 143
Cherrywood. OL9—2D 62
Cherrywood Clo. M28—2F 69
Chertsey Clo. M18—2G 103
Chertsey Clo. OL2—5F 35
Cherwell Av. OL10—2C 30
Cherwell Clo. OL8—2A 78
Cherwell Clo. SK8—6C 142
Chesham Av. BL1—3A 24
Chesham Av. M22—1A 140
Chesham Av. M31—4A 96
Chesham Av. OL11—6D 32
Chesham Clo. SK9—5C 158
Chesham Cres. BL9—2E 29
Chesham Fold Rd. BL9—2F 29
Chesham Ho. M5—3F 85
Chesham Pl. WA14—3E 137
Chesham Rd. BL9—1D 28
Chesham Rd. M30—5E 83

Chesham Rd. OL4—3G 65
Chesham Rd. SK9—5C 158
Chesham St. BL3—5F 37
Cheshire Clo. BL0—3F 5
Cheshire Rd. M31—6B 110
Cheshire Rd. SK15—6G 81
Cheshire Sq. SK15—6G 81
Cheshires, The. OL5—2F 81
Cheshire St. OL5—3F 81
Chesney Av. OL9—1E 77
Chesshyre Av. M4—4H 87 & 5H 163
Chessington Rise. M27—6G 57
Chester Av. BL3—3B 40
Chester Av. M25—2E 59
Chester Av. M31—4G 97
Chester Av. M33—2D 124
Chester Av. OL11—5C 18
Chester Av. SK15—2H 93
Chester Av. SK16—6C 92
Chester Av. WA15—3H 137
Chester Clo. BL3—3B 40
Chester Clo. M30—4B 110
Chester Clo. SK9—6A 152
Chester Dri. BLO—5C 4
Chesterfield Gro. OL6—2B 92
Chesterfield St. OL4—3F 65
Chesterfield Way. M34—1F 121
Chestergate. SK3 & SK1—2F 131
Chester Pl. OL2—3B 48
Chester Rd. M29—3A 68
Chester Rd. M32, M16 & M15
    —2C 114 & 6A 164
Chester Rd. SK7—6D 144
    (Hazel Grove)
Chester Rd. SK7 & SK12—6F 153
    (Woodford & Poynton)
Chester Rd. WA16 & WA14—6A 136
Chester Sq. OL6—3G 91
Chester St. BL1—4B 24
Chester St. BL9—1E 29
Chester St. M15 & M1—6D 86 &
    4H 165
Chester St. M25—4E 59
Chester St. M27—4E 71
Chester St. M34—5F 105
Chester St. OL9—4A 64
Chester St. OL11—5A 20
Chester St. SK3—2F 131
Chesterton Dri. BL3—2C 36
Chesterton Gro. M35—3A 90
Chesterton Rd. M23—3D 126
Chesterton Rd. OL1—5F 49
Chesterton Wlk. M23—4E 127
Chester Wlk. BL1—3A 24
    (off Boardman St.)
Chester Walks. BL6—2G 133
Chestnut Av. BL8—6A 14
Chestnut Av. BL9—3F 29
Chestnut Av. M21—1H 115
Chestnut Av. M25—2D 58
Chestnut Av. M28—1F 69
Chestnut Av. M30—4B 110
Chestnut Av. M35—2G 89
Chestnut Av. SK8—6A 130
Chestnut Clo. BL3—3F 37
Chestnut Clo. OL4—1H 65
Chestnut Clo. SK9—6A 152
Chestnut Clo. SK15—5E 93
Chestnut Ct. SK7—3F 143
Chestnut Cres. OL8—1E 79
Chestnut Dri. M33—2F 125
Chestnut Dri. SK12—4F 155
Chestnut Gdns. M34—5E 105
Chestnut Gro. M26—1F 57
Chestnut Gro. M35—5F 77
Chestnut Pl. OL16—3B 20
Chestnut Rd. M30—1C 82
Chestnut St. OL9—6F 63
Chestnut Vs. SK4—1E 131
Chestnut Wlk. M31—6B 110
Chestnut Way. OL15—3D 8
Chesworth Clo. SK1—3H 131
Chesworth St. M35—4H 89
Chesworth Fold. SK1—3H 131
Chesworth Wlk. M15—6C 86
    (off Jackson Cres.)
Chetham Clo. M5—6H 85
Chetwyn Av. BL7—4E 11

Chetwyn Av. OL2—3A 48
Chetwynd Av. M31—5E 97
Chetwynd Clo. M33—3G 113
Chevin Gdns. SK7—6A 144
Chevington Dri. M9—5F 75
Chevington Dri. SK4—6H 117
Chevington Gdns. BL1—2A 24
Cheviot Av. OL2—4A 48
Cheviot Av. OL8—6C 64
Cheviot Av. SK8—3B 142
Cheviot Clo. BLO—5E 5
Cheviot Clo. BL8—6B 10
Cheviot Clo. BL8—2G 27
Cheviot Clo. M6—2E 85
Cheviot Clo. M24—1D 62
Cheviot Clo. OL9—4G 63
Cheviot Clo. OL16—5G 21
Cheviot Clo. SK4—6F 119
Cheviot Ct. OL8—5C 64
Cheviot Rd. SK7—4B 144
Cheviots Rd. OL2—5E 35
Cheviot St. M3—2D 86 & 1H 161
Chevithorne Clo. WA14—5D 124
Chevril Clo. M15—1E 101 & 5A 166
Chevron Clo. M6—3H 85
Chevron Clo. OL11—2B 32
Chew Brook Dri. OL3—4F 53
Chew Vale. OL3—4F 53
Chew Vale. SK16—6D 92
Chew Valley Rd. OL3—3E 53
Chichester Clo. OL15—6D 8
Chichester Cres. OL9—6G 47
Chichester Rd. M15—2C 100 &
    6G 165
Chichester Rd. SK6—1A 134
Chichester St. OL16—4A 20
Chichester Way. M34—6G 105
Chidlow Av. M20—2E 117
Chidwall Rd. M22—3H 139
Chief St. OL4—3E 65
Chigwell Clo. M22—6B 128
Chilcombe Wlk. M9—4G 61
    (off Brockford Dri.)
Chilcote Av. M33—5F 113
Chilham Rd. M28—1G 69
Chilham Rd. M30—1H 83
Chilham St. BL3—4F 37
Chilham St. M27—5E 71
Chillington Wlk. M34—6E 105
Chillingworth St. M8—5C 74
Chilmark Dri. M23—5G 127
Chiltern Av. M31—4A 96
Chiltern Av. SK8—3B 142
Chiltern Clo. M28—3G 69
Chiltern Clo. OL2—5D 34
Chiltern Clo. SK7—4B 144
Chiltern Dri. BL2—6D 24
Chiltern Dri. BL8—1H 27
Chiltern Dri. SK7—7F 71
Chiltern Dri. OL2—3A 48
Chiltern Dri. SK2—1A 144
Chiltern Dri. WA15—3H 137
Chiltern Gdns. M33—3C 126
Chiltern Rd. BLO—5E 5
Chilton Av. OL9—3G 63
Chilton Dri. M24—2C 62
Chilworth St. M14—5F 101
Chime Bank. M8—4D 74
Chimney Hall St. SK4—5G 119
China La. BL1—4B 24
China La. M1—4F 87 & 5C 162
Chingford Wlk. M13—3B 102
    (off St John's Rd.)
Chinley Av. M10—3A 76
Chinley Av. M32—3A 98
Chinley Clo. M33—6D 114
Chinley Clo. SK4—6D 118
Chinley Clo. SK7—2G 143
Chinley St. M6—6F 73
Chinwell View. M19—6C 102
Chip Hill Rd. BL3—3D 36
Chippendale Pl. OL6—6A 80
Chippenham Av. SK2—4D 132
Chippenham Ct. M4—3H 87 & 4G 163
Chippenham Rd. M4—3G 87 & 4H 163
Chipping Fold. OL16—6F 21
Chipping Rd. BL1—3D 22
Chipstead Wlk. M12—2A 102

Chirmside St. BL8—4H 27
Chirton Wlk. M10—4A 76
Chiseldon Clo. BL3—2A 38
    (off Bantry St.)
Chiselhurst St. M8—3C 74
Chisholme Clo. BL8—1H 13
Chisholm St. M11—6F 89
Chisledon Av. M8—5B 74
Chislehurst Av. M31—4E 97
Chislehurst Clo. BL8—4H 27
Chisolm Ct. SK1—2H 131
Chiswick Dri. M26—2B 40
Chiswick Rd. M20—6G 117
Chisworth Clo. SK7—2G 143
Chisworth St. BL2—2D 24
Chisworth Wlk. M34—1G 121
Choir St. M7—1C 86
Chokeberry Clo. WA14—3D 124
Cholmondeley Av. WA14—2G 125
Cholmondeley Rd. M6—1B 84
Cholsey Av. M7—4F 73
Chomlea. WA14—1D 136
Chomlea Manor. M6—1C 84
Choral Gro. M7—6H 73
Chorley Clo. BL8—4F 27
Chorley Hall Clo. SK9—5F 159
Chorley Hall La. SK9—5F 159
Chorley Old Rd. BL1—3D 22
Chorley Old Rd. BL6 & BL1—
    2A 22
Chorley Rd. M27—2E 71
Chorley Rd. M33—1E 127
Chorley St. BL1—5A 24
Chorley St. M27—3F 99
Chorley Wood Av. M19—3B 118
Chorlton Dri. SK8—5A 130
Chorlton Fold. M30—6D 70
    (in two parts)
Chorlton Fold. SK6—4A 122
Chorlton Grn. M21—1G 115
Chorlton Gro. SK1—4B 132
Chorlton Pl. M21—6H 99
Chorlton Rd. M16 & M15—3B 100 &
    6E 165
Chorlton St. M1—5E 87 & 1B 166
Chorlton St. M16—2A 100
Chretien Rd. M22—1B 128
Chrisleton Av. SK4—4F 119
Christ Chu. Av. M5—3H 85
Christchurch Clo. BL2—2H 25
Christchurch La. BL2—2H 25
Christchurch Rd. M33—4E 113
Christie Rd. M32—4E 99
Christie St. SK1—3A 132
Christine St. OL2—6F 35
    (in two parts)
Christleton Way. SK9—2H 151
Christopher Acre. OL11—2A 18
Christopher St. M5—4G 85
Christopher St. M10—1F 89
Chronnell Dri. BL2—5G 25
Chudleigh Clo. SK7—2A 144
Chudleigh Clo. WA14—5D 124
Chudleigh Rd. M8—1C 74
Chulsey St. BL3—3F 37
Church Av. BL3—3G 37
Church Av. M6—3D 84
Church Av. M10—6C 76
Church Av. M24—1D 46
Church Av. M34—1G 121
Church Av. SK9—5E 151
Church Av. SK14—1D 122
Church Bank. BL1—6C 24
Churchbank. SK15—2H 93
Church Bank. WA14—3D 136
Church Brow. M24—6A 46
Church Brow. SK14—6B 106
    (Hyde)
Church Brow. SK14—4C 108
    (Mottram)
Church Brow. WA14—3D 136
Church Clo. M34—6F 91
Church Clo. SK9—4H 151
Church Ct. BLO—1A 4
Church Ct. OL9—4A 64
Church Ct. SK16—4H 91
Church Croft. BL9—3F 43
Churchdale Rd. M9—5D 60

Church Dri. M25—5E 59
Churchfield Clo. M26—6F 41
Churchfield Rd. M6—6B 72
Churchfields. M34—6E 91
Churchfields. OL3—5A 52
Churchfields. WA14—4D 136
Churchfield Wlk. M11—5C 88
    (off Outrington Dri.)
Churchgate. BL1—6B 24
Churchgate. M31—6G 97
Churchgate. SK1—2H 131
Churchgate Bldgs. M1—5G 87 & 1E 163
Church Grn. M6—2F 85
Church Grn. M26—3B 42
Church Gro. M30—4G 83
Church Gro. SK7—3E 145
Churchill Av. BL2—4D 26
Churchill Av. M16—5B 100
Churchill Clo. OL10—5G 31
Churchill Ct. M6—3F 85
Churchill Cres. SK6—6G 103
Churchill Cres. SK8—6B 134
Churchill Dri. BL3—4C 40
Churchill Rd. WA14—4F 125
Churchill St. BL2—6E 25
Churchill St. OL4—3E 65
Churchill St. OL12 & OL11—2E 19
    (in two parts)
Churchill St. SK4—6F 119
Churchill St. E. OL4—3E 65
Churchill Way. M6—3G 85
Churchill Way. M17—6C 84
Church La. BLO—1A 4
Church La. M7—2G 73
Church La. M9—3F 75
    (in two parts)
Church La. M19—3B 118
Church La. M25—5E 59
    (Prestwich)
Church La. M25—1C 58
    (Whitefield)
Church La. M33—2G 113
Church La. OL1—2D 64
Church La. OL3—6D 52
Church La. OL16—4H 19
Church La. SK6—5D 134
    (Marple)
Church La. SK6—1A 134
    (Romiley)
Church La. SK7—5E 153
Church La. SK9—4G 159
Churchley Clo. SK3—5C 130
Churchley Rd. SK3—4C 130
Church Manor. SK4—5D 118
Church Meadow. BL9—3F 43
Church Meadow. OL3—4G 67
Church Meadows. BL2—2H 25
Church M. M34—4E 105
Church Pl. OL1—2D 64
Church Pl. OL10—3F 31
Church Rd. BLO—1G 5
Church Rd. BL1—3E 23
Church Rd. BL4—1G 55
Church Rd. M22—2B 128
Church Rd. M24—2D 62
Church Rd. M26—1A 56
Church Rd. M28—6F 55
Church Rd. M30—3H 83
Church Rd. M31—6B 96
Church Rd. M33—5D 114
Church Rd. OL2—1F 49
Church Rd. OL3—4G 67
    (Greenfield)
Church Rd. OL3—1F 53
    (Uppermill)
Church Rd. OL16—5B 20
Church Rd. SK4—1F 131
Church Rd. SK8—5D 142
    (Cheadle Hulme)
Church Rd. SK8—6E 129
    (Gatley)
Church Rd. SK9—3H 151
    (Handforth)
Church Rd. SK9—5B 158
    (Wilmslow)
Church Rd. SK14—3F 109
Church Rd. E. M33—5D 114
Church Rd. W. M33—5C 114

Churchside Clo. M9—1F 75
Church Stile. OL16—4H 19
(in two parts)
Churchstoke Wlk. M23—4E 127
Church St. BL2—4C 26
(Ainsworth)
Church St. BL2—6H 11
(Bradshaw)
Church St. BL3—4H 39
(Farnworth)
Church St. BL4—1G 55
(Kearsley, in two parts)
Church St. BL8—1F 27
Church St. BL9—2E 29
Church St. M4—3E 87 & 4B 162
Church St. M26—4H 41
Church St. M27—3H 71
(Pendlebury)
Church St. M27—3E 71
(Swinton)
Church St. M30—3G 83
(in three parts)
Church St. M32—6C 98
Church St. M34—6E 91
Church St. M35—4B 90
(Droylsden)
Church St. M35—3F 77
(Failsworth)
Church St. OL1—2D 64
Church St. OL2—3B 48
Church St. OL3—3G 51
Church St. OL4—4A 66
Church St. OL5—2F 81
Church St. OL6—3H 91
Church St. OL10—3F 31
Church St. OL11—4G 19
Church St. OL12—1C 6
Church St. OL15—4E 9
Church St. OL16—1F 35
(Newhey)
Church St. OL16—6B 8
(Smallbridge)
Church St. SK4—6F 119
(in two parts)
Church St. SK6—4G 121
(Bredbury)
Church St. SK6—5D 134
(Marple)
Church St. SK8—5H 129
Church St. SK9—2E 159
Church St. SK14—6B 106
Church St. SK14—3H 109
Church St. SK16—4H 91
Church St. WA14—6F 125
Church St. E. M26—4A 42
(in two parts)
Church St. E. OL4—1A 66
Church Ter. M33—3A 114
Church Ter. OL1—2D 64
Church Ter. OL16—6G 21
Church Ter. SK4—1F 131
Church Ter. SK9—3H 151
Churchtown Av. BL2—6H 25
Churchwood Rd. M20—6F 117
Churnet St. M10—6F 75
Churston Av. M9—5G 61
Churston Av. SK7—3H 143
Churton Av. M14—5F 101
Churton Av. M33—6H 113
Churton Rd. M18—4E 103
Churwell Av. SK4—5B 118
Cicero St. M9—3H 75

Cicero St. OL1—6E 49
Cilder's Villa. OL4—5D 66
Cinder Hill La. OL1—3G 47
Cinnamon Clo. OL12—3F 19
Cinnamon St. OL12—3F 19
Cipher St. M4—2C 87
Circle Ct. M32—3H 97
Circle, The. M32—3H 97
Circuit, The. M20—4F 117
Circuit, The. SK3—5D 130
Circuit, The. SK8—6C 142
Circuit, The. SK9—6E 159
(Alderley Edge)
Circuit, The. SK9—4A 158
(Wilmslow)
Circular Rd. M20—4F 117
Circular Rd. M25—1F 73
Circular Rd. M34—5E 105
Cirencester Clo. M28—3C 54
Ciss La. M31—5G 97
City Av. M34—5E 105
City Course Trading Est. M11
—5C 88
City Gdns. M34—5D 104
City Rd. M15—1A 100 & 6B 164
City Rd. M28—3C 68
City Rd. E. M15—6D 86 & 3G 165
City Wlk. M27—3H 71
Civic Wlk. OL10—3F 31
Clacton Wlk. M13—1G 101
(off Ardeen Wlk.)
Clague St. M11—3C 88
Claife Av. M10—1B 76
Clammerclough Rd. BL4—1H 55
Clandon Av. M30—3D 82
Clandon Clo. M12—1H 101 & 6H 167
Clapgate. SK6—2F 133
Clapgate Rd. OL11—2A 18
Clapham St. M10—3C 76
Clara Gorton Ct. OL16—5B 20
Clara St. OL9—5A 64
Clara St. OL11—6H 19
Clara St. OL12—4H 7
Clare Av. SK9—4G 151
Clare Clo. BL8—6D 14
Clare Ct. SK1—2A 132
Claremont Av. M20—4E 117
Claremont Av. SK4—4F 125
Claremont Av. SK6—5A 134
Claremont Av. WA14—3F 125
Claremont Dri. M28—4D 54
Claremont Gro. M20—6E 117
Claremont Gro. WA15—2G 137
Claremont Range. M18—3H 103
Claremont Rd. M6—5A 72
Claremont Rd. M16 & M14—4C 100
Claremont Rd. M33—4B 114
Claremont Rd. OL11—4E 19
Claremont Rd. OL16—6E 21
Claremont Rd. SK2—6B 132
Claremont Rd. SK8—5C 142
Claremont St. M35—3F 77
Claremont St. OL6—1C 92
(in two parts)
Claremont St. OL8—1D 78
Claremont St. OL9—6A 48
Clarence Arc. OL6—3H 91
Clarence Av. M17—6H 83
Clarence Av. M25—2E 59
Clarence Av. M33—6G 113
Clarence Av. OL8—5B 64
Clarence Ct. BL1—5A 24
Clarence Clo. SK9—3D 158
Clarence Gro. M15—3C 100
Clarence Rd. M13—4A 102
Clarence Rd. M27—4C 70
Clarence Rd. OL6—1A 92
Clarence Rd. SK4—4D 118
Clarence Rd. WA15—2H 137
Clarence St. BL1—5B 24
(in two parts)
Clarence St. BL4—6G 39
Clarence St. M2—4D 86 & 6H 161
Clarence St. M7—1A 86
Clarence St. OL2—4E 49
Clarence St. OL12—1F 19
Clarence St. SK14—3C 106

Clarence St. SK15—4C 92
Clarendon Av. SK4—6D 118
Clarendon Av. WA15—6G 125
Clarendon Cres. M30—2H 83
Clarendon Cres. M33—4D 114
Clarendon Gdns. M30—2H 83
Clarendon Gro. BL2—1D 38
Clarendon Pl. SK14—5C 106
Clarendon Rd. BL2—6E 25
Clarendon Rd. M16—5A 100
Clarendon Rd. M27—3F 71
Clarendon Rd. M30—2H 83
(Eccles)
Clarendon Rd. M30—2D 110
(Irlam)
Clarendon Rd. M31—4A 96
Clarendon Rd. M33—5D 114
Clarendon Rd. M34—6A 90
(Audenshaw)
Clarendon Rd. M34—5H 105
(Denton)
Clarendon Rd. SK7—2F 145
Clarendon Rd. SK14—4B 106
Clarendon Rd. W. M21—5H 99
Clarendon St. BL3—3A 38
Clarendon St. BL9—1E 29
Clarendon St. M15—1D 100 & 5G 165
(in two parts)
Clarendon St. M25—1D 58
Clarendon St. OL3—3F 81
Clarendon St. OL16—1H 33
Clarendon St. SK5—6H 119
Clarendon St. SK14—4B 106
(in two parts)
Clarendon St. SK16—5G 91
(in two parts)
Clare Rd. M19—1C 118
Clare St. M5—5H 119
Clare St. M5—4A 86 & 6B 160
Clare St. M34—3E 105
Claribel St. M11—5A 88
Claridge Rd. M21—5G 99
Clarion St. M4—2G 87 & 2E 163
Clark Av. M18—2G 103
Clarke Av. M6—6H 85
Clarke Brow. M24—6A 46
Clarke Cres. M28—3A 54
Clarke Cres. WA15—2B 138
Clarke Ind. Est. M42—1B 6
Clarkenwell Clo. OL1—1C 64
Clarkes Croft. BL9—2G 29
Clarke's La. OL12—3F 19
Clarke St. BL1—5G 23
Clarke St. BL4—2G 55
Clarke St. M4—3G 87 & 4F 163
Clarke St. OL7—5F 91
Clarke St. OL10—3F 31
Clarke St. OL16—1B 20
Clarke St. WA14—4F 125
Clarkethorn Ter. SK5—6G 119
Clarksfield Rd. OL4—3G 65
Clarksfield St. OL4—3G 65
Clark's Hill. M25—5E 59
Clarkson Clo. M24—2E 61
Clarkson Clo. M34—5D 104
Clark Way. SK14—4A 106
Clatford Wlk. M9—4F 75
(off Fernclough Rd.)
Claude Av. M27—3D 70
Claude Rd. M21—2G 115
Claude St. M8—2C 74
Claude St. M27—3D 70
Claude St. M30—2D 82
Claudia Sq. SK15—6G 81
Claughton Av. BL2—6H 25
Claughton Av. M28—3E 69
Claughton Rd. BL8—6H 13
Clavendon Rd. M26—6E 27
Claverham Wlk. M23—4E 127
Claverton Rd. M23—1E 139
Claxton Av. M9—6F 61
Claybank Dri. BL8—4F 13
Clay Bank St. OL10—2E 31
Claybrook Wlk. M11—4C 88
Clayburn Rd. M15—1C 100 & 5F 165
Clay Croft Ter. OL15—2E 9
Claydon Dri. M26—2B 40

Clayfield Dri. OL11—3B 18
Claygate Dri. M9—4F 61
Clayhill Wlk. M9—2F 75
Claylands Clo. SK14—3F 109
Clay La. M23—1F 139
Clay La. OL11—3H 17
Clay La. SK9—3F 151
(Handforth)
Clay La. SK9—5A 158
(Wilmslow)
Clay La. WA15—6B 126
Claymore St. M18—1G 103
Clay St. BL7—4E 11
Clay St. OL8—5C 64
Clay St. OL15—4D 8
Claythorpe Wlk. M8—1A 74
Clayton Av. BL2—2E 39
Clayton Av. M20—5F 117
Claytonbrook Rd. M11—5E 89
Clayton Clo. BL8—4F 27
Clayton Clo. M15—2C 100
Clayton Hall Rd. M11—3E 89
Clayton Ind. Est. M11—4E 89
Clayton La. M11—5D 88
Clayton La. S. M12—6C 88
Clayton's Clo. OL4—2B 66
Clayton St. BL2—2E 39
Clayton St. M11—2D 88
(in two parts)
Clayton St. M34—5F 105
Clayton St. M35—4F 77
Clayton St. OL9—6G 63
Clayton St. OL12—1B 20
Clayton St. SK16—5B 92
Cleadon Av. M18—3E 103
Cleadon Dri. BL8—6C 14
Cleadon Dri. S. BL8—6C 14
Cleavley St. M30—3D 82
Clee Av. M13—5B 102
Cleethorpes Av. M9—6D 60
Cleeve Rd. M23—1G 127
Cleeve Rd. OL4—3G 65
Cleeve Way. SK8—1D 152
Clegg Hall Rd. OL15—1D 20
Clegg Pl. OL6—1B 92
Clegg's Bldgs. BL1—6A 24
Clegg's Ct. M3—3D 86 & 4G 161
Clegg's La. M28—5C 54
Clegg St. BL2—6E 25
Clegg St. M25—2D 58
Clegg St. M35—4H 89
(Droylsden)
Clegg St. OL1—3D 64
Clegg St. OL4—3D 64
(Oldham)
Clegg St. OL4—3C 66
(Springhead)
Clegg St. OL12—3G 7
Clegg St. OL15—2D 8
Clegg St. OL16—6G 21
Clegg St. SK6—6F 121
Cleggswood Av. OL15—6E 9
Clelland St. BL4—2G 55
Clematis Wlk. M27—1E 71
Clement Ct. OL16—5B 20
Clementina St. OL12—2H 19
Clement Pl. OL12—3G 19
Clement Pl. OL15—4G 9
Clement Rd. SK6—4F 135
Clement Royds St. OL12—3G 19
Clements St. M11—6G 89
Clement Stott Clo. M9—5H 61
Clement St. SK4—6G 119
Cleminson St. M3—3B 86 & 4C 160
Clemshaw Clo. OL10—4E 31
Clerewood Av. SK8—6F 141
Clerke St. BL9—3D 28
Clerk's Ct. M5—3B 84
Clevedon Av. M31—5A 98
Clevedon Rd. OL9—6G 47
Clevedon St. M9—4G 75
Cleveland Av. M6—2C 84
Cleveland Av. M19—5D 102
Cleveland Av. SK14—5A 106
Cleveland Clo. BL0—6E 5
Cleveland Clo. M27—1G 71
Cleveland Dri. OL16—5G 21
Cleveland Gdns. BL3—3F 37

Cleveland Gro. OL2—4A 48
Cleveland Rd. M8—2D 74
Cleveland Rd. SK4—5C 118
Cleveland Rd. WA15—2H 137
Clevelands Clo. OL2—5E 35
Cleveland St. BL3—3F 37
Cleveleys Av. BL2—5E 25
Cleveleys Av. BL9—5C 28
Cleveleys Av. M21—1A 116
Cleveleys Av. OL16—2H 33
Cleveleys Av. SK8—4F 141
Cleveleys Gro. M7—4A 74
Cleves Clo. OL10—4E 31
Cleworth Rd. M24—5H 45
Cleworth Wlk. M15—6B 86 & 4C 164
Clibarn St. M8—5D 74
Clifden Dri. M22—3C 140
Cliff Av. BL9—1C 14
Cliff Av. M7—5G 73
Cliffbrook Gro. SK9—5H 151
Cliff Cres. M7—4H 73
Cliffdale Rd. M8—2C 74
Cliffe Dale. SK15—5D 92
Cliffe St. OL15—5H 9
Cliff Grange. M7—4H 73
Cliff Gro. SK4—5D 118
Cliff Hill. OL2—4H 35
Cliff Hill Rd. M7—4H 35
Cliffmere Clo. SK8—2B 142
Cliff Mt. BL0—2D 4
Clifford Av. M34—2E 105
Clifford Av. WA15—5A 126
Clifford Ct. M15—2C 100
Clifford Ct. SK2—6B 132
Clifford Rd. BL3—5E 37
Clifford Rd. SK9—3C 158
Clifford St. SK12—3C 154
Clifford St. M27—3H 71
Clifford St. M30—4D 82
Clifford St. OL11—6H 19
Cliff Rd. BL9—2D 42
Cliff Rd. SK9—1E 159
Cliff Side. SK9—1E 159
Cliff St. OL16—2B 20
Clifton Av. M14—1H 117
Clifton Av. M30—2F 83
Clifton Av. OL4—4F 65
Clifton Av. SK8—3E 141
Clifton Av. WA15—6G 125
Clifton Clo. M16—2B 100
Clifton Clo. OL4—4F 65
Clifton Clo. OL10—4E 31
Clifton Ct. BL4—5D 38
Clifton Ct. M27—5E 57
Clifton Ct. SK4—6D 118
Clifton Cres. OL2—4E 49
Clifton Dri. M27—1A 72
 (Clifton)
Clifton Dri. M27—2D 70
 (Swinton)
Clifton Dri. SK6—4D 134
Clifton Dri. SK8—6D 128
 (Gatley)
Clifton Dri. SK8—3E 141
 (Heald Green)
Clifton Dri. SK9—5B 158
Clifton Gro. M27—1C 70
Clifton Ho. Rd. M27—5E 57
Clifton Lodge. SK2—6A 132
Clifton Pk. Rd. SK2—6A 132
Clifton M16—2B 100
Clifton Rd. M21—1A 116
Clifton Rd. M24—1D 46
Clifton Rd. M25—5C 58
Clifton Rd. M30—2F 83
Clifton Rd. M31—5C 96
Clifton Rd. M33—6B 114
Clifton Rd. SK4—6C 118
Clifton St. BL1—5A 24
Clifton St. BL4—5D 38
 (Farnworth)
Clifton St. BL4—2H 55
 (Kearsley)
Clifton St. BL9—1D 28
Clifton St. M10—2B 88
Clifton St. M16—2B 100
Clifton St. M29—3A 68
Clifton St. M35—2G 77

Clifton St. OL6—2G 91
Clifton St. OL16—5F 21
Clifton St. SK9—5G 159
Clifton View. M27—5E 57
Clifton Vs. M35—2G 77
Cliftonville Dri. M27 & M6—5G 71
Cliftonville Rd. OL16—5A 34
Clifton Wlk. M24—4F 45
Clinton Av. M14—5D 100
Clinton Gdns. M14—5E 101
Clinton Ho. M5—4F 85
Clinton St. OL6—1B 92
Clinton Wlk. OL4—3E 65
Clippers Quay. M5—1G 99
Clipsley Cres. OL4—3B 50
Cliston Wlk. SK7—3A 144
Clitheroe Clo. OL10—2F 31
Clitheroe Dri. BL8—3F 27
Clitheroe Rd. M13—4B 102
Clito St. M9—3H 75
Clive Av. M25—6C 42
Cliveley Wlk. M27—3H 71
Clive Rd. M35—4E 77
Clive St. BL1—6B 24
Clive St. M4—2F 87 & 2C 162
Clive St. OL7—6E 79
Clive St. OL8—1B 78
 (in two parts)
Clivia Gro. M7—5H 73
Cloak St. M1—6E 87 & 3B 166
Clock Ho. Av. M35—2G 89
Clockhouse M. M35—2G 89
Clock Houses. SK15—3G 93
Clock Tower Clo. M28—6B 54
Cloister Clo. SK16—1A 106
Cloister Rd. SK4—1H 129
Cloisters, The. OL16—2B 20
Cloisters, The. SK8—6C 130
Cloister St. BL1—3G 23
Clopton Wlk. M15—1C 100 & 5F 165
 (in four parts)
Closeburn Wlk. M11—5B 88
Close, The. BL2—2D 24
Close, The. BL8—5C 14
Close, The. M24—4B 46
Close, The. M34—3D 104
Close, The. SK6—2F 135
Close, The. SK15—1D 92
 (in two parts)
Close, The. WA14—6E 125
 (Altrincham)
Close, The. WA14—1E 137
 (Bowdon)
Clothorn Rd. M20—5F 117
Cloudberry Wlk. M31—6D 110
Cloudstock Gro. M28—4A 54
Clough. OL2—1H 49
Clough Av. M33—2F 125
Clough Av. SK6—4G 135
Clough Av. SK9—5F 151
Clough Bank. M9—1F 75
Clough Bank. OL15—1E 9
Clough Ct. M24—5B 46
Clough Croft. OL4—3G 67
Clough Dri. M25—5D 58
Clough End Rd. SK14—6A 108
Clough Field. OL15—5E 9
Cloughfield Av. M5—5H 85
Cloughfield Dri. M5—5H 85
Clough Ga. OL8—1B 78
Clough Ga. SK14—1C 122
Clough La. M25—5D 58
Clough La. OL4—3F 67
Clough Meadow. BL1—1B 36
Clough Meadow. SK6—4A 122
Clough Meadow Rd. M26—4E 41
Clough Pk. Av. OL4—3G 67
Clough Rd. M9—3H 75
Clough Rd. M24—5A 46
Clough Rd. M35—3A 90
 (Droylsden)
Clough Rd. M35—4G 77
 (Failsworth)
Clough Rd. OL1—4H 49

Clough Rd. OL2—1H 49
Clough Rd. OL15—1E 9
Cloughs Av. OL9—1D 62
Clough Side. M9—2H 75
Clough Side. SK6—4F 135
Clough St. BL4—2H 55
Clough St. M10—6C 76
Clough St. M24—5B 46
Clough St. M26—6A 42
Clough St. OL12—3A 8
Clough, The. BL1—6C 22
Clough, The. SK5—3B 120
Cloughton Wlk. M10—6D 76
Clough Top Rd. M9—1A 76
Clough Wlk. M25—5D 58
Clough Wlk. SK5—3B 120
Clovelly Av. OL8—1A 78
Clovelly Rd. M21—1A 116
Clovelly Rd. M27—4C 70
Clovelly Rd. SK2—3C 132
Clovelly St. M10—6D 76
Clovelly St. OL11—2B 32
Clover Av. SK3—6F 131
Cloverbank Av. M19—5H 117
Clover Cres. OL8—6H 65
Clover Croft. M33—2D 126
Cloverdale Sq. BL1—4E 23
Cloverfield Wlk. M28—6F 55
 (off Bolton Rd.)
Clover Hall Cres. OL16—2C 20
Cloverley. M33—1B 126
Cloverley Dri. WA15—1A 138
Clover Rd. SK6—6C 122
Clover Rd. WA15—6A 126
Clover St. OL12—3G 19
Clover View. OL16—3C 20
Clowes St. M3—3C 86 & 4F 161
Clowes St. M7—6H 73
Clowes St. M12—1B 102
 (in two parts)
Clowes St. OL9—1H 77
Club St. M11—6H 89
Clumber Clo. SK12—4E 155
Clumber Rd. M18—3H 103
Clumber Rd. SK12—4E 155
Clunton Av. BL3—2F 37
Clutha Rd. SK3—1H 143
Clwyd Av. SK3—4F 131
Clyde Av. M25—5B 58
Clyde Ct. OL16—5D 20
Clyde Rd. M20—5D 116
Clyde Rd. M26—2F 41
Clyde Rd. SK3—4E 131
Clydesdale Rise. OL3—2D 52
Clydesdale St. OL8—6H 65
Clyde St. BL1—3A 24
Clyde St. OL1—6G 49
Clyde St. OL7—4F 91
Clyde Ter. M26—2F 41
Clyne Ho. M32—3F 99
Clyne St. M32—2F 99
Clysbarton St. SK7—4F 143
Coach Ho., The. SK9—4H 159
Coach Rd. M22—6A 140
Coach Rd. SK14—2C 108
Coach St. BL2—2C 38
Coalbrook Wlk. M12—4A 88
 (off Aden Clo.)
Coalburn St. M12—1C 102
Coal Pit La. OL4—4F 51
Coalshaw Grn. Rd. OL9—6G 63
Coatbridge St. M11—3E 89
Cobalt Av. M31—1H 97
Cobb Clo. M8—6A 60
Cobbett's Way. SK9—5C 158
Cobble Bank. M9—6E 61
Cobblers Yd. SK9—5G 159
Cobden St. BL1—2H 23
Cobden St. BL7—1B 10
Cobden St. BL9—2E 29
Cobden St. M6—1G 85
Cobden St. M9—3G 75
Cobden St. M26—1F 41
Cobden St. OL4—1H 65
Cobden St. OL6—3B 92
Cobden St. OL9—2H 63
Cobden St. OL10—4F 31
Coberley Av. M31—3B 96

Cob Hall Rd. M32—6C 98
Cobham Av. BL3—4H 37
Cobham Av. M10—6C 62
Coblers Hill. OL3—2H 51
Cobourg St. M1—5F 87 & 1C 166
Coburg Av. M7—1B 86
Cochrane Av. M12—2A 102
Cochrane St. BL3—2B 38
Cochrane St. OL1—1E 65
Cock Brow. SK14—2G 123
Cock Clod St. M26—4A 42
Cockcroft St. M9—2F 75
Cocker Hill. SK15—3E 93
Cocker Mill La. OL2—2D 48
Cockers La. SK15—5H 93
Cocker St. M28—5C 54
Cockey Moor Rd. BL2 & BL8—4D 26
Cockhall La. OL12—4G 7
Cock Hollow. BL9—1E 29
Cocklinstones. BL8—2H 27
Cockroft Rd. M5—3H 85
Codale Dri. BL2—4H 25
Coddington Av. M11—5G 89
Cody Ct. M5—5E 85
Coe St. BL3—2B 38
Coghlan Clo. M11—3D 88
Cohen St. M10—6G 75
Coke St. M8—3B 74
Colbeck Clo. M15—1C 100 & 5E 165
Colborne Av. M30—3D 82
Colborne Av. SK5—4H 103
Colborne Av. SK6—1H 133
Colbourne Av. M8—1B 74
Colbourne Gro. SK14—4A 108
Colbourne Way. SK14—4A 108
Colby Wlk. M10—4A 76
Colchester Av. BL2—5G 25
Colchester Av. M25—1G 73
Colchester Clo. M23—2E 127
Colchester Dri. BL4—6B 38
Colchester Pl. SK4—6D 118
Colchester St. M10—1H 87
Colchester Wlk. OL1—2D 64
Colclough Clo. M10—5B 76
Coldfield Dri. M23—5F 127
Cold Greave Clo. OL16—1G 35
Coldhurst Hollow Est. OL1—6C 48
Coldhurst St. OL1—1C 64
Coldstream Av. M9—5F 61
Coldstream Ho. M16—2A 100
Coldwall St. OL12—3F 19
Colebrook Dri. M10—5A 76
Colebrook Rd. WA15—5A 126
Coleby Av. M16—3A 100
Coleby Av. M22—4D 140
Coledale Dri. M24—5E 45
Coleford Clo. BL1—1A 38
Coleford Wlk. M16—4C 100
 (off Maclure Clo.)
Colegate Cres. M14—1F 117
Colenso Gro. SK4—6D 118
Colenso Rd. BL2—6F 25
Colenso St. OL8—6B 64
Coleport Clo. SK8—4C 142
Coleridge Av. M24—4C 46
Coleridge Av. M26—4E 41
Coleridge Clo. SK5—6G 103
Coleridge Dri. OL15—1F 21
Coleridge Rd. BL8—1H 13
Coleridge Rd. M16—4A 100
Coleridge Rd. OL1—3H 49
Coleridge Rd. SK5—6G 103
Coleridge St. M10—1E 89
Coleridge Way. SK5—6G 103
Colesbourne Clo. M28—3C 54
Coleshill St. M10—3H 75
Colesmere Wlk. M10—2D 76
Cole St. M9—3H 75
Colgate La. M5—1G 99
Colgrove Av. M10—1C 76
Colindale Av. M9—5G 61
Colindale Clo. BL3—2G 37
Colin Rd. SK4—5F 119
Colinton Clo. BL3—2H 37
Colinwood Clo. BL9—4D 42
Coll Dri. M31—2F 97
College Av. M35—5H 89
College Av. OL8—6B 64

College Clo. BL3—1A 38
College Clo. SK25—5A 132
College Clo. SK9—1C 158
College Croft. M30—3H 83
College Dri. M16—5A 100
College Land. M3—4D 86 & 5G 161
College Rd. M16—4A 100
College Rd. M30—3A 84
College Rd. OL8—5B 64
College Rd. OL12—4F 19
College Way. BL3—1H 37
Collen Cres. BL8—5B 14
Collett St. OL1—1G 65
Colley St. M32—2F 99
Colley St. OL16—2A 20
Collie Av. M6—6G 73
Collier Av. OL16—4F 21
Collier Clo. SK14—6A 108
Collier Hill. OL8—6B 64
Collier Hill Av. OL8—6A 64
Collier's Ct. OL11—4H 33
Collier St. M3—5C 86 & 2E 165
(Manchester)
Collier St. M3—2C 86 & 2F 161
(Salford)
Collier St. M6—5D 72
Collier St. M26—4H 41
Collier St. M27—4E 71
Collier Wlk. SK14—6A 108
Colliery St. M11—4C 88
(in two parts)
Collin Av. M18—3E 103
Collingburn Av. M5—6H 85
Collingburn Ct. M5—6H 85
Colling Clo. M30—6E 95
Collinge Av. M24—1C 62
Collinge St. BL8—1H 27
Collinge St. M24—2D 62
Collinge St. OL2—6F 35
Collinge St. OL10—3E 31
Collingham St. M8—1E 87
Collings St. BL1—3A 24
Colling St. BL0—4D 4
Collington Clo. M12—2C 102
Collingwood Av. M35—2G 89
Collingwood Clo. SK12—4G 155
Collingwood Dri. M27—4H 71
Collingwood Rd. M19—6B 102
Collingwood St. OL11—5C 32
Collingwood Way. OL1—1D 64
Collins St. BL8—1F 27
Collop Dri. OL10—6G 31
Coll's La. OL3—3F 51
Collyhurst Av. M28—1G 69
Collyhurst Rd. M10—1F 87
Collyhurst St. M10—1G 87
Colmar Way. SK14—5B 106
Colmore Av. M20—6H 117
Colmore Dri. M9—5A 62
Colmore Gro. BL2—1D 24
Colmore St. BL2—2D 24
Colnbrook Clo. M5—3H 85
Colne St. OL11—4D 32
Colonial Rd. SK2—5A 132
Colshaw Clo. E. M26—3F 41
Colshaw Clo. S. M26—3F 41
Colshaw Dri. SK9—6H 151
Colshaw Rd. M23—1G 139
Colshaw Wlk. SK9—6H 151
Colson Dri. M24—2H 61
Colt Hill La. OL3—1H 67
Coltness Wlk. M10—6C 76
Colts Acre. M5—6A 86
(off Bramble Av.)
Coltsfoot Dri. WA14—3D 124
Columbia Av. M18—3H 103
Columbia Rd. BL1—5G 23
Columbia St. OL8—5D 64
Columbine Clo. OL12—6C 6
Columbine St. M11—6F 89
Columbine Wlk. M31—6D 110
Colville Dri. BL8—4H 27
Colville Gro. M33—2G 125
Colville Gro. WA15—5A 126
Colville Rd. OL1—6B 48
Colwell Av. M32—5B 98
Colwell Wlk. M9—4D 60
Colwick Av. WA14—5G 125

Colwith Av. BL2—4G 25
Colwood Wlk. M8—5B 74
(off Elizabeth St.)
Colwyn Av. M14—1A 118
Colwyn Av. M24—3A 62
Colwyn Cres. SK5—4H 119
Colwyn Gro. BL1—4H 23
Colwyn Rd. M27—4C 70
Colwyn Rd. SK7—5G 143
Colwyn Rd. SK8—4A 142
Colwyn St. M6—2F 85
Colwyn St. OL7—5E 79
Colwyn St. OL9—2B 64
Colwyn St. OL11—3B 32
Colwyn Ter. OL7—5E 79
Colyton Wlk. M22—2D 140
Combe Clo. M11—2D 88
Combermere Av. M20—2E 117
Combermere Clo. SK8—1B 142
Combermere St. SK16—4A 92
Combs Bank. SK13—6F 109
(off Melandra Castle Rd.)
Combs Fold. SK13—5F 109
(off Brassington Cres.)
Combs Gdns. SK13—6F 109
(off Brassington Cres.)
Combs Gro. SK13—5F 109
(off Brassington Cres.)
Combs Lea. SK13—6F 109
(off Brassington Cres.)
Combs M. SK13—5F 109
(off Brassington Cres.)
Combs Ter. SK13—6F 109
(off Melandra Castle Rd.)
Combs Way. SK13—5F 109
Comer Ter. M33—5A 114
Comet St. M1—4F 87 & 6D 162
Commercial Av. SK8—2A 152
Commercial Brow. SK14—3C 106
Commercial Rd. OL1—3D 64
Commercial Rd. SK7—2D 144
Commercial St. M15—6C 86 & 3F 165
Commercial St. OL9—3A 64
Commercial St. SK14—4C 106
Common La. N. M31—4F 111
Common Side Rd. M28—4B 68
Como Wlk. M18—1D 102
Compass St. M11—6E 89
Compstall Av. M14—5F 101
Compstall Gro. M18—1G 103
Compstall Rd. SK6—1A 134
(in two parts)
Compton Clo. M31—6G 95
Compton Dri. M23—3G 139
Compton St. SK15—4F 93
Compton Way. M24—2C 62
Comrie Wlk. M23—6G 127
Comus St. M5—5A 86 & 1A 164
Concastrian Ind. Est. M9—4E 75
Concert La. M2—4E 87 & 6A 162
Concord Bus. Pk. M22—4C 140
Concord Pl. M6—6E 73
Concord Way. SK16—5A 92
(in two parts)
Condor Clo. M35—2C 90
Condor Pl. M6—6E 73
Conduit St. OL1—4H 49
Conduit St. OL6—3A 92
Conduit St. SK14—1H 109
Conewood Wlk. M13—1G 101 & 5F 167
Coney Gro. M23—4G 127
Coneymead. SK15—1E 93
Congham Rd. SK3—3E 131
Congleton Av. M14—5E 101
Congleton Clo. SK9—6G 159
Congleton Rd. SK9—5G 159
Congou St. M1—4G 87 & 1E 167
Congreave St. OL1—1C 64
Conifer Wlk. M31—6C 110
Coningsby Dri. M9—3F 75
Conisborough. OL11—5G 19
Conisborough Pl. M25—2F 59
Coniston Av. BL4—1A 54
Coniston Av. M9—3F 75
Coniston Av. M25—1D 58
Coniston Av. M28—4C 54
Coniston Av. M33—1C 126
Coniston Av. OL8—6B 64
Coniston Av. SK14—3A 106

Coniston Clo. BL0—1E 5
Coniston Clo. BL3—3A 40
Coniston Clo. M34—5B 104
Coniston Clo. OL9—2G 63
Coniston Dri. BL9—6C 28
Coniston Dri. M24—5G 45
Coniston Dri. SK9—3G 151
Coniston Dri. SK15—1E 93
Coniston Gro. M28—5C 54
Coniston Gro. OL2—1B 48
Coniston Gro. OL7—1G 91
Coniston Gro. OL10—5F 31
Coniston Rd. M27—5F 71
Coniston Rd. M31—5C 110
(Partington)
Coniston Rd. M31—1A 112
(Urmston)
Coniston Rd. M32—4C 98
Coniston Rd. SK5—3H 119
Coniston Rd. SK6—5B 146
Coniston Rd. SK8—5F 129
Coniston St. BL1—2B 24
Coniston St. M6—1H 85
Coniston St. M10—6C 76
Coniston Wlk. WA15—6D 126
Conmere Sq. M15—6D 86 & 4H 165
Connaught Av. M19—2B 118
Connaught Av. M25—1E 59
Connaught Av. OL16—2H 33
Connaught Clo. SK9—1F 159
Connaught Pl. M6—3F 85
Connaught Sq. BL2—3D 24
Connaught St. BL8—4H 27
Connaught St. OL8—3C 64
Connel Clo. BL2—1H 39
Connell Rd. M23—5G 127
Connell Way. OL10—2H 31
Connery Cres. OL6—5H 79
Connie St. M11—5E 89
Connington Av. M9—2F 75
Connington Clo. OL2—3A 48
Connor Way. SK8—1D 140
Conquest Clo. M12—1B 102
Conrad Clo. OL1—3A 50
Conrad St. BL1—5A 24
Conran St. M9—4F 75
Consett Av. M23—5G 127
Consiber Clo. BL2—2C 10
Consort Av. OL2—1A 48
Constable Clo. BL1—4H 23
Constable Dri. SK6—3F 135
Constable Dri. SK9—1H 159
Constable St. M18—1G 103
Constable Wlk. M34—2G 121
Constable Wlk. OL1—3H 49
Constance Gdns. M5—4F 85
Constance Rd. BL3—3G 37
Constance Rd. M31—6D 110
Constance St. M15—6C 86 & 3F 165
Constantine Rd. OL16—4H 19
Constantine St. OL4—3H 65
Consul St. M22—2C 128
Convamore Rd. SK7—6F 143
Convent St. OL4—5G 65
Conway Av. BL1—4E 23
Conway Av. M25—2D 58
Conway Av. M27—6H 57
Conway Av. M30—1D 110
Conway Clo. BL0—3D 4
Conway Clo. M16—4G 99
Conway Clo. M24—2A 62
Conway Clo. M25—2D 58
Conway Clo. OL10—2C 30
Conway Cres. BL8—1H 13
Conway Dri. BL9—3H 29
Conway Dri. SK7—4C 144
Conway Dri. SK15—2E 93
Conway Dri. WA15—5C 126
Conway Gro. OL9—6F 47
Conway Rd. M31—3F 97
Conway Rd. M33—6D 114
Conway Rd. SK8—3A 142
Conway St. BL4—2F 55
Conway St. SK5—5G 119
Conway Towers. SK5—2C 120
Conyngham Rd. M14—3H 101
Cooke St. BL4—2G 55
Cooke St. M34—4E 105

Cooke St. M35—3F 77
Cooke St. SK7—2D 144
Cooke St. SK14—2D 106
Cooks Croft. OL4—2C 66
Cook St. BL9—3D 28
Cook St. M3—3C 86 & 4E 161
Cook St. M30—3E 83
Cook St. M34—1F 105
Cook St. OL4—2G 65
Cook St. OL16—2B 20
Cook St. SK3—2G 131
Cook Ter. OL16—2B 20
Cook Ter. SK16—4H 91
(off Astley St.)
Coomassie St. M26—4G 41
Coomassie St. OL10—3E 31
Coombes Av. SK6—6D 134
Coombes Av. SK14—6D 106
Coombes St. SK2—6B 132
Co-operation St. M35—2F 77
Co-operative St. M6—3F 85
Co-operative St. M26—3G 41
Co-operative St. M28—4A 54
Co-operative St. OL2—6F 35
Co-operative St. OL3—1F 53
Co-operative St. OL4—3B 66
Co-operative St. SK7—2E 145
Cooper Fold. M24—3A 46
Cooper Ho. M15—1E 101 & 6A 166
Cooper La. M9—4F 61
Cooper La. M24—4H 45
Cooper Rd. M30—2C 110
Coopers Fold. SK8—1B 152
Coopers Row. BL1—6B 24
Cooper St. BL1—4B 24
Cooper St. BL9—3C 28
Cooper St. M2—4E 87 & 6H 161
Cooper St. M32—6D 98
Cooper St. OL4—2C 66
Cooper St. OL12—5B 8
Cooper St. SK1—4H 131
Cooper St. SK7—2F 145
Cooper St. SK16—4H 91
Cooper Ter. OL16—3B 20
Coop St. BL1—1A 24
Coop St. M4—3F 87 & 3C 162
Coop Ter. OL16—4D 20
Copage Dri. SK6—5G 121
Cope Bank. BL1—4G 23
Cope Bank E. BL1—4G 23
Cope Bank W. BL1—3F 23
Cope Clo. M11—6G 89
Copeland Av. M27—2A 72
Copeland Clo. M24—6E 45
Copeland M. BL1—6E 23
Copeland St. SK14—2B 106
Copeman Clo. M13—1G 101 & 6E 167
Copenhagen Sq. OL16—3A 20
Copenhagen St. OL16—3A 20
Cope St. BL1—4G 23
Copgrove Rd. M21—2H 115
Copgrove Wlk. M22—6C 140
Copley Av. SK15—3G 93
Copley Pk. M. SK15—3G 93
Copley Rd. M21—5G 99
Copley St. OL2—5G 35
Copley St. SK15—3G 93
Copperas La. M35—5G 89
Copperas St. M4—3E 87 & 4B 162
Copperbeech Dri. M22—2C 128
Copperfield Ct. WA14—2E 137
Copperfield Rd. SK8—2D 152
Copperfield Rd. SK10—5D 154
Copperfields. BL6—3A 36
Copperfields. SK9—1F 159
Copper La. M25—3G 57
Copperways. M20—4F 117
Coppice Clo. SK6—4H 121
Coppice Clo. SK12—1E 157
Coppice Dri. M22—2B 128
Coppice Dri. OL12—2C 6
Coppice Dri. SK12—1E 157
Coppice La. SK12—1E 157
Coppice Rd. SK12—4G 155
Coppice St. BL9—2B 29
Coppice St. OL8—4B 64
(in two parts)

Coppice, The. BL0—5C 4
Coppice, The. BL2—6H 11
Coppice, The. M24—3B 62
Coppice, The. M27—6C 70
Coppice, The. M28—3H 69
Coppice, The. WA15—5B 138
Coppice Wlk. M34—5D 104
Copping St. M12—1B 102
Coppins, The. SK9—5B 158
Coppleridge Dri. M8—2C 74
Copplestone Dri. M33—4E 113
Cop Rd. OL1—3G 49
Copse Av. M22—2C 140
Copse Dri. BL9—5F 15
Copse, The. BL7—1G 11
Copse, The. SK6—3G 147
Copse, The. WA15—6D 138
Copse Wlk. OL15—4D 8
Copson St. M20—2F 117
Copster Av. OL8—6C 64
Copster Hill Rd. OL8—6C 64
Copster Pl. OL8—6C 64
Copthall La. M8—3B 74
Copthorne Cres. M13—5A 102
Copthorne Dri. BL2—1G 39
Copthorne Wlk. BL8—6H 13
Coptrod Head Clo. OL12—5E 7
Coral Av. M45—4C 142
Coral Rd. SK8—4C 142
Coral St. M13—6G 87 & 4E 167
Coram St. M18—1H 103
Corbar Rd. SK2—6A 132
Corbett St. M11—3C 88
(in two parts)
Corbett St. OL16—3A 20
Corbridge Wlk. M8—5D 74
Corbrook Rd. OL9—6E 47
Corby St. M12—1C 102
Corcoran Clo. OL10—2E 31
Corcoran Dri. SK6—1D 134
Corda Av. M22—3B 128
Corday La. M25—1H 59
Cordingley Av. M35—5H 89
Cordova Av. M34—4H 103
Corelli St. M10—1B 88
Corfe Clo. M31—6G 95
Corfe Cres. SK7—4C 144
Corinthian Av. M7—6G 73
Corinth Wlk. M28—1F 69
Corkland Clo. OL6—3B 92
Corkland Rd. M21—1H 115
Corkland St. OL6—3C 92
Corks La. SK12—2H 157
Cork St. BL9—3E 29
Cork St. M12—5H 87 & 1H 167
Cork St. OL6—2A 92
Corley Av. SK3—4B 130
Corley Wlk. M11—4B 88
Cormallon Gro. M35—4G 77
Cormoran Clo. M28—6E 55
Cormorant Wlk. M12—1C 102
Cornall St. BL8—2A 28
Cornbrook Arches. M15—6A 86 &
4B 164
Cornbrook Clo. OL12—3A 8
Cornbrook Ct. M15—1B 100 & 6C 164
Cornbrook Gro. M16—2B 100
Cornbrook Pk. Rd. M15—1A 100 &
5B 164
Cornbrook Rd. M15—1A 100 & 5A 164
Cornbrook St. M16 & M15—2B 100
Cornbrook Way. M16—2B 100
Corn Clo. M13—2G 101
Cornell St. M4—3F 87 & 3D 162
Corner Croft. SK9—5D 158
Corner St. OL6—3A 92
Cornet St. M7—5H 73
Corn Exchange. M4—3D 86
& 3H 161
Cornfield. SK15—1A 108
Cornfield Clo. BL9—4F 15
Cornfield Dri. M33—6F 115
Cornfield Dri. M22—2A 140
Cornfield Rd. SK6—6C 122
Cornfield St. OL16—6F 21
Cornford Av. M18—4D 102
Cornhey Rd. M33—1E 125
Cornhill Av. M31—4D 96

Corn Hill La. M34—2A 104
Cornhill Rd. M31—3D 96
Cornhill St. OL1—5H 49
Cornishway. M22—4A 140
Cornishway Ind. Est. M22—5B 140
Corn Mill Clo. OL12—5A 8
Corn St. M35—5C 76
Corn St. OL4—2E 65
Cornwall Av. M19—1D 118
Cornwall Clo. BL9—5E 29
Cornwall Clo. SK6—6C 146
Cornwall Cres. OL3—3B 52
Cornwall Cres. SK5—3C 120
Cornwall Dri. BL9—5D 28
Cornwall Rd. M30—4B 110
Cornwall Rd. M35—2A 90
Cornwall St. SK8—5F 141
Cornwall St. M11—6F 89
Cornwall St. M30—4E 83
Cornwall St. OL9—4H 63
Cornwell Clo. SK9—1G 159
Cornwood Clo. M8—4B 74
Corona Av. OL8—6B 64
Corona Av. SK14—4C 106
Coronation Av. OL10—5G 31
Coronation Av. SK14—6C 106
Coronation Av. SK16—1D 106
Coronation Bldgs. M4—1F 87
Coronation Gdns. M26—2E 41
Coronation Rd. M26—2E 41
Coronation Rd. M35—2H 89
(Droylsden)
Coronation Rd. M35—5E 77
(Failsworth)
Coronation Rd. OL6—5G 79
Coronation Sq. BL3—4B 40
Coronation Sq. M12—5G 87 & 2F 167
Coronation Sq. M34—6D 90
Coronation St. BL1—1B 38
(off Gt. Moor St.)
Coronation St. M5—5H 85 & 1A 164
Coronation St. M11—5E 89
Coronation St. M27—2G 71
Coronation St. M34—4C 104
Coronation St. SK5—5G 119
Coronation Vs. OL12—3H 7
Coronation Wlk. M26—2E 41
Corporation Cotts. M31—3G 111
Corporation Rd. M30—3G 83
Corporation Rd. M34—2D 104
Corporation Rd. OL11—5F 19
Corporation St. BL1—6B 24
& 4H 161
Corporation St. M24—1A 62
Corporation St. SK1—1H 131
Corporation St. M14—5B 106
Corporation St. SK15—4E 93
Corporation Yd. SK4—6C 118
Corporation Yd. SK5—1H 119
Corran Clo. M30—3D 82
Corrie Clo. M34—6F 105
Corrie Cres. BL4—4D 56
Corrie Clo. BL4—5D 56
Corrie Rd. M27—6G 57
Corrie St. M28—5C 54
Corrie Way. SK6—3E 121
Corrigan St. M18—1G 103
Corringham Rd. M19—2E 119
Corring Way. BL1—1D 24
Corrin Rd. BL2—2D 38
Corris Av. M9—4C 60
Corry St. OL10—3G 31
Corson St. BL3—5F 39
(in two parts)
Corston Wlk. M10—5B 76
Corwen Clo. OL8—1H 77
Corwen St. M9—3G 75
Cosgrove Cres. M35—6E 77
Cosgrove Rd. M35—6E 77
Cosham Rd. M22—2D 140
Costabeck Wlk. M10—1F 89
Costobadie Clo. SK14—4B 108
Cotaline Clo. OL11—2B 32
Cotall Wlk. M7—1C 86
Cotefield Av. BL3—4B 38
Cotefield Clo. SK6—6D 134
Cotefield Rd. M22—3H 139

Cote Grn. Rd. SK6—2F 135
Cote Grn La. SK6—2F 135
Cote La. OL5—6G 67
Cote La. OL15—3D 8
Cotford Rd. BL1—6D 10
Cotham St. M3—1D 86
Cotman Dri. SK6—3G 135
Cotswold Av. M31—4B 96
Cotswold Av. OL2—5D 34
Cotswold Av. OL9—4G 63
Cotswold Av. SK7—4B 144
Cotswold Clo. BL0—5E 5
Cotswold Clo. M25—4G 59
Cotswold Cres. BL8—2G 27
Cotswold Cres. OL16—4G 21
Cotswold Dri. M6—2F 85
Cotswold Dri. OL2—4H 47
Cotswold Rd. SK4—6F 119
Cottage Gdns. SK6—6D 120
Cottage Grn. M8—3F 135
Cottage, The. OL10—3E 45
Cottage Wlk. OL12—5C 6
Cottam Cres. SK6—3F 135
Cottam Gro. M27—4G 71
Cottam St. BL8—2A 28
Cottam St. OL1—1B 64
Cottenham La. M7 & M3—1C 86 &
1F 161
Cottenham St. M13—1F 101 & 5D 166
Cotteridge Wlk. M11—5B 88
Cotterill Clo. M23—2C 126
Cotter St. M12—6G 87 & 3E 167
Cottesmore Dri. M8—3E 75
Cottesmore Gdns. WA15—5C 138
Cottingham Dri. OL6—1A 92
Cottonfield Rd. M20—3G 117
Cotton Hill. M20—4G 117
Cotton La. M20—3F 117
Cotton La. OL11—1C 32
Cotton St. BL1—3H 23
Cotton St. M4—3F 87 & 4D 162
Cotton St. SK14—4C 106
Cotton St. E. OL6—3G 91
Cotton St. W. OL6—3G 91
Cotton Tree Clo. OL4—1H 65
Cotton Tree St. SK4—2G 131
Cottonwood Dri. M33—4E 113
Cottrell Rd. WA15—6D 138
Cottrill St. M6—3H 85
Coucill Sq. BL4—1G 55
Coulsden Dri. M9—6F 61
Coulthart St. OL6—2H 91
Coulthurst St. BL0—3D 4
Coulton Clo. OL1—1E 65
Coulton Wlk. M6—3F 85
Councillor La. SK8—5B 130
Councillor St. M12—4A 88
Countess Av. SK8—2A 142
Countess Gro. M7—6G 73
Countess La. M26—2D 40
Countess Pl. M25—5F 59
Countess Rd. M20—6F 117
Countess St. OL6—3B 92
Countess St. SK2—6H 131
Counthill Dri. M8—1A 74
Counthill Rd. OL4—6H 49
Counting Ho. Rd. SK12—2H 157
Count St. OL16—6A 20
County Av. OL6—1C 92
County Rd. M28—5C 54
County St. M2—4D 86
County St. OL8—1A 78
Coupland Dri. OL4—3B 50
Coupland St. M15—2E 101
Coupland St. OL12—1C 6
Coupland St. E. M15—1E 101 & 6B 166
Courier St. M18—6G 89
Course View. OL4—6A 66
Court Dri. M10—1G 89
Courtfield Av. M9—5F 61
Courthill St. SK1—3A 132
Court Ho. Way. OL10—3F 31
(off Longford St.)
Court St. BL2—6C 24
Court St. OL3—1F 53
Court, The. M25—5F 59
Cousin Fields. BL7—4G 11
Covall Wlk. M8—5D 74
Covell Rd. SK12—2E 155

Covent Garden. SK1—2H 131
Coventry Av. SK3—4B 130
Coventry Gro. OL9—6G 47
Coventry Rd. M26—2F 41
Coventry St. OL11—5H 19
Coverdale Av. BL1—5E 23
Coverdale Av. OL2—2A 48
Coverdale Clo. OL10—4E 31
Coverdale Cres. M12—1H 101 & 5H 167
Coverham Av. OL4—5H 65
Coverhill Rd. OL4—6D 66
Covert Rd. M22—6C 128
Covert Rd. OL4—6H 65
Cove, The. WA15—2H 137
Cowan St. M10—3H 87 & 4H 163
Cowburn St. M3—2D 86 & 1H 161
Cowburn St. OL10—4G 31
Cowdals Rd. BL6—3A 36
Cowesby St. M14—4E 101
Cowhill La. OL6—2A 92
Cowie St. OL2—5F 35
Cow La. M5—4A 86 & 6B 160
Cow La. M33—3E 115
Cow La. M35—4E 77
Cow La. OL4—2G 65
Cow La. SK7—1D 144
Cow La. SK9—2F 159
Cow La. WA14—6A 124
Cow La. WA15—6H 137
Cowley Gro. SK14—4B 108
Cowley Rd. BL1—6D 10
Cowling St. M27—3D 72
Cowling St. OL8—5D 64
Cowlishaw. OL2—2E 49
Cowlishaw La. OL2—2E 49
Cowlishaw Rd. SK14 & SK6—4D 122
Cowm Pk. Way N. OL12—3G 7
Cowm Pk. Way S. OL12—1C 6
Cowm Top La. OL11—4D 32
(in two parts)
Cowper St. M24—1D 62
Cowper St. OL6—2A 92
Cowper Wlk. M11—4E 88
Cox Grn. Rd. BL7—1C 10
Coxton Rd. M22—4C 140
Coxwold Gro. BL3—4G 37
Crabbe St. M4—1E 87 & 1B 162
Crab La. M9—5D 60
Crabtree Av. SK12—2H 157
Crabtree Av. WA15—6D 138
Crabtree La. M11—5F 89
(in two parts)
Crabtree Rd. OL1—1F 65
Crabtree St. BL9—2F 29
Craddock Rd. M33—1C 126
Craddock St. OL5—2D 80
Cradley Av. M11—5F 89
Crag Av. BL9—1D 14
Cragg Pl. OL15—4F 9
Cragg Rd. OL1—5F 47
(in two parts)
Crag La. BL9—1D 14
Craig Av. BL8—4H 27
Craig Av. M31—4C 96
Craig Clo. SK4—2D 130
Craigend Dri. M9—4G 75
Craig Hall. M30—2D 110
Craighall Av. M19—1B 118
Craighall Rd. BL1—5C 10
Craigie St. M8—6B 74
Craiglands. OL16—3H 33
Craiglands Av. M10—5A 76
Craigmore Av. M20—5B 116
Craigner Ct. M27—4A 72
Craig Rd. M18—3E 103
Craig Rd. SK4—2B 130
Craig Wlk. OL8—4C 64
Craigwell Av. M20—6G 117
Craigwell Rd. M25—1A 74
Craigwell Wlk. M13—6F 87 & 4C 166
Crail Pl. OL10—4B 30
Cramer St. M10—6H 75
Crammond Clo. M10—5D 76
Cramond Clo. BL1—4H 23
Cramond Wlk. BL1—4H 23
Crampton Dri. WA15—5C 138
Crampton La. M31—2G 111
(in three parts)

Cranage Rd. M19—1D 118
Cranage Way. SK9—2H 151
Cranark Clo. BL1—6E 23
Cranberry Clo. WA14—3D 124
Cranberry Rd. M31—6D 110
Cranberry St. OL4—3F 65
Cranbourne Av. SK8—3D 142
Cranbourne Clo. OL7—1G 91
Cranbourne Ct. SK4—5D 118
Cranbourne Rd. M16—3A 100
Cranbourne Rd. M21—1H 115
Cranbourne Rd. OL7—1G 91
Cranbourne Rd. OL11—5A 18
Cranbourne Rd. SK4—5D 118
Cranbourne St. M5—4A 86 & 6A 160
Cranbourne Ter. OL6—6F 79
Cranbrook Clo. BL1—4B 24
(off Lindfield Dri.)
Cranbrook Dri. M25—1G 73
Cranbrook Pl. OL4—3G 65
Cranbrook Rd. M18—4G 103
Cranbrook Rd. M30—1C 82
Cranbrook St. M26—2A 42
Cranbrook St. OL4—3F 65
Cranbrook St. OL7—1H 91
Cranbrook Wlk. OL9—3G 63
Crandon Ct. M27—1G 71
Crandon Dri. M20—3G 129
Crane St. BL3—4F 37
Crane St. M12—5G 87 & 2F 167
Cranfield Wlk. M10—3A 88
Cranford Av. M20—5H 117
Cranford Av. M25—5C 42
Cranford Av. M32—4F 99
Cranford Av. M33—3C 114
Cranford Clo. M25—5C 42
Cranford Clo. M27—5H 71
Cranford Dri. M30—4D 94
Cranford Gdns. M31—4A 96
Cranford Gdns. SK6—4D 134
Cranford Rd. M31—4A 96
Cranford Rd. SK9—6E 151
Cranford St. BL3—5G 37
Cranham Clo. BL8—2H 27
Cranham Clo. M28—3C 54
Cranham Rd. M23—3G 139
Cranleigh Av. SK4—5B 118
Cranleigh Dri. M28—3G 69
Cranleigh Dri. M33—2C 126
(Brooklands)
Cranleigh Dri. M33—4A 114
(Sale)
Cranleigh Dri. SK7—5G 145
Cranleigh Dri. SK8—5B 130
Cranlington Dri. M8—5B 74
Cranmer Ct. OL10—4E 31
Cranmere Av. M19—5E 103
Cranmere Dri. M33—1F 125
Cranmer Rd. M20—5F 117
Cranston Dri. M20—3F 129
Cranston Dri. M33—6E 115
Cranston Gro. SK8—6D 128
Cranswick St. M14—4E 101
Crantock Dri. SK8—5G 141
Crantock St. SK5—2H 93
Crantock St. M12—4D 102
Cranwell Dri. M19—5A 118
Cranworth St. SK15—4F 93
Craston Rd. M13—5A 102
Crathie Ct. BL1—4F 23
Craven Av. M5—5H 85
Craven Clo. M5—5H 85
Craven Dri. M5—1G 99
Craven Dri. WA14—3E 125
Craven Gdns. OL11—6G 19
Cravenhurst Av. M10—1D 88
Craven Pl. BL1—3C 22
Craven Pl. M11—3E 89
Craven Rd. SK5—3H 119
Craven Rd. WA14—4E 125
(in two parts)
Craven St. BL9—2F 29
Craven St. M5—4A 86 & 6B 160
Craven St. M6—5D 72
Craven St. M35—4A 90
Craven St. OL1—6C 48
Craven St. OL6—5H 79
Craven Ter. M33—5C 114

Cravenwood Rd. M8—3C 74
Crawford Av. BL2—1D 38
Crawford Av. M28—3H 69
Crawford Sq. OL16—4C 30
Crawford St. BL2—1D 38
Crawford St. M10—6C 76
Crawford St. M30—2F 83
Crawford St. OL6—3B 92
Crawford St. OL16—6A 20
Crawley Av. M22—2B 140
Crawley Av. M30—2A 84
Crawley Gro. SK2—4B 132
Crawley Way. OL9—3G 63
Craybridge Rd. M12—1H 101 & 5H 167
Craydon St. M11—5D 88
Crayfield Rd. M19—1D 118
Crayford Rd. M10—1D 88
Cray, The. OL16—5E 21
Cray Wlk. M13—6F 87 & 4C 166
Creation Way. M24—3E 45
Creden Av. M22—2D 140
Crediton Clo. M15—2D 100
Crediton Clo. WA14—5D 124
Crediton Dri. BL2—6A 26
Creel Clo. M9—5D 60
Cresbury St. M12—5H 87 & 2G 167
Crescent. M5—3H 85 & 4A 160
Crescent Av. BL1—5H 23
Crescent Av. BL4—3E 55
Crescent Av. M8—3C 74
Crescent Av. M25—1F 73
Crescent Av. M27—3A 72
Crescent Clo. SK3—6H 131
Crescent Clo. SK16—4A 92
Crescent Ct. M21—6F 99
Crescent Ct. M33—6B 114
Crescent Dri. M28—4D 54
Crescent Gro. M19—6C 102
Crescent Gro. M25—1F 73
Crescent Gro. SK8—5G 129
Crescent Pk. SK4—1D 130
Crescent Range. M14—4G 101
Crescent Rd. BL3—3C 38
Crescent Rd. BL4—3H 55
Crescent Rd. M8—3B 74
Crescent Rd. OL9—1E 77
Crescent Rd. OL11—1B 32
Crescent Rd. SK1—6B 120
Crescent Rd. SK8—5G 129
Crescent Rd. SK9—4H 159
Crescent Rd. SK16—4A 92
Crescent Rd. WA14—5C 124
Crescent Rd. WA15—3G 137
Crescent St. M8—3E 75
Crescent, The. BL2—1H 25
Crescent, The. BL3—5B 40
Crescent, The. BL7—4E 11
Crescent, The. M19—6C 102
Crescent, The. M24—1G 61
Crescent, The. M25—5F 59
Crescent, The. M26—2D 40
Crescent, The. M30—3F 95
Crescent, The. M31—5B 96
Crescent, The. M35—4H 89
Crescent, The. OL5—2D 80
Crescent, The. OL12—1C 6
Crescent, The. SK3—1A 144
Crescent, The. SK6—5D 120
Crescent, The. SK8—5G 129
Crescent, The. SK16—5A 92
Crescent, The. WA14—6C 124
Crescent, The. WA15—4H 125
Crescent View. SK16—4A 92
(off Astley St.)
Crescent Way. SK3—6A 132
Cresgarth Ho. SK3—1A 144
Cressfield Way. M21—2B 116
Cressingham Rd. BL3—3E 37
Cressingham Rd. M32—5B 98
Cressington Clo. M5—3E 85
Cresswell Gro. M20—4E 117
Crestfield. M28—5C 54
Crestfold. M28—5C 54
Crest St. M3—2E 87
Crest, The. M35—6A 90
Crest, The. OL2—1E 49
Crestwood Wlk. M10—5E 75
Crete St. OL8—5D 64

Crewe Rd. M23—3E 127
Crib Fold. OL3—5A 52
Crib La. OL3—5A 52
Criccieth Rd. SK3—4C 130
Criccieth Way. M16—3D 100
Crickets La. OL6—2A 92
Cricket St. BL3—2H 37
Cricket St. M34—3G 105
Cricket View. OL16—6F 21
Cricklewood Rd. M22—3A 140
Crimble La. OL11 & OL10—6A 18
Crimbles Dri. OL4—1A 66
(in two parts)
Crimble St. OL12—4F 19
Crime La. M35 & OL8—4B 78
Crimsworth Av. M16—5H 99
Crinan Sq. OL10—4B 30
Crinan Way. BL2—1H 39
Cringle Dri. BL3—3C 36
Cringle Dri. SK8—2G 141
Cringleford Wlk. M12—2A 102
Cringle Hall Rd. M19—1B 118
Cringle Rd. M19—2D 118
Cringle St. M10—5A 76
Cripple Ga. La. OL11—4E 33
Crispin Rd. M22—5C 140
Critchley Clo. SK14—6D 106
Criterion St. SK5—5H 103
Croal St. BL1—1H 37
Croal Wlk. M25—6F 43
Croasdale St. BL1—4B 24
(in two parts)
Crocker Wlk. M9—4G 75
Crocus St. BL1—1B 24
Crocus Wlk. M7—5H 73
(off Hilton St. N.)
Croftacres. BL0—3A 4
Croft Av. M25—1B 60
Croft Bank. M7—6G 73
Croft Bank. M18—2G 103
Croft Bank. OL12—3H 7
Croft Bank. SK15—1H 93
Croft Brow. OL8—1C 78
Croft Clo. WA15—1C 148
Croft Dri. BL8—5G 13
Crofters Brook. M26—3A 42
Crofters Grn. SK9—3C 158
Crofters Hall Wlk. M10—4B 76
Crofters, The. M33—6F 115
Croft Ga. BL2—1G 25
Croft Gates Rd. M24—2F 61
Croft Gro. M28—4B 54
Crofthead. OL15—2F 9
Croft Head Dri. OL16—4F 21
Crofthill Ct. OL12—5B 8
Croft Hill Rd. M10—2A 76
Croftlands. BL0—6C 4
Croftlands Rd. M22—1C 140
Croft La. BL3—2D 38
Croft La. BL9—2E 43
Croft La. M26—3A 42
Crofton Av. WA15—2A 126
Crofton St. M14—4F 101
Crofton St. M16—3B 100
Crofton St. OL8—6C 64
(in two parts)
Croft Rd. M33—1D 126
Croft Rd. SK8—2D 142
Croft Rd. SK9—5B 158
Crofts Bank Rd. M31—3E 97
Croftside Av. M28—6G 55
Croftside Clo. M28—6G 55
Croftside Gro. M28—6G 55
Croft Sq. OL12—6A 8
Croft St. BL3—3D 38
Croft St. BL9—3E 29
Croft St. M7—6G 73
Croft St. M11—3D 88
Croft St. M28—4B 54
Croft St. M35—2G 77
Croft St. OL5—3E 81
Croft St. OL12—6A 8
Croft St. SK14—5A 106
Croft St. SK15—3F 93
Croft, The. BL9—1E 43
Croft, The. OL8—1C 78
Croft, The. SK2—5B 132

Croft, The. SK14—1H 109
Cromar Rd. SK7—2F 145
Cromarty Av. OL9—6F 63
Cromarty Sq. OL10—4C 30
Cromarty Wlk. M11—4B 88
Crombie Av. M22—4B 128
Cromdale Av. BL1—5F 23
Cromdale Av. SK7—2F 145
Cromer Av. BL2—4E 25
Cromer Av. M20—3F 117
Cromer Av. M34—4A 104
Cromer Ind. Est. M24—6B 46
Cromer Rd. BL8—6C 14
(in two parts)
Cromer Rd. M33—6C 114
Cromer Rd. SK8—5A 130
Cromer St. M11—4F 89
Cromer St. M24—6B 46
Cromer St. OL12—3G 19
Cromer St. SK1—1B 132
Cromford Av. M32—4B 98
Cromford Bank. SK13—5F 109
(off Grassmoor Cres.)
Cromford Clo. BL1—4A 24
Cromford Clo. SK13—5F 109
(off Grassmoor Cres.)
Cromford Ct. M4—3E 87
(off Arndale Cen.)
Cromford Courts. M4—3E 87 & 4A 162
Cromford Fold. SK13—5F 109
(off Grassmoor Cres.)
Cromford Gdns. BL1—3B 24
Cromford Grn. SK13—5F 109
(off Grassmoor Cres.)
Cromford Gro. SK13—5F 109
(off Grassmoor Cres.)
Cromford Lea. SK13—5F 109
Cromford Pl. SK13—5F 109
(off Grassmoor Cres.)
Cromford St. OL1—1E 65
Cromford Way. SK13—5F 109
Cromhall Wlk. M8—5C 74
Cromhurst St. M8—4B 74
Cromley Dri. SK6—1C 156
Cromley Rd. SK2—2A 144
Cromley Rd. SK6—6C 146
Crompton Av. BL2—5G 25
Crompton Av. OL16—2H 33
Crompton Clo. BL1—1C 24
Crompton Clo. M26—6H 41
Crompton Clo. SK6—4D 134
Crompton Ho. M27—3E 71
Crompton Rd. M19—1C 118
Crompton Rd. M26—1A 56
Cromptons St. OL2—4C 48
Crompton St. BL1—5C 24
Crompton St. BL4—2G 55
Crompton St. BL9—3C 28
Crompton St. M27—3E 71
Crompton St. M28—4A 54
(Greenheys)
Crompton St. M28—1H 69
(Walkden)
Crompton St. OL1—1C 64
Crompton St. OL2—4B 48
(Royton, in three parts)
Crompton St. OL2—6F 35
(Shaw)
Crompton St. OL6—1C 92
Crompton St. OL2—3A 64
Crompton Vale. BL2—5F 25
Crompton Way. BL1 & BL2—1B 24
Crompton Way. OL2—1F 49
Cromwell Av. M16—5A 100
Cromwell Av. SK6—4B 134
Cromwell Av. SK8—5E 129
Cromwell Ct. M6—1H 85
Cromwell Ct. M30—2C 110
Cromwell Gro. M7—6G 73
Cromwell Gro. M19—6C 102
Cromwell Range. M14—5H 101
Cromwell Rd. M6—1G 85
Cromwell Rd. M25—5G 59
(Prestwich)
Cromwell Rd. M25—5B 42
(Whitefield)
Cromwell Rd. M27—2E 71

Cromwell Rd. M30—3E 83
(Eccles)
Cromwell Rd. M30—2C 110
(Irlam)
Cromwell Rd. M32—6E 99
Cromwell Rd. OL2—1A 48
Cromwell Rd. SK6—3D 120
Cromwell Rd. SK7—1F 153
Cromwell St. BL1—6A 24
Cromwell St. OL1—3D 64
Cromwell St. OL10—4F 31
Cromwell St. SK4—6F 119
*Crondale Wlk. M13—1G 101
(off Watkin Clo.)
Crondall St. M14—4E 101
Cronefield Wlk. M16—4D 100
Cronkeyshaw Rd. OL12—2G 19
Cronshaw St. M19—1D 118
Crookhill Dri. M8—4B 74
Crookhilley Way. SK1—6A 120
Crook St. BL3—1B 38
Crook St. M26—4H 41
Crook St. OL16—3A 20
Crook St. SK14—5B 106
Croom Wlk. M10—2H 87 & 2G 163
Crosby Av. M28—1H 69
*Crosby Ho. BL1—5B 24
(off Haydock St.)
Crosby Rd. BL1—5F 23
Crosby Rd. M6—6B 72
Crosby Rd. M10—6C 76
Crosby Rd. M26—6E 27
Crosby St. OL12—1H 19
Crosby St. SK2—4H 131
Crosfield Gro. M18—2F 103
Crossacres Rd. M22—2B 140
Cross Av. M25—3E 59
Crossbank Av. OL4—2B 66
Crossbank Clo. M13—2H 101
Crossbank St. OL8—3C 64
(in two parts)
Crossbank Way. M24—6H 45
Crossby Clo. M24—4H 61
Cross Bri. Rd. SK14—5E 107
Crosscliffe Clo. M16—3D 100
Crossdale Rd. BL2—5G 25
Crossdale Rd. M9—5H 61
Crossefield Rd. SK8—2C 142
Crossen St. BL3—2E 39
Crossfell Av. M9—4D 60
Crossfield Av. BL9—1C 14
Crossfield Clo. OL12—2A 8
Crossfield Clo. SK15—4E 93
Cross Field Dri. M26—4E 41
Crossfield Dri. M27—2E 71
Crossfield Dri. M28—4H 69
Crossfield Gro. SK2—1B 144
Crossfield Gro. SK6—2F 135
Crossfield Pl. OL11—6A 20
Crossfield Rd. M30—3G 95
Crossfield Rd. OL12—3A 8
Crossfield Rd. SK9—3H 151
Crossfield Rd. WA15—3B 138
Crossfields. BL7—3G 11
Crossfield St. BL9—3D 42
Crossford Ct. M33—3C 114
Crossford Dri. BL3—2C 36
Crossford St. M32—6D 98
Crossgate Av. M22—5B 128
Crossgate M. SK4—6A 118
Crossgates Rd. OL16—4F 21
Cross Glebe St. OL6—2A 92
Cross Gro. WA15—3H 125
Crosshill. OL11—6H 19
Crosshill Clo. M16—3D 100
Cross Hill Wlk. BL3—2C 36
Cross Hope St. OL6—1B 92
Cross Keys St. M4—3F 87 & 3C 162
Cross Knowle View. M31—3B 96
Crossland Rd. M21—1G 115
Crossland Rd. M35—3B 90
Crosslands Rd. M28—5B 68
Cross La. BL8—4C 4
Cross La. M5—4G 85
Cross La. M18—2F 103
Cross La. M26—3A 42

Cross La. M35—1D 90
Cross La. SK6—6C 134
Cross La. SK9—1H 159
Cross La. W. M31—6D 110
Cross Lees. OL12—6G 7
Crossley Cres. OL6—5H 79
Crossley Est. OL9—3H 63
Crossley Rd. M19 & SK4—2B 118
Crossley Rd. M33—3A 114
Crossley St. BL3—4A 40
Crossley St. M18—1D 102
Crossley St. OL2—5C 48
(Royton)
Crossley St. OL2—6G 35
(Shaw)
Crossley St. OL16—5E 21
Crossley St. SK15—3D 92
Crossley St. SK16—4B 92
Crossmead Dri. M9—4G 61
Crossmoor Cres. SK6—1A 134
Crossmoor Dri. BL2—5D 24
Crossnoor Gro. SK6—1A 134
Cross Ormrod St. BL3—1H 37
Cross Rd. M21—1H 115
Cross Rd. SK8—6F 141
Cross St. BL1—5B 24
Cross St. BL3—4B 40
Cross St. BL4—6F 39
(Farnworth)
Cross St. BL4—4B 56
(Kearsley)
Cross St. BL7—4D 10
Cross St. BL9—3D 28
Cross St. M2—4D 86 & 5H 161
Cross St. M3—3C 86 & 3F 161
Cross St. M16—2B 100
Cross St. M24—1H 61
(in two parts)
Cross St. M25—5C 42
Cross St. M26—4H 41
Cross St. M27—1B 72
Cross St. M28—4E 67
Cross St. M31—6E 97
Cross St. M32—5D 98
Cross St. M33—4B 114
Cross St. M34—2E 105
Cross St. OL4—3A 66
(Lees)
Cross St. OL4—2F 65
(Oldham)
Cross St. OL4—3C 66
(Springhead)
Cross St. OL5—1E 81
Cross St. OL6—3G 91
Cross St. OL10—4G 31
Cross St. OL11—3D 32
Cross St. OL16—4D 20
Cross St. SK14—2H 109
(Hadfield)
Cross St. SK14—3F 109
(Hollingworth)
Cross St. SK14—5B 106
(Hyde)
Cross St. SK15—1H 93
Cross St. WA14—1F 137
Cross, The. SK14—2H 109
Crosswaite Rd. SK2—5D 132
Crossway. M20—6F 117
Crossway. M35—6A 90
Crossway. SK2—1A 144
Crossway. SK7—2G 153
Crossway Rd. M33—2H 125
Cross Ways. OL8—2E 79
Croston Clo. M16—2B 100
Croston Clo. OL9—2A 64
Croston Clo. Rd. BL9—2A 16
Crostons Rd. BL8—2B 28
Croston St. BL3—3G 37
Croston St. S. M16—3B 100
Croston Wlk. M11—4A 88
Croton St. SK4—1A 130
Croughton Clo. M11—6F 89
Crowbank Wlk. M10—6A 76
Crowborough Wlk. M15—2E 101
Crowbrook Gro. SK9—6H 151
Crowcombe Wlk. M16—3C 100
Crowcroft Rd. M13 & M12—4B 102
Crowden Rd. M10—1B 76

Crow Hill. SK15—6G 81
Crow Hill N. M24—3H 61
Crowhill Rd. OL7—1F 91
Crow Hill S. M24—3H 61
Crow Hill View. OL4—5A 66
*Crowhurst Wlk. M23—4E 127
(off Sandy La.)
Crowland Gdns. SK8—1D 152
Crowland Rd. BL2—3E 25
Crowland Rd. M23—2F 139
Crowland St. OL8—5G 65
Crow La. BL0—3E 5
Crowley La. OL4—8H 49
Crowley Rd. M9—3H 75
Crowley Rd. WA15—5B 126
Crowneast St. OL11—4E 19
Crown Gdns. OL16—6A 20
Crown Hill. OL5—3F 81
Crown Ind. Est. M44—3G 87
Crown Ind. Est. WA14—4G 125
Crown La. M4—2E 87 & 2B 162
Crown M. SK2—1C 144
Crown Pas. WA15—5B 126
Crown Point Av. M10—6C 76
Crown Rd. OL10—3D 30
Crown Royal Ind. Est. SK1—3H 131
Crown Sq. M3—4C 86 & 6F 161
Crown St. BL1—6B 24
Crown St. M3—3C 86 & 3E 161
Crown St. M15—6C 86 & 3E 165
Crown St. M34—3E 105
Crown St. M35—3F 77
Crown St. OL2—6F 35
Crown St. OL6—3H 91
Crown St. OL16—6A 20
Crown St. SK6—4F 121
(Bredbury)
Crown St. SK6—2D 146
(Marple)
Crownswood Dri. SK15—5F 81
Crowsdale Pl. SK2—1E.145
Crowshaw Dri. OL12—6E 7
Crowther Av. M5—5G 85
Crowther Ct. OL15—5C 8
Crowther Gdns. M5—5G 85
Crowther St. M18—2F 103
Crowther St. OL15—4C 8
Crowther St. OL16—1H 33
Crowther St. SK1—2H 131
Crowthorn Dri. M23—3G 139
Crowthorn Rd. OL7—4F 91
Crowthorn Rd. SK4—2F 119
Crowton Av. M33—1F 125
Croxdale Clo. OL7—6C 78
*Croxdale Wlk. M9—4F 61
(off Claygate Dri.)
Croxton Av. OL16—3B 20
Croxton Clo. M33—6F 113
Croxton Clo. SK6—6C 134
Croxton Wlk. M13—1G 101 & 5E 167
Croyde Clo. BL2—2H 25
Croyde Clo. M22—6D 140
Croydon Av. OL2—1A 48
Croydon Dri. M10—1D 88
Croydon Sq. OL11—5D 32
Crummock Clo. BL3—4H 39
Crummock Dri. M24—4G 45
Crummock Gro. BL4—2A 54
Crummock Rd. SK8—2F 141
Crumpsall Cres. M8—3C 74
Crumpsall La. M8—2B 74
Crumpsall St. BL1—2A 24
Crumpsall Vale. M9—1E 75
Crundale Rd. BL1—5E 11
Cruttenden Rd. SK2—1D 144
Cryer St. M18—1C 90
Cuba St. M24—1C 62
Cubley Rd. M7—3A 74
Cuckoo Gro. M25—3F 59
Cuckoo La. BL9—3G 29
Cuckoo La. M25—3F 59
Cuddington Av. M20—1E 117
Cuddington Cres. SK3—5F 131
Cuddington Way. SK9—2H 151
Cudworth Rd. M9—4C 60
Cuerdon Wlk. M22—3C 128
Culand St. M12—1A 102

Culbert Av. M20—6G 117
Culcheth Av. SK6—5D 134
Culcheth La. M10—6C 76
Culcheth Rd. WA14—2F 137
Culcombe Wlk. M13—2G 101
Culford Clo. M12—1A 102
Culgaith Wlk. M9—4F 75
Culham Clo. BL1—6A 24
Cullen Gro. M9—6H 61
Cullercoats Wlk. M12—4D 102
Culmere Rd. M22—4B 140
Culmington Clo. M15—2C 100
Culross Av. BL3—1C 36
Culross Av. M10—2E 77
Culvercliff Wlk. M3—5C 86 & 1F 165
Culverden Av. M6—5D 72
Culverden Wlk. M6—5D 72
Culver Rd. SK3—6F 131
Culvert St. OL4—1A 66
Culvert St. OL16—3H 33
Cumber Clo. SK9—5A 158
Cumber Dri. SK9—5A 158
Cumberland Av. M27—1F 71
Cumberland Av. M30—5A 110
Cumberland Av. OL10—3C 30
Cumberland Av. SK5—5C 120
Cumberland Av. SK16—5C 92
Cumberland Clo. BL9—1C 42
Cumberland Dri. OL1 & OL2—6B 48
Cumberland Gro. OL7—1H 91
Cumberland Rd. M9—2F 75
Cumberland Rd. M31—6E 97
Cumberland Rd. M33—1C 126
Cumberland Rd. OL11—3F 33
Cumberland St. M7—1B 86
Cumberland St. SK15—3D 92
Cumber La. SK9—4A 158
Cumbrae Gdns. M5—4D 84
Cumbrae Rd. M19—6E 103
Cumbria Ct. M25—2D 72
Cumbria Clo. M13—1G 101 & 6E 167
Cumbrian Clo. OL2—5D 34
Cumbria Wlk. M6—1H 85
Cummings St. OL8—1A 78
Cunard Clo. M13—1G 101 & 5E 167
Cundall Wlk. M23—2F 127
Cundey St. BL1—4G 23
Cundiff Ct. M19—6E 103
Cundiff Rd. M21—3H 115
Cundy St. SK14—3C 106
Cunliffe Av. BL0—5C 4
Cunliffe Brow. BL1—3F 23
Cunliffe Dri. M33—6C 114
Cunliffe Dri. OL2—6G 35
Cunliffe St. BL3 1B 38
Cunliffe St. M26—4A 42
Cunliffe St. SK3—3E 131
Cunliffe St. SK14—3A 106
Cunnah's Gro. M16—2H 99
Cunningham Dri. BL9—6F 43
Cunningham Dri. M22—5E 141
Cunningham Way. OL1—1D 64
Curate St. SK1—2A 132
Curlew Clo. OL11—4B 18
Curlew Dri. M30—3E 95
Curlew Rd. OL4—5A 66
Curlew Wlk. M12—2A 102
Currier La. OL6—3A 92
Curtels Clo. M28—4C 70
Curtis Gro. SK14—2H 109
Curtis Rd. SK4—1C 130
Curtis St. BL3—5G 37
Curtis St. M19—6E 103
Curzon Av. M14—3A 102
Curzon Clo. OL11—3F 33
Curzon Dri. WA15—5B 126
Curzon Grn. SK2—3D 132
Curzon Rd. BL1—6G 23
Curzon Rd. M7—4H 73
Curzon Rd. M32—4A 98
Curzon Rd. M33—4B 114
Curzon Rd. OL6—1B 92
Curzon Rd. SK2—4D 132
Curzon Rd. SK8—6F 141
Curzon St. SK5—5E 155
Curzon St. OL1—2D 64
Curzon St. OL5—2E 81

Cutgate Clo. M23—2E 127
Cutgate Rd. OL12—2D 18
Cuthbert Av. M19—5D 102
Cuthbert Mayne Ct. OL16—5G 19
Cuthbert Rd. SK8—5A 130
Cuthbert St. BL3—5F 37
Cuthill Wlk. M10—1F 89
Cutland St. M10—5A 76
Cut La. OL12—2B 18
Cutler Hill Rd. M35—4H 77
Cutler St. OL9—2A 64
Cutnook La. M30—2D 94
Cycle St. M11—5D 88
Cyclone St. M11—5B 88
Cygnus Av. M7—2A 86 & 1B 160
Cymbal Ct. SK5—6H 119
Cynthia Dri. SK6—6D 134
Cypress Av. OL9—1H 63
Cypress Clo. SK3—3E 131
Cypress Gro. BL4—2H 55
Cypress Gro. M34—4G 105
Cypress Rd. M30—1C 82
Cypress Rd. M25—2A 90
Cypress Rd. OL4—1H 65
Cypress St. M9—4F 75
Cypress St. M24—2C 62
Cypress Wlk. M33—3E 113
Cypress Way. SK6—6E 147
Cyprus Clo. OL4—4F 85
Cyprus Clo. OL4—3H 65
Cyprus St. M32—6D 98
Cyril St. BL3—2C 38
Cyril St. M14—4F 101
Cyril St. OL2—6G 35
Cyrus St. M10—3H 87 & 4H 163

Daccamill Dri. M27—4F 71 b
Dacre Av. M16—5H 99
Dacre Clo. M24—6D 44
Dacre Rd. OL11—1F 33
Dacres Av. OL3—5H 67
Dacres Dri. OL3—5H 67
Dacres Rd. OL3—5H 67
Daffodil Clo. OL12—6E 7
Daffodil Rd. BL4—6C 38
Daffodil St. BL1—6D 10
Dagenham Rd. M14—3G 101
Dagmar St. M28—5E 55
Dagnall Av. M21—2H 115
Dahila Clo. OL12—6D 6
Daimler St. M8—5C 74
Dain Clo. SK16—5C 92
Daine Av. M23—2H 127
Dainton St. M12—5H 87 & 2H 167
Daintry Clo. M15—1D 100 & 5G 165
Daintry Rd. OL9—2A 64
Dairybrook Gro. SK9—6A 152
Dairyground Rd. SK7—6G 143
Dairy Ho. La. SK7—4C 152
Dairyhouse La. WA14—5C 124
Dairy St. OL9—2H 63
Daisy Bank Av. M27—5A 72
Daisy Hill Ct. OL4—1A 66
(off Howard St.)
Daisy St. SK1—4H 131
Daisy Av. BL4—6C 38
Daisy Av. M13—3A 102
Daisy Bank. M10—6C 76
Daisy Bank. SK14—1A 122
Daisybank La. SK8—4E 141
Daisy Bank Rd. M14—3H 101
Daisyfield Ct. BL8—4A 28
Daisy Hill Clo. M33—5F 115
Daisy Hill Rd. OL5—2F 81
Daisy M. SK3—1F 143
Daisy Row. OL15—6D 8
Daisy St. BL3—3G 37
Daisy St. BL8—3A 28
Daisy St. OL9—1G 63
(Chadderton)
Daisy St. OL9—2B 64
(Oldham)
Daisy St. OL12—3G 19
Daisy Way. SK6—6D 146
Dakerwood Clo. M10—6C 76
Dakota Av. M5—5E 85

Dalbeattie St. M9—2G 75
Dalberg St. M12—6H 87 & 4G 167
Dalbury Dri. M10—6E 75
Dalby Av. M27—4E 71
Dalby Gro. SK1—2A 132
Dale Av. M30—2E 83
Dale Av. OL5—6G 67
Dale Av. SK7—5H 143
Dale Bank M. M27—4D 56
Dalebeck Clo. M25—1G 59
Dalebeck Wlk. M25—1G 59
Dalebrook Av. SK16—1B 106
Dalebrook Clo. BL3—3A 40
Dalebrook Rd. M33—1C 126
Dale Ct. M34—5F 105
Dale End. OL8—1E 79
Dalefields. OL3—3H 51
Daleford Sq. M13—6F 87 & 4D 166
Dalegarth Av. BL1—6A 22
Dale Gro. M30—3C 110
Dale Gro. OL7—6E 79
Dale Gro. WA15—4H 125
Dalehead Clo. M18—1H 103
Dalehead Dri. OL2—6H 35
Dale Ho. M24—6B 46
Dale Ho. OL2—1F 49
Dale Ho. Fold. SK12—3G 155
Dale La. OL3—2H 51
Dale M. M24—5B 46
Dale Rd. SK6—5B 134
Dales Av. M8—1B 74
Dales Av. M25—6B 42
Dales Brow. BL1—5D 10
Dales Brow. M27—5D 70
Dalesfield Cres. OL5—2G 81
Dales Gro. M28—2H 69
Dales La. M25—6B 42
Dalesman Wlk. M15—1E 101
(off Wilmott St.)
Dales Pk. Dri. M27—5D 70
Dale Sq. OL2—3D 48
Dale Sq. WA14—4F 125
Dale St. BL0—1E 5
Dale St. BL1—5B 24
(in two parts)
Dale St. BL4—6G 39
Dale St. BL8—1A 28
Dale St. M1—4F 87 & 5C 162
(in two parts)
Dale St. M24—2B 62
Dale St. M25—6C 42
Dale St. M26—5G 41
(in two parts)
Dale St. M27—5E 71
Dale St. OL2—1F 49
Dale St. OL6—5C 80
Dale St. OL16—5F 21
(Milnrow)
Dale St. OL16—4C 20
(Rochdale)
Dale St. SK3—5F 131
Dale St. SK15—4D 92
Dale St. WA14—4F 125
Dale St. E. OL6—3G 91
Dale St. W. OL6—3G 91
Dale W. Ind. Est. M26—5G 41
Dalewood Av. M25—6B 42
Dale View. M34—2G 121
Dale View. OL16—1F 21
Dale View. SK14—1B 122
Dalham Av. M9—1A 76
Dalkeith Av. SK5—2H 119
Dalkeith Gro. BL3—2D 36
Dalkeith Rd. SK5—2H 119
Dalkeith Sq. OL10—4C 30
Dallas St. M5—5E 85
Dalley Av. M7—1B 86
Dallimore Rd. M23—5E 127
Dalmahoy Clo. M10—3C 76
Dalmain Wlk. M8—5B 74
Dalmeny Ter. OL11—1F 33
Dalmorton Rd. M21—1B 116
Dalny St. M19—6D 102
Dalry Wlk. M23—5G 127
Dalston Av. M35—3H 77
Dalston Dri. M20—1F 129
Dalston Dri. SK7—2E 153

Dalston Gdns. BL1—4A 24
(off Gladstone St.)
Dalton Av. M14—5E 101
Dalton Av. M25—2E 59
Dalton Av. M27—6A 58
Dalton Av. M32—3H 97
Dalton Av. OL16—4D 20
Dalton Clo. BL0—5C 4
Dalton Clo. OL16—4D 20
Dalton Dri. M27—4B 72
Dalton Gdns. M31—4D 96
Dalton Gro. SK4—5E 119
Dalton Rd. M9—4F 61
Dalton Rd. M24—2D 60
Dalton St. BL8—3A 28
(in two parts)
Dalton St. M4 & M10—1F 87
Dalton St. M30—2F 83
Dalton St. M33—3C 114
Dalton St. M35—3C 77
Dalton St. OL1—2F 65
Dalton St. OL9—2H 63
Daltrey St. OL1—1E 65
Dalveen Av. M31—3E 97
Dalveen Dri. WA15—4H 125
Dalymount Clo. BL2—3D 24
Damask Av. M3—3B 86 & 3C 160
Dame Hollow. SK8—6H 141
Damery Ct. SK7—5G 143
Damery Rd. SK7—5G 143
Dame St. OL9—1B 64
Dam Head Dri. M9—6G 61
Damien St. M12—5C 102
Damside. SK14—1H 109
Damson Wlk. M31—6B 110
Dan Bank. SK6—5A 134
Danbury Wlk. M23—3D 126
Danby Clo. SK14—3D 106
Danby Ct. OL1—1C 64
Danby Pl. SK14—3D 106
Danby Rd. BL3—4A 38
Danby Rd. SK14—3D 106
Danby Wlk. M9—2G 75
(off Polworth Rd.)
Dane Av. M31—5D 110
Dane Av. SK3—3C 130
Dane Bank Dri. SK12—1H 157
Danebank Wlk. M13—6F 87 & 4D 166
Dane Clo. SK7—2F 143
Danecroft Clo. M13—1H 101 & 6G 167
Dane Dri. SK9—3G 159
Danefield Ct. SK8—5H 141
Danefield Rd. M33—3C 114
Dane Hill Clo. SK12—2H 157
Daneholme Rd. M19—4A 118
Dane M. M33—3B 114
Dane Rd. M33—3B 114
Dane Rd. M34—5A 104
Dane Rd. Ind. Est. M33—3C 114
Danesbury Rise. SK8—6H 129
Danesbury Rd. BL2—1D 24
Daneshill. M25—3F 59
Daneshot St. M34—5B 104
Danes La. OL12—1A 6
Danesmoor Dri. BL9—1F 29
Danesmoor Rd. M20—4E 117
Danes Rd. M14—5H 101
Danes, The. M8—2B 74
Dane St. M11—6G 89
Dane St. OL4—2G 65
Dane St. OL5—6F 67
Dane St. OL11—4G 19
Danesway. M25—1H 73
Danesway. M27—4A 72
Daneswood Av. M9—5H 61
Daneswood Clo. OL12—1C 6
Daneswood Clo. OL12—1B 6
Danett Clo. M12—1D 102
Dane Wlk. SK5—4H 119
Dan Fold. OL1—2C 64
Danforth Gro. M19—1D 118
Daniel Adamson Rd. M31—6B 110
Daniel Adamson Rd. M5—4D 84
Daniel Fold. OL12—1D 18
Daniel's La. SK1—1G 131
Daniel St. OL1—1F 65
Daniel St. OL2—4E 49
Daniel St. OL10—3D 30

Daniel St. OL12—3H 7
Daniel St. SK7—3E 145
Danisher La. OL8—3D 78
Dannywood Clo. SK14—1A 122
Danson St. M10—2A 88
Dantall Av. M9—6A 62
Dante Clo. M30—1A 84
Danty St. SK16—4H 91
Dantzic St. M4—3E 87 & 3A 162
Danwood Clo. M34—5H 105
Darbishire St. BL1—4C 24
Darby Rd. M30—3B 111
Darbyshire Clo. BL1—5G 23
Darbyshire Ho. WA15—4C 126
Darbyshire Wlk. M26—4H 41
Darcy Wlk. M14—3E 101
Darden Clo. SK4—6A 118
Darell Wlk. M8—5D 74
Darenth Clo. M15—1D 100 & 6G 165
Daresbury Av. M31—3H 95
Daresbury Av. WA15—6G 125
Daresbury Clo. M33—6F 115
Daresbury Clo. SK3—6F 131
Daresbury Rd. M21—6F 99
Daresbury St. M8—3C 74
Darfield Wlk. M10—2H 87 & 2G 163
Dargai St. M11—4F 89
Dargle Rd. M33—3B 114
Darian Av. M22—5B 140
Dark La. M12—5H 87 & 2G 167
Dark La. OL3—1G 51
Dark La. OL5—1F 81
(in two parts)
Dark La. SK6—6D 120
Dark La. WA14—2A 124
Darlbeck Wlk. M21—4A 116
Darley Av. BL4—6G 39
Darley Av. M21 & M20—3H 115
(in two parts)
Darley Av. M30—5E 83
Darley Av. SK8—6F 129
Darley Ct. BL1—3G 23
Darley Gro. BL4—6G 39
Darley Rd. M16—4H 99
Darley Rd. OL11—1F 33
Darley Rd. SK7—6F 145
Darley St. BL1—4H 23
Darley St. M11—4B 88
Darley St. M32—3D 98
Darley St. M33—5B 114
Darley St. SK4—6E 119
Darley Ter. BL1—4A 24
Darlington Clo. BL8—6B 14
Darlington Rd. M20—3E 117
Darlington Rd. OL11—1F 33
Darlington St. M4—3G 87 & 3F 163
Darliston Av. M9—4C 60
Darlton Wlk. M9—3G 75
Darnall Av. M20—1E 117
Darnbrook Dri. M22—4H 139
Darncombe Clo. M16—3D 100
Darnley Av. M28—2E 69
Darnley St. M16—3B 100
Darnton Rd. OL6 & SK15—1C 92
Darras Rd. M18—4E 103
Darsham Wlk. M16—3C 100
Dart Clo. OL9—1F 63
Dartford Av. M30—3D 82
Dartford Av. SK5—3B 120
Dartford Clo. M12—1H 101 & 6H 167
Dartford Rd. M31—6E 97
Dartington Clo. M23—5D 126
Dartington Clo. SK7—2H 143
Dartmouth Cres. SK5—4C 120
Dartmouth Rd. M21—1A 116
Dartmouth Rd. M25—2E 59
Dartnall Clo. SK12—1E 157
Darton Av. M10—2A 88
Darvel Clo. BL2—1H 39
Darwell Av. M30—5E 83
Darwen Rd. BL7—2C 10
Darwen St. M16—1A 100 & 6A 164
Darwin Gro. SK7—1G 153
Darwin St. BL1—3H 23
Darwin St. OL4—4G 65
Darwin St. SK14—2E 107

Dashwood Rd. M25—4E 59
Dashwood Wlk. M12—1C 102
Datchet Ter. OL11—1F 33
Dauntesey Av. M27—3B 72
Davehall Av. SK9—2D 158
Davenfield Gro. M20—6F 117
Davenfield Rd. M20—6F 117
Davenham Rd. M33—3G 113
Davenham Rd. SK5—5H 103
Davenham Rd. SK9—3H 151
Davenhill Rd. M19—1C 118
Davenport Av. M20—2F 117
Davenport Av. M26—1F 41
Davenport Av. SK9—5B 158
Davenport Dri. SK6—3H 121
Davenport Fold. BL2—2A 26
Davenport Fold Rd. BL2—1A 26
Davenport Ho. SK7—1F 153
Davenport La. WA14—4E 125
Davenport Lodge. SK2—6H 131
Davenport Pk. Rd. SK2—6A 132
Davenport Rd. SK7—2D 144
Davenport Rd. WA14—4E 125
Davenport St. BL1—5A 24
Davenport St. M34—5E 91
Davenport St. M35—4G 89
Davenport Ter. M9—4G 75
Daventry Rd. M21—1B 116
Daventry Rd. OL11—1F 33
Daventry Way. OL11—2F 33
Daveylands. SK9—2G 159
Davey La. SK4—4G 159
David Brow. BL3—5E 37
David M. M14—2G 117
David Pegg Wlk. M10—5B 76
David's Farm Clo. M24—2C 62
David's La. OL4—2B 66
Davidson Dri. M24—3B 62
David's Rd. M35—3G 89
David St. BL8—2A 28
(in two parts)
David St. M34—5G 105
David St. OL1—3C 64
David St. OL12—2H 19
David St. SK15—1G 119
David St. N. OL12—2H 19
Davies Av. SK8—1F 147
Davies Rd. M31—6E 111
Davies Rd. SK6—6D 120
Davies Sq. M14—3E 101
Davies St. BL4—2A 56
Davies St. OL1—1B 64
Davies St. OL7—4F 91
Davis St. M30—4G 83
Davy Av. M27—1B 72
Davyhulme Circ. M31—3E 97
Davyhulme Rd. M31—3A 96
Davyhulme Rd. M32—4C 98
Davyhulme Rd. E. M32—4D 98
Davyhulme Rd. La. OL12—2B 20
Davylands. M31—2B 96
Davy St. M10—1F 49
Daw Bank. SK3—2G 131
Dawes St. BL3—1B 38
Dawley Clo. BL3—1G 37
Dawley Flats. OL10—3E 31
(off Brunswick St.)
Dawlish Av. M35—3G 89
Dawlish Av. OL9—6F 47
Dawlish Av. SK5—4C 120
Dawlish Av. SK8—5B 142
Dawlish Clo. SK7—6H 143
Dawlish Clo. SK14—4A 108
Dawlish Clo. WA3—6A 110
Dawlish Rd. M21—1A 116
Dawlish Rd. M33—4G 113
Dawnay St. M11—5D 88
Dawn St. OL2—1F 49
Dawson La. BL1—6A 24
Dawson Rd. SK8—5H 141
Dawson Rd. WA14—4F 125
Dawson St. BL9—1E 29
(in two parts)
Dawson St. M3—5B 86 & 2C 164
(Manchester)
Dawson St. M3—3D 86 & 3G 163
(Salford)

Dawson St. M27—3G 71
Dawson St. OL4—4A 66
(Lees)
Dawson St. OL4—3H 65
(Oldham)
Dawson St. OL10—3E 31
Dawson St. OL12—3H 19
Dawson St. SK1—6B 120
Dawson St. SK14—6C 106
Day Dri. M35—5F 77
Day Gro. SK14—4C 108
Daylesford Clo. SK8—1H 141
Daylesford Cres. SK8—1H 141
Daylesford Rd. SK8—1H 141
Deacon Av. M27—2E 71
Deacon Clo. WA14—4C 136
Deacons Clo. SK1—2A 132
Deacons Cres. BL8—6A 14
Deacon's Dri. M6—5B 72
Deacon St. OL16—2B 20
Deal Av. SK5—4B 120
Deal Clo. M10—6D 76
Dealey Rd. BL3—3E 37
Deal St. BL3—4B 38
Deal St. M3—3C 86 & 4F 161
Deal St. SK14—5C 106
Deal St. N. BL9—2F 29
Deal St. S. BL9—3F 29
(in two parts)
Deal Wlk. OL9—3G 63
Dean Av. M10—5B 76
Dean Av. M16—4H 99
Deanbank Av. M19—1B 118
Dean Bank Dri. OL16—4H 33
Dean Clo. BL0—2A 4
Dean Clo. BL4—1B 54
Dean Clo. M15—1B 100 & 6C 164
Dean Clo. M25—2B 58
Dean Clo. M31—5D 110
Dean Clo. SK6—6G 151
Dean Ct. BL1—5C 24
Dean Ct. M15—1B 100 & 6C 164
Deancourt. OL11—1F 33
Dean Ct. SK16—4H 91
Dean Dri. SK9—6G 151
Dean Dri. WA14—4C 136
Deane Av. BL3—2F 37
Deane Av. SK8—6B 130
Deane Av. WA15—6A 126
Deane Chu. Clough. BL3—2E 37
Deane Chu. La. BL3—3F 37
Deane Rd. BL3—2G 37
Deanery Gdns. M7—3H 73
Deanery Way. SK1—1G 131
Deane Wlk. BL3—1A 38
(in two parts)
Dean Ho. BL1—5B 24
Dean La. M10—4B 76
Dean La. SK7—5D 144
Dean Moor Rd. SK7—3A 144
Dean Rd. M3—2C 86 & 2F 161
Dean Rd. M30—3C 110
Dean Rd. SK9—4A 152
Dean Row Rd. SK9—6G 151
Deanscourt Av. M27—4E 71
Deansgate. BL1—6A 24
Deansgate. M3—5C 86 & 2F 165
(in two parts)
Deansgate. M26—4H 41
Deansgate La. WA14 & WA15 —4G 125
Deanshut Rd. OL8—1E 79
Deans Rd. M27—4D 70
Dean St. BL1—5B 24
Dean St. M1—4F 87 & 5C 162
Dean St. M26—4F 41
Dean St. M35—4E 77
Dean St. OL5—2D 80
Dean St. OL6—2G 91
Dean St. OL16—2B 20
Dean St. SK15—3E 93
Deansway. M27—3E 71
Deanswood Dri. M9—4C 60
Dean Ter. OL6—2F 79
Dean Wlk. M24—5F 45
Deanwater Clo. M13—6F 87 & 4D 166
Deanwater Ct. M32—1D 114

Deanway. M10—3A 76
Deanway. M31—5H 95
Deanway. SK9—6G 151
Deanway Trading Est. SK9—4H 151
Dearden Av. M28—4C 54
Dearden Fold. BL8—4A 28
Deardens St. BL8—4A 28
Dearden St. BL3—3A 40
Dearden St. OL15—3F 9
Dearden Wlk. M15—1C 100 & 6F 165
Dearnley Clo. OL15—5C 8
Dearnley Pas. OL12—5C 8
Debdale Av. M18—3H 103
Debdale La. M18—3H 103
Debenham Av. M10—1E 89
Debenham Ct. BL4—2F 55
Debenham Rd. M32—5A 98
De Brook Ct. M31—6A 96
Dee Av. WA15—6D 126
Deepcar St. M19—5C 102
Deepdale. OL4—3H 65
Deepdale Av. M20—1E 117
Deepdale Av. OL2—5A 34
Deepdale Av. OL16—5C 20
Deepdale Clo. SK5—6H 103
Deepdale Ct. M9—6B 62
Deepdale Dri. M27—4B 72
Deepdale Rd. BL2—5G 25
Deeping Av. M16—5B 100
Deeplish Cotts. OL11—6H 19
Deeplish Rd. OL11—6H 19
Deeplish St. OL11—6H 19
Deeply Vale La. BL0—1A 16
Deeracre Av. SK2—5C 132
Deerfold Clo. M18—2F 103
Deerhurst Dri. M8—5B 74
Deeroak Clo. M18—1D 102
Deerpark Rd. M16—4C 100
Defence St. M3—1H 37
Deganwy Gro. SK5—4H 119
Deighton Av. M20—1E 117
Delacourt Rd. M14—1E 117
De Lacy Dri. BL2—4D 24
Delafield Av. M12—5C 102
Delaford Clo. SK3—6H 143
Delaford Wlk. M10—1F 89
Delahays Dri. WA15—3B 138
Delahays Range. M18—3H 103
Delahays Rd. WA15—3B 138
Delaine Rd. M20—3G 117
Delamare Av. OL2—5H 35
Delamere Av. M6—5A 72
Delamere Av. M25—1B 58
Delamere Av. M27—1H 71
Delamere Av. M32—5D 98
Delamere Av. M33—6E 115
Delamere Clo. M34—4A 122
Delamere Clo. SK7—2G 145
Delamere Clo. SK15—5G 81
Delamere Ct. M9—4C 60
Delamere Gdns. BL1—2H 23
Delamere Rd. M19—1C 118
Delamere Rd. M31—5B 96
Delamere Rd. M34—5B 104
Delamere Rd. OL16—1A 34
Delamere Rd. SK6—2H 121
Delamere Rd. SK7—2G 145
Delamere Rd. SK8—6F 129
Delamere St. M11—6H 89
Delamere St. OL6—2H 91
Delamere St. OL8—4F 65
Delamer Rd. WA14—2E 137
Delaunays Rd. M8 & M9—2C 74
Delaunays Rd. M33—5H 113
Delaware Wlk. M9—4F 75
Delboeth Av. M31—3A 96
Delft Wlk. M6—6E 73
Delfur Rd. SK7—6H 143
Delhi Rd. M30—1D 110
Dellar St. OL12—2E 19
Dell Av. M27—4B 72
Dellcot Clo. M6—6H 71
Dellcot Clo. M25—1H 73
Dellcot La. M28—6H 69
Dell Gdns. OL12—1D 18

Dell Meadow. OL12—4C 6
Dell Rd. OL12—6B 6
Dell Side. SK6—6E 121
Dellside Gro. M28—6G 55
Dell Side Way. OL12—1E 19
Dell, The. BL2—6G 11
Delph Brook Way. BL7—1B 10
Delph La. BL2—2H 25
Delph La. OL3—2H 51
Delph New Rd. OL3—4G 51
Delph Rd. BL3—2H 37
Delph St. OL16—5F 21
Delside Av. M10—3A 76
Delta Clo. OL2—5A 48
Delta Rd. M34—6E 91
Delta Wlk. M10—4A 76
Delvino St. M15—2D 100
Delvino Wlk. M14—3E 101
Delwood Gdns. M22—2B 140
De Massey Clo. SK6—3H 121
Demesne Clo. SK15—4G 93
Demesne Cres. SK15—4G 93
Demesne Dri. SK15—3G 93
Demesne Rd. M16—5C 100
Demmings Ind. Est. SK8—6B 130
Demmings Rd. SK8—6B 130
Demmings, The. SK8—6B 130
Dempsey Dri. BL9—5F 43
Denbigh Clo. SK7—5C 144
Denbigh Dri. OL2—1D 48
Denbigh Pl. M6—3G 85
(in two parts)
Denbigh Rd. BL2—2D 38
Denbigh Rd. M27—1G 71
Denbigh Rd. M34—6F 105
Denbigh St. OL5—3F 81
Denbigh St. OL8—6D 64
Denbigh St. SK4—6F 119
Denbigh Wlk. M15—2C 100
Denbury Dri. WA14—6D 124
Denbury Grn. SK7—4A 144
Denbury Wlk. M9—4E 75
(off Westmere Dri.)
Denbydale Way. OL2—3A 48
(in two parts)
Denby La. SK4—5F 119
Denby Rd. SK16—6A 92
Dencombe St. M13—3B 102
Dene Av. BL8—5C 14
Dene Bank. BL2—6G 11
Dene Brow. M34—1H 121
Dene Ct. SK4—1E 131
Dene Dri. M24—2H 61
Denefield Clo. SK6—2F 135
Denefield Pl. M30—2H 83
Deneford Rd. M20—1E 129
Dene Hollow. SK5—6A 104
Denehurst Rd. OL11—3D 18
Denehurst St. M12—1B 102
Dene Pk. M20—6E 117
Dene Rd. M20—6E 117
Dene Rd. W. M20—6D 116
Deneside. M10—5F 75
Deneside Cres. SK7—2F 145
Deneside Wlk. M9—2G 75
(off Dalbeattie St.)
Dene St. BL2—6G 11
Denesway. M33—6G 113
(in two parts)
Deneway. SK4—1E 131
Deneway. SK6—5D 146
Deneway. SK7—6E 143
Deneway Clo. SK4—1E 131
Deneway M. SK4—1E 131
Denewell Clo. M13—1H 101 & 6G 167
Denewood Ct. SK9—3D 158
Denham Clo. BL1—5E 11
Denham Dri. M30—6E 95
Denham Dri. SK7—6F 143
Denham St. M13—3H 101
Denham St. M26—1F 41
Den Hill Dri. OL4—3B 66
Denhill Rd. M15—2C 100
Denholme Rd. OL11—1F 33
Denholm Rd. M20—3G 129
Denhurst Rd. OL15—3F 9
Denis Av. M16—5C 100
Denison Rd. M14—4G 101

Denison Rd. SK7—5E 145
Deniston Rd. SK4—4D 118
Den La. OL3—1F 53
Den La. OL4—2B 66
Denman Wlk. M8—5B 74
(off Ermington Dri.)
Denmark Rd. M15—3D 100
Denmark Rd. M33—3B 114
Denmark St. OL4—2G 65
Denmark St. OL9—1A 64
Denmark St. OL16—3A 20
Denmark St. WA14 & WA15
—1F 137
Denmark Way. OL9—1A 64
Denmore Rd. M10—6D 62
Dennington Dri. M31—3E 97
Dennison Av. M20—2F 117
Dennison Rd. SK8—5D 142
Denshaw Av. M34—2D 104
Denshaw Clo. M19—6A 118
Denshaw Rd. OL3—1E 51
Densmead Wlk. M10—2G 87 & 2F 163
Densmore St. M35—4F 77
Denson Rd. WA15—3B 126
Denstone Av. M30—2G 83
Denstone Av. M33—6G 113
Denstone Cres. BL2—3G 25
Denstone Rd. M6—6B 72
Denstone Rd. M31—4E 97
Denstone Rd. SK5—6H 103
Denstone Wlk. M9—6G 61
(off Dam Head Dri.)
Dent Clo. SK5—3C 120
Dentdale Clo. BL1—1B 36
Dentdale Wlk. M22—5A 140
Denton La. OL9—4G 63
Denton Relief Rd. M34—3D 104
Denton Rd. BL2—1B 40
Denton Rd. M34—2E 105
Denton St. BL9—1D 28
Denton St. OL10—4E 31
Denton St. OL12—2H 19
Denver Av. M10—2H 87 &
1H 163
Denver Dri. WA15—5A 126
Denver Rd. OL11—1F 33
Denville Cres. M22—2C 140
Denyer Ter. SK16—4H 91
Depleach Rd. SK8—6H 129
Deptford Av. M23—2G 139
De Quincey Clo. WA14—2F 125
De Quincey Rd. WA14—2F 125
Deramore Clo. OL6—2C 92
Deramore St. M14—4F 101
Derby Av. M6—3E 85
Derby Clo. M30—4A 110
Derby Ct. M33—6C 114
Derby Ct. OL9—4A 64
Derby Gro. M19—6D 102
Derby Ho. M15—2F 101
Derby Range. SK4—5D 118
Derby Rd. M14—2G 117
Derby Rd. M25—3E 59
Derby Rd. M26—1A 56
Derby Rd. M31—4F 97
Derby Rd. M33—3G 113
Derby Rd. OL6—2B 92
Derby Rd. SK4—5E 119
Derby Rd. SK14—3C 106
Derbyshire Av. M32—4A 98
Derbyshire Cres. M32—4B 98
Derbyshire Grn. M32—5D 98
Derbyshire Gro. M32—4A 98
Derbyshire La. M32—5C 98
Derbyshire La. W. M32—4A 98
Derbyshire Rd. M31—2A 24
Derbyshire Rd. M31—1F 89
Derbyshire Rd. M33—5C 114
Derbyshire St. M11—6E 89
Derbyshire St. M26—4G 41
Derby St. BL0—3F 5
Derby St. BL3—3H 37
Derby St. BL9—3D 28
Derby St. M8—6A 74
Derby St. M25—5E 59
Derby St. M34—4D 104
(in two parts)
Derby St. M35—2G 77

Derby St. OL5—3F 81
Derby St. OL7—6E 79
Derby St. OL9—6H 63
(Chadderton)
Derby St. OL9—4A 64
(Oldham)
Derby St. OL10—3D 30
Derby St. OL11—6A 20
Derby St. SK3—3F 131
Derby St. SK6—5D 134
Derby St. SK15—2F 93
Derby St. WA14—6G 125
Derby Way. SK6—5D 134
Dereham Clo. BL8—6D 14
Derg St. M6—3F 85
Derker St. OL1—1E 65
Dermont Murphy Clo. M20—3D 116
Dernford Av. M19—4B 118
Derrett Clo. M11—5C 88
Derrick Walker Ct. OL11—6F 19
Derry Av. M22—1C 140
Derry St. OL1—3D 64
Derville Wlk. M9—3F 75
(off Alderside Rd.)
Derwen Rd. SK3—4G 131
Derwent Av. M21—4B 116
Derwent Av. M25—1F 59
Derwent Av. M35—4G 89
Derwent Av. OL7—1G 91
Derwent Av. OL10—4F 31
Derwent Av. WA15—6D 126
Derwent Clo. BL3—4H 39
Derwent Clo. M21—4B 116
Derwent Clo. M25—1F 59
Derwent Clo. M28—1D 68
Derwent Clo. M31—5D 110
Derwent Clo. M34—5B 104
Derwent Av. BL4—4B 56
Derwent Dri. BL9—6B 28
Derwent Dri. M33—1A 126
Derwent Dri. OL2—5E 35
Derwent Dri. OL9—2G 63
Derwent Dri. OL15—1F 21
Derwent Dri. SK7—2E 153
Derwent Dri. SK9—2G 151
Derwent Ind. Area. M5—5A 86 &
2B 164
Derwent Rd. BL4—1B 54
Derwent Rd. M24—4G 45
Derwent Rd. M31—5A 96
Derwent Rd. M32—4D 98
Derwent Rd. OL16—5H 21
Derwent Rd. SK6—5C 146
Derwent St. M5—5A 86 & 2B 164
Derwent St. M8—5E 75
Derwent St. M35—3F 89
Derwent St. OL12—2H 19
Derwent Ter. SK15—1E 93
Derwent Wlk. M25—1F 59
Derwent Wlk. OL4—2H 65
Desford Av. M21—6A 100
Design St. BL3—3F 37
Desmond Rd. M22—1C 140
Destructor Rd. M27—2E 71
De Traffords, The. M30—4F 95
Dettingen St. M6—5B 72
Deva Clo. SK7—4D 144
Deva Clo. SK12—3B 154
Devaney Wlk. M34—6E 105
Deva Sq. OL9—4A 64
Devas St. M15—2E 101
Deverill Av. M18—3H 103
Devine Clo. M3—3B 86 & 3C 160
Devine Clo. OL2—1B 48
Devisdale Ct. WA14—2D 136
Devisdale Rd. WA14—1D 136
Devoke Av. M28—1G 69
Devoke Gro. BL4—1A 54
Devon Av. M19—1B 118
Devon Av. M25—6C 42
Devon Clo. BL3—3B 40
Devon Clo. M6—2A 84
Devon Clo. OL2—6D 34
Devon Clo. SK5—5C 120
Devon Dri. BL2—4C 26
Devon Dri. OL3—3B 52
Devonport Cres. OL2—3D 48
Devon Rd. M30—4B 110
Devon Rd. M31—6A 96

Devon Rd. M35—2A 90
(Droylsden)
Devon Rd. M35—5E 77
(Failsworth)
Devonshire Clo. M31—5G 97
Devonshire Clo. OL10—3C 30
Devonshire Ct. M7—3H 73
Devonshire Ct. SK2—6A 132
Devonshire Dri. M28—5A 68
Devonshire Dri. SK9—4H 159
Devonshire Pk. Rd. SK2—6A 132
Devonshire Pl. M25—4E 59
Devonshire Rd. BL1—4F 23
Devonshire Rd. M6—2A 84
Devonshire Rd. M21—1A 116
Devonshire Rd. M28—3E 55
Devonshire Rd. M30—3G 83
Devonshire Rd. OL11—3F 33
Devonshire Rd. SK4—1D 130
Devonshire Rd. SK7—5F 145
Devonshire Rd. WA15—4F 125
Devonshire St. M7—5H 73
Devonshire St. M12—1H 101 & 6G 167
Devonshire St. E. M35—5D 76
Devonshire St. N. M12—6H 87 & 4H 167
Devonshire St. S. M13—2H 101 &
6G 167
Devon St. BL2—6C 24
Devon St. BL4—5F 39
Devon St. BL9—5D 28
Devon St. M27—1F 71
Devon St. OL9—5H 63
Devon St. OL11—5H 19
Dewar Clo. M11—4C 88
Dewar St. M11—5C 88
Dewberry Clo. M27—1E 71
Dewes Av. M27—1H 71
Dewey St. M11—6F 89
Dewhirst Rd. OL12—5F 7
(in three parts)
Dewhirst Way. OL12—5F 7
Dewhurst Clo. BL7—1B 10
Dewhurst Clough Rd. BL7—1B 10
Dewhurst Rd. BL2—2G 25
Dewhurst St. M8—1D 86
Dewhurst St. OL10—3G 31
De Wint Av. SK6—3F 135
Dew Meadow Clo. OL12—1G 19
Dewsnap La. SK14—1B 108
Dewsnap La. SK16—1A 106
Dew Way. M9—2B 64
Dexter Rd. M9—4C 60
Deyne Av. M14—3G 101
Deyne Av. M25—5F 59
Deyne St. M6—3E 85
Dial Ct. BL4—6F 39
Dial Pk. Rd. SK2—1D 144
Dial Rd. SK2—6C 132
Dial Rd. WA15—5C 138
Dialstone La. SK2—4C 132
Diamond Clo. OL6—1B 92
Diamond St. OL6—1B 92
Diamond St. SK2—5A 132
Diamond Ter. SK6—1D 146
Dibberford Wlk. M40—4C 100
Dibden Wlk. M23—6G 127
Dicken Grn. OL11—1F 33
Dicken Grn. La. OL11—1F 33
Dickens Clo. SK8—2D 152
Dickens La. SK12—4D '54
Dickenson Rd. M14 & M13—4G 101
Dickens Rd. M30—4F 83
Dickens St. OL1—3A 50
Dickinson Clo. BL1—4A 24
Dickinson St. BL1—4A 24
Dickinson St. M1—5D 86 & 1H 165
Dickinson St. M3—2C 86
Dickinson St. OL4—2F 65
Dickinson Ter. BL1—4A 24
(off Dickinson St.)
Dickins St. OL10—3D 30
Didcot Rd. M22—4A 140
Didley Sq. M12—6C 88
Didsbury Pk. M20—5F 129
Didsbury Rd. SK4—1H 129
Digby Rd. OL11—1F 33
Digby Wlk. M11—4B 88
(off Albert St.)

Dig Ga. La. OL16—2C 34
Diggles La. OL11—5A 18
(in two parts)
Diggle St. OL2—1F 49
Diggle Wlk. SK15—5G 81
Digsby Ct. M20—5F 117
Dijon St. BL3—3G 37
Dilham Ct. BL1—5G 23
Dillicar Wlk. M9—4F 75
Dillmoss Wlk. M15—1B 100 & 6D 164
Dillon Dri. M12—2A 102
Dilston Clo. M13—1G 101 & 6F 167
Dilworth Clo. OL10—3B 30
Dilworth Ct. SK2—6E 133
Dilworth Ho. M15—2F 101
Dilworth St. M15—2F 101
Dinas Wlk. M11—1C 100
(off Ipstone Clo.)
Dingle Av. M34—5H 105
Dingle Av. OL2—4G 35
Dingle Av. SK9—6A 158
Dingle Bank Rd. SK7—3F 143
Dinglebrook Gro. SK9—6A 152
Dingle Clo. SK6—1B 134
Dingle Dri. M35—2B 90
Dingle Gro. SK8—5D 128
Dingle Hollow. SK6—1C 134
Dingle Rd. M24—3G 61
Dingle Ter. OL6—1F 79
Dingle, The. SK7—4E 143
Dingle, The. SK14—3C 122
Dingle Wlk. BL1—5B 24
Dining Room St. M11—6C 88
Dinmore Ct. SK2—6D 132
Dinmor Rd. M22—4B 140
Dinnington Dri. M8—5B 74
Dinorwic Clo. M8—1C 74
Dinsdale Clo. M10—3H 163
Dinsdale Dri. BL3—2H 37
Dinslow Wlk. M8—4B 74
Dinting Av. M20—2E 117
Dinting La. SK13—5H 109
Dinting Lodge Ind. Est. SK13
—5H 109
Dinting Rd. SK13—5H 109
Dinting Vale. SK13—5G 109
Dinton St. M15—6A 86 & 4B 164
Dinwoodie Clo. M15—1E 101 & 5A 166
Dipton Wlk. M8—5E 75
(off Smedley Rd.)
Dirty La. OL4—6D 50
Dirty La. WA14—6A 136
Dirty Leech. OL12—3F 7
Disley Av. M20—3D 116
Disley St. OL11—1C 32
Disley Wlk. M34—6G 105
Distaff Rd. SK12—3B 154
Ditton Mead Clo. OL12—1B 20
Ditton Wlk. M23—5F 127
Division St. BL3—3B 38
Division St. OL12—1B 20
Dixon Av. M7—5H 73
Dixon Clo. M33—1D 126
Dixon Closes. OL11—4B 18
Dixon Ct. SK8—6H 129
Dixon Dri. M27—5E 57
Dixon Fold. M25—6C 42
Dixon Fold. OL11—5A 18
Dixon Rd. M34—6H 105
Dixon St. M6—5G 72
Dixon St. M10—5B 76
(in two parts)
Dixon St. M24—5A 46
Dixon St. M30—1D 110
Dixon St. OL1—1C 64
Dixon St. OL4—1A 66
Dixon St. OL6—1B 92
Dixon St. OL11—1D 32
Dobb Hedge Clo. WA15—1C 148
Dobbinets La. WA15 & M23
—1E 139
Dobcross Clo. M13—5C 102
Dobcross New Rd. OL3—6A 52
Dobhill St. BL4—1F 55
Dobran Wlk. OL1—4H 49
Dobroyd St. M8—3C 74
Dobsen St. BL1—3H 23
Dobson Clo. M13—1H 101 & 6G 167
Dobson Ct. M10—1D 88

Dobson Rd. BL1 –6G 23
Dockray Ho. SK8—6A 142
Doctor Dam Cotts. OL12—1H 17
Doctor Fold La. OL10—1D 44
Doctor La. OL4—6E 51
Doctor La. Head Cotts. OL4—6E 51
Doddington La. M5—5G 85
Doddington Wlk. M34—6E 105
Dodd St. M5—3D 84
Dodge Fold. SK2—5E 133
Dodge Hill. SK4—1G 131
Dodgson St. OL16—5A 20
Dodington Clo. M16—3D 100
Dodworth Clo. M15—1D 100 &6G 165
Doe Hey Gro. BL4—5D 38
Doe Hey Rd. BL3—5D 38
Doffcocker Brow. BL1—4D 22
Doffcocker La. BL1—4D 22
Dogford Rd. OL2—2B 48
Dolbey St. M5—4E 85
Dolefield. M3—4C 86 & 5F 16¹
Dollis Wlk. M11—5B 88
Dollond St. M9—2G 75
Dolman Wlk. M8—5B 74
Dolphin Pl. M12—6G 87 & 4F 167
Dolphin St. M12—6G 87 & 4F 167
Dolwen Wlk. M10—6B 76
Doman St. BL3—2B 38
Dombey Rd. SK12—5D 154
Domett St. M9—1E 75
Dominic Clo. M23—2E 127
Donald Av. SK14—6D 106
Donald St. M1—5E 87 & 2A 166
Dona St. SK1—3A 132
Don Av. M6—3C 84
Doncaster Av. M20—2E 117
Doncaster Clo. BL3—4H 39
Doncaster Wlk. OL1—2D 64
Donhead Wlk. M13—1G 101 &6F 167
Donkey La. SK9—4D 158
Donlan St. M18—1H 103
Donleigh St. M10—5D 76
Donnington. OL11—5G 19
Donnington Av. SK8—5B 130
Donnington Gdns. M28—6F 55
Donnington Rd. M18—2G 103
Donnington Rd. M26—2C 40
Donnison St. M12—1C 102
Donovan Av. M10—1G 87
Don St. BL3—4H 37
Don St. M24—6C 46
Doodson Av. M30—5E 95
Doodson Sq. BL4—1F 55
Dooley La. SK6—4H 133
Dooleys La. SK9—5H 149
Dorac Av. SK8—1G 15¹
Dora St. BL0—5C 4
Dorchester Av. BL2—4G 25
Dorchester Av. M25—1G 73
Dorchester Av. M31—4H 97
Dorchester Av. M34—6F 105
Dorchester Clo. SK9—1G 159
Dorchester Clo. WA15—2C 138
Dorchester Ct. M33—1B 126
Dorchester Ct. SK8—4D 142
Dorchester Dri. M23—2E 127
Dorchester Dri. OL2—5B 48
Dorchester Gro. OL10—5E 31
Dorchester Pde. SK7—4B 144
Dorchester Rd. SK7—4B 144
Dorclyn Av. M31—5F 97
Dorfield Clo. SK6—6E 121
Doric Av. SK6—6D 120
Doric Clo. M11—4B 88
Doris Av. BL2—6F 25
Doris Rd. SK3—3E 131
Doris St. M24—5A 46
Dorking Av. M10—1D 88
Dorking Clo. SK1—4B 132
Dorlan Av. M18—3H 103
Dorland Gro. SK2—4B 132
Dorman St. M11—6F 89
Dormer St. BL1—2B 24
Dorney St. M18—2F 103
Dorning Rd. M42—4G 71
Dorning St. BL4—1H 55
Dorning St. BL8—1H 27

Dorning St. M30—4F 83
Dornton Wlk. M8—5B 74
  (off Waterloo Rd.)
Dorothy Rd. SK7—2F 145
Dorothy St. BL0—4D 4
Dorothy St. M8—4B 74
Dorrington Rd. M33—5F 113
Dorrington St. SK3—4C 130
Dorris St. M19—1D 118
Dorrit Clo. SK12—5E 155
Dorset Av. BL4—1E 55
Dorset Av. M14—5E 101
Dorset Av. M34—5C 90
Dorset Av. OL2—6D 34
Dorset Av. OL3—3C 52
Dorset Av. SK5—4C 120
Dorset Av. SK7—3F 143
Dorset Av. SK8—6E 131
Dorset Clo. BL4—1E 55
Dorset Clo. OL10—4C 30
Dorset Dri. BL9—5E 29
Dorset Rd. M19—6E 103
Dorset Rd. M30—4B 110
Dorset Rd. M35—2H 89
  (Droylsden)
Dorset Rd. M35—5F 77
  (Failsworth)
Dorset Rd. WA14—6D 124
Dorset St. BL2—6C 24
Dorset St. M27—1F 71
Dorset St. M32—5D 98
Dorset St. OL6—3B 92
Dorset St. OL9—4A 64
Dorset St. OL11—5H 19
Dorstone Clo. M10—6C 76
Dorwood Av. M9—4E 61
Dougall Wlk. M12—1C 102
Doughty Av. M30—2H 83
Dougill St. BL1—4F 23
Douglas Av. BL8—3H 27
Douglas Av. M32—4D 98
Douglas Clo. M25—6G 43
Douglas Clo. M35—5B 90
Douglas Grn. M6—6E 73
Douglas Rd. M28—5C 70
Douglas Rd. SK3—1G 143
Douglas Rd. SK7—2E 145
Douglas Sq. OL10—4B 30
Douglas St. BL0—3D 4
Douglas St. BL1—6C 10
Douglas St. M7—5H 73
Douglas St. M10—4A 76
Douglas St. M27—4G 71
Douglas St. M35—4G 77
Douglas St. OL1—1E 65
Douglas St. OL6—2C 92
  (in two parts)
Douglas St. SK14—5C 106
Douglas St. Bk. BL0—3D 4
Douglas Wlk. M33—4E 113
Douro St. M10—6H 75
Douthwaite Dri. SK6—2C 134
Dove Bank Rd. BL3—3A 40
Dovecote. M35—2D 90
Dovecote La. M28—6A 54
Dovecote La. OL4—1B 66
Dovecote M. M21—1G 115
Dovedale Av. M20—2E 117
Dovedale Av. M25—6H 59
Dovedale Av. M30—2G 83
Dovedale Av. M35—1F 97
Dovedale Av. M35—3G 89
Dovedale Clo. SK6—6C 146
Dovedale Dri. OL12—3B 8
Dovedale Rd. BL2—4H 25
Dovedale Rd. SK2—4D 132
Dovedale St. M35—4E 77
Dove Dri. BL9—1F 29
Dovehouse Clo. M25—1C 58
Doveleys Rd. M6—1C 84
Dovercourt Av. SK4—5B 118
Dover Gro. BL3—1H 37
Dove Rd. BL3—3F 37
Dover Pk. M31—3F 97
Dover Rd. M27—1G 71
Dover St. BL4—5E 39
Dover St. M13—1F 101 & 6C 166

Dover St. M30—3D 82
Dover St. OL9—4A 64
Dover St. OL16—1B 20
Dover St. SK5—1G 119
Dovestone Cres. SK16—6D 92
Dovestone Wlk. M10—2E 77
Doveston Gro. M33—3B 114
Doveston Rd. M33—3B 114
Dove St. BL1—1A 24
Dove St. OL4—4G 65
Dove St. OL11—4F 19
Dove Wlk. BL4—1B 54
Dove Wlk. M8—5D 74
Dow Field. BL8—2F 27
Dow La. BL8—2F 27
Dowling St. M19—6E 103
  (in two parts)
Dowling St. OL11—5H 19
Downesway. SK9—5F 159
Downfield Clo. BL0—3C 4
Downfields. SK5—6A 104
Downgate Wlk. M8—5C 74
Down Grn. Rd. BL2—2G 25
Downhall Grn. BL1—5B 24
Downham Av. BL2—5E 25
Downham Chase. WA15—5B 126
Downham Clo. OL2—5A 48
Downham Cres. M25—6H 59
Downham Gdns. M25—6A 60
Downham Gro. M25—6A 60
Downham Rd. OL10—3C 30
Downham Rd. SK4—4F 119
Downham Wlk. M23—3E 127
Downing Clo. OL7—5D 78
Downing St. M1—6F 87 & 3D 166
Downing St. OL7—6D 78
Downley Dri. M4—3G 87 & 3F 163
Downs Dri. WA14—3G 125
Downshaw Rd. OL7—5E 79
Downs, The. M24—3B 62
  (in two parts)
Downs, The. M25—1E 73
Downs, The. SK8—2H 141
Downs, The. WA14—2E 137
Dowry Rd. OL4—2A 66
Dowry St. OL8—6D 64
Dowson Rd. SK14—2B 122
Dowson St. BL2—6C 24
Dow St. SK14—2B 106
Doyle Av. SK6—6D 120
Doyle Clo. OL1—3A 50
Doyle Rd. BL3—4C 36
Draba Brow. BL0—3E 5
Drake Av. BL4—2F 55
Drake Av. M30—3C 110
Drake Clo. OL1—1D 64
Drake Ct. SK5—5G 119
Drake Rd. OL15—6G 9
Drake Rd. WA14—3D 124
Drake St. OL16—4H 19
Draxford Ct. SK9—3E 159
Draycott St. BL1—3A 24
Draycott St. E. BL1—3A 24
Drayfields. M35—3D 90
Drayton Clo. BL1—3H 23
Drayton Clo. M33—1F 125
Drayton Dri. SK8—6F 141
Drayton Gro. WA15—1A 138
Drayton Manor. M20—3F 129
Drayton Wlk. M16—2B 100
Drefus Av. M11—3E 89
Dresden St. M10—3C 76
Dresser Cen., The. M11—6D 88
Drewett St. M10—1A 88
Dreyfus St. M12—4E 101
Driffield St. M14—4E 101
Driffield St. M30—5E 83
Drill Wlk. M4—3G 87
  (off Kirby Wlk.)
Drinkwater Rd. M25—2D 72
Driscoll St. M13—4B 102
Drive, The. BL0—2A 4
Drive, The. BL9—6F 15
Drive, The. M7—2G 73
Drive, The. M20—6G 117
Drive, The. M25—5F 59
Drive, The. M33—2G 125
Drive, The. SK5—5C 120

Drive, The. SK6—6D 120
  (Bredbury)
Drive, The. SK6—5C 134
  (Marple)
Drive, The. SK8—1E 143
Drive, The. WA15—5D 138
Droitwich Rd. M10—1H 87
Dronfield Rd. M6—1D 84
Dronfield Rd. M22—3B 128
Droughts La. M25—1H 59
Droylesden Rd. M34—4B 90
Droylsden Rd. M10—5C 76
Drummond St. BL1—1A 24
Drury La. OL9—6G 63
Drury St. M19—6C 102
Dryad Clo. M27—1F 71
Drybrook Clo. M13—2A 102
Dryburgh Av. BL1—1H 23
Dry Clough La. OL3—2E 53
Dryclough Wlk. OL2—4C 48
Dryden Av. M27—4D 70
Dryden Av. SK8—5A 130
Dryden Clo. SK6—1D 146
Dryden Clo. SK16—6F 93
Dryden Rd. M16—4A 100
Dryden St. M13—1G 101 & 6E 167
Dryden Way. M34—1G 121
Drygate Wlk. M9—4G 75
  (off Orpington Rd.)
Dryhurst Dri. SK12—1H 157
Dryhurst La. SK12—1H 157
Dryhurst Wlk. M15—1E 101 & 6A 166
Drymoss. OL8—2E 79
Drywood Av. M28—6A 70
Ducal St. M4—1F 87 & 1C 162
Duchess Pk. Clo. OL2—5F 35
Duchess Rd. M8—3D 74
Duchess St. OL2—5E 35
Duchess Wlk. BL3—3F 37
Duchy Av. M28—3F 69
Duchy Bank. M6—5B 72
Duchy Rd. M6—5C 72
Duchy St. M6—2F 85
  (in two parts)
Duchy St. SK3—4F 131
Ducie Av. BL1—6G 23
Ducie Pl. M5—4A 86 & 6A 160
Ducie St. BL0—2D 4
Ducie St. M1—4F 87 & 6C 162
Ducie St. M25—1D 58
Ducie St. M26—2F 41
Ducie St. OL8—1D 78
Duckshaw La. BL4—1E 55
Duckworth Ho. M6—1F 85
Duckworth Rd. M25—6D 58
Duckworth St. BL3—3G 37
Duckworth St. BL9—1E 29
  (in two parts)
Duckworth St. OL2—6G 35
Duddon Av. BL2—4H 25
Duddon Clo. M25—1G 59
Duddon Wlk. M24—5G 45
Dudley Av. BL2—4E 25
Dudley Av. M25—1D 58
Dudley Clo. M15—2C 100
Dudley Rd. M16—5B 100
Dudley Rd. M27—2F 71
Dudley Rd. M30—5B 110
Dudley Rd. M33—3C 114
Dudley Rd. WA15—4B 126
Dudley St. M7 & M8—4A 74
Dudley St. M30—4E 83
Dudley St. M34—3E 105
Dudley St. OL4—3H 65
Dudlow Wlk. M15—1B 100 & 6D 164
Duerden St. BL3—5E 37
Duffield Ct. M15—2E 101
Duffield Gdns. M24—4H 61
Duffield Rd. M6—6B 72
Duffield Rd. M24—4H 61
Duffins Clo. OL12—6D 6
Dufton Wlk. M22—4C 140
Dufton Wlk. M24—5G 45
Dugdale Av. M9—5G 61
Duke Av. SK8—1B 152
Duke Clo. M16—2B 100
Duke Ct. M16—2B 100

Dukefield St. M22—3C 128
Duke Pl. M3—5C 86 & 2E 164
Duke Rd. SK14—2D 106
Dukes All. BL1—6B 24
  (off Ridgeway Gdns.)
Duke's Av. BL3—3A 40
Dukes Platting. OL6—6B 80
Duke's Ter. SK16—4H 91
  (off Astley St.)
Duke St. BL0—5C 4
Duke St. BL1—5A 24
  (in two parts)
Duke St. BL2—4C 26
Duke St. M3—5C 86 & 2E 165
  (Manchester)
Duke St. M3—3D 86 & 3G 161
  (Salford)
Duke St. M26—5H 41
Duke St. M28—4C 54
Duke St. M30—1E 83
Duke St. M34—4E 105
Duke St. M35—4B 90
  (Droylsden)
Duke St. M35—3G 77
  (Failsworth)
Duke St. OL2—1G 49
Duke St. OL5—2G 81
Duke St. OL6—2H 91
Duke St. OL10—3D 30
Duke St. OL12—2H 19
  (in two parts)
Duke St. OL15—4E 9
Duke St. SK1—2H 131
Duke St. SK9—4H 159
Duke St. SK15—4D 92
Duke St. N. BL1—5A 24
Duke's Wharf. M28—6H 69
Dukinfield Rd. SK14—2A 106
Dulford St. M7—5B 74
Dulford Wlk. M13—2G 101
  (off Plymouth Gro.)
Dulgar St. M11—5D 88
Dulverton St. M10—5B 76
Dulwich St. M4—2F 87 & 1C 162
Dumbarton Clo. SK5—3H 119
Dumbarton Dri. OL10—4C 30
Dumbarton Rd. SK5—2H 119
Dumbell St. M27—1F 71
Dumber La. M33—3H 113
Dumers Clo. M26—3B 42
Dumers La. M26 & BL9—3B 42
Dumfries Wlk. OL10—4C 30
Dumplington Circ. M31—6F 83
Dunbar Av. M23—2G 139
Dunbar Gro. OL10—5B 30
Dunbar St. OL1—1C 64
Dunblaine Av. SK4—6F 119
Dunblane. OL11—6H 19
Dunblane Av. BL3—2C 36
Dunblane Gro. OL10—5C 30
Duncan Edward Ho. M6—2F 85
  (off Sutton Dwellings)
Duncan Edwards Ct. M10—6B 76
  (off Eddie Colman Clo.)
Duncan Rd. M13—4B 102
  (in two parts)
Duncan St. BL1—5B 24
Duncan St. M5—5A 86 & 1A 164
Duncan St. M7—4G 73
Duncan St. OL2—4E 49
Duncan St. SK16—1A 106
Dunchurch Clo. BL6—1B 36
Dunchurch Rd. M33—5G 113
Dun Clo. M3—3B 86 & 3D 160
Duncombe Clo. SK7—2A 144
Duncombe Dri. M10—4B 76
Duncombe Rd. BL3—4A 38
Duncombe St. M7—5A 74
Dundee. M30—3G 83
  (off St Andrews Ct.)
Dundee Clo. OL10—4B 30
Dundee La. BL0—3D 4
Dundonald Rd. M20—6G 117
Dundonald St. SK8—6C 142
Dundonald St. SK2—5H 131
Dundraw Clo. M24—6D 44
Dundrennan Clo. SK12—2D 154
Dunecroft. M34—3G 105

Dunedin Rd. BL8—1H 13
Dunelm Dri. M33—2D 126
Dungeon Wlk. SK9—2E 159
Dunham Lawn. WA14—1D 136
Dunham Rise. WA14—1E 137
Dunham Rd. M31—1A 124
Dunham Rd. SK9—2H 151
Dunham Rd. WA14—5A 136
Dunham St. OL4—1A 66
Dunkeld Gdns. M23—5F 127
Dunkeld Rd. M23—5F 127
Dunkerley Av. M35—4F 77
Dunkerleys Clo. M8—3B 74
Dunkerley St. OL2—3B 48
Dunkerley St. OL4—1G 65
Dunkerley St. OL7—6E 79
Dunkery Rd. M22—4B 140
Dunkirk Clo. M34—5A 104
Dunkirk La. SK14—2H 105
Dunkirk Rise. OL12—4G 19
Dunkirk Rd. M25—6D 42
Dunkirk St. M35—4B 90
Dunley Clo. M12—2C 102
Dunlin Clo. BL2—2C 38
Dunlin Clo. OL11—4B 18
Dunlin Clo. SK2—6G 133
Dunlin Clo. SK12—3A 154
Dunlin Dri. M30—4E 95
Dunlin Wlk. WA14—3D 124
Dunlop Av. OL11—1E 33
Dunlop St. M3—4D 86 & 5G 161
Dunmail Dri. M24—4G 45
Dunmere Wlk. M9—4E 75
  (off Mannington Dri.)
Dunmore Rd. SK8—5F 129
Dunmow Ct. SK2—6E 133
Dunmow Wlk. M23—1G 127
Dunnerdale Wlk. M18—2E 103
Dunnisher Rd. M23—6H 127
Dunnock Clo. SK2—6F 133
Dunollie Rd. M28—6E 115
Dunoon Clo. OL10—4C 30
Dunoon Dri. BL1—6A 10
Dunoon Rd. SK5—2H 119
Dunoon Wlk. M9—4F 75
Dunrobin Clo. OL10—5C 30
Dunscar Clo. M25—2B 58
Dunsfold Dri. M23—3D 126
Dunsford Ct. OL4—3B 66
Dunsley Av. M10—1D 76
Dunsmore Clo. M16—3B 100
Dunsop Dri. BL1—2D 22
Dunsop Wlk. M15—1D 100 & 6G 165
Dunstable. OL12—3G 19
  (off Spotland Rd.)
Dunstable St. M19—6D 102
Dunstall Rd. M22—6C 128
Dunstan St. BL2—6E 25
Dunstar Av. M34—6E 91
Dunster Av. M9—5G 61
Dunster Av. M27—1H 71
Dunster Av. OL11—6G 19
Dunster Av. SK5—4C 120
Dunster Clo. SK7—4C 144
Dunster Dri. M31—6G 95
Dunster Pl. M28—4B 68
Dunster Rd. M28—4B 68
Dunsters Av. BL8—6C 14
Dunsterville Ter. OL11—6G 19
  (off New Barn La.)
Dunston St. M11—5E 89
Dunton Grn. SK5—3B 120
Dunton Towers. SK5—3B 120
  (off Dunton Grn.)
Dunvegan Clo. OL10—4A 30
Dunvegan Rd. SK7—4F 145
Dunwood Av. OL2—5G 35
Dunworth St. M14—4F 101
Durant St. M4—2F 87 & 2C 162
Durban Clo. OL2—1E 49
Durban Rd. BL1—6C 10
Durban Lawn. OL7—4E 91
Durban St. OL8—6A 64
Durban St. OL11—3C 32
Durden M. OL2—1F 49
Durham Av. M31—4G 97
Durham Clo. BL3—3B 40

Durham Clo. M27—1F 71
Durham Clo. SK6—2G 133
Durham Cres. M35—5G 77
Durham Dri. BL0—6D 4
Durham Dri. BL9—5E 29
Durham Dri. OL6—3H 79
Durham Gro. M30—3A 110
Durham Rd. M6—6A 72
Durhams Pas. OL15—4E 9
Durham St. BL1—3B 24
Durham St. M26—2A 42
Durham St. M35—5A 90
Durham St. OL9—5A 64
  (in two parts)
Durham St. OL11—5H 19
Durham St. SK5—5G 103
Durham St. Bri. OL11—6A 20
Durham Wlk. M34—6F 105
Durham Wlk. OL10—3C 30
Durley Av. M8—4D 74
Durley Av. WA15—4B 126
Durling St. M12—6G 87 & 3F 167
Durnford Av. M31—4A 98
Durnford Clo. OL12—1H 17
Durnford St. M24—6H 45
Durnford Wlk. M22—2H 139
Durn St. OL15—3G 9
Durrington Wlk. M10—6C 62
  (off Sawston Wlk.)
Dutton St. M3—2D 86 & 1H 161
Duty St. BL1—2A 24
Duxbury Av. BL2—6A 12
Duxbury Av. BL3—2A 40
Duxbury Dri. BL9—3G 29
Duxbury Sq. M15—2E 101
Duxbury St. BL1—3H 23
Duxford Lodge. M8—1B 74
Duxford Wlk. M10—6C 62
Dyche St. M4—2F 87 & 2C 162
Dye Ho. La. OL16—6A 8
Dye La. SK6—1H 133
Dyers Ct. OL15—3E 9
Dyer St. M5—6A 86 & 3B 164
Dyer St. M11—5C 88
Dymchurch St. M10—1E 89
Dysarts Clo. OL5—6G 67
Dysart St. OL6—3B 92
Dysart St. SK2—6B 132
Dyserth Gro. SK5—4H 119
Dyson Clo. BL4—1F 55
Dyson Gro. OL4—1B 66
Dyson St. BL4—2F 55
Dyson St. OL1—3D 64
Dyson St. OL5—1D 80
Dystelegh Rd. SK12—1H 157

Eades St. M6—2G 85
Eadingall St. M11—5C 88
Eadington St. M8—2C 74
Eafield Av. OL16—4F 21
Eafield Clo. OL16—4F 21
Eafield Gro. OL15—6C 8
Eafield Rd. OL16—2C 20
Eagar St. M10—5C 76
Eagle Dri. M6—8E 73
Eagle Mill Ct. OL3—2G 51
Eagles Nest. M25—6E 59
Eagle St. BL2—6C 24
Eagle St. M4—3E 87 & 3B 162
Eagle St. OL9—2C 64
Eagle Technology Pk. OL11—1G 33
Eagley Brow. BL1—5D 10
Eagley Ct. BL7—4E 11
Eagley Dri. BL8—4G 27
Eagley Way. BL1—4D 10
Ealees. OL15—4G 9
Ealees Rd. OL15—4G 9
Ealing Av. M14—5G 101
Ealing Pl. M19—3C 118
Eames Av. M26—1A 56
Eamont Wlk. M9—4E 75
Earby Gro. M9—6H 61
Earle St. SK7—3G 143
Earlesden Cres. M28—3C 54
Earle St. OL7—3F 91
Earl Rd. BL0—3D 4
Earl Rd. SK4—5E 119

Earl Rd. SK8—2A 152
Earlscliffe Ct. WA14—1D 136
Earlston Av. M34—4A 104
Earl St. BL0—3F 5
Earl St. BL3—2C 38
Earl St. BL9—3D 28
Earl St. M7—1B 86
Earl St. M25—5G 59
Earl St. M34—5E 91
  (Audenshaw)
Earl St. M34—3A 104
  (Denton)
Earl St. OL5—2D 80
Earl St. OL10—3E 31
Earl St. OL11—5C 32
Earl St. SK3—3F 131
Earlswood Wlk. BL3—3B 38
Earlswood Wlk. M18—1E 103
Earl Ter. SK16—4H 91
  (off Astley St.)
Earl Wlk. M12—2B 102
Early Bank. SK15—6G 93
Early Bank Rd. SK16—1F 107
Earney St. WA14—1F 137
Earnshaw Av. OL12—6E 7
Earnshaw Av. SK1—2B 132
Earnshaw St. BL3—4F 37
Earnshaw St. M10—5G 75
Earnshaw St. OL7—6D 78
Earnshaw St. SK14—3F 109
Easby Clo. SK8—1D 152
Easby Clo. SK12—2D 154
Easby Rd. M24—4H 45
Easedale Clo. M31—4B 96
Easedale Rd. BL1—5E 23
Easington Wlk. M10—5A 76
E. Aisle Rd. M17—3C 98
East Av. M19—2B 118
East Av. M25—5C 42
East Av. SK8—4G 141
East Av. SK15—2E 93
  (in two parts)
E. Bank Rd. BL0—6C 4
  (in two parts)
Eastbank St. BL1—3B 24
Eastbourne Gro. BL1—3B 24
Eastbourne St. OL8—5F 65
Eastbourne St. OL11—6H 19
Eastbrook Av. M26—3A 42
Eastburn Av. M10—2G 87 & 1F 163
Eastbury Ct. M7—4F 73
E. Central Dri. M27—4H 71
Eastchurch Clo. BL4—2F 55
Eastcote Av. M11—5G 89
Eastcote Rd. SK5—4H 119
Eastcote Wlk. BL4—6G 39
Eastcourt Wlk. M13—1G 101 & 5E 167
East Cres. M24—2H 61
Eastdale Pl. WA14—4F 125
E. Downs Rd. SK8—2B 142
E. Downs Rd. WA14—3E 137
East Dri. BL9—3F 43
East Dri. M6—6C 72
East Dri. M21—6F 99
East Dri. M27—4H 71
East Dri. SK6—2D 146
Easterdale. OL4—3G 65
Eastern Av. M27—6B 58
Eastern By-Pass. M11—3E 89
  (in two parts)
Eastern Circ. M19—3C 118
Eastfield. M6—1E 85
Eastfield Av. M10—2A 88
Eastfield Av. M24—2A 62
Eastfields. M26—2F 41
Eastford Sq. M40—1G 87
E. Garth Wlk. M9—6G 61
Eastgate. OL12—2G 19
Eastgate St. OL7—4G 91
E. Gate St. OL16—3H 19
E. Grange Av. M11—2E 89
East Gro. M13—2G 101
Eastgrove Av. BL1—5C 10
Eastham Av. BL9—5E 15
Eastham Av. M14—6F 101
Eastham Way. M28—4D 54
Eastham Way. SK9—2H 151
Easthaven Av. M11—2E 89

E. Hill St. OL4 —3E 65
Eastholme Dri. M19—2D 118
Easthope Clo. M20—2F 117
E. Lancashire Rd. M28—5A 68
E. Lancashire Rd. M28 & M27
　　　　　　　　　—3G 69
Eastlands Rd. M9—4F 61
East Lea. M14—4G 105
Eastleigh Av. M7—3A 74
Eastleigh Rd. M10—2H 87 & 1G 163
Eastleigh Gro. BL1 —5A 24
Eastleigh Rd. M25— 6A 60
(in two parts)
Eastleigh Rd. SK8 —4F 141
E. Lynn Dri. M28—6A 56
East Meade. BL3—5A 38
E. Meade. M21—2H 115
E. Meade. M25—1H 73
E. Meade. SE7 5E 7*
East M. BL2—1F 25
Eastmoor Dri. M10—6D 76
Eastmoor Gro. BL3—5F 37
E. Newton St. M4—2G 87 & 2F 163
Eastnor Clo. M15—1B 100 & 6C 164
Easton Clo. M24—3C 62
Easton Dri. SK8—6C 130
Easton Rd. M35—3G 89
E. Ordsall La. M5 & M3—4B 86 & 6C 160
E. Over. SK6—3G 133
Eastpark Clo. M13—1G 101 & 5F 167
E. Philip St. M3—2C 86 & 1F 161
East Rd. M12—4C 102
East Rd. M18—4D 102
East Rd. M22—1A 150
East Rd. M31—1H 97
East Rd. M32—3B 98
East Rd. SK15—5G 81
Eastry Av. SK5—3B 120
East St. BL0—1A 4
East St. BL9—4D 28
East St. M2—5D 86 & 1H 165
East St. M26—4H 41
East St. M34—1F 105
East St. OL6—1B 92
East St. OL12—3A 8
East St. OL15—4G 9
East St. OL16—4D 20
(Firgrove, in two parts)
East St. OL16—3A 20
(Rochdale)
East St. SK3—3F 131
E. Union St. M16—1A 100 & 6B 164
East Vale. SK6—6E 135
E. View. BL0—1E 5
E. View. BL9—6E 5
East View. M24—1H 61
East View. M33—6B 114
Eastville Gdns. M19—4A 118
East Wlk. BL7—1B 10
Eastward Av. SK9—3C 158
East Way. BL1—2D 24
Eastway. M24—6H 45
Eastway. M31—4A 96
Eastway. M33—1H 125
Eastway. OL2—1F 49
Eastwood Av. M10—2F 77
Eastwood Av. M28—6C 54
Eastwood Av. M31—5F 97
Eastwood Av. M35—4G 89
Eastwood Clo. BL9—3F 29
Eastwood Ct. BL9—3F 29
Eastwood Dri. SK3—1F 143
Eastwood Rd. M10—2E 77
Eastwood St. M34—6D 90
Eastwood St. OL15—4F 9
Eastwood Ter. BL1—5D 22
Eastwood View. SK15—4F 93
Eaton Clo. M27—1F 71
Eaton Clo. SK8—2B 142
Eaton Clo. SK12—4G 155
Eaton Ct. WA14—4E 137
Eaton Dri. OL7—1F 91
Eaton Dri. SK9—4F 159
Eaton Dri. WA15—3A 126
Eaton Rd. M8—2B 74
Eaton Rd. M33—5A 114
Eaton Rd. WA14—4E 137
Eaversham St. OL1—1C 64

Eavesford Wlk. M15—1C 100 & 5E 165
Eaves La. OL9—4G 63
Ebbdale Clo. SK1—3A 132
Ebberstone St. M14—5E 101
Ebden St. M1—5F 87 & 1C 166
Ebenezer St. M15—6D 86 & 4H 165
Ebenezer St. OL6—2A 92
Ebnall Wlk. M14—2H 117
Ebor Clo. OL2—5E 35
Ebor Rd. M22—1C 140
Ebor St. OL15—4F 9
Ebsworth St. M10—3A 76
Ebury St. M26—3F 41
Eccles Bri. Rd. SK6—6D 134
Eccles By-Pass. M30—2F 83
Eccles Clo. M11—5E 89
Eccleshall Clo. M15—1E 101 & 5A 166
Eccleshall St. M11 4E 89
(in two parts)
Eccles New Rd. M5—3B 84
Eccles Old Rd. M5—3A 84
Eccles Old Rd. M6—2B 84
Eccles Rd. M27—5F 71
Eccles St. BL0—3D 4
Eccleston Av. BL2—4D 24
Eccleston Av. M14—6F 101
Eccleston Av. M27—4D 70
Eccleston Clo. BL8—4G 27
Eccleston Pl. M7—3H 73
Eccleston Rd. SK3—1F 143
Eccleston St. M35—3G 77
Eccleston Way. SK9—3H 151
Eccups La. M9—1A 158
Echo St. M1—5F 87 & 2C 166
Eckersley Rd. BL1—2A 24
Eckersley St. BL3—3G 37
Eckford St. M8—5D 74
Eclipse Clo. OL16—4C 20
Edale Av. M10—3A 76
Edale Av. M31—6D 96
Edale Av. M34—6D 90
(Audenshaw)
Edale Av. M34 —1F 121
(Denton)
Edale Av. SK5—6A 104
Edale Bank. SK13—5G 109
Edale Clo. M30—6E 95
Edale Clo. SK7—4E 145
Edale Clo. SK8—6H 141
Edale Clo. SK13—5G 109
Edale Clo. WA14—4E 137
Edale Cres. SK13—5G 109
Edale Fold. SK13—5G 109
(off Edale Cres.)
Edale Gro. M33—1G 125
Edale Gro. OL6—5C 80
Edale Rd. BL3—3E 37
Edale Rd. BL4—2E 55
Edale Rd. M32—4B 98
Edale St. M35—4E 77
Eddie Colman Clo. M10—6B 76
Eddie Colman Ct. M6—2G 85
(off Meyrick Rd.)
Eddisbury Av. M20—1D 116
Eddisbury Av. M31—3H 95
Edditch Gro. BL2—6E 25
Eddystone Clo. M5—4G 85
Eden Av. BL0—2A 4
Eden Av. BL1—2A 24
Eden Av. SK6—6C 146
Edenbridge Rd. M10—1D 88
Edenbridge Rd. SK8—1D 142
Eden Clo. M15—1E 101 & 6A 106
Eden Clo. OL10—2D 30
Eden Clo. SK1—3A 132
Eden Clo. SK8—3A 158
Edendale Dri. M22—4B 140
Edenfield Av. M21—5B 116
Edenfield La. M28—6H 69
Edenfield Rd. M25—6A 60
Edenfield Rd. OL11 & OL12—1G 17
Edenfield Rd. OL12—1E 17
Edenfield St. OL12—2E 19
Eden Gro. BL1—2H 23
Edenhall Av. M19—1B 118
Edenham Wlk. M10—1D 76
Edenhurst Dri. WA15—6B 126

Edenhurst Rd. SK2 —5B 132
Eden Lodge. BL1—2A 24
Eden Pl. M33—4B 114
Eden Pl. SK8—5H 129
Edensor Dri. WA15—2C 138
Eden St. BL0—3A 4
Eden St. BL1 —1A 24
Eden St. OL1—2C 64
Eden St. OL12—3F 19
Edenvale. M28—4C 68
Eden Waugh Gdns. OL12 —6D 6
Eden Way. OL2—5E 35
Edgar St. BL0—4D 4
Edgar St. BL3—1A 38
Edgar St. OL16—1C 20
Edgar St. W. BL0—4D 4
Edgedale Av. M19—4A 118
Edgefield Av. M9—5G 61
Edge Fold Rd. M28—2F 69
Edge Hill. SK15—4F 93
Edge Hill Av. OL2—5C 48
Edgehill Chase. SK9—2H 159
Edgehill Ct. M32—5E 99
Edgehill Cres. M27—4D 70
Edge Hill Rd. BL3—4F 37
Edgehill Rd. M6—2C 84
Edge Hill Rd. OL2—4C 48
Edgehill St. M4—3E 87 & 4B 162
Edge La. BL1—1A 22
Edge La. M11 & M35—3F 89
Edge La. M32 & M21—6D 98
Edge La. SK14—3A 108
Edge La. Rd. OL1—1D 64
Edge La. St. OL2—3C 48
Edgeley Fold. SK3—4E 131
Edgeley Rd. M31—1C 112
Edgeley Rd. SK3—4C 130
Edgeley Rd. Trading Est. SK3
　　　　　　　　　—4C 130
Edgemoor. WA14—3C 136
Edgemoor Clo. M26—2E 41
Edgemoor Dri. OL11—6B 18
Edge St. M4—3E 87 & 4B 162
Edge View. OL1—6E 47
Edgeview Wlk. M13—6F 87 & 4D 166
Edgeware Av. M25—5B 60
Edgeware Rd. M30—1C 82
Edgeware Rd. OL9—6E 63
Edgeway. SK9—4E 159
Edgeworth Av. BL2—4D 26
Edgeworth Clo. OL10—3C 30
Edgeworth Dri. M14—2A 118
Edgmont Av. BL3—3H 37
Edgware Rd. M10—1D 88
Edgworth Dri. BL8—4G 27
Edilom Rd. M8—1A 74
Edinburgh. M30—3G 83
(off St Andrews Ct.)
Edinburgh Clo. SK8—5B 130
Edinburgh Dri. SK6—4A 122
Edinburgh Rd. BL3—5A 40
Edinburgh Sq. M10—1H 87
Edinburgh Way. OL11—1D 32
Edison Rd. M30—4E 83
Edison St. M11—6G 89
Edith Av. M14—4E 101
Edith Cavell Clo. M14—4E 89
Edith Cliff Wlk. M10—2F 77
Edith St. BL1—1G 37
Edith St. BL4—2F 55
Edith St. OL8—6D 64
Edleston Gro. SK9—6A 152
Edlin Clo. M12—2A 102
Edlingham. OL11—5G 19
Edlington Wlk. M10—5C 76
Edmonds St. M24—6B 46
Edmonton Rd. M10—1C 88
Edmonton Rd. SK2—1A 144
Edmund Clo. SK4—6G 119
Edmunds Pas. OL15—2E 9
Edmund St. BL1—5B 24
Edmund St. M6—2E 85
Edmund St. M26—3A 42

Edmund St. M35— 4A 90
(Droylsden)
Edmund St. M35— 3F 77
(Failsworth)
Edmund St. OL2—6G 35
Edmund St. OL12—3F 19
Edmund St. OL16—5F 21
Edna St. SK14—6B 106
Edson Rd. M8—6B 60
Edward Av. M6—2C 84
Edward Av. M21—1F 115
Edward Av. OL15—6D 8
Edward Av. SK6—6E 121
Edward Charlton Rd. M16—5G 99
Edward Onyon Ct. M6—2E 85
Edward Rd. M9—4F 61
Edward Rd. OL2—1E 49
Edwards Clo. SK6—6C 134
Edwards Ct. M22—2B 140.
Edward St. BL3—2H 37
Edward St. BL4—5D 38
Edward St. BL9—4D 28
Edward St. M7—1C 86
Edward St. M9—3G 75
Edward St. M24—5A 46
Edward St. M24—4E 59
Edward St. M26—5H 41
(Radcliffe)
Edward St. M26—1B 56
(Stoneclough)
Edward St. M33—5E 115
Edward St. M34—6D 90
(Audenshaw)
Edward St. M34—3F 105
(Denton)
Edward St. M35—5A 90
(Droylsden)
Edward St. M35—4E 77
(Failsworth)
Edward St. OL6—3C 92
Edward St. OL9—2G 63
(Chadderton)
Edward St. OL9—3A 64
(Oldham)
Edward St. OL12—3H 7
Edward St. OL16—3A 20
Edward St. SK1—3H 131
Edward St. SK6—2E 135
Edward St. SK14—1A 106
(in two parts)
Edward St. SK16—1A 106
Edwards Way. SK6—6C 134
Edwin Rd. M11—3A 88
Edwin St. BL9—3C 28
Edwin St. SK1—3B 132
Edzell Wlk. M11—4E 89
Eeasbrook. M31—6F 97
Egbert St. M10—4A 76
Egerton Barn Cottage. BL7—1C 10
Egerton Clo. OL10—4F 31
Egerton Ct. M21—2F 115
Egerton Ct. M28—3A 70
Egerton Ct. SK3—1H 143
Egerton Cres. M20—2F 117
Egerton Cres. OL10—4E 31
Egerton Dri. M33—4B 114
Egerton Dri. WA15—2A 138
Egerton Gro. M28—6F 55
Egerton M. M3—4B 86 & 5D 160
Egerton M. M35—5A 90
Egerton Pk. M28—4B 70
Egerton Pl. OL2—1E 49
Egerton Rd. M14—1H 117
Egerton Rd. M25—2D 58
Egerton Rd. M28—6F 55
Egerton Rd. M30—1F 83
Egerton Rd. SK3—6A 132
Egerton Rd. SK9—6F 151
Egerton Rd. WA15—2A 138
Egerton Rd. N. M16 & M21—5A 100
Egerton Rd. N. SK4—4E 119
Egerton Rd. S. M21—1A 116
Egerton Rd. S. SK4—5E 119
Egerton St. BL4—6E 39
Egerton St. M3—4B 86 & 5D 160
Egerton St. M15—6B 86 & 3D 164
Egerton St. M22—2E 61
Egerton St. M25—5G 59

Egerton St. M26—5G 41
Egerton St. M30—3D 82
Egerton St. M34—2D 104
Egerton St. M35—4B 90
Egerton St. OL1—2D 64
Egerton St. OL5—1E 81
Egerton St. OL6—2A 92
Egerton St. OL10—4E 31
Egerton St. OL15—4G 9
Egerton Ter. M14—2H 117
Egerton Vale. BL7—1B 10
Eggington St. M10—6E 75
Egham Ct. BL2—4D 24
Egham Ho. BL3—5F 37
Egmont St. M6—5C 72
Egmont St. M8—3C 74
Egmont St. OL5—3E 81
Egremont Av. M20—2E 117
Egremont Clo. M25—6E 43
Egremont Ct. M7—3G 73
Egremont Gro. SK3—3D 130
Egremont Rd. OL16—1C 34
Egret Dri. M30—4E 95
Egyptian St. BL1—4B 24
Egypt La. M25—6H 43
Eight Acre. M25—2A 58
Eighth Av. OL8—2B 78
Eighth St. M17—1D 98
Eileen Gro. M14—5G 101
Eileen Gro. W. M14—5F 101
Elaine Av. M9—1B 76
Elbain Wlk. M10—6C 76
Elberton Wlk. M8—4B 74
(off Landfield Dri.)
Elbe St. M12—5G 87 & 2F 167
Elbow La. OL11—5A 20
Elbow St. M9—6C 102
Elbow St. Trading Est. M19
—6D 102
Elbut La. BL9—6D 16
Elcho Ct. WA14—2D 136
Elcho Rd. WA14—2D 136
Elcot Clo. M10—6E 75
Elderberry Wlk. M31—6C 110
Elderburn Dri. M10—5F 75
Elder Clo. SK2—3D 132
Eldercot Gro. BL3—3E 37
Eldercot Rd. BL3—3E 37
Elderfield Dri. SK6—5F 121
Elder Gro. M10—1F 77
Elder Mt. Rd. M9—1F 75
Elder Rd. OL4—3A 66
Elder St. OL16—6B 20
Elder Wlk. M33—3E 113
Elderwood. OL9—2E 63
Eldon Clo. M34—6E 91
Eldon Pl. M30—4E 83
Eldon Precinct. OL8—4C 64
Eldon Rd. M30—5E 95
Eldon Rd. SK3—4E 131
Eldon St. BL2—4D 24
Eldon St. BL9—1D 28
Eldon St. OL8—4D 64
Eldridge Dri. M10—6A 76
Eleanor Rd. M21—1F 115
Eleanor Rd. M22—5C 48
Eleanor St. BL1—6E 11
Eleanor St. OL1—1B 64
Elevator Rd. M17—1E 99
Eleventh St. M17—1C 98
Elf Mill Clo. SK3—5G 131
Elf Mill Ter. SK3—5G 131
Elford Gro. M18—3A 104
Elgar St. M12—3C 102
Elgin Av. M20—6H 117
Elgin Dri. M33—6E 115
Elgin Rd. OL4—3G 65
Elgin Rd. SK16—1A 106
Elgin St. BL1—3G 23
Elgin St. OL7—1G 91
(in two parts)
Elgin St. OL11—6A 20
Elgin St. SK15—4F 93
Elgol Clo. SK3—6H 131
Elgol Ct. OL10—4C 30
Elgol Dri. BL3—1C 36
Elham Wlk. M10—1G 87

Elim St. OL15—2G 9
Eliot Rd. M30—4F 83
Eliot Wlk. M24—4C 46
Elisie St. BL0—5C 4
Eli St. OL9—6G 63
Elitex Ho. M7—1C 86
Eliza Ann St. M10—1G 87
Elizabeth Ann St. M30—4E 83
Elizabethan Way. OL16—5F 21
Elizabeth Av. M34—2E 105
Elizabeth Av. OL2—4A 48
Elizabeth Av. OL9—6G 63
Elizabeth Av. SK1—3H 131
Elizabeth Av. SK12—2H 157
Elizabeth Av. SK15—3E 93
Elizabeth Ct. M14—1H 117
Elizabeth Ct. SK4—1E 131
Elizabeth Gro. OL2—6F 35
Elizabeth Rd. M31—5D 110
Elizabeth Slinger Rd. M20—5D 116
Elizabeth St. BL0—2A 4
Elizabeth St. M8—5B 74
Elizabeth St. M25—5G 59
(Prestwich)
Elizabeth St. M25—2D 58
(Whitefield)
Elizabeth St. M26—4G 41
Elizabeth St. M27—2F 71
Elizabeth St. M34—4D 104
Elizabeth St. OL6—1H 91
Elizabeth St. OL9—1B 64
Elizabeth St. OL10—3E 31
Elizabeth St. OL11—2C 32
Elizabeth St. OL15—5C 8
Elizabeth St. SK14—4B 106
Eliza St. BL0—3F 5
Eliza St. M33—4B 114
Elkstone Av. M28—3C 54
Ellanby Clo. M14—4F 101
Elland Clo. BL9—5F 43
Ellaston Dri. M31—5F 97
Ellastone Rd. M6—1C 84
Ellbourne Rd. M9—6C 60
Ellenbrook Clo. M12—1D 102
Ellenbrook Rd. M22—5B 140
Ellenbrook Rd. M28—3D 68
Ellenbrook St. M12—1D 102
Ellendale Grange. M28—3D 68
Ellen Gro. BL4—4C 56
Ellenhall Clo. M9—3F 75
Ellenroad St. OL16—1E 35
Ellenrod La. OL12—1C 18
Ellens Pl. OL15—6D 8
Ellen St. BL1—2G 23
(in two parts)
Ellen St. M35—5B 90
Ellen St. OL9—1B 64
Ellen St. SK4—6F 119
Ellen Wilkinson Cres. M12—2C 102
Elleray Clo. BL3—4C 40
Elleray Rd. M6—6B 72
Elleray Rd. M24—4H 61
Ellerby Av. M27—6G 57
Ellesmere Av. M28—6E 55
Ellesmere Av. M30—2G 83
Ellesmere Av. OL6—4G 79
Ellesmere Av. SK6—5D 134
Ellesmere Clo. M28—6D 54
Ellesmere Clo. SK16—5C 92
Ellesmere Dri. SK8—6C 130
Ellesmere Pl. M15—1B 100 & 6D 164
Ellesmere Pl. WA14—1F 137
Ellesmere Rd. BL3—4G 37
Ellesmere Rd. M21—6A 100
Ellesmere Rd. M30—1G 83
Ellesmere Rd. SK3—4C 130
Ellesmere Rd. WA14—5F 125
Ellesmere Rd. N. SK4—4E 119
Ellesmere Rd. S. M21—1A 116
Ellesmere St. BL4—1F 55
Ellesmere St. M15—6B 86 & 4C 164
Ellesmere St. M27—2G 71
(Pendlebury)
Ellesmere St. M27—4D 70
(Swinton)
Ellesmere St. M28—6D 54

Ellesmere St. M30—4F 83
(in two parts)
Ellesmere St. M35—3F 77
Ellesmere St. OL11—6H 19
Ellesmere Ter. M14—1F 117
Ellesmere Wlk. BL4—1F 55
Elliot Sq. OL1—1E 65
Elliot St. BL1—2G 23
Elliott Av. SK14—2B 106
Elliott Dri. M33—5G 113
Elliott St. BL4—2E 55
Elliott St. OL4—3A 66
Elliott St. OL12—3A 20
Ellis Cres. M28—6D 54
Ellis Fold. OL12—1A 18
Ellishaw Row. M5—4F 85
Ellisland Wlk. M10—4A 76
Ellis La. M24—6D 44
Ellison Clo. SK14—2F 109
Ellis St. BL3—2H 37
Ellis St. BL8—3H 27
Ellis St. M7—1C 86
Ellis St. SK14—5D 106
Elliston Sq. M12—1C 102
Ellon Wlk. M11—4E 89
Ellor St. M6—2F 85
Ellwood Rd. SK1—2B 132
Elm Av. M26—1F 57
Elmbank Av. M20—5C 116
Elmbank Rd. M24—1C 62
Elm Beds Rd. SK12—5A 156
Elmbridge Wlk. BL3—2H 37
Elmbridge Wlk. M10—5A 76
Elm Clo. M31—6D 110
Elm Clo. SK12—4F 155
Elm Clo. SK14—3C 108
Elm Ct. SK1—3B 132
Elm Cres. M28—4A 70
Elm Cres. SK9—4H 159
Elmdale Av. SK8—3F 141
Elmdale Wlk. M15—6E 87 & 4A 166
Elm Dri. M32—6B 98
Elmfield Av. M22—3C 128
Elmfield Clo. SK9—4H 159
Elmfield Dri. SK6—5C 134
Elmfield Rd. M34—5C 90
Elmfield Rd. SK3—6H 131
Elmfield Rd. SK9—4H 159
Elmfield St. BL1—2B 24
(in three parts)
Elmfield St. M8—5C 74
Elmgate Gro. M19—6C 102
Elm Gro. BL4—1D 54
Elm Gro. BL7—3E 11
Elm Gro. M20—6F 117
Elm Gro. M25—3E 59
Elm Gro. M27—1B 70
Elm Gro. M31—5G 97
Elm Gro. M33—3B 114
Elm Gro. M34—2D 104
Elm Gro. M35—3F 89
Elm Gro. OL4—3D 66
Elm Gro. OL6—6G 79
Elm Gro. OL11—6G 19
(in two parts)
Elm Gro. OL12—4A 8
Elm Gro. OL16—2E 35
Elm Gro. SK9—4H 159
(Alderley Edge)
Elm Gro. SK9—4G 151
(Handforth)
Elm Gro. SK14—5D 106
Elmhurst Dri. M19—4B 118
Elmin Wlk. M15—6C 86 & 4F 165
Elmley Clo. SK2—6G 133
Elmore Wood. OL15—3C 8
Elm Pk. Ga. OL12—6B 6
Elm Pk. Gro. OL12—6B 6
Elm Pk. Vale. OL12—6B 6
Elm Pk. View. OL12—6B 6
Elm Pk. Way. OL12—6B 6
Elmridge Dri. WA15—5C 138
Elm Rd. BL3—5B 40
Elm Rd. BL4—4H 55
Elm Rd. M20—5E 117
Elm Rd. OL8—2B 78
Elm Rd. SK6—6D 146
Elm Rd. SK8—6E 129

Elm Rd. SK15—2H 93
Elm Rd. WA15—2G 137
Elm Rd. S. SK3—4C 130
Elms Clo. M25—5D 42
Elmscott Wlk. M13—2H 101
Elmsdale Av. M9—4F 61
Elmsfield Av. OL11—2A 18
Elmsleigh Rd. SK8—3E 141
Elmsmere Rd. M20—6H 117
Elms Rd. M25—6D 42
Elms Rd. SK4—5D 118
Elms Sq. M25—6C 42
Elms St. M25—6C 42
Elmstead Av. M20—3E 117
Elmsted Clo. SK8—2D 142
Elms, The. OL5—2D 80
Elms, The. OL15—5C 8
Elms, The. SK9—3C 158
Elmstone Gro. BL1—4B 24
Elm St. BL0—2B 4
Elm St. BL0—3F 5
Elm St. BL4—6F 39
Elm St. BL9—3F 29
Elm St. M24—6C 46
Elm St. M27—2E 71
Elm St. M30—4F 83
Elm St. M35—3F 77
Elm St. OL10—3F 31
Elm St. OL12—2H 19
(Rochdale)
Elm St. OL12—3H 7
(Whitworth)
Elm St. OL15—1F 21
Elm St. SK6—5F 121
Elmsway. SK6—1C 156
Elmsway. SK7—6E 143
Elmsway. WA15—5B 138
Elmswood Av. M14—5D 100
Elmsworth Av. M19—6D 102
Elmton Rd. M9—5G 61
Elm Tree Clo. M35—4H 77
Elm Tree Clo. SK15—5E 93
Elm Tree Dri. M22—2B 140
Elmtree Dri. SK4—1D 130
Elm Tree Dri. SK16—6D 92
Elm Tree Rd. SK6—6C 120
Elmwood. M28—6A 70
Elmwood. M33—5E 113
Elmwood Dri. OL2—2A 48
Elmwood Gro. BL1—5G 23
Elmwood Gro. BL4—3E 55
Elmwood Gro. M9—4H 75
Elmwood Lodge. M20—5E 117
Elrick Wlk. M11—4D 88
Elsa Rd. M19—6E 103
Elsdon. OL11—6H 19
Elsdon Dri. M18—1F 103
Elsdon Gdns. BL2—4D 24
Elsdon Rd. M13—5B 102
Elsfield Clo. BL1—3H 23
Elsham Dri. M28—6D 54
Elsham Gdns. M18—3D 102
Elsie St. BL4—1E 55
Elsie St. M9—3G 75
Elsinore Av. M30—6E 95
Elsinore Clo. M35—4H 77
Elsinore Rd. M16—3G 99
Elsinore St. BL2—2D 24
Elsinor Ter. M31—5H 97
Elsma Rd. M10—1G 89
Elsmore Rd. M14—6E 101
Elson Clo. SK14—2B 122
Elson Dri. SK14—2B 122
Elson St. BL8—1H 27
Elstead Wlk. M9—6C 60
Elsted Rd. OL3—4G 67
Elston Wlk. M15—1D 100 & 5H 165
Elstree Av. M10—1D 88
Elstree Gro. SK3—3F 131
Elswick Av. BL3—2F 37
Elswick Av. M21—4B 116
Elswick Av. SK7—6G 143
Elsworth Dri. BL1—1B 24
Elsworth St. M3—2E 87
Elterwater Clo. BL8—1H 27
Eltham Av. SK2—6C 132
Eltham Dri. M31—2E 97
Eltham St. M19—5C 102

Elton Av. BL4—1B 54
Elton Av. M19—1C 118
Elton Bank. SK13—6F 109
(off Brassington Cres.)
Elton Clo. M25—1E 59
Elton Clo. SK9—6A 152
Elton Clo. SK13—6F 109
(off Brassington Cres.)
Elton Dri. SK7—5D 144
Elton Lea. SK13—6F 109
(off Langsett La.)
Elton Pl. SK13—6F 109
(off Brassington Cres.)
Elton Rd. M33—1G 125
Elton Sq. BL8—3A 28
Elton St. BL2—6C 24
Elton St. M7—2B 86 & 1D 160
Elton St. M32—2F 99
Elton St. 0L11—4C 32
Eltons Yd. M7—2B 86 & 1D 160
Elton Vale Rd. BL8—3H 27
Elvate Cres. M8—6B 74
Elverdon Clo. M15—2C 100
Elverston St. M22—2C 128
Elverston Way. 0L9—1A 64
Elvey St. M10—6H 75
Elvington Cres. M28—3E 69
Elvington Wlk. M15—1E 101 & 5A 166
Elvira Clo. M35—4H 77
Elwick Clo. M16—4D 100
Elworth Way. SK9—3H 151
Elwyn Av. M22—4B 128
Ely Av. M32—4H 97
Ely Clo. M28—3D 68
Ely Cres. M35—6F 77
Ely Dri. BL8—1B 28
Ely Gdns. M31—5G 97
Ely Gro. BL1—4A 24
Ely Pas. M4—2G 87 & 2E 163
Elysian St. M11—5E 89
Ely St. 0L9—4H 63
Embankment Footway. SK3
    —4F 131
Embassy Wlk. M18—3F 103
Embden Wlk. M15—2D 100
(in two parts)
Ember St. M11—3F 89
Emblem St. BL3—2H 37
Embleton Wlk. M18—1E 103
Emerald Rd. M22—6D 140
Emerald St. BL1—2B 24
Emerald St. M34—4E 105
Emerson Av. M30—2A 84
Emerson Dri. M24—6H 45
Emerson St. M5—3D 84
Emery Av. M21—3A 116
Emery Clo. SK4—5C 118
Emily Beavan Clo. M11—4D 88
Emily Pl. M35—4H 69
Emley St. M19—6D 102
Emlyn Gro. SK8—5C 130
Emlyn St. BL4—6E 39
Emlyn St. M27—3D 70
Emlyn St. M28—6E 55
Emmanuel Clo. BL3—2H 37
(off Emmanuel Pl.)
Emmanuel Ct. 0L6—1H 91
Emmanuel Pl. BL3—2H 37
Emma St. B8—6D 64
Emma St. 0L12—3G 19
Emmaus Wlk. M6—2F 85
Emmerson St. M27—2F 71
Emmett St. E. M10—6G 75
Emmott St. 0L1—3D 64
Emperor St. SK1—1A 132
Empire Rd. BL2—5F 25
Empire St. M3—1D 86
Empress Av. SK6—6D 134
Empress St. M15—1A 100 & 6B 164
Empress Dri. SK4—5F 119
Empress St. BL1—4F 23
Empress St. M8—3B 74
Empress St. M16—1A 100 & 6A 164
Emsworth Clo. BL2—4D 24
Emsworth Dri. M33—2C 126
Ena St. BL3—4C 38
Ena St. 0L1—6G 49
Enbridge St. M5—5G 85

Encombe Pl. M3—3B 86 & 4C 160
Endcott Clo. M18—1D 102
Enderby Rd. M10—2C 76
Ending Rake. 0L12—5C 6
Endon Rd. M21—1D 116
Endon St. BL1—4F 23
Endsleigh Rd. M20—3G 117
Endsley Av. M28—2E 69
Endsor Clo. M16—4D 100
Energy St. M10—2A 88
Enfield Av. M19—3C 118
Enfield Av. 0L8—6C 64
Enfield Clo. BL1—4A 24
Enfield Clo. BL9—2D 42
Enfield Clo. M30—5F 83
Enfield Clo. 0L11—3A 18
Enfield Dri. M11—3E 89
Enfield Ho. M30—5F 83
Enfield Rd. M27—5E 71
Enfield Rd. M30—1F 83
Enfield St. M28—4F 55
Enfield St. SK14—2C 122
Enford Av. M22—3G 139
Engell Clo. M18—2F 103
Engels Ho. M30—5F 83
(off Trafford Rd.)
Engine Fold Rd. M28—6C 54
Engine St. 0L9—5H 63
Engledene. BL1—5B 10
Englefield Gro. M18—3F 103
Enid Clo. M7—6A 74
Enid St. M7—6A 74
Enmore Wlk. M7—5A 74
Ennerdale Av. BL2—4H 25
Ennerdale Av. M21—5B 116
Ennerdale Av. M27—5F 71
Ennerdale Av. 0L2—6A 34
Ennerdale Clo. BL3—4H 39
Ennerdale Dri. BL9—4E 43
Ennerdale Dri. M33—4G 113
Ennerdale Dri. SK8—2F 141
Ennerdale Dri. WA15—3A 126
Ennerdale Gdns. BL2—4G 25
Ennerdale Gro. BL4—1A 54
Ennerdale Gro. 0L7—6D 78
Ennerdale Rd. M24—5H 45
Ennerdale Rd. M31—6C 110
Ennerdale Rd. M32—4C 98
Ennerdale Rd. 0L11—1B 32
Ennerdale Rd. SK1—4B 132
Ennerdale Rd. SK6—5H 121
Ennerdale Ter. SK15—2E 93
Ennis Clo. M23—6E 127
Ennismore Av. M30—3A 84
Enoch St. M10—6G 75
Enstone Dri. M10—2D 76
Enterprise Ho. M5—6F 85
Enterprise Trading Est. M17
    —5A 84
Enticott Rd. M30—4A 110
Entron Ho. 0L2—6D 34
Entwisle Av. M31—3D 96
Entwisle Rd. 0L16—3A 20
Entwisle Row. BL4—1F 55
Entwisle St. BL4—6F 39
Entwistle St. BL2—5D 24
Entwistle St. M26—5H 41
Entwistle St. M27—2D 70
Entwistle St. 0L16—5E 21
Enver Rd. M8—3D 74
Enville Rd. M6—5C 72
Enville Rd. M10—2B 76
Enville Rd. WA14—2E 137
Enville St. M34—6E 91
Enville St. 0L6—2A 92
Enys Wlk. M6—6E 73
Epping Clo. 0L6—4G 79
Epping Clo. 0L9—1E 63
Epping Dri. M33—4E 113
Epping Rd. M34—5B 104
Epping Wlk. M15—1E 101 & 6A 166
Eppleworth Rise. M27—6G 57
Epsley Clo. M15—1E 101 & 6A 166
Epsom Av. M19—3B 118
Epsom Av. M33—1E 125
Epsom Clo. 0L11—3B 18
Epsom Clo. SK7—3F 145
Epsom M. M7—5H 73

Epsom Wlk. 0L9—2A 64
Epworth Gro. BL3—4G 37
(in two parts)
Equitable St. 0L4—1H 65
Equitable St. 0L11—5A 20
Equitable St. 0L16—6F 21
Erasmus St. M10—2H 87
Era St. BL2—6G 25
Era St. M33—5B 114
Erica Av. 0L4—3B 50
Erica Clo. SK5—1A 120
Erica Dri. M19—5A 118
Eric Brook Clo. M14—4E 101
Eric St. M5—4F 85
Eric St. 0L4—2G 65
Eric St. 0L15—3E 9
Erindale Wlk. M10—5F 75
Erin St. M11—6G 89
Erith Clo. SK5—3B 120
Erith Rd. 0L4—3G 65
Eriesmere Av. M34—3G 105
Erley Rd. M27—4A 72
Erlington Av. M16—4H 99
Erman's Bldgs. M27—1F 71
Ermen Rd. M30—5E 83
Ermington Dri. M8—5E 74
Erneley Clo. M12—4D 102
Ernest St. BL1—1H 37
(in two parts)
Ernest St. M25—5D 58
Ernest St. SK2—5D 132
Ernest St. SK8—5G 129
Ernest Ter. 0L12—2B 20
Enlouen Av. BL1—5E 23
Ernocroft Gro. M18—1G 103
Ernocroft La. SK6—5H 123
Ernocroft Rd. SK6—1F 135
Errington Clo. SK2—5D 132
Errington Clo. BL3—2D 36
Errington Dri. M7—1B 86
Errol Av. M9—4C 60
Errol Av. M22—1A 140
Errwood Cres. M19—1C 118
Errwood Rd. M19—4B 118
Erskine Clo. BL3—2C 36
Erskine Rd. M31—6D 110
Erskine St. M15—1B 100 & 6D 164
Erskine St. SK6—6F 123
Erwin St. M10—5B 76
Eryngo St. SK1—2H 131
Escott Wlk. M16—3D 100
Esher Dri. M33—2C 126
Esk Clo. M31—3C 96
Eskdale. SK8—1G 141
Eskdale Av. BL2—3H 25
Eskdale Av. M20—2E 117
Eskdale Av. 0L2—6B 34
Eskdale Av. 0L3—4F 53
Eskdale Av. 0L8—5B 64
Eskdale Av. 0L11—2B 32
Eskdale Av. SK6—4H 121
Eskdale Av. SK7—2E 153
Eskdale Clo. BL9—4E 43
Eskdale Dri. M24—4H 45
Eskdale Dri. WA15—4C 126
Eskdale Gro. BL4—1B 54
Eskdale M. 0L3—4F 53
Eskdale Ter. SK15—1E 93
Eskrick St. BL1—4H 23
Esmond Rd. M8—4C 74
Esmont Dri. M24—4G 45
Esplanade, The. 0L16—4G 19
Essex Av. BL9—4A 30
Essex Av. M20—5F 117
Essex Av. M35—2A 90
Essex Clo. M35—6F 77
Essex Clo. 0L2—6D 34
Essex Dri. BL9—5D 28
Essex Gdns. M30—5A 110
Essex Pl. M27—1F 71
Essex Rd. M18—3H 103
Essex Rd. M31—1G 97
Essex Rd. SK5—5C 120
Essex St. M2—4D 86 & 5H 161
Essex St. 0L11—5H 19
Essex Wlk. M15—2B 100

Essex Way. M15—2B 100
Essingdon St. BL3—3H 37
(in two parts)
Essington Wlk. M34—6E 105
Estate St. 0L8—5D 64
Estate St. 0L8—5D 64
Esther St. 0L4—2H 65
Esther St. 0L15—4D 8
Eston St. M13—2H 101
Eswick St. M11—4E 89
Etchells Rd. SK8—4H 141
Etchells St. M35—5C 76
Etchells St. SK1—2H 131
Ethel Av. M9—4F 61
Ethel Av. M27—3F 71
Ethel Ct. 0L16—5B 20
Ethel St. BL3—1H 37
Ethel St. 0L8—6D 64
Ethel St. 0L12—3H 7
Ethel St. 0L16—5B 20
Ethel Ter. M19—6C 102
Etherlow Way. SK14—2G 109
Etherly Clo. M30—5E 95
Etherow Av. SK6—1C 134
Etherow Gro. M10—1F 77
Etherstone St. M8—2B 75
Eton Av. 0L8—6C 64
Eton Clo. M16—2B 100
Eton Clo. 0L11—5D 18
Eton Ct. M16—2B 100
Eton Hill Rd. M26—3A 42
Eton Way N. M26—2A 42
Eton Way S. M26—2A 42
Etropway. M22—2B 140
Etruria Clo. M13—2H 101
Ettington Clo. BL8—2G 27
Ettrick Clo. M11—5F 89
Euclid Clo. M11—4A 88
Europa Trading Est. M26—2B 56
Europa Way. M26—2A 56
Eustace St. BL3—4C 38
Eustace St. 0L9—6H 47
Euston Av. M9—6A 62
Euxton Clo. BL8—4G 27
Evans Rd. M30—4C 82
Evans St. M3—2C 86 & 2F 161
Evans St. M7—1C 86
Evans St. M24—1B 62
Evans St. 0L1—1D 64
Evans St. 0L6—1B 92
Evan St. M10—6G 75
Evanton Wlk. M9—4G 75
(off Nethervale Dri.)
Eva Rd. SK3—4C 130
Eva St. M14—4G 101
Eva St. 0L12—1A 20
Evelyn St. M14—1H 117
Evelyn St. 0L1—6F 49
Evening St. M35—3F 77
Evenley Clo. M11—6F 89
Everard Clo. M28—3E 69
Everard St. M5—6A 86 & 3B 164
Everdingen Wlk. 0L1—4H 49
Everest Av. 0L7—6F 79
Everest Clo. SK14—3E 107
Everest Rd. SK14—3E 107
Everest St. 0L11—3G 33
Everett Ct. M20—3F 117
Everett Rd. M20—3E 117
Everglade. 0L8—2E 79
Evergreen Wlk. M33—3E 113
Everitt St. BL1—3A 24
Everleigh Clo. BL2—6A 12
Everleigh Dri. M8—5B 74
Eversden Ct. M7—1C 86
Eversley Ct. M33—1B 126
Eversley Rd. M20—6E 117
Everton Rd. 0L8—5B 64
Everton Rd. SK5—5H 103
Everton St. M27—3E 71
Every St. BL0—3F 5
Every St. BL9—1D 28
Every St. M4—4H 87 & 6G 163
Evesham Av. M23—4D 126
Evesham Av. SK4—6D 118
Evesham Clo. BL3—1H 37
Evesham Clo. M24—4B 62

Evesham Dri. BL4—5D 38
Evesham Gro. M33—5E 115
Evesham Gro. OL6—4G 79
Evesham Rd. M9—1A 76
Evesham Rd. M24—4A 62
Evesham Rd. SK8—6C 130
Evesham Wlk. BL3—2H 37
Evesham Wlk. M24—4B 62
Evesham Wlk. OL8—4C 64
Eveside Clo. SK8—1D 142
Eve St. OL8—1D 78
Evington Av. M11—6A 90
Ewan St. M18—1F 103
Ewart Av. M5—4G 85
Ewart St. BL1—3A 24
Ewhurst Av. M27—5D 70
Ewing Clo. M8—2C 74
Ewood. OL8—3E 79
Ewood Dri. BL8—5G 27
Exbourne Rd. M22—4A 140
Exbridge Wlk. M10—1F 89
Exbury. OL12—3G 19
  (off Spotland Rd.)
Exbury St. M14—2H 117
Exchange St. BL0—2A 4
Exchange St. BL1—6B 24
Exchange St. M2—4D 86
Exchange St. OL4—2F 65
Exchange St. SK3—2G 131
Exeter Av. BL3—2D 24
Exeter Av. BL4—6B 38
Exeter Av. M26—2D 40
Exeter Av. M30—1A 84
Exeter Av. M34—6F 105
Exeter Clo. M12—1A 102
Exeter Clo. SK8—5B 142
Exeter Ct. M24—6H 45
Exeter Dri. M30—5F 95
Exeter Dri. OL6—4H 79
Exeter Rd. M31—3F 97
Exeter Rd. SK5—4C 120
Exeter St. OL11—6A 20
Exeter Wlk. SK7—6H 143
Exford. OL11—1E 33
Exford Clo. M10—2H 87 & 1G 163
Exford Clo. SK5—3H 119
Exford Dri. BL2—1A 40
Exford Wlk. M10—2H 87 & 2G 163
Exhall Clo. M28—3C 54
Exit Rd. E. M22—6H 139
Exit Rd. W. M22—6H 139
Exmoor Clo. OL6—4G 79
Exmoor Wlk. M23—2G 139
Exmouth Av. SK5—4C 120
Exmouth Pl. OL16—1H 33
Exmouth Rd. M33—4F 113
Exmouth Sq. OL16—2G 33
Exmouth St. OL16—1H 33
Exmouth Wlk. M16—4D 100
Express Trading Est. BL4—3F 55
Exton Wlk. M16—3C 100
Eyam Clo. SK13—5F 109
  (off Eyam La.)
Eyam Fold. SK13—5G 109
  (off Langsett La.)
Eyam Gdns. SK13—5G 109
  (off Eyam M.)
Eyam Grn. SK13—5F 109
  (off Eyam La.)
Eyam Gro. SK2—6D 132
Eyam La. SK13—5F 109
  (off Eyam La.)
Eyam La. SK13—5F 109
Eyam M. SK13—5G 109
Eyam Rd. SK7—5E 145
Eyebrook Rd. WA14—3C 136
Eynford Av. SK5—3B 120

Faber St. M4—2E 87 & 1B 162
Factory Brow. M24—2E 61
Factory La. M3—4B 86 & 5C 160
Factory La. M9—2E 75
Factory La. SK12—6H 147
Factory St. BL0—2E 5
Factory St. M24—1H 61

Factory St. M26—4H 41
Failsworth Rd. M35—4H 77
Faircres. BL2—2G 25
Faircres Rd. SK6—5C 146
Fairbairn St. M11—3B 88
Fairbank Av. M14—3F 101
Fairbank Dri. M24—5F 45
Fairbottom Clo. OL1—2D 64
Fairbottom Wlk. M35—5A 90
Fairbourne Clo. SK9—5C 158
Fairbourne Dri. SK9—5C 158
Fairbourne Dri. WA15—2B 126
Fairbourne Rd. M19—6E 103
Fairbourne Rd. M34—5E 105
Fairbrother St. M5—6A 86 & 4A 164
Fairclough St. BL3—3B 38
Fairclough St. M11—3C 88
Fairfax Av. M20—5F 117
Fairfax Av. WA15—5A 128
Fairfax Clo. SK6—4B 134
Fairfax Dri. OL15—6D 8
Fairfax Dri. SK9—5C 158
Fairfax Rd. M25—4E 59
Fairfield Av. M35—5A 90
Fairfield Av. SK6—5G 121
Fairfield Av. SK8—3B 142
Fairfield Ct. M13—3H 101
Fairfield Ct. M35—5A 90
Fairfield Dri. BL9—1H 29
Fairfield Rd. BL4—2E 55
Fairfield Rd. M11—6G 89
Fairfield Rd. M24—6G 45
Fairfield Rd. M30—4A 110
Fairfield Rd. M35—5G 89
Fairfield Rd. WA15—6C 126
Fairfields. BL7—3D 10
Fairfield Sq. M35—5A 90
Fairfield St. M1 & M12—5F 87 & 1D 166
Fairfield St. M6—6B 72
Fairfield View. M34—6A 90
Fairford Clo. SK5—4H 119
Fairford Dri. BL3—2A 38
Fairford Way. SK5—4H 119
Fairford Way. SK9—2G 159
Fairham Wlk. M4—4H 87 & 6H 163
Fairhaven Av. M21—1H 115
Fairhaven Av. M25—2B 58
Fairhaven Clo. M25—2B 58
Fairhaven Clo. SK7—5H 143
Fairhaven Rd. BL1—2B 24
Fairhaven St. M12—1B 102
Fairhills Rd. M30—1D 110
Fairholme Av. M31—6E 97
Fairholme Rd. M20—3G 117
Fairholme Rd. SK4—6E 119
Fairhope Av. M6—1B 84
Fairhurst Dri. M28—1B 68
Fairisle Clo. M11—4B 88
Fairland Pl. BL3—2D 36
Fairlands Pl. OL11—3H 33
Fairlands Rd. BL9—4F 15
Fairlands Rd. M33—1H 125
Fairlands St. OL11—3H 33
Fairlands View. OL11—3H 33
Fairlawn. SK4—6F 119
Fairlawn Clo. M14—3E 101
Fairlea. M34—5G 105
Fairlea Av. M20—1G 129
Fairlee Av. M34—4C 90
Fairleigh Av. M6—2C 84
Fairless Rd. M30—4F 83
Fairlie Av. BL3—2D 36
Fairlie Dri. WA15—3B 126
Fairman Clo. M16—4D 100
Fairmead Rd. M23—2A 128
Fairmile Dri. M20—3G 129
Fairmount Av. BL2—5G 25
Fairmount Rd. M27—5B 70
Fairoak Ct. BL3—2H 37
Fair Oak Rd. M19—4B 118
Fairstead Wlk. M11—6H 89
Fair St. BL3—5G 37
Fair St. M1—4G 87 & 6E 163
Fair St. M27—2G 71
Fairthorne Gro. OL7—4F 91
Fair View. OL15—2G 9

Fairview Av. M19—5B 102
Fairview Av. M34—6A 104
Fairview Clo. OL12—1E 63
Fairview Clo. OL12—1G 17
Fairview Clo. SK6—4D 134
Fairview Dri. SK6—4D 134
Fairview Rd. M34—5A 104
Fairview Rd. WA15—6C 126
Fairway. M25—1H 73
Fairway. M27—4A 72
Fairway. M35—5A 90
Fair Way. OL11—4B 32
Fairway. OL12—2C 6
Fairway. OL16—5G 21
Fairway. SK7—1F 153
Fairway. SK8—1E 141
Fairway Av. BL2—1A 26
Fairway Av. M23—4D 126
Fairway Cres. OL12—1B 48
Fairway Dri. M33—1G 125
Fairway Rd. BL9—4D 42
Fairway Rd. OL4—5A 66
Fairway, The. M10—4C 76
Fairway, The. SK2—4D 132
Fairwood Rd. M23—4D 126
Fairy La. M8—6A 74
Fairy La. M33—5F 115
Fairy St. BL8—3A 28
Fairywell Clo. SK9—6A 152
Fairywell Dri. M23—4D 126
Fairywell Dri. M33—2A 126
Fairywell Rd. WA15—3B 126
Faith St. BL1—4E 23
Falcon Av. M31—5G 97
Falcon Clo. BL9—1E 29
Falcon Clo. M5—4C 84
Falcon Clo. OL12—1H 17
Falcon Ct. M15—2C 100
Falcon Cres. M27—1H 71
Falcon Dri. M28—4C 54
Falcon Dri. M30—3F 95
Falcon Dri. OL9—1A 64
Falcon St. BL1—5B 24
Falcon St. OL4—6C 64
Falconwood Chase. M28—5D 68
Falfield Dri. M8—6D 74
Falinge Fold. OL12—2F 19
Falinge Rd. OL12—2F 19
Falkirk. OL11—1F 33
Falkirk Dri. BL2—1H 39
Falkirk St. OL4—2G 65
Falkirk Wlk. M23—3G 139
Falkland Av. M10—1A 88
Falkland Av. OL11—3E 19
Falkland Clo. OL4—5A 50
Falkland Rd. BL2—6A 26
Fall Bank. SK4—2E 119
Fallons Rd. M28—2C 70
Fallow Wlk. M15—1C 100 & 6E 165
Fallowfield. SK5—4A 104
Fallowfield Dri. OL12—1F 19
Fallow Fields Dri. SK5—4A 104
Fallows, The. OL9—4G 63
Falls Gro. SK8—2E 141
Falmer Clo. BL8—4C 14
Falmer Dri. M18—1H 103
Falmer Dri. M22—4B 140
Falmouth Av. M31—4A 96
Falmouth Av. M33—4F 113
Falmouth Cres. SK5—4C 120
Falmouth Rd. M30—5F 95
Falmouth St. M10—2B 88
Falmouth St. OL8—5D 64
Falmouth St. OL11—6A 20
Falsgrave Clo. M10—6A 76
Falshaw Dri. BL9—2E 15
Falside Wlk. M10—6C 76
Falston Av. M10—1D 76
Falstone Av. BL0—5E 5
Falterley Rd. M23—3E 127
Fancroft Rd. M22—4A 128
Fane Wlk. M9—6D 60
Faraday Av. M8—5C 74
Faraday Av. M27—1B 72
Faraday Dri. BL1—4A 24

Faraday Ho. BL1—4A 24
  (off Faraday Dri.)
Faraday St. M1—3F 87 & 4C 162
Farcroft Av. M26—1A 42
Farcroft Clo. M23—3F 127
Far Cromwell Rd. SK6—3D 120
Fardale. OL2—1F 49
Farden Dri. M23—3D 126
Fareham Ct. M16—2B 100
Farewell Clo. OL11—3C 32
Fargner St. M11—4F 89
Far Hey Clo. M26—4E 41
Farholme. OL2—5A 48
Faringdon. OL11—5G 19
Faringdon Wlk. BL3—2A 38
Farington Av. M20—2E 117
Farlands Dri. M20—4F 129
Far La. M18—3F 103
Farley Av. M18—3A 104
Farley Ct. SK8—2B 142
Farley Rd. M33—1C 126
Farley Way. SK5—6G 103
Farman St. BL3—4H 37
Farm Av. M32—3A 98
Farm Clo. SK4—3E 119
Farmers Clo. M33—6G 115
Farmer St. SK4—6F 119
Farmfield. M33—3G 113
Farmfold. SK9—3D 150
Farm La. M25—1A 60
Farm La. M28—6H 69
Farm La. SK14—1B 122
Farm Rd. OL8—3A 78
Farmside Av. M30—4E 95
Farmside Pl. M19—6C 102
Farmstead Clo. M35—4A 78
Farm St. M35—5D 76
Farm St. OL1—6H 47
Farm St. OL10—5G 31
Farm Wlk. OL15—4D 8
Farm Wlk. OL16—2C 20
Farm Wlk. WA14—3A 136
Farmway. M24—2H 61
Farm Yd. M19—6C 102
Farnborough Rd. BL1—5C 10
Farnborough Rd. M10—2H 87 & 1G 163
Farncombe Clo. M23—4D 126
Farndale Sq. M28—6E 55
Farndale Wlk. M9—3G 75
  (off Up. Conran St.)
Farndon Av. SK7—1F 145
Farndon Clo. M33—6E 115
Farndon Dri. WA15—5A 126
Farndon Rd. SK5—5G 103
Farnham Av. M9—4F 61
Farnham Clo. BL1—4A 24
Farnham Clo. SK8—6C 142
Farnham Dri. M30—6E 95
Farnhill Wlk. M23—2E 127
Farnley Clo. OL12—1B 18
Farnsworth Av. OL7—6F 79
Farnsworth Clo. OL7—6F 79
Farnsworth St. M11—6F 89
Farnworth Dri. M14—5G 101
Farnworth & Kearsley By-Pass.
  BL4—5F 39
Farnworth St. BL3—3G 37
Farnworth St. OL10—3E 31
Farrand Rd. OL8—1H 77
Farrant Rd. M12—3C 102
Farrar Rd. M35—5H 89
Farrell St. M7—2C 86 & 1E 161
Farrer Rd. M13—4B 102
Far Ridings. SK6—6B 122
Farriers La. OL11—1B 32
Farringdon Dri. M26—2E 41
Farringdon St. M6—2E 85
Farrowdale Av. OL2—1F 49
Farrow St. OL2—1F 49
  (in two parts)
Farrow St. E. OL2—1F 49
  (off Market St.)
Farr St. SK3—3F 131
Farwood Dri. M16—2A 100
Fastnet St. M11—5C 88
Fatherford Clo. OL3—2D 52
Faulkenhurst M. OL1—6A 48
Faulkenhurst St. OL1—6A 48

Faulkner Dri. WA15—1A 138
Faulkner Rd. M32—5E 99
Faulkner St. BL3—2A 38
Faulkner St. OL16—4H 19
Faulkner St. M1—5E 87 & 1A 166
Faversham Brow. OL1—1C 64
Faversham St. M40—4B 76
Fawborough Rd. M23—2F 127
Fawcett St. BL2—6D 24
Fawley Av. SK14—6B 106
Fawley Gro. M22—1A 140
Fawns Keep. SK9—2G 159
Fawns Keep. SK15—1A 108
Fay Av. M9—6B 62
Faywood Dri. SK6—5E 135
Fearney Side. BL3—4H 39
Fearnhead Clo. BL4—1G 55
Fearnhead St. BL3—3G 37
Fearn St. OL10—3E 31
Featherstall Rd. OL15—4D 8
Featherstall Rd. N. OL9 & OL1
—2B 64
Featherstall Rd. S. OL9—3A 64
Featherstone Sq. OL15—4E 9
February St. M13—2G 101
Federation St. M4—3E 87 & 3A 162
Federation St. M25—4D 58
Feldom Rd. M23—1F 127
Fellbrigg Clo. M18—4E 103
Felling Clo. M14—3F 101
Felling Wlk. M14—3F 101
(off Felling Clo.)
Fellpark Rd. M23—1G 127
Fells Gro. M28—2H 69
Fellside. BL2—2A 26
Fellside. OL1—2C 64
Fell St. BL8—3A 28
Felltop Dri. SK5—1A 120
Fell Wlk. BL9—1C 42
Felside Clo. BL8—2H 13
Felskirk Rd. M22—5A 140
Felsted. BL1—5C 22
Felt Ct. M34—5C 104
Feltham St. M12—1C 102
Felthorpe Dri. M8—5B 74
Felton Av. M22—2B 140
Felton Clo. BL9—2E 43
Felton Wlk. BL1—3A 24
Fencegate Av. SK4—4F 119
Fence St. SK2—1D 144
Fenchurch Av. M10—1E 89
Fencot Dri. M12—3C 102
Fenella St. M13—3A 102
Fenham Clo. M10—6E 75
Fenmore Av. M18—4D 102
Fennel St. M4—3D 86 & 3H 161
Fenners Clo. BL3—4H 37
Fenney St. M7—6H 73
Fenside Rd. M22—6C 128
Fensom Clo. M11—5B 88
Fenstock Wlk. M10—1F 89
Fentewan Wlk. SK14—4A 108
Fenton Av. SK7—1C 144
Fenton M. OL11—6G 19
Fenton St. BL8—2A 28
Fenton St. M12—2C 102
Fenton St. OL2—2F 49
Fenton St. OL4—3F 65
Fenton St. OL11—6G 19
Fenwick Clo. M15—1E 101 & 6A 166
Fenwick Dri. SK4—6A 118
Fenwick St. OL12—4G 19
Ferdinand St. M10—1H 87
Fereday St. M28—5F 55
Ferguson Ct. M19—1B 118
Fernacre. M33—4C 114
Fernaley St. SK14—4C 106
Fern Av. M31—5C 96
Fernbank. M26—1G 57
Fern Bank. SK15—5G 93
Fern Bank Clo. SK15—5G 93
Fern Bank Dri. M23—3E 127
Fern Bank St. M34—3F 105
Fern Bank St. SK14—1C 122
Fernbray Av. M19—5H 119
Fernbrook Clo. M13—2H 101

Fernbrook Wlk. M8—4B 74
(off Hillbrow Wlk.)
Fern Clo. M24—1D 62
Fern Clo. OL4—3B 66
Fernclose. M41—4H 159
Fern Clough. BL1—6D 22
Fernclough Rd. M9—4F 75
Fern Cres. SK15—4G 93
Ferndale Av. M25—2A 58
Ferndale Av. OL16—5A 34
Ferndale Av. SK2—1B 144
Ferndale Clo. OL4—5H 65
Ferndale Gdns. M19—3A 118
Ferndale Rd. M33—1B 126
Ferndene Rd. M20—4F 117
Ferndene Rd. M25—2G 59
Ferndown Av. OL9—2D 62
Ferndown Av. SK7—4C 144
Ferndown Rd. BL2—2G 25
Ferndown Rd. M23—3D 126
Ferney Field Rd. OL9—2F 63
Ferngate Dri. M20—3F 117
Ferngrove E. BL9—6H 15
Ferngrove W. BL9—1F 29
Fernham Gro. M7—4F 73
Fernhill. SK6—5F 135
Fernhill Av. BL3—3E 37
Fernhill Dri. M18—3D 102
Fern Hill La. OL12—6A 6
Fernhills. BL7—1C 10
Fernhill St. BL9—2D 28
Fernhurst Gro. BL1—4A 24
Fernhurst Rd. M20—4G 117
Fernhurst St. OL1—6A 48
Fernie St. M4—2E 87 & 1A 162
Fern Isle Clo. OL12—3B 6
Fern Lea. SK8—4F 141
Fernlea. WA15—4H 137
Fernlea Av. OL1—6A 48
Fernlea Clo. SK14—3G 109
Fernlea Cres. M27—4E 71
Fernleaf St. M14—3E 101
Fern Lea Gro. M28—5B 54
Fernleigh Av. M19—6E 103
Fernleigh Dri. M16—2A 100
Fernley Av. M34—5G 105
Fernley Rd. SK2—5B 132
Ferns Gro. BL1—6F 23
Fernside. M26—2C 56
Fernside Av. M20—4H 117
Fernside Gro. M28—5G 55
Fernstead. BL3—1G 37
Ferns, The. SK5—6H 119
Fern St. BL0—3F 5
(in two parts)
Fern St. BL3—1G 37
Fern St. BL4—6G 39
Fern St. BL9—2D 28
Fern St. M8—1E 87
Fern St. OL8—4B 64
Fern St. OL9—1G 63
Fern St. OL11—5G 19
Fern St. OL12—3A 8
Fern St. SK14—2E 107
Fernthorpe Av. OL3—6C 52
Fern View. WA15—6E 127
Fernwood. SK6—4F 135
Fernwood Av. M18—4F 103
Ferrand Rd. OL15—2F 9
Ferring Wlk. OL9—3H 63
Ferris St. M11—5F 89
Ferryhill Rd. M30—5E 95
Ferry Rd. M30—5E 95
(in two parts)
Ferry St. M11—5A 88
Fetter La. M1—4E 87 & 6B 162
Fettler Clo. M27—5E 71
Fiddlers La. M30—4F 95
Field Bank Gro. M19—6D 102
Field Clo. SK6—6B 134
Field Clo. SK7—3F 153
Field Cres. SK14—1F 109
Fieldcroft. OL11—4D 18
Fielden Av. M21—6H 99
Fielden Rd. M20—4D 116
Fielden St. OL15—1E 21

Fieldfare Av. M10—1D 88
Fieldhead. SK9—1H 159
Fieldhead Av. BL8—3G 27
Fieldhead Av. OL11—4D 18
Fieldhead M. SK9—1H 159
Fieldhead Wlk. M15—1C 100 & 5E 165
Fieldhouse La. SK6—5E 135
Fieldhouse Rd. OL12—1H 19
Fielding Av. SK12—5E 155
Fielding St. M24—5A 46
Fielding St. M30—4E 83
Field La. OL6—6H 79
Field Pl. M20—6F 117
Field Rd. M33—3G 113
Field Rd. OL16—4D 20
Fields Ct. SK14—6G 107
Fields Farm Clo. SK14—6H 107
Fields Farm Rd. SK14—6G 107
Fields Farm Wlk. SK14—6H 107
Fields New Rd. OL9—5G 63
Fields, The. SK6—2G 133
Field St. M6—3F 85
Field St. M18—1G 103
Field St. M35—5H 89
(Droylsden)
Field St. M35—4E 77
(Failsworth)
Field St. SK6—6F 121
Field St. SK14—2B 106
Fieldsway. OL8—1C 78
Field Vale Dri. SK5—6A 104
Fieldvale Rd. M33—2G 125
Field View Wlk. M16—6D 100
Field Wlk. M31—6C 110
Field Wlk. WA15—2B 138
Fieldway. OL16—2H 33
Fife Av. OL9—5F 63
Fifth Av. BL1—6F 23
Fifth Av. BL3—3H 39
Fifth Av. BL9—1H 29
Fifth Av. M11—3E 89
Fifth Av. OL8—1A 78
Fifth Av. BL1—1D 22
Fifth St. M17—2D 98
Filbert St. OL1—6G 49
Filby Wlk. M10—1A 88
Fildes St. M24—2D 62
Fildes St. M35—2G 77
Filey Av. M16—5B 100
Filey Av. M31—3C 96
Filey Dri. M6—5B 72
Filey Rd. M14—1H 117
Filey Rd. SK2—4C 132
Filey St. OL16—6A 8
Filtcroft St. OL4—5G 65
Filton Av. BL3—2H 37
Filton Wlk. M9—4E 75
(off Westmere Dri.)
Finance St. OL15—4C 8
Finborough Clo. M16—3C 100
Finch Av. BL4—2B 54
Finchcroft. OL1—2C 64
Finchdale Dri. WA15—4B 138
Finchley Av. M10—1E 89
Finchley Gro. M10—2A 76
Finchley Rd. M14—1F 117
Finchley Rd. WA15—2G 137
Findlay Vs. M9—4F 75
Findon Rd. M23—5G 127
Finger Post. BL3—3A 40
Finghall Rd. M31—5D 96
Finishing Wlk. M4—4G 87 & 5F 163
Finland Rd. SK3—4F 131
Finlan Rd. M24—2D 46
Finlay St. BL4—1F 55
Finney Bank Rd. M33—3A 114
Finney Clo. SK9—5G 151
Finney Dri. M21—2G 115
Finney St. SK9—5G 151
Finney Ho. M6—2F 85
(off Sutton Dwellings)
Finney La. SK8—5E 141
Finney St. BL3—3B 38
Finningley Rd. M9—3D 60
Finsbury Av. M10—1E 89
Finsbury Clo. OL8—5F 65
Finsbury Rd. SK5—1G 119
Finsbury St. OL11—6F 19

Finstock Clo. M30—4D 82
Fintry Gro. M30—4F 83
Fir Av. SK7—5G 143
Firbank Rd. M23—6G 127
Fir Bank Rd. OL2—1B 48
Firbeck Dri. M4—3H 87 & 3G 163
Fir Clo. SK12—4E 155
Fircroft St. SK3—1H 143
Fircroft Rd. OL8—1E 79
Firdale Av. M10—2E 77
Firdale Wlk. OL9—2A 64
Firdon Wlk. M9—4G 75
(off Nethervale Dri.)
Firecrest Clo. M28—3D 68
Fire Sta. Sq. M5—3H 85 & 4A 160
Fire Sta. Yd. OL11—5H 19
Firethorn Av. M19—3B 118
Firethorn Wlk. M33—4E 113
(in two parts)
Fir Gro. M19—6C 102
Fir Gro. OL9—1H 63
Firgrove Av. OL16—3D 20
Firgrove Gdns. OL16—3D 20
Fir La. OL2—1B 48
Fir Rd. BL4—1D 54
Fir Rd. M27—5E 71
Fir Rd. M34—4G 105
Fir Rd. SK6—6C 134
Fir Rd. SK7—4G 143
Firs Av. M16—4H 99
Firs Av. M35—4E 77
Firs Av. OL6—6F 79
Firsby Av. SK6—5F 121
Firsby St. M19—6C 102
Firs Gro. SK8—1E 141
Firs Rd. M33—5E 113
(in three parts)
Firs Rd. SK8—2E 141
First Av. BL3—3A 40
First Av. BL8—5H 13
First Av. M11—3F 89
First Av. M17—2D 98
First Av. M27—6D 70
First Av. OL8—1B 78
First Av. SK10—6D 154
First Av. SK15—6G 81
Firs, The. SK9—4D 158
Firs, The. WA14—2D 136
Fir St. BL0—2F 5
Fir St. BL1—3B 24
Fir St. BL3—3F 39
Fir St. M6—3F 85
Fir St. M10—1H 87
Fir St. M16—3A 100
Fir St. M26—5H 41
Fir St. M30—3A 110
(Cadishead)
Fir St. M30—4F 83
(Eccles)
Fir St. M35—4E 77
Fir St. OL2—1B 48
Fir St. OL10—4G 31
Fir St. SK4—1G 131
First St. BL1—1D 22
Firs Way. M33—6E 113
Firswood Dri. M27—5E 71
Firswood Dri. OL2—1H 47
Firswood Mt. SK8—1E 141
Firth Clo. M7—5H 73
Firth Rd. M20—6F 117
Firth St. OL1—3D 64
Fir Tree Av. M28—6D 68
Firtree Av. M33—5E 113
Fir Tree Av. OL8—1D 78
Fir Tree Clo. SK16—5D 92
Fir Tree Cres. SK16—5D 92
Fir Tree La. SK14—2C 106
Fir Tree La. SK16—6D 92
Firvale Av. SK8—4F 141
Firwood Av. BL4—2E 55
Firwood Av. M31—5A 98
(in two parts)
Firwood Clo. SK2—3C 132
Firwood Ct. M30—2G 83
Firwood Cres. M26—6H 41
Firwood Fold. BL2—2E 25
Firwood Gro. BL2—3D 24
Firwood La. BL2—2D 24

Firwood Pk. OL9—2E 63
Firwood Stables. BL2—2E 25
Firwood St. M24—2D 62
Fiscall Way. M35—4E 77
Fishbourne Av. M14—4G 101
Fisherfield. OL12—2B 18
Fishermore Rd. M31—5A 96
Fisher St. OL1—1D 64
Fishwick St. OL16—5A 20
Fistral Av. SK8—5G 141
Fistral Cres. SK15—2H 93
Fitchfield Wlk. M28—6F 55
(off Emlyn St.)
Fitton Av. M21—3H 115
Fitton Cres. M27—6F 57
Fitton Hill Rd. OL8—5E 65
Fitton St. BL3—3A 38
Fitton St. M24—3E 63
Fitton St. OL2—3D 48
(Royton)
Fitton St. OL2—5D 34
(Shaw)
Fitton St. OL16—3A 20
Fitzgerald Clo. M25—1D 72
Fitzgerald Way. M6—2F 85
Fitzhugh St. BL1—6E 11
Fitzroy St. M35—5B 90
Fitzroy St. OL7—5F 91
Fitzroy St. SK15—1H 93
Five Fold Pk. OL9—3B 64
Five Quarters. M26—2E 41
Flag Croft Dri. M23—6H 127
Flagg Wood Av. SK6—4B 134
Flag Row. M4—2F 87 & 1C 162
Flake La. OL2—2B 48
Flamborough Wlk. M14—3F 101
Flamingo Clo. M12—1C 102
Flamstead Av. M23—5E 127
Flannel St. OL12—3A 20
Flashfields. M25—2D 72
Flash St. M10—5C 76
Flatley Clo. M15—1E 101 & 6A 162
Flavian Wlk. M11—5D 88
(off Herne St.)
Flaxcroft Rd. M22—2H 139
Flaxfield Av. SK15—3H 93
Flaxman Rise. OL1—4H 49
Flaxpool Clo. M16—3C 100
Flax St. BL0—5C 4
Flax St. M3—2B 86 & 2C 160
Flaxwood Wlk. M22—2H 139
Fleece St. OL4—2F 65
Fleece St. OL16—4H 19
Fleeson St. M14—4G 101
Fleet Ho. BL1—4A 24
(off Nottingham Dri.)
Fleet St. M18—1H 103
Fleet St. OL4—2G 65
Fleet St. OL6—3G 91
(in two parts)
Fleet St. OL11—5C 32
Fleet St. SK14—3C 106
Fleetwood Rd. M28—6C 54
Fleming Pl. OL9—3B 64
Fleming Rd. M22—3B 140
Flemish Rd. M34—5H 105
Fletcher Av. M27—6G 57
Fletcher Clo. OL9—3B 64
Fletcher Clo. OL10—3F 31
Fletcher Dri. SK12—1D 156
Fletcher Fold. BL9—1D 42
Fletchers Pas. OL15—3E 9
Fletcher's Pl. OL15—3E 9
(off Hare Hill Rd.)
Fletcher's Rd. OL15—6C 8
Fletchers Sq. OL15—3F 9
(off Sutcliffe St.)
Fletcher St. BL3—2A 38
(Bolton)
Fletcher St. BL3—4B 40
(Little Lever)
Fletcher St. BL4—1F 55
Fletcher St. BL9—3E 29
Fletcher St. M10—6H 75
Fletcher St. M26—3A 42

Fletcher St. OL6—2A 92
Fletcher St. OL11—6A 20
Fletcher St. SK1—2H 131
Fletsand Rd. SK9—3F 159
Flexbury Wlk. M10—6D 76
Flint Clo. M11—3D 88
Flint Gro. M30—3A 110
Flint St. BL9—2D 28
Flint St. M35—3B 90
Flint St. SK3—3G 131
Flitcroft Ct. BL3—3B 38
Flixton Rd. M31—1A 112
(Carrington)
Flixton Rd. M31—6B 96
(Flixton)
Flixton Wlk. M13—2H 101
Floatshall Rd. M23—5F 127
Floats Rd. M23—1E 139
(in two parts)
Flora Dri. M7—1B 86
Floral Av. M19—1D 118
Floral Ct. M7—5H 73
Flora St. BL3—3H 37
Flora St. OL1—2C 64
Florence Av. BL1—1B 24
Florence Ct. SK3—5D 130
Florence Pk. Ct. M20—5G 117
Florence St. BL3—3H 37
Florence St. M30—4D 82
Florence St. M33—3B 114
Florence St. M35—3B 90
(Droylsden)
Florence St. M35—3F 77
(Failsworth)
Florence St. OL16—5B 20
Florence St. SK4—1G 131
Florence Way. SK14—2F 109
Florida St. OL8—4C 64
Florist St. SK3—4G 131
Flowery Bank. OL8—5F 65
Flowery Field. SK2—1A 144
Floyd Av. M21—3A 116
Foden La. SK7—4F 153
Foden Wlk. SK9—5H 151
Fogg La. BL3—3F 39
Fog La. M20 & M19—5F 117
Fold Av. M35—3B 90
Fold Cres. SK15—5H 81
Fold Gdns. OL12—6B 6
Fold Grn. OL9—3G 63
Fold M. SK7—2E 145
Fold Rd. M26—2C 56
Folds Rd. BL1—5C 24
Fold St. BL4—1G 55
Fold St. BL9—3B 28
Fold St. M10—3A 76
Fold St. OL10—2G 31
Fold, The. M9—6F 61
Fold, The. M31—4C 96
Fold View. BL7—2C 10
Fold View. OL8—1E 79
Foleshill Av. M9—4F 75
Foley Gdns. OL16—6G 31
Foley Wlk. M22—5C 140
Foliage Cres. SK5—4B 120
Foliage Gdns. SK5—4C 120
Foliage Rd. SK5—5B 120
Folkestone Rd. M11—3F 89
Folkestone Rd. E. M11—3F 89
Folkestone Rd. W. M11—2E 89
Follows St. M18—1F 103
Folly La. M27—6D 70
Folly Wlk. OL12—2H 19
Fonthill Gro. M23—2H 125
Fontwell Clo. M16—4A 100
Fontwell La. OL1—6E 49
Fontwell Rd. BL3—5A 40
Fontwell Wlk. M10—1D 76
Foot Mill Cres. OL12—1F 19
Foot Wood Cres. OL12—1F 19
Forber Cres. M18—4F 103
Forbes Clo. M33—1D 126
Forbes Clo. SK1—3B 132
Forbes Pk. SK7—6F 143
Forbes Rd. SK1—2B 132
Forbes St. SK6—5F 121
Fordbank Rd. M20—1E 129

Fordel Wlk. M7—1C 86
Ford Gdns. OL11—5D 18
Ford Gro. SK14—2C 108
Fordham Gro. BL1—5G 23
Ford La. M6—1G 85
Ford La. M22 & M20—2C 128
(in two parts)
Ford Lodge. M20—1F 129
Ford's La. SK7—1F 153
Ford St. M3—3B 86 & 4D 160
Ford St. M7—6G 73
Ford St. M12—6H 87 & 4G 167
Ford St. M26—1A 56
Ford St. OL16—4A 20
Ford St. SK3—2F 131
Ford St. SK16—1A 106
Foreland Clo. M10—6F 75
Forest Dri. M33—1G 125
Forester Dri. SK15—4E 93
Forester Hill Av. BL3—4B 38
(in two parts)
Forester Hill Clo. BL3—4B 38
Forest Gdns. M31—6B 110
Forest Range. M19—6C 102
Forest Rd. BL1—2F 23
Forest St. M30—1C 82
Forest St. OL6—1A 92
Forest St. OL8—6D 64
Forest View. OL12—1F 19
Forest Way. BL7—4G 11
Forfar St. BL1—6C 10
Forge Ind. Est. OL4—2F 65
Forge La. M11—2B 88
Forge St. OL4—2F 65
Formby Av. M21—2B 116
Formby Dri. SK8—5F 141
Formby Rd. M6—5C 72
Forrester Dri. OL2—5H 35
Forrester Ho. M12—1C 102
(off Blackwin St.)
Forrester St. M28—3A 70
Forrest Rd. M34—6H 105
Forrest St. M11—3B 88
Forshaw Av. M18—1H 103
Forshaw St. M34—3D 104
Forston Wlk. M8—5D 74
Forsyth St. OL12—1A 18
Fortescue Rd. SK2—4D 132
Fortgate Wlk. M13—1H 101 & 6H 167
Forth Pl. M26—2F 41
Forth Rd. M26—2F 41
Forton Av. BL2—6G 25
Fortran Clo. M5—4G 85
Fort Rd. M25—1H 73
Fortrose Av. M9—6D 60
Fortuna Gro. M19—1B 118
Fortune St. BL3—2D 38
Fortyacre Dri. SK6—6E 121
Forum Gro. M7—6A 74
Fosbrook Av. M20—5G 117
Foscarn Dri. M23—6H 127
Foster Ct. BL9—1H 29
Foster La. BL2—4F 25
Foster St. M5—4D 84
Foster St. M26—4F 41
Foster St. M34—4F 105
Foster St. OL4—2G 65
Foster Ter. BL1—4A 24
(off Barnwood Dri.)
Fotherby Dri. M9—6F 61
Foulds Av. BL8—3G 27
Foundry La. M4—3F 87 & 3C 162
Foundry St. BL3—2B 38
(Bolton)
Foundry St. BL3—4A 40
(Little Lever)
Foundry St. BL9—3D 28
Foundry St. M26—4G 41
Foundry St. OL8—3C 64
Foundry St. OL10—3E 31
Foundry St. SK16—5A 92
(in two parts)
Fountain Av. WA15—3B 138
Fountain Clo. SK12—4D 154
Fountain Pl. M25—2D 58
Fountain Pl. SK12—3D 154
Fountains Av. BL2—4E 25

Fountain Sq. SK12—1G 157
Fountains Rd. M32—4H 97
Fountains Rd. SK8 & SK7—1D 152
Fountain St. BL8—3A 28
Fountain St. BL9—3E 29
Fountain St. M2—4E 87 & 6A 162
Fountain St. M24—1H 61
Fountain St. M30—5F 83
Fountain St. OL1—2C 64
Fountain St. OL6—1C 92
Fountain St. SK14—4D 106
Fountain St. N. BL9—3E 29
Fountains Wlk. OL9—4G 63
Fount Rd. M15—1C 100 & 5F 165
Fouracres. M23—6G 127
Fouracres Rd. M23—6F 127
Four Lanes. SK14—3C 108
Four Lanes Way. OL11—2G 17
Fourth Av. BL1—6F 23
Fourth Av. BL3—3H 39
Fourth Av. BL9—1H 29
Fourth Av. M11—2E 89
Fourth Av. M17—1C 98
Fourth Av. M27—6D 70
Fourth Av. OL8—2A 78
Fourth Av. OL9—4G 63
Fourth Av. SK15—5G 81
Fourth St. BL1—1D 22
Fourways Wlk. M10—1B 76
Fourways. M17—1A 98
Four Yards. M2—4D 86 & 6H 161
Fovant Cres. SK5—6G 103
Fowey Wlk. M23—6G 127
Fowey Wlk. SK14—4A 108
Fowler Av. M18—6H 89
Fowler St. OL8—6A 64
Fownhope Av. M33—6H 113
Fownhope Rd. M33—6H 113
Foxall St. M24—2E 61
Fox Bank Ct. SK3—3F 131
Foxbank St. M13—3A 102
Fox Bench Clo. SK8—1E 153
Foxbench Wlk. M21—2B 116
Fox Clo. WA15—5H 125
Foxcroft St. OL16—4D 8
Foxdale St. M11—4E 89
Foxdenton La. M24 & OL9—3E 63
Foxdenton Wlk. M34—6E 105
Foxfield Clo. BL8—6B 14
Foxfield Rd. M23—2F 139
Foxford Wlk. M22—3C 140
Foxglove Ct. OL12—6D 6
Foxglove Dri. BL9—2H 29
Foxglove Dri. WA14—3D 124
Foxglove Wlk. M31—6D 110
Foxhall Rd. M34—6H 105
Foxhall Rd. WA15—5G 125
Foxham Wlk. M7—5A 74
Foxhill. OL2—5C 34
Foxhill Chase. SK2—6G 133
Foxhill Dri. SK15—5G 93
Foxhill Rd. M30—4B 82
Fox Hill Rd. OL11—5D 32
Foxholes Clo. OL12—2A 20
Foxholes Rd. OL12—2A 20
Foxholes Rd. SK14—1A 122
Foxlair Rd. M22—2H 139
Foxland Rd. SK8—1F 141
Foxley Wlk. M12—2C 102
Fox Platt Rd. OL5—2D 80
Fox Platt Ter. OL5—3E 81
Fox St. BL9—2D 28
Fox St. M30—3H 83
Fox St. OL8—1A 78
Fox St. OL10—3E 31
Fox St. OL16—5E 21
(Milnrow)
Fox St. OL16—3B 20
(Rochdale)
Fox St. SK3—3F 131
Foxton St. M24—2E 61
Foxton Wlk. M23—3G 139
Foxwell Wlk. M8—5D 74
Foxwood Gdns. M19—6A 118
Foynes Clo. M10—6F 75
Framingham Rd. M33—6A 114
Frampton Clo. M24—2B 62
Fram St. M6—3E 85

Fram St. M9—3H 75
Frances Av. SK8—5E 129
Francesca Wlk. M18—1E 103
Frances St. M35—4F 77
Frances St. OL1—6E 49
(in two parts)
Frances St. OL1—5B 8
Frances St. SK3—3G 131
Frances St. SK8—5A 130
Frances St. SK14—4A 106
Frances St. W. SK14—4A 106
Francis Av. M28—1H 69
Francis Av. M30—3G 83
Francis Rd. M20—4G 117
Francis Rd. M30—1D 110
Francis St. BL1—3H 23
Francis St. BL4—6E 39
Francis St. M3—2D 86 & 1G 161
Francis St. M29—3A 68
Francis St. M30—4C 110
(Cadishead)
Francis St. M30—2F 83
(Eccles)
Francis St. M34—1H 121
Francis Ter. SK16—4A 92
(off Astley St.)
Francis Thompson Dri. OL6—2H 91
Frandley Wlk. M13—6F 87 & 3D 166
Frankby Clo. M27—4A 72
Frank Cowin Ct. M7—1B 86
Frankford Av. BL1—3G 23
Frankford Sq. BL1—3G 23
Frank Hulme Ho. M32—6E 99
Frankland Clo. M11—3D 88
Franklin Av. M35—4A 90
Franklin Rd. M18—1G 103
Franklin St. M30—3F 83
Franklin St. OL1—1C 64
Franklin St. OL16—6B 20
Franklin Ter. OL15—4E 9
(off William St.)
Franklyn Av. M31—5A 96
Franklyn Clo. M34—5A 104
Frank Price Ct. M22—2A 140
Frank St. BL1—3H 23
Frank St. BL9—4D 28
Frank St. M1—6D 86 & 3A 166
Frank St. M6—1G 85
Frank St. M35—4E 77
Frank St. OL1—1F 65
Frank St. SK14—5C 106
Frank Swift Wlk. M14—4E 101
Frankton Rd. M25—2D 58
Franton Rd. M11—3D 88
Fraser Av. M33—6E 115
Fraser Ho. BL1—4H 23
(off Kirk Hope Dri.)
Fraser Rd. M8—2B 74
Fraser Rd. M17—2D 98
Fraser St. M27—2G 71
Fraser St. OL2—5E 35
Fraser St. OL6—2A 92
Fraser St. OL16—1H 33
Fraternitas Ter. M35—2G 89
Freckleton Av. M21—5A 116
Freckleton Dri. BL8—5F 27
Freda Wlk. M11—4B 88
Frederick Av. OL2—2F 49
Frederick Rd. BL4—1G 55
Frederick Rd. M6 & M7—2H 85
Frederick St. BLO—4D 4
Frederick St. BL4—1F 55
Frederick St. M3—3C 86 & 3E 161
Frederick St. M34—2E 105
Frederick St. OL6—3C 92
Frederick St. OL8—4A 64
Frederick St. OL9—1H 63
Frederick St. OL15—3E 9
Fred Tilson Clo. M14—4E 101
Freehold St. OL11—6G 19
Freeland Wlk. M11—5E 89
Freeman Av. OL6—2B 92
Freeman Rd. SK16—1A 106
Freemantle St. SK3—3F 131
Freeman Wlk. M15—1E 101 &
             6A 166
Freestone Clo. BL8—1B 28
Freetown Clo. M14—3E 101
Freetrade St. OL11—6G 19

Fremantle Av. M18—4F 103
French Av. OL1—6G 49
French Av. SK15—4G 93
French Barn La. M9—6E 61
French Gro. BL3—2F 39
French St. SK15—4G 93
Frensham Wlk. M23—1F 139
Freshfield. SK8—5F 141
Freshfield Av. BL3—5H 37
Freshfield Av. M25—3G 59
Freshfield Av. SK14—6B 106
Freshfield Clo. SK6—2F 135
Freshfield Gro. BL3—5B 38
Freshfield Rd. SK4—1B 130
Freshfields. M26—2D 40
Freshfield Wlk. M11—3E 89
Freshford Wlk. M22—4H 139
Freshpool Way. M22—5C 128
Freshwater Dri. M34—1H 121
Freshwater St. M18—1G 103
Fresia Av. M28—6B 54
Frew Clo. M10—1B 76
Frewland Av. SK3—1H 143
Freya Gro. M5—5A 86 & 2B 164
Friarmere Rd. OL3—2G 51
Friars Clo. M29—2A 68
Friars Clo. SK9—1B 158
Friar's Ct. M5—3B 84
Friars Cres. OL11—3F 33
Friar's Rd. M33—5B 114
Friar's Rd. SK9—2A 68
Frieston. OL12—3G 19
(off Spotland Rd.)
Frieston Rd. WA14—3G 125
Friezland Clo. SK15—5G 81
Friezland La. OL3—5E 53
Frimley Gdns. M22—2B 140
Frinton Av. M10—6D 62
Frinton Clo. M33—2H 125
Frinton Rd. BL3—4F 37
Frobisher Clo. M13—2H 101
Frobisher Pl. SK5—5G 119
Frobisher Rd. OL15—6G 9
Frodesley Wlk. M12—1B 102
Frodsham Av. SK4—6E 119
Frodsham Rd. M33—1E 127
Frodsham St. M14—4F 101
Frodsham Way. SK9—3A 152
Frogley St. BL2—2D 24
Frogmore Av. SK14—2C 122
Frome Av. M31—6D 96
Frome Av. SK2—6C 132
Frome Dri. M8—4D 74
Frome St. OL4—3G 65
Frostlands Rd. M16—4C 100
Frost St. M4—4H 87 & 5H 163
Frost St. OL8—5C 64
Frowde Wlk. M16—3C 100
Froxmer St. M18—1E 103
Fuchsia Gro. M7—5H 73
Fulbeck Wlk. M7—6A 74
Fulford St. M16—4A 100
Fulham Av. M10—6B 76
Fulham St. OL4—3G 65
Fullbrook Dri. SK8—1B 152
Fullerton Rd. SK4—1D 130
Full Pot La. OL11—3A 18
Fulmar Clo. SK12—3A 154
Fulmar Dri. M33—1E 125
Fulmar Dri. SK2—6F 133
Fulmards Clo. SK9—2F 159
Fulmer Gdns. OL11—4B 18
Fulmead Wlk. M8—5B 74
(off Kilmington Dri.)
Fulmer Dri. M4—3G 87 & 3F 163
Fulmere Ct. M27—5D 70
Fulneck Sq. M35—5A 90
Fulshaw Av. SK9—3D 158
Fulshaw Ct. SK9—4D 158
Fulshaw Hall Cotts. SK9—4D 158
Fulshaw Pk. Rd. SK9—5D 158
Fulshaw Pk. Rd. S. SK9—5C 158
Fulshaw Wlk. M13—6F 87 &
             4D 166
Fulstone M. SK2—5B 132
Fulthorpe Wlk. M9—4G 61
Fulton Ct. M15—2E 101
(off Brackenbury Wlk.)

Fulton's Ct. OL4—3A 66
Fulwood Av. M9—5H 61
Fulwood Clo. BL8—4F 27
Furbarn La. OL1—3H 17
Furbarn Rd. OL1—4H 17
Furlong Rd. M22—2H 139
Furnace St. SK14—3A 106
Furnace St. SK16—4H 91
Furness Av. BL2—3D 24
Furness Av. M25—1E 59
Furness Av. OL7—6D 78
Furness Av. OL8—5G 65
Furness Av. OL10—2E 31
Furness Av. OL15—3E 9
Furness Clo. OL5—1E 21
Furness Clo. SK12—3C 154
Furness Gro. SK4—2C 130
Furness Quay. M5—6G 85
Furness Rd. BL1—6F 23
Furness Rd. M14—6G 101
Furness Rd. M24—4H 45
Furness Rd. M31—4F 97
Furness Rd. SK8—1E 153
Furness Sq. BL2—3D 24
Furnival Clo. M34—5A 104
Furnival Rd. M18—2E 103
Furnival St. SK5—5H 103
Furnwood Gro. SK9—1F 159
Further Field. OL11—2H 17
Further Hey Clo. OL4—2A 66
Further La. SK14—4A 108
Further Pitts. OL11—4E 19
Furtherwood Rd. OL1—6A 48
Furze La. OL4—6H 49
(in two parts)
Furze Wlk. M31—6E 111
Fyfield Wlk. M8—5D 74
Fylde Av. BL2—6G 25
Fylde Av. SK8—5G 141
Fylde Rd. SK4—1C 130
Fylde St. BL3—5F 39
Fylde St. E. BL3—5F 39

Gable Av. SK9—2D 158
Gable Ct. M34—1F 105
Gable Dri. M24—6G 45
Gables, The. M33—6B 114
(Brooklands)
Gables, The. M33—4C 114
(Sale)
Gable St. BL2—6H 11
Gable St. M11—5B 88
Gabriels, The. OL2—6D 34
Gabriel Wlk. M16—4D 100
Gaddum Rd. M20—6G 117
Gaddum Rd. WA14—4C 136
Gail Av. SK4—1F 131
Gail Clo. M35—6E 77
Gail Clo. SK9—4H 159
Gainford Av. SK8—1F 141
Gainford Gdns. M10—2B 76
Gainford Rd. SK5—6H 103
Gainford Wlk. BL3—3A 38
Gainsboro Rd. M34—4D 90
Gainsborough Av. BL3—6G 37
Gainsborough Av. M20—3G 117
Gainsborough Av. M32—4F 99
Gainsborough Av. OL8—5C 64
Gainsborough Clo. SK9—1G 159
Gainsborough Dri. OL11—2E 33
Gainsborough Dri. SK8—5B 130
Gainsborough Rd. BLO—2B 14
Gainsborough Rd. BL9—6E 47
Gainsborough St. M7—4A 74
Gainsborough Wlk. M34—6E 105
Gainsborough Wlk. SK14—
             2C 106
Gairlock Av. M32—5B 98
Gair Rd. SK5—5H 119
Gair St. SK14—3B 106
Gaitskell Clo. M12—4A 88
Galbraith Rd. M20—6G 117
Gale Dri. M24—5F 45
Galena St. OL11—1E 33
Gale Rd. M25—6D 58
Gales Ter. OL11—6G 19
Gale St. OL10—3D 30

Gale St. OL12—6E 7
Galey St. BL1—3I 22
Galgate Clo. BL8—4F 27
Galgate Clo. M15—6C 86 & 4E 165
Galgate St. M16—3H 99
Galindo St. BL2—1E 25
Galland St. OL4—1H 65
Galloway Clo. BL3—2C 36
Galloway Clo. OL10—4B 30
Galloway Dri. M27—5F 57
Galloway Rd. M27—5D 70
Gallowsclough Rd. SK15—1A 108
Galston St. M11—5C 88
Galsworthy Av. M8—5C 74
Galvin Rd. M9—6D 60
Galway St. OL1—3D 64
Galway Wlk. M23—3F 139
Gambleside Clo. M28—3D 68
Gambrel Bank Rd. OL6—5F 79
Gambrell Gro. OL6—5F 79
Game St. OL4—4G 65
Games Wlk. M22—4H 139
Gamma Wlk. M11—3D 88
Gandy La. OL12—5C 6
Gan Eden. M7—3A 74
Ganesmoor Clo. M12—1A 102
Gantock Wlk. M14—4G 101
Ganton Av. M25—2B 58
Garbrook Av. M9—4E 61
Garden Av. M32—4D 98
Garden Av. M35—3B 90
Garden City. BLO—1A 14
Garden Clo. M34—1F 105
Garden Clo. OL15—6E 9
Gardenia Sq. M12—1H 101 & 6G 167
Garden La. M3—3C 86 & 3F 161
(in two parts)
Garden La. WA14—6F 125
Garden M. SK14—4F 9
(off Industry St.)
Garden Row. OL10—1D 30
Gardens, The. BL1—5D 10
Gardens, The. M2—3D 86 & 4H 161
Gardens, The. M30—1A 84
Garden St. BLO—3E 5
Garden St. BL4—1G 55
Garden St. BL8—4H 13
Garden St. BL9—6E 5
Garden St. M4—3E 87 & 4A 162
Garden St. M30—4G 83
Garden St. M34—1F 105
Garden St. OL1—2E 65
Garden St. OL4—4B 66
Garden St. OL10—2E 31
Garden St. OL16—1F 35
Garden St. SK2—6C 132
Garden St. SK14—3C 106
Garden Ter. OL2—6A 34
Garden View. M33—3B 114
Garden Wlk. M31—6C 110
Garden Wlk. M34—4G 105
Garden Wlk. OL6—1A 92
Garden Wall Clo. M5—5A 86 & 2A 164
Garden Way. OL15—1F 21
Gardner. M30—3G 83
Gardner Grange. SK5—5C 120
Gardner Rd. M25—5D 58
Gardner St. M6—1G 85
Gardner St. M12—1D 102
Garfield Av. M19—6D 102
Garfield Clo. OL11—3A 18
Garfield Gro. BL3—2H 37
Garfield St. M5—1G 99
(in two parts)
Garforth Av. M4—3G 87 & 3F 163
Garforth St. OL9—2A 64
Gargrave Av. BL1—3D 22
Gargrave St. M27—3D 72
Gargrave St. OL4—3F 65
Garland Rd. M22—2C 140
Garlick St. M18—2F 103
Garlick St. OL9—3C 64
(in two parts)
Garlick St. SK14—4D 106
Garner Av. WA15—2A 126
Garner Clo. WA14—3F 137
Garner Dri. M5—2D 84
Garner Dri. M30—2E 83

Garnet St. OL1—1F 65
Garnett Clo. SK14—4B 108
Garnett Rd. SK14—4B 108
Garnett St. BL0—3D 4
Garnett St. BL1—2A 24
Garnett St. M7—5B 74
Garnett St. SK1—2H 131
Garnett Way. SK14—4B 108
(off Garnett Clo.)
Garnet Wolseley Av. M5—6H 85
Garnham Wlk. M9—.G 61
Garratt Way. M18—2E 103
Garret Gro. OL2—6G 35
Garrett Hall Rd. M28—4A 68
Garrett La. M28—4A 68
Garrett Wlk. SK3—3E 131
Garron Wlk. M22—3G 139
Garrowmore Wlk. M9—6G 61
Garsdale St. M1—6E 87 & 3B 166
Garsden Wlk. M23—1F 139
Garside Gro. BL1—3G 23
Garside Hey Rd. BL8—5B 14
Garside St. BL1—6A 24
Garside St. M34—5F 105
Garside St. SK14—6C 106
Garstang Av. BL2—1G 39
Garstang Dri. BL8—4F 27
Garstang Ho. M15—2F 101
Garston Clo. SK4—6E 119
Garston St. BL9—1E 29
Garswood Dri. BL8—5B 14
Garswood Rd. BL3—5A 38
Garswood Rd. M14—5D 100
Garth Av. WA15—5G 125
Garth Heights. SK9—2F 159
Garthland Rd. SK7—2F 145
Garthorne Clo. M16—3B 100
Garthorp Rd. M23—2E 127
Garth Rd. M22—1B 140
Garth Rd. SK2—4C 132
Garth Rd. SK6—4G 115
Garth, The. M5—3D 84
Garthwaite Av. OL8—5C 64
Gartland Wlk. M8—3E 75
Garton Wlk. M9—4G 61
Gartside Gdns. M13—6F 87 & 4D 166
Gartside St. M3—4C 86 & 6F 161
Gartside St. OL3—3G 51
Gartside St. OL4—4F 65
Gartside St. OL7—4E 91
Garwick Rd. BL1—2F 23
Garwood St. M15—6D 86 & 4G 165
Gascoyne St. M14—4F 101
Gaskell Clo. OL15—3E 9
Gaskell Rise. OL1—2A 50
Gaskell Rd. M30—4F 83
Gaskell Rd. WA14—5F 125
Gaskell St. BL1—5H 23
Gaskell St. M10—6C 76
Gaskell St. M27—1F 71
Gaskell St. SK16—4H 91
Gaskill St. OL10—3C 30
Gas St. BL1—6A 24
Gas St. BL4—6F 39
Gas St. OL6—2H 91
Gas St. OL10—3F 31
Gas St. OL11—4G 19
Gas St. SK4—2G 131
Gas St. SK14—2F 109
Gaston Wlk. M9—4F 61
(off Claygate Dri.)
Gatcombe M. SK9—3D 158
Gatcombe Sq. M14—4G 101
Gateacre Wlk. M23—3E 127
Gate Fold Precinct. BL2—6H 11
Gatehead Croft. OL3—4H 51
Gatehead M. OL3—4H 51
Gatehead Rd. OL3—5H 51
Gatehouse Rd. M28—5C 54
Gate Keeper Fold. OL7—4F 79
Gatemere Clo. M28—3D 68
Gate Rd. M32—3A 98
Gatesgarth Rd. M24—5E 45
Gateshead Clo. M14—3F 101
Gateside Wlk. M9—4G 61
(off Brockford Dri.)
Gate St. M11—5E 89

Gate St. OL11—6H 19
Gate St. SK16—1G 105
Gateway Ind. Est. M1—5F 87
Gateway Rd. M18—1E 103
Gathill Clo. SK8—4B 142
Gathurst St. M18—1G 103
Gatley Av. M14—6E 101
Gatley Brow. OL1—1C 64
Gatley Grn. SK8—6E 129
Gatley Rd. M33—6E 115
Gatley St. SK8—6F 129
Gatling Av. M12—5C 102
Gatwick Av. M23—5H 127
Gatwick Clo. BL8—4C 14
Gavel Wlk. M24—6G 45
Gavin Av. M5—4G 85
Gawsworth Av. M20—2G 129
Gawsworth Clo. OL2—6D 34
Gawsworth Clo. SK3—6F 131
Gawsworth Clo. SK7—2G 153
Gawsworth Clo. SK12—5F 155
Gawsworth Clo. WA15—5D 126
Gawsworth Ct. M9—4C 60
(off Deanswood Dri.)
Gawsworth Rd. M33—1E 127
Gawsworth Way. M34—6G 105
Gawsworth Way. SK9—3A 152
Gawthorpe Clo. BL9—2E 43
Gaydon Rd. M33—5F 113
Gayford Wlk. M9—4G 61
(off Brockford Dri.)
Gayrigg Wlk. M9—4F 75
Gaythorne St. BL1—2F 24
Gaythorn St. M5—4A 86 & 5B 160
Gayton Wlk. M10—1D 76
Gaywood Wlk. M10—5E 75
Gazebo Clo. M28—6B 54
Gee Cross Fold. SK14—2D 122
Gee La. M30—2D 82
Gee St. SK3—4F 131
Gellifield La. OL3—6D 52
Gendre St. BL7—3C 10
Geneva Rd. SK7—2G 143
Geneva Ter. OL11—3E 19
Geneva Wlk. M8—5D 74
Geneva Wlk. OL9—3A 64
Genista Gro. M7—6H 73
(off Hilton St. N.)
Geoff Bent Wlk. M10—5B 76
Geoffrey St. BL0—5C 4
Geoffrey St. BL9—1E 29
George Barton St. BL2—4D 24
George Ct. SK16—4H 91
(off Astley St.)
George La. SK6—5G 121
George Leigh St. M4—3F 87 &
                         4D 162
George Rd. BL0—4D 4
George's Clo. SK12—4E 155
George Sq. OL1—3C 64
George's Rd. M33—6B 114
Georges Rd. SK4—1F 131
George's Rd. E. SK12—4E 155
George's Rd. W. SK12—4D 154
George St. BL3—3B 38
George St. BL4—2G 55
  (Farnworth)
George St. BL4—2D 54
  (New Bury)
George St. BL9—3D 28
George St. M1—5D 86 & 1H 165
  (in two parts)
George St. M3—4B 86 & 5C 160
George St. M8—3A 74
George St. M15—1A 100
George St. M25—2F 73
  (Prestwich)
George St. M25—6C 42
  (Whitefield)
George St. M26—4F 41
George St. M30—4E 83
  (Eccles)
George St. M30—4F 95
  (Irlam)
George St. M31—5G 97
George St. M34—4G 105
George St. M35—3F 77
George St. OL1—3C 64

George St. OL2—5G 35
George St. OL5—1E 81
George St. OL6—2A 92
George St. OL9—2G 63
George St. OL10—2D 30
George St. OL12—1C 6
George St. OL15—3F 9
George St. OL16—4E 21
  (Firgrove)
George St. OL16—6B 8
  (Hurstead)
George St. OL16—3A 20
  (Rochdale, in two parts)
George St. SK1—1A 132
George St. SK6—1F 135
George St. SK9—5G 159
George St. SK15—3E 93
George St. WA14—1F 137
George St. E. SK1—3B 132
George St. W. SK1—3B 132
George St. W. SK14—4A 106
Georgiana St. BL4—5D 38
Georgiana St. BL9—4D 26
Georgina Ct. BL3—4F 37
Georgina St. BL3—5F 37
Gerald Av. M8—3C 74
Gerald Rd. M6—6E 73
Germain Clo. M9—4E 61
German Bldgs. SK1—5A 132
Gerrard Av. WA15—3A 126
Gerrards Clo. M30—5E 95
Gerrards Gdns. SK14—2C 122
Gerrards Hollow. SK14—2B 122
Gerrard St. BL4—1G 55
Gerrard St. M6—2H 85
Gerrard St. OL11—3G 33
Gerrard St. SK15—4F 93
Gertrude St. M5—5G 85
Gervis Clo. M10—6F 75
Ghyll Gro. M28—1G 69
Gibb La. SK6—1H 147
Gibbon Av. M22—3B 140
Gibbon St. BL3—2H 37
Gibbon St. M11—5C 88
Gibb Rd. M28—4B 70
Gibbs St. M3—4B 86 & 5C 160
Gibb St. OL4—3H 65
Gib La. M23—4A 128
Gib La. Cottages. M23—4H 127
Gibraltar La. M34—1H 121
Gibraltar St. BL3—1H 37
Gibraltar St. OL4—4H 65
Gibsmere Clo. WA15—5D 126
Gibson Av. M18—6H 89
Gibson Gro. M28—6C 54
Gibson La. M26—6C 54
Gibson Pl. M3—2E 87 & 1A 162
Gibsons Rd. SK4—5D 118
Gibson St. BL2—4E 25
Gibson St. OL4—3G 65
Gibson St. OL16—3C 20
Gibwood Rd. M22—3A 128
Giddings St. M1—5G 87 & 1F 167
Gidlow St. M18—1G 103
Gifford Av. M9—5H 61
Gifford Wlk. SK7—3A 144
Gigg La. BL9—6C 28
Gilbertbank. SK6—5G 121
Gilbert Rd. WA15—4G 137
Gilbert St. M6—4F 85
Gilbert St. M15—6C 86 & 3F 165
Gilbert St. M30—5D 82
Gilbert White Rd. WA14—1B 136
Gilcrest Rd. M30—3C 110
Gilda Brook Rd. M30—3A 84
  (in two parts)
Gilda Cres. Rd. M30—2A 84
Gilda Rd. M28—4A 68
Gildenhall. M35—4G 77
Gilden Wlk. M9—4G 61
Gilderdale Dri. M9—3D 60
Gilderdale St. BL3—3C 38
Gildridge Rd. M16—6C 100
Gilesgate. M14—4G 101
  (off Grelley Wlk.)
Giles St. M12—3C 102
Gill Bent Rd. SK8—1C 152
Gillbrook Rd. M20—6F 117

Gillemere Gro. OL2—6G 35
Giliford Av. M9—2H 75
Gillingham Rd. M30—3D 82
Gillingham Sq. M11—4B 88
  (off Jobling St.)
Gill St. M9—3H 75
Gill St. SK1—6B 120
Gillwood Dri. SK6—2F 133
Gilman Clo. M9—1E 75
Gilmerton Dri. M10—6C 76
Gilmore St. SK3—4G 131
Gilmour St. M24—1A 62
Gilmour Ter. M9—2H 75
Gilnow Gdns. BL1—1G 37
Gilnow Gro. BL1—1H 37
Gilnow La. BL3—1G 37
Gilnow Rd. BL1—1H 37
Gilpin Rd. M31—5H 97
Gilpin Wlk. M24—6F 45
Giltbrook Av. M10—1H 87
Gilwell Dri. M23—1F 139
Gin Croft La. BL0—4E 3
Gingham Pk. M26—2E 41
Gipsy La. OL11—2C 32
Girton St. BL2—6F 25
Girton St. M7—1C 86
Girton Wlk. M10—2D 76
Girvan Av. M10—1D 76
Girvan Clo. BL3—4G 37
Girvan Wlk. OL10—4B 30
Gisborne Dri. M6—6D 72
Gisburn Av. BL1—3C 22
Gisburn Dri. BL8—2E 27
Gisburn Dri. OL11—2G 33
Gisburne Av. M10—1D 76
Gisting Wlk. M9—5F 75
Givendale Dri. M8—1C 74
Glade Brow. OL4—3C 66
Gladeside Rd. M22—1A 140
Glade St. BL1—6G 23
Glade, The. BL1—4H 23
Glade, The. SK4—2C 130
Gladstone Clo. BL1—3A 24
Gladstone Clo. M15—3C 100
Gladstone Ct. B¹ ¹—6E 39
Gladstone Cres. OL11—2F 33
Gladstone Gro. SK4—6C 118
Gladstone Ho. OL12—3A 8
Gladstone Rd. BL4—6E 39
Gladstone Rd. M30—3D 83
Gladstone Rd. M31—5G 97
Gladstone Rd. WA14—5F 125
Gladstone St. BL1—3A 24
Gladstone St. BL9—2F 29
Gladstone St. M27—3G 71
Gladstone St. OL4—3F 65
Gladstone St. SK2—1C 144
Gladstone Ter. OL3—5E 53
Gladville Dri. SK8—5C 130
Gladwyn Av. M20—5C 116
Gladys St. BL3—5F 39
Gladys St. M5—6G 85
Gladys St. M16—3A 100
Glaisdale. OL4—2H 65
Glaisdale Clo. BL2—3D 24
Glaisdale St. BL2—3D 24
Glaister La. BL2—4F 25
Glamis Av. M11—2D 88
Glamis Av. M32—5A 98
Glamis Av. OL10—6G 17
Glamorgan Pl. OL9—4A 64
Glandon Dri. SK8—5E 143
Glanford Av. M9—6C 60
Glanton Wlk. M10—2D 76
Glanvor Rd. SK3—3E 131
Glasshouse St. M4—2G 87 & 2E 163
Glasson Wlk. OL9—3G 63
Glass St. BL4—2G 55
Glass St. M11—4B 88
Glastonbury. OL12—3G 19
  (off Spotland Rd.)
Glastonbury Av. SK8—1D 152
Glastonbury Av. WA15—3B 138
Glastonbury Dri. SK12—3D 154
Glastonbury Gdns. M26—2E 41
Glastonbury Rd. M32—4H 97
Glaswen Gro. SK5—5H 119

Glazebrook Clo. OL10—4E 31
Glazebrook La. WA3—4A 110
Glazebury Dri. M23—6H 127
Glazedale Av. OL2—3A 48
Glaze Wlk. M25—5G 43
Gleave Clo. WA15—1G 137
Gleaves Rd. M30—4G 83
Gleave St. BL1—5B 24
(off Bark St.)
Gleave St. M33—3B 114
Glebe Ho. M24—5A 46
(off Rochdale Rd.)
Glebeland Rd. BL3—2F 37
Glebelands Rd. M23—5F 127
Glebelands Rd. M25—4E 59
Glebelands Rd. M33—3G 113
Glebelands Rd. E. M25—4F 59
Glebe La. OL1—3A 50
Glebe Rd. M31—5F 97
Glebe St. BL2—1C 38
Glebe St. M26—4H 41
Glebe St. M34—3F 105
Glebe St. OL2—6F 35
Glebe St. OL6—2A 92
Glebe St. OL9—6G 63
Glebe St. SK1—2A 132
Gleden St. M10—3A 88
(in two parts)
Gledhall St. SK15—3E 93
Gledhill Av. M5—6G 85
Gledhill Clo. OL2—4E 35
Gledhill St. M20—2F 117
Gledhill Way. BL7—2E 11
Glemsford Clo. M10—5B 76
Glenarm Wlk. M22—3C 140
Glenart. M30—2G 83
Glen Av. BL3—2F 37
Glen Av. BL4—3B 56
Glen Av. M9—2G 75
Glen Av. M27—3D 70
Glen Av. M28—3A 70
Glen Av. M33—3A 114
Glenavon Dri. OL2—5D 34
Glenavon Dri. OL12—6D 6
Glenbarry Clo. M13—1F 101 & 6D 166
Glenbarry St. M12—5H 87
& 2H 167
Glenbeck Rd. M25—6C 42
Glenboro Av. BL8—3H 27
Glen Bott St. BL1—3H 23
Glenbourne Pk. SK7—2F 153
Glenbrook Rd. M9—4C 60
Glenburn St. BL3—4H 37
Glenby Av. M22—2D 140
Glenby Est. OL9—3A 64
Glencar Dri. M10—1D 76
Glencastle Rd. M18—2E 103
Glencoe. BL2—6D 24
Glencoe Clo. OL10—4B 30
Glencoe Dri. BL2—1H 39
Glencoe Dri. M33—1E 125
Glencoe Pl. OL11—4F 19
Glencoe St. OL8—1A 78
Glen Dale. M27—1H 71
Glendale Av. BL9—4D 42
Glendale Av. M19—3B 118
Glendale Clo. M28—4B 68
Glendale Clo. OL10—3F 31
Glendale Dri. BL3—1D 36
Glendale Rd. M28—4B 68
Glendale Rd. M30—2A 84
Glendene Av. M35—2C 90
Glendene Av. SK7—2F 153
Glenden Foot. OL12—1F 19
Glendevon Clo. BL3—2D 36
Glendevon Pl. M25—2F 59
Glendinning St. M6—3E 85
Glendon Cres. OL6—4F 79
Glendore. M5—3C 84
Glendower Dri. M10—6E 75
Gleneagles. BL3—4D 36
Gleneagles Av. M11—3E 89
Gleneagles Av. OL10—5F 31
Gleneagles Clo. SK7—6H 143
Gleneagles Clo. SK9—1G 159

Gleneagles Rd. M31—3A 96
Gleneagles Rd. SK8—4G 141
Glenfield. WA14—1D 136
Glenfield Dri. SK12—4D 154
Glenfield Rd. SK4—5F 119
Glenfield Sq. BL4—5D 38
Glenfyne Rd. M6—6B 72
Glen Gdns. OL12—6F 7
Glengarth Dri. BL6 & BL1—1A 36
Glen Gro. M24—2C 62
Glen Gro. OL2—2B 48
Glenhaven Av. M31—5E 97
Glenholme Rd. SK7—6F 143
Glenhurst Rd. M19—4A 118
Glenlea Dri. M20—3F 129
Glenluce Wlk. BL3—2C 36
Glenmere Clo. M25—3D 58
Glenmere Rd. M20—3G 129
Glenmoor Rd. SK1—3A 132
Glenmore Av. BL4—5C 38
Glenmore Av. M20—5C 116
Glenmore Clo. BL3—2C 36
Glenmore Clo. OL11—6A 18
Glenmore Dri. M8—4D 74
Glenmore Dri. M35—3H 77
Glenmore Gro. SK16—5A 92
Glenmore Rd. BL0—1H 13
Glenmore St. BL9—4C 28
Glenolden St. M11—3F 89
Glenpark Wlk. M9—4G 75
(off Orpington Rd.)
Glenridding Clo. OL1—6E 49
Glenridge Clo. BL1—3B 24
Glen Rise. WA15—6A 126
Glen Rd. OL4—3G 65
Glen Royd. OL12—2E 19
Glenroy Way. M9—4G 61
Glensdale Dri. M10—2E 77
Glenshee Dri. BL3—2D 36
Glenside Av. M18—4F 103
Glenside Dri. BL3—5B 38
Glenside Dri. SK6—4H 121
Glenside Gro. M28—5G 55
Glen St. M5—6G 85
Glen, The. M24—3B 62
Glenthorn Av. M9—3F 61
Glenthorne Dri. OL7—1G 91
Glenthorne Rd. BL1—4A 24
Glenthorn Gro. M33—6B 114
Glentrees M. BL1—5E 23
Glentrool M. BL1—6E 23
Glent View. SK15—1E 93
Glentwood. WA14—4G 137
Glen View. OL2—2B 48
Glen View. OL12—3G 7
Glenville Wlk. SK15—4E 93
Glenville Way. M34—5G 105
Glenwood Av. SK14—2B 106
Glenwood Dri. M9—4G 75
Glenwood Dri. M24—5C 46
Glenwood Gro. SK2—2B 144
Glenwyn Av. M9—5G 61
Globe La. BL7—1B 10
Globe La. SK16—6G 91
Globe La. Ind. Est. SK16
—1H 105
Globe Sq. SK16—6G 91
Glodwick. OL4—4F 65
Glodwick Rd. OL4—4F 65
Glossop Rd. SK6—3F 135
Glossop St. SK13—6F 109
Glossop Ter. M10—6D 62
Gloster St. BL2—6C 24
Gloucester Av. M19—1D 118
Gloucester Av. M25—1E 59
Gloucester Av. OL10—5E 31
Gloucester Av. OL12—5B 8
Gloucester Av. SK6—5D 134
Gloucester Clo. OL6—3H 79
Gloucester Dri. M33—5F 113
Gloucester Dri. OL3—3C 52
Gloucester Ho. M7—5H 73
Gloucester Pl. M6—2G 85
Gloucester Rise. SK16—6E 93
Gloucester Rd. M6—1C 84
Gloucester Rd. M24—3A 62
Gloucester Rd. M31—5F 97

Gloucester Rd. M34—5A 104
Gloucester Rd. M35—2A 90
Gloucester Rd. SK6—6G 121
Gloucester Rd. SK12—3D 154
Gloucester Rd. SK14—1C 122
Gloucester St. M1—6D 86 & 3H 165
Gloucester St. M5—5A 86 & 2A 164
Gloucester St. M6—1G 85
Gloucester St. SK3—4F 131
Gloucester St. N. OL9—4A 64
Gloucester St. S. OL9—4A 64
Glover Av. M8—5D 74
Glover Ct. M8—3B 74
Glover Field. M7—5H 73
(off Devonshire St.)
Glyn Av. WA15—3A 138
Glyneath Clo. M11—4B 88
Glynis Clo. SK3—5H 131
Glynis Glo. SK3—5H 131
Glynne St. BL4—1E 55
Glyn Gdns. M20—5B 116
Glynrene Dri. M27—2C 70
Glynwood Pk. BL4—6E 39
G.Mex Cen. M2—5D 86 & 1G 165
Gnat Bank. OL11—6B 18
Goats Ga. Ter. M25—5B 42
Godbert Av. M21—4A 116
Goddard La. SK14—1H 109
Goddard St. OL8—5D 64
Godfrey Av. M35—2F 89
Godfrey Range. M18—3H 103
Godfrey Rd. M6—6A 72
Godlee Dri. M27—4E 71
Godley Clo. M11—5E 89
Godley St. SK14—3D 106
Godson St. OL1—6C 48
Godwin St. M18—1G 103
Goit Pl. OL16—4H 19
Golborne Av. M20—2D 116
Golborne Dri. OL2—5F 35
Golborne Ho. BL1—5B 24
Golborne Ho. OL2—5F 35
(off Cowie St.)
Goldbrook Clo. OL10—4G 31
Goldcraft Clo. OL10—4G 31
Goldcrest Clo. M22—6D 128
Goldcrest Clo. M28—4D 68
Goldenhill Av. M11—2E 89
Golden Sq. M30—4F 83
(off Golden St.)
Golden St. M30—4F 83
Goldfinch Dri. BL9—6A 16
Goldfinch Way. M35—2C 90
Goldie Av. M22—3D 140
Goldrill Av. BL2—5H 25
Goldrill Gdns. BL2—5H 25
Goldsmith Av. OL1—3A 50
Goldsmith Rd. SK5—6F 103
Goldsmith St. BL3—3H 37
Goldsmith Way. M34—2G 121
Goldstien Rd. BL6—3A 36
Gold St. M1—4E 87
Goldsworthy Rd. M31—4A 96
Goldwick Wlk. M23—2E 127
Golf Rd. M33—5F 115
Golf Rd. WA15—2H 137
Gomer Wlk. M8—5E 75
Gooch Clo. M16—4C 100
Gooden Pl. BL4—5E 39
Gooden St. OL10—4G 31
Goodiers Dri. M5—5G 85
Goodier St. M10—6H 75
Goodier St. M33—5A 114
Goodiers View. SK14—2D 106
Good Intent. OL16—6G 21
Goodison Clo. BL9—4F 43
Goodlad St. BL8—1H 27
Goodley Hill Rd. SK14—4F 107
Goodman St. M9—3G 75
Goodrich. OL11—5G 19
Goodridge Av. M22—3A 140
Goodwill Clo. M27—4F 71
Goodwin St. BL1—5C 24
Goodwood Av. M23—3D 126
Goodwood Av. M33—5E 113
Goodwood Clo. BL3—4H 39
Goodwood Ct. M7—5H 73
(off Bury New Rd.)

Goodwood Cres. WA15—5C 126
Goodwood Dri. M27—4H 71
Goodwood Dri. OL7—1F 49
Goodwood Rd. SK6—6C 134
Goodworth Wlk. M10—4A 76
(off Hanson Rd.)
Goole St. M11—5C 88
Goosecote Hill. BL7—1C 10
Goose Grn. WA14—1F 137
Goosehouse Grn. SK6—6B 122
Goose La. OL12—4H 19
Goostrey Clo. SK9—6A 152
Goostrey Av. M20—1E 117
Gorden St. OL11—6A 20
Gorden Ter. M9—3G 75
Gordon Av. BL3—2G 37
Gordon Av. M19—6D 102
Gordon Av. M33—3B 114
Gordon Av. OL4—3F 65
Gordon Av. OL9—6G 63
Gordon Av. SK7—2D 144
Gordon Pl. M20—4F 117
Gordon Rd. M27—5C 70
Gordon Rd. M30—2F 83
Gordon St. BL9—1C 28
Gordon St. M7—1B 86
Gordon St. M16—2B 100
Gordon St. M18—1G 103
Gordon St. OL2—6G 35
(in two parts)
Gordon St. OL4—4A 66
(Lees)
Gordon St. OL4—3C 66
(Springhead)
Gordon St. OL6—1B 92
Gordon St. OL9—5F 63
Gordon St. OL16—1F 35
Gordon St. SK4—1G 131
Gordon St. SK14—5C 106
Gordon St. SK15—4F 93
Gordon Way. OL10—4B 30
Gore Av. M5—3D 84
Gore Av. M35—3H 77
Goredale Av. M18—4G 103
Gore Cres. M5—2D 84
Gore Dri. M5—2D 84
Gorelan Rd. M18—2F 103
Gore St. BL9—3G 29
Gore St. M1—4F 87 & 6C 162
Gore St. M3—4C 86 & 5E 161
Gore St. M6—2G 85
Goring Av. M18—1F 103
Gorrells Clo. OL11—2D 32
Gorrell St. OL11—6A 20
Gorrells Way. OL11—2D 32
(in two parts)
Gorrells Way Ind. Est. OL11
—2D 32
Gorse Av. M32—4F 99
Gorse Av. M35—3C 90
Gorse Av. OL5—2G 81
Gorse Av. OL8—6G 65
Gorse Av. SK6—5C 134
Gorse Bank. BL9—2G 29
Gorse Cres. M32—4F 99
Gorse Dri. M28—3B 54
Gorse Dri. M32—4F 99
Gorse Field Clo. M26—3G 41
Gorsefield Dri. M27—4F 71
Gorsefield Hey. SK9—1H 159
Gorse Hall Clo. SK16—6D 92
Gorse Hall Dri. SK15—4D 92
Gorse Hall Rd. SK16—6D 92
Gorselands. SK8—2D 152
Gorse La. M32—4F 99
Gorse Pit. BL9—2G 29
Gorse Rd. M27—5E 71
Gorse Rd. M28—1G 69
Gorse Rc. OL16—5G 21
Gorses Mt. BL2—2E 39
Gorse Sq. M31—6B 110
Gorse St. M32—4E 99
Gorse St. OL9—5F 63
Gorse, The. WA14—5D 136
Gorseway. SK5—5B 120
Gorsey Av. M22—6A 128
Gorsey Bank. OL15—2G 9
Gorsey Bank Rd. SK3—3C 130

Gorsey Brow. M31—5H 97
Gorsey Brow. SK6—1G 133
Gorsey Brow. SK14—6C 108
Gorsey Brow St. SK1—2A 132
Gorsey Clough Dri. BL8—6H 13
Gorsey Clough Wlk. BL8—6H 13
Gorsey Dri. M22—1A 140
Gorseyfields. M35—5A 90
Gorsey Hill St. OL10—4F 31
Gorsey La. OL6—5A 80
Gorsey La. WA14—6D 124
Gorsey Mt. St. SK1—2A 132
Gorsey M. M22—1A 140
Gorsey Rd. SK9—2C 158
Gorsey Way. OL6—5A 80
Gorston Wlk. M22—5A 140
Gort Clo. BL9—6E 43
Gorton Cres. M34—5C 104
Gorton Cross Cen. M18—2F 103
Gorton Gro. M28—4E 55
Gorton La. M12 & M18—6C 88
Gorton Rd. M11—5B 88
Gorton Rd. SK5—2H 119
Gorton St. BL2—1C 38
Gorton St. BL4—2D 54
Gorton St. M3—3D 86 & 3G 161
Gorton St. M10—1G 87
Gorton St. M30—4C 82
Gorton St. OL7—4F 91
Gorton St. OL9—3H 63
Gorton St. OL10—3G 31
Gortonvilla Wlk. M12—1B 102
Gosforth Clo. BL8—6C 14
Gosforth Clo. OL1—6E 49
Gosforth Wlk. M22—5A 140
Goshen La. BL9—1D 42
Gosling Clo. M16—4D 100
Gosport Sq. M7—6H 73
Gosport Wlk. M8—5E 75
(off Smeaton St.)
Goss Hill St. OL4—3G 65
Gotha Clo. M13—1G 101 &
5F 167
Gotherage Clo. SK6—1C 134
Gotherage La. SK6—1C 134
Gothic Clo. SK6—1D 134
Gough St. OL10—3G 31
Gough St. SK3—2F 131
Goulden Rd. M20—3E 117
Goulden St. M4—3F 87 & 3C 162
Goulden St. M6—3E 85
Goulder Rd. M18—4G 103
Gould St. M34—4E 105
Gould St. M34—2F 87 & 1C 162
Gould St. OL1—1F 65
Gourham Dri. SK8—3B 142
Govan St. M22—2C 128
Gowan Dri. M24—6F 45
Gowanlock's St. BL1—3A 24
Gowan Rd. M16—6C 100
Gower Av. SK7—2C 144
Gowerdale Rd. SK5—4C 120
Gower Rd. SK4—5F 119
Gower Rd. SK14—6B 106
Gowers St. OL16—3B 20
Gower St. BL1—5H 23
Gower St. BL4—6E 39
Gower St. M27—2E 71
Gower St. OL1—2E 65
Gower St. OL6—2A 92
Gowran Pk. OL4—3H 65
Gowy Clo. SK9—5A 152
Goya Rise. OL1—3H 49
Goyt Av. SK6—1D 146
Goyt Cres. SK6—6F 121
Goyt Cres. SK6—6F 121
Goyt Rd. SK1—6D 146
Goyt Rd. SK6—1D 146
Goyt St. SK12—2H 157
Goyt Valley. SK6—1E 133
Goyt Valley Rd. SK6—6F 121
Goyt Valley Wlk. SK6—6F 121
Grace St. OL12—1A 20
Grac_ Wlk. M4—4H 87 & 6H 163
Gracie Av. OL1—6F 49
Gradwell St. SK3—3F 131
Gradwell Wlk. M15—2C 100
Grafton Av. M30—1A 84
Grafton Ct. M15—2B 100

Grafton Ct. OL1—3A 50
(off Grafton St.)
Grafton Ct. OL6—5B 20
Grafton Mall. WA14—1F 137
Graftons, The. WA14—1F 137
Grafton St. BL1—5H 23
Grafton St. BL9—5D 28
Grafton St. M13—2F 101
Grafton St. M35—3G 77
Grafton St. OL1—3A 50
Grafton St. OL6—3B 92
(in two parts)
Grafton St. OL16—5B 20
Grafton St. SK4—6G 119
Grafton St. SK14—4B 106
Grafton St. SK15—2H 93
Grafton St. WA14—1F 137
Graham Cres. M30—5A 110
Graham Dri. SK12—6G 147
Graham Rd. M6—1C 84
Graham Rd. SK1—3B 132
Graham St. BL1—5B 24
Graham St. M11—5C 88
Graham St. OL7—4F 91
Grainger Av. M12—4C 102
Grains Rd. OL2—1G 49
Grains Rd. OL3—1C 50
Gralam Clo. M33—2E 127
Grammar School Rd. OL8—1H 77
Grampian Clo. OL9—4G 63
Grampian Way. OL2—5D 34
Granada Rd. M34—4H 103
Granary La. M28—6H 69
Granary Way. M33—1H 125
Granby Houses. M1—5E 87 &
2B 166
Granby Rd. M27—4C 70
Granby Rd. M32—6D 96
Granby Rd. SK2—6B 132
Granby Rd. SK8—5D 142
Granby Rd. WA15—2B 126
Granby Row. M1—5E 87 & 2B 166
Granby St. BL8—1F 27
Granby St. OL9—6G 63
Grandale St. M14—4D 101
Grandidge St. OL11—6G 19
Grand Union Way. M30—5F 83
Grange Av. BL3—4C 40
Grange Av. M19—1B 118
Grange Av. M27—1D 70
Grange Av. M30—1F 83
Grange Av. M31—5A 96
Grange Av. M32—5D 98
Grange Av. M34—5H 105
Grange Av. OL8—5A 64
Grange Av. OL16—1D 34
Grange Av. SK4—4F 119
Grange Av. SK8—2B 142
Grange Av. WA15—4B 126
(Altrincham)
Grange Av. WA15—3A 138
(Hale)
Grange Clo. SK14—6D 106
Grange Ct. OL8—5B 64
Grange Ct. WA14—4E 137
Grange Cres. M31—6E 97
Grange Dri. M9—6H 61
Grange Dri. M30—1F 83
Grangeforth Rd. M8—3B 74
Grange Gro. M25—1D 58
Grange La. M20—1F 129
Grange La. OL3—1H 51
Grange Mill Wlk. M10—4B 76
Grange Pk. Av. OL6—5B 80
Grange Pk. Av. SK8—6H 129
Grange Pk. Av. SK9—1D 158
Grange Pk. Rd. BL7—5G 11
Grange Pk. Rd. M9—6H 61
Grange Pk. Rd. SK8—6H 129
Grange Pl. M30—4B 110
Grange Rd. BL3—2F 37
Grange Rd. BL4—6C 38
Grange Rd. BL7—4G 11
Grange Rd. BL8—3H 27
Grange Rd. M21—5G 99
Grange Rd. M24—1D 46
Grange Rd. M28—4A 68
Grange Rd. M30—1C 82
Grange Rd. M31—6E 97

Grange Rd. M33—5H 113
Grange Rd. OL12—2H 7
Grange Rd. SK7—2H 143
Grange Rd. WA14—4E 137
Grange Rd. WA15—4B 126
Grange Rd. N. SK14—5D 106
Grange Rd. S. SK14—6D 106
(in two parts)
Grange St. M6—3E 85
Grange St. M35—5D 76
Grange St. OL9—2C 64
Grange St. OL12—1H 19
Grange, The. M14—4G 101
Grange, The. SK14—6D 106
Grangethorpe Dri. M19—2A 118
Grangethorpe Rd. M14—5G 101
Grangethorpe Rd. M31—6E 97
Grange Wlk. M24—5G 45
Grangeway. SK9—3H 151
Grangewood. BL7—4G 11
Grangewood Dri. M9—4F 75
Granite St. OL1—1F 65
Gransden Dri. M8—5E 75
Granshaw St. M10—2A 88
Gransmoor Av. M11—6H 89
Gransmoor Rd. M11—6H 89
Grantchester Pl. BL4—6B 38
Grantchester Way. BL2—4G 25
Grant Clo. M9—1F 75
Grant Ct. BL0—2D 4
Grantham Clo. BL1—4A 24
Grantham Dri. BL8—6D 14
Grantham Rd. SK4—1E 131
Grantham St. M14—4E 101
Grantham St. OL4—2E 65
Granton OL11—6H 19
Grant St. BL3—2C 38
Grant St. BL4—5D 38
Grant St. OL11—3D 32
Granville Av. M7—3A 74
Granville Av. M16—5A 100
Granville Clo. OL9—2A 64
Granville Ct. M16—4A 100
Granville Ct. OL16—2F 35
Granville Gdns. M20—1E 129
Granville Rd. BL3—4G 37
Granville Rd. M14—1G 117
Granville Rd. M31—4G 97
Granville Rd. M34—4B 90
Granville Rd. SK8—6D 130
Granville Rd. SK9—4C 158
Granville Rd. WA15—5C 126
Granville St. BL4—5F 39
Granville St. M27—3F 71
Granville St. M28—6E 55
Granville St. M30—2F 83
Granville St. OL6—3B 92
Granville St. 'L9—1A 64
Granville Ter. OL6—3B 92
Granville Wlk. OL9—1A 64
Grasdene Av. M9—6G 61
Grasmere Av. BL3—3A 40
Grasmere Av. BL4—2B 54
Grasmere Av. M25—2A 58
Grasmere Av. M27—1C 70
Grasmere Av. M31—6A 96
Grasmere Av. OL10—5F 31
Grasmere Av. SK4—3G 119
Grasmere Clo. SK15—1E 93
Grasmere Cres. M30—2D 82
Grasmere Cres. SK6—4C 134
Grasmere Cres. SK7—5G 143
Grasmere Gro. OL7—1F 91
Grasmere Rd. M27—5F 71
Grasmere Rd. M31—6C 110
Grasmere Rd. M32—4D 96
Grasmere Rd. M33—1C 126
Grasmere Rd. OL2—1A 48
Grasmere Rd. OL4—3G 65
Grasmere Rd. SK8—2F 141
Grasmere Rd. SK9—5F 159
Grasmere Rd. WA15—5C 126
Grasmere St. M12—4D 102
Grasmere St. OL12—2H 19
Grasmere Wlk. M24—5H 45
Grason Av. SK9—6G 151
Grasscroft. SK5—3C 120
Grasscroft Clo. M14—5D 100
Grasscroft Rd. SK15—4E 93

Grassfield Av. M7—5G 73
Grassholm Dri. SK2—5G 133
Grassingham Gdns. M6—2F 85
Grassington Av. M10—2A 76
Grassington Ct. BL8—1F 27
Grassington Pl. BL2—4C 24
Grass Mead. M34—1H 121
Grassmere St. BL1—2B 24
Grassmoor Cres. SK13—5F 109
Grathome Wlk. BL3—3A 38
Gratrix Av. M5—6H 85
Gratrix St. M18—3G 103
Gratrix St. M33—6F 115
Gravel Bank Rd. SK6—3H 121
Gravel La. M3—3C 86 & 4F 161
(in two parts)
Gravel La. SK9—5B 158
Gravel Walks. OL4—2F 65
Graver La. M10—6D 76
Graves St. M26—1F 41
Gray Clo. SK14—4B 108
Gray Ho. BL1—5A 24
(off Gray St.)
Graymar Rd. M28—5C 54
Graymarsh Dri. SK12—5E 155
Graysands Rd. WA15—2H 137
Grayson Av. M25—1E 59
Grayson Rd. M28—5D 54
Grayson Way. OL3—3F 53
Gray St. BL1—5A 24
(in two parts)
Graythorpe Wlk. M5—4G 85
Graythorp Wlk. M14—4F 101
Graythwaite Rd. BL1—3D 22
Greame St. M14—4D 100
Gt. Ancoats St. M4—3F 87 & 4C 162
Gt. Arbour Way. M24—6H 45
Gt. Bent Clo. OL12—5B 8
Gt. Bridgewater St. M-5C 86&2F 165
Gt. Cheetham E. M7 & M8—5A 74
Gt. Cheetham St. W. M7—6G 73
Gt. Clowes St. M7 & M3—5G 73
& 1D 160
Gt. Ducie St. M3—2D 86 & 1G 161
Gt. Egerton St. SK1—2G 131
Greatfield Rd. M22—2H 139
Gt. Flatt. OL12—2D 18
Gt. Gable Clo. OL1—1E 65
Gt. Gates Clo. OL11—1G 33
Gt. Gates Rd. OL11—2G 33
Gt. George St. M3—3B 86 & 4C 160
Gt. George St. OL16—5H 19
Gt. Hall Clo. M26—3G 41
Gt. Holme. BL3—3B 38
Gt. Howarth. OL12—5H 7
Gt. Howarth Rd. OL12—5A 8
Gt. Jackson St. M15—6C 86 & 3E 165
Gt. John St. M3—5C 86 & 1E 165
Gt. Jones St. M12—1C 102
Great Lee. OL12—6D 6
Gt. Lee Wlk. OL12—6D 6
Gt. Marlborough St. M1—6E 87 &
3A 166
Gt. Marld Clo. BL1—3D 22
Gt. Meadow. OL2—4C 34
Gt. Moor St. BL3 & BL1—1B 38
Gt. Moor St. SK2—6B 132
Gt. Newton St. M10—6C 76
Gt. Norbury St. SK14—4A 106
Gt. Portwood St. SK1—1H 131
Gt. Southern St. M14—4F 101
Greatstone Clo. M26—4D 40
Greatstone Rd. M32 & M16—3F 99
Gt. Stones Clo. BL7—1C 10
Gt. Underbank. SK1—2H 131
Gt. Western St. M14—3D 100
Greave. SK6—5B 122
Greave. OL11—3D 18
Greave Fold. SK6—5B 122
Greave Rd. SK1—3C 132
Greaves Av. BL2—1A 26
Greaves Av. M35—5D 76
Greaves Ro. SK9—2A 58
Greaves St. OL1—2D 64
Greaves St. OL2—6G 35
Greaves St. OL4—3B 66
Greaves St. OL5—1E 81
Grebe Clo. SK12—3B 154
Grebe Wlk. SK2—1G 145

Grecian Cres. BL3—3B 38
Grecian St. M7—6G 73
Grecian St. N. M7—5G 73
Grecian Ter. M7—6G 73
Greeba Rd. M23—5E 127
Greek St. M1—6F 87 & 3C 166
Greek St. SK3—3G 131
Greenacre La. M28—6H 69
Greenacre Rd. M27—5D 70
Greenacres Ct. OL12—5B 8
Greenacres Dri. M19—5A 118
Greenacres Rd. OL4—2F 65
Green Av. BL3—4D 38
Green Av. M27—4F 71
Green Av. M28—4A 54
Green Bank. BL2—2G 25
Green Bank. BL4—6E 39
Greenbank. OL12—4C 6
(off Tonacliffe Rd.)
Green Bank. SK14—2F 119
Greenbank Av. M27—5D 70
Greenbank Av. OL3—6C 52
Greenbank Av. SK4—1A 130
Greenbank Av. SK8—6E 129
Greenbank Cres. SK6—6D 134
Greenbank Dri. OL15—6D 8
Greenbank Rd. BL3—2F 37
(in two parts)
Greenbank Rd. M6—2E 85
Green Bank Rd. M26—2F 41
Greenbank Rd. M33—4G 113
Greenbank Rd. OL12—1H 19
Greenbank Rd. SK6—2F 135
Greenbank Rd. SK8—5E 129
Greenbank Ter. M24—6C 46
Greenbank Ter. SK4—1G 131
Green Beech Clo. SK6—4C 134
Greenbooth Clo. SK16—6D 92
Greenbooth Rd. OL12—1H 17
Green Bri. Dri. OL11—1F 33
Green Bri. La. OL3—4F 53
Greenbrook Clo. BL9—1E 29
Greenbrook St. BL9—1E 29
Greenbrow Pde. M23—1G 139
Greenbrow Rd. M23—6G 127
Greenburn Dri. BL2—3G 25
Green Clo. SK8—5E 129
Greencourt Dri. M28—5B 54
Green Courts. WA14—2D 136
Green Croft. SK6—6B 122
Greencroft Rd. M30—1D 82
Greendale Gro. M34—1H 121
Green Dri. BL6—6A 22
Green Dri. M19—6B 102
Green Dri. SK9—5H 151
Green Dri. WA15—4A 126
Green End. M34—1H 121
Green End Rd. M19—4A 118
Greenfield Av. M30—5C 82
Greenfield Av. M31—5F 97
Greenfield Clo. BL4—4G 27
Greenfield Clo. SK3—5G 131
Greenfield Clo. WA15—5C 126
Greenfield Ct. OL10—4F 31
Greenfield La. OL2—1F 49
Greenfield La. OL11—1G 33
Greenfield La. OL16—6B 8
Greenfield Rd. M28—5D 54
Greenfield St. M34—6D 90
Greenfield St. OL11—1G 33
Greenfield St. SK14—5B 106
Greenfield Ter. M31—5A 96
Green Fold. M18—1H 103
Greenfold Av. BL4—2D 54
Greenford Clo. SK8—1D 142
Greenford Rd. M8—4C 74
Green Gables Clo. SK8—4F 141
Greengate. M3—2C 86 & 2E 161
(in two parts)
Greengate. M10 & M24—6C 62
Green Ga. SK4—1B 122
Green Ga. WA15—1D 148
Greengate Clo. OL12—5B 8
Greengate La. BL2—5H 25
Greengate La. M25—5E 59
Greengate Lawns. M3—2C 86 & 2E 161

Greengate Rd. M34—3G 105
Greengate St. M24—3D 62
Greengate St. OL4—3E 65
(in three parts)
Greenhalgh Moss La. BL8—6B 14
Greenhalgh St. M35—5C 76
Greenhalgh St. SK4—1G 131
Greenhalgh Wlk. M4—3G 87
(off Jackroom Dri.)
Greenhall Rd. SK9—3E 159
Greenham Rd. M23—1F 127
Greenhead Fold. SK6—2G 133
Greenhead Wlk. BL3—3A 38
Greenheys. BL2—2G 25
Greenheys Cres. BL8—2H 13
Greenheys La. M15—1A 100
Greenheys Rd. M28—3A 54
Green Hill. M25—5E 59
Greenhill Av. BL3—2F 37
Greenhill Av. BL4—2E 55
Greenhill Av. M33—3A 114
Greenhill Av. OL2—4C 34
Greenhill Av. OL12—3G 19
Greenhill Cotts. OL5—1F 81
Greenhill La. BL3—3D 36
Greenhill Pas. OL1—3E 65
Green Hill Pl. SK3—4F 131
Greenhill Rd. BL8—4G 27
Greenhill Rd. M8—4C 74
Greenhill Rd. M24—2C 62
Green Hill Rd. SK14—4D 106
Greenhill Rd. WA15—5C 126
Greenhill St. M15—2D 100
Green Hill St. SK3—4F 131
Greenhill Ter. M24—2D 62
Green Hill Ter. SK3—4F 131
Greenhill Terraces. OL4—3E 65
Greenhill Wlk. SK12—1H 157
Greenholme Clo. M10—2D 76
Greenhow St. M35—3H 89
Greenhurst Cres. OL8—1E 79
Greenhurst La. OL6—5A 80
Greenhurst Rd. OL6—4H 79
Green Hythe Rd. SK8—1G 151
Greening Rd. M19—5D 102
Greenland Rd. BL3—4B 38
Greenland St. M6—3E 85
Greenland St. M8—4B 74
Green La. BL3—4B 38
Green La. BL4—2A 56
Green La. M18—1F 103
Green La. M24—5B 46
(Middleton)
Green La. M24—2D 62
(Middleton Junction)
Green La. M25—6C 42
Green La. M30—4C 110
(Cadishead)
Green La. M30—3E 83
(Eccles)
Green La. M33—3G 113
Green La. M35—1G 89
Green La. OL3—3G 51
Green La. OL4—5B 50
Green La. OL5—5D 66
Green La. OL6—6F 79
Green La. OL8—1B 78
Green La. OL10—3G 31
Green La. OL12—3G 19
Green La. OL16—3A 20
Green La. SK4—6D 118
Green La. SK6—2H 133
Green La. SK7—2D 144
Green La. SK9—5F 159
(Alderley Edge)
Green La. SK9—2E 159
(Wilmslow)
Green La. SK12—3H 157
(Disley)
Green La. SK12—3A 156
(Poynton)
Green La. SK14—6E 107
(Godley Green)
Green La. SK14—3H 109
(Hadfield)
Green La. SK14—1F 109
(Hollingworth)

Green La. SK14—5E 107
(Hyde)
Green La. WA15—2B 138
Green La. N. WA15—6B 126
Greenlaw Ct. M16—4D 100
Greenlea Av. M18—4F 103
Greenleach La. M28—3G 69
Greenleaf Clo. M28—5B 68
Greenleas. BL6—1A 36
Greenlees St. OL12—3H 19
Green Meadow. OL12—5B 8
Green Meadows. SK6—4D 134
Green Meadows Dri. SK6—4D 134
Green Meadow Wlk. M22—4C 140
Greenmount Ct. BL1—5E 23
Green Mt. Dri. BL8—1H 13
Greenmount Dri. OL10—6H 31
Greenmount Ho. BL1—6E 23
Greenmount La. BL1—4D 22
Greenmount Pk. BL4—2A 56
Greenoak. M26—2C 56
Greenoak Dri. M28—4E 55
Greenoak Dri. M33—2C 126
Greenock Clo. BL3—2C 36
Greenock Dri. OL10—4B 30
Green Pk. Clo. BL8—2H 13
Greenpark Rd. M22—2B 128
Green Pastures. SK4—2H 129
Green Rd. M31—6C 110
Greenroyd Av. BL2—3G 25
Greenroyde. OL11—6G 19
Greenshank Clo. OL11—4B 18
Greenside. BL4—6E 39
Greenside. M28—6A 70
Greenside. SK4—2C 130
Greenside Av. BL4—3H 55
Greenside Av. OL4—5H 49
Greenside Clo. BL8—1D 12
Greenside Clo. SK16—5E 93
Greenside Ct. M30—2F 83
Greenside Cres. M35—3H 89
Greenside Dri. BL8—2B 14
Greenside Dri. M30—6D 94
Greenside Dri. WA14—4G 137
Greenside La. M35—2G 89
Greenside Pl. M34—1G 121
Greenside St. BL2—4C 26
Greenside St. M11—5D 88
Greenside Way. M24—4C 62
Greenson Dri. M24—2G 61
Greenstead Av. M8—3C 74
Greens, The. OL12—4G 7
Greenstone Dri. M6—6D 72
Green St. BL0—2B 4
Green St. BL1—6B 24
Green St. BL4—6E 39
Green St. BL8—1H 27
(Bury)
Green St. BL8—1F 27
(Walshaw)
Green St. M14—2H 117
Green St. M24—6B 46
Green St. M26—4G 41
(in two parts)
Green St. M30—5D 82
Green St. M32—1C 114
Green St. M35—4E 77
Green St. OL8—3B 64
Green St. OL9—6H 63
Green St. SK3—5H 131
Green St. SK9—5G 159
Green St. SK14—6C 106
Green, The. BL8—2H 13
Green, The. M27—1H 71
Green, The. M28—6A 70
Green, The. M31—5D 110
Green, The. OL8—6E 65
Green, The. SK4—5E 119
Green, The. SK6—2E 147
Green, The. SK8—5B 142
Green, The. SK9—4A 152
Green, The. SK15—1H 93
Green, The. WA15—4C 126
Greenthorne Av. SK4—2F 119
Greenthorn Wlk. M15—2D 100
(off Botham Clo.)
Green Tree Gdns. SK6—1H 133
Greenvale. OL11—3A 18

Greenvale Cotts. OL15—1H 9
Greenvale Dri. SK8—5G 129
Greenview Dri. M20—3G 129
Green Villa Pk. SK9—5B 158
Green Wlk. M16—4A 100
Green Wlk. M32—5B 98
Green Wlk. SK8—5E 129
Green Wlk. WA14—2C 136
Green Wlk. WA15—4H 125
Green Walks. M25—6G 59
Green Way. BL1—2C 24
Greenway. M22—3C 128
Greenway. M24—4H 61
Greenway. OL2—4D 34
Green Way. OL11—4B 32
Greenway. SK6—2C 134
Greenway. SK7—1F 153
Greenway. SK9—3E 159
Greenway. SK14—6B 106
Greenway. WA14—6C 124
Greenway Av. M19—1D 118
Greenway Clo. BL1—1C 24
Greenway Clo. BL8—2H 27
Greenway Clo. M33—6G 113
Greenway Dri. OL5—1D 80
Greenway Rd. SK8—1G 151
Greenway Rd. WA15—3H 125
Greenways. M10—2D 76
Greenways. OL7—5D 78
Greenwich Clo. M10—1F 89
Greenwich Clo. OL11—5B 18
Greenwood Av. M27—2H 71
Greenwood Av. M28—5E 55
Greenwood Av. OL6—5G 79
(in two parts)
Greenwood Av. SK2—5C 132
Greenwood Clo. M28—4A 68
Greenwood Clo. WA15—6D 126
Greenwood Dri. SK9—1G 159
Greenwood Gdns. SK6—6F 121
Greenwood Pl. OL15—4F 9
(off Hare Hill Rd.)
Greenwood Rd. M22—2H 139
Greenwoods La. BL2—1H 25
Greenwood St. BL4—1F 55
Greenwood St. M6—1F 85
Greenwood St. OL4—1G 65
(Oldham, in two parts)
Greenwood St. OL8—1D 78
Greenwood St. OL15—4F 9
Greenwood St. WA14—1F 137
Greenwood Vale. BL1—2A 24
Greer St. M11—5E 89
Gregge St. OL10—4G 31
Gregory Av. BL2—5G 25
Gregory Av. SK6—2A 134
Gregory St. M12—1B 102
Gregory St. OL8—6A 64
Gregory St. SK14—2C 106
Gregson Field. BL3—3A 38
(in two parts)
Gregson Rd. SK5—3G 119
Gregson St. OL1—3D 64
Gregson Way. SK5—3H 119
Greg St. SK5—4G 119
Grelley Wlk. M14—4F 101
Grendale Av. SK1—2B 132
Grendale Av. SK7—4E 145
Grendale Dri. M16—2A 100
Grendon Av. OL8—5C 64
Grendon St. BL3—4G 37
Grendon Wlk. M12—1C 102
Grenfell Rd. M20—6E 117
Grenfell St. M20—6E 117
Grenham Av. M15—1B 100 & 5C 164
Grenville St. SK3—3F 131
Grenville Rd. SK7—2C 144
Grenville St. SK15—1H 93
Grenville St. SK16—5A 92
Gresford Clo. M21—1G 115
Gresham Clo. M25—2B 58
Gresham Dri. OL9—2A 64
Gresham St. BL1—2B 24
Gresham St. M34—3F 105
Gresham Wlk. SK4—6G 119
Gresty Av. M22—4D 140

Greswell St. M34—3E 105
Greta Av. SK8—1G 151
Gretney Wlk. M15—2D 100
Gretton Clo. M13—3A 102
Greville St. M13—3A 102
Grey Clo. SK6—5G 121
Grey Friar Ct. M3—2C 86 & 1E 161
Greyfriars Rd. M22—3H 139
Greyhound Dri. M6—6G 73
Greylands Clo. M33—5H 113
Greylands Rd. M20—3G 129
Grey Mare La. M11—4B 88
Greymont Rd. BL9—5F 15
Grey Rd. WA14—6D 124
Greyscroft Dri. M23—1G 139
Greysham Ct. M16—5C 100
Greystoke Av. M19—6E 103
Greystoke Av. M33—6B 114
Greystoke Av. WA15—5D 126
Greystoke Cres. M25—5C 42
Greystoke Dri. BL1—5B 10
Greystoke Dri. M24—5F 45
Greystoke Dri. SK9—4G 159
Greystoke La. M35—5D 76
Greystoke St. SK1—2A 132
Greystone Av. M21—1D 116
Greystone Wlk. SK4—2F 119
Grey St. M12—1A 102
Grey St. M24—6H 45
Grey St. M25—5G 59
Grey St. M26—4H 41
Grey St. M34—4D 104
Grey St. OL6—3A 92
Grey St. SK15—4G 93
Greyswood Av. M8—4B 74
Greythorne Rd. BL1—1D 22
Greywood Av. BL9—3F 29
Grierson St. BL1—2A 24
Grierson Wlk. M16—3C 100
Griffe La. BL9—3G 43
Griffin Clo. BL9—1F 29
Griffin Ct. M3—3C 86 & 4E 161
Griffin Gro. M19—1C 118
Griffin St. M7—5G 73
Griffiths Clo. M7—1B 86
Griffiths St. M10—6C 76
Grimes Cotts. OL12—2B 18
Grimes St. OL12—2B 18
Grime St. BL0—5C 4
Grimscott Clo. M9—2H 75
Grimshaw Av. M35—3G 77
Grimshaw La. M10—6H 75
Grimshaw La. M24—1A 62
Grimshaw St. M35—3E 77
Grimshaw St. SK1—2A 132
Grimstead Clo. M23—5E 127
Grindall Av. M10—1B 76
Grindleford Gdns. SK13—5G 109
 (off Buxton M.)
Grindleford Gro. SK13—5G 109
 (off Edale Cres.)
Grindleford Lea. SK13—5G 109
 (off Edale Cres.)
Grindleford Wlk. M21—4B 116
Grindleford Wlk. SK13—5G 109
 (off Edale Cres.)
Grindle Grn. M30—5E 83
Grindley Av. M21—4B 116
Grindlow St. M13—2A 102
Grindon Av. M7—4E 73
Grindrod Clo. OL12—4G 7
Grindrod St. M26—3F 41
 (in two parts)
Grindrod St. OL12—2G 19
Grindsbrook Rd. M26—6F 27
Grinton Av. M13—5A 102
Grisdale Dri. M24—5G 45
Grisdale Rd. BL3—2G 37
Grisebeck Way. OL1—2C 64
Grisedale Av. OL2—5A 34
Grisedale Ct. M9—5A 62
Grisedale Rd. OL11—1B 32
Gritley Wlk. M22—4A 140
Grizebeck Clo. M18—1E 103
Grizedale Clo. BL1—3D 22
Grizedale Clo. SK15—4G 81
Grizedale Rd. SK6—5H 121

Groby Ct. WA14—1E 137
Groby Pl. WA14—6E 125
Groby Rd. M21—1H 115
Groby Rd. M34—6E 91
Groby Rd. WA14—1D 136
Groby Rd. N. M34—5D 90
Groby St. OL8—6E 65
Groby St. SK15—4G 93
Groomsport Dri. M8—6A 74
Groom St. M1—6F 87 & 3C 166
Grosvenor Av. M25—6C 42
Grosvenor Clo. M28—4E 55
Grosvenor Clo. SK9—5D 158
Grosvenor Ct. M7—3H 73
Grosvenor Ct. M33—4H 113
Grosvenor Ct. OL7—4G 91
Grosvenor Cres. SK14—6A 106
Grosvenor Dri. M28—4E 55
Grosvenor Dri. SK12—4C 154
Grosvenor Gdns. M7—1B 86
Grosvenor Gdns. M22—5C 128
Grosvenor Gdns. SK15—4E 93
Grosvenor Ho. M33—5H 113
Grosvenor Ho. M. M8—1B 74
Grosvenor Pl. OL7—4G 91
Grosvenor Rd. M16—5B 100
Grosvenor Rd. M25—6C 42
Grosvenor Rd. M27—4H 71
Grosvenor Rd. M28—4E 55
Grosvenor Rd. M30—2C 82
Grosvenor Rd. M31—5E 97
Grosvenor Rd. M33—4H 113
Grosvenor Rd. SK4—6C 118
 (in two parts)
Grosvenor Rd. SK6—4D 134
Grosvenor Rd. SK8—1E 143
Grosvenor Rd. SK14—6B 106
Grosvenor Rd. WA14—6G 125
Grosvenor Sq. M7—1B 86
Grosvenor Sq. M15—6E 87 & 4A 166
Grosvenor Sq. M33—5H 113
Grosvenor Sq. SK15—4E 93
Grosvenor St. BL2—1C 38
Grosvenor St. BL3—3A 40
Grosvenor St. BL4—1G 55
Grosvenor St. BL9—5D 28
Grosvenor St. M1—6E 87 & 4B 166
Grosvenor St. M25—5G 59
Grosvenor St. M26—3F 41
Grosvenor St. M27—1F 71
Grosvenor St. M32—5D 98
Grosvenor St. M34—3D 104
Grosvenor St. OL7—4F 91
 (in two parts)
Grosvenor St. OL10—4E 31
Grosvenor St. OL11—4C 32
Grosvenor St. SK15—3H 131
Grosvenor St. SK7—2D 144
Grosvenor St. SK15—4E 93
 (in two parts)
Grosvenor Way. OL2—5B 48
Grotton Hollow. OL4—3C 66
Grotton Meadows. OL4—4D 66
Grouse St. OL12—2H 19
Grove Arc. SK9—2E 159
Grove Av. M35—6E 77
Grove Av. SK9—2D 158
Grove Clo. M14—4G 101
Grove Cotts. OL3—1D 52
Grove Ct. M33—5D 114
Grove Ct. SK7—2E 145
Grove Hill. M28—5B 68
Grove Ho. M15—2F 101
Grovehurst. M27—5B 70
Grove La. M20—6E 117
Grove La. SK8—1C 152
Grove La. WA15—4H 125
 (Altrincham)
Grove La. WA15—2A 138
 (Hale)
Grove M. M28—6F 55
Grove Pk. M33—5H 113
Grove Rd. M24—5B 46
Grove Rd. OL3—2F 53
Grove Rd. SK15—1H 93
Grove Rd. WA15—2G 137
Grove St. BL1—3H 23
Grove St. BL4—1G 55

Grove St. BL9—1G 29
Grove St. M7—6A 74
Grove St. M35—5H 89
Grove St. OL1—2E 65
 (in two parts)
Grove St. OL3—4F 53
Grove St. OL7—6C 78
Grove St. OL10—3G 31
Grove St. OL11—6G 19
Grove St. SK7—2E 145
Grove St. SK9—2E 159
Grove St. SK16—4B 92
Grove Ter. OL4—1A 66
Grove, The. BL2—2D 38
Grove, The. BL3—4B 40
Grove, The. M20—2F 129
Grove, The. M30—4H 83
Grove, The. M31—6B 96
Grove, The. M33—6B 114
Grove, The. OL2—1E 49
Grove, The. OL3—6H 51
Grove, The. SK2—4G 131
Grove, The. SK8—1C 152
Grove, The. SK14—3H 109
Grove, The. WA14—6F 125
Grovewood Clo. OL7—6C 78
Grundey St. SK7—3E 145
Grundy Av. M25—1C 72
Grundy La. BL9—4E 29
Grundy Rd. BL4—2G 55
Grundy St. M28—6H 55
Grundy St. OL1—2E 65
Grundy St. SK4—1A 130
Guardian Ct. M33—4A 114
Guest Rd. M25—3E 59
Guide La. M34—1F 105
Guide Post Sq. M13—1H 101 & 6G 167
Guide St. M5—4C 84
Guido St. BL1—3H 23
Guido St. M35—4E 77
Guild Av. M30—4C 66
Guildford Av. SK8—6C 142
Guildford Clo. SK1—4B 132
Guildford Dri. OL6—4G 79
Guildford Rd. BL1—3F 23
Guildford Rd. M6—1B 84
Guildford Rd. M19—5D 102
Guildford Rd. M31—3G 97
Guildford Rd. SK16—6E 93
Guildford St. OL16—4A 20
 (in two parts)
Guildhall Clo. M15—2E 101
Guild St. BL7—4E 11
Guilford Rd. M30—4D 82
Guiness Ho. OL16—5B 20
Guinness Rd. M17—5H 83
Guinness Rd. Trading Est. M17
 —5A 84
Guiseley Clo. BL9—3E 15
Gullane Clo. M10—4C 76
Gull Clo. SK12—4B 154
Gunson Ct. M10—2G 87 & 1F 163
Gunson St. M10—2G 87 & 2F 163
Gun St. M4—3F 87 & 4D 162
Gurner Av. M5—6H 85
Gurney St. M4—4H 87 & 5H 163
Gurth St. BL2—6D 24
Gutter La. BL0—2D 4
Guy Fawkes St. M5—6H 85
Guy St. M8—4B 74
Guywood La. SK6—6A 122
Gwelo St. M11—3C 88
Gwenbury Av. SK1—2B 132
Gwendore Av. M8—6B 60
Gwladys St. SK15—5G 81
Gwynant Pl. M20—2G 117
Gylden Clo. SK14—1F 107
Gypsy La. SK2—5C 132
Gypsy Wlk. SK2—5C 132

Hackberry Clo. WA14—3D 124
Hacken Bri. Rd. BL3—3E 39
Hacken La. BL3—3E 39
Hackford Clo. BL1—5G 23
Hackford Clo. BL8—6D 14

Hacking St. BL9—3E 29
Hacking St. M7—5A 74
Hacking St. M25—5E 59
Hackle St. M11—3E 89
Hackleton Clo. M4—4H 87 & 5H 163
Hackness Rd. M21—1F 115
Hackney Av. M10—1E 89
Hackwood Wlk. M8—4B 74
 (off Levenhurst Rd.)
Haddington Dri. M9—6G 61
Haddock St. M26—5G 41
Haddon Av. M10—2F 77
Haddon Clo. BL9—2E 43
Haddon Clo. SK6—1C 156
Haddon Clo. SK9—4F 159
Haddon Grn. SK13—5F 109
 (off Haddon M.)
Haddon Gro. M33—5A 114
Haddon Gro. SK5—2G 119
Haddon Gro. WA14—4H 125
Haddon Hall Rd. M35—3G 89
Haddon Ho. M5—2D 84
Haddon Lea. SK13—5F 109
 (off Grassmoor Cres.)
Haddon M. SK13—5F 109
Haddon Rd. M21—4B 116
Haddon Rd. M27—5C 70
Haddon Rd. M30—5D 82
Haddon Rd. SK7—4E 145
Haddon Rd. SK8—6G 141
Haddon St. M6—6F 73
Haddon St. M32—3D 98
Haddon Way. M34—6G 105
Haddon Way. OL2—5G 35
Hadfield Av. OL9—4H 63
Hadfield Cres. OL6—6A 80
Hadfield Rd. SK14—3G 109
Hadfield St. M7—5A 74
Hadfield St. M16—1A 100 & 6B 164
Hadfield St. OL8—6C 64
Hadfield St. SK16—6G 91
Hadfield Ter. OL6—6A 80
Hadleigh Clo. BL1—5E 11
Hadley Av. M13—5A 102
Hadley Clo. SK8—4B 142
Hadley St. M6—6F 73
Hadlow Clo. M10—2A 88
Hadlow Grn. SK5—3B 120
Hadwin St. BL1—4B 24
Hafton Rd. M7—5F 73
Hag Bank La. SK12—1H 157
Hag End Brow. BL2—2E 39
Haggate. OL2—4A 48
Haggate Cres. OL2—4A 48
Hags, The. BL9—2E 43
Hague Ho. OL8—4D 64
Hague Pl. SK15—3D 92
Hague Rd. M20—4E 117
Hague Rd. SK14—6D 108
Hague St. M10—6H 75
Hague St. OL4—1A 66
Hague St. OL6—1A 92
Haig Av. M30—5A 110
Haigh Av. SK4—4G 119
Haigh Hall Clo. BL0—5D 4
Haigh La. OL9 & OL1—6E 47
Haigh Pk. SK4—4G 119
Haigh St. BL1—5B 24
Haigh St. OL11—5A 20
Haig Rd. BL8—3H 27
Haig Rd. M32—4D 98
Haile Dri. M28—5B 68
Hailsham Clo. BL8—4C 14
Hailsham St. M11—3B 88
Hail St. BL0—5C 4
Haldene Wlk. M8—5B 74
Haldon Rd. M20—4H 117
Hale Av. SK12—5D 154
Hale Bank Av. M20—2D 116
Hale Ct. WA14—2F 137
Hale Grn. Ct. WA15—2A 138
Hale La. M35—3E 77
Hale Low Rd. WA15—2H 137
Hale Rd. WA14 & WA15—2F 137
Hales Clo. M35—3H 89
Halesden Rd. SK4—4F 119
Halesworth Wlk. M10—1G 87
Haletop. M22—3B 140

Hale Wlk. SK8—1C 142
Haley Clo. SK5—1H 119
Haley St. M8—4C 74
Half Acre. M26—1E 41
Half Acre Dri. OL11—5E 19
Half Acre Grn. SK9—1E 159
Half Acre La. M25—3F 59
(in two parts)
Half Acre La. OL11—5D 18
Half Acre M. OL11—5D 18
Halfacre Rd. M22—1A 140
Half Acre Rd. OL11—5D 18
Half Edge La. M30—2G 83
Half Moon La. SK2—5D 132
Halford Dri. M10—3B 76
Half St. M3—2C 86 & 2F 161
Half St. M24—6H 45
Halifax Rd. OL4—2B 50
Halifax Rd. OL12 & OL16—2B 20
Halifax Rd. OL15 & HX6—4G 9
Halifax St. BL1—4A 24
Haliwell St. BL1—3H 23
Hallam Rd. M10—6B 76
Hallam St. M26—3B 42
Hallam St. SK2—5A 132
Hall Av. M14—4H 101
Hall Av. M33—3G 113
Hall Av. SK15—6E 81
Hall Av. WA15—4H 125
Hall Bank. M30—3C 82
Hallbottom Pl. SK14—2D 106
Hallbottom St. SK14—2D 106
Hall Clo. SK14—2C 108
Hall Coppice, The. BL7—2B 10
Hall Cotts. OL3—3F 53
Hallcroft. M31—5D 110
Hallcroft Gdns. OL16—5E 21
Hall Dri. M24—2H 61
Hall Dri. SK14—2C 108
Halle Mall. M4—3E 87
(off Arndale Cen.)
Halle Sq. M4—3E 87
(off Arndale Cen.)
Hall Farm Av. M31—4D 96
Hall Fold. OL12—1B 6
Hall Fold. SK14—2H 109
Hall Gdns. OL12—1E 19
Hallgate Dri. SK8—3E 141
Hallgate Rd. SK1—3B 132
Hall Grn. Clo. SK16—4A 92
Hall Grn. Rd. SK16—4A 92
Hall Gro. M14—4H 101
Hall Gro. SK8—5G 129
Halliday Ct. OL15—5C 8
Halliday Rd. M10—6B 76
Halliford Rd. M10—5A 76
Hallington Clo. BL3—3A 38
Hall i' th' Wood La. BL1—1C 24
Hall i' th' Wood La. BL2—2D 24
Halliwell Av. OL8—6C 64
Halliwell Ind. Est. BL1—2H 23
(off Regan St.)
Halliwell La. M8—4B 74
Halliwell Rd. BL1—2G 23
Halliwell Rd. M25—2D 72
Halliwell St. M3—3E 87 &
3A 162
Halliwell St. M8—4B 74
Halliwell St. OL9—2G 77
Halliwell St. OL12—3G 19
(in two parts)
Halliwell St. OL15—4G 9
Halliwell St. OL16—4E 21
Hallkirk Wlk. M10—1D 76
Hall La. BL4—5F 39
(in two parts)
Hall La. M23—5H 127
Hall La. M31—5D 110
Hall La. SK6—3H 121
Hallman La. M22—6B 140
Hall Meadow. SK8—4A 142
Hall Moss La. SK7—2D 152
Hall Moss Rd. M9—5A 62
Hallows Av. M21—4A 116
Hall Rd. M14—4H 101
Hall Rd. OL6—6G 79

Hall Rd. SK7—4F 143
Hall Rd. SK9—4A 152
(Handforth)
Hall Rd. SK9—2D 158
(Wilmslow)
Hall Rd. WA14—4E 137
Hallroyd Brow. OL1—1C 64
Hall's Pl. OL4—3B 66
Hallstead Av. M28—5A 54
Hallstead Gro. M28—5A 54
Hall St. BL3—5F 39
(in two parts)
Hall St. BL8—1A 28
(Bury)
Hall St. BL8—1F 27
(Walshaw)
Hall St. BL9—1C 14
Hall St. M2—5D 86 & 1H 165
Hall St. M24—1A 62
Hall St. M26—1F 41
Hall St. M27—1F 71
Hall St. M35—5D 76
Hall St. OL2—3B 48
Hall St. OL4—2F 65
Hall St. OL10—4G 31
Hall St. OL12—1C 6
Hall St. SK1—2A 132
Hall St. SK8—5G 129
Hall St. SK14—4H 105
Hallsville Rd. M19—6E 103
Hallsworth Rd. M30—4C 82
Hallwood Av. M6—6A 72
Hallwood Rd. M23—5G 127
Hall Wood Rd. SK9—5H 151
Hallworth St. OL11—1E 33
Hallworth Av. M34—4B 90
Hallworth Rd. M8—3D 74
Halmore Rd. M10—3H 87 &
3G 163
Halsall Clo. BL9—5F 15
Halsall Dri. BL3—5A 38
Halsbury Clo. M12—1A 102
Halsey Clo. OL9—1E 77
Halsey Wlk. M8—4B 74
Halshaw La. BL4—2H 55
Halsmere Dri. M9—6G 61
Halstead Av. M6—1D 84
Halstead Av. M21—2G 115
Halstead Dri. M30—6F 95
Halstead Gro. SK8—1D 140
Halstead St. BL2—6C 24
Halstead St. BL9—6G 15
Halstead Wlk. BL9—6G 15
Halstock Wlk. M10—6F 75
(off Carslake Rd.)
Halston Clo. M15—2C 100
Halstone Av. SK9—5B 158
Halton Dri. WA15—2B 124
Halton Flats. OL10—3E 31
(off Pitt St.)
Halton Ho. M5—4F 85
Halton Rd. M11—3E 89
Halton St. BL2—6D 24
Halton St. SK14—4D 106
Halvard Av. BL9—5F 15
Halvard Ct. BL9—5F 15
Halvis Gro. M16—4H 99
Hambledon Clo. BL3—2D 36
Hamble M. M7—4F 73
Hambleton Clo. BL8—4F 27
Hambleton Dri. M23—1G 139
Hambleton Dri. M33—4F 113
Hambleton Rd. SK8—5G 141
Hambleton Wlk. M33—4F 113
Hambridge Clo. M8—4C 74
Hamel St. BL3—4H 37
Hamel St. SK14—2D 106
Hamer Bldgs. OL10—3D 30
Hamer Clo. OL7—4G 91
Hamer Ct. OL16—2B 20
Hamer Dri. M16—2B 100
Hamer Hall Cres. OL12—1A 20
Hamer Hill. M9—6E 61
Hamer La. OL16—2B 20
Hamer St. BL0—1B 14
Hamer St. M26—3A 42
Hamer Ter. BL9—6E 5
(off Ruby St.)
Hamerton Rd. M10—1G 87

Hamilcar Av. M30—3G 83
Hamilton Av. M30—5B 110
(Cadishead)
Hamilton Av. M30—4G 83
(Eccles)
Hamilton Av. OL2—4H 47
Hamilton Clo. BL8—2H 27
Hamilton Ct. BL3—4B 40
Hamilton Ct. M33—5B 114
Hamilton Cres. SK4—2D 130
Hamilton Gro. M16—2B 100
Hamilton Ho. WA14—6F 125
Hamilton Lodge. M14—4G 101
Hamilton M. M25—6E 59
Hamilton M. M30—2D 82
Hamilton Pl. OL7—4F 91
Hamilton Rd. M13—4B 102
Hamilton Rd. M25—6E 59
(Prestwich)
Hamilton Rd. M25—1C 58
(Whitefield)
Hamilton Sq. SK4—6G 119
Hamilton St. BL1—6C 10
Hamilton St. BL9—1D 28
Hamilton St. M7—4H 73
Hamilton St. M16—2B 100
Hamilton St. M27—2D 70
Hamilton St. M30—2D 82
Hamilton St. OL4—3E 65
Hamilton St. OL7—4F 91
Hamilton St. OL9—2G 63
Hamilton St. SK15—3D 92
Hamilton Way. OL10—4A 30
Hamlet Dri. M33—3G 113
Hamlet, The. BL6—5A 22
Hammerstone Rd. M18—1E 103
Hammett Rd. M33—1G 113
Hammond Av. SK4—4G 119
Hammond Flats. OL10—3E 31
(off Ashton St.)
Hamnet Clo. BL1—6E 11
Hamnett St. M11—4F 89
Hamnett St. SK14—4B 106
Hamon Rd. WA15—1G 137
Hampden Ct. M30—3F 83
Hampden Cres. M18—2E 103
Hampden Gro. M30—3F 83
Hampden Rd. M33—4A 114
Hampden Rd. M25—5F 59
Hampden Rd. OL2—1H 49
Hampden St. OL10—4F 31
Hampden St. OL11—5H 19
Hampshire Clo. BL9—5E 29
Hampshire Clo. SK5—4C 120
Hampshire Rd. M35—2A 90
Hampshire Rd. OL9—4H 63
Hampshire Rd. SK5—4C 120
Hampshire St. M7—4H 73
Hampshire Wlk. M8—5D 74
Hampson Clo. M30—4D 82
Hampson Cres. SK9—3G 151
Hampson Fold. M26—3F 41
Hampson Mill La. BL9—2D 42
Hampson Pl. OL6—5A 80
Hampson Rd. M32—5C 98
Hampson Rd. OL6—5A 80
Hampson St. M5—4A 86 & 6B 160
Hampson St. M10—1H 87
Hampson St. M26—3G 41
Hampson St. M27—2G 71
Hampson St. M30—4D 82
Hampson St. M33—5D 114
Hampson St. M35—3A 90
Hampson St. SK1—3B 132
Hampson St. Trading Est. M5
—4B 86 & 5C 160
Hampstead Av. M31—6A 96
Hampstead Dri. SK2—6C 132
Hampstead La. SK2—6B 132
Hampton Gro. BL9—5F 15
Hampton Gro. SK8—3A 142
Hampton Gro. WA14—2H 125
Hampton Pl. M15—1B 100 &
6D 164
Hampton Rd. BL3—4C 38
Hampton Rd. M21—6F 99
Hampton Rd. M30—5B 110
Hampton Rd. M31—6F 97
Hampton Rd. M35—3G 77

Hampton St. OL8—5B 64
Hamsell Rd. M13—6G 87 & 4E 167
Hanbury St. M10—1B 88
Hancock Clo. M14—4F 101
Hancock St. M30—1D 114
Handel M. M33—5C 114
Handel St. BL1—2H 23
Handforth Gro. M13—5A 102
Handforth Rd. SK5—4H 119
Handforth Rd. SK9—5A 152
Handle Av. M31—5C 96
Handle St. OL12—1B 6
Handley Av. M14—6F 101
Handley Clo. SK3—6E 131
Handley Rd. SK7—2G 143
Handley St. BL9—5D 28
Handley St. OL12—3F 19
Hands La. OL11—4C 18
Handsworth St. M12—6H 87 & 3H 167
Hanging Birch. M24—2D 60
Hanging Bri. M3—3D 86
(off Cateaton St.)
Hanging Chaddar La. OL2—6A 34
Hanging Ditch. M4—3D 86 & 4H 161
Hanging Lees Clo. OL16—1G 35
Hankinson Clo. M31—6D 110
Hankinson Wlk. M15—2C 100
Hankinson Way. M6—2G 85
Hanley Clo. M24—4A 62
Hanley Clo. SK12—2H 157
Hanlith M. M19—1B 118
Hanlon St. M8—2F 73
Hannah Baldwin Clo. M11—5B 88
Hannah St. M12—5C 102
Hannerton Rd. SK2—5H 35
Hannet Rd. M22—3B 140
Hanover Ct. M7—4F 73
Hanover Ct. BL3—2F 37
(off Greenbank Rd.)
Hanover Ct. M7—4H 73
Hanover St. M28—5B 70
Hanover Cres. M14—3H 101
Hanover Gdns. M7—3A 74
Hanover Ho. M4—4F 37
Hanover Rd. WA14—4D 124
Hanover St. BL1—6A 24
Hanover St. M4—3E 87 & 3A 162
Hanover St. OL5—1E 81
Hanover St. OL11—3C 32
Hanover St. OL15—4E 9
Hanover St. SK15—3D 92
Hanover St. N. M34—5E 91
Hanover St. S. M34—5E 91
Hanover Ter. SK5—6H 119
Hansdon Clo. M8—5C 74
Hansen Wlk. M22—3A 140
Hanslope Wlk. M9—3G 75
(off Swainsthorpe Dri.)
Hanson Clo. M24—6A 46
Hanson Rd. M10—4A 76
Hanson St. BL9—1D 28
Hanson St. M24—1B 62
(in two parts)
Hanson St. OL4—2G 65
Hanworth Clo. M13—6F 87 & 4D 166
Hapsford Wlk. M10—6A 76
Hapton Av. M32—6D 98
Hapton Pl. SK4—6G 119
Hapton St. M19—5C 102
Harbern Clo. M30—1F 83
Harborne Wlk. BL8—2H 13
Harboro Ct. M33—6H 113
Harboro Gro. M33—5H 113
Harboro Rd. M33—4G 113
Harboro Way. M33—5H 113
Harbour Farm Rd. SK14—1C 106
Harbour La. OL16—6F 21
Harbour La. N. OL16—5F 21
Harbour M. Ct. BL7—3F 11
Harbourne Av. M28—3E 69
Harbourne Clo. M28—3E 69
Harburn Wlk. M22—5C 140
Harcombe Rd. M20—3G 117
Harcourt Av. M31—6H 97
Harcourt Clo. M31—6H 97
Harcourt St. M33—3A 114
Harcourt Rd. WA14—5F 125

220 Manchester

Harcourt St. BL4—5F 39
Harcourt St. M28—4F 55
  (in two parts)
Harcourt St. M32—4E 99
Harcourt St. OL1—1F 65
Hardberry La. SK2—5E 133
Hardcastle Av. M21—3A 116
Hardcastle Gdns. BL2—5G 11
  (in two parts)
Hardcastle Rd. SK3—4F 131
Hardcastle St. BL1—3B 24
Hardcastle St. OL1—2D 64
Harden Dri. BL2—3F 25
Harden Hills. OL2—5H 35
Harden Pk. SK9—6D 158
Hardfield Rd. M24—4A 62
Hardfield St. OL10—3F 31
Hardicker St. M19—2D 118
Hardie Av. BL4—2D 54
Harding St. M3—3D 86 & 3G 161
Harding St. M4—4H 87 & 6H 163
Harding St. M6—1G 85
Harding St. SK1—2B 132
Harding St. SK14—2B 106
Hardman Av. M25—1H 73
Hardman Av. SK6—6G 121
Hardman Clo. M26—1F 41
Hardman La. M35—3E 77
Hardmans. BL7—4D 10
Hardman's La. BL7—3D 10
Hardmans M. M25—3D 58
Hardman's Rd. M25—3D 58
Hardman St. BL2—2G 55
  (in two parts)
Hardman St. BL9—1D 28
Hardman St. M3—4C 86 & 6F 161
Hardman St. M26—1F 41
Hardman St. M35—4D 76
Hardman St. OL9—6H 63
Hardman St. OL10—3F 31
Hardman St. OL16—6G 21
Hardman St. SK3—2F 131
Hardon Gro. M13—5B 102
Hardshaw Clo. M13—1F 101 & 5D 166
Hardwick Clo. M26—2B 40
Hardwick Rd. SK6—1D 156
Hardwicke Rd. SK12—3F 155
Hardwicke St. OL11—1E 33
Hardwick Rd. M31—6E 111
Hardwick St. OL7—3F 91
Hardy Av. M21—1G 115
Hardy Dri. SK7—6F 143
Hardy Dri. WA15—4H 125
Hardy Gro. M27—6D 70
Hardy Gro. M28—3H 69
Hardy La. M21—3H 115
Hardy Mill Rd. BL2—1H 25
Hardy St. M30—5D 82
Hardy St. OL4—4E 65
Hardy St. OL6—5A 80
Harebell Av. M28—6B 54
Harebell Clo. OL12—6D 6
Harecastle Av. M30—5G 83
Haredale Dri. M8—5D 74
Hare Dri. BL9—3F 43
Harefield Av. OL11—6A 20
Harefield Dri. M20—1E 129
Harefield Dri. OL10—3H 31
Harefield Dri. SK9—4E 159
Harefield Rd. SK9—3A 152
Harehill Clo. M13—6F 87 & 3D 166
Hare Hill Ct. OL15—3F 9
Hare Hill Rd. OL15—3E 9
Hare Hill Rd. OL15—5G 107
Hare Hill Wlk. SK14—5G 107
Hareshill Rd. OL10—5D 30
Hare St. OL11—6H 19
Harewood Av. M33—5F 113
Harewood Av. OL11—1H 17
Harewood Clo. OL11—2H 17
Harewood Ct. M9—4C 60
  (off Deanswood Dri.)
Harewood Ct. M33—6C 114
Harewood Dri. OL2—2A 48
Harewood Dri. OL11—2G 17
Harewood Gro. SK5—1G 119
Harewood Rd. M30—5F 95
Harewood Rd. OL2—5G 35

Harewood Rd. OL11—1G 17
Harewood Wlk. M34—6G 105
Harewood Way. M27—1F 71
Harewood Way. OL11—2G 17
Harford Clo. SK7—4A 144
Hargate Clo. BL9—1C 14
Hargate Dri. M30—4E 95
Hargate Dri. WA15—4A 138
Hargrave Clo. M9—3E 61
Hargreaves Ho. BL3—1A 38
Hargreaves Rd. WA15—5C 126
Hargreaves St. BL1—3A 24
Hargreaves St. M4—2E 87 & 1B 162
Hargreaves St. OL1—2D 64
Hargreaves St. OL9—3A 64
Hargreaves St. OL11—1C 32
Harington Rd. SK8—5H 141
Harkness St. M12—6G 87 & 4F 167
Harland Dri. M8—4D 74
Harlech Av. M25—2F 59
Harlech Clo. M15—2E 101
Harlech Dri. SK7—4C 144
Harleen Gro. SK2—4D 132
Harlesden Cres. BL3—2G 37
Harleston St. M11—6C 88
Harley Av. BL2—4D 26
  (Bolton)
Harley Av. BL2—2G 25
  (Harwood)
Harley Av. M14—4A 102
Harley Ct. M24—6H 45
Harley Rd. M24—6H 45
Harley Rd. M33—4B 114
Harley St. M11—5F 89
Harley St. OL6—2H 91
Harling Rd. M22—4B 128
Harlington Clo. M23—4D 126
Harlow Dri. M18—4F 103
Harlyn Av. SK7—6H 143
Harmer Clo. M10—6A 76
Harmol Gro. OL7—5D 78
Harmony St. OL4—3E 65
Harmsworth Dri. SK4—4D 118
Harmsworth St. M6—3E 85
Harold Av. M18—3H 103
Harold Av. SK16—4B 92
Haroldene St. BL2—3D 24
Harold Lees Rd. OL10—2H 31
Harold Priestnall Clo. M10—5B 76
Harold St. BL1—3H 23
Harold St. M16—1A 100 & 5B 164
Harold St. M24—6G 45
Harold St. M25—5D 58
Harold St. M35—4E 77
Harold St. OL9—2B 64
Harold St. OL16—1C 20
Harold St. SK1—3B 132
Haroman Rd. SK5—1H 119
Harper Fold Rd. M26—4D 40
Harper Grn. Rd. BL4—5D 38
Harper Pl. OL6—2A 92
Harper Rd. M22—4C 128
Harper's La. BL1—3F 23
Harper Sq. OL2—6G 35
Harper St. BL4—5D 38
Harper St. OL6—2A 92
Harper St. OL8—5C 64
Harper St. OL11—6G 19
Harper St. SK3—4G 131
Harpford Clo. BL2—2A 40
Harpford Dri. BL2—2A 40
Harp Rd. M17—5A 84
Harp St. M11—6G 89
Harp Trading Est. M17—5A 84
Harpurhey District Cen. M9—3G 75
Harpurhey Rd. M8 & M9—3E 75
Harridge Av. OL12—6C 6
  (in two parts)
Harridge Av. SK15—3H 93
Harridge Bank. OL12—1E 19
Harridge St. OL12—6C 6
Harridge, The. OL12—6C 6
Harriet St. BL3—5F 37
Harriet St. M28—6F 55
Harriet St. OL16—4A 20
Harriett St. M30—4C 110
Harringay Rd. M10—6B 76
Harrington Rd. WA14—6D 124

Harrington St. M18—2G 103
Harris Av. M31—2F 97
Harris Av. M34—4B 104
Harris Clo. M34—4B 104
Harris Clo. OL10—4A 30
Harris Dri. BL9—5F 43
Harris Dri. SK14—3E 107
Harrison Av. M19—5D 102
Harrison Clo. OL12—2B 18
Harrisons Dri. SK6—4A 122
Harrison St. M4—4H 87 & 6G 163
Harrison St. M7—1B 86
Harrison St. M28—5C 54
Harrison St. M30—5D 82
Harrison St. OL1—3D 64
Harrison St. SK14—1D 122
Harrison St. SK15—3D 92
Harris St. BL3—1A 38
Harris St. M8—1C 86
Harrod Av. SK4—4G 119
Harrogate Av. M25—1H 73
Harrogate Dri. SK5—1G 119
Harrogate Rd. SK5—1G 119
Harrogate Sq. BL8—4F 27
Harroil Ga. M27—4G 71
Harrop Ct. OL3—2D 52
Harrop Ct. Rd. OL3—2D 52
Harrop Edge La. OL3—3A 52
Harrop Edge Rd. SK14—3A 108
Harrop Grn. La. OL3—2C 52
Harrop Rd. WA15—3G 137
Harrop St. BL3—3E 37
Harrop St. M18—1H 103
Harrop St. M28—6D 54
Harrop St. SK1—4A 132
Harrop St. SK15—3E 93
Harrow Av. M19—3C 118
Harrow Av. OL11—5C 18
Harrowby Ct. BL4—1D 54
Harrowby Dri. M10—6F 75
Harrowby Fold. BL4—1E 55
Harrowby La. BL4—1E 55
Harrowby Rd. BL1—3D 22
Harrowby Rd. BL3—4E 37
Harrowby Rd. M27—4E 71
Harrowby St. BL4—1E 55
Harrow Clo. BL9—2D 42
Harrowdene Wlk. M9—3F 75
Harrow Dri. M33—1A 126
Harrowgate Clo. M11—6G 89
Harrow M. OL2—6F 35
Harrow Rd. BL1—5F 23
Harrow Rd. M33—1A 126
Harrow St. M8—2D 74
Harrow St. OL11—3H 33
Harrycroft Rd. SK6—4H 121
Harry Hall Gdns. M7—1A 86
Harry Rd. SK5—1H 119
Harry St. OL2—5C 48
Harry St. OL9—3A 64
Harry St. OL11—2B 32
Harry Thorneycroft Wlk. M11
  —5A 88
Harrytown. SK6—1G 133
Hart Av. M33—5F 115
Hart Av. M35—4B 90
Hart Cl. OL5—1D 80
Hart Dri. BL9—3F 43
Harter St. M1—5E 87 & 1A 166
Hartfield Clo. M13—1G 101 & 5E 167
Hartfield Wlk. BL2—5E 25
Hartford Av. OL10—2D 30
Hartford Av. SK4—3F 119
Hartford Av. SK9—4C 158
Hartford Clo. OL10—2D 30
Hartford Gdns. WA15—6D 126
Hartford Grange. OL8—5B 64
Hartford Rd. M31—3G 97
Hartford Rd. M33—1F 125
Hartford Sq. OL9—3A 64
Hartford St. M34—2E 105
Hartford Wlk. M9—4E 75
  (off Westmere Dri.)
Hart Hill Dri. M5—2D 84
Harthill St. M8—6B 74
Hartingdon Clo. M31—5G 97
Hartington Ct. OL2—3C 48

Hartington Dri. M11—2D 88
Hartington Dri. SK7—5E 145
Hartington Rd. BL1—6G 23
Hartington Rd. M21—1H 115
Hartington Rd. M30—2C 82
Hartington Rd. SK2—6D 132
Hartington Rd. SK6 & SK12—6C 146
Hartington Rd. SK7—1G 153
Hartington Rd. WA14—3F 125
Hartington St. M14—4D 100
Hartis Av. M7—5A 74
Hartland Av. M31—5A 98
Hartland Clo. SK2—3C 132
Hartland Clo. SK12—2D 154
Hartland St. OL10—3F 31
Hartlebury. OL11—5G 19
Hartlepool Clo. M14—4F 101
Hartley Av. M25—6G 59
Hartley Gro. M30—3F 95
Hartley La. OL11—1E 33
Hartley Pl. OL16—4D 20
Hartley Rd. M21—6G 99
Hartley Rd. WA14—6E 125
Hartley St. M10—3H 75
Hartley St. OL10—3F 31
Hartley St. OL12—2D 18
  (Rochdale)
Hartley St. OL12—3A 8
  (Wardle)
Hartley St. OL15—4E 9
Hartley St. OL16—4D 20
Hartley St. SK3—3F 131
Hartley St. SK15—2H 93
Hartley Ter. OL11—2E 33
Hartley Ter. OL15—4E 9
  (off William St.)
Hartley Ter. SK15—2H 93
Hart Mill Clo. OL5—1D 80
Harton Av. M18—3E 103
Harton Clo. OL2—1E 49
Hart Rd. M14—5E 101
Hartshead Av. OL6—5G 79
Hartshead Av. SK15—2A 94
Hartshead Clo. M11—6A 90
Hartshead Cres. M35—5A 78
Hartshead Rd. OL6—5G 79
Hartshead St. OL4—3B 66
Hartshead View. SK14—6D 106
Hartsop Dri. M24—5E 45
Hartspring Av. M27—4G 71
Hart St. BL1—5B 24
Hart St. M1—5E 87 & 1B 166
  (in two parts)
Hart St. M35—3A 90
Hart St. WA14—6G 125
Hartswood Clo. M34—3G 105
Hartswood Rd. M20—3H 117
Hartwell Clo. BL2—2E 25
Hartwell Clo. M11—5B 88
Harty. M30—3G 83
Harvard Clo. SK6—4A 122
Harvard St. OL11—1G 33
Harvest Clo. M6—6C 72
Harvest Clo. M33—6G 115
Harvey Clo. M11—5B 88
Harvey Ct. OL15—3G 9
Harvey St. BL1—2H 23
Harvey St. BL8—2A 28
Harvey St. OL12—2B 20
Harvey St. SK1—2H 131
Harvin Gro. M34—5G 105
Harvington Wlk. M15—2E 101
  (off Persian Clo.)
Harwich Clo. M19—6D 102
Harwich Clo. SK5—3C 120
Harwick Gro. OL10—4A 30
Harwin Clo. OL12—6D 6
Harwood Clo. SK4—1A 130
Harwood Cres. BL8—4G 13
Harwood Dri. BL8—4G 27
Harwood Gdns. OL10—4F 31
Harwood Gro. BL2—4D 24
Harwood Meadows. BL2—2H 25
Harwood Pk. OL10—4F 31
Harwood Rd. BL2—4C 26

Harwood Rd. BL8—6E 13
Harwood Rd. M19—3A 118
Harwood Rd. SK4—1A 130
Harwood St. BL1—5B 24
Harwood St. OL15—4D 8
Harwood St. SK4—6F 119
Harwood Vale. BL2—2G 25
Harwood Vale Ct. BL2—2G 25
Harwood Wlk. BL8—4G 13
Haseley Clo. SK12—2E 155
Haselhurst Wlk. M23—1F 127
Haslam Brow. BL9—5C 28
Haslam Ct. BL3—2F 37
Haslam Hey Clo. BL8—3E 27
Haslam Rd. SK3—5G 131
Haslam St. BL3—2H 37
Haslam St. BL9—1E 29
Haslam St. M24—2C 62
Haslam St. OL12—3F 19
Haslemere Av. WA15—1C 148
Haslemere Dri. SK8—4C 142
Haslemere Rd. M20—3H 117
Haslemere Rd. M31—6D 96
Hassall Av. M20—1D 116
Hassall St. M26—2C 42
Hassall St. SK15—4F 93
Hassall Way. SK9—2A 152
Hassop Av. M7—4E 73
Hassop Clo. M11—4A 88
Hassop Rd. SK5—6A 104
Hastings Av. M21—1G 115
Hastings Av. M25—2F 59
Hastings Clo. M25—2F 59
Hastings Clo. SK1—4B 132
Hastings Clo. SK8—3E 143
Hastings Ct. Sk3—3C 130
Hastings Dri. M31—4A 96
Hastings Rd. BL1—5F 23
Hastings Rd. M25—4G 59
Hastings Rd. M30—1C 82
Hastings St. OL11—6H 19
Haston Clo. SK5—5H 119
Hasty La. M15—6E 139
(in two parts)
Hatchett Rd. M22—4B 140
Hatchmere Clo. SK8—1B 142
Hatchmere Clo. WA15—5D 126
(in two parts)
Hateley Rd. M16—4G 99
Hatfield. OL11—1E 33
Hatfield Av. M19—3B 118
Hatfield Rd. BL1—4G 23
Hathaway Clo. SK8—6F 141
Hathaway Dri. BL1—6E 11
Hathaway Gdns. SK6—6F 121
Hathaway Rd. BL9—4E 43
Hatherleigh Wlk. BL2—1H 39
Hatherley Rd. M20—3H 117
Hatherlow. SK6—1G 133
Hatherlow La. SK7—3D 144
Hatherop Clo. M30—4D 82
Hathersage Av. M6—2D 84
Hathersage Cres. SK13—5G 109
Hathersage Rd. M13—3G 101
Hathersage St. OL9—3A 64
Hathersage Way. M34—1G 121
Hathershaw La. OL8—6D 64
Hatro Ct. M31—6A 98
Hattersley Ind. Est. SK14—6H 107
Hattersley Rd. E. SK14—5A 108
Hattersley Rd. W. SK14—5G 107
Hattersley Wlk. M34—4G 107
Hatter St. M4—3F 87 & 3C 162
Hatton Av. M7—2B 86
Hatton Gro. BL1—6E 11
Hatton's Ct. M3—3D 86 & 4G 161
Hattons Rd. M17—1B 98
Hatton St. M12—4C 102
Hatton St. SK4 & SK1—1G 131
Haugh Fold. OL16—1G 35
Haugh Hill Rd. OL4—4A 50
Haugh La. OL16—1G 35
Haugh Sq. OL16—1G 35
Haughton Clo. SK6—3G 121
Haughton Dri. M22—1B 128
Haughton Grn. M34—1G 121
Haughton Hall Rd. M34—4F 105
Haughton St. M34—2F 105

Haughton St. SK14—6C 106
Havana Clo. M11—4B 88
(in two parts)
Haveley Circ. M22—6A 128
Haveley Rd. M22—6A 128
Havelock Dri. M7—1B 86
Havelock St. OL8—4D 64
Havenbrook Gro. BL0—6C 4
Haven Clo. M26—2D 40
Haven Clo. SK3—3F 67
Haven Clo. SK7—4C 144
Haven Dri. M35—2G 89
Haven La. OL4—5A 50
Haven St. M6—3E 85
Haven, The. BL3—4A 40
Haven, The. M14—2H 137
Haverfield Rd. M9—6G 61
Haverford St. M12—1A 102
Havergate Walks. SK2—1F 145
Haverhill Gro. BL2—3D 24
Haversham Rd. M8—1A 74
Havers Rd. M18—2G 103
Haverton Dri. M22—3H 139
Havisham Clo. BL6—3A 36
Hawarden Av. M16—5A 100
Hawarden Rd. WA14—5F 125
Hawarden St. BL1—6C 10
Haw Clough La. OL3—3G 53
Hawdraw Grn. SK2—5E 133
Hawes Av. BL4—1A 54
Hawes Av. M14—2A 118
Hawes Av. M27—5F 71
Hawes Clo. BL8—6B 14
Hawes Clo. SK2—4A 132
Haweswater Clo. M34—5A 104
Haweswater Dri. M24—5G 45
Hawkchurch Wlk. M16—4C 100
Hawk Clo. BL9—1F 29
Hawker Av. BL3—4H 37
Hawkesheath Clo. BL7—2C 10
Hawke St. OL6—2B 92
Hawke St. SK15—4G 93
Hawk Grn. Clo. SK6—2D 146
Hawk Grn. Rd. SK6—2D 146
Hawkhurst Rd. M13—4B 102
Hawkins St. SK5—5G 119
Hawkins Way. OL15—6G 9
Hawk Rd. M30—4E 95
Hawkshaw Ct. M5—4G 85
Hawkshaw La. BL8—1D 12
Hawkshead Dri. BL3—4E 37
Hawkshead Dri. M24—6G 45
Hawkshead Dri. OL2—1B 48
Hawkshead Rd. M8—5D 74
Hawkshead Rd. OL2—5E 35
Hawksley St. OL8—6A 64
Hawksmoor Clo. M15—1C 100 & 6F 165
Hawkstone Av. M25—2B 58
Hawkstone Av. M35—2G 89
Hawkstone Clo. BL2—2G 25
Hawkswick Dri. M23—1G 127
Hawk Yd. La. OL3—4H 53
Hawley Dri. WA15—5B 138
Hawley Grn. OL12—1F 19
Hawley La. WA15—5B 138
Hawley St. M19—1D 118
Haworth Av. BL0—1B 14
Haworth Clo. BL9—1D 42
Haworth Dri. M26—4H 41
Haworth Dri. M32—4H 97
Haworth St. BL8—1E 27
Haworth St. M26—4H 41
Haworth St. OL1—6C 48
Haworth Wlk. M26—4H 41
Hawsworth Clo. M15—2E 101
Hawthorn Av. BL0—3B 4
Hawthorn Av. BL0—1A 14
Hawthorn Av. BL8—1A 28
Hawthorn Av. M26—6H 41
Hawthorn Av. M28—2G 69
Hawthorn Av. M30—2F 83
Hawthorn Av. M31—6H 97
Hawthorn Av. SK6—5B 134
Hawthorn Av. SK9—2D 158
Hawthorn Av. WA15—4H 125
Hawthorn Bank. BL2—1G 25
Hawthorn Bank. SK14—3H 109
Hawthorn Clo. WA15—4H 125

Hawthorn Cres. BL8—4H 13
Hawthorn Cres. OL2—1F 49
Hawthorn Cres. OL8—1D 78
Hawthorn Dri. M6—1B 84
Hawthorn Dri. M19—2B 118
Hawthorn Dri. M27—4A 72
Hawthorn Dri. M30—4B 110
Hawthorn Dri. SK15—5D 92
Hawthorne Av. BL4—1D 54
Hawthorne Dri. M28—4A 70
Hawthorne Gro. OL7—4F 91
Hawthorne Gro. OL9—1H 63
Hawthorne Gro. SK6—5E 121
Hawthorne Gro. SK12—3A 156
Hawthorne Gro. SK14—1F 109
Hawthorne La. OL16—1E 35
Hawthorne Rd. BL3—2F 37
Hawthorne St. BL3—2F 37
Hawthorn Gro. SK4—6D 118
Hawthorn Gro. SK7—1E 153
Hawthorn Gro. SK9—2E 159
Hawthorn Gro. SK14—6B 106
Hawthorn La. M21—1F 115
Hawthorn La. M33—3F 113
Hawthorn La. SK9—2D 158
Hawthorn Lodge. SK3—1H 143
Hawthorn Pk. SK9—2D 158
Hawthorn Rd. BL4—4B 56
Hawthorn Rd. M10—2E 77
Hawthorn Rd. M33—1D 114
Hawthorn Rd. M34—4B 104
Hawthorn Rd. M35—3C 90
(in two parts)
Hawthorn Rd. OL8—1H 77
Hawthorn Rd. OL11—5A 18
Hawthorn Rd. SK4—1B 130
Hawthorn Rd. SK8—6E 129
Hawthorn Rd. WA15—2G 137
Hawthorn Rd. S. M35—3C 90
Hawthorns, The. M34—1D 104
Hawthorn St. M18—1F 103
Hawthorn St. M34—1E 105
Hawthorn St. SK9—3D 158
Hawthorn Ter. SK4—6D 118
Hawthorn Ter. SK9—3D 158
Hawthorn Wlk. M31—6C 110
Hawthorn Wlk. OL15—4D 8
Hawthorn Wlk. SK9—2D 158
Hawthorpe Gro. OL3—1F 53
Haxby Rd. M18—4F 103
Haybarn Rd. M23—4H 127
Hayburn Rd. SK2—3C 132
Haycock Clo. SK15—6H 93
Hay Croft. SK8—5E 143
Hayden Ct. M10—6F 75
(off Sedgeford Rd.)
Haydn Av. M14—3F 101
Haydn St. BL1—3H 23
Haydock Av. M33—1D 124
Haydock Dri. M28—5D 68
Haydock Dri. SK7—3F 145
Haydock Dri. WA15—6B 126
Haydock Ho. BL1—5B 24
Haydock La. BL7—2E 11
(in two parts)
Haydock St. BL1—5B 24
Haydock Wlk. OL9—2A 64
Haye's Rd. M30—4C 110
Hayeswater Circ. M31—4E 97
Hayeswater Rd. M31—4E 97
Hayfield Av. SK6—5G 121
Hayfield Clo. BL8—2H 13
Hayfield Clo. M24—4C 46
Hayfield Clo. OL4—3B 50
Hayfield Rd. M6—1B 84
Hayfield Rd. SK6—5G 121
Hayfield St. M33—4A 114
Hayfield Wlk. M34—1G 121
Hayfield Wlk. WA15—5C 126
Haygrove Wlk. M9—3F 75
Hayley St. M13—3A 102
Hayling Rd. M33—4G 113
Haymans Wlk. M13—6F 87 & 4D 166
Haymarket Clo. M13—2G 101 & 6F 167
Haymarket St. BL9—3C 28
Haymarket, The. BL9—3D 28
Haymill Av. M28—3C 54
Haymond Clo. M6—5E 73

Haynes St. BL3—4F 37
Haynes St. OL12—3H 19
Haysbrook Av. M28—5B 54
Haythorp Av. M22—2C 140
Hayward Av. BL3—4C 40
Hayward St. BL3—4A 40
Hayward St. BL8—2A 28
Hayward Way. SK14—4B 108
(off Garnett Clo.)
Hazel Av. BL0—2B 14
Hazel Av. BL8—6H 13
Hazel Av. BL9—3F 29
Hazel Av. M16—5B 100
Hazel Av. M26—1A 56
Hazel Av. M27—4G 71
Hazel Av. M28—4A 54
Hazel Av. M33—6B 114
Hazel Av. OL6—5A 80
Hazel Av. OL16—2E 35
Hazel Av. SK6—1B 134
Hazel Av. SK8—6A 130
Hazelbadge Clo. SK12—3C 154
Hazelbadge Rd. SK12—3C 154
Hazelbank Av. M20—2F 117
Hazelbottom Rd. M8—4D 74
Hazel Clo. M35—3C 90
Hazel Clo. SK6—1C 146
Hazelcroft Gdns. SK9—6G 159
Hazel Dene Clo. BL9—6D 28
Hazeldene Rd. M10—2E 77
Hazel Dri. M22—5E 141
Hazel Dri. SK2—5D 132
Hazel Dri. SK12—4F 155
Hazel Gro. BL4—1D 54
Hazel Gro. M5—3C 84
Hazel Gro. M26—1F 57
Hazel Gro. M31—5G 97
Hazel Gro. OL9—1H 63
Hazel Hall La. BL0—2B 14
Hazelhurst Clo. BL0—5D 4
Hazelhurst Clo. BL1—3A 24
Hazelhurst Fold. M28—4C 70
Hazelhurst M. OL9—6F 63
Hazelhurst Rd. M28—5B 70
Hazelhurst Rd. OL6—5B 80
Hazelhurst Rd. SK15—1E 93
Hazel La. OL8—1B 78
Hazelmere Av. M30—1D 82
Hazel Mt. BL7—1C 10
Hazel Rd. M24—5B 46
Hazel Rd. M27—1F 59
Hazel Rd. SK8—4D 142
Hazel Rd. WA14—6F 125
Hazel St. BL0—5C 4
Hazel St. M34—1E 105
Hazel St. SK7—2E 145
Hazel View. SK6—2D 146
Hazel Wlk. M31—6C 110
Hazelwell. M33—6B 114
Hazelwood. OL9—1E 63
Hazelwood Av. BL2—2G 25
Hazelwood Ct. M31—4F 97
Hazelwood Dri. BL9—4F 15
Hazelwood Dri. M34—1F 105
Hazelwood Rd. BL1—3F 23
Hazelwood Rd. SK2—1A 144
Hazelwood Rd. SK7—2F 145
Hazelwood Rd. SK9—1G 159
Hazelwood Rd. WA15—3G 137
Headingley Ct. M14—2H 117
(off Ladybarn La.)
Headingley Dri. M16—4G 99
Headingley Rd. M14—2H 117
Headingley Way. BL3—4H 37
Headlands Dri. M25—1E 73
Headlands Rd. SK7—4H 143
Headlands St. OL12—2G 19
Heady Hill Ct. OL10—3C 30
Heady Hill Rd. OL10—3C 30
Heald Av. M14—4F 101
Heald Clo. OL12—6C 6
Heald Clo. OL15—6E 9
Heald Dri. WA14—3E 137
Heald Dri. OL12—6C 6
Heald Gro. M14—4F 101
Heald Gro. SK8—4E 141
Heald La. OL15—5E 9

Heald Pl. M14—3F 101
(in two parts)
Heald Rd. WA14—3E 137
Healds Grn. OL1—4F 47
Heald St. SK1—1A 132
Healdwood Rd. SK6—5A 122
Healey Av. OL10—2G 31
Healey Clo. OL12—5D 6
Healey Av. M7—3G 73
Healey Clo. M23—1F 127
Healey Dell. OL12—5B 6
Healey Gro. OL12—4C 6
Healey Hall M. OL12—5C 6
Healey La. OL12—6E 7
Healey Stones. OL12—5D 6
Healing St. OL11—6A 20
Heanor Av. M34—1G 121
Heap Brow. BL9—4H 29
Heape St. OL11—4C 32
Heaplands. BL8—2H 13
Heap Rd. OL12—1H 17
Heaps Farm Ct. SK15—5H 93
Heap St. BL3—2A 38
Heap St. BL9—4H 29
Heap St. M25—2D 58
Heap St. M26—4H 71
Heap St. M4—2G 65
Heapworth Av. BL0—3D 4
Heapy Clo. BL8—4F 27
Heath Av. BL0—2B 14
Heath Av. M7—1A 86 & 1B 160
Heath Av. M31—4G 97
Heathbank M. M9—4E 61
Heathbank Rd. SK3—4D 130
Heathbank Rd. SK8—6B 142
Heathcliffe Wlk. M13—1G 101 & 6F 167
Heath Clo. BL3—5F 37
Heathcote Av. SK4—6E 119
Heathcote Gdns. SK6—1C 134
Heathcote Rd. M18—3E 103
Heath Cotts. BL5—5B 10
Heath Cres. SK2—6H 131
Heather Av. M30—3B 110
Heather Av. M35—3C 90
Heather Av. OL2—5H 35
Heather Bank. BL8—4G 13
Heather Brow. SK15—6H 93
Heather Clo. OL4—6A 50
Heather Clo. OL10—5F 31
Heather Ct. WA12—2D 136
Heather Dale Dri. M8—5C 74
Heatherfield. BL1—6B 10
Heatherfield Ct. SK9—1H 159
Heather Gro. M35—5B 90
Heather Gro. SK14—1F 109
Heather Lea. M34—5G 105
Heather Rd. WA14—4G 137
Heathers Av. OL5—2G 81
Heathersett Dri. M9—4F 75
Heatherside. SK5—6A 104
Heatherside Rd. BL0—2D 4
Heather St. M11—3D 88
Heather Wlk. M31—6B 110
Heatherway. M14—3F 101
Heatherway. M33—4F 113
Heatherway. SK6—5C 134
Heath Farm La. M31—6E 111
Heathfield. BL2—1H 25
Heathfield. BL4—6G 39
Heathfield. M28—6H 69
Heathfield. SK9—4D 158
Heathfield Av. M34—5D 104
Heathfield Av. SK4—4E 119
Heathfield Av. SK8—6F 129
Heathfield Clo. M33—5F 115
Heathfield Dri. BL3—5F 37
Heathfield Dri. M27—4G 71
Heathfield Dri. M29—2A 68
Heathfield Rd. BL9 & M25—4D 42
Heathfield Rd. SK2—5H 131
Heathfields Rd. OL3—1G 53
Heathfield St. M10—6B 76
Heath Gdns. M6—1F 85
Heathland Rd. M7—3F 73
Heathlands Dri. M25—2E 73
Heathland Ter. SK3—4G 131
Heath Rd. OL12—3A 8
Heath Rd. SK2—5H 131

Heath Rd. WA14—3F 137
Heath Rd. WA15—3H 125
Heathside Gro. M28—6G 55
Heathside Pk. Rd. SK3—3B 130
Heathside Rd. M20—4G 117
Heathside Rd. SK3—4C 130
Heath St. M8—4B 74
Heath St. OL11—5F 19
Heath, The. M24—3B 62
Heath, The. OL7—4E 79
Heath View. M7—3E 73
Heath View. WA14—2F 137
Heathwood. OL3—1G 53
Heathwood Rd. M19—5A 118
Heatley Clo. M34—5B 104
Heatley Rd. OL16—5D 20
Heatley Way. SK9—3H 151
Heaton Av. BL1—4D 22
Heaton Av. BL2—6A 12
Heaton Av. BL3—3A 40
Heaton Av. BL4—1E 55
Heaton Av. SK7—2F 143
Heaton Clo. BL9—2E 43
Heaton Ct. BL1—6D 22
Heaton Ct. M9—6C 60
Heaton Ct. M33—6C 114
Heaton Ct. SK4—5D 118
Heaton Ct. Gdns. BL1—6C 22
Heaton Dri. BL9—2E 43
Heaton Fold. BL9—5C 28
Heaton La. SK4—2G 131
Heaton Moor Rd. SK4—6D 118
Heaton Pk. Rd. M9—4C 60
Heaton Pl. SK4—1A 130
Heaton Rd. BL2—2B 40
Heaton Rd. BL6—2A 36
Heaton Rd. M20—2G 117
Heaton Rd. SK4—6E 119
Heaton St. Heys Rd.—4E 59
Heaton St. M7—4A 74
Heaton St. M24—2D 60
Heaton St. M25—5F 59
Heaton St. M26—5G 41
Heaton St. M34—4D 104
Heaton St. OL16—6G 21
Heaton Towers. SK4—1G 131
(off Wilkinson Rd.)
Heaviley Gro. SK2—5A 132
Hebble Butt Clo. OL16—5E 21
Hebburn Dri. BL8—6C 14
Hebburn Wlk. M14—3F 101
Hebden Av. M6—2C 84
Hebden Av. SK6—5G 121
Hebden St. BL1—5A 24
Hebden Wlk. M15—2D 100
(off Arnott Cres.)
Heber Pl. OL15—4F 9
(off Victoria St.)
Heber St. M26—4G 41
Hebron St. OL2—4E 49
Hector Av. OL16—3B 20
Hector Rd. M13—4B 102
Heddon Clo. SK4—6A 118
Heddon Wlk. M8—5E 75
(off Smedley Rd.)
Hedgehog Ho. M5—5F 85
Hedgelands Wlk. M33—4E 113
Hedge Rows. OL12—4G 7
Hedges St. M35—3G 77
Hedley St. BL1—3G 23
Hedley Wlk. M8—4B 74
(off Halliwell La.)
Heginbottom Cres. OL6—6G 79
Heights Av. OL12—1G 19
(in three parts)
Heights Clo. OL12—1G 19
Heights La. OL1—5F 47
Heights La. OL3—1F 51
Heights La. OL12—2G 19
Helena St. M6—6A 72
Helen St. BL4—1F 55
Helen St. M7—6G 73
Helen St. M11—4D 88
Helen St. M30—5D 82
Helensville Av. M6—6D 72
Helga St. M10—1H 87
Helias Clo. M28—6B 54

Hellidon Clo. M12—1H 101 & 5G 167
Helmclough Way. M28—3E 69
Helmet St. M1—5G 87 & 1F 167
Helmsdale Av. BL3—1D 36
Helmsdale Clo. BL0—5C 4
Helmshore Av. OL4—5A 50
Helmshore Ho. OL2—5F 35
(off Helmshore Way)
Helmshore Rd. BL8—3C 4
Helmshore Wlk. M13—6F 87 & 4D 166
Helmshore Way. OL2—5F 35
Helrose St. M10—6C 76
Helsby Gdns. BL1—1B 24
Helsby Rd. M33—1E 127
Helsby Wlk. M12—5A 88
Helsby Way. SK9—3H 151
Helston Clo. SK7—6H 143
Helston Clo. SK14—6H 107
Helston Dri. OL2—3D 48
Helston St. M10—1B 88
Helston Wlk. SK14—6H 107
Helthorn St. M10—6C 76
Helton Wlk. M24—6D 44
Helvellyn Av. M24—5F 45
Helvellyn Wlk. OL1—6E 49
Hembury Av. M19—3B 118
Hemington Dri. M9—4F 75
Hemlock Av. OL8—6C 64
Hemming Dri. M30—4G 83
Hemmons Rd. M12—5D 102
Hempcroft Rd. WA15—6C 126
Hempshaw La. SK1 & SK2—4H 131
(in two parts)
Hemptonstall Wlk. M18—2E 103
Hemsby Clo. BL3—3E 37
Hemsley St S. M9—3G 75
Hemsley St. M9—2G 75
Hemsworth Rd. BL1—5H 23
Hemsworth Rd. M18—4F 103
Henbury Dri. SK6—3H 121
Henbury La. SK8—1B 152
Henbury Rd. SK9—3H 151
Henbury St. M14—4E 101
Henbury St. SK2—1C 144
Henderson Av. M27—2F 71
Henderson St. M19—1D 118
Henderson St. OL12—1B 20
Henderson St. OL15—4E 9
Henderville St. OL15—3E 9
Hendham Clo. SK7—3A 144
Hendham Dri. WA14—6D 124
Hendham Vale. M9—4E 75
Hendham Wlk. SK7—4A 144
Hendon Dri. BL9—2D 42
Hendon Dri. SK3—4C 130
Hendon Rd. M9—5E 61
Hendriff Pl. OL12—2G 19
Henfield Wlk. M22—2A 140
Hengist St. BL2—6E 25
Henley Av. M16—4H 99
Henley Av. M30—3C 110
Henley Av. SK8—3A 142
Henley Clo. BL8—5G 27
Henley Dri. OL7—1F 91
Henley Dri. WA15—4H 125
Henley Pl. M19—3C 118
Henley St. OL1—1B 64
Henley St. OL9—6G 63
Henley St. OL12—2G 19
Henley Ter. OL11—6G 19
Henlow Wlk. M10—1D 76
Hennelly St. SK14—3C 106
Hennicker St. M28—2F 69
Henniker St. BL3—5E 37
Henniker St. M27—5E 71
Hennon St. BL1—4H 23
Henrietta St. BL3—3F 37
Henrietta St. M16—3A 100
Henrietta St. OL6—6F 79
Henry Cres. M16—2A 100
Henry Herman St. BL3—4E 37
(in two parts)
Henry Lee St. BL3—4G 37
Henry Sq. OL6—5E 79
Henry St. BL0—2F 5
Henry St. M4—3F 87 & 4D 162
(in two parts)

Henry St. M16—2A 100
Henry St. M24—1H 61
Henry St. M25—4G 59
Henry St. M30—4E 83
Henry St. M35—4A 90
(Droylsden)
Henry St. M35—4F 77
(Failsworth)
Henry St. OL11—5H 19
Henry St. OL12—2A 8
Henry St. OL15—6D 8
Henry St. SK1—3B 132
Henry St. SK14—5B 106
Henshaw La. OL9—1F 77
Henshaw St. M32—5D 98
Henshaw St. OL1—2C 64
Henshaw Wlk. BL1—4A 24
(off Ewart St.)
Henshaw Wlk. M13—6F 87 & 4D 166
Henson Gro. WA15—1A 138
Henthorn St. OL1—1E 65
Henthorn St. OL2—1F 49
Henton Wlk. M10—1G 87
Henwick Hall Av. BL0—5D 4
Henwood Rd. M20—4G 117
Hepley Rd. SK2—4G 155
Hepple Clo. SK4—6A 118
Heppleton Rd. M10—1D 76
Hopple Wlk. OL7—6C 78
Hepton St. OL1—1C 64
Hepworth St. SK14—2C 122
Heraldic Ct. M6—6E 73
Herbert St. BL3—4B 40
Herbert St. M8—6B 74
Herbert St. M25—5D 58
Herbert St. M26—2F 41
Herbert St. M32—5D 98
Herbert St. M34—3G 105
Herbert St. M35—4H 89
Herbert St. OL6—6H 49
Herbert St. OL9—2H 63
Herbert St. SK3—4F 131
Hereford Clo. OL2—6D 34
Hereford Clo. OL6—4H 79
Hereford Clo. SK6—2G 133
Hereford Clo. SK9—4A 152
Hereford Ct. SK5—4C 120
Hereford Cres. BL3—3A 40
Hereford Dri. BL9—5D 28
Hereford Dri. M25—6G 59
Hereford Dri. M27—5F 71
Hereford Gro. M31—5E 97
Hereford Rd. BL1—5F 23
Hereford Rd. M30—6G 71
Hereford Rd. SK5—4C 120
Hereford Rd. SK8—1C 142
Hereford St. BL1—3B 24
Hereford St. M33—5B 114
(in two parts)
Hereford St. OL9—4H 63
Hereford St. OL11—6A 20
Hereford Wlk. M34—6F 105
Hereford Wlk. SK6—6G 133
Hereford Way. M24—5C 46
Hereford Way. SK15—6H 93
Herevale Grange. M28—4D 68
Herevale Hall Dri. BL0—5D 4
Heristone Av. M34—4E 105
Herle Dri. M22—4A 140
Hermitage Av. SK6—1D 134
Hermitage Ct. WA15—2H 137
Hermitage Gdns. SK6—1D 134
Hermitage Rd. WA15—2H 137
Hermon Av. OL8—5C 64
Herne St. M11—5C 88
Heron Av. BL4—1B 54
Heron Av. SK16—6C 92
Heron Ct. M6—2B 84
Herondale Clo. M10—6B 76
Heron Dri. M30—4E 95
Heron Dri. M34—4C 90
Heron Dri. SK12—4A 154
Heron St. M27—2G 71
Heron St. OL8—5A 64
Heron St. SK3—3F 131
Heron's Way. BL2—1C 38
Herries St. OL6—1B 92
Herristone Rd. M8—1C 74

Herschel St. M10—3A 76
Hersey St. M6—3E 85
Hersham Wlk. M9—2G 75
(off Huncote Dri.)
Herston Wlk. M7—5B 74
Hertford Av. M30—3A 110
Hertford Rd. M9—2F 75
Hertfordshire Pk. Clo. OL2—5E 35
Hertford St. OL7—4G 91
Hesford Av. M9—4H 75
Hesketh Av. BL1—6D 10
Hesketh Av. M20—6E 117
Hesketh Av. OL2—2E 49
Hesketh Rd. M33—6H 113
Hesketh Rd. OL16—4C 20
Hesketh St. SK4—5G 119
(in two parts)
Hesketh Wlk. BL4—1F 55
Hesketh Wlk. M24—5G 45
Heslington St. M14—3D 100
Hessel St. M5—4D 84
Hester Wlk. M15—1E 101 & 6A 166
Heston Av. M13—5A 102
Heston Dri. M31—4E 97
Heston Gro. SK8—5G 141
Heswall Av. M20—2F 117
Heswall Dri. BL8—6G 13
Heswall Rd. SK5—6H 103
Hetherington Wlk. M12—3C 102
Hetton Av. M13—5A 102
Heversham Av. OL2—6H 35
Heversham Wlk. M18—2E 103
(off Beyer Clo.)
Hewart Clo. M10—6E 75
Hewart Dri. BL9—2G 29
Hewitt Av. M34—4H 103
Hewitt St. M15—6C 86 & 2F 165
Hewlett Ct. BL0—1A 14
Hewlett Rd. M21—6G 99
Hewlett St. BL2—6C 24
Hexham Av. BL1—4D 22
Hexham Clo. M33—6F 113
Hexham Clo. SK2—6E 133
Hexham Rd. M18—4E 103
Hexworth Wlk. SK7—3A 144
Hey Bottom La. OL12—4F 7
Heybrook. OL12—2B 20
Heybrook Clo. M25—1G 59
Heybrook Rd. M23—6H 127
Heybrook St. OL16—3B 20
Heybrook Wlk. M25—1G 59
Hey Cres. OL4—2B 66
Hey Croft. M25—2A 58
Heyden Bank SK13—5F 109
(off Grassmoor Cres.)
Heyden Fold. SK13—5F 109
(off Grassmoor Cres.)
Heyden Ter. SK13—5F 109
Heyes Av. WA15—4B 126
Heyes Dri. WA15—4B 126
Heyes La. SK9—4G 159
Heyes La. WA15—4B 126
Heyes Leigh. WA15—3B 126
Heyes Ter. WA15—3B 126
Hey Flake La. OL3—1G 51
Heyford Av. M10—1D 76
Hey Head Cotts. BL2—6D 12
Hey Head La. OL15—1F 9
Heyheads New Rd. SK15—4G 81
Heyland Rd. M23—5G 127
Hey La. OL3—6C 52
Heyridge Dri. M22—2B 128
Heyrod St. M1—5G 87 & 1E 167
Heyrod St. SK15—6F 81
Heyrose Wlk. M15—1B 100 &
                                  6D 164
Heys Av. M23—2G 127
Heys Av. M27—1C 70
Heys Av. SK6—6C 122
Heysbank Rd. SK12—1H 157
Heys Clo. N. M27—1C 70
Heys Clo. SK3—3D 130
Heyscroft Rd. M20—3G 117
Heyscroft Rd. SK4—1C 130
Heysham Av. M20—2D 116
Heyshaw Wlk. M23—2E 127
Heyside. OL4—2E 49
Heyside Av. OL2—4E 49
Heyside Way. BL9—4D 28

Heys La. OL10—3C 30
Heys La. SK6—6C 122
Heys Rd. M25—4E 59
Heys Rd. OL6—2B 92
Heys St. BL8—3B 28
Heys, The. SK5—6A 104
Hey St. OL16—3B 20
Heys View. M25—5F 59
Heywood Av. M27—1H 71
Heywood Av. OL4—1C 66
Heywood Bus. Pk. OL10—5C 30
Heywood Clo. M24—2C 60
Heywood Clo. SK9—4H 159
Heywood Fold Rd. OL4—2B 66
Heywood Gdns. BL3—3A 38
Heywood Gdns. M25—5F 59
Heywood Gro. M33—3B 114
Heywood Hall Rd. OL10—2F 31
Heywood Ho. M6—2C 84
Heywood Ho. OL8—4D 64
Heywood La. OL4—2C 66
Heywood Old Rd. M24—6C 44
Heywood Pk. View. BL3—3A 38
Heywood Rd. M25—6F 59
Heywood Rd. M33—6B 114
Heywood Rd. OL11—3B 32
Heywood Rd. SK9—4H 159
Heywood's Hollow. BL1—2A 24
Heywood St. BL1—5B 24
Heywood St. BL3—4B 40
Heywood St. BL9—4E 29
Heywood St. M8—4C 74
Heywood St. M27—3E 71
Heywood St. M35—4D 76
Heywood St. OL4—1A 66
Heywood Way. M6—2F 85
Heyworth Av. SK6—6B 122
Heyworth St. M5—4E 85
Hibbert Av. M34—2E 105
Hibbert Av. SK14—6C 106
Hibbert Cres. M35—4G 77
Hibbert La. SK6—6D 134
Hibbert St. BL1—3B 24
Hibbert St. M14—4G 101
Hibbert St. OL4—2A 66
Hibbert St. SK4 & SK5—4G 119
Hibernia St. BL3—2G 37
Hibernia Way. M32—2A 98
Hibson Av. OL12—1H 17
Hibson Clo. OL12—3A 8
Hickenfield Rd. SK14—2D 106
Hicken Pl. SK14—2D 106
Hickton Dri. WA14—5D 124
Higginshaw La. OL1 & OL2—5E 49
Higginshaw Rd. OL1—6D 48
Higginson Rd. SK5—2G 119
Higham La. SK14—1D 122
Higham St. SK8—4C 142
Higham View. M6—2G 85
Higham Wlk. M10—2H 87 & 1H 163
High Ash Gro. M34—6D 90
High Av. BL2—5G 25
High Bank. BL7—4D 10
High Bank. M18—2G 103
Highbank. M27—3A 72
High Bank. M34—5B 104
High Bank. WA14—6F 125
High Bank Av. SK15—6H 93
Highbank Clo. M30—3B 110
High Bank Cres. M25—6G 59
Highbank Cres. OL4—4G 67
Highbank Dri. M20—3F 129
High Bank Gro. M25—6G 59
High Bank La. BL6—6A 22
Highbank Rd. BL9—3D 42
High Bank Rd. M27—3H 71
High Bank Rd. M35—5H 89
Highbank Rd. OL16—1G 35
High Bank Rd. SK14—4D 106
High Bankside. SK1—2H 131
High Bank St. BL2—6E 25
Highbank Trading Est. M11
                                  —6F 89
High Barn Clo. OL11—6G 19
High Barn La. OL12—1B 6
(Hallfold)
High Barn La. OL12—2G 7
(Whitworth)
Highbarn Rd. M24—2A 62

High Barn Rd. OL2—3D 48
High Barn St. OL2—3C 48
High Bent Av. SK8—1C 152
High Birch Ter. OL11—1B 32
Highbridge Clo. BL2—1A 40
High Brindle. M6—1F 85
Highbrook Gro. BL1—4B 24
Highbury. SK4—1B 130
Highbury Av. M30—6E 95
Highbury Av. M31—5A 96
Highbury Rd. M16—6C 100
Highbury Rd. SK4—3E 119
Highbury Way. OL2—2B 48
Highclere Av. M8—5B 74
Highclere Rd. M8—5B 74
Highcrest Av. SK8—6D 128
Highcroft. SK14—2C 122
Highcroft Av. M20—5C 116
High Croft Clo. SK16—5E 93
Highcroft Rd. SK6—6A 122
Highcroft Way. OL12—5F 7
Highdales Rd. M23—6H 127
High Elm Dri. WA15—5C 138
High Elm Rd. WA15—5C 138
High Elms. SK8—2D 152
Higher Ainsworth Rd. M26—6E 27
Higher Ardwick. M12—6G 87 & 4F 167
Higher Arthurs La. OL3—3F 53
Higher Bank Rd. OL15—6E 9
Higher Barlow Row. SK1—3H 131
Higher Barn Rd. SK14—3G 109
Higher Bents La. SK6—6F 121
Higher Bri. St. BL1—4B 24
Higher Bury St. SK4—1F 131
Higher Calderbrook. OL15—6G 9
Higher Calderbrook Rd. OL15—6G 9
Higher Cambridge St. M15—1E 101
                                  & 5A 166
Higher Carr La. OL3—2F 53
Higher Chatham St. M15—1E 101 &
                                  5A 166
Higher Cleggswood Av. OL15—6E 9
Higher Crimble. OL11—1H 31
Higher Croft. M30—5E 83
Higher Croft. OL2—3A 58
Higher Croft. M30—5E 83
Higher Crossbank. OL4—1B 66
Higher Cross La. OL3—2G 53
Higher Darcy St. BL2—2E 39
Higher Dean St. M26—4E 41
Higher Downs. WA14—2E 137
Higher Dunscar. BL7—2C 10
Higher Fold. OL2—2E 49
Higher Fulwood. OL1—3H 49
Higher Grn. M41—6C 94
Higher Grn. OL6—1A 92
Higher Henry St. SK14—6B 106
Higher Hillgate. SK1—3H 131
Higher Ho. Clo. OL9—5G 63
Higher Kinders. OL3—3F 53
Higher La. OL2—1C 58
Higher La. SK12—6H 157
Higher Lee St. OL8—3B 64
Higher Lime Rd. OL8—3A 78
Higher Lodge. OL12—1H 17
Higher Lomax La. OL10—3C 30
Higher Market St. BL4—1G 55
(in two parts)
Higher Mill Rd. SK15—3F 93
Higher Ormond St. M15—1E 101 &
(in two parts)   5B 166
Higher Pit La. M26—5E 27
Higher Ridings. BL7—3D 10
(in two parts)
Higher Rise. OL2—4E 35
Higher Rd. M31—5F 97
Higher Row. BL9—2F 29
Higher Shady La. BL7—4F 11
Higher Shore Rd. OL15—2C 8
Higher Summerseat. BL0—1B 14
Higher Swan La. BL3—3H 37
Higher Tame St. SK15—3F 93
Higher Turf La. OL4—1D 66
Higher Turf Pk. OL2—4C 48
Higher Wharf St. OL7—3H 91
Higher Wheat La. OL16—3C 20
Higher Wood St. M24—6H 45
Higher York St. M13—1F 101 &
                                  5C 166
Highfield. M20—1F 129

Highfield. M33—6C 114
Highfield Av. BL2—2A 26
Highfield Av. M26—6A 42
Highfield Av. M28—4B 68
Highfield Av. M33—6C 114
Highfield Av. OL10—3C 30
Highfield Av. SK6—1F 133
Highfield Clo. M32—1C 114
Highfield Clo. SK3—1H 143
Highfield Clo. SK14—1H 107
Highfield Ct. M25—4F 59
Highfield Cres. SK9—6G 151
Highfield Dri. M24—2H 61
Highfield Dri. M27—4A 72
Highfield Dri. M30—1F 83
Highfield Dri. M31—4E 97
Highfield Dri. OL2—5C 48
Highfield Dri. OL5—3E 81
Highfield Est. SK9—6G 151
Highfield Ho. BL4—1B 54
Highfield Ho. SK3—6H 131
Highfield La. M26—4D 42
Highfield Pk. SK4—1B 130
Highfield Pk. Rd. SK6—5F 121
Highfield Parkway. SK7—3F 153
Highfield Pl. M18—3H 103
Highfield Pl. M25—4E 59
Highfield Range. M18—3H 103
Highfield Rd. BL0—3A 4
Highfield Rd. BL1—3F 23
Highfield Rd. BL4—1A 54
Highfield Rd. M6—2F 85
Highfield Rd. M8—4B 74
Highfield Rd. M19—6E 103
Highfield Rd. M25—3E 59
Highfield Rd. M28—4B 54
Highfield Rd. M30—1F 83
Highfield Rd. M32—1C 114
Highfield Rd. OL11—2A 18
Highfield Rd. OL16—5G 21
Highfield Rd. SK6—5D 134
(Marple)
Highfield Rd. SK6—5F 135
(Mellor)
Highfield Rd. SK7—2H 143
(Bramhall)
Highfield Rd. SK7—3G 145
(Hazel Grove)
Highfield Rd. SK8—4A 142
Highfield Rd. SK12—3A 154
Highfield Rd. WA15—6B 126
(Altrincham)
Highfield Rd. WA15—3A 138
(Hale)
Highfield Rd. Ind. Est. M28—3B 54
Highfield St. BL4—3A 56
Highfield St. M24—1B 62
Highfield St. M34—1F 105
(Audenshaw)
Highfield St. M34—2E 105
(Denton)
Highfield St. OL9—2C 64
(in two parts)
Highfield St. SK3—3E 131
Highfield St. SK6—6F 121
Highfield St. SK16—4H 91
Highfield St. W. SK16—4H 91
Highfield Ter. M9—3F 75
Highfield Ter. OL4—5H 49
Highfield Ter. OL7—4D 78
Highgate. BL3—5A 36
Highgate Av. M31—3C 96
Highgate Cres. M18—3F 103
Highgate Dri. M28—4A 54
High Gate Dri. OL6—6H 33
Highgate La. M28—4A 54
Highgate La. OL12—3C 6
Highgate Rd. WA14—1D 136
Highgrove Clo. BL1—1B 24
Highgrove M. SK9—3D 158
High Gro. Rd. OL4 & OL3—4G 67
High Gro. Rd. SK8—6G 129
High Houses. BL1—5B 10
High Hurst Clo. M24—1E 61
Highland Rd. BL7—3F 11
Highlands. OL2—4A 48
Highlands. OL15—6E 9
Highlands Dri. SK2—5F 133

Highlands Rd. OL2—4A 48
(Royton)
Highlands Rd. OL2—5D 34
(Shaw)
Highlands Rd. OL11—6A 18
Highlands Rd. SK2—5F 133
Highlands, The. OL5—2D 80
Highland View. OL5—1E 81
Highland Wlk. M10—5D 76
High La. M21—1G 115
High La. SK6—4H 121
High Lea. SK8—6G 129
High Lea. SK9—5H 159
High Lee La. OL4—4D 50
High Legh Rd. M11—5F 89
High Level Rd. OL11—5H 19
High Meadow. BL7—3F 11
Highmeadow. M26—6F 41
High Meadow. SK8—5A 142
High Meadows. SK6—6A 122
Highmead St. M18—2F 103
Highmead Wlk. M16—2B 100
High Moor Cres. OL4—6A 50
Highmore Dri. M9—6G 61
High Mt. BL2—2G 25
Highnam Wlk. M22—4G 139
High Peak Rd. OL6—5C 80
High Peak Rd. OL12—3C 6
High Peak St. M10—5B 76
High Rid La. BL6—4A 22
Highshore Dri. M8—4B 74
High Stile La. OL3—5D 52
High Stile St. BL4—2G 55
Highstone Dri. M8—5E 75
High St. Altrincham, WA14—1F 137
High St. Bolton, BL3—3H 37
High St. Bury, BL8—2F 27
High St. Cheadle, SK8—5H 129
High St. Dearnley, OL15—4D 8
High St. Delph, OL3—3H 51
High St. Droylesden, M35—4A 90
High St. Hazel Grove, SK7 145
High St. Heywood, OL10—3D 30
High St. Hyde, SK14—4D 106
High St. Lees, OL4—3A 66
High St. Little Lever, BL3—4B 40
High St. Manchester, M4—4E 87 &
5A 162
High St. Middleton, M24—5A 46
High St. Mossley, OL5—1F 81
High St. Oldham, OL1—2D 64
High St. Rochdale, OL12—3H 19
High St. Royton, OL2—3B 48
High St. Shaw, OL2—1F 49
High St. Stalybridge, SK15—
5C 92
High St. Stockdale, SK1—2H 131
High St. Uppermill, OL3—6B 52
High St. Worsley, M28—6E 55
High View. M25—6F 59
Highview St. BL1—5C 10
High View St. BL3—3G 37
Highview Wlk. M9—6G 61
Highwood. OL11—2A 18
Highworth Clo. BL3—2A 38
Highworth Rd. M10—1D 76
Higson Av. M21—2H 115
Higson Av. M30—5E 83
Higson Av. SK6—1F 133
Higson St. BL2—6C 24
Hilary Av. OL2D 78
Hilary Av. SK8—5H 141
Hilary Clo. SK4—1F 131
Hilary Gro. BL4—2E 55
Hilary Rd. M22—4A 140
Hilary St. OL11—4D 32
Hilbre Av. OL1 & OL2—5B 48
Hilbre Av. OL2—5B 48
Hilbre Rd. M19—1B 118
Hilbre Way. SK9—3H 151
Hilbury Av. M9—2F 75
Hilda Av. BL8—5H 13
Hilda Av. SK8—6A 130
Hilda Gro. SK5—5H 119
Hilda Rd. SK14—2B 122
Hilda St. OL9—2B 64
(in two parts)
Hilda St. OL10—2F 31
Hilda St. SK5—5H 119

Hilden Ct. M16—3B 100
Hilden St. BL2—1C 38
Hilditch Clo. M23—5H 127
Hiley Rd. M30—5B 82
Hillam Clo. M31—6H 97
Hillary Av. OL7—6F 79
Hillary Rd. SK14—2E 107
Hillbank Clo. BL1—2G 23
Hillbank St. M24—1D 46
Hill Barn La. OL3—4D 52
Hillbrook Av. M10—1B 76
Hillbrook Rd. SK1—3C 132
Hillbrook Rd. SK7—1F 153
Hillbrow Wlk. M8—4B 74
Hillbury Rd. SK7—4H 143
Hill Carr M. WA14—1D 136
Hill Clo. OL4—4G 65
Hillcote Wlk. M18—1D 102
Hill Cot Rd. BL1—6D 10
Hillcourt Rd. SK6—6C 146
(High Lane)
Hillcourt Rd. SK6—5A 122
(Romiley)
Hill Cres. M9—6C 60
Hillcrest. M6—2A 84
Hillcrest. M24—4H 45
Hillcrest. SK14—2D 122
Hill Crest Av. SK4—1C 130
Hillcrest Cres. OL10—2C 30
Hillcrest Dri. M19—2E 118
Hillcrest Dri. M34—6H 105
Hillcrest Rd. M25—1D 72
Hillcrest Rd. M29—3A 68
Hillcrest Rd. OL11—3D 32
(in two parts)
Hillcrest Rd. SK2—5C 132
Hillcrest Rd. SK7—3H 143
Hillcroft. OL8—2E 79
Hillcroft Clo. M8—3C 74
Hillcroft Ho. M6—2F 85
Hillcroft Rd. WA14—6C 124
Hilldale Av. M9—5F 61
Hill Dri. SK9—4A 152
Hillel Ho. M15—2E 101
Hill End. SK6—5B 122
Hillend La. SK14—6B 108
Hillend Pl. M23—1G 127
Hillend Rd. M23—1G 127
Hill End Rd. OL3—2H 51
Hillfield. M5—3D 84
Hillfield Clo. M13—2H 101
Hillfield Dri. BL2—4D 24
Hillfield Dri. M28—4C 68
Hillfield Wlk. BL2—4D 24
Hillfoot Wlk. M15—1B 100 & 5D 164
Hillgate Av. M5—6H 85
Hillgate St. OL6—1A 92
Hillhead Wlk. M8—5C 74
(off Barnsdale Dri.)
Hillier St. M9—3G 75
Hillier St. N. M9—3G 75
Hillingdon Clo. OL8—2H 77
Hillingdon Dri. M9—1B 76
Hillingdon Rd. M25—2B 58
Hillingdon Rd. M32—6E 99
Hillington Rd. M33—5G 113
Hillington Rd. SK3—3E 131
Hillkirk St. M11—4A 88
Hill La. M9—6F 61
Hillman Clo. M10—6F 75
Hill. Mt. SK16—5E 93
Hill Rise. BL0—5C 4
Hill Rise. SK6—1H 133
Hill Rise. WA14—6C 124
Hillsborough Dri. BL9—4F 43
Hills Ct. BL8—1H 27
Hillsdale Gro. BL2—2G 25
Hillsdide Clo. M10—2A 76
Hill Side. BL1—6D 22
Hill Side. SK6—4A 122
Hillside Av. BL4—2D 54
Hillside Av. BL7—2F 11
Hillside Av. M7—3E 73
Hillside Av. M25—5C 42
Hillside Av. M28—5E 55
Hillside Av. OL2—2C 48
(Royton)

Hillside Av. OL2—6H 35
(Shaw)
Hillside Av. OL3—4B 52
Hillside Av. OL4—4C 66
(Grotton)
Hillside Av. OL4—2G 65
(Oldham)
Hillside Av. SK14—3D 122
Hillside Av. SK15—5H 81
Hillside Clo. BL2—6A 12
Hillside Clo. BL3—5B 36
Hillside Clo. SK7—6A 144
Hillside Clo. SK14—4G 109
Hillside Ct. BL1—6D 22
Hill Side Ct. M25—6E 59
Hillside Cres. BL9—5F 15
Hillside Cres. OL6—6B 80
Hillside Dri. M24—6B 46
Hillside Dri. M27—5B 72
Hillside Gro. SK6—2F 135
Hillside Rd. BL0—4C 4
Hillside Rd. SK2—4D 132
Hillside Rd. WA15—2A 138
Hillside St. BL3—2H 37
Hillside View. M34—2G 121
Hillside View. OL16—5G 21
Hillside Wlk. OL5—2D 6
Hillside Way. OL12—4G 7
Hills La. BL9—5G 43
Hillsley Wlk. M10—2H 87 &
                              1H 163
Hillstone Av. OL12—5C 6
Hillstone Clo. BL8—1H 13
Hill St. BL8—1F 27
Hill St. BL9—6E 5
Hill St. M6—2F 85
Hill St. M7—5H 73
(in two parts)
Hill St. M20—2F 117
Hill St. M24—4A 46
Hill St. M26—6H 41
(Outwood)
Hill St. M26—3F 41
(Radcliffe)
Hill St. OL2—1G 49
Hill St. OL4—2F 65
Hill St. OL7 & OL6—3G 91
Hill St. OL10—3E 31
Hill St. OL16—4A 20
Hill St. SK6—1H 133
Hill St. SK14—1D 122
Hill St. SK16—4H 91
Hill St. WA14—3E 125
Hilltop. BL3—3A 40
Hilltop. OL12—4C 6
Hill Top. SK6—6H 121
Hill Top. WA15—5A 138
Hilltop Av. M9—6F 61
Hill Top Av. M25—5F 59
(Prestwich)
Hilltop Av. M25—1F 59
(Whitefield)
Hill Top Av. SK8—4C 142
Hilltop Av. SK9—1E 159
Hilltop Ct. M8—1B 74
Hill Top Ct. SK8—4D 142
Hilltop Dri. BL8—5G 13
Hill Top Dri. OL11—3F 33
Hill Top Dri. SK6—5A 134
Hill Top Dri. WA15—3A 138
Hilltop Gro. M25—1F 59
Hill Top La. OL3—2C 50
Hill Top Rd. M28—5F 55
Hill View. SK15—1H 107
Hillview Ct. BL1—1A 24
Hillview Rd. BL1—1A 24
Hillview Rd. M34—6A 104
Hillwood Av. M8—6B 60
Hillyard St. BL8—2A 28
Hilly Croft. BL7—3D 10
Hilmarton Clo. BL2—6A 12
Hilrose Av. M31—5H 97
Hilson Ct. M35—4A 90
Hilton Arc. OL1—2D 64
Hilton Av. M31—5F 97
Hilton Bank. M28—6D 54
Hilton Cres. M25—1F 73
Hilton Cres. M28—5D 68

Hilton Cres. OL6—6G 79
Hilton Dri. M25—1F 73
Hilton Dri. M30—4A 110
Hilton Fold La. M24—6B 46
Hilton Gro. SK12—3D 154
Hilton La. M25—2D 72
Hilton La. M28—6D 54
Hilton Lodge. M25—1F 73
Hilton Rd. BL9—3D 28
Hilton Rd. SK7—3H 143
Hilton Rd. SK12—6F 147
(Disley)
Hilton Rd. SK12—2A 156
(Poynton, in two parts)
Hiltons Farm Clo. M34—1E 105
Hilton Sq. M27—3G 71
Hilton St. BL2—6E 25
Hilton St. BL9—1D 28
Hilton St. M1—4F 87
Hilton St. M4 & M1—3E 87 & 4B 162
Hilton St. M7—5H 73
Hilton St. M24—5H 45
Hilton St. M28—5C 54
Hilton St. OL1—1G 65
Hilton St. SK3—3F 131
Hilton St. SK14—2D 106
Hilton St. N. M7—5H 73
Hilton Wlk. M24—1E 61
(in two parts)
Himley Rd. M11—2E 89
Hincaster Wlk. M18—2E 103
Hinchcliffe St. OL12—3F 19
Hinchcliffe Wlk. M16—3C 100
Hinchcombe Clo. M28—3C 54
Hinckley St. M11—5B 88
Hindburn Clo. M25—6F 43
Hindburn Dri. M28—3C 68
Hindburn Wlk. M25—6F 43
Hindell Ter. OL3—3H 51
(off King St.)
Hinde St. M10—3A 76
Hindhead Wlk. M10—1F 89
Hind Hill St. OL10—4F 31
Hindle Dri. OL2—4A 48
Hindle St. M26—4G 41
Hindley Av. M22—3H 139
Hindley Clo. OL7—4F 91
Hindley St. BL4—1E 55
Hindley St. OL7—4F 91
(in two parts)
Hindley St. SK1—3H 131
Hindsford Clo. M23—2E 127
Hinds La. M26 & BL8—6A 28
Hind St. BL2—6E 25
Hinkler Av. BL3—4A 38
Hinstock Cres. M18—2F 103
Hinton. OL12—3G 19
(off Spotland Rd.)
Hinton Clo. OL11—5A 18
Hinton St. M4—2F 87 & 2D 162
Hinton St. OL8—4D 64
Hinton St. SK1—2B 132
Hipley Clo. SK6—4G 121
Hirons La. OL4—4C 66
Hirst Av. M28—4E 55
Hitchen Clo. SK16—6D 92
Hitchen Dri. SK16—6D 92
Hitchen Wlk. M13—2H 101
Hive St. OL8—1H 77
Hobart Clo. SK7—3H 153
Hobart St. BL1—3H 23
Hobart St. M18—2F 103
Hobbs Mill. M8—1A 74
Hobson Ct. M34—1E 105
Hobson Cres. M34—1E 105
Hobson Moor Rd. SK14—1B 108
Hobson St. M11—6A 90
Hobson St. M35—5C 76
Hobson St. OL1—3D 64
Hobson St. SK5—5H 103
Hockley Clo. SK12—4G 155
Hockley Rd. M23—5F 127
Hockley St. SK12—4F 155
Hodder Av. OL15—3D 8
Hodder Bank. SK2—6E 133
Hodder Sq. M15—1D 100 &
                              6G 165
Hodder Way. M25—1G 59
(in three parts)

Homestead Gdns. OL12—5B 8
Homestead Rd. SK12—1G 157
Homestead, The. M35—4H 113
Homewood Av. M22—2B 128
Homewood Rd. M22—2A 128
Honduras St. OL4—2F 65
Honey Hill. OL4—4B 66
Honey St. M8—1E 87
Honeysuckle Wlk. M33—4F 113
Honeysuckle Way. OL12—6D 6
Honeywell La. OL8—6D 64
Honeywood Clo. BL0—6C 4
Honford Rd. M22—1A 140
Honister Dri. M24—5G 45
Honister Dri. M9—4H 75
Honister Way. OL11—1B 32
Honiton Av. SK14—5G 107
Honiton Clo. OL9—6E 47
Honiton Clo. OL10—5E 31
Honiton Ct. SK14—5H 107
Honiton Dri. BL2—1A 40
Honiton Gro. M26—2D 40
Honiton Wlk. SK14—5H 107
Honiton Way. WA14—5C 124
Honor St. M13—4B 102
Honsham Wlk. M23—2E 127
Hood Clo. M29—2A 68
Hood Sq. OL4—4C 66
Hood St. M4—3F 87 & 4D 162
Hoole Clo. SK8—6C 130
Hooley Bri. Ind. Est. OL10—1E 31
Hooley Clough. OL10—1F 31
Hooley Range. SK4—6D 118
Hooper St. M12—5H 87 & 2H 167
Hooper St. OL4—3E 65
Hooper St. SK1—2G 131
Hooton St. BL3—4G 37
Hooton St. M10—2B 88
Hopcroft Clo. M9—3D 60
Hope Av. BL2—1D 38
Hope Av. M28—5E 55
Hope Av. M32—4B 98
Hope Av. SK9—4G 151
Hopecourt Clo. M6—1C 84
Hope Cres. M6—2C 84
Hopedale Clo. M11—4B 88
Hopedale Rd. SK5—3H 119
Hopefield St. BL3—1G 37
Hopefold Dri. M28—1G 69
Hope Hey La. M28—4B 54
Hope La. SK10—6D 154
Hope Pk. Rd. M25—6F 59
Hope Rd. M14—3H 101
Hope Rd. M25—1E 73
Hope Rd. M33—6B 114
Hopes Carr. SK1—2H 131
Hope St. BL0—4D 4
Hope St. BL2—6A 12
Hope St. BL4—1G 55
Hope St. M1—4E 87 & 6C 162
Hope St. M5—4A 86 & 5A 160
Hope St. M7—4H 73
Hope St. M20—2F 117
Hope St. M27—3G 71
(Pendlebury)
Hope St. M27—4D 70
(Swinton)
Hope St. M28—5C 54
Hope St. M30—3H 83
Hope St. M34—2F 105
Hope St. OL1—1F 65
Hope St. OL2—6F 35
Hope St. OL6—1B 92
Hope St. OL10—5H 31
Hope St. OL12—3H 19
Hope St. SK4—2F 131
Hope St. SK7—2D 144
Hope St. SK16—5H 91
(in two parts)
Hope Ter. SK16—5H 91
Hopgarth Wlk. M10—6D 76
Hopkin Av. OL1—1F 65
Hopkins Field. WA14—4D 136
Hopkinson Av. M34—2D 104
Hopkinson Clo. OL3—1F 53
Hopkinson Rd. M9—4F 61
Hopkins St. M12—4C 102

Hopkins St. SK14—3C 106
Hopkin St. OL1—2D 64
Hoppet La. M35—3C 90
Hopton Av. M22—2C 140
Hopton Ct. M15—1E 101 & 5A 166
Hopwood Av. M30—2F 83
Hopwood Av. OL10—5F 31
Hopwood Clo. BL9—4D 42
Hopwood Ct. M24—3A 46
Hopwood Ct. OL12—6D 34
Hopwood Rd. M24—3A 46
Hopwood St. M3—3C 86 & 3F 161
Hopwood St. M10—5B 76
Hopwood St. M27—3G 71
Horace Barnes Clo. M14—4E 101
Horace Gro. SK4—5G 119
Horace St. BL1—3H 23
Horatio St. M18—1H 103
Horbury Av. M18—4F 103
Horbury Dri. BL8—3A 28
Horden Wlk. OL2—3C 48
(off Shaw St.)
Hordron Clo. M15—1C 100 & 5E 165
Horeb St. BL3—2H 37
Horley Clo. BL8—4C 14
Horlock Ct. M6—2H 85
Hornbeam Clo. M33—4E 113
Hornbeam Ct. M6—2G 85
Hornbeam Rd. M19—5D 102
Hornby Av. M9—4G 61
Hornby Dri. BL3—5B 36
Hornby Rd. M32—3F 99
Hornby St. BL9—6F 15
Hornby St. M8—1D 86
Hornby St. M24—1A 62
Hornby St. OL8—4B 64
Hornby St. OL10—4F 31
Horncastle Clo. BL8—6D 14
Horncastle Rd. M10—1B 76
Hornchurch Ct. M15—1D 100
(off Bonsall St.)
Horne Dri. M4—3G 87 & 4F 163
Horne St. BL9—5C 28
Hornet Clo. OL11—2G 33
Hornsea Clo. BL8—3F 27
Hornsea Clo. OL9—6F 47
Hornsea Rd. SK2—6G 133
Hornsea Wlk. M11—4C 88
Horridge Fold. BL7—1C 10
Horridge Fold Av. BL5—5D 36
Horridge St. BL8—1H 27
Horrobin La. BL7—1G 11
Horrocks Fold Av. BL1—5B 10
Horrocks St. BL3—2E 37
Horrocks St. M26—2A 42
Horsa St. BL2—4D 24
Horsedge St. OL1—1D 64
Horsefield Av. OL12—3C 6
Horsefield Clo. M21—2C 116
Horsefield Way. SK6—3E 121
Horseshoe La. BL7—3E 11
Horseshoe La. SK9—4G 159
Horsfield St. BL3—3E 37
Horsforth La. OL3—5E 53
Horsham Av. SK7—4C 144
Horsham Clo. BL8—4C 14
Horsham St. M6—3E 85
Horstead Wlk. M19—5C 102
Horton Av. BL1—5C 10
Horton Rd. M14—5E 101
Horton St. SK1—4A 132
Hortree Rd. M32—5E 99
Horwood Cres. M20—4H 117
Hoscar Dri. M19—2B 118
Hoskins Clo. M12—2C 102
Hospital Av. M30—3G 83
Hospital Rd. BL7—3D 10
Hospital Rd. M27—4H 71
Hotel Rd. M22—6A 140
Hotel St. BL1—6B 24
Hothersall Rd. SK5—1H 119
Hothersall St. M7—2C 86 & 1E 161
Hotspur Clo. M14—1E 117
Houghend Av. M21—3A 116
Hough End Cen. M21—2C 116
Houghend Cres. M21—1C 116
Hough Fold Way. BL2—6H 11
Hough Hall Rd. M10—3H 75

Hough Hill Rd. SK15—4E 93
(in two parts)
Hough La. BL7—4D 10
Hough La. M24—3F 47
Hough La. SK9—5G 159
Hough La. SK14—1D 106
Hough Rd. M20—2E 117
Hough St. BL3—2E 37
Hough St. M10—6G 75
Houghton Av. OL8—1B 78
Houghton La. M27—6D 70
Houghton St. BL3—2A 38
Houghton St. BL9—4C 28
Houghton St. M27—5B 72
Houghton St. OL2—5C 48
Hough Wlk. M7—2A 86 & 1B 160
Houldsworth Av. WA14—4G 125
Houldsworth Sq. SK5—2G 119
Houldsworth St. M1—3F 87 & 4C 162
Houldsworth St. M26—2F 41
Houldsworth St. SK5—2G 119
Hounslow Ho. BL1—4A 24
Houseley Av. OL9—6G 63
Houson St. OL8—4D 64
Houston Pk. M5—4F 85
Hove Clo. BL8—2G 13
Hoveden St. M8—1D 86
Hove Dri. M14—2A 118
Hove St. BL3—2G 37
Hovey Clo. M8—4B 74
Hoviley. SK14—4C 106
Hoviley Brow. SK14—4C 106
Hovingham St. OL16—3B 20
Hovington Gdns. M19—3A 118
Hovis St. M11—5E 89
Howard Av. BL3—3E 37
Howard Av. BL4—2H 55
Howard Av. M30—2F 83
Howard Av. SK4—3E 119
Howard Av. SK8—4C 142
Howard Clo. SK6—1G 133
Howard Ct. OL6—2A 92
Howard Dri. WA15—4A 138
Howard Hill. BL9—2E 43
Howard La. M34—3F 105
Howard Pl. OL16—3H 19
Howard Pl. SK14—5B 106
Howard Rd. M22—2B 128
Howard's La. OL5—1H 93
Howard Spring Wlk. M8—3B 74
Howard St. BL1—4B 24
Howard St. M5—5G 85
Howard St. M8—1D 86
Howard St. M12—5G 87 & 2E 167
Howard St. M26—4H 41
Howard St. M32—5D 98
Howard St. M34—1F 105
(Audenshaw)
Howard St. M34—2E 105
(Denton)
Howard St. OL2—6E 35
Howard St. OL4—1A 66
Howard St. OL7—1G 91
Howard St. OL12—3H 19
Howard St. SK1—1H 131
Howard St. SK15—1G 93
Howard Way. OL15—6G 9
Howarth Av. M28—4C 70
Howarth Clo. M11—4C 88
Howarth Cross St. OL16—1B 20
Howarth Dri. M30—6D 94
Howarth Grn. OL12—6A 8
Howarth Pl. OL11—6F 19
Howarth Sq. OL12—3A 20
Howarth St. M16—3A 100
Howarth St. OL15—3F 9
Howbridge Clo. M28—3E 69
Howbro Dri. OL7—6C 78
Howbrook Wlk. M15—1D 100 & 6H 165
Howclough Clo. M28—1H 69
Howclough Dri. M28—1H 69
Howcroft Clo. BL1—5A 24
Howcroft St. BL3—3H 37
Howden Clo. SK5—5G 103
Howden Rd. M9—4E 61
Howe Dri. BL0—1B 14
Howell Croft N. BL1—6B 24
Howell Croft S. BL1—6B 24

Howells Av. M33—4B 114
Howell's Yd. BL1—6B 24
Howe St. M7—4G 73
Howe St. OL7—5F 91
Howgill St. M11—4F 89
How La. BL9—5E 15
How Lea Dri. BL9—5F 15
Howsin Av. BL2—1D 24
Howton Clo. M12—3C 102
Howty Clo. SK9—6H 151
Hoxton Clo. SK6—5G 121
Hoy Dri. M31—2F 97
Hoylake Clo. M10—3D 76
Hoylake Rd. M33—1F 127
Hoylake Rd. SK3—3C 130
Hoyland Clo. M12—1B 102
Hoyle Av. OL8—4C 64
Hoyle's Ter. OL16—5E 21
Hoyle St. BL1—1A 24
Hoyle St. M12—5G 87 & 2F 167
Hoyle St. M24—3C 62
Hoyle St. M26—6A 42
Hoyle St. OL12—2H 7
Hoyle Wlk. M13—1G 101 & 5E 167
Hubert Worthington Ho. SK9
                                    —5G 159
Huccllecote Av. M22—3A 140
Hucklow Av. M23—3G 139
Hucklow Bank. SK13—5F 109
(off Grassmoor Cres.)
Hucklow Clo. SK13—5F 109
(off Grassmoor Cres.)
Hucklow Fold. SK13—5F 109
(off Grassmoor Cres.)
Hucklow Lanes. SK13—5F 109
(off Grassmoor Cres.)
Hudale Clo. M15—1C 100 & 5E 165
Huddart Clo. M5—5H 85
Huddersfield Rd. OL1 & OL4—2F 65
Huddersfield Rd. OL3—3H 51
(Delph)
Huddersfield Rd. OL3—4B 52
(Diggle)
Huddersfield Rd. OL16—1F 35
Huddersfield Rd. SK15, OL5 & OL3
                                    —6G 81
(Mossley)
Huddersfield Rd. SK15—3F 93
(Stalybridge)
Huddleston St. M11—6C 88
Hudgar La. BL9—1E 29
Hudson Rd. BL3—4F 37
Hudson Rd. SK14—2C 122
Hudsons Pas. OL15—2A 10
Hudson St. OL9—1G 77
Hudsons Wlk. OL11—4D 18
Hudswell. M25—1C 58
Huges St. BL3—2G 29
Hughes St. BL1—3G 23
(in two parts)
Hughes St. M11—5A 88
Hughes Way. M30—5C 82
Hugh Fold. OL4—4A 66
Hugh Lupus St. BL1—1A 24
Hugh Oldham Dri. M7—5G 73
Hugh St. BL3—3G 37
Hugh St. OL16—2H 33
Hughtrede St. OL16—2H 33
Hugo St. BL4—5D 38
Hugo St. M10—4A 76
Hugo St. OL11—3D 32
Hulbert St. BL8—4A 28
Hulbert St. M24—6B 46
Hullard Clo. M16—2A 100
Hull Mill La. OL3—2H 51
Hull Sq. M3—3B 86 & 3C 160
Hully St. SK15—3D 92
Hulme Hall Av. SK8—5C 142
Hulme Hall Cres. SK8—5C 142
Hulme Hall La. M10 & M11—1A 88
Hulme Hall Rd. M15—6B 86 & 3C 164
Hulme Hall Rd. SK8—3C 142
Hulme Pl. M5—3A 86 & 4B 160
Hulme Rd. BL2—5A 12
Hulme Rd. M26—2C 56
Hulme Rd. M33—6D 114
Hulme Rd. M34—4B 104
Hulme Rd. SK4—3F 119

Manchester 227

Hulme's La. M34—1E 121
Hulmes Rd. M10 & M35—6E 77
Hulmes Rd. M35—1H 89
Hulme St. BL1—5B 24
Hulme St. BL8—2B 28
Hulme St. M5—4A 86 & 5B 160
Hulme St. M15 & M1—6C 86 & 4F 165
(in three parts)
Hulme St. OL6—1B 92
Hulme St. OL8—5C 64
Hulme St. SK1—4B 132
Hulme Wlk. M15—1C 100 & 6E 165
(in three parts)
Hulton Av. M28—6C 54
Hulton Clo. BL3—3E 37
Hulton Dri. BL4—2E 37
Hulton Dri. M16—3C 100
Hulton La. BL3—5E 37
Hulton La. Est. BL3—4E 37
Hulton St. M5—6G 85
Hulton St. M34—3E 105
Hulton St. M35—4E 77
Humber Dri. BL9—3F 15
Humber Rd. OL16—5G 21
Humberstone Av. M15—6C 86 &
5G 165
Humber St. M5—4D 84
Humber St. M8—4C 74
Hume St. M19—1D 118
Hume St. OL16—5A 20
Humphrey Booth's Gdns. M6—2E 85
Humphrey Cres. M31—5H 97
Humphrey La. M31—5A 98
Humphrey Pk. M31—5A 98
Humphrey Rd. M16—2H 99
Humphrey St. SK7—2G 143
Humphrey St. M8—3B 74
Humps M. OL1—2E 65
Huncoat Av. SK4—3F 119
Huncote Dri. M9—2G 75
Hungerford Wlk. M23—4D 126
Hunger Hill. OL12—3B 8
Hunger Hill Av. BL3—5C 36
Hunger Hill La. OL12—1B 18
Hunmanby Av. M15—6D 86 & 4G 165
Hunstanton Dri. BL8—6D 14
Hunston Rd. M33—6H 113
Hunt Av. OL7—6F 79
Hunters Clo. SK9—6B 152
Hunters Ct. SK15—6H 93
Hunters Grn. BL0—6B 4
Hunters Hill. BL9—3F 43
Hunters Hill La. OL3—1B 52
Hunter's La. M12—2C 102
Hunters La. OL1—2D 64
Hunters La. OL16—3H 19
Hunters M. M33—4A 114
Hunters M. SK9—2F 159
Hunterson Av. M30—3A 84
Hunter St. M24—6A 46
Hunters View. SK9—4G 151
Hunt Fold Dri. BL8—1H 13
Hunt Hill Rd. M26—3F 41
Huntingdon Av. M20—2E 117
Huntingdon Cres. SK5—4C 120
Huntingdon Wlk. BL1—3A 24
Huntingdon Way. M34—6F 105
Hunt La. OL9—2F 63
Huntley Mt. Rd. BL9—1F 29
Huntley Rd. M8—1A 74
Huntley Rd. SK3—4D 130
Huntley St. BL9—2F 29
Huntley Way. OL10—4A 30
Huntly Chase. SK9—2G 159
Hunton Av. OL6—3C 92
Hunt Rd. SK14—2E 107
Huntroyde Av. BL2—4E 25
Hunt's Bank App. M3—3D 86 & 3H 161
Huntsham Clo. WA14—5D 124
Huntsman Dri. M30—2D 110
Hunts Rd. M6—6B 72
Hunt St. M9—2F 75
Hunt St. SK3—3E 131
Huntsworth Wlk. M13—2H 101
Hurdlow Av. M7—4E 73
Hurdlow Grn. SK13—6F 109
(off Brassington Cres.)

Hurdlow Lea. SK13—6F 109
(off Brassington Cres.)
Hurdlow M. SK13—6F 109
Hurdlow Wlk. M9—4F 75
Hurdlow Way. SK13—6F 109
(off Brassington Cres.)
Hurdsfield Rd. SK2—1D 144
Hurford Av. M18—1F 103
Hurlbote Clo. SK9—2H 151
Hurley Dri. SK8—3A 142
Hurlston Rd. BL3—5H 37
Hurst Av. M33—6E 113
Hurst Av. SK8—1E 153
Hurst Bank. OL6—1C 92
Hurstbank Av. M19—5H 117
Hurstbourne Av. M11—2D 88
Hurstbrook Clo. OL6—1A 92
Hurst Ct. M23—1F 139
Hurst Ct. OL6—6H 79
Hurst Cross. OL6—6H 79
Hurstead. OL12—5B 8
Hurstead Grn. OL12—5B 8
Hursted Rd. OL16—5F 21
Hurstfield Ind. Est. SK5—3G 119
Hurstfield Rd. M28—3D 68
Hurst Fold. M30—4F 95
(off Fiddlers La.)
Hurstfold Av. M19—6H 117
Hurst Grn. Clo. BL8—5F 27
Hurst Gro. OL6—6A 80
Hurst Hall Dri. OL6—6A 80
Hurst Head Rd. SK8—6D 142
Hursthead Wlk. M13—6F 87 & 4D 166
Hurst Lea Ct. SK9—4G 159
Hurstmead Ter. M20—1F 129
(off South Rd.)
Hurst St. BL3—4G 37
Hurst St. BL4—6E 39
Hurst St. BL9—3E 29
Hurst St. M28—3E 55
Hurst St. OL9—2B 64
Hurst St. OL11—6A 20
Hurst St. SK5—2G 119
Hurstvale Av. SK8—4F 141
Hurstville Rd. M21—3H 115
Hurst Wlk. M23—3G 139
Hurstway Dri. M9—6G 61
Hurstwood Gro. SK2—6F 133
Hurstwood Wlk. M6—3G 85
Hus St. M35—5H 89
Husteads La. OL3—6G 51
Hutchinson Rd. OL11—2H 17
Hutchinson St. M26—3A 42
Hutchinson St. OL11—5D 18
Hutchinson Way. M26—5G 41
Hutton Av. M28—5B 68
Hutton Wlk. M13—1G 101
(off Copeman Clo.)
Huxley Av. M8—5C 74
Huxley Clo. SK7—6G 143
Huxley Dri. SK7—6G 143
Huxley St. BL1—3G 23
Huxley St. OL4—4G 65
Huxley St. WA14—4F 125
Huxton Grn. SK7—4A 144
Hyacinth Clo. SK3—6F 131
Hyacinth Wlk. M31—6C 110
Hydebank. SK6—2B 134
Hyde By-Pass. SK14—4A 106
Hyde Dri. M28—1G 69
Hyde Fold Clo. M19—3B 118
Hyde Gro. M13—2G 101
Hyde Gro. M28—1E 69
Hyde Gro. M33—5B 114
Hyde Pk. Pl. OL16—4C 20
Hyde Pl. M13—2G 101
Hyde Rd. M12 & M18—6G 87 & 4F 167
Hyde Rd. M24—3E 63
Hyde Rd. M28—1E 69
Hyde Rd. M34—3F 105
Hyde Rd. SK6—4G 121
Hyde St. SK14—4B 108
Hyde Sq. M24—1G 61
Hydes Ter. SK15—3F 93
Hyde St. BL3—4G 37
Hyde St. M15—2B 100 & 6E 165
(in two parts)
Hyde St. M35—1C 90

Hyde St. OL1—3D 64
Hyde St. SK16—5B 92
Hydon Brook Wlk. OL11—1C 32
Hydrangea Clo. M33—4E 113
Hyldavale Av. SK8—5F 129
Hylton Dri. OL7—6D 78
Hylton Dri. SK8—5E 143
Hyman Goldstone Wlk. M8—4B 74
Hyndman Ct. M5—4D 84
Hypatia St. BL2—5D 24
Hythe Clo. M14—4G 101
Hythe Rd. SK3—3D 130
Hythe St. BL3—3E 37
Hythe Wlk. OL9—3H 63

Ibberton Wlk. M9—2H 75
(off Carnaby St.)
Ibsley. OL12—3G 19
(off Spotland Rd.)
Ice Ho. M28—6B 54
Iceland St. M6—3E 85
Idiona St. BL1—2H 23
Ilex Gro. M7—5H 73
Ilford St. M11—3D 88
Ilfracombe Rd. SK2—3C 132
Ilfracombe St. M10—5D 76
Ilkestone Wlk. M10—4A 76
(off Halliford Rd.)
Ilkeston Wlk. M34—1G 121
Ilkley Av. M31—3C 96
Ilkley Clo. BL2—6E 25
Ilkley Clo. OL9—3H 63
Ilkley Cres. SK5—1G 119
Ilkley St. M10—2D 76
Ilk St. M11—3D 88
Illingworth Av. SK15—4G 93
Illona Dri. M7—3E 73
Ilminster. OL11—5G 19
Ilminster Wlk. M9—4G 61
(off Eastlands Rd.)
Ilthorpe Wlk. M10—5A 76
Imogen Ct. M5—5A 86 & 2B 164
Imperial Ter. M33—3A 114
Ina Av. BL1—4D 22
Ince Clo. M20—2F 117
Ince Clo. SK4—6G 119
Ince St. SK4—6G 119
Inchcape Dri. M9—5D 60
Inchfield Clo. OL11—3A 18
Inchfield Rd. M10—2A 76
Inchley Rd. M13—6F 87 & 4C 166
Inchwood M. OL4—3A 50
Incline Rd. OL8—1H 77
Independant St. BL1—5C 24
Independent St. BL3—4A 40
India St. BL9—6E 5
Indigo St. M6—6D 72
Indigo Wlk. M6—5D 72
Indoor Mkt. OL16—4H 19
Industrial St. BL0—1E 5
Industry Rd. OL12—2H 19
Industry St. OL9—5G 63
Industry St. OL11—2A 18
Industry St. OL12—3H 7
Industry St. OL15—4F 9
Infant St. M25—5G 59
Infirmary St. BL1—6B 24
Ingham Rd. WA14—3F 125
Inghams La. OL15—4F 9
Ingham St. BL9—4E 29
Ingham St. M10—1G 89
Ingham St. OL1—2E 65
Inghamwood Clo. M8—4B 74
Ingleby Av. M9—5G 61
Ingleby Clo. OL2—5E 35
Ingleby Ct. M32—6E 99
Ingleby Way. OL2—5E 35
Ingledene Av. M7—2A 74
Ingledene Ct. M7—2A 74
Ingledene Gro. BL1—3E 23
Ingle Dri. SK2—4C 132
Inglefield. OL11—2B 18
Inglehead Clo. M34—5G 105
Ingle Rd. SK8—5C 130
Ingles Fold. M28—4D 68
Ingleton Av. M8—1D 74

Ingleton Clo. BL2—1F 25
Ingleton Clo. BL8—1H 27
Ingleton Clo. OL2—2B 48
Ingleton Clo. SK8—5G 129
Ingleton Gdns. OL2—2B 48
Ingleton Rd. SK3—3E 131
Inglewhite Clo. BL9—5B 28
Inglewood Clo. OL7—6D 78
Inglewood Rd. OL9—6D 46
Inglewood Wlk. M13—1G 101
(off Brunswick St.)
Inglis St. OL15—3F 9
Ingoe Clo. OL10—2H 31
Ingoldsby Av. M13—3H 101
Ingram Dri. SK4—6A 118
Ingres Wlk. OL1—3G 49
Ings Av. OL12—1D 18
Ings La. OL12—1D 18
Inkerman St. M10—5F 75
(off Topley St.)
Inkerman St. OL12—2H 19
Inkerman St. SK14—3B 106
Ink St. OL16—4H 19
Inman St. BL9—5C 28
Inman St. M34—4F 105
Innes St. M12—4D 102
Innis Av. M10—6C 76
Institute St. BL1—6B 24
Instow Clo. M13—1H 101
Instow Clo. OL9—6F 47
Intake La. OL3—6E 53
Invar Rd. M28—2D 70
Inverbeg Dri. BL2—6A 26
Invergarry Wlk. M11—4E 89
Inverlael Av. BL1—5F 23
Inverness Av. M9—5A 62
Inverness Ct. OL8—5D 64
Inverness Rd. SK16—6A 92
Inver Wlk. M10—1D 76
Inwood Wlk. M8—5E 75
Inworth Wlk. M8—4B 74
(off Highshore Dri.)
Iona Pl. BL2—3E 25
Iona Way. M31—2F 97
Ipstone Clo. M15—1C 100 & 5E 165
Ipswich St. OL11—6H 19
Ipswich Wlk. M12—2A 102
(off Martindale Cres.)
Ipswich Wlk. M34—6G 105
Iqbal Clo. M12—2C 102
Irby Wlk. SK8—1C 142
Ireby Clo. M24—5E 45
Iredine St. M11—4E 89
Irene Av. SK14—2C 106
Iris Av. BL4—6C 38
(Farnworth)
Iris Av. BL4—4H 55
(Kearsley)
Iris Av. M11—5F 89
Iris St. BL0—3D 4
Iris St. OL8—6D 64
Iris Wlk. M31—6D 110
Irkdale St. M8—5E 75
Irk Pl. M8—4E 75
Irk Way. M25—5F 43
Irlam Av. M30—4F 83
Irlam-Cadishead By-Pass. M30
—2E 111
Irlam Rd. M31—6F 95
Irlam Rd. M33—4C 114
Irlams Sq. M6—6B 72
Irlam St. BL1—2A 24
Irlam St. M10—6G 75
Irlam Wharf Rd. M30—3E 111
Irma St. BL1—2B 24
Ironmonger La. OL1—3D 64
Iron St. M10—2A 88
Iron St. M34—4F 105
Irvin Dri. M22—5E 141
Irvine. OL11—1E 33
Irvine Av. M28—5C 68
Irving Clo. SK2—2A 144
Irving St. BL1—3A 24
Irving St. OL8—1H 77
Irvin St. M10—5C 76
Irwell Av. M28—5D 54
Irwell Av. M30—4H 83

Irwell Clo. M26—5H 41
Irwell Gro. M30—4H 83
Irwell Pl. M5—3A 86
Irwell Pl. M30—4H 83
Irwell St. BL0—3E 5
Irwell St. BL9—3C 28
Irwell St. M3—3B 86 & 4D 160
Irwell St. M6—5E 73
Irwell St.—1C 86
Irwell St. M26—1A 56
  (Prestolee)
Irwell St. M26—5H 41
  (Radcliffe)
Irwell Ter. BL9—6B 28
Irwin Dri. SK9—2G 151
Irwin Rd. WA14—3E 125
Irwin St. M34—4E 105
Isaac Clo. M5—5G 85
Isaac St. BL1—5G 23
Isabella St. OL12—1H 19
Isabel Wlk. BL3—2H 37
Isaiah St. OL8—5D 64
Isa St. BL0—5C 4
Isca St. M11—4B 88
Isel Wlk. M24—5F 45
Isherwood Clo. OL10—4F 31
Isherwood Dri. SK6—5B 134
Isherwood Rd. M31—3B 112
Isherwood St. OL10—4G 31
Islington Rd. SK2—1C 144
Islington St. M3—4B 86 & 5C 160
Isobel Bailey Lodge. M16—2B 100
Isobel Clo. M30—4D 82
Isobel Wlk. M10—6C 91
Ivanhoe Ct. BL3—5E 39
Ivanhoe St. BL3—5E 39
Ivanhoe St. OL1—6G 49
Iveagh Ct. OL16—5B 20
Ivor St. OL11—2B 32
Ivory St. M4—1F 87
Ivory Way. OL1—2D 64
Ivy Bank. OL12—2H 7
Ivy Bank Clo. BL1—6C 10
Ivy Bank Rd. BL1—6C 10
Ivybridge Clo. M13—2H 101
Ivy Clo. M35—2H 89
Ivy Clo. OL2—6F 35
Ivy Cotts. M34—2G 121
Ivy Cotts. OL12—2F 19
Ivy Ct. M21—1H 115
Ivycroft. SK14—3G 109
Ivy Dri. M24—2H 61
Ivygreen Dri. OL4—3B 66
Ivygreen Rd. M21—1F 115
Ivy Gro. BL4—1D 54
  (Farnworth)
Ivy Gro. BL4—2H 55
  (Kearsley)
Ivy Gro. M28—5B 54
Ivy Leaf Sq. M7—5A 74
Ivylea Rd. M19—5A 118
Ivylodge Clo. SK15—1H 93
Ivy Rd. BL1—4G 23
Ivy Rd. BL8—3H 27
Ivy Rd. SK12—4E 155
Ivy St. BL3—3G 37
Ivy St. M10—3A 76
Ivy St. M30—4F 83
Ivy Ter. OL15—5H 9
Ivy Villa. OL4—4B 66
Ivy Wlk. M31—6B 110

Jackdaw Rd. BL8—1H 13
Jackie Brown Wlk. M10—6F 75
Jack La. M31—1G 111
  (Flixton)
Jack La. M31—5G 97
  (Urmston)
Jack La. M35—3B 90
  (in two parts)
Jack McCann Ct. OL16—3A 20
Jackman Av. OL10—6F 31
Jackroom Dri. M4—3G 87 & 4E 163
Jackson Av. SK16—5B 92
Jackson Clo. BL8—2H 27
Jackson Clo. OL8—4C 64

Jackson Ct. M21—6F 99
Jackson Ct. M31—5C 96
Jackson Cres. M15—1C 100 & 5E 165
Jackson Gdns. M34—5D 104
Jackson Pit. OL1—3C 64
Jackson Pl. OL16—3B 20
Jacksons Edge Rd. SK6 & SK12
  —6E 147
Jacksons La. SK7—4A 144
Jackson's Row. M2—4D 86 & 6G 161
Jackson St. BL4—1F 55
  (Farnworth)
Jackson St. BL4—2H 55
  (Kearsley)
Jackson St. M24—6B 46
Jackson St. M25—2D 58
Jackson St. M26—5H 41
Jackson St. M28—5E 55
Jackson St. M32—5C 98
Jackson St. M33—4D 114
Jackson St. M35—5D 76
Jackson St. OL4—2F 65
  (Oldham)
Jackson St. OL4—3B 66
  (Springhead)
Jackson St. OL12—3A 8
Jackson St. OL16—5B 20
Jackson St. SK8—5A 130
Jackson St. SK14—5B 106
Jackson St. SK14—4C 108
Jack St. BL2—4E 25
Jacobsen Av. SK14—3D 106
Jacob's Ladder. OL5—2E 81
James Andrew St. M24—6B 46
James Bentley Wlk. M10—6C 91
James Brindley Basin. M1—4G 87
James Butterworth Ct. OL16
  —4B 20
James Butterworth St. OL16
  —5B 20
James Clo. SK16—5C 92
James Corbett Rd. M5—4C 84
James Hill St. OL15—4F 9
James Leech St. SK3—3H 131
James Leigh St. M1—5E 87 & 2A 166
Jameson St. M13—3B 32
James Rd. OL2—5F 35
James St. BL3—4B 40
James St. BL4—1H 55
James St. BL7—1B 10
James St. BL9—4E 29
James St. M3—4B 86 & 5C 160
James St. M10—2H 87 & 1H 163
James St. M25—6C 58
James St. M26—6G 41
James St. M33—5D 114
  (Audenshaw)
James St. M34—3G 105
  (Denton)
James St. M35—3B 90
  (Droylsden)
James St. M35—3G 77
  (Failsworth)
James St. OL2—2E 49
James St. OL4—6H 49
James St. OL10—2F 31
James St. OL12—3H 7
James St. OL12—5A 8
  (Great Howarth)
James St. OL12—3A 20
  (Rochdale)
James St. OL15—5C 8
James St. OL16—4D 20
James St. SK3—4G 131
James St. SK6—4G 121
James St. SK6—5E 135
James St. S. OL9—2G 63
Jammy La. OL9—3A 64
Jane St. OL9—3H 63
Jane St. OL12—3G 19
Japan St. M8—4B 74
Jarmain St. M12—6C 88
Jarrold St. M11—6C 88
Jarvis St. M11—5B 88
Jarvis St. OL4—3E 65
Jarvis St. OL12—2H 19
Jasmine Av. M35—3C 90

Jasmine Wlk. M31—6D 110
Jasper Wlk. M16—3C 100
Jauncey St. BL3—2G 37
Jay St. M14—4F 101
Jayton Av. M20—4F 129
Jean Clo. M19—5C 102
Jean St. M19—5C 102
Jedburgh Av. KL1—5D 160
Jedburgh Sq. M8—2B 74
Jefferson Way. OL5—6F 7
Jeffreys Dri. SK16—5B 92
Jeffrey Wlk. OL10—3C 30
Jehlum Clo. M8—4D 74
Jellicoe Av. M30—3C 110
Jenkyn Wlk. M11—4B 88
Jenner Clo. M15—1C 100 & 5F 165
Jennings Av. M5—5G 85
Jennings Clo. M5—5G 85
Jennings Clo. SK14—2F 107
Jennings St. SK3—4F 131
Jennison Clo. M18—1D 102
Jenny Beck Gro. BL3—3A 38
Jenny La. SK7—4G 153
Jenny St. OL8—1A 78
Jepheys Pl. OL12—2H 19
Jepheys St. OL12—2H 19
Jepson St. SK2—5A 132
Jericho Rd. BL9—1A 30
Jermyn St. OL12—3A 20
Jerrold St. OL15—4F 9
Jersey Clo. M19—2B 118
Jersey Pl. SK4—1A 130
Jersey Rd. SK5—5H 119
Jersey St. M4—3F 87 & 4D 162
Jersey St. OL6—1H 91
Jerusalem Pl. M2—5D 86 & 1G 165
Jervas Wlk. OL1—3G 49
Jesmond Av. M25—1F 73
Jesmond Dri. BL8—6C 14
Jesmond Gro. SK8—5D 142
Jesmond Rd. BL1—1F 23
Jesmond St. M35—5C 76
Jesmond Wlk. M9—4F 61
  (off Claygate Dri.)
Jespersen St. OL1—2D 64
Jessamine Av. M7—1B 86
Jessel Clo. M13—1G 101 & 5E 167
Jessie St. BL3—2G 37
Jessie St. M10—5A 76
Jessop Dri. SK6—3D 134
Jessop St. M18—2F 103
Jethro St. BL2—5E 25
  (Bolton)
Jethro St. BL2—1E 25
  (Bradshaw)
Jetson St. M18—1H 103
Jevington. OL11—1F 33
Jevington Wlk. M13—1G 101
  (off Dilston Clo.)
Jimmy McMullen Wlk. M14
  —4E 101
Jinnah Clo. M11—5E 89
Joan St. M10—4A 76
Jobling St. M11—5B 88
Jocelyn St. M10—5G 75
Joddrell St. M3—4C 86 & 6F 161
Joel La. SK14—2D 122
Johannesburg Dri. M23—1F 139
Johannesburg Gdns. M23—1F 139
John Ashworth St. OL12—2B 20
John Atkinson Ct. M5—3D 84
John Av. SK8—6A 130
John Booth St. OL4—4B 66
John Bromley St. BL1—5C 24
John Brown St. BL1—5A 24
John Cross St. BL3—3A 38
John Dalton St. M2—4D 86 & 5G 161
John Dalton St. M3—3B 86 & 3C 160
John Dalton St. SK14—2G 109
John Foran Clo. M10—5B 76
John Henry St. OL12—1H 7
John Heywood St. M11—3D 88
John Kemble Ct. OL11—1D 32
John Kennedy Gdns. SK14—4C 108
John Kennedy Rd. SK14—4B 108
John Knott St. OL4—3B 66
John Lee Fold. M24—6A 46

John Lester Ct. M6—2G 85
  (off Meyrick Rd.)
John Nash Cres. M15—1C 100 & 1F 165
Johnny King Clo. M10—6F 75
John Robinson Wlk. M10—4A 76
Johns Clo. M21—1H 115
John Shepley St. SK14—5C 106
John Smeaton Ct. M1—4G 87 & 6E 163
Johnson Av. OL12—2A 50
Johnsonbrook Rd. SK14 & SK16
  —2A 106
Johnson Fold Av. BL1—3C 22
Johnson Gro. M24—1G 61
Johnson's Sq. M10—1H 87
Johnson St. BL1—1B 38
Johnson St. M3—3C 86 & 4F 161
Johnson St. M15—1B 100 & 6C 164
Johnson St. M26—5G 41
Johnson St. M27—5B 72
John's Pl. SK6—1A 134
Johnston. OL12—3G 19
  (off Spotland Rd.)
Johnston Av. OL15—6D 8
John Stone Ct. M32—4A 98
John St. BL3—4B 40
John St. BL4—1G 55
John St. BL7—4E 11
John St. BL9—2D 28
John St. M3—3C 86 & 3F 161
John St. M4—3E 87 & 4B 162
John St. M7—1B 86
John St. M25—1A 60
John St. M27—3G 71
John St. M28—5F 55
John St. M30—4C 110
  (Cadishead)
John St. M30—4D 82
  (Eccles)
John St. M33—4B 114
John St. M34—3F 105
John St. M35—2F 77
  (Failsworth)
John St. OL2—3B 48
  (Royton)
John St. OL2—2E 49
  (Shaw)
John St. OL4—3C 66
John St. OL8—3C 64
John St. OL10—3F 31
John St. OL12—3H 7
John St. OL15—4E 9
John St. OL16—3H 19
  (Rochdale)
John St. OL16—6A 8
  (Smallbridge)
John St. SK1—2H 131
  (in two parts)
John St. SK6—4G 121
  (Bredbury)
John St. SK6—6F 123
  (Compstall)
John St. SK6—6E 135
  (Marple)
John St. SK6—1A 134
  (Romiley)
John St. SK7—2D 144
John St. SK14—4B 106
  (in two parts)
John St. SK15—6E 81
John St. WA14—1F 137
John St. E. OL7—4F 91
  (in two parts)
John St. W. OL7—5F 91
John William St. M11—4E 89
John William St. M30—3H 83
Joiner St. M4—4E 87 & 5B 162
Joiner St. M5—4A 86 & 5B 160
Join Rd. M33—5D 114
Jolly Brows. BL2—2F 25
Jonas St. M7—2C 86 & 1E 161
Jones Sq. SK1—4A 132
Jones St. M6—2F 85
Jones St. M9—3G 75
Jones St. M26—3H 41
Jones St. OL1—1E 65
Jones St. OL2—5C 48

Jones St. OL16—5A 20
Jones St. SK14—2H 109
Jonquil Dri. M28—1B 68
Jopson St. M24—6B 46
Jordan Av. OL2—4G 35
Jordan St. M15—6C 86 & 3F 165
Joseph Dean Ct. M10—4A 76
Josephine Dri. M27—4G 71
Joseph Mamlock Ho. M8—2A 74
Joseph St. BL4—6F 39
Joseph St. BL9—2E 29
Joseph St. M24—6H 45
Joseph St. M26—5H 41
Joseph St. M30—4D 82
Joseph St. M34—5B 104
Joseph St. M35—3F 77
Joseph St. OL12—1F 19
Joseph St. OL15—3F 9
Joseph St. SK4—2E 131
Joseph St. SK6—5E 135
Joshua La. M24—2D 62
Josslyn Rd. M5—2D 84
Jo St. M5—4G 85
Joule Clo. M5—5G 85
Joules Ct. SK1—2H 131
Joule St. M9—2G 75
Jowett St. OL1—6G 49
Jowett St. SK5—5H 119
Jowett's Wlk. OL7—3F 91
Jowkin La. OL11—4H 17
Joyce St. M10—4B 76
Joynson Av. M7—1B 86
Joynson St. M10—1A 88
Joynson St. M33—4B 114
Joy St. BL0—3D 4
Joy St. OL12—6F 7
Jubilee. OL2—3G 35
Jubilee Av. M26—6A 42
Jubilee Av. SK16—4B 92
Jubilee Clo. M30—2F 83
Jubilee Ct. OL1—3H 49
Jubilee Ct. SK5—5H 103
Jubilee Ho. BL1—1A 38
Jubilee Houses. M28—6E 55
Jubilee Rd. M24—6B 46
Jubilee St. BL3—4G 37
Jubilee St. M3—2D 86 & 1H 161
Jubilee St. M6—3F 85
Jubilee St. OL2—1G 49
Jubilee Ter. M24—5B 46
Jubilee Wlk. OL12—2H 7
Jubilee Way. BL9—3B 28
Judith St. OL12—6C 6
Judson Av. M21—3A 116
Julian Ho. OL1—2D 64
Julia St. M3—2D 86 & 1G 161
Julia St. OL12—3G 19
Julius St. M19—1D 118
Junction Rd. BL3—2D 36
Junction Rd. SK1 & SK4—4H 131
Junction Rd. SK3—4H 131
Junction Rd. W. BL6—2A 36
Junction St. M24—3D 62
Junction St. OL6—2A 92
Junction St. OL8—5C 64
Junction St. SK14—2A 106
June Av. SK4—1D 130
June St. OL7—3G 91
Juniper Bank. SK5—1A 120
Juniper Clo. OL4—3B 50
Juniper Cres. M35—5G 89
Juno St. OL1—6E 49
Jupiter Wlk. M10—6A 76
Jura Clo. SK16—5B 92
Jura Dri. M31—2G 97
Jurby Av. M9—5E 61
Jury St. M8—1D 86
Justin Clo. M13—6F 87 & 4C 166
Jutland Av. OL11—3E 19
Jutland St. M1—4F 87 & 6D 162

Kale St. M13—6F 87 & 3D 166
Kalmia Av. M7—6H 73
 (off Hilton St. N.)
Kansas Av. M5—5E 85
Kara St. M6—3E 85
Kate St. BL0—3D 4

Kate St. M9—2F 75
Kathan Clo. OL16—4B 20
Katherine Ho. OL6—2G 91
Katherine Rd. SK2—6C 132
Katherine St. OL7 & OL6—3F 91
Kathkin Av. M15—1D 74
Kathleen Gro. M14—5G 101
Kathleen St. OL12—4F 19
Kay Av. SK6—6D 120
Kay Brow. BL0—3E 5
Kay Brow. OL10—3E 31
Kayes Av. SK1—2B 132
Kayfields. BL2—1G 25
Kayley Ind. Est. OL7—3F 91
Kays Gdns. M3—3B 86 & 3D 160
Kay St. BL0—3A 4
Kay St. BL1—4B 24
Kay St. BL3—4A 40
Kay St. BL9—2E 29
 (Bury)
Kay St. BL9—6E 5
 (Summerseat)
Kay St. M6—5D 72
Kay St. M11—5B 88
Kay St. OL10—3E 31
Kay St. OL11—6G 19
Kay St. SK15—4E 93
Kay St. SK16—5C 92
Kays Wood Rd. SK6—5B 134
Keal Dri. M30—3E 95
Keane St. OL7—2G 91
Kean Pl. M30—4F 83
Kearsley Dri. BL3—4D 38
Kearsley Hall Rd. M26—2C 56
Kearsley Mt. BL4—3B 56
Kearsley Rd. M8—1C 74
Kearsley Rd. M26—1C 56
Kearsley St. M30—3D 82
Kearsley Vale. M26—1B 56
Kearton Dri. M30—3A 84
Keary Clo. M18—1F 103
Keats Av. M34—1G 121
Keats Av. M35—3A 90
Keats Ct. M7—4F 73
Keats Cres. M26—3E 41
Keats Fold. SK16—6F 93
Keats Rd. BL8—1H 13
Keats Rd. M30—4F 83
Keats Rd. OL1—6F 49
Keats Wlk. BL1—3A 24
Keb La. OL8—3E 79
Keble Av. OL8—6C 64
Kedington Clo. M10—6E 75
Kedleston Av. M14—3A 102
Kedleston Grn. SK2—4D 132
Kedleston Wlk. M34—6F 105
Keele Clo. M20—2G 87 & 1F 163
Keele Clo. SK2—5B 132
Keeley Clo. M10—1E 89
Keepers Dri. OL12—1A 18
Keighley Av. M35—2A 90
Keighley Clo. BL8—3F 27
Keighley St. BL1—3G 23
Keilder M. BL1—6E 23
Keith Dri. SK3—4D 130
Keith Wlk. M10—2H 87 & 2G 163
Kelboro Av. M34—6D 90
Kelbrook Ct. SK2—6E 133
Kelbrook Rd. M11—5D 88
Kelby Av. M23—4H 127
Kelday Wlk. M8—5E 75
 (off Smeaton St.)
Keld Clo. BL8—6B 14
Keld Wlk. M18—2E 103
Kelfield Av. M23—1G 127
Kelham Wlk. M10—2C 76
Kellbrook Cres. M7—2F 73
 (in two parts)
Kellet's Row. M28—4E 55
Kellet St. OL16—3B 20
Kellett St. BL1—5D 10
Kellett Wlk. M11—3D 88
Kelling Wlk. M15—6B 86 & 4D 164
Kelmarsh Clo. M11—6F 89
Kelmscott Lodge. M31—4D 96
 (off Cornhill Rd.)
Kelsall Clo. SK3—5F 131
Kelsall Dri. M35—2H 89

Kelsall Dri. WA15—5C 126
Kelsall St. BL2—6E 25
Kelsall St. M12—1B 102
Kelsall St. M33—5A 114
Kelsall St. OL9—3B 64
Kelsall St. OL16—3H 19
Kelsall Way. SK9—2H 151
Kelsal Rd. SK8—6C 130
Kelsey Flats. OL10—3E 31
 (off Fearn St.)
Kelsey Wlk. M9—4D 60
Kelso Clo. OL8—2D 78
Kelson Av. OL7—6E 79
Kelstern Av. M13—4A 102
Kelstern Sq. M13—4A 102
Kelverlow St. OL4—2G 65
Kelvin Av. M24—2D 60
Kelvin Av. M33—5B 114
Kelvindale Dri. WA15—4C 126
Kelvin Gro. M8—5C 74
Kelvington Dri. M9—5F 75
Kelvin St. M4—3E 87 & 4B 162
Kelvin St. OL7—5F 91
Kelwood Av. BL9—6B 16
Kemble Av. M23—2A 128
Kemmel Av. M22—6C 128
Kemnay Wlk. M11—4E 89
Kempley Clo. M12—1B 102
Kemp Rd. SK6—3G 135
Kempsey Ct. OL9—2H 63
Kempsey St. OL9—2H 63
Kempsey Wlk. M10—2D 76
Kempster St. M7—1B 86
Kempston Gdns. BL1—3A 24
Kemp St. M24—1H 61
Kemp St. SK14—3C 106
Kempton Av. BL3—5A 40
Kempton Av. M33—6F 113
Kempton Clo. M35—3C 90
Kempton Clo. SK7—4G 145
Kempton Rd. M19—1C 118
Kempton Way. OL9—2A 64
Kemsing Wlk. M5—4G 85
Kenchester Av. M11—5F 89
Kendal Av. M31—3A 96
Kendal Av. M33—6C 114
Kendal Av. M34—6G 105
Kendal Clo. OL10—5G 31
Kendal Clo. WA15—6D 126
Kendal Dri. BL9—6B 28
Kendal Dri. OL2—6H 35
Kendal Dri. SK7—2E 153
Kendal Gdns. SK6—5H 121
Kendal Gro. M25—1D 58
Kendal Gro. M28—1H 69
Kendall Rd. M8—6B 60
Kendal Rd. BL0—1H 13
Kendal Rd. BL1—5G 23
Kendal Rd. M6—6A 72
Kendal Rd. M28—4A 68
Kendal Rd. M32—4D 98
Kendal Rd. W. BL0—1H 13
Kendal Ter. SK16—4A 92
 (off Astley St.)
Kendal Wlk. M24—6G 45
Kendon Gro. M34—4E 105
Kendon Wlk. M8—6A 74
Kendrew Rd. BL3—3E 37
Kendrew Wlk. M9—2G 75
Kenford Wlk. M8—5B 74
Kenilworth. OL11—5G 19
Kenilworth Av. M20—4D 116
Kenilworth Av. M25—3E 59
Kenilworth Av. M27—6H 57
Kenilworth Av. OL9—6E 47
Kenilworth Av. SK8—2C 142
Kenilworth Av. SK9—4H 151
Kenilworth Clo. M26—1F 41
Kenilworth Clo. OL4—4B 66
Kenilworth Clo. SK6—3D 134
Kenilworth Dri. SK7—5D 144
Kenilworth Gro. M34—5C 90
Kenilworth Rd. M31—6G 95

Kenilworth Rd. M33—5G 113
Kenilworth Rd. OL16—5A 34
Kenilworth Rd. SK3—4B 130
Kenilworth Sq. BL1—4F 23
Kenion Rd. OL11—5D 18
Kenion St. OL16—4H 19
Kenley Lodge. SK7—6F 143
Kenley Wlk. M8—5E 75
 (off Smedley Rd.)
Kenmay Av. BL3—1D 36
Kenmere Gro. M10—2B 76
Kenmor Av. BL8—5G 27
Kenmore Clo. M25—1F 59
Kenmore Dri. WA15—2A 138
Kenmore Gro. M30—3B 110
Kenmore Rd. M22—4A 128
Kenmore Rd. M25—1F 59
Kenmore Rd. M33—1E 125
Kenmore Way. M25—1F 59
Kennard Clo. M9—2H 75
Kennard Pl. WA14—5G 125
Kennedy Dri. BL3—4C 40
Kennedy Dri. BL9—5F 43
Kennedy Rd. M5—3C 84
Kennedy St. BL2—6E 25
Kennedy St. M2—4D 86 & 6H 161
Kennedy St. OL8—4C 64
Kennedy Way. M34—5D 104
Kennedy Way. SK4—1E 131
Kennerley Ct. SK2—6A 132
Kennerley Lodge. SK3—6H 131
Kennerley Rd. SK2—6A 132
Kennerley's La. SK9—2D 158
Kennet Flats. OL10—3E 31
 (off Meadow Clo.)
Kenneth Sq. M7—5A 74
Kennett Rd. M23—2G 139
Kenninghall Rd. M22—2B 140
Kennington Av. M10—1D 88
Kennington Fold. BL3—4H 37
Kenside Wlk. M16—4D 100
Kensington Av. M14—3H 101
Kensington Av. OL2—1A 48
Kensington Av. OL9—1E 63
Kensington Av. SK14—6C 106
Kensington Clo. BL8—2H 13
Kensington Clo. OL16—5G 21
Kensington Ct. M7—3G 73
Kensington Ct. M34—3B 104
Kensington Ct. SK9—3D 158
Kensington Ct. SK14—6C 106
Kensington Dri. BL8—5G 27
Kensington Dri. M5—2D 84
Kensington Gdns. SK14—6D 106
Kensington Gdns. WA15—4H 137
Kensington Gro. M34—3B 104
Kensington Gro. SK15—4E 93
Kensington Gro. WA14—3G 125
Kensington Pl. BL1—6A 24
 (off Kensington St.)
Kensington Rd. M21—5G 99
Kensington Rd. M35—3H 77
Kensington Rd. OL8—5B 64
Kensington Rd. SK3—4D 130
Kensington St. BL1—6A 24
Kensington St. M14—4E 101
Kensington St. OL11—1E 33
Kensington St. SK14—6C 106
Kenslow Av. M8—1B 74
Kensworth Clo. BL1—4H 23
Kensworth Clo. M23—5D 126
Kensworth Dri. BL1—4H 23
Kent Av. M35—4G 89
Kent Av. OL9—3G 63
Kent Av. SK8—6E 131
Kent Clo. M28—1D 68
Kent Clo. OL3—3C 52
Kent Ct. BL1—5A 24
Kent Dri. BL4—3B 56
Kent Dri. BL9—5D 28
Kentford Dri. M10—1G 87
Kentford Gro. BL4—1E 55
Kentford Rd. BL1—4A 24
Kent Gro. M35—5F 77
Kentleigh Wlk. SK14—4A 108
Kentmere Av. OL12—6H 7

Kentmere Ct. M9—5A 62
Kentmere Dri. M24—4G 45
Kentmere Gro. BL4—2B 54
Kentmere Rd. BL2—4H 25
Kentmere Rd. WA15—5C 126
Kentmore Clo. SK4—1A 130
Kenton Av. M18—3E 103
Kenton Clo. BL1—4H 23
Kenton Clo. M34—6D 90
Kenton Rd. OL2—6E 35
Kenton St. OL8—4F 65
Kent Rd. M30—4A 110
Kent Rd. M31—6C 110
Kent Rd. M34—5A 104
Kent Rd. SK3—3D 130
Kent Rd. E. M14—4H 101
Kent Rd. W. M14—4G 101
Kentsford Dri. M26—2B 40
Kentstone Av. SK4—6H 117
Kent St. BL1—5A 24
Kent St. M2—4D 86 & 5H 161
Kent St. M7—1B 86
Kent St. M27—1F 71
Kent St. OL8—5D 64
Kent St. OL11—5H 19
Kentucky St. OL4—3G 65
Kent Wlk. OL10—4C 30
Kenwick Dri. M10—1E 77
Kenwood Av. M19—3B 118
Kenwood Av. SK7—2F 153
Kenwood Av. SK8—5E 129
Kenwood Av. WA15—3H 137
Kenwood Clo. M32—5E 99
Kenwood Ct. M32—6E 99
Kenwood La. M28—6H 69
Kenwood Rd. BL1—2F 23
Kenwood Rd. M32—6E 99
Kenwood Rd. OL1—6A 48
Kenwood Rd. SK5—5G 103
Kenworthy Av. OL6—6H 79
Kenworthy La. M22—1B 128
Kenworthy St. OL16—4C 20
Kenworthy St. SK15—4E 93
(in two parts)
Kenworthy Ter. OL16—4C 20
Kenwright St. M4—3E 87 & 3B 162
Kenwyn St. M10—2A 88
Kenyon Av. M33—1E 127
Kenyon Av. SK16—6C 92
Kenyon Clo. SK14—2D 106
Kenyon Fold. OL11—6A 18
Kenyon Gro. M28—5A 54
Kenyon La. M10—3A 76
Kenyon La. M24—6B 46
Kenyon La. M25—5G 59
Kenyon Rd. BL2—2B 40
Kenyon St. BL0—2E 5
Kenyon St. BL9—2E 29
Kenyon St. M18—1G 103
Kenyon St. M26—4H 41
Kenyon St. OL6—2G 91
Kenyon St. OL10—3E 31
Kenyon St. SK1—6H 119
Kenyon St. SK16—5H 91
Kenyon Ter. M28—6A 54
Kenyon Way. BL8—6H 13
Kenyon Way. M28—5A 54
Keppel Rd. M21—6H 99
Kepple St. OL6—2A 92
Kepwick Dri. M22—4C 140
Kerenhappuch St. BL0—3D 4
(off Buchanan St.)
Kerfield Wlk. M13—6F 87 & 4D 166
Kerfoot Clo. M22—3C 128
Kermoor Av. BL1—5C 10
Kerne Gro. M23—2G 127
Kerrera Dri. M5—4D 84
Kerridge Dri. SK6—5F 61
Kerridge Wlk. M16—4D 100
(off Peachey Clo.)
Kerrier Clo. M30—3A 84
Kerr St. M9—6F 61
Kerry Gro. BL2—5D 24
Kerry Wlk. M23—2F 139
Kersal Av. M27—3A 72
Kersal Av. M28—5D 54
Kersal Bank. M7—3G 73

Kersal Bar. M7—2G 73
Kersal Clo. M25—2E 73
Kersal Crag. M7—2G 73
Kersal Dri. WA15—4C 126
Kersal Gdns. M7—2G 73
Kersal Hall Av. M7—3E 73
Kersal Rd. M25—2D 72
Kersal Vale Ct. M7—3E 73
Kersal Vale Rd. M7—2D 72
Kersal View. M6—1F 85
Kersall Wlk. M10—5A 76
Kersh Av. M19—1D 118
Kershaw Av. BL3—3A 40
Kershaw Av. M25—1D 72
Kershaw Av. M33—1E 127
Kershaw Dri. OL9—6D 62
Kershaw Gro. M34—5B 90
Kershaw La. M34—5B 90
Kershaw Rd. M35—4F 77
Kershaws Pas. OL15—5C 8
Kershaw St. BL2—6G 11
Kershaw St. BL3—2H 37
Kershaw St. BL9—3E 29
Kershaw St. M35—4H 89
Kershaw St. OL2—2B 48
(Royton)
Kershaw St. OL2—6F 35
(Shaw, in two parts)
Kershaw St. OL4—1G 65
Kershaw St. OL7—5F 91
Kershaw St. OL10—3D 30
Kershaw St. OL12—3H 19
Kershaw Wlk. M12—1H 101
Kershope Gro. M5—5G 85
Kersley St. M10—2B 88
Kersley St. OL4—3E 65
Kerwin Wlk. M11—5C 88
Kerwood Dri. OL2—4C 48
Kesteven Rd. M9—4F 75
Keston Av. M9—6A 62
Keston Av. M35—4G 89
Keston Cres. SK5—3B 120
Keston Rd. OL1—6G 49
Kestor St. BL2—5C 24
Kestrel Av. BL4—2B 54
Kestrel Av. M27—1H 71
Kestrel Av. M28—4C 54
Kestrel Av. M34—4C 90
Kestrel Av. OL4—4G 65
Kestrel Clo. M25—3E 59
Kestrel Clo. SK6—2E 147
Kestrel Dri. BL9—1F 29
Kestrel Dri. M30—4E 95
Kestrel M. OL11—4B 18
Kestrel Rd. M17—5H 83
Kestrel St. BL1—5C 24
Kestrel Wlk. M12—1C 102
Keswick Av. M31—6A 96
Keswick Av. M34—3D 104
Keswick Av. OL7—6D 78
Keswick Av. OL8—5E 65
Keswick Av. OL9—2G 63
Keswick Av. SK8—2F 141
Keswick Av. SK14—3A 106
Keswick Clo. M13—2H 101
Keswick Clo. M24—5F 45
Keswick Clo. M30—4B 110
Keswick Clo. SK15—1E 93
Keswick Ct. M24—5F 45
Keswick Dri. BL9—6B 28
Keswick Dri. SK7—2E 153
Keswick Gro. M6—2F 85
Keswick Rd. M28—1H 69
Keswick Rd. SK4—2F 119
Keswick Rd. SK6—5C 146
Keswick Rd. WA15—5D 126
Keswick St. BL1—3B 24
Keswick St. OL11—3B 32
Kesworthy Clo. SK14—5A 108
Ketley Wlk. M22—2D 140
Kettering Rd. M19—5D 102
Kettleshulme Wlk. SK9—6A 152
Kettleshume Way. SK12—5F 155
Kettlewell Wlk. M18—2E 103
Ketton Clo. M11—6G 89
Keverlow La. OL8—1G 79
Kevin Av. OL2—5C 48

Kevin Ct. SK2—1B 144
Kevin St. M19—1D 118
Kew Av. SK14—6C 106
Kew Dri. M31—3C 96
Kew Dri. SK8—3A 142
Kew Gdns. M10—2D 4
Kew Rd. M35—3G 77
Kew Rd. OL4—3F 65
(in two parts)
Kew Rd. OL11—2G 33
Key Ct. M34—1G 121
Keyhaven Wlk. M10—6E 75
Keymer St. M11—3A 88
Keynsham Rd. M11—2D 88
Key West Clo. M11—4B 88
Keyworth Wlk. M10—1A 88
Khartoum St. M11—3F 89
Khartoum St. M16—3B 100
Kibboth Crew. BL0—2D 4
Kibworth Clo. M25—1B 58
Kibworth Wlk. M9—4G 61
(off Brockford Dri.)
Kidacre Wlk. M10—4A 76
Kidderminster Way. M9—6F 47
Kidnall Wlk. M9—2H 75
Kid St. M24—6H 45
Kiel Clo. M30—5G 83
Kielder Sq. M5—4F 85
Kilbride Av. BL2—1H 39
Kilburn Av. M9—3F 61
Kilburn Clo. SK8—6F 141
Kilburn Rd. M26—3D 40
Kilburn Rd. SK3—4E 131
Kilburn St. OL1—6G 49
Kildale Clo. BL3—3C 36
Kildare Cres. OL11—3F 33
Kildare Rd. M21—1B 116
Kildare Rd. M27—4E 71
Kildare St. BL4—2E 55
Kildonan Dri. BL3—1D 36
Killer St. BL0—2E 5
Killon St. BL9—4E 29
Kilmaine Dri. BL3—2A 40
Kilmarsh Wlk. M8—4B 74
Kilmington Dri. M8—5B 74
Kilmory Dri. BL2—1H 39
Kiln Bank La. OL12—3G 7
Kiln Brow. BL7—3G 11
Kiln Croft. SK6—2F 133
Kilner Clo. BL9—3F 43
Kilnerdeyne Ter. OL12—5G 19
Kilner Wlk. M10—1G 87
Kilnfield. BL7—3D 10
Kiln Hill Clo. OL1—5F 47
Kiln Hill La. OL1—5F 47
Kilnhurst Wlk. BL1—5H 23
Kiln La. OL16—5F 21
Kiln La. SK14—2H 109
Kilnsey Wlk. M10—2E 103
Kilnside Dri. M9—4F 75
Kiln St. BL0—0D 4
Kiln St. BL3—4A 40
Kilnwick Clo. M18—4D 102
Kilsby Clo. BL4—5D 38
Kilsby Clo. BL6—1B 36
Kilsby Wlk. M10—1H 87
Kilton Wlk. M10—1G 87
Kilvert Dri. M33—4H 113
Kilvert St. M17—2F 99
Kilworth Av. M33—6H 113
Kilworth Dri. BL6—2B 36
Kilworth St. OL11—1D 32
Kimberley Av. SK6—1H 133
Kimberley Rd. BL1—6C 10
Kimberley St. M7—4A 74
Kimberley St. OL8—6A 64
Kimberley St. SK3—4G 131
Kimberley Wlk. M15—6B 86 & 4D 164
Kimble Clo. BL8—1H 13
Kimbolton Clo. M12—6C 88
Kimmel Wlk. M23—5F 127
Kinburn Rd. M19—1H 129
Kincardine Rd. M13—6F 87 & 4C 166
Kincraig Clo. BL3—3C 36
Kincraig Clo. M11—4D 88
Kinder Av. OL4—4H 65
Kinder Av. OL6—5C 80

Kinder Dri. SK6—5E 135
Kinder Fold. SK15—1H 107
Kinder Gro. SK6—1C 134
Kinder Ho. M5—2D 84
Kinders Cres. OL3—4F 53
Kinders La. OL3—4F 53
Kinders M. OL3—4F 53
Kinder St. SK3—4G 131
Kinder St. SK15—3E 93
Kinderton Av. M20—2F 117
Kinder Way. M24—5H 45
Kineton Wlk. M13—1G 101
(off Lauderdale Cres.)
King Albert St. OL2—6F 35
Kingcombe Wlk. M9—3G 75
King Edward Rd. SK14—2C 122
King Edward St. M5—5H 85
King Edward St. M19—6D 102
King Edward St. M30—3E 83
Kingfisher Av. M34—4C 90
Kingfisher Clo. M12—2A 102
Kingfisher Dri. BL4—2B 54
Kingfisher Dri. BL9—1F 29
Kingfisher Rd. SK2—1F 145
King George Rd. SK14—6C 106
Kingham Dri. M4—3G 87 & 3F 163
Kingholm Gdns. BL1—4H 23
King La. OL1—3A 50
Kingmoor Av. M26—3H 41
Kings Av. M8—3C 74
Kings Av. M25—5C 42
Kings Av. SK8—1E 141
Kingsbridge Av. BL2—4D 26
Kingsbridge Clo. SK14—5G 107
Kingsbridge Clo. SK6—4C 134
Kingsbridge Rd. M9—4E 75
Kingsbridge Rd. OL8—4F 65
Kingsbridge Wlk. SK14—5G 107
Kingsbrook Rd. M16—1C 116
Kingsbury Av. BL1—4E 23
Kingsbury Rd. M11—3E 89
Kingscliffe St. M9—3G 75
King's Clo. M18—1H 103
Kings Clo. SK7—3H 143
King's Clo. SK9—3D 158
Kings Ct. WA14—1F 137
Kingscourt Av. BL1—3G 23
King's Cres. M16—4H 99
Kingsdale Rd. M18—3A 104
Kingsdown Dri. BL1—4B 24
Kingsdown Rd. M22—4A 140
Kingsdown Wlk. SK5—4B 120
King's Dri. M24—1G 61
King's Dri. SK4—6C 118
Kings Dri. SK8—2C 142
Kingsfield Dri. M20—6G 117
Kingsfold Av. M10—1G 87
Kingsfold Clo. BL2—1G 39
Kingsford St. M5—3D 84
King's Ga. BL1—6A 24
Kingsgate Rd. M22—4A 140
Kings Gro. M32—4F 99
Kings Gro. OL12—5A 8
Kingsheath Av. M11—2D 88
Kingsholme Rd. M22—3A 140
Kingsland Clo. M10—2H 87 & 1H 163
Kingsland Rd. BL4—2D 54
Kingsland Rd. OL11—1B 32
Kingsland Rd. M24—4C 130
Kingsland Wlk. M10—2H 87 & 1G 163
Kings La. M32—4F 99
Kings La. OL1—2A 50
Kingslea Rd. M20—4G 117
Kingsleigh. M25—6F 43
Kingsleigh Rd. SK4—5A 118
Kingsley Av. M7—4E 73
Kingsley Av. M9—4H 75
Kingsley Av. M25—2E 59
Kingsley Av. M31—5E 97
Kingsley Av. M32—4F 99
Kingsley Av. SK4—5G 119
Kingsley Av. SK9—5G 151
Kingsley Clo. M34—6D 104
Kingsley Clo. OL6—6B 80
Kingsley Ct. M5—4G 85

Kingsley Dri. OL4—2A 66
Kingsley Dri. SK8—2C 142
Kingsley Gro. M34—5C 90
Kingsley Rd. M22—3B 128
Kingsley Rd. M24—5B 46
Kingsley Rd. M27—2D 70
Kingsley Rd. M28—5E 55
Kingsley Rd. OL4—3G 65
Kingsley Rd. WA15—4B 126
Kingsley St. BL1—3H 23
Kingsley St. BL3—3H 27
Kings Lynn Clo. M20—6F 117
Kingsmead M. M9—4E 61
Kingsmere Av. M19—6B 102
Kingsmill Av. M19—1D 118
Kingsnorth Clo. BL1—4B 24
Kingsnorth Rd. M31—3A 96
King Sq. OL8—3C 64
Kings Rd. M21—1A 116
King's Rd. M25—1G 73
Kings Rd. M26—6F 27
Kings Rd. M30—3C 110
King's Rd. M32 & M16—6E 99
Kings Rd. M33—4H 113
King's Rd. M34—2A 104
King's Rd. OL2—1E 49
King's Rd. OL6—1A 92
King's Rd. OL8—4D 64
Kings Rd. OL9—6E 63
Kings Rd. OL16—6B 20
Kings Rd. SK6—6G 121
Kings Rd. SK7—2E 145
Kings Rd. SK8—2B 142
King's Rd. SK9—1B 158
Kings Ter. M32—4F 99
Kings Ter. SK16—4H 91
Kingston Arc. SK14—5A 108
Kingston Av. BL2—4E 25
Kingston Av. M20—2F 129
Kingston Av. OL1—6F 49
Kingston Av. OL9—5G 63
Kingston Clo. M7—3H 73
Kingston Clo. OL2—5F 35
Kingston Ct. M20—2F 129
Kingston Dri. M31—1D 112
Kingston Dri. M33—4D 114
Kingston Dri. OL2—1A 48
Kingston Gdns. SK14—4H 105
Kingston Gro. M9—5H 61
Kingston M. M35—4H 77
Kingston Pl. SK8—3A 142
Kingston Rd. M20—2F 129
Kingston Rd. M26—1A 42
Kingston Rd. M35—4H 77
Kingston Rd. SK9—2G 131
Kingston St. SK3—2F 131
King St. BL0—3E 5
King St. BL1—6A 24
King St. BL2—6H 11
King St. BL4—1F 55
King St. BL7—3D 10
King St. M2—4D 86 & 5G 161
(in two parts)
King St. M3—3C 86 & 3F 161
King St. M6—6B 72
King St. M7—4A 74
King St. M24—6A 46
King St. M26—5H 41
King St. M30—4H 83
King St. M32—6D 98
King St. M34—1F 105
(Audenshaw)
King St. M34—4F 105
(Denton)
King St. M35—5A 90
(Droylsden, in two parts)
King St. M35—5D 76
(Failsworth)
King St. OL1 & OL8—2C 64
King St. OL2—3B 48
King St. OL3—3H 51
King St. OL4—3B 66
King St. OL5—2F 81
King St. OL10—4F 31
King St. OL12—2H 7
King St. OL16—4H 19
King St. SK14—2F 109
(Hollingworth)

King St. SK14—4B 106
(Hyde)
King St. SK15—3E 93
King St. SK16—4H 91
King St. E. OL11—5H 19
King St. E. SK1—1H 131
King St. S. OL11—6G 19
(in two parts)
King St. W. M3—4D 86 & 5G 161
King St. W. SK3—2G 131
Kings Wlk. M35—5A 90
Kingsway. BL4—3H 55
Kingsway. M24—3B 62
Kingsway. M27—5A 72
Kingsway. M31—3G 97
Kingsway. M32—6C 98
Kingsway. OL16—6B 20
Kingsway. S1—1H 131
Kingsway. SK6—6E 121
Kingsway. SK7—3H 143
Kingsway. SK8, M20 & M19
—2G 141
Kingsway. SK16—6C 92
Kingsway. WA14—6F 125
Kingsway Av. M19—6B 102
Kingsway Bldgs. M19—4A 118
Kingsway Clo. OL8—4C 64
Kingsway Cres. M19—4A 118
Kingsway Pk. M31—2E 97
(in five parts)
Kingswear Dri. BL1—4G 23
Kingswood Av. BL1—4D 22
Kingswood Gro. SK5—6H 103
Kingswood Rd. M14—1H 117
Kingswood Rd. M24—4H 45
Kingswood Rd. M25—4D 58
Kingswood Rd. M30—1D 82
Kingthorpe Gdns. BL3—3B 38
King William St. M5—5G 85
King William St. M30—2C 82
King William St. Enterprise Zone.
M5—5G 85
Kinlett Wlk. M10—1D 76
Kinley Clo. M12—1B 102
Kinloch Dri. BL1—6F 23
Kinloch Gdns. OL8—5D 64
Kinloch Dri. M11—3C 88
Kinloch St. OL8—5E 65
Kinmel Av. SK5—5C 120
Kinmount Wlk. M9—5F 75
(off Lathbury Rd.)
Kinnaird Cres. SK1—3B 132
Kinnaird Rd. M20—4F 117
Kinnerley Gro. M28—2C 68
Kinross Av. SK2—2A 144
Kinross Dri. BL3—2D 36
Kinross Rd. M14—4A 102
Kinsale Wlk. M23—2F 139
Kinsbury Wlk. M10—1G 87
Kinsey Av. M23—4F 127
Kintore Av. SK7—2F 145
Kintore Wlk. M10—6E 75
(off Keyhaven Wlk.)
Kintyre Av. M5—4D 84
Kintyre Dri. BL3—2C 36
Kinver Clo. BL3—4G 37
Kinver Rd. M10—1C 76
Kipling Av. M34—2G 121
Kipling Av. M35—2A 90
Kipling Clo. SK2—4E 133
Kipling Rd. OL1—5F 49
Kipling St. M7—5H 73
Kippax St. M14—4F 101
Kirby Av. M27—6D 70
Kirby Av. OL9—6D 62
Kirby Wlk. M4—3G 87 & 5F 163
Kirby Wlk. OL2—5F 35
Kirkbank St. OL9—2B 64
(in two parts)
Kirkby Av. M10—1D 76
Kirkby Av. M33—1C 126
Kirkby Dri. M33—1C 126
Kirkby Rd. BL1—5F 23
Kirkdale Av. M10—1D 76
Kirkdale Dri. OL2—2A 48
Kirkebrok Rd. BL3—3E 37
Kirkfell Dri. SK6—5C 146
Kirkfell Wlk. OL1—6D 48

Kirkgate Clo. M10—2G 87 & 2F 163
Kirkhall La. BL1—5G 23
Kirkham Av. M18—1F 103
Kirkham Clo. M34—4F 105
Kirkham Rd. SK8—5G 141
Kirkham St. BL2—4D 24
Kirkham St. M5—4E 85
Kirkham St. M28—4C 54
Kirkham St. OL9—2C 64
Kirkhaven Sq. M10—1A 88
Kirkhill Wlk. M10—1D 76
Kirkholt Wlk. M9—6G 61
Kirk Hope Dri. BL1—4H 23
Kirk Hope Wlk. BL1—4H 23
Kirklands. BL2—3F 25
Kirklands. M33—1A 126
Kirklee Av. OL9—6G 47
Kirklee Rd. OL11—3D 32
Kirklees St. BL8—4H 13
Kirklees Wlk. M25—1F 59
Kirkley St. SK14—6B 106
Kirkman Av. M30—5E 83
Kirkmanshulme La. M12 & M18
—3B 102
Kirkman St. BL9—4D 42
Kirk Rd. M19—2D 118
Kirkstall. OL12—3G 19
(off Spotland Rd.)
Kirkstall Av. OL10—2E 31
Kirkstall Av. OL15—2E 9
Kirkstall Clo. SK12—3D 154
Kirkstall Gdns. M26—2E 41
Kirkstall Rd. M24—4H 45
Kirkstall Rd. M31—4D 96
Kirkstall Sq. M13—1G 101 & 5E 167
Kirkstead Clo. M11—5C 88
Kirkstead Rd. SK8—6E 143
Kirkstile Pl. M27—5E 57
Kirkstone Av. M28—2H 69
Kirkstone Clo. OL1—6D 48
Kirkstone Dri. M24—5G 45
Kirkstone Dri. OL2—1B 48
Kirkstone Rd. M10—1C 76
Kirkstone Rd. SK14—2A 106
Kirk St. M18—2F 103
Kirktown Wlk. M11—5E 89
Kirkwall Dri. BL2—2D 38
Kirkway. M9—5A 62
Kirkway. M24—2A 62
Kirkway. OL11—3F 33
Kirkwood Dri. M10—1G 87
Kirtley Av. M30—2F 83
Kirtlington Clo. OL2—2E 49
Kirton Wlk. M9—4E 61
Kitchener Av. M30—5A 110
Kitchener St. BL3—4D 38
Kitchen St. BL8—4H 27
Kitchen St. OL16—3A 20
Kitepool St. M30—1C 82
Kitter St. OL12—6H 7
Kitt's Moss La. SK7—1F 153
Knacks La. OL12—4A 6
Knarr Barn La. OL3—4F 51
Knarr La. OL3—5G 51
Kneller Wlk. OL1—3G 49
Knight Cres. M24—4F 45
Knightley Wlk. M10—6F 75
Knightsbridge. M4—3E 87
(off Arndale Cen.)
Knightsbridge. SK1—1H 131
Knightsbridge Clo. M7—3H 73
Knights Clo. M25—4F 59
Knight's Ct. M5—3A 84
Knight St. BL8—3A 28
Knight St. M20—1F 129
Knight St. OL7—3F 91
Knight St. SK4—6C 106
Kniveton Rd. M12—6B 88
Kniveton St. SK14—4D 106
Knob Hall Gdns. M23—2F 139
Knole Av. SK12—3F 155
Knoll St. M7—4H 73
Knoll St. OL11—2B 32
Knoll, The. M2—1H 49
Knoll, The. OL5—2D 80
Knoll, The. WA14—6D 124
Knott Fold. SK14—1B 122

Knott Hill La. OL3—4G 51
Knott La. BL1—3D 22
Knott La. SK14—1B 122
Knott Lanes. OL8—5A 66
Knott St. M5—4D 84
Knott St. OL7—4F 91
Knowe Av. M22—4B 140
Knowe Av. OL7—1F 91
Knowl Clo. M34—5A 104
Knowldale Way. M12—2A 102
Knowle Av. OL7—1F 91
Knowle Dri. M25—1E 73
Knowle Gorn. SK9—4G 151
Knowle Pk. SK9—4G 151
Knowle Rd. SK6—5G 135
Knowles Ct. M6—2A 84
Knowles Edge St. BL1—3G 23
Knowles Pl. M15—6D 86
Knowles St. M26—3G 41
Knowl Hill Dri. OL12—1A 18
Knowl Rd. OL2—1G 49
Knowl Rd. OL16—4D 20
Knowls La. OL4—4B 66
Knowls, The. OL8—2A 78
Knowl St. OL8—1A 78
Knowl St. SK15—3F 93
Knowl Syke St. OL12—2A 8
Knowl Top La. OL3—2H 53
Knowl View. BL8—5A 14
Knowl View. OL15—1F 21
Knowsley. OL4—2C 66
Knowsley Av. M5—5H 85
Knowsley Av. M31—3E 97
Knowsley Av. OL4—2C 66
Knowsley Cres. SK1—3B 132
Knowsley Dri. M27—5D 70
Knowsley Dri. OL4—2C 66
Knowsley Grange. BL1—6B 22
Knowsley Grn. M5—5H 85
(off Knowsley Av.)
Knowsley Grn. OL4—2C 66
Knowsley Rd. BL1—3F 23
Knowsley Rd. BL2—4C 26
Knowsley Rd. M25—1D 58
Knowsley Rd. SK1—3B 132
Knowsley Rd. SK7—5E 145
Knowsley St. BL1—5B 24
Knowsley St. BL9—4C 28
Knowsley St. M8—1D 86
Knowsley St. OL12—3G 19
Knowsley Ter. OL4—2C 66
Knowsley Ter. SK1—3B 132
Knutsford Av. M16—3B 100
Knutsford Av. M33—5E 115
Knutsford Av. SK4—2F 119
Knutsford Rd. M18—2E 103
Knutsford Rd. WA16 & SK9—6A 158
Knutsford St. M6—3E 85
Knutsford View. WA15—5C 138
Knutshaw Cres. BL3—5B 36
Knypersley Av. SK2—4C 132
Kranj Way. OL1—2D 64
Krokus Sq. OL9—2G 63
Kyleakin Ct. OL10—4B 30
Kyle Ct. SK7—4F 145
Kylemore Av. BL3—2F 37
Kyle Rd. SK7—4F 145
Kynder St. M34—4F 105

Laburnham Vs. OL8—2E 79
Laburnum Av. BL8—4H 13
Laburnum Av. M25—2D 58
Laburnum Av. M27—5E 71
Laburnum Av. M30—5C 82
Laburnum Av. M34—4C 90
Laburnum Av. M35—5F 77
Laburnum Av. OL2—1F 49
Laburnum Av. OL6—5G 79
Laburnum Av. OL9—6H 47
Laburnum Av. SK14—1B 122
Laburnum Av. SK15 & SK16—5D 92
Laburnum Dri. BL9—6E 43
Laburnum Gro. M25—3E 59
Laburnum Gro. M29—2A 68
Laburnum Rd. OL2—1F 49
Laburnum La. OL16—2E 35
Laburnum La. WA15—5G 137

Laburnum Pk. BL2—6F 11
Laburnum Rd. BL4—1D 54
Laburnum Rd. M18—3F 103
Laburnum Rd. M24—1C 62
Laburnum Rd. M28—1G 69
Laburnum Rd. M30—4B 110
Laburnum Rd. M31—3D 96
Laburnum Rd. M34—4H 103
Laburnum Rd. OL8—3A 78
Laburnum St. BL1—5H 23
Laburnum St. M6—3F 85
Laburnum Ter. OL11—1E 33
Laburnum Vs. M31—5G 97
  (off Cavendish Rd.)
Laburnum Wlk. M33—4E 113
Laburnum Way. OL15—4D 8
Laburnum Way. SK3—3D 130
Lacey Av. SK9—6F 151
Lacey Clo. SK9—6F 151
Lacey Ct. SK9—6F 151
Lacey Grn. SK9—1E 159
Lacey Clo. SK9—6G 151
Lackford Dri. M10—1G 87
Lacrosse Av. OL8—5A 64
Lacy Gro. M32—6D 98
Lacy St. M32—6D 98
Lacy St. SK1—3H 131
Lacy Wlk. M12—5A 88
Ladbrooke Clo. M20—1A 92
Ladbrooke Rd. OL6—6F 79
Ladcastle Rd. OL3—3E 53
Ladhill La. OL3—4F 53
Ladybarn Ct. M20—2H 117
  (off Ladybarn Shopping Cen.)
Ladybarn Cres. M14—2H 117
Ladybarn Cres. SK7—1H 153
Ladybarn La. M14—1H 117
Ladybarn Rd. M14—1H 117
Ladybarn Shopping Cen. M20
  —2H 117
Ladybower. SK8—2E 143
Lady Bri. Brow. BL1—6D 22
Ladybridge Cres. M28—3E 69
Lady Bri. La. BL1—6D 22
Ladybridge Rd. SK8—3D 142
Ladybrook Av. WA15—3B 126
Ladybrook Gro. SK9—5H 151
Ladybrook Rd. SK7—4E 143
Ladyfield St. SK9—2E 159
Ladyfield Ter. SK9—2F 159
Ladyhouse Clo. OL16—6G 21
Lady Ho. Fold. OL16—1D 34
  (off Ashfield La.)
Ladyhouse La. OL16—1D 34
  (in two parts)
Lady Kelvin Rd. WA14—5E 125
Ladylands Av. M11—3E 89
Ladymere Dri. M28—3D 68
Lady Rd. OL4—3A 66
Ladys Clo. SK12—3E 155
Ladyshore Clo. M5—3F 85
Ladyshore Rd. BL3—5C 40
Lady's Incline. SK12—3E 155
Ladysmith Av. BL9—6G 15
Ladysmith Dri. OL6—6B 80
Ladysmith Rd. M20—6G 117
Ladysmith Rd. OL6—6B 80
Ladysmith Rd. SK15—1E 93
Ladysmith St. OL8—6A 64
Ladysmith Rd. SK3—4G 131
Ladysmith, The. OL6—6B 80
Ladythorn Av. SK6—6E 135
Ladythorn Cres. SK7—1H 153
Ladythorne Av. M25—1E 73
Ladythorne Dri. M25—1E 73
Ladythorne Dri. M25—1E 73
Ladythorn Gro. SK7—6H 143
Ladythorn Rd. SK7—6G 143
Ladywell Av. M28—5C 54
Ladywell Clo. SK7—3A 144
Ladywell Gro. M28—4C 54
Ladywell Trading Est. M5—3B 84
Lagan Wlk. M22—3B 140
Lagos Clo. M14—3E 101
Laindon Rd. M14—3A 102
Lake Bank. OL15—6E 9
Lake Dri. M24—2H 61
Lakeland Ct. M24—5F 45

Lakeland Cres. BL9—1C 42
Lakeland Dri. OL2—5A 34
Lakelands Dri. BL3—2D 36
Lakenheath Dri. BL1—5D 10
Lake Rd. M34—3F 105
Lake Rd. SK15—1D 92
Lakeside. BL9—2D 42
Lake Side. OL15—1G 21
Lakeside. SK14—1H 109
Lakeside Av. BL3—5C 38
Lakeside Av. M28—4F 55
Lakeside Av. OL7—1F 91
Lakeside Clo. M18—1H 103
Lakeside Dri. SK12—2E 155
Lakeside Grn. SK2—5C 132
Lakeside Grn. SK2—5C 132
Lakeside Way. BL9—4D 28
Lakes Rd. SK6—5E 135
Lakes Rd. SK16—5A 92
Lake St. BL3—2B 38
Lake St. M11—3B 88
Lake St. SK2—6B 132
Lakeswood Clo. SK4—5B 118
Lake View. M9—1A 76
Lake View. OL15—2D 8
Lakin St. M10—4A 76
Laleham Grn. SK7—2F 143
Lamb Clo. M12—2B 102
Lamb Ct. M3—3C 86 & 4E 161
Lambert Dri. M33—3F 113
Lamberton Dri. M23—5E 127
Lambert St. OL7—4F 91
Lambeth Av. M35—3H 77
Lambeth Gro. SK6—4G 121
Lambeth Rd. M10—1E 89
Lambeth Rd. SK5—1H 119
Lambeth Ter. OL11—6F 19
Lamb La. M3—3C 86 & 4E 161
Lambourn Clo. BL3—2A 38
Lambourn Clo. SK12—3D 154
Lambourne Clo. M22—5B 140
Lambourne Gro. OL16—6F 21
Lambourn Rd. M31—3H 95
Lambrook Wlk. M10—1F 89
Lambs Fold. SK4—4F 119
Lambton Rd. M21—1D 116
Lambton Rd. M28—5C 70
Lambton St. BL3—5G 37
Lambton St. M30—1D 82
Lamburn Av. M10—1D 76
Lamb Wlk. M34—2G 121
Lamorna Clo. M7—3F 73
Lamphey Clo. BL1—5B 22
Lamport Clo. M1—6F 87 & 3C 166
Lamport Ct. M1—6F 87
  (off Lamport Clo.)
Lampson St. M8—1C 86
Lamsholme Clo. M19—5C 102
Lanark Av. M22—3B 128
Lanark Clo. OL10—4B 30
Lanark Clo. SK7—3G 145
Lanbury Dri. M8—4B 74
Lancashire Ct. OL9—4A 64
Lancashire Hill. SK4 & SK5—6G 119
Lancashire St. M10—6H 75
Lancaster Av. BL0—5C 4
Lancaster Av. BL4—6B 38
Lancaster Av. M24—2C 62
Lancaster Av. M25—2E 59
Lancaster Av. M31—4G 97
Lancaster Av. M35—4E 77
Lancaster Av. SK15—2E 93
Lancaster Clo. BL1—6C 24
Lancaster Clo. SK6—2G 133
Lancaster Clo. SK7—5D 144
Lancaster Ct. M10—1E 89
Lancaster Dri. BL3—3B 40
Lancaster Dri. BL9—3F 15
Lancaster Dri. M25—1G 73
Lancaster Ho. M7—3G 73
Lancaster Rd. M6—5H 71
Lancaster Rd. M20—6E 117
Lancaster Rd. M30—4A 110
Lancaster Rd. M34—6F 105
Lancaster Rd. M35—2H 89
Lancaster Sq. OL2—2B 48
Lancaster St. M26—4E 41
Lancaster St. OL5—2D 80
Lancaster St. OL9—5G 63

Lancaster St. SK1—1A 132
Lancaster Ter. BL1—3A 24
  (off Boardman St.)
Lancaster Wlk. OL11—1H 17
Lancaster Wlk. BL1—3A 24
Lancastrian Ho. M25—2G 73
Lancelot Rd. M22—3D 140
Lancelyn Dri. SK9—1G 159
Lanchester Dri. BL3—2H 37
Lanchester St. M10—2A 88
Lancing Av. M20—6H 117
Lancing Wlk. OL9—3G 63
Landacre Dri. M28—5D 68
Landcross Rd. M14—6G 101
Landells Wlk. M10—6A 76
Lander Gro. M9—6H 61
Landfall Wlk. M8—6A 74
Landfield Dri. M8—4B 74
Land La. SK9—4F 159
Landor Ct. M34—4H 103
Landore Clo. M26—3H 41
Landos Ct. M10—2G 87 & 2F 163
Landos Rd. M10—2G 87 & 2F 163
Landsberg Rd. M35—3H 77
Landsberg Ter. M35—3H 77
Landsdowne Dri. M28—2E 69
Landseer Dri. SK6—4H 133
Landseer St. OL4—4E 65
Lands End Rd. M24—2D 60
Landstead Dri. M10—3A 88
Lane Brow. OL4—4D 66
Lane End. M30—4H 83
Lane End. OL10—5H 31
Lane End Rd. M19—5H 117
Lane Ends. SK6—6B 122
Lanegate. SK14—1B 122
Lane Head Rd. OL4—5B 66
Lanesfield Wlk. M8—3E 75
  (off Crescent Rd.)
Laneside Av. OL2—6H 35
Laneside Dri. SK7—4A 144
Laneside Rd. M20—3G 129
Laneside Wlk. OL16—4F 21
Lane, The. BL1—6B 22
Langcliffe Wlk. M18—2E 103
Langdale Av. M19—1D 118
Langdale Av. OL8—5B 64
Langdale Av. OL16—5A 34
Langdale Clo. M34—6E 105
Langdale Clo. SK6—5C 146
Langdale Clo. SK8—2G 141
Langdale Clo. WA15—6G 125
Langdale Ct. M8—5D 74
Langdale Dri. BL9—4E 43
Langdale Dri. M24—4H 45
Langdale Dri. M28—2H 69
Langdale Rd. M14—3H 101
Langdale Rd. M31—6C 110
Langdale Rd. M32—4C 98
Langdale Rd. M33—2G 125
Langdale Rd. SK4—3E 119
Langdale Rd. SK6—4H 121
Langdale Rd. SK7—2E 153
Langdale St. BL3—4A 38
Langdale St. BL4—2D 55
Langdale Ter. SK15—1E 93
Langden Clo. OL2—5E 35
Langdon Clo. BL1—4H 23
Langfield Av. M16—4B 100
Langfield Cres. M35—3C 90
Langfield Wlk. M5—3F 85
Langford Dri. M30—6E 95
Langford Gdns. BL3—3A 38
Langford Rd. M20—3E 117
Langford Rd. SK4—5E 119
Langford St. M34—4F 105
Langham Clo. BL1—5E 11
Langham Ct. M20—5D 116
Langham Ct. M32—3A 98
Langham Gro. WA15—3B 126
Langham Rd. M6—3F 85
Langham Rd. OL8—5C 64
Langham Rd. SK4—2D 130
Langham Rd. WA14—3D 136
Langham St. OL7—6E 79
Langham St. Ind. Est. OL7—6E 79

Langholm Clo. M15—6B 86 & 4D 164
Langholm Dri. BL2—1H 39
Langholme Pl. M30—3D 82
  (in two parts)
Langley. OL11—1F 33
Langley Av. M24—3G 45
Langley Av. M25—3F 59
Langley Av. OL4—4D 66
Langley Av. OL4—4D 66
Langley Clo. SK7—4B 144
Langley Clo. M31—5G 97
Langley Clo. M21—5G 99
Langley Cres. M25—3F 59
Langley Dri. BL3—2G 37
Langley Dri. M28—5B 68
Langley Dri. SK9—4A 152
Langley Gdns. M25—3F 59
Langley Ga. M25—3F 59
Langley Grn. M25—3F 59
Langley Hall Rd. M25—3F 59
Langley Ho. M24—4A 46
Langley La. M24—3E 45
Langley Rd. M14—6G 101
Langley Rd. M25—4E 59
Langley Rd. M27 & M6—3D 72
Langley Rd. M33—6G 113
Langness St. M11—4E 89
Lango St. M16—3A 100
Langport Av. M12—1A 102
Langroyd Wlk. M8—4B 74
  (off Highshore Dri.)
Langsett Av. M6—2C 84
Langsett Av. SK13—6F 109
  (off Langsett La.)
Langsett Grn. SK13—6F 109
  (off Langsett La.)
Langsett Gro. SK13—6F 109
  (off Langsett La.)
Langsett La. SK13—6F 109
Langsett Lea. SK13—6F 109
  (off Langsett La.)
Langsett Ter. SK13—6F 109
Langshaw Rd. BL3—2G 37
Langshaw St. M6—4F 85
Langshaw St. M16—3A 100
Langshaw Wlk. BL3—2G 37
Langside Av. M9—5G 61
Langside Dri. BL3—3C 36
Langston Grn. SK7—4A 144
Langston Dri. M3—2D 86 & 1G 161
Langthorne St. M19—1D 118
Langthorne Wlk. BL3—1H 37
Langton Dri. BL9—5E 29
Langton St. M6—3E 85
Langton St. M24—1A 62
Langton St. OL10—2F 31
Langton Ter. OL11—1E 33
Langtree Clo. M28—3D 68
Langworthy Av. M28—4D 54
Langworthy Rd. M6—1F 85
Langworthy Rd. M10—4A 76
Lanhill Dri. M8—5E 75
Lanreath Wlk. M8—5D 74
  (off Geneva Wlk.)
Lansdale Gdns. M19—4A 118
Lansdale St. BL4—1G 55
Lansdale St. M28—4F 55
Lansdale St. M30—5C 82
Lansdown Clo. SK8—6E 143
Lansdowne Av. M34—4C 90
Lansdowne Rd. M6—1B 134
Lansdowne Clo. BL2—4D 24
Lansdowne Ct. OL9—3H 63
Lansdowne Ho. M20—1F 129
Lansdowne Rd. BL2—3D 24
Lansdowne Rd. M30—2F 83
Lansdowne Rd. M31—1A 112
Lansdowne Rd. M33—3A 114
Lansdowne Rd. OL9—3A 64
Lansdowne Rd. WA14—5F 125
Lansdowne Rd. N. M31—6A 96
Lansdowne St. OL11—4E 19
Lapford Clo. M11—6F 89
Lapwing Clo. OL11—4A 18
Lapwing Clo. SK16—1E 93
Lapwing La. M20—4E 117
Lapwing La. M20—4E 117
Lapwing La. SK5—2B 120
Larch Av. M26—6H 41

Leicester St. OL4—3F 65
Leicester St. OL7—1H 91
Leicester St. OL11—6A 20
Leicester St. SK5—5H 103
Leigh Av. M27—6D 70
Leigh Av. SK6—6C 134
Leighbrook Rd. M14—1F 117
Leigh Clo. BL8—4G 13
Leigh Clo. SK6—3H 121
Leigh Fold. SK14—2C 106
Leigh La. BL8—2G 27
Leigh Rd. M7—3H 73
Leigh Rd. M28—5D 68
Leigh Rd. SK9—4A 158
Leigh Rd. WA15—3G 137
Leighs Cottages. WA15—1B 138
Leigh St. BL4—1F 55
Leigh St. BL8—1F 27
Leigh St. M7—3H 73
Leigh St. OL10—3E 31
Leigh St. OL16—4D 20
Leigh St. SK14—5C 106
Leighton Av. BL1—5F 23
Leighton Av. OL15—1F 21
Leighton Dri. SK6—3G 135
Leighton Rd. M16—3A 100
Leighton St. M10—3A 76
Leinster Rd. M27—4E 71
Leinster St. BL4—1E 55
Leisure Cres. OL11—2C 32
Leith Av. M33—5E 115
Leith Rd. M33—5E 115
Lemnos St. OL1—2E 65
Lena St. BL1—3B 24
Lena St. M1—4F 87 & 6C 162
Lenchford Clo. M1—6F 87 & 3D 166
Len Cox Wlk. M4—3F 87 & 4C 162
Leng Rd. M10—6D 76
Lenham Av. M30—3D 82
Lenham Clo. SK5—3B 120
Lenham Gdns. BL2—1G 39
Lenham Towers. SK5—3B 120
Lenham Wlk. M22—5B 140
Lennie Rd. M31—6F 83
Lennox Gdns. BL3—2D 36
Lennox St. M34—1E 105
Lennox St. OL6—2A 92
Lennox Wlk. OL10—4B 30
Lenora St. BL3—3F 37
Lenten Gro. OL10—6G 31
Lenthall Wlk. M8—4B 74
(off Lanbury Dri.)
Lentmead Dri. M10—2A 76
Lenton Gdns. M22—6C 128
Lentworth Wlk. M15—1C 100 & 5E 165
Leominster Dri. M22—2C 140
Leominster Rd. M24—3B 62
Leonardin Clo. OL2—5D 34
Leonard St. BL3—4A 38
Leonard St. OL11—4C 32
Leopold Av. M20—3E 117
Leopold St. OL11—4F 19
Lepp Cres. BL8—5C 14
Lepton Wlk. M9—5G 61
Leroy Dri. M9—1G 75
Lerryn Dri. SK7—4F 143
Lesley Rd. M32—6A 98
Leslie Av. BL9—4D 42
Leslie Av. OL9—6H 63
Leslie Gro. WA15—5A 126
Leslie Hough Way. M6—1H 85
Leslie St. BL4—2D 24
Leslie St. M14—4F 101
Lester Rd. M28—5A 54
Lester St. M32—5D 98
Letchworth Av. OL11—6A 20
Letchworth St. M14—4F 101
Letcombe Ct. M7—4F 73
Letham St. OL8—1D 78
Levedale Rd. M9—5G 61
Leven Clo. BL4—4B 56
Levenhurst Rd. M8—4B 74
Levens Clo. SK8—2F 141
Levens Dri. BL2—4G 25
Levenshulme Rd. M18—3F 103
Levens Rd. SK7—3C 144
Levens St. M6—6F 73
Levens St. M10—4A 76

Levens Wlk. OL9—4G 63
Leven Wlk. M23—5G 127
Leven Wlk. M25—1G 59
Lever Av. M27—1H 71
Lever Dri. BL3—2A 38
Lever Edge La. BL3—5G 37
Leverett Clo. WA14—6C 124
Lever Gdns. BL3—3A 40
Lever Gro. BL2—2C 38
Lever Hall Rd. BL2—6F 25
Leverhulme Av. BL3—4C 38
Lever Pl. M15—2C 100
Lever St. BL2—2C 38
Lever St. BL3—3A 38
(Bolton)
Lever St. BL3—3A 40
(Little Lever)
Lever St. BL9—2D 28
Lever St. M1—4E 87 & 5B 162
Lever St. M24—6A 46
Lever St. M26—2F 41
Lever St. SK7—3D 144
Lever Wlk. M24—2H 61
Levington Dri. OL8—3E 79
Levi St. BL1—4D 22
Lewes Av. M34—6F 105
Lewes Wlk. OL9—3H 63
Lewis Av. M9—2G 75
Lewis Av. M31—2F 97
Lewis Dri. OL10—4B 30
Lewisham Av. M10—1D 88
Lewisham Clo. OL2—1A 48
Lewis Rd. M35—3G 89
Lewis Rd. SK5—6H 103
Lewis St. M10—2H 87 & 1H 163
Lewis St. M30—4F 83
Lewis St. OL2—1F 49
Lewis St. OL10—2G 31
Lewis St. SK14—4C 106
Lewtas St. M30—4G 83
Lexton Av. M8—1D 74
Leybourne Av. M19—5D 102
Leybourne M. M7—5A 74
Leybourne St. BL1—3A 24
Leybrook Rd. M22—2A 140
Leyburn Av. M31—6C 96
Leyburn Av. M32—4C 98
Leyburn Av. OL2—3B 48
Leyburn Clo. M26—1C 58
Leyburne Rd. SK2—5D 132
Leyburn Gro. BL4—6F 39
Leyburn Gro. SK6—1A 134
Leyburn Rd. M10—1C 76
Leycett Dri. M23—2G 127
Leyden Wlk. M23—1G 139
Ley Dri. OL10—6G 31
Leyfield Av. SK6—1A 134
Leyfield Ct. SK6—1A 134
Leyfield Rd. OL16—5D 20
Ley Hey Av. SK6—4D 134
Ley Hey Rd. SK6—4D 134
Leyland Av. M20—6H 117
Leyland Av. M30—3F 95
Leyland Av. SK8—5F 129
Leyland St. BL3—3D 42
Ley La. SK6—2G 135
Leys Rd. WA14—3G 125
Leyton Av. M10—4B 76
Leyton Clo. BL4—6C 38
Leyton Dri. BL9—2D 42
Leyton St. OL12—1H 19
Library La. OL9—1B 64
Library Wlk. M2—4D 86
Libra St. BL1—3H 23
Lichens Cres. OL8—6E 65
Lichfield Av. BL2—3D 24
Lichfield Av. OL6—3H 79
Lichfield Av. SK5—2G 119
Lichfield Av. WA15—2C 138
Lichfield Clo. BL4—6C 38
Lichfield Clo. M26—2D 40
Lichfield Dri. BL8—1B 28
Lichfield Dri. M8—4D 74
Lichfield Rd. M25—1G 73
Lichfield Rd. M27—5F 71
Lichfield Rd. OL9—6G 47
Lichfield Rd. M26—2D 40

Lichfield Rd. M30—1H 83
Lichfield Rd. M31—3F 97
Lichfield St. M6—6E 73
Lichfield Ter. OL16—1A 34
Lichfield Wlk. SK6—2G 133
Lidbrook Wlk. M12—1A 102
Liddington Hall Dri. BL0—5D 4
Lidgate Gro. BL4—1E 55
Lidgate Gro. M20—6E 117
Lidgett Clo. M28—4E 55
Lidiard St. M8—2C 74
Liffey Av. M22—2C 140
Lifton Av. M10—1A 88
Light Alders La. SK12—6E 147
Lightbirches La. OL5—1D 80
Lightborne Rd. M33—5F 113
Lightbounds Rd. BL1—2D 22
Lightbourne Av. M27—4F 71
Lightbowne Rd. M10—5A 76
Lightburn Av. OL15—5C 8
Lightburne Av. BL1—6F 23
Lightfoot Wlk. M11—4B 88
Lighthorne Av. SK3—4B 130
Lighthorne Gro. SK3—4B 130
Lighthorne Rd. SK3—4B 130
Lighthouse. OL15—6G 9
Light Oaks Rd. M6—1B 84
Lightowlers La. OL15—2H 9
Lightwood. M28—3D 68
Lightwood Clo. BL4—6G 39
Lignum Av. OL9—1H 63
Lilac Av. BL9—6B 28
Lilac Av. M27—3G 71
Lilac Av. OL16—2E 35
Lilac Av. SK14—1B 122
Lilac Ct. M6—3G 85
Lilac Gro. M10—2A 76
Lilac Gro. M25—3E 59
Lilac Gro. OL9—1H 63
Lilac La. OL8—1B 78
Lilac Rd. OL11—3F 33
Lilac Rd. WA15—2A 138
Lilac St. SK2—5H 131
Lilac View Clo. OL2—1G 49
Lilac Wlk. M31—6C 110
Lila St. M9—4H 75
Liley St. OL16—4A 20
Lilford Clo. M12—1C 102
Lilian St. M16—3A 100
Lillian Gro. SK5—1H 119
Lilly St. BL1—5H 23
Lilly St. SK14—1D 122
Lilmore Av. M10—5C 76
Lilstock Wlk. M9—6G 61
Lily Av. BL4—6D 38
Lily Clo. SK3—6F 131
Lily Hill St. M25—5C 42
Lily La. M9—4H 75
Lily La. OL6—5F 79
Lily Lanes. OL6—3A 80
Lily St. M24—1C 62
Lily St. M30—4D 82
Lily St. OL2—3D 48
Lily St. OL16—6C 48
Lily St. OL2—3D 48
Lily St. OL16—5F 21
Lily Thomas Ct. M11—6F 89
Lima St. BL9—2F 29
Lime Av. M25—2D 58
Lime Av. M27—5C 70
Lime Av. M31—5D 96
Lime Bank St. M12—5H 87 & 2H 167
Limebrook Clo. M11—6G 89
Lime Clo. SK16—1B 106
Lime Ct. M6—2G 85
Lime Cres. M16—3H 99
Lime Ditch Rd. M35—2G 77
Limefield. M24—1G 61
Limefield. OL16—4E 21
Limefield Av. BL4—6F 39
Limefield Brow. BL9—4F 15
Limefield Clo. BL1—1F 23
Limefield Ct. M7—2H 73
Limefield Rd. BL1—1F 23
Limefield Rd. BL9—4F 15
Limefield Rd. M7—2H 73
Limefield Rd. M26—4D 40
Limefield Ter. M19—6C 102

Lime Gdns. M24—1G 61
Lime Gdns. SK16—5H 91
Lime Ga. OL8—1A 78
Lime Grn. OL8—2B 78
Lime Grn. Rd. OL8—3A 78
Lime Gro. BL0—2F 5
Lime Gro. BL9—4F 15
Lime Gro. M15—2F 101
Lime Gro. M16—3H 99
Lime Gro. M25—3E 59
Lime Gro. M28—2F 69
Lime Gro. M34—3F 105
Lime Gro. OL2—1B 48
Lime Gro. OL6—6G 79
Lime Gro. OL10—2E 31
Lime Gro. OL15—3D 8
Lime Gro. SK8—5H 129
Lime Gro. SK15—5C 92
Lime Gro. WA15—4B 126
Limehurst Av. OL7—5E 79
Limehurst Rd. OL7—5E 79
Limekiln La. M12—5H 87 & 1G 167
Lime Kiln La. SK6—6E 135
Lime La. OL8 & M35—2A 78
(in two parts)
Lime Pl. SK16—5H 91
Lime Rd. M32—6D 98
Limerston Dri. M10—6H 75
Limeside Rd. OL8—1A 78
Limestead Av. M8—3C 74
Limes, The. OL5—2D 80
(Fox Platt)
Limes, The. OL5—2G 81
(Mossley)
Lime St. BL4—1G 55
Lime St. BL9—5F 15
Lime St. M10—2H 87 & 1H 163
Lime St. M30—4F 83
Lime St. OL1—6A 48
Lime St. OL11—1C 32
Lime St. SK6—5E 121
Lime St. SK16—5H 91
(in two parts)
Lime Tree Clo. M31—6G 97
Lime Tree Gro. M35—4H 77
Limetrees Rd. M24—1H 61
Limetree Wlk. M11—4B 88
Lime Wlk. M31—6B 110
Lime Wlk. SK9—6H 151
Limley Gro. M21—2A 116
Linacre Av. BL3—5A 38
Linby St. M15—6C 86 & 4E 165
Lincoln Av. BL3—5A 40
Lincoln Av. M19—6D 102
Lincoln Av. M30—5A 110
Lincoln Av. M32—4H 97
Lincoln Av. M34—6F 105
Lincoln Av. SK8—5F 129
Lincoln Clo. OL6—3H 79
Lincoln Clo. OL11—5A 20
Lincoln Ct. M7—2A 74
Lincoln Ct. M10—1D 88
Lincoln Dri. BL9—5D 28
Lincoln Dri. M25—1G 73
Lincoln Dri. OL15—5D 8
Lincoln Dri. WA15—6B 126
Lincoln Grn. SK5—3B 120
Lincoln Gro. BL2—1H 25
Lincoln Gro. M13—2G 101
Lincoln Gro. M33—5E 115
Lincoln Minshull Clo. M23—1F 127
Lincoln Rise. SK6—2G 133
Lincoln Rd. BL1—5F 23
Lincoln Rd. M24—4C 62
Lincoln Rd. M27—4E 71
Lincoln Rd. M35—5G 77
Lincoln Rd. SK9—6A 152
Lincoln St. BL1—4B 24
Lincoln St. M13—3B 102
Lincoln St. M30—4E 83
Lincoln St. OL9—4H 63
Lincoln St. OL11—5A 20
Lincoln Towers. SK1—3H 131
Lincoln Wlk. OL10—3C 30
Lincombe Rd. M22—5A 140
Lincroft St. M14—3E 101
Linda Dri. SK7—3D 144

Lindale. SK14—2A 106
Lindale Av. BL1—5D 22
Lindale Av. BL9—4E 43
Lindale Av. M10—1D 76
Lindale Av. M31—4B 96
Lindale Av. OL2—5A 34
Lindale Av. OL9—3G 63
Lindale Clo. M28—4A 68
Lindale Dri. M24—4G 45
Lindale Rise. OL2—6H 35
Lindale Rd. M28—4A 68
Lindbury Av. M28—5B 68
Linden Av. BL0—3F 5
Linden Av. BL3—2A 40
Linden Av. M6—5C 72
Linden Av. M33—5H 113
Linden Av. M34—6D 90
Linden Av. OL4—1H 65
Linden Av. WA15—6G 125
Linden Clo. BL0—3A 4
Linden Croft. OL8—5A 64
Linden Dri. M5—5D 85
Linden Dri. E. M5—5H 85
Linden Gro. M5—5G 85
Linden Gro. M14—1H 117
Linden Gro. M30—4B 110
Linden Gro. SK2—1B 144
Linden Gro. SK7—3F 153
Linden Lea. M33—1B 126
Linden M. M28—5B 68
Linden Pk. M19—1B 118
Linden Rd. M20—5E 117
Linden Rd. M28—5B 68
Linden Rd. M34—4G 105
Linden Rd. SK8—2C 142
Linden Rd. SK15—6H 93
Linden St. M27—4D 70
Linden Wlk. BL2—6F 11
Linden Way. SK6—6E 147
Lindenwood. OL9—1E 63
Lindeth Av. M18—3F 103
Lindfield Dri. BL1—4A 24
Lindfield Est. N. SK9—3D 158
Lindfield Est. S. SK9—3D 158
Lindfield Rd. SK5—6H 103
Lindinis Av. M5—3G 85
Lindisfarne. OL12—3G 19
(off Spotland Rd.)
Lindisfarne Clo. M33—2B 126
Lindisfarne Dri. SK12—2D 154
Lindisfarne Pl. BL2—3E 25
Lindisfarne Rd. OL7—6C 78
Lindley St. BL3—4B 40
Lindley St. BL3—3B 56
Lindley Wood Rd. M14—1A 118
Lindon Av. M34—5D 104
Lindon Clo. M28—4G 1C5
Lindon Way. M35—5G 89
Lindop Rd. WA15—4H 137
Lindow Clo. BL8—5B 14
Lindow Ct. SK9—1B 158
Lindow Fold Dri. SK9—5A 158
Lindow La. SK9—2B 158
Lindow Pde. SK9—3C 158
Lindow Rd. M16—4A 100
Lindow St. M33—6F 115
Lindrick Av. M25—3B 58
Lindrick Clo. M10—4C 76
Lindrick Ter. BL3—2H 37
Lindsay Av. M19—6B 102
Lindsay Av. M27—4E 71
Lindsay Av. SK8—4D 142
Lindsay Clo. OL4—5H 49
Lindsay Rd. M19—1B 118
Lindsay St. SK15—3F 93
Lindsell Rd. WA14—3E 125
Lindsgate Dri. WA15—4B 126
Lindside Wlk. M9—6G 61
Lind St. M10—3A 88
Lindum Av. M16—3A 100
Lindum Ct. OL10—3G 31
Lindum St. M14—4F 101
Lindwall Clo. M23—1H 127
Lindy Av. M27—6F 57
Linear Walkway. M30—1G 83
Linehan Clo. SK4—1H 129
Lineholme. OL2—5A 48
Lines Rd. M30—1D 110

Lines Rd. M35—4B 90
Linfield Clo. BL2—1F 25
Linfield St. M11—4D 88
Linford Av. M10—1C 76
Lingard Clo. M34—5C 90
Lingard La. SK6—4D 120
Lingard Rd. M22—2B 128
Lingard St. SK5—1H 119
Lingaro Ter. M34—5C 90
Lingbeck Cres. M15—2C 100
Lingcrest Clo. M19—2E 119
Lingdale Rd. SK8—3B 142
Lingfield Av. M33—1D 124
Lingfield Av. SK7—3F 145
Lingfield Clo. BL4—2E 55
Lingfield Clo. BL8—4C 14
Lingfield Rd. M11—3E 89
Lingfield Wlk. OL9—2A 64
Lingholme Dri. M24—5E 45
Lingmell Clo. BL1—5D 22
Lingmell Clo. M24—5F 45
(in two parts)
Lingmell Clo. M31—3C 96
Lingmoor Clo. M24—5E 45
Lingmoor Rd. BL1—4D 22
Lingmoor Wlk. M15—1D 100 & 6H 165
Linhope Clo. SK4—6A 118
Link Av. M31—6A 98
Linkfield Dri. M28—5B 68
Link La. OL8—1C 78
Link Rd. M33—2F 125
Link Rd. OL4—2B 66
Links Av. M35—6F 77
Links Cres. M25—1A 74
Linksfield. M34—2F 105
Linkside Av. OL2—2B 48
Links Pl. OL6—5A 80
Links Rise. M31—3C 96
Links Rd. BL2—1A 26
Links Rd. BL3—4D 36
Links Rd. OL10—5F 31
Links Rd. SK6—1D 146
(Marple)
Links Rd. SK6—6B 122
(Romiley)
Links Rd. SK9—6B 158
Links, The. M10—4C 76
Links View. M25—2E 73
Links View. OL11—5D 18
Links View Ct. M25—2B 58
Linksway. M25—1H 73
Linksway. M27—5G 71
Linksway. OL9—1A 64
Linksway. SK8—1E 141
Linksway Clo. SK4—4C 118
Linksway Dri. BL9—4E 43
Link, The. OL2—5D 34
Link, The. SK5—3C 120
Link, The. SK9—4H 151
Linley Dri. OL4—5H 65
Linley Rd. M33—4B 114
Linley Rd. SK8—5D 142
Linley St. M26—2C 42
Linnell Dri. OL11—3A 18
Linnet Clo. M34—4C 90
Linnet Clo. SK2—6F 133
Linnet Dri. BL9—1F 29
Linnet Dri. M30—4E 95
Linnet Hall. BL8—4E 27
Linnet Hill. OL11—5E 19
Linnett Clo. M12—3B 102
Linney Gro. BL0—1A 14
Linney La. OL2—6G 35
Linney Rd. SK7—3F 143
Linn St. M8—2C 74
Linnyshaw Ind. Est. M28—6H 55
Linnyshaw La. M28—5G 55
Linslade Gdns. BL3—2A 38
Linslade Wlk. M9—4F 75
(off Foleshill Av.)
Linsley St. M3—3C 86 & 3F 161
Linstead Dri. M8—5B 74
Linthorpe Wlk. BL3—3F 37
Linton Av. BL9—6F 15
Linton Av. M34—4A 104
Linton Clo. M4—5H 87 & 1G 167

Linton Rd. M33—3C 114
Linton Wlk. M7—3D 72
Linwood Gro. M12—5C 102
Lion Brow. M9—1F 75
Lion Fold La. M9—6F 61
Lions Dri. M27—3F 71
Lion St. M9—1F 75
Lisbon St. OL12—3E 19
Lisburn Av. M21—6A 100
Lisburn Av. M33—6A 114
Lisburn La. M20—5D 132
Lisburne Clo. SK2—5D 132
Lisburne Ct. SK2—5D 132
Lisburne La. SK2—5D 132
Lisburn Rd. M10—3A 76
Liscard Av. M14—6F 101
Lisetta Av. OL4—4F 65
Liskeard Av. OL2—4D 48
Liskeard Clo. OL16—2C 20
Liskeard Rd. SK7—6H 143
Lisle St. OL12—3A 20
Lismore Av. BL3—2D 36
Lismore Rd. SK16—6B 92
Lismore Wlk. M22—5C 140
Lismore Way. M31—2G 97
Lissadel St. M6—1G 85
Lisson Gro. WA15—3G 137
Lister Rd. M24—3D 60
Lister St. BL3—4F 37
Liston St. SK16—5D 92
Litcham Clo. M1—6F 87 & 3C 166
Litchfield Gro. M28—4A 70
Litherland Rd. BL3—5A 38
Litherland Rd. M33—6E 115
Lit. Ancoats St. M1—3F 87 & 4C 162
Lit. Bank St. OL4—3F 65
Littlebourne Wlk. BL1—5E 11
Lit. Bridge St. M3—2D 86 & 2G 161
Littlebrook Clo. SK14—3H 109
Lit. Brook Clo. SK8—1E 143
Lit. Brook Rd. M33—2E 125
Lit. Brow. BL7—4E 11
Lit. Clegg Rd. OL15—1E 21
Littledale St. OL12—3G 19
(in two parts)
Lit. David St. M1—5E 87 & 1B 166
Lit. Ees La. M33—3H 113
Lit. Egerton St. SK1—1G 131
Littlefields. SK14—3C 108
Lit. Flatt. OL12—2D 18
Littlegreen Ho. M6—2F 85
Lit. Harwood Lee. BL2—2F 25
Littlehaven Clo. M12—2A 102
Lit. Hey St. OL2—3E 49
Littlehills Clo. M24—6G 45
Lit. Holme St. M4—4H 87 & 4H 163
Lit. Holme Wlk. BL3—3B 38
Lit. John St. M3—4C 86 & 6E 161
Little La. M9—5D 60
Lit. Lever St. M1—4F 87 & 5C 162
Lit. Meadow. BL7—4D 10
Lit. Meadow Rd. WA14—1D 136
Littlemoor Cotts. SK1—3B 132
Littlemoor La. OL4—1G 65
Littlemoor Rd. SK14—5C 108
Little Moss La. M27—1F 71
Littlemoss Rd. M35—2C 90
Lit. Oak Clo. OL4—3A 66
Lit. Peter St. M15—6C 86 & 3F 165
Lit. Pitt St. M1—4F 87
Lit. Quay St. M3—4C 86 & 6F 161
Littler Av. M21—3B 116
Lit. Stones Rd. BL7—1C 10
Little St. OL16—1C 20
Little St. SK2—3B 132
Littleton Rd. M7 & M6—3D 72
Littletown. OL8—5A 64
Lit. Underbank. SK1—2H 131
Lit. Western St. M14—4F 101
Littlewood Av. BL9—6F 15
Littlewood Rd. M22—1A 140
Littlewood St. M6—3E 85
Litton Bank. SK13—6G 109
(off Litton M.)
Littondale Clo. OL2—2C 48

Litton Fold. SK13—6G 109
(off Riber Bank)
Litton Gdns. SK13—6G 109
Litton M. SK13—6G 109
Liverpool Clo. SK5—2G 119
Liverpool Rd. M3—5B 86 & 1D 164
Liverpool Rd. M30—5D 82
Liverpool Rd. WA3 & M30—6A 110
Liverpool St. M5 & M6—3D 84 & 5A 160
Liverpool St. SK5—2G 119
(in two parts)
Liverstudd Av. SK5—1H 119
Liverton Ct. M9—4D 60
Liverton Dri. M9—4D 60
Livesey St. M4—2G 87 & 1E 163
Livesey St. M19—1D 118
Livesey St. OL1—1G 65
Livingstone Av. OL5—2D 80
Livingstone St. OL4—4A 66
(Lees)
Livingstone St. OL4—3C 66
(Springhead)
Livsey Ct. BL1—4B 24
Livsey La. OL10—3C 30
Livsey St. M25—1D 58
Livsey St. OL16—4A 20
Lizard St. M1—4F 87 & 5C 162
Lizmar Ter. M9—3H 75
Llanberis Rd. SK8—4A 142
Llanfair Rd. SK3—3E 131
Lloyd Av. SK8—5E 129
Lloyd Rd. M19—2D 118
Lloyd's Ct. WA14—1F 137
Lloyd's Gdns. WA14—2F 137
Lloyd Sq. WA14—1F 137
Lloyd St. M2—4D 86 & 6G 161
Lloyd St. OL10—4F 31
Lloyd St. OL11—1D 32
Lloyd St. OL12—4G 7
Lloyd St. SK14—6F 119
Lloyd St. WA14 & WA15—1F 137
Lloyd St. N. M15—3E 101
Lloyd St. S. M14—6E 101
Lobden Cres. OL12—2C 6
Lobelia Av. BL4—6C 38
Lobley Clo. OL12—1B 20
Lochawe Clo. OL10—4C 30
Lochinver Gro. OL10—4C 30
Lochmaddy Clo. SK7—4F 145
Lock Clo. OL10—5G 31
Lockett Gdns. M3—3B 86 & 3D 160
Lockett St. M6—6E 73
Lockett St. M8—1C 86
Lockhart Clo. M12—2C 102
Lockhart St. OL16—6B 20
Lockingate St. OL6—5F 79
Locking Ga. Rise. OL4—6A 50
Lock La. BL6 & BL3—3A 36
Lock La. M31—6B 110
Lock Rd. WA14—5E 125
Lockside. SK6—5E 135
Locksley Clo. SK4—1B 130
Lockstock Ct. SK9—3H 119
Lockton Clo. M1—6F 87 & 3D 166
Lockton Clo. SK5—3H 119
Lockton St. M12—4D 102
Lockwood St. M12—4D 102
Loddon Wlk. M9—3G 75
Lodge Av. M31—5G 97
Lodge Bank. SK14—1H 109
Lodge Bank Rd. OL15—6D 8
Lodge Brow. M26—5H 41
Lodge Clo. SK16—6C 92
Lodge Ct. M22—6C 128
Lodge Ct. SK4—1B 130
Lodge Ct. SK14—3C 108
Lodge Farm Clo. SK7—3G 143
Lodge Grn. SK16—6C 92
Lodge La. OL3—2G 51
(in two parts)
Lodge La. SK14—3B 106
Lodge La. SK16—5B 92
Lodgepole Clo. M30—5B 82
Lodge Rd. M26—5H 41
Lodges, The. M28—3A 70
Lodge St. BL0—3E 5
Lodge St. BL9—2E 29

Lodge St. M10—6G 75
Lodge St. M24—6A 46
Lodge St. OL7—4F 91
Lodge St. OL12—3A 8
Lodge St. OL15—3F 9
Lodge St. SK14—2C 106
Lodge, The. SK14—1H 109
Loen Cres. BL1—2G 23
Logan St. BL1—6C 10
Logwood Av. BL8—2B 28
Loisine Clo. OL11—2B 32
Lois St. OL9—2G 77
Lomas Clo. M19—6A 118
Lomas St. M24—6B 46
Lomas St. M35—2G 77
Lomas St. SK3—4F 131
Lomax St. BL1—3A 24
Lomax St. BL4—5E 39
Lomax St. BL8—2H 13
Lomax St. BL9—2E 29
Lomax St. M1—4G 87 & 5E 163
Lomax St. M26—5G 41
Lomax St. OL12—2H 19
Lomax St. OL15—2E 9
Lombard Clo. SK6—5F 121
Lombard Gro. M14—1G 117
Lombard St. OL1—2C 64
Lombard St. OL12—3F 19
Lombardy Ct. M6—2G 85
Lomond Av. M32—4D 98
Lomond Clo. SK2—2A 144
Lomond Dri. BL8—1H 27
Lomond Lodge. M8—1B 74
Lomond Pl. BL3—1C 36
Lomond Rd. M22 & SK8—3D 140
Lomond Ter. OL16—1A 34
London Pl. SK1—2H 131
London Rd. M1—4F 87 & 6C 162
London Rd. OL7—6F 49
London Rd. SK7—2D 144
London Rd. SK9—5G 159
London Rd. N. SK12—3E 155
London Rd. S. SK12—5D 154
London Sq. SK1—2H 131
London St. BL3—3A 38
London St. M6—1H 85
London St. M25—2D 58
Longacres Dri. OL12—4H 7
Longacres La. OL12—3H 7
Longacres Rd. WA15—6C 138
Longacre St. M1—4G 87 &
                        6E 163
Longbow Ct. M7—6H 73
Longbridge Rd. M17—1A 98
Long Causeway. BL4—2F 55
Longcliff Wlk. BL4—3A 24
Longcrag Wlk. M15—2E 101
  (off Moston La.)
Longcroft Dri. WA14—1D 136
Longcroft Gro. M23—4F 127
Longcroft Gro. M34—5B 90
Long Croft La. SK8—5A 142
Longdale Clo. OL2—3A 48
Longdale Dri. SK14—4C 108
Longdell Wlk. M9—3G 75
  (off Moston La.)
Longden Av. OL4—4A 50
Longden Rd. M12—5C 102
Longden St. BL1—5G 23
Longfellow Av. BL3—4F 37
Longfellow Cres. OL1—3H 49
Longfellow St. M6—1A 86
Longfellow Wlk. M34—2G 121
Longfield. BL9—6G 15
Longfield. M25—4E 59
Longfield Av. M31—6E 97
Longfield Av. SK8—6G 141
Longfield Av. WA15—5C 126
Longfield Clo. SK14—1C 106
Longfield Cotts. M31—5D 96
  (off Stamford Rd.)
Longfield Cres. OL4—6G 49
Longfield Dri. M31—5D 96
Longfield Gdns. M30—5B 110
Longfield Pk. OL2—1E 49
Longfield Rd. BL3—5E 37
Longfield Rd. M23—3F 127
Longfield Rd. OL2—1E 49

Longfield Rd. OL11—3E 19
Longford Av. BL1—3G 23
Longford Av. M32—5E 99
Longford Clo. M32—4E 99
Longford Cotts. M32—5F 99
Longford Ho. M14—3A 102
Longford Pl. M14—3A 102
Longford Rd. M21—6G 99
Longford Rd. M32—4D 98
Longford Rd. SK5—6H 103
Longford Rd. W. M19 & SK5
                        —6F 103
Longford St. M18—1F 103
Longford St. OL10—3F 31
Longford Trading Est. M32—4D 98
Long Grain Pl. SK2—6D 132
Longham Clo. M11—4A 88
Longham Clo. SK7—4E 143
Long Hey. WA15—2A 138
Longhey Rd. M22—6B 128
Long Hill. OL11—1D 32
Longhill Wlk. M10—5A 76
Longhirst Clo. BL1—2F 23
Longhope Rd. M22—2H 139
Longhurst La. SK6—5F 135
Longhurst Rd. M9—5D 60
Long La. BL2—2F 39
Long La. OL3—5A 52
  (Dobcross)
Long La. OL3—3H 53
  (Tunstead)
Long La. OL9—6F 63
Long La. SK12—3H 157
Long Levens Rd. M22—3A 140
Longley Dri. M28—5B 70
Longley La. M22 & SK8—3B 128
Longley St. OL1—3D 64
Longley St. OL2—2F 49
Longmead Av. SK7—3D 144
Longmeade Gdns. SK9—3F 159
Long Meadow. BL7—4G 11
Longmeadow. SK8—6E 143
Long Meadow. SK14—1D 106
Longmeadow Gro. M34—5E 105
Long Meadow Pas. SK14—4B 106
Longmead Rd. M6—6B 72
Longmere Av. M22—2B 140
Long Millgate. M3—3D 86 &
                        3H 161
Longnor Grn. SK13—5F 109
  (off Longnor M.)
Longnor M. SK13—5F 109
Longnor Rd. SK7—5E 145
Longnor Rd. SK8—5H 141
Longport Av. M20—2D 116
Longridge. BL7—3G 11
Longridge Av. SK15—1E 93
Longridge Cres. BL1—3D 22
Longridge Dri. BL8—5G 27
Longridge Pl. M4—3D 86 & 4H 161
Long Row. SK12—4F 155
Long Rushes. OL2—5D 34
Longshaw Av. M27—2F 71
Longshaw Dri. M28—5C 54
Longshaw Ford Rd. BL1—1D 22
Longshut La. SK1—4H 131
Longshut La. W. SK1—4H 131
Long Sides Rd. WA15—6C 138
Longsight. BL0—6C 4
Longsight. BL2—6A 12
Longsight Ind. Est. M12—3B 102
Longsight La. BL2—2F 25
Longsight La. SK8—2B 152
Longsight Rd. M18—4D 102
Longsight St. SK4—1F 131
Longsons, The. SK5—6H 119
Longson St. BL1—4C 24
Long St. M18—1G 103
Long St. M24—6A 46
  (in two parts)
Long St. M27—4F 71
Longton Av. M20—4E 117
Longton Rd. M6—6A 72
Longton Rd. M9—4E 61
Longton St. BL3—4D 42
Longtown Gdns. BL1—3A 24
  (off Gladstone St.)
Longview Dri. M27—2C 70

Long Wlk. M31—6B 110
Longwall Av. M28—3D 68
  (in two parts)
Longwood Av. SK2—5B 132
Longwood Clo. SK6—6C 122
Long Wood Rd. M17—1B 98
Longwood Rd. M22—2C 140
Long Wood Rd. Est. M17—1A 98
Longworth Clo. M31—6A 96
Longworth Rd. BL7—1A 10
Longworth St. BL2—6E 25
Longworth St. M3—5C 86 & 1F 164
Lonsdale Av. M27—6D 70
Lonsdale Av. M31—3D 96
Lonsdale Av. OL16—6B 20
Lonsdale Av. SK5—4H 103
Lonsdale Gro. BL4—1E 55
Lonsdale Rd. M19—5D 102
Lonsdale Rd. OL8—1A 78
Lonsdale St. BL8—3A 28
Lonsdale St. M10—5C 76
Loom St. M4—3F 87 & 4D 162
Loonies Ct. SK1—2H 131
Lord Byron Sq. M5—4F 85
Lord Derby Rd. SK14—3C 122
Lord Kitchener Ct. M33—3B 114
Lord La. M35—1G 89
  (Droylsden)
Lord La. M35—4F 77
  (Failsworth)
Lord Napier Dri. M5—6H 85
Lord North St. M10—1A 88
Lord's Av. M5—3D 84
Lordsfield Av. OL7—1H 91
Lordship Clo. M9—2H 75
Lordsmead St. M15—1B 100 &
                        5D 164
Lord's Stile La. BL7—4F 11
Lords St. M30—3A 110
Lord St. BL3—4B 40
Lord St. BL4—1G 55
Lord St. BL9—3D 28
  (Bury)
Lord St. BL9—3G 29
  (Heap Bridge)
Lord St. M7—1A 86
Lord St. M3 & M4—1D 86 &
                        1A 162
Lord St. M25—6C 42
Lord St. M26—6A 41
Lord St. M34—3G 109
Lord St. OL1—1D 64
  (in three parts)
Lord St. OL6—1H 91
Lord St. OL15—4G 9
Lord St. SK1—2H 131
Lord St. SK14—3F 109
Lord St. SK16 & SK15—5D 92
Loreto Wlk. M15—2D 100
  (off Moss Side Shopping Cen.)
Loretto Rd. M31—6H 97
Lorgill Clo. SK3—1H 143
Loring St. M10—6C 76
Lorland Rd. SK3—4D 130
Lorna Gro. SK8—5D 128
Lorna Rd. SK8—3D 142
Lorne Av. OL2—4H 47
Lorne Gro. M31—5G 97
Lorne Gro. SK3—5G 131
Lorne Rd. M14—1G 117
Lorne St. BL1—6B 24
Lorne St. BL4—5E 39
Lorne St. M13—2G 101
Lorne St. M30—5D 82
Lorne St. OL5—2E 81
Lorne St. OL8—5C 64
Lorne St. OL10—4F 31
Lorne St. OL12—6H 7
Lorne Way. OL16—4B 30
Lorraine Clo. OL10—5G 31
Lorraine Rd. WA15—6A 126
Lorton Clo. M24—5E 45
Lorton Clo. M28—5B 68
Lorton Gro. BL2—5H 25
Lostock Av. M19—6D 102
Lostock Av. M31—4D 96
Lostock Av. M33—5E 115
Lostock Av. SK7—4B 144

Lostock Av. SK12—3B 154
Lostock Clo. OL10—2D 30
Lostock Ct. M32—3H 97
Lostock Dene. BL6—5F 15
Lostock Dri. BL9—5F 15
Lostock Gro. M32—4B 98
Lostock Hall Rd. SK12—4B 154
Lostock Junct. La. BL6—1A 36
Lostock Rd. M5—2E 85
Lostock Rd. M31—3E 97
Lostock Rd. SK9—3H 151
Lostock Rd. SK12—5D 154
Lostock St. M10—2H 87 & 2G 163
Lostock Wlk. M25—5G 43
Lottery St. SK3—2F 131
Lottie St. M27—3G 71
Loughfield. M31—5C 96
Loughman Wlk. M15—1C 100 & 5E 165
Loughrigg Av. OL2—5A 34
Louisa St. BL1—3A 24
Louisa St. M11—5F 89
Louisa St. M28—5F 55
Louis Av. BL9—1D 28
Louise Clo. OL12—6H 7
Louise Gdns. OL12—6A 8
Louise St. OL12—6H 7
  (in three parts)
Louvaine Av. BL1—1D 22
Louvaine Clo. M18—1G 103
Louvain St. M35—4E 77
Lovalle St. BL1—4A 24
Lovat Rd. BL2—6A 26
Love La. BL0—4B 4
Love La. SK4—1G 131
Lovell Ct. M8—1B 74
Lovell Dri. SK14—3D 106
Lovers La. OL4—3E 67
Lovers Wlk. WA15—1G 137
Lovett Wlk. M22—3C 128
Low Bank. OL12—6A 8
Lowbrook La. OL4—6B 50
  (in two parts)
Lowcock St. M7—1C 86
Low Crompton Rd. OL2—1B 48
Lowcross Rd. M10—5A 76
Lowe Grn. OL2—2C 48
Lwr. Alma St. SK16—4H 91
Lwr. Bamford Clo. M24—5A 46
Lwr. Bank. M34—2F 105
Lwr. Bank Clo. SK14—4H 109
Lwr. Bank St. BL9—3C 28
Lwr. Barn Rd. SK14—3G 109
Lwr. Bennett St. SK14—3A 106
Lwr. Bents La. SK6—5F 121
Lwr. Bridgeman St. BL2—1C 38
Lwr. Broadacre. SK15—1A 108
Lwr. Brooklands Pde. M8—1A 74
Lwr. Broughton Rd. M7—6G 73 & 1C 160
Lwr. Bury St. SK4—1F 131
Lwr. Byrom St. M3—5C 86 & 1E 165
Lwr. Calderbrook. OL15—6G 9
Lwr. Carr La. OL3—3F 53
Lwr. Carrs. SK1—2H 131
Lwr. Chatham St. M1 & M15—6E 87 & 3A 166
  (in two parts)
Lwr. Crimble. OL11—1G 31
Lwr. Croft. M25—3A 58
Lowercroft Rd. BL8—3E 27
Lwr. Crossbank. OL4—1B 66
Lwr. Darcy St. BL2—2E 39
Lwr. Dingle. OL3—3G 49
Lwr. Edge Av. OL1—1C 64
Lwr. Falinge. OL12—3G 19
Lowerfield. M34—5G 105
Lowerfield Dri. SK2—6F 133
Lowerfields. OL3—6A 52
Lowerfields. OL8—5F 65
Lwr. Fold. SK6—3F 135
Lowerfold Av. OL2—3E 49
Lowerfold Clo. OL12—5C 6
Lowerfold Cres. OL12—5C 6
Lowerfold Dri. OL12—5C 6
Lowerfold Way. OL12—5C 6
Lwr. Fullwood. OL1—2H 49
Lwr. Goodwin Clo. BL2—2G 25
Lower Grn. M6—1F 85
Lwr. Green. M24—4H 61
Lwr. Green. OL6—1A 92

Lower Grn. OL12—2E 19
Lwr. Hague. SK12—5H 147
Lwr. Hardman St. M3—4C 86 & 6F 161
Lwr. Healey La. OL12—1G 19
Lwr. Hey La. OL5—6G 67
Lwr. Hillgate. SK1—2H 131
Lwr. House Dri. BL6—6A 22
Lwr. House St. OL1—1F 65
Lwr. House Wlk. BL7—3E 11
Lwr. Jowkin La. OL11—4H 17
Lwr. Knoll Rd. OL3—2C 52
Lower La. OL16—2A 34
Lwr. Lime Rd. OL8—3A 78
Lwr. Marlands. BL7—3D 10
Lwr. Mead. BL7—2D 10
Lwr. Mill Cotts. SK4—6G 119
Lwr. Moat Clo. SK4—6G 119
Lwr. Monton Rd. M30—3G 83
Lwr. Mosley St. M2—5D 86 & 2G 165
Lwr. Moss La. M15—6B 86 & 4D 164
Lwr. Moss La. M25—1D 58
Lwr. New Rd. M28—2C 68
Lwr. Ormond St. M1 & M15—6E 87
   (in two parts)   & 3A 166
Lwr. Park Cres. SK12—1C 154
Lwr. Park Rd. M14—3G 101
Lwr. Park Rd. SK12—2B 154
   (in three parts)
Lwr. Rawson St. BL4—6G 39
Lwr. Seedley Rd. M6—2E 85
Lwr. Sheriff St. OL12—1G 19
Lwr. Standrings. OL11—3C 18
Lower St. BL4—2E 55
Lower St. OL16—1G 33
Lwr. Strines Rd. SK6—6E 135
Lwr. Sutherland St. M27—3E 71
Lwr. Tenterfield. OL11—1H 17
Lwr. Tong. BL7—4D 10
Lwr. Turf La. OL4—2C 66
Lwr. Tweedale St. OL11—5H 19
Lwr. Vickers St. M10—2H 87 & 2H 163
Lwr. Victoria St. OL9—2H 63
Lwr. Wharf St. OL6—3H 91
Lwr. Wheat End. OL16—3B 20
Lwr. Woodhill Rd. BL8—2B 28
   (in two parts)
Lwr. Wood La. BL2—4D 24
Loweside Av. BL1—1A 36
Lowes Rd. BL9—5F 15
Lowestead Rd. M14—3G 101
Lowestern Clo. BL7—2C 10
Lowes, The. WA14—4D 136
Lowestoft St. M14—5F 101
Lowe St. M26—3F 41
Lowe St. M34—4H 105
Lowe St. SK1—2H 131
Loweswater Rd. SK8—2F 141
Loweswater Ter. SK15—1E 93
Lowfell Wlk. M18—4F 103
Lowfield Av. M35—2H 89
Lowfield Av. OL6—6B 80
Lowfield Gro. SK2—4H 131
Lowfield Rd. SK3—5G 131
Lowfield Wlk. M9—6G 61
   (off White Moss Rd.)
Lowgill Wlk. M18—2F 103
Low Hill. OL12—6A 8
Lowhouse Clo. OL16—4G 21
Lowick Av. BL3—4C 38
Lowick Clo. SK7—3D 144
Lowick Grn. SK6—3F 121
Lowland Gro. OL7—5E 79
Lowland Rd. SK2—1B 144
Lowlands Clo. M24—4B 62
Low Lea Rd. SK6—4F 135
Lowndes Clo. SK2—5B 132
Lowndes La. SK2—4B 132
Lowndes St. BL1—5F 23
Lowndes Wlk. M13—1G 101 & 6E 167
Lownorth Rd. M22—5C 140
Lowood Av. M31—3B 96
Lowood Clo. OL16—5F 21
Lowrey Wlk. M9—4G 75
   (off Broadwell Dri.)
Lowry. M30—3G 83
Lowry Dri. M27—2F 71
Lowry Dri. SK6—3F 135
Lowry Gro. SK14—4B 108

Lowry Lodge. M16—2B 100
Lowry Wlk. BL1—4H 23
Lowside Av. SK6—3A 122
Lowside Dri. OL4—4F 65
Low's Pl. OL12—1A 20
Lows, The. OL4—4F 65
   (in two parts)
Low St. BL0—3E 5
Lowther Av. M18—4D 102
Lowther Av. OL2—5A 34
Lowther Av. WA15—5A 126
Lowther Ct. M25—6D 58
Lowther Cres. M24—6F 45
Lowther Gdns. M31—4H 95
Lowther Rd. M8—2C 74
Lowther Rd. M25—6D 58
Lowther Rd. OL11—1E 33
Lowther St. BL3—5C 38
   (in two parts)
Lowthorpe St. M14—4E 101
Lowton Av. M9—4H 75
Lowton Ho. BL1—5B 24
   (off Gray St.)
Lowton Rd. M33—1F 125
Lowton St. M26—3G 41
Low Wood Clo. SK7—4E 143
Low Wood Rd. M34—3A 104
Loxford Ct. M15—1D 100 & 5H 165
Loxford Gdns. M15—1D 100 & 1H 165
Loxford St. M15—1D 100 & 5H 165
Loxham St. BL3 & BL4—5F 39
Loxton Wlk. M7—5A 74
Loyalty Pl. SK1—2H 131
Loynd St. BL0—3F 5
Lubeck St. M9—3G 75
Lucas Rd. BL4 & M28—1C 54
Lucas St. BL9—2E 29
Lucas St. OL4—2F 65
Lucas Wlk. M11—5B 88
Lucerne Clo. OL9—3A 64
Lucerne Rd. SK7—2G 143
Lucien Clo. M12—2A 102
Lucknow St. OL11—6H 19
Lucy St. BL1—4E 23
Lucy St. BL4—1F 55
Lucy St. M7—6H 73
Lucy St. M15—1B 100 & 6C 164
Lucy St. SK3—3G 131
Ludford Gro. M33—1H 125
Ludgate Hill. M4—2F 87 & 2C 162
Ludgate Rd. M10—1E 89
Ludgate Rd. OL11—3G 33
Ludgate St. M4—2E 87 & 2B 162
Ludlow Av. M25—3F 59
Ludlow Av. M27—1G 71
Ludlow Pk. OL4—3H 65
Ludlow Rd. SK2—3C 132
Ludlow Towers. SK5—2C 120
Ludwell Wlk. M8—5C 74
Lugano Rd. SK7—2G 143
Luke Kirby Ct. M27—2F 71
Luke Rd. M35—4B 90
Luke St. BL3—2A 38
Luke Wlk. M8—5D 74
Lullington Rd. M6—1D 84
Lulworth Av. M31—5B 96
Lulworth Clo. BL8—5C 14
Lulworth Cres. M35—3H 77
Lulworth Gdns. M23—3F 127
Lulworth Rd. BL3—4E 37
Lulworth Rd. M24—5A 46
Lulworth Rd. M30—2E 83
Lumb Carr Av. BL0—5C 4
Lumb Carr Rd. BL8—6C 4
Lumb Clo. SK7—1G 153
Lumber La. M28—3G 69
Lumb Ho. SK7—1G 153
Lumb La. M34—4C 90
Lumb La. M35—2C 90
   (in three parts)
Lumb La. SK7—1G 153
Lumley Clo. M14—3F 101
Lumn Gro. BL9—3F 15
Lumn Hollow. SK14—5C 106
Lumn Rd. SK14—5C 106
Lumn's La. M27—1A 72
Lumsden St. BL3—2A 38
Luna St. M4—3F 87 & 4C 162

Lundale Wlk. M10—5A 76
Lund Av. M26—1H 57
Lund St. M16—1A 100 & 6A 164
Lundy Av. M21—4A 116
Lunedale Grn. SK2—5D 132
Lune Dri. M25—1E 59
Lune Gro. OL10—2D 30
Lune St. BL8—5C 64
Lune Wlk. M25—1E 59
Lune Wlk. M35—5B 90
Lune Way. SK5—4H 119
Lunn Av. M18—1H 103
Lupin Av. BL4—6C 38
Lupton St. M3—3B 86 & 4D 160
Lupton St. M34—3F 105
Lupton Wlk. M15—1D 100 & 5G 165
Lurden Wlk. OL9—5H 63
Lurgan Av. M33—6C 114
Lutener Av. WA14—3E 125
Luton Dri. M23—1G 139
Luton Rd. SK5—1H 119
Luton St. BL3—3C 38
Luton St. BL8—4H 27
Luxhall Wlk. M10—6B 76
Luxor Gro. M34—4H 103
Luzley Rd. OL5 & OL6—3D 80
Luzley Rd. SK15—2F 93
Lyceum Pas. OL16—4H 19
Lychgate M. SK4—1A 130
Lydbrook Clo. BL1—1A 38
Lydden Av. M11—2F 89
Lydford. OL11—5G 19
Lydford Gdns. BL2—2H 39
Lydford St. M6—6F 73
Lydford Wlk. M13—1G 101
   (off Torquay Clo.)
Lydgate Av. BL2—5G 25
Lydgate Clo. M25—6E 43
Lydgate Clo. M34—6H 105
Lydgate Dri. OL4—4G 65
Lydgate Rd. M33—1C 126
Lydgate Rd. M35—2G 89
Lydgate Wlk. M25—6E 43
Lydiat La. SK9—6G 159
Lydney Av. SK8—6G 141
Lydney Rd. M31—4H 95
Lyefield Wlk. OL16—5B 20
Lyme Av. SK9—6F 151
Lymefield Dri. M28—4C 68
Lymefield Gro. SK2—5B 132
Lyme Gro. M35—4H 89
Lyme Gro. SK1—4H 131
   (Marple)
Lyme Gro. SK6—6D 134
   (Marple)
Lyme Gro. SK6—1B 134
   (Romiley)
Lyme Gro. WA14—1E 137
Lyme Rd. SK7—4E 145
Lyme Rd. SK12—6E 147
   (Disley)
Lyme Rd. SK12—4B 156
   (Poynton)
Lyme St. SK4—1A 130
Lyme St. SK7—2D 144
Lyme Ter. SK16—4H 91
Lymewood Dri. SK9—1H 159
Lymewood Dri. SK12—1G 157
Lymington Clo. M24—4B 62
Lymington Rd. M23—2D 126
Lymm Clo. M28—6C 54
Lymm Clo. SK3—5F 131
Lymm Rd. WA13 & WA14—5A 136
Lymm Wlk. SK8—6C 130
Lyncombe Clo. SK8—1D 152
Lyndale Av. M27—5D 70
Lyndale Av. SK5—4H 103
Lyndale Dri. OL15—3E 9
Lyndene Av. M28—3A 70
Lyndene Gdns. SK8—5F 129
Lyndene Rd. M22—6B 128
Lyndhurst Av. M25—6A 60
Lyndhurst Av. M30—4F 95
Lyndhurst Av. M31—3E 97
Lyndhurst Av. M33—6H 113
Lyndhurst Av. M34—4E 105

Lyndhurst Av. OL6—6F 79
Lyndhurst Av. OL9—4F 63
Lyndhurst Av. OL11—5D 32
Lyndhurst Av. SK6—5F 121
Lyndhurst Av. SK7—4C 144
Lyndhurst Clo. SK9—4A 158
Lyndhurst Dri. WA15—3A 138
Lyndhurst Gdns. M24—1G 61
Lyndhurst Rd. M20—5E 117
   (in two parts)
Lyndhurst Rd. M32—5B 98
Lyndhurst Rd. OL8—6D 64
Lyndhurst Rd. SK5—5G 103
Lyndhurst St. M5—3E 85
Lyndhurst View. SK16—4A 92
Lyndon Clo. BL8—5H 13
Lyndon Clo. OL4—1D 66
Lyndon Rd. M30—5D 94
Lyne Edge Cres. SK16—6D 92
Lyne Edge Rd. SK15—5D 92
Lyne Edge Rd. SK16—6E 93
Lyne Gro. M33—6C 114
Lyneham Wlk. M8—5B 74
Lyneham Wlk. M9—4G 61
Lyne View. SK14—1D 106
Lyngard Clo. SK9—6A 152
Lyngarth Ho. WA14—5G 125
Lyngate Clo. SK1—3A 132
Lyn Gro. OL10—2D 30
Lynham Dri. OL10—5F 31
Lynmouth Av. M20—3E 117
Lynmouth Av. M31—1D 112
Lynmouth Av. OL2—4A 48
Lynmouth Av. OL8—6D 64
Lynmouth Av. SK5—2G 119
Lynmouth Clo. M26—3A 42
Lynmouth Clo. OL9—6E 47
Lynmouth Ct. M25—6D 58
Lynmouth Gro. M25—6D 58
Lynn Av. M33—3D 114
Lynn Dri. M35—3G 89
Lynnfield Ho. WA14—6F 125
Lynn St. OL9—5A 64
Lynnwood Dri. OL11—3D 18
Lynnwood Rd. M19—1H 129
Lynroyle Way. OL11—2D 32
Lynside Wlk. M22—6C 140
Lynslade Av. M31—4B 96
Lynsted Av. BL3—4C 38
Lynthorpe Av. M30—3B 110
Lynthorpe Rd. M10—6D 62
Lynton Av. M27—2F 71
Lynton Av. M30—3C 110
Lynton Av. M31—5G 95
Lynton Av. OL2—4A 48
Lynton Av. OL8—1A 78
Lynton Av. SK14—5G 107
Lynton Clo. OL9—6F 47
Lynton Cres. M28—2F 69
Lynton Dri. M19—2B 118
Lynton Dri. M25—3G 59
Lynton Dri. SK6—5C 146
Lynton Gro. WA15—6H 125
Lynton La. SK9—4G 159
Lynton Lee. M26—3A 42
Lynton M. SK9—4G 159
Lynton Pk. Rd. SK8—5B 142
Lynton Rd. BL3—5G 37
Lynton Rd. M21—6G 99
Lynton Rd. M27—2F 71
Lynton Rd. M29—3A 68
Lynton Rd. SK4—4E 119
Lynton Rd. SK8—6F 129
Lynton St. M14—5F 101
Lyntonvale Av. SK8—5E 129
Lynton Wlk. SK14—5G 107
Lyn Town Trading Est. M30—3F 83
Lyntown Trading Est. OL11—2D 32
Lynway Dri. M20—4F 117
Lynwell Rd. M30—3F 83
Lynwood. WA15—3A 138
Lynwood Av. BL3—5D 38
Lynwood Av. M16—5A 100
Lynwood Av. M30—3F 83
Lynwood Ct. M8—1B 74
Lynwood Dri. OL4—1H 65
Lynwood Gro. BL2—1F 25

Lynwood Gro. M33—4C 114
Lynwood Gro. M34—4C 90
Lynwood Gro. SK4—3E 119
Lyon Gro. M28—3A 70
Lyon Rd. BL4—4G 55
Lyon Rd. WA14—4E 125
Lyon's Fold. M33—3B 114
Lyons Rd. M17—6A 84
Lyon St. M27—4E 71
Lyon St. OL2—6F 35
Lyon Way. SK5—3G 119
Lysander Clo. M14—1F 117
Lytham Av. M21—2A 116
Lytham Clo. OL6—5A 80
Lytham Dri. OL10—4E 31
Lytham Dri. SK7—6A 144
Lytham Rd. M19—6B 102
Lytham Rd. M31—5G 95
Lytham Rd. SK8—4F 141
Lytham St. OL12—6E 7
Lytham St. SK3—5H 131
Lytherton Av. M30—5B 110
Lyth St. M5—5B 86 & 1C 164
Lyth St. M24—1H 117
Lytton Av. M8—5C 74
Lytton Rd. M35—3A 90
Lytton St. BL1—3H 23

Mabel Av. BL3—4C 38
Mabel Av. M28—4A 70
Mabel Rd. M35—2G 77
Mabel's Brow. BL4—2G 55
(in two parts)
Mabel St. BL1—5G 23
Mabel St. OL12—1F 19
Mabfield Rd. M14—6G 101
Mabledon Clo. SK8—5H 141
Mable St. M10—6D 76
Mabs Ct. OL6—3B 92
Macaulay Way. M34—1G 121
Macaulay Clo. SK16—6E 93
Macauley Rd. M16—5H 99
Macauley Rd. SK5—6F 103
Macauley St. OL2—3C 48
Macauley St. OL11—3D 32
McCall Wlk. M11—3D 88
Maccles Ct. OL15—3E 9
Macclesfield Rd. SK7—6E 145
Macclesfield Rd. SK9—5G 159
(Alderley Edge)
Macclesfield Rd. SK9—2F 159
(Wilmslow)
McConnell Rd. M10—4A 76
Macdonald Av. BL4—2C 54
Macdonald Rd. M30—2C 110
Macdonald St. OL8—5D 64
McDonna St. BL1—2G 23
McDowall Wlk. M8—1D 74
Macefin Av. M21—5B 116
Macfarren St. M12—4C 102
McKean St. BL3—3C 38
Mackenzie Gro. BL1—1H 23
Mackenzie Rd. M7—5F 73
Mackenzie St. BL1—6B 10
Mackenzie St. M12—4C 102
Mackeson Dri. OL6—1C 92
Mackeson Rd. OL6—1C 92
Mackintosh Way. OL1—2D 64
Maclaren Dri. M8—1A 74
Maclaren Ho. M6—2F 85
(off Sutton Dwellings)
McLean Dri. M30—3E 95
Maclure Clo. M16—4C 100
Macnair St. SK6—6E 135
McNaught St. OL16—5B 20
McOwen Pl. OL16—4A 20
McOwen St. OL16—4A 20
Madam Wood Rd. M28—6B 54
Maddison Rd. M35—4H 89
Madeley Clo. WA14—5G 137
Madeley Dri. OL9—3A 64
Madeley Gdns. BL1—3A 24
Madeley Gdns. OL12—2F 19
Madeline St. BL3—5F 39
Maden Wlk. OL9—1H 63

Madison Av. M34—5C 90
Madison Av. SK8—3C 142
Madison Gdns. M35—4E 77
Madison St. M18—1G 103
Madras Rd. SK3—4E 131
Mafeking Av. BL9—6G 15
Mafeking Rd. BL2—6G 25
Mafeking St. OL8—6A 64
Magdala St. OL1—1C 64
Magdala St. OL10—5G 31
Magdalen Wlk. M15—6C 86 &
                              4F 165
Magda Rd. SK2—6C 132
Magna Carta Ct. M6—5H 71
Magnolia Clo. M31—6C 110
Magnolia Clo. M33—3E 113
Magnolia Ct. M6—3G 85
Magnolia Ct. M33—4E 113
(off Magnolia Clo.)
Magnolia Dri. M8—5C 74
Magpie Clo. M35—2C 90
Magpie Wlk. M11—4B 88
Mahogony Wlk. M33—4E 113
Mahood St. SK3—4F 131
Maida St. M12—5D 102
Maiden Clo. OL7—5E 79
Maiden M. M27—4F 71
Maidford Clo. M4—4H 87 & 5H 163
Maidstone Av. M21—6G 99
Maidstone M. M21—6G 99
Maidstone Rd. SK4—6H 117
Maidstone Wlk. M34—6G 105
Main Av. M17—3C 98
Main Av. M19—2B 118
Maine Rd. M14—5E 101
Mainhill Wlk. M10—6C 76
Mainprice Clo. M6—1F 85
Main Rd. M27—6B 58
Main Rd. OL9—2A 64
Main St. M35—3F 77
Main St. SK14—3B 106
Mainwaring Dri. SK9—1G 159
Mainway. M24—3H 61
Mainway E. M24—3C 62
Mainwood Rd. WA15—6C 126
Mainwood Sq. M13—6F 87
Maismore Rd. M22—4G 139
Maismore Rd. M22—4H 139
Maitland Av. M21—4A 116
Maitland Clo. OL12—6A 8
Maitland St. SK1—4B 132
Maitland Wlk. OL9—1H 63
Major St. BL0—3D 4
Major St. M1—5E 87 & 1B 166
Major St. OL16—5F 21
Makant St. BL1—2G 23
Makepiece Wlk. M8—1A 74
Makin Ct. OL10—4F 31
Makin St. M1—5E 87 & 2A 166
Malakoff St. SK15—4C 92
Malbrook Wlk. BL3—3B 38
Malbrook Wlk. M13—1G 101
(off Ardeen Wlk.)
Malby St. OL1—1D 64
Malcom Av. M27—6G 57
Malcom Dri. M27—1G 71
Malcom St. OL11—2D 32
Malden Gro. M23—4G 127
Maldon Clo. SK2—5G 133
Maldon Cres. M27—5F 71
Maldon Dri. M30—1G 83
Maldon St. OL11—6H 19
Maldwyn Av. BL3—5F 37
Maldwyn Av. M8—1C 74
Malford Dri. M8—5B 74
Malgam Dri. M20—3F 129
Malham Clo. OL2—3B 48
Malham Gdns. BL3—4G 37
Mallaig Wlk. M11—5E 89
Mallard Clo. OL8—1B 78
Mallard Clo. SK2—6G 133
Mallard Clo. SK16—6C 92
Mallard Ct. SK8—5F 141
Mallard Cres. SK12—3A 154
Mallard Grn. WA14—3D 124
Mallard Wlk. M1—5E 87 & 2A 166
Mallet Cres. BL1—3D 22

Malley Wlk. M9—6G 61
(off Greendale Dri.)
Malling Rd. M23—1G 139
Mallison St. BL1—2B 24
Mallory Dri. OL7—6F 79
Mallory Ct. WA14—2E 137
Mallory Rd. SK14—2E 107
Mallory Wlk. M23—3D 126
Mallowdale. M28—3D 68
Mallowdale Clo. BL1—6B 22
Mallowdale Clo. M15—1D 100 & 5G 165
Mallowdale Rd. SK2—6E 133
Mallow Wlk. M31—6D 110
Mall, The. BL9—3D 28
Mall, The. M30—3H 83
Mall, The. M34—5B 106
Mall, The. SK14—5B 106
Mall, The. SK15—1A 108
Malmesbury Clo. SK12—3D 154
Malmesbury Rd. SK8—1D 152
Malpas Clo. SK8—1C 142
Malpas Clo. SK9—6A 152
Malpas Dri. WA14—2G 125
Malpas St. M12—1C 102
Malpas St. OL1—2D 64
Malpas Wlk. M16—2B 100
Malsham Rd. M23—1F 127
Malta Clo. M24—1D 62
Malta St. M4—4H 87 & 5G 163
Malta St. OL4—3H 65
Maltby Dri. BL3—4G 37
Maltby Rd. M23—5F 127
Malton Av. BL3—3E 37
Malton Av. M21—1H 115
Malton Av. M25—5D 42
Malton Av. OL9—6F 47
Malton Clo. M25—5D 42
Malton Dri. SK7—6D 144
Malton Dri. WA14—5C 124
Malton Rd. M28—4A 68
Malton Rd. SK4—5C 118
Malton St. OL8—4B 64
Malt St. M15—6B 86 & 4C 164
Malus Ct. M6—2G 85
Malvern Av. BL1—4E 23
Malvern Av. BL9—6F 15
Malvern Av. M31—4D 96
Malvern Av. M35—3C 90
Malvern Av. OL6—4G 79
Malvern Clo. BL4—1B 54
Malvern Clo. M25—4G 59
Malvern Clo. M27—5B 72
Malvern Clo. OL2—4A 48
(Royton)
Malvern Clo. OL2—6D 34
(Shaw)
Malvern Clo. OL16—4G 21
Malvern Clo. SK4—6F 119
Malvern Dri. WA14—6D 124
Malvern Gro. M6—2C 84
Malvern Gro. M20—3E 117
Malvern Gro. M28—6F 55
Malvern Rd. M24—4H 61
Malvern Row. M15—1B 100 & 6C 164
Malvern St. M15—1B 100 & 6C 164
Malvern St. OL8—4B 64
Malvern St. E. OL11—4E 19
Malvern St. W. OL11—4E 19
Manby Rd. M18—3D 102
Manby Sq. M18—3D 102
Manchester Ind. Cen. M3—5B 86 &
                              1D 164
Manchester International Airport.
         M22, SK9 & WA15—2H 149
(Ringway)
Manchester International Bus. Cen.
                    M22—6E 141
Manchester New Rd. M24—4G 61
Manchester New Rd. M31—5D 110
Manchester Old Rd. BL9—4C 28
Manchester Old Rd. M24—2D 60
Manchester Rd. BL0 & BL9—3G 5
Manchester Rd. BL2 & BL3—1C 38
Manchester Rd. BL4—1G 55
(Farnworth)
Manchester Rd. BL4 & M27—3A 56
(Kearsley)

Manchester Rd. BL5—6A 36
Manchester Rd. BL9 & M25—4C 28
Manchester Rd. M21 & M16—1G 115
(in two parts)
Manchester Rd. M28 & M27—6F 55
(Walkden)
Manchester Rd. M31—5D 110
Manchester Rd. M34—3A 104
Manchester Rd. M34 & OL7—6A 90
Manchester Rd. M35—4G 89
Manchester Rd. OL2—2E 49
Manchester Rd. OL3—5H 67
Manchester Rd. OL5—5E 81
Manchester Rd. OL8 & OL9—1H 77
Manchester Rd. OL10—3E 45
Manchester Rd. OL11—2C 32
Manchester Rd. OL11 & OL12—6F 19
(in three parts)
Manchester Rd. SK4—3E 119
Manchester Rd. SK8—3H 129
Manchester Rd. SK9—2E 159
Manchester Rd. SK14—1G 109
(Hollingworth)
Manchester Rd. SK14—4H 105
(Hyde)
Manchester Rd. WA3—6A 110
Manchester Rd. WA14—5F 125
Manchester Rd. E. M28—5C 54
Manchester Rd. N. M34—3C 104
Manchester Rd. S. M34—3C 104
Manchester Science Pk. M5.
(off Lloyd St. N.)   —2E 101
Manchester St. M16—2A 100
Manchester St. OL8 & OL9—4B 64
Manchester St. OL10—3F 31
Manchet St. OL11—4B 32
Mancroft Av. BL3—3H 37
Mancroft Wlk. M1—6F 87 & 3C 166
Mancunian Rd. M34—1G 121
Mancunian Way. M15, M1 & M12
                —6C 86 & 4E 165
Mandalay Gdns. SK6—4B 134
Mandarin Grn. WA14—3D 124
Mandarin Wlk. M6—2G 85
Mandeville St. M19—1D 118
Mandley Av. M10—1D 76
Mandley Clo. BL3—2A 40
Mandley Pk. Av. M8—4A 74
Mandon Clo. M26—2E 41
Manesty Clo. M24—5E 45
Manet Wlk. OL1—3H 49
Mangle St. M1—4F 87 & 5C 162
Manifold Dri. SK6—1D 156
Manifold St. M6—6F 73
Manilla Wlk. M11—4B 88
Manipur St. M11—5B 88
Manley Av. M27—5E 57
Manley Clo. BL9—1C 14
Manley Clo. SK3—5E 131
Manley Gro. SK7—1G 153
Manley Rd. M21 & M16
                —6A 100
Manley Rd. M33—2G 125
Manley Rd. OL8—5C 64
Manley Rd. OL11—2C 32
(in two parts)
Manley Row. BL5—6A 36
Manley St. M7—5H 73
Manley Ter. BL1—1A 24
Manningham Rd. BL3—2F 37
Mannington Dri. M9—4E 75
Mannock St. OL8—3B 64
Manor Av. BL3—4C 40
Manor Av. M16—5B 100
Manor Av. M33—6F 97
Manor Av. M33—4F 113
Manor Clo. M34—5H 105
Manor Clo. OL4—3G 67
Manor Clo. OL9—1A 64
Manor Clo. SK8—5E 143
Manor Clo. SK9—3B 158
Manor Ct. M32—6B 98
Manor Ct. M33—4F 113
Manordale Wlk. M10—5F 75
Manor Dri. M21—5B 116
Manor Dri. M28—3A 54
Manor Dri. OL2—4C 48
Manor Farm Clo. OL7—5D 78

Marlheath Wlk. M15—6C 86
(off Jackson Cres.)
Marlhill Clo. SK2—6E 133
Marlhill Ct. SK2—6E 133
Marlinford Dri. M10—6C 76
Marlor Ct. OL10—3D 30
Marlor St. M34—3E 105
Marlow Clo. BL2—4H 25
Marlow Clo. M31—3D 96
(in four parts)
Marlow Clo. SK8—3B 142
Marlow Dri. M27—5E 71
Marlow Dri. M30—4E 95
Marlow Dri. SK9—2G 151
Marlow Dri. WA14—3B 136
Marlowe Dri. M20—5F 117
Marlowe Wlk. M34—2G 121
Marlowe Walks. SK6—1E 133
Marlow Rd. M9—2H 75
Marlton Wlk. M9—6G 61
(off Leconfield Dri.)
Marlwood Rd. BL1—3D 22
Marmaduke St. OL9—1B 64
Marmion Dri. M21—1G 115
Marne Av. M22—6C 128
Marne Av. OL6—6B 80
Marne Cres. OL11—4E 19
Marnland Gro. BL3—3C 36
Maroon Rd. M22—6D 140
Marple Av. BL1—1C 24
Marple Ct. SK1—4A 132
Marple Gro. M32—4C 98
Marple Hall Dri. SK6—4B 134
Marple Old Rd. SK2—5G 133
Marple Rd. SK2—4D 132
Marquis Av. BL9—1C 28
Marquis Dri. SK8—6H 141
Marquis St. M19—6F 103
Marrick Av. SK8—6G 129
Marriott's Ct. M2—4E 87 & 5A 162
Marriott St. M20—3F 117
Marriott St. SK1—3H 131
Mars Av. BL3—4G 37
Marsden Clo. OL5—1D 80
Marsden Clo. OL7—6C 78
Marsden Clo. OL16—5A 34
Marsden Ct. M4—3E 87
(off Arndale Cen.)
Marsden Dri. WA15—5C 126
Marsden Rd. BL1—6A 24
Marsden Rd. SK6—6A 122
Marsden's Sq. OL15—3F 9
(off Sutcliffe St.)
Marsden St. BL9—2D 28
Marsden St. M2—4D 86 & 5H 161
Marsden St. M24—2C 62
Marsden St. M28—4B 68
(Mosley Common)
Marsden St. M28—1B 70
(Worsley)
Marsden St. M30—2E 83
Marsden St. SK14—3H 109
Marsden Wlk. M26—3F 41
Marsden Way. M4—3E 87
(off Arndale Cen.)
Marsett Clo. OL12—2B 18
Marsett Wlk. M23—1F 127
Marshall Ct. OL1—1C 64
Marshall Rd. M19—6C 102
Marshall St. M4—3F 87 & 3C 162
Marshall St. M34—3E 105
Marshall St. OL16—4C 20
Marsham Clo. M13—2A 102
Marsham Clo. OL4—4D 66
Marsham Dri. SK6—6E 135
Marsham Rd. SK7—4B 144
Marshbrook Rd. M31—4E 97
Marshdale Rd. BL1—5D 22
Marshfield Rd. WA15—6C 126
Marshfield Wlk. M13—1G 101
(off Lauderdale Cres.)
Marsh Fold La. BL1—5G 23
Marsh La. BL3—3B 40
Marsh La. BL4—1C 54
Marsh Rd. BL3—3A 40
Marsh Rd. M28—5D 54
Marsh St. BL1—3A 24
Marsh St. M28—1H 69

Marsland Av. WA15—3B 126
Marsland Clo. M34—4B 104
Marsland Rd. M33—6A 114
Marsland Rd. M34—4B 160
Marsland Rd. SK6—4C 134
Marsland Rd. WA15—5B 126
Marsland St. SK1—6H 119
(in two parts)
Marsland St. SK7—3D 144
Marsland St. N. M8—4B 74
Marsland St. S. M8—4B 74
Marsland Ter. SK1—3B 132
Mars St. OL9—2A 64
Marston Clo. M25—1G 59
Marston Dri. M30—5F 95
Marston Rd. M7—3A 74
Marston Rd. M32—5E 99
Marston St. M10—6F 75
Marsworth Dri. M4—3G 87 & 4F 163
Martens Rd. M30—4C 110
Marthall Dri. M33—1E 127
Marthall Way. SK9—2A 152
Martham Dri. SK2—6G 133
Martha's Ter. OL16—6A 8
Martha St. BL3—3H 37
Martha St. OL1—1B 64
Martin Av. BL3—4C 40
Martin Av. BL4—2B 54
Martin Av. OL4—3G 65
Martin Clo. M34—2F 105
Martin Clo. SK2—6G 133
Martindale Clo. OL2—2C 48
Martindale Cres. M12—1A 102
Martindale Cres. M44—4F 45
Martindale Gdns. BL1—3A 24
Martindale Way. M35—2D 90
Martin Dri. M30—3E 95
Martin Gro. BL4—2H 55
Martin La. OL12—2D 18
Martin Rd. M27—1H 71
Martinsclough. BL6—1A 36
Martinscroft Rd. M23—6H 127
Martin St. BL9—2H 29
Martin St. M5—3D 84
Martin St. M34—6F 91
Martin St. SK14—5C 106
Martlesham Wlk. M4—3E 87 & 4B 162
Martlet Av. OL11—4A 18
Martlet Clo. M14—6F 101
Martlets Av. SK12—1G 157
Martock Av. M22—2C 140
Marton Av. BL2—5E 25
Marton Av. M20—1G 116
Marton Ga. M25—1H 73
Marton Grn. SK3—5F 131
Marton Gro. SK4—3G 119
Marton Pl. M33—5A 114
Marton Way. SK9—2A 152
Marvic Ct. M13—4A 102
Marwood Clo. M26—1A 56
Marwood Clo. WA14—5D 124
Marwood Dri. M23—2F 139
Mary Anne Clo. OL7—5E 79
Maryfield Ct. M16—1C 116
Maryland Av. BL2—6F 25
Marylon Dri. M22—3C 128
Mary St. BL0—4D 4
Mary St. BL4—2F 55
Mary St. BL9—5F 15
Mary St. M3—2D 86 & 1G 161
Mary St. M34—3G 105
Mary St. M35—3B 90
Mary St. OL10—3E 31
Mary St. OL16—5B 8
Mary St. SK8—5H 129
Mary St. SK14—4B 106
Mary St. SK16—4H 91
Masbury Clo. BL1—4C 10
Masefield Av. M25—6D 58
Masefield Av. M26—3E 41
Masefield Clo. SK16—6F 93
Masefield Cres. M35—4A 90
Masefield Dri. BL4—2D 54
(in two parts)
Masefield Gro. SK5—6G 103
Masefield Rd. BL3—3B 40
Masefield Rd. M35—4A 90
Masefield Rd. OL1—5F 49
Mason Gdns. BL3—1A 38

Mason Row. BL7—1B 10
Mason St. BL9—3E 29
Mason St. M4—3F 86 & 4D 160
Mason St. M4—3F 87 & 3C 162
Mason St. OL10—3D 30
Mason St. OL16—4H 19
Massey Av. M35—3H 77
Massey Av. OL6—5G 79
Massey Croft. OL12—1C 6
Massey Rd. M33—5E 115
Massey Rd. WA15—1G 137
Massey St. BL9—2E 29
Massey St. M5—3A 86 & 4B 160
Massey St. SK9—5G 159
Massey Wlk. M22—4D 140
Massie St. SK8—5H 129
Matham Wlk. M15—1E 101
(off Chevril Clo.)
Mather Av. M25—1G 73
(Prestwich)
Mather Av. M25—5D 42
(Whitefield)
Mather Av. M30—3G 83
Mather Clo. M25—6D 42
Mather Fold Rd. M28—2D 68
Mather Rd. BL9—4F 15
Mather Rd. M30—3G 83
Mather St. BL3—1A 38
Mather St. BL4—1G 55
Mather St. M26—4G 41
Mather St. M35—4E 77
Mather Way. M6—2E 85
Matley Clo. SK14—2F 107
Matley Gro. SK5—3C 120
Matley La. SK14 & SK15—2F 107
Matley Pk. La. SK15—1H 107
Matlock Av. M7—4E 73
Matlock Av. M20—3D 116
Matlock Av. M31—1D 112
Matlock Av. M34—1G 121
Matlock Av. OL6—5B 80
Matlock Bank. SK13—6G 109
(off Riber Bank)
Matlock Clo. BL4—6G 39
Matlock Clo. M33—5C 114
Matlock Dri. SK7—5E 145
Matlock Gdns. SK13—6G 109
(off Riber Bank)
Matlock La. SK13—6G 109
(off Riber Bank)
Matlock M. WA14—6G 125
Matlock Pl. SK13—6G 109
(off Riber Bank)
Matlock Rd. M32—4A 98
Matlock Rd. SK5—6A 104
Matlock Rd. SK8—6G 141
Matlock St. M30—5E 83
Matson Wlk. M22—3G 139
Matt Busby Clo. M27—4H 71
Matterdale Ter. SK15—1E 93
Matthew Moss La. OL11—1B 32
Matthews Av. BL4—2H 55
Matthews La. M12 & M19—5C 102
Matthew's St. M12—6B 88
Matthew St. BL4—5E 39
Matthew St. SK6—5E 135
Matthias Ct. M3—2B 86 & 2C 160
Maudsley St. BL9—4C 28
Maud St. BL2—6G 11
Maud St. OL12—1A 20
Mauldeth Clo. SK4—6C 118
Mauldeth Rd. SK4—6C 118
Mauldeth Rd. M20 & M19—2G 117
(Withington & Burnage)
Mauldeth Rd. SK4 & M19—4B 118
(Heaton Mersey & Green End)
Mauldeth Rd. W. M21 & M20
—3A 116
Maunby Gdns. M28—6E 55
Maureen Av. M8—3C 74
Maurice Clo. SK16—5C 92
Maurice Dri. M6—1F 85
Maurice Pariser Wlk. M8—4B 74
Maurice Rd. OL11—5H 19
Maurice St. M6—1F 85
Maveen Ct. SK2—1A 144
Maveen Gro. SK2—1A 144
Mavis Gro. OL16—5G 21

Mavis St. OL11—4C 32
Mawdsley Dri. M8—3E 75
Mawdsley St. BL1—6B 24
Maxton Ho. BL4—1G 55
Maxwell St. SK2—6C 132
Maxwell St. BL1—1A 24
Maxwell St. BL9—2F 29
Max Woosnam Wlk. M14—4E 101
Mayall St. OL5—2E 81
Mayall St. S. OL4—2G 65
Mayan Av. M3—3B 86 & 3C 160
May Av. SK4—1D 130
May Av. SK8—1D 152
Maybank Clo. M15—2D 100
Maybank Bl. BL3—2H 37
Mayberth Av. M8—1C 74
Maybrook Wlk. M9—3F 75
Mayburn Clo. M24—4C 62
Maybury St. M18—1G 103
Maycroft. SK5—3B 120
Maycroft Av. M20—4G 117
May Dri. M19—3B 118
Mayering Ct. SK4—5E 119
Mayer St. SK2—4C 132
Mayes Gdns. M4—4H 87 & 6G 163
Mayes St. M4—3E 87 & 3A 162
(in two parts)
Mayfair Av. M6—2B 84
Mayfair Av. M25—2D 58
Mayfair Av. M26—3D 40
Mayfair Av. M31—5D 96
Mayfair Clo. SK16—5E 93
Mayfair Cres. M35—3H 77
Mayfair Dri. M30—5E 95
Mayfair Dri. M33—1G 125
Mayfair Dri. OL2—5B 48
Mayfair Gdns. OL11—6F 19
Mayfair Gro. M25—2E 59
Mayfair Pk. M20—6D 116
Mayfair Rd. M22—2C 140
Mayfield. BL2—6H 11
Mayfield. M26—5E 41
Mayfield Av. BL3—4D 38
Mayfield Av. BL4—2E 55
Mayfield Av. M27—5C 70
Mayfield Av. M28—6F 55
Mayfield Av. M32—6B 98
Mayfield Av. M33—5E 115
Mayfield Av. M34—2G 121
Mayfield Av. OL4—2C 66
Mayfield Av. SK5—4H 119
Mayfield Clo. BL0—1A 14
Mayfield Clo. WA15—5B 126
Mayfield Ct. WA15—5B 126
Mayfield Gro. M18—3H 103
Mayfield Gro. SK5—3H 119
Mayfield Gro. SK9—4B 158
Mayfield Rd. BL0—1A 14
Mayfield Rd. M7—2F 73
Mayfield Rd. M16—4C 100
Mayfield Rd. OL1—6F 49
Mayfield Rd. SK6—2F 135
Mayfield Rd. SK7—3G 153
Mayfield Rd. WA15—5B 126
Mayfield St. M34—2E 105
Mayfield St. OL16—2B 20
(in two parts)
Mayfield Ter. M33—5A 114
Mayfield Ter. OL16—2B 20
Mayford Rd. M19—5C 102
Maygate. OL1—1B 64
Mayhill Dri. M6—1A 84
Mayhill Dri. M28—3A 70
Mayhurst Av. M21—5B 116
Mayorlowe Av. SK5—5C 120
Mayor's Rd. WA15—1G 137
Mayor St. BL1 & BL3—1H 37
Mayor St. BL8—2A 28
Mayor St. OL9—2A 64
Mayo St. M12—5H 87
May Pl. OL11—1G 33
(off Oldham Rd.)
May Pl. OL15—5C 8
Maypool Dri. SK5—3H 119
May Rd. M16—4B 100
May Rd. M27—5H 71
May Rd. SK8—1D 152

Maysmith M. M7—5H 73
May St. BL2—6C 24
May St. M10—6C 76
(in two parts)
May St. M26—4G 41
May St. M30—1E 83
May St. OL8—5A 64
May St. OL10—5G 31
(in two parts)
Mayton St. SK5—1C 88
Mayville Dri. M20—4F 117
May Wlk. M31—6C 110
Maywood. SK9—5B 158
Maywood Av. M20—3F 129
Maze Ct. OL1—1C 64
Maze St. BL3—2E 39
Meachin Av. M21—3A 116
Meade Clo. M31—5E 97
Meade Gro. M13—4B 102
Meade Hill Rd. M25—6A 60
Meade, The. BL3—5A 38
Meade, The. M21—2H 115
Meade, The. SK9—1F 159
Meadfoot Av. M25—6G 59
Meadfoot Rd. M18—1F 103
Meadland Gro. BL1—1B 24
Meadon Av. M27—2H 71
Meadow Av. SK14—6C 106
Meadow Av. WA15—2B 138
Meadow Bank. BL9—5C 28
Meadow Bank. M21—2G 115
Meadow Bank. SK4—1D 130
Meadow Bank. SK6—6F 121
Meadow Bank. SK14—1F 109
Meadow Bank. WA15—4A 126
Meadow Bank Ct. M32—6A 98
Meadowbank Rd. BL3—5F 37
Meadowbrook Clo. BL6—4A 36
Meadow Brow. SK9—4G 159
Meadow Clo. BL3—5B 40
Meadow Clo. M32—6E 99
Meadow Clo. M34—2G 121
Meadow Clo. OL5—6G 67
Meadow Clo. OL10—3E 31
Meadow Clo. SK6—5D 146
(High Lane)
Meadow Clo. SK6—4G 121
(Woodley)
Meadow Clo. SK9—5B 158
Meadow Clo. WA15—2B 138
Meadow Cotts. OL12—2H 7
Meadow Ct. M6—2B 84
Meadow Ct. WA15—2C 138
Meadow Croft. M25—3A 58
Meadowcroft. M26—2F 41
Meadowcroft. M38—3H 114
Meadow Croft. SK7—2E 145
Meadowcroft. SK14—3C 108
Meadowcroft La. OL11—5B 18
Meadowfield. BL6—6A 22
Meadowfield Clo. SK13—4H 109
Meadowfield Dri. M28—5D 68
Meadow Fold. OL3—1G 53
Meadowgate. M28—3H 69
Meadowgate. M31—6F 97
Meadowgate Rd. M6—2B 84
Meadow Head Av. OL12—3D 6
Meadow La. BL2—6A 26
Meadow La. M28—6H 69
Meadow La. M34—1G 121
Meadow La. OL1—1C 78
Meadow La. SK12—1H 157
Meadow La. SK16—5B 92
Meadow Rise. OL2—4E 35
Meadow Rd. M7—2A 86 & 1B 160
Meadow Rd. M24—3G 61
Meadow Rd. M31—6F 97
Meadowside. M21—3H 115
Meadowside. OL16—1G 35
Meadowside. SK7—3E 143
Meadowside Av. BL2—5E 25
(in two parts)
Meadowside Av. M22—1B 140
Meadowside Av. M28—5G 55
Meadowside Av. M30—5E 95
Meadowside Gro. M28—6G 55
Meadows La. BL2—2H 25
Meadows Rd. M33—3C 114

Meadows Rd. SK4—2E 119
Meadows Rd. SK8—5B 142
(Cheadle Hulme)
Meadows Rd. SK8—4F 141
(Heald Green)
Meadows, The. M24—3B 62
Meadows, The. M25—5F 59
Meadows, The. M26—2E 41
Meadows, The. M30—3C 110
Meadows, The. OL3—2F 53
Meadows, The. OL4—3C 66
Meadows, The. SK14—3H 109
Meadow St. M16—3C 100
Meadow St. OL8—2H 77
Meadow St. SK2—6C 132
Meadow St. SK14—6C 106
Meadow, The. BL1—6A 22
Meadow, The. OL12—4G 7
Meadow View. OL12—2C 18
Meadow Wlk. M31—6C 110
Meadow Wlk. OL15—4D 8
Meadow Wlk. SK6—6F 121
Meadow Way. BL8—5G 13
Meadow Way. BL9—1C 14
Meadow Way. M10—2A 76
Meadow Way. SK9—5B 158
Meadow Way. WA15—2B 138
Meads Gro. BL4—1A 54
Meads, The. OL9—3G 63
Mead, The. M5—3D 84
Meadway. BL0—1E 5
Meadway. BL4—6H 39
Meadway. BL9—1D 42
Meadway. M33—6G 113
Mead Way. M34—1F 121
Meadway. OL9—1E 77
Meadway. OL11—1C 32
Meadway. SK6—5D 146
Meadway. SK7—2G 153
Meadway. SK12—2B 154
Meadway. SK15—1A 108
Meadway. SK16—6C 92
Meadway Clo. M33—1G 125
Meadway Rd. SK8—2D 142
Mealhouse Brow. OL12—3E 19
(in two parts)
Meanwood Fold. OL12—3F 19
Meddings Clo. SK9—5F 159
Medina Clo. SK8—1D 142
Medley Clo. OL12—2H 19
Medlar St. OL12—2H 19
Medlock Av. M25—1G 59
Medlock Way. OL4—3A 66
Medway Clo. M5—2D 84
Medway Clo. OL8—6A 64
Medway Cres. WA14—5E 125
Medway Dri. BL4—4B 56
Medway Rd. M28—3D 68
Medway Rd. OL2—5E 35
Medway Rd. OL8—6A 64
Medway, The. OL10—2D 30
Medway Wlk. M10—2H 87 & 1G 163
Meech St. M11—5E 89
Meek St. OL1—5E 49
Meersbrook Rd. SK3—3C 130
Mee's Sq. M30—5F 83
Melandra Castle Rd. SK13—6F 109
Melandra Cres. SK14—5A 108
Melanie Dri. SK5—1H 119
Melba St. M11—5G 89
Melbecks Wlk. M23—1E 127
Melbourne Av. M32—5D 98
Melbourne Clo. OL11—3G 33
Melbourne M. M7—6H 73
Melbourne Rd. BL3—2F 37

Melbourne Rd. OL11—3G 33
Melbourne Rd. SK7—1G 153
Melbourne St. M7—6H 73
Melbourne St. M9—3G 75
Melbourne St. M15—6C 86 & 3F 165
Melbourne St. M27—3H 71
Melbourne St. M34—5E 105
Melbourne St. OL9—2H 63
Melbourne St. SK5—1H 119
Melbourne St. SK15—3E 93
Melbourne St. N. OL6—1A 92
Melbourne St. S. OL6—1A 92
Melbourne Wlk. M5—5H 85
Melbury. OL11—1F 33
Melbury Av. M20—5H 117
Melbury Rd. SK8—1D 152
Meldon Rd. M13—5A 102
Meldreth Dri. M12—3B 102
Meldrum St. OL8—5D 64
Meldrum Wlk. OL8—5D 64
Melford Av. M10—3G 77
Melford Ho. BL1—4A 24
(off Nottingham Dri.)
Melford Rd. SK7—4F 145
Melfort Av. M32—6E 99
Meliden Cres. BL1—4F 23
Meliden Cres. M22—2C 140
Mellalieu St. M24—6G 45
Mellalieu St. OL2—5C 48
Mellalieu St. OL10—2E 31
Melland Av. M21—4A 116
Melland Rd. M18—4E 103
Meller Rd. M13—5B 102
Melling Av. OL9—6E 47
Melling Av. SK4—3G 119
Melling Rd. OL4—3G 65
Melling St. M12—3C 102
Mellington Av. M20—3F 129
Mellish Wlk. M8—6B 74
Mellor Brow. OL10—3E 31
Mellor Clo. M16—2B 100
Mellor Clo. OL6—2C 92
Mellor Ct. SK2—4E 133
Mellor Dri. BL9—6B 28
Mellor Dri. M28—2E 69
Mellor Gro. BL1—4F 23
(in two parts)
Mellor Ho. OL2—3C 48
(off Royton Hall Wlk.)
Mellor Rd. OL6—3C 92
(in two parts)
Mellor Rd. SK8—4D 142
Mellors Rd. M17—6B 84
Mellor St. M10—2H 87 & 2G 163
Mellor St. M25—5D 58
Mellor St. M26—5H 41
(in two parts)
Mellor St. M30—4F 83
Mellor St. M32—3E 99
Mellor St. M35—4H 89
(Droylsden)
Mellor St. M35—5D 76
(Failsworth)
Mellor St. OL2—2B 48
Mellor St. OL4—3A 66
Mellor St. OL8—1A 78
Mellor St. OL11 & OL12—3F 19
Mellor Way. OL9—5H 63
Mellowdew St. OL1—3A 50
Mellowstone Dri. M21—1D 116
Melloy Pl. M8—1E 87
Melmerby Ct. M5—4F 85
Melrose. OL12—3G 19
(off Spotland Rd.)
Melrose Av. BL1—4E 23
Melrose Av. BL8—2A 28
Melrose Av. M20—6G 117
Melrose Av. M30—1C 82
Melrose Av. M33—5B 114
Melrose Av. OL10—2E 31
Melrose Av. OL15—2E 9
Melrose Av. SK3—4B 130
Melrose Clo. M25—5D 42
Melrose Ct. OL9—5G 63
Melrose Cres. SK3—1F 143
Melrose Cres. WA15—4B 138
Melrose Gdns. M26—2E 41
Melrose Rd. BL3—4H 39

Melrose Rd. M26—2E 41
Melrose St. BL9—1B 14
Melrose St. OL1—6F 49
Melrose St. OL11—4F 19
Melsomby Rd. M23—1G 127
Meltham Av. M20—3E 117
Meltham Clo. SK4—2A 130
Meltham Pl. BL3—3G 37
Meltham Rd. SK4—2A 130
Melton Av. M31—4H 95
Melton Av. M34—4A 104
Melton Clo. M28—1E 69
Melton Clo. OL10—4D 30
Melton Dri. BL9—2E 43
Melton St. M7—2A 74
Melton St. M9—2H 75
Melton St. M26—3F 41
Melton St. OL10—4D 30
Melton St. SK5—5H 119
Melverley Rd. M9—4C 60
Melville Clo. M11—6G 89
Melville Rd. BL4—3H 55
Melville Rd. M30—4A 110
Melville Rd. M32—4B 98
Melville St. BL3—3C 38
Melville St. M3—3B 86 & 4D 160
Melville St. OL4—4A 66
Melville St. OL6—2H 91
Melville St. OL11—5G 21
Melvin Av. M22—1C 140
Memorial Rd. M28—1F 69
Menai Gro. SK8—5C 130
Menai Rd. SK3—5G 131
Menai St. BL3—3F 37
Mendip Av. M22—1D 140
Mendip Clo. BL2—6A 26
Mendip Clo. OL2—4A 48
Mendip Clo. OL9—4H 63
Mendip Clo. SK4—6G 119
Mendip Clo. SK8—6F 141
Mendip Ct. SK4—6G 119
Mendip Cres. BL8—2G 27
Mendip Dri. BL2—1A 40
Mendip Dri. OL16—5G 21
Mendips Clo. OL2—5D 34
Menston Av. M10—2E 77
Mentmore Rd. OL16—4D 20
Mentone Cres. M22—1C 140
Mentone Rd. SK4—6D 118
Mentor St. M13—4B 102
Mercer La. OL11—3A 18
Mercer Rd. M35—3B 90
Mercer Rd. OL10—6F 31
Mercer St. M18—2F 103
Mercer St. M19—6D 102
Merchants Quay. M5—1F 99
Mercian Way. OL6—2H 91
Mercian Way. SK3—4F 131
Mercia St. BL3—2G 37
Mercury Way. M31—2H 97
Mere Av. M6—3E 85
Mere Av. M24—3A 62
Mere Av. M35—5G 89
Mere Clo. M33—6F 115
Mere Clo. M34—4B 104
Mereclough Av. M28—2H 69
Meredew Av. M27—5E 71
Meredith St. BL3—4B 38
Meredith St. M14—2H 117
Mere Dri. M20—5F 117
Mere Dri. M27—1G 71
Merefield Rd. WA15—6C 126
Merefield Ter. OL11—6G 19
Mere Fold. M28—6D 54
Mere Gdns. BL1—5A 24
Merehall Clo. BL1—5A 24
Merehall Dri. BL1—4A 24
Merehall St. BL1—4H 23
Mereland Av. M20—5G 117
Mere La. OL11—6H 19
Merepool Clo. SK6—4B 134
Mere Side. SK15—1D 92
(in four parts)
Mereside Clo. SK8—1B 142
Mereside Gro. M28—6G 55
Mereside Wlk. M15—1B 100 & 5D 164
Mere St. OL11—5H 19
(in three parts)

Mere, The. OL6—5A 80
Mere, The. SK8—1B 142
Mere Wlk. BL1—5A 24
Merewood Av. M22—5B 128
Merfield Av. OL11—6G 19
Meriden Clo. M26—1F 41
Meriden Gro. BL6—1B 36
Merinall Clo. OL16—4C 20
Meriton Rd. SK9—3G 151
Meriton Wlk. M18—3D 102
Merlewood. BL0—2B 4
Merlewood Av. M19—2E 119
Merlewood Av. M34—4B 90
Merlewood Av. OL3—1F 53
Merlewood Dri. M27—5C 70
Merlin Clo. OL8—3E 79
 (in two parts)
Merlin Clo. OL15—1G 21
Merlin Clo. SK2—5G 133
Merlin Dri. M27—1H 71
Merlin Gro. BL1—4F 23
 (in two parts)
Merlin Rd. M30—3E 95
Merlin Rd. OL16—5F 21
Merlyn Av. M20—5G 117
Merlyn Av. M33—3C 114
Merlyn Av. M34—5E 105
Merlyn Ct. M20—5E 117
Merrick Av. M22—1C 140
Merrick St. OL10—4G 31
Merridale, The. WA15—5A 138
Merridge Wlk. M8—5B 74
Merrill St. M4—4H 87 & 5H 163
Merriman Clo. M16—3C 100
Merriman Hall. OL16—1B 20
Merrion St. BL4—5E 39
Merrow Wlk. M1—6F 87
 (off Grosvenor St.)
Merrybent Clo. SK2—6D 132
Merry Bower Rd. M7—3A 74
Merrydale Av. M30—1G 83
Mersey Bank. SK14—2H 109
Merseybank Av. M21—4A 116
Mersey Bank Rd. SK14—3H 109
Mersey Clo. M25—6F 43
Mersey Cres. M20—6B 116
Mersey Dri. M25—6F 43
Mersey Dri. M31—5E 111
Mersey Ho. SK3—4C 130
Mersey Meadows. M20—6D 116
Mersey Rd. M20—6D 116
Mersey Rd. M33—3B 114
Mersey Rd. SK4—1B 130
 (in two parts)
Mersey Rd. N. M35—2G 77
Mersey Sq. M25—6F 43
Mersey Sq. SK1—2G 131
Mersey St. SK1—1A 132
Mersey St. SK1—1A 132
Mersey View. M31—1A 112
Merseyway. SK1—2G 131
Merston Dri. M20—3G 129
Mersy Ct. M33—4E 115
Mersy St. SK1—2H 131
Merton Av. OL8—6B 64
Merton Av. SK6—5G 121
Merton Av. SK7—5F 145
Merton Clo. BL3—2G 37
Merton Dri. M35—4G 89
Merton Gro. OL9—6D 62
Merton Gro. WA15—5B 126
Merton Rd. M25—4G 59
Merton Rd. M33—3A 114
Merton Rd. SK3—4D 130
Merton Rd. SK12—3B 154
Merton St. BL8—2B 28
Merton Wlk. M9—4G 75
 (off Trongate Wlk.)
Merville Av. M10—2H 75
Mervyn Rd. M7—5E 73
Merwell Rd. M31—6A 96
Merwood Av. SK8—5H 141
Merwood Gro. M14—3A 102
Mesnefield Rd. M7—3E 73
 (in two parts)
Mesne Lea Gro. M28—3G 69
Mesne Lea Rd. M28—2G 69
Metcalfe St. OL16—4D 20

Metcalfe Ter. BL2—4D 26
Metfield Pl. BL1—5G 23
Metfield Wlk. M10—1D 76
Methuen St. M12—4D 102
Methwold St. BL3—3G 37
Metroplex Bus. Pk. M5—5E 85
Metropolitan Ho. OL1—3D 64
Mevagissey Wlk. OL4—1G 65
Mews, The. M10—2B 88
Mews, The. M25—6F 59
Mews, The. M33—6C 114
Mews, The. SK8—6F 129
Meyer St. SK3—5H 131
Meyrick Rd. M6—2G 85
Miall St. OL11—5H 19
Micawber Rd. SK12—5E 155
Michaels Hey Pde. M23—3C 126
Michael St. M24—1H 61
Michael Wife La. BL0—1H 4
Michigan Av. M5—5F 85
Mickleby Wlk. M10—2H 87 & 2G 163
Micklehurst Av. M20—5C 116
Micklehurst Grn. SK2—6E 133
Micklehurst Rd. OL5—3F 81
Midbrook Wlk. M22—4H 139
Middlebourne St. M6—3E 85
Middlebrook Dri. BL6—1A 36
Middlefell St. SK5—5F 39
Middlefield. OL8—3E 79
Middle Field. OL11—2A 18
Middlefields. SK8—1D 142
Middlegate. M10—6D 62
Middle Ga. OL8—1C 78
Middle Grn. OL6—1A 92
Middleham St. M14—5E 101
Middle Hill. OL12—5F 7
Middle Hillgate. SK1—3H 131
Middle Holly Gro. OL3—4C 52
Middle Rd. M31—1G 97
Middlesex Dri. BL9—5D 28
Middlesex Rd. M9—1F 75
Middlesex Rd. SK5—3B 120
Middlesex Wlk. OL9—3B 64
Middlestone Dri. M9—4F 75
Middle St. OL12—4G 7
Middleton Av. M35—4F 77
Middleton Clo. M26—6F 27
Middleton Dri. BL9—4Q 42
Middleton Gdns. M24—1H 61
Middleton Old Rd. M9—6F 61
Middleton Rd. M8 & M24—2B 74
Middleton Rd. OL2—4H 47
Middleton Rd. OL9—6E 47
Middleton Rd. OL10—5G 31
Middleton Rd. SK5—5H 103
Middleton View. M24—1B 62
Middleton Way. M24—1H 61
Middleway. OL4—4D 66
Middlewich Wlk. M18—2E 103
Middlewood Dri. SK4—2C 130
Middle Wood La. OL12—3C 8
Middlewood Rd. SK12—4G 155
Middlewood St. M5—4A 86 & 6B 160
Middlewood View. SK6—5B 146
Middlewood Wlk. M9—4F 75
Midfield Ct. M7—4A 74
Midford Av. M30—3D 82
Midford Dri. BL1—4C 10
Midford Wlk. M8—5C 74
Midge Hall Dri. OL11—5C 18
Midgley Av. M18—1G 103
Midgley Gro. OL6—1C 92
Midgley St. M27—5D 70
Midgrove. OL3—3H 51
Midgrove La. OL3—4H 51
Midhurst Av. M10—1D 88
Midhurst Clo. BL1—4A 24
Midhurst Clo. SK8—5B 142
Midhurst St. OL11—6H 19
Midhurst Way. OL9—3H 63
Midland Cotts. SK7—4A 146
Midland Rd. SK5—5H 103
Midland Rd. SK7—1G 143
Midland St. M12—6H 87 & 3H 167
Midland Ter. WA14—3F 137

Midland Wlk. SK7—2G 143
 (in two parts)
Midlothian St. M11—3D 88
Midmoor Wlk. M9—6G 61
 (off Levedale Rd.)
Midville Rd. M11—2E 89
Midway. SK8—2D 152
Midway. SK12—5D 154
Milan St. M7—5A 74
Milbourne Rd. BL9—5F 15
Milburn Av. M23—1H 127
Milburn Dri. BL2—5H 25
Milbury Dri. OL15—1G 21
Milden Clo. M20—5G 117
Mildred Av. M25—1G 73
Mildred Av. OL2—5C 48
Mildred Av. OL4—4D 66
Mildred St. M7—6G 73
Mile End La. SK2—6B 132
Mile La. BL8—4F 27
Miles St. BL4—1E 55
Miles St. M12—6C 88
Miles St. OL1—1F 65
Miles St. SK14—5D 106
Milford Clo. M28—4F 55
Milford Brow. OL4—2A 66
Milford Cres. OL15—3F 9
Milford Dri. M19—2D 118
Milford Gro. SK2—4C 132
Milford Rd. BL2—1H 25
Milford Rd. BL3—4A 38
Milford St. M6—3E 85
Milford St. M9—5D 60
Milking La. BL3—5G 37
Milkstone Pl. OL11—5H 19
Milkstone Rd. OL11—5H 19
 (in two parts)
Milk St. BL0—4D 4
Milk St. M2—4E 87 & 5A 162
Milk St. OL4—2G 65
Milk St. OL11—5H 19
Milk St. SK14—5B 106
Milkwood Gro. M18—3F 103
Millais St. M10—3A 76
Millard St. OL9—2G 63
Millard Wlk. M18—3F 103
Millbank Ct. OL10—3D 30
Millbank St. M1—4G 87 & 6E 163
Millbank St. OL10—3D 30
Millbeck Ct. M24—5F 45
Millbeck Gro. BL3—3A 38
Millbeck Rd. M24—5F 45
Millbrook Av. M34—5D 104
Millbrook Bank. OL11—2H 17
Millbrook Gro. SK9—6H 151
Millbrook Ho. BL4—1G 55
Mill Brook Ind. Est. M23—5E 127
Millbrook Rd. M23—3E 127
Millbrook St. SK1—3H 131
Millbrook Towers. SK1—3H 131
Mill Brow. M9—1E 75
Mill Brow. M28—5H 69
Mill Brow. OL1—5G 47
Mill Brow. OL6—2G 79
Mill Brow. SK6—3H 135
Mill Brow Rd. SK6—3H 135
Millbrow Ter. OL1—5G 47
Mill Ct. M31—5G 97
Mill Croft. BL1—5H 23
Millcroft. OL2—1G 49
Mill Croft Clo. OL11—1G 17
Millerhouse. OL2—2F 49
Miller Rd. OL8—6C 64
Millers Brook Clo. OL10—2F 31
Millers Clo. M33—6G 115
Miller's Ct. M5—3A 84
Millers St. M30—3E 83
Miller St. M4—2E 87 & 2A 162
Miller St. M26—1F 41
Miller St. OL6—1H 91
Miller St. OL10—3F 31
Millet St. BL0—2F 5
Millett St. BL9—3B 28
Millfield Dri. M28—5D 68

Millfield Gro. OL16—5B 20
Millfield Rd. BL2—6A 26
Millfield Wlk. M10—1C 76
Millfold. OL12—3H 7
Mill Fold Rd. M24—1H 61
Millford Av. M31—5A 96
 (in two parts)
Millford Gdns. M31—5A 96
Millford St. OL12—2H 19
Millgate. BL7—1B 10
Millgate. OL3—3H 51
Mill Ga. OL8—6B 64
Mill Ga. OL16—1B 20
Millgate. SK1—1H 131
Millgate Cen. OL3—3H 51
Millgate La. M20—2F 129
 (in two parts)
Millgate Ter. OL12—1H 7
Mill Gro. St. M12—5H 87 & 2G 167
Millhall Clo. M15—2C 100
Millhead Av. M10—3A 88
Mill Hill. M28—3A 54
Mill Hill Av. SK7—6D 144
Mill Hill Caravan Pk. BL1—5C 24
 (off Mill Hill St.)
Mill Hill Gro. SK14—5B 108
Mill Hill Hollow. SK12—6D 144
Mill Hill St. BL2—5C 24
Mill Hill Ter. BL2—5C 24
Mill Hill Way. SK14—5B 108
Millhouse Av. M23—1G 139
Mill Ho. Clo. OL12—5B 8
Millington Wlk. M15—1B 100
 (off Shawheath Clo.)
Mill La. BL2—5C 24
Mill La. BL8—1H 27
Mill La. M22—2C 128
Mill La. M34 & SK14—6H 105
Mill La. M35—4C 76
Mill La. OL2—3A 48
Mill La. OL3—6F 51
Mill La. OL5—1E 81
Mill La. OL9—3H 91
Mill La. OL9—5A 64
Mill La. SK5—6H 103
 (North Reddish)
Mill La. SK5—2A 120
 (Reddish Vale)
Mill La. SK6—4G 133
 (Chadkirk)
Mill La. SK6—4G 121
 (off Hyde Rd)
Mill La. SK6—3G 121
 (off Lambeth Gro., in two parts)
Mill La. SK7—5F 145
Mill La. SK8—5H 129
 (Cheadle)
Mill La. SK8—2D 142
 (Cheadle Hulme)
Mill La. WA15—3D 148
Millom Av. M23—2H 127
Millom Clo. OL16—2C 20
Millom Ct. WA15—5D 126
Millom Dri. BL9—5E 43
Millom Pl. SK8—2F 141
Millow St. M4—2E 87 & 2A 162
Millpool Wlk. M9—3F 75
 (off Alderside Rd.)
Millrise. OL1—1C 64
Mill Rd. BL9—3F 15
Mill Rd. SK9—2E 159
Mills Hill Rd. M24—6D 46
Mills St. M25—1D 58
Mills St. OL10—3D 30
Mills St. OL12—4H 7
Millstone Clo. SK12—2F 155
Millstone Rd. BL1—4D 22
Millstream La. M10—1G 89
Mill St. BL0—5C 4
Mill St. BL1—6C 24
Mill St. BL4—1E 55
Mill St. BL7—3D 10
Mill St. M6—1G 85
Mill St. M11—2B 88
Mill St. M26—5H 41
 (in two parts)
Mill St. M28—4C 68
 (Boothstown)

Mill St. M28—3A 54
(Greenheys)
Mill St. M35—4D 76
Mill St. OL2—3B 48
Mill St. OL3—1F 53
Mill St. OL5—2E 49
Mill St. OL15—6D 8
Mill St. SK6—4G 121
(in two parts)
Mill St. SK7—2D 144
Mill St. SK9—2E 159
Mill St. SK14—2C 106
Mill St. SK15—4G 93
Mill St. WA14—6G 125
Milltown Clo. M26—5H 41
Milltown St. M26—5H 41
Millview. OL3—3C 52
Millwall Clo. M18—2F 103
Millway. WA15—6C 138
Millway Wlk. M10—6C 76
Millwood Ct. BL9—1D 42
Millwood View. SK15—3F 93
Millwright St. M10—6B 76
Mill Yd. BL9—2E 29
Milly St. M31—5E 97
Milne Clo. M12—1C 102
Milner Av. BL9—6F 15
Milner Av. WA14—4D 124
Milner St. M16—3B 100
Milner St. M26—4E 41
Milner St. M27—3F 71
Milner St. OL12—1C 6
Milne St. OL1—5E 49
Milne St. OL2—1F 49
Milne St. OL9—6A 48
(Busk)
Milne St. OL9—2H 63
(Chadderton)
Milne St. OL9—4A 64
(Oldham)
Milne St. OL11—3C 32
Milnrow Clo. M13—6F 87 & 3D 166
Milnrow Rd. OL2—6F 35
Milnrow Rd. OL15—1F 21
Milnrow Rd. OL16—4H 19
Milnthorpe Rd. BL2—5G 25
Milnthorpe St. M6—6F 73
Milnthorpe Way. M12—1A 102
Milo St. M9—6F 61
Milsom Av. BL3—4G 37
Milstead Wlk. M10—6A 76
Milton Av. BL3—4F 37
(Bolton)
Milton Av. BL3—3B 40
(Little Lever)
Milton Av. M5—3D 84
Milton Av. M30—3C 110
Milton Av. M35—4A 90
Milton Av. SK15—1H 93
Milton Clo. M32—4E 99
Milton Clo. SK6—1D 146
Milton Clo. SK16—6F 93
(in two parts)
Milton Ct. M7—2A 74
Milton Cres. BL4—3D 54
Milton Cres. SK8—6G 129
Milton Dri. M33—3A 114
Milton Dri. M33—3G 63
Milton Dri. SK12—3D 154
Milton Dri. WA15—2A 126
Milton Gro. M16—5A 100
Milton Gro. M33—3A 114
Milton Mt. M18—3F 103
Milton Pl. M6—2H 85
Milton Rd. M25—4D 40
Milton Rd. M25—3D 40
Milton Rd. M27—2D 70
Milton Rd. M32—4E 99
Milton Rd. M34—4D 90
Milton Rd. SK7—6G 143
Milton St. BL0—3D 4
Milton St. BL8—2B 28
Milton St. M7—1C 86
Milton St. M24—6H 45
Milton St. M30—3F 83
Milton St. M34—3E 105
Milton St. OL2—2C 48
Milton St. OL5—1E 81

Milton St. OL16—3H 19
Milton St. SK14—3B 106
Milton View. OL5—1E 81
Milverton Av. SK14—5G 107
Milverton Clo. BL6—2B 36
Milverton Dri. SK7—2D 152
Milverton Rd. M14—3H 101
Milverton Wlk. SK14—5G 107
Milwain Dri. SK4—3E 119
Milwain Rd. M19—1B 118
Milwain Rd. M32—6C 98
Mimosa Dri. M27—1F 71
Mincing St. M4—2E 87 & 2B 162
Minden Clo. BL8—3H 27
Minden Clo. M20—5G 117
Minden Pde. BL9—3D 28
Minden St. M6—5C 72
Minehead Av. M20—2D 116
Minehead Av. M31—1D 112
Minerva Rd. BL4—6B 38
Minerva Rd. OL6—3A 92
Minerva Ter. BL2—6D 24
Minerva Ter. OL15—4E 9
(off William St.)
Mine St. OL10—1E 31
Minford Clo. M10—5B 76
Minnie St. BL3—4G 37
Minnie St. OL12—3H 7
Minoan Gdns. M7—6G 73
Minorca Av. M11—3F 89
Minorca Clo. OL11—3A 18
Minorca St. BL3—3A 38
Minor St. M35—3G 77
(in two parts)
Minor St. OL8—4C 64
Minor St. OL11—4C 32
Minshull St. M1—4E 87 & 6B 162
Minshull St. S. M1—5F 87 & 1C 166
Minsmere. SK2—6F 133
Minsmere Wlk. M8—5B 74
(off Alderford Pde.)
Minstead Wlk. M22—3H 139
Minster Clo. BL2—3E 25
Minster Dri. SK8—6C 130
Minsterley Pde. M22—4A 140
Minster Rd. BL2—3E 25
Minster Way. OL9—6G 47
Minton St. OL4—4E 65
Minto St. OL7—1G 91
(in two parts)
Mintridge Clo. M11—6G 89
Mint St. BL0—3A 4
Mirabel St. M3—2D 86 & 2G 161
Miranda Ct. M5—5A 86 & 2B 164
Mirfield Av. M9—5F 61
Mirfield Av. OL8—5C 64
Mirfield St. SK4—1D 130
Mirfield Dri. M24—6H 45
Mirfield Dri. M30—1F 83
Mirfield Dri. M31—3E 97
Mirfield Rd. M9—5F 61
Miriam St. BL3—3F 37
Miriam St. M35—5D 76
Mission St. OL10—3E 31
Missouri Av. M5—4E 85
Mistletoe Grn. M3—2B 86 & 2D 160
Mistral Ct. M7—2G 73
Mitcham Av. M9—6A 62
Mitchell Gdns. M22—1C 140
Mitchell Hey. OL12—4G 19
Mitchell St. BL8—1A 28
Mitchell St. M10—6B 76
Mitchell St. M24—6H 45
Mitchell St. M30—2E 83
Mitchell St. OL1—1B 64
Mitchell St. OL12—3F 19
Mitchell St. OL16—6A 8
Mitcheson Gdns. M6—2F 85
Mitford Ct. M14—2G 117
Mitford Rd. M14—2G 117
Mitford St. M32—6C 98
Mitre Rd. M13—3B 102
Mitre St. BL1—1A 24
Mitre St. BL8—2B 28
Mitton Clo. BL8—3E 27
Mitton Clo. OL10—3B 30

Mizpah Gro. BL8—3H 27
Mizzy Rd. OL12—2G 19
Moadlock. SK6—5A 122
Moat Av. M22—6A 128
Moat Gdns. M22—1A 140
Moat Hall Av. M30—5C 82
Moat Rd. M22—1A 140
Moat Wlk. S05—2C 120
Mobberley Clo. M19—5A 118
Mobberley Rd. BL2—5F 25
Mocha Pde. M7—2B 86
Modbury Clo. SK7—4A 144
Modbury Wlk. M8—5C 74
Mode Hill La. M25—1G 59
Mode Hill Wlk. M25—1G 59
Mode Wheel Rd. M6—5C 84
Mode Wheel Rd. S. M5—5D 84
Moelfre Dri. SK8—6E 143
Moffat Clo. BL2—1H 39
Moffat Ct. SK16—4H 91
Moisant St. BL3—4H 37
Mold St. BL1—2A 24
Mold St. OL1—1C 64
Molesworth St. OL1—1E 65
Molesworth St. OL16—4A 20
Mollets Wood. M34—2G 105
Mollington Rd. M22—5C 140
Molyneux Rd. M19—6E 103
Molyneux St. OL12—3F 19
Mona Av. M32—4C 98
Mona Av. SK8—4H 141
Monaco Dri. M22—1B 128
Monarch Trading Est. M17—1F 99
Monart Rd. M9—2G 75
Mona St. BL1—3A 24
Mona St. M6—1G 85
Mona St. SK14—5C 106
Moncrieffe St. BL3—2C 38
Monde Trading Est. M17—1A 98
Mond Rd. M30—3F 95
Money Ash Rd. WA15—2F 137
Monfa Av. SK2—1A 144
Monica Av. M8—6B 60
Monica Ct. M30—2H 83
Monica Gro. M19—1B 118
Monks Clo. M8—1D 74
Monk's Ct. M5—3B 84
Monksdale Av. M31—5D 96
Monks Hall Gro. M30—2H 83
Monks La. BL2—3F 25
Monkswood. OL1—2C 64
Monkton Av. M18—3E 103
Monkwood Dri. M9—3G 75
Monmouth Av. BL9—6F 15
Monmouth Av. M24—6C 46
Monmouth St. M24—6C 46
Monmouth St. OL11—5H 19
Monsal Av. M7—4E 73
Monsal Av. SK2—4D 132
Monsall Clo. BL9—5E 43
Monsall Rd. M10—5G 75
Monsall St. M10—5G 75
Monsall St. OL8—6C 64
Mons Av. OL11—3E 19
Monsanto St. M33—5C 114
Montagu Ho. SK3—3F 131
(off East St.)
Montague Rd. M16—2G 99
Montague Rd. M33—5B 114
Montague Rd. OL6—3B 92
Montague St. BL3—4F 37
Montague Way. SK15—3E 93
Montagu Rd. SK2—4D 132
Montagu St. SK6—1F 135
Montana Sq. M11—6G 89
Montcliffe Cres. M16—6D 100
Monteagle St. M9—6F 61
Montford St. M5—4F 85
Montgomery. OL11—5G 19
Montgomery Dri. BL9—5F 43
Montgomery Rd. M13—5B 102
Montgomery St. OL8—1H 77
Montgomery Way. M26—2C 40
Monton Av. M30—2G 83
Monton Fields Rd. M30—2E 83
Monton Grn. M30—1E 83

Monton La. M30—3G 83
Montonmill Gdns. M30—2E 83
Monton Rd. M30—2F 83
(in two parts)
Monton Rd. SK5—5C 120
Monton St. BL3—4A 38
Monton St. M14—3E 101
(in two parts)
Monton St. M26—4F 41
Montpellier Rd. M22—3B 140
Montreal St. M19—6D 102
Montreal St. OL8—5D 64
Montrose. M30—3G 83
(off St Andrews Ct.)
Montrose Av. BL0—1A 14
Montrose Av. BL2—4E 25
Montrose Av. M20—4E 117
Montrose Av. M32—5B 98
Montrose Av. SK2—2A 144
Montrose Av. SK16—6A 92
Montrose Dri. BL7—4F 11
Montrose Gdns. OL2—3D 48
Montrose Ho. OL8—5D 64
Montrose St. OL11—4C 32
Montserrat Brow. BL1—3B 22
Montserrat Rd. BL1—3C 22
Monyash St. SK13—6F 109
(off Monyash M.)
Monyash Gro. SK13—6F 109
(off Monyash M.)
Monyash Lea. SK13—6F 109
(off Monyash M.)
Monyash M. SK13—6F 109
Monyash Pl. SK13—6F 109
(off Monyash M.)
Monyash Way. SK13—6G 109
(off Ashford M.)
Moon Gro. M14—4H 101
Moon St. OL9—2A 64
Moor Bank La. OL16—1B 34
Moorbottom Rd. BL8—3A 4
Moorby Av. M19—5A 118
Moorby St. OL1—1E 65
Moorby Wlk. BL3—2B 38
Moor Clo. M26—2E 41
Moorclose St. M24—1C 62
Moorclose Wlk. M9—4F 75
(off Heathersett Dri.)
Mcorcock Av. M27—3H 71
Moor Cres. BL3—3C 52
Moorcroft. BL0—3A 4
Moorcroft. OL11—2F 33
Moorcroft Dri. M19—5B 118
Moorcroft Rd. M23—2F 127
Moorcroft Sq. SK14—1C 106
Moorcroft St. M35—4A 90
Moorcroft St. OL8—1A 78
Moorcroft Wlk. M19—5A 118
Moordale Av. OL4—6A 50
Moordale St. M20—4E 117
Moordown Clo. M8—5D 74
Moor Edge Rd. OL5 & OL3—1H 81
Mooredge Ter. OL2—5C 48
Moore Ho. M30—5F 83
Moor End. M22—3B 128
Moor End Av. M7—3G 73
Moor End Ct. M7—3G 73
Moore St. OL16—4H 19
Moore Wlk. M34—2G 121
Moorfield. M7—2G 73
Moorfield. M28—4B 68
(Mosley Common)
Moorfield. M28—3H 69
(Worsley)
Moorfield Av. M14—2G 117
Moorfield Av. M34—6G 105
Moorfield Av. OL15—2E 9
Moorfield Av. SK15—6H 93
Moorfield Clo. M27—5D 70
Moorfield Clo. M30—4F 83
(Eccles)
Moorfield Clo. M30—4F 95
(Irlam)
Moorfield Dri. SK9—4B 158
Moorfield Dri. SK14—2C 106
Moorfield Gro. BL2—4D 24
Moorfield Gro. M33—6C 114
Moorfield Gro. SK4—5D 118

Moorfield Pde. M30—4F 95
Moorfield Pl. OL12—2G 19
Moorfield Rd. M6—1D 84
Moorfield Rd. M20—5D 116
Moorfield Rd. M27—5C 70
Moorfield Rd. M30—4F 95
Moorfield Rd. OL8—1H 77
Moorfield St. M20—2F 117
(in two parts)
Moorfield St. OL2—6F 35
Moorfield St. SK14—2F 109
Moorfield Ter. SK14—2F 109
Moorfield Ter. SK15—4G 81
Moorfield View. OL15—3E 9
Moorfield Wlk. M31—5F 97
Moorgate. BL2—6H 11
Moorgate. BL9—2D 28
Moorgate Av. M20—2D 116
Moorgate Av. OL11—4C 58
Moorgate Ct. BL2—4D 24
Moorgate Dri. SK15—5G 81
Moor Ga. La. OL15—2C 8
Moorgate Rd. M26—5E 27
Moorgate Rd. SK15—5G 81
Moorgate St. OL3—1F 53
Moorhead St. M4—2F 87 & 2D 162
Moorhey Rd. M28—3B 54
(in two parts)
Moorhey St. OL4—3F 65
Moor Hill. OL11—2B 18
Moorhill Ct. M7—2G 73
Moorhouse Fold. OL16—5E 21
Moorings, The. M28—6A 70
Moorland Av. M8—1B 74
Moorland Av. M33—6C 114
Moorland Av. M35—4G 89
Moorland Av. OL11—3B 18
Moorland Av. OL12—2C 6
Moorland Av. OL16—5G 21
Moorland Cres. OL12—2C 6
Moorland Dri. M28—3B 54
Moorland Dri. SK8—5B 142
Moorland Gro. BL1—3E 23
Moorland Rd. M20—6F 117
Moorland Rd. SK2—1B 144
(in two parts)
Moorland Rd. SK15—6G 81
Moorlands Av. M31—4D 96
Moorlands Cres. OL5—2F 81
Moorlands Rd. OL5—6G 67
Moorland St. OL2—6F 35
Moorland St. OL12—2G 19
Moorland St. OL15—2G 9
Moorlands View. BL3—5E 37
Moorland Ter. OL12—2C 18
Moor La. BL3 & BL1—1A 38
Moor La. M7—3D 72
Moor La. M23—1G 127
Moor La. M31—4C 96
Moor La. OL3—5C 52
Moor La. OL12—1B 18
Moor La. SK7—3F 153
Moor La. SK9—4A 158
Moor Nook. M33—6D 114
Moor Pk. Av. OL11—3B 32
Moor Pk. Rd. M20—2G 129
Moor Rd. BL8—3C 4
Moor Rd. M23—2E 127
Moor Rd. OL15—6G 9
Moorsbrook Gro. SK9—6A 152
Moorsholme Av. M10—4A 76
Moorside. OL5—2G 81
Moorside. OL11—2F 33
Moorside. OL15—3H 9
Moorside Av. BL1—3E 23
(in two parts)
Moorside Av. BL2—4D 26
Moorside Av. BL4—2D 54
Moorside Av. M35—2C 90
Moorside Av. OL4—3B 50
Moorside Ct. M33—5B 114
Moorside Cres. M35—3C 90
Moorside Ho. WA15—4C 126
Moorside La. M34—3G 105
(in two parts)
Moorside Lodge. M27—3D 70
Moorside Rd. BL8—5G 13
Moorside Rd. M7—2G 73

Moorside Rd. M27—4C 70
Moorside Rd. M31—4A 96
Moorside Rd. SK4—1C 130
Moorside St. M35—3B 90
Moor St. BL9—2D 28
Moor St. M27—4F 71
Moor St. M30—4D 82
Moor St. OL1—2F 65
Moor St. OL2—1E 49
Moor St. OL10—3D 30
Moors View. BL0—3D 4
Moorton Av. M19—2B 118
Moorton Pk. M19—2B 118
Moortop Clo. M9—4E 61
Moor Way. BL8—1D 12
Moorway. SK9—4B 158
Moorway Dri. M9—5A 62
Moorwood Dri. M33—6G 113
Mora Av. OL9—6H 47
Moran Wlk. M15—1D 100 & 6H 165
Morar Dri. BL2—6A 26
Morar Rd. SK16—6B 92
Mora St. M9—3H 75
Moravian Clo. SK16—4A 92
Moravian Field. M35—5A 90
Moray Clo. BL0—5C 4
Moray Rd. OL9—5G 63
Moray Wlk. OL8—5D 64
Morden Av. M11—3E 89
Morecombe Clo. M10—5B 76
Moresby Dri. M20—3B 129
Morestead Wlk. M10—1F 163
Moreton Av. M25—6D 42
Moreton Av. M32—5D 98
Moreton Av. M33—6G 113
Moreton Av. SK7—2G 153
Moreton Dri. BL8—2H 27
Moreton Dri. SK9—4A 152
Moreton La. SK2—4C 132
Moreton St. OL9—1F 63
Moreton Wlk. SK2—4C 132
Morgan Pl. SK15—5H 119
Morgan St. OL15—4F 9
Morillon Rd. M30—3E 95
Morland Rd. M16—3A 100
Morley Av. M14—6E 101
Morley Av. M27—5E 71
Morley Grn. Rd. SK9—5A 150
Morley Ho. M6—2F 85
(off Sutton Dwellings)
Morley Rd. M26—3D 40
Morley St. BL3—1H 37
Morley St. BL9—5D 28
Morley St. M25—1D 58
Morley St. OL4—6A 50
Morley St. OL16—2B 20
Morley Way. OL3—4F 53
Morna Wlk. M12—5H 87 & 1H 167
Morningside Clo. M35—5A 90
Morningside Dri. M20—3G 129
Mornington Av. SK8—1H 141
Mornington Clo. OL1—1C 64
Mornington Cres. M14—1E 117
Mornington Rd. BL1—5F 23
Mornington Rd. M33—4D 114
Mornington Rd. OL11—3F 33
Mornington Rd. SK8—1H 141
Morpeth Clo. OL7—1E 91
Morpeth St. M27—5E 71
Morpeth Wlk. M12—2A 102
Morrell Rd. M22—3B 128
Morris Fold Dri. BL6—1A 36
Morris Grn. BL3—5G 37
Morris Grn. La. BL3—4G 37
Morris Grn. St. BL3—5G 37
Morris Gro. M31—1A 112
Morrison St. BL3—4A 38
Morrison Wlk. M10—6A 76
(off Eldridge Dri.)
Morris St. BL1—6C 24
Morris St. M20—2F 117
Morris St. M26—2C 42
Morris St. OL4—4E 65
Morrowfield Av. M8—4B 74
Morrwell Rd. M22—2C 128
Morse Rd. M10—6B 76

Mortar St. OL4—1G 65
(in two parts)
Mort Ct. BL1—2G 23
Mortfield Gdns. BL1—5H 23
Mortfield La. BL1—5H 23
(in two parts)
Mort Fold. M28—4C 54
Mortimer Av. M9—5G 61
Mortimer St. OL1—6E 49
Mortlake Clo. M28—6B 54
Mortlake Dri. M10—6B 76
Mort La. M29—2A 68
Morton Dri. SK12—3F 155
Morton St. BL2—6C 24
Morton St. M24—5A 46
Morton St. M26—5H 41
Morton St. M35—4C 76
Morton St. OL16—4A 20
Morton St. SK4—5G 119
Morton Ter. SK6—4H 121
Mort St. BL4—1D 54
Morven Av. SK7—2F 145
Morven Dri. M23—6G 127
Morven Gro. M22—6H 25
Morville Rd. M6—6A 72
Morville Rd. M21—6B 100
Moschatel Wlk. M31—6E 111
Moscow Rd. SK3—4F 131
Moscow Rd. E. SK3—4F 131
Mosedale Clo. M23—5E 127
Mosedale Rd. M24—5F 45
Moseldene Rd. SK2—6D 132
Moseley Grange. SK8—2B 142
Moseley Rd. M14 & M19—1H 117
Moseley Rd. SK8—2B 142
Moseley St. SK3—3G 131
Mosley Arc. M1—4E 87
(off Piccadilly Plaza)
Mosley Av. BL0—1B 14
Mosley Av. BL9—6F 15
Mosley Clo. WA15—4H 125
Mosley Comn. Rd. M29 & M28
—3A 68
Mosley Rd. M17—1C 98
Mosley Rd. WA15—5B 126
Mosley Rd. N. M17—6C 84
Mosley Rd. S. WA15—5C 126
Mosley St. M2—4E 87 & 6A 162
Mosley St. M26—2F 41
Mossack Av. M22—4B 140
Moss Av. OL15—5C 20
Moss Bank. M8—3C 74
Moss Bank. OL2—1F 49
Moss Bank. SK6—4G 135
Moss Bank. SK7—2E 153
Moss Bank Av. M35—3C 90
Moss Bank Clo. BL1—1H 23
Mossbank Clo. SK14—3G 109
Moss Bank Gro. M27—1D 70
Mossbank Gro. OL10—2E 31
Moss Bank Rd. M27—1D 70
Moss Bank Trading Est. M28
—5G 55
Moss Bank Way. BL1—4C 22
Mossbray Av. M19—5H 117
Moss Bri. Rd. OL16—6B 20
Mossbrook Dri. M28—3A 54
Moss Brook Rd. M9—4G 75
Moss Clo. M26—2D 40
Moss Clo. OL7—4E 91
Mossclough Ct. M9—4G 75
Moss Colliery Rd. M27—6E 57
Mosscot Clo. M13—6F 87 & 3D 166
Moss Croft Clo. M31—4A 96
Mossdale Rd. M23—2F 127
Mossdale Rd. M33—2G 125
Mossdown Rd. OL2—4E 49
Mossfield Clo. BL9—1G 29
Mossfield Clo. SK4—1D 130
Mossfield Dri. M9—5A 62
Mossfield Grn. M30—3G 95
Mossfield Rd. BL4—1D 54
(Farnworth)
Mossfield Rd. M27—1E 71
Mossfield Rd. WA15—5D 126
Moss Ga. Rd. OL2—5D 34
(in two parts)

Moss Grange Av. M16—3B 100
Moss Grn. M31—3B 112
Moss Gro. BL9—2F 29
Moss Gro. OL2—4C 34
Mossgrove Av. WA15—4H 125
Mossgrove St. OL8—1B 78
Mosshall Clo. M15—1B 100 & 5D 164
Moss Hall Rd. BL9 & OL10—4H 29
Moss Hey Dri. M23—2A 128
Moss Hey St. OL2—1F 49
Moss Ho. La. M28—6B 54
Moss Ind. Est. OL16—6B 20
Mossland Clo. OL10—5F 31
Mossland Gro. BL3—5B 36
Moss La. BL1—2E 23
Moss La. BL4—4B 56
Moss La. M24—4H 61
(in two parts)
Moss La. M25—1D 58
Moss La. M27—1D 70
Moss La. M28—5G 55
(in two parts)
Moss La. M30—4B 110
Moss La. M31—2F 97
Moss La. M31 & WA13—6D 110
Moss La. M33—6F 113
(Sale)
Moss La. M33—1E 125
(Woodhouses)
Moss La. OL2—4E 49
Moss La. OL7—1D 90
(in two parts)
Moss La. OL12—1B 6
Moss La. OL16—5A 20
Moss La. SK7—2D 152
Moss La. SK9—5H 159
(Alderley Edge)
Moss La. SK9—2B 150
(Wilmslow)
Moss La. WA14 & WA15—1F 137
(Altrincham)
Moss La. WA15—4H 125
(Timperley)
Moss La. E. M15 & M14—3C 100
Moss Lane Ind. Est. M25—6D 42
Moss Lane Trading Est. M25
—6E 43
Moss La. W. M15—3B 100
Moss Lea. BL1—1H 23
Mosslee Av. M8—6B 60
Mossley Rd. OL5 & OL4—5F 67
Mossley Rd. OL6—2A 92
Moss Lodge La. OL7—3D 90
Moss Lynn. OL4—2C 66
Moss Manor. M33—6G 113
Moss Meadow Rd. M6—1C 84
Mossmere Rd. SK8—1C 142
Moss Mill St. OL16—6B 20
Moss Nook Ind. Area. M22—5D 140
Moss Pk. Rd. M32—5A 98
Moss Pl. BL9—5C 28
Moss Rd. BL4—2C 55
(in two parts)
Moss Rd. M30—6A 94
Moss Rd. M32—3C 98
Moss Rd. M33—5D 112
Moss Rd. SK9—4H 159
Moss Rose. SK9—4H 159
Moss Row. BL9—4D 28
Moss Row. OL11—2H 17
Moss Shaw Way. M26—2D 40
Moss Side. BL6—6A 14
Moss Side Cres. M15—2D 100
Moss Side La. OL16—6C 20
Moss Side Rd. M30—3B 110
Moss Side Shopping Cen. M15
—2D 100
Moss St. BL4—6G 39
Moss St. BL9—3C 28
(Bury)
Moss St. BL9—1D 14
(Summerseat)
Moss St. M7—6H 73
Moss St. M34—4B 90
Moss St. M35—3B 90
Moss St. OL4—1A 66
Moss St. OL10—3E 31
Moss St. OL16—5B 20

Moss St. SK3—2F 131
Moss St. SK14—2F 109
Moss St. E. OL6—2H 91
Moss St. W. OL7—3F 91
Moss Ter. OL6—3G 91
Moss Ter. OL6—5B 20
Moss, The. M24—3B 62
Moss Vale Cres. M32—3H 97
Moss Vale Rd. M31—5G 97
Moss Vale Rd. M32—4H 97
Moss View Rd. BL2—5G 25
Moss View Rd. M31—6E 111
Mossway. M24—4H 61
Moss Way. SK5—3G 113
Mosswood Clo. M20—3F 129
Moston Bk. Av. M9—4G 75
Moston La. M9—3F 75
Moston La. M10—3A 76
Moston La. E. M10—1E 77
Moston Rd. M24—3D 62
Moston St. M8—4B 74
Moston St. SK5—2H 119
Mostyn Av. M14—1A 118
Mostyn Av. SK8—3A 142
Mostyn St. SK7—4B 144
Mostyn St. SK15 & SK16—5D 92
Motcombe Farm Rd. SK8—4F 141
Motcombe Gro. SK8—2E 141
Motcombe Rd. SK8—3E 141
Motherwell Av. M19—6C 102
Motive St. BL3—1A 38
Motlow Wlk. M23—3D 126
Motor St. M3—4D 86 & 5G 161
Mottershead Av. BL3—3A 40
Mottershead Rd. M22—2H 139
Mottram Av. M21—4A 116
Mottram Clo. SK8—6C 130
Mottram Dri. WA15—6A 126
Mottram Fold. SK1—3H 131
Mottram Moor. SK14—3C 108
Mottram Old Rd. SK14—1D 122
Mottram Old Rd. SK15—4G 93
Mottram Rd. M33—6E 115
Mottram Rd. SK9—5H 159
Mottram Rd. SK14—6B 108
  (Broadbottom)
Mottram Rd. SK14—5C 106
  (Hyde)
Mottram St. SK15—3F 93
Mottram St. SK1—3H 131
Mottram Towers. SK1—3H 131
Mottram Way. SK1—3H 131
  (off Mottram Fold)
Mough La. OL9—6D 62
Mouldsworth Av. M20—2E 117
Mouldsworth Av. SK4—3F 119
Moulton St. M8—1C 86
Moulton St. Precinct. M8—1C 86
Mountain Ash. OL12—6B 6
Mountain Ash M33—4E 113
Mountain Ash Clo. OL12—6B 6
Mountain Gro. M28—5E 55
Mountain La. M20—1F 89
Mountain St. M28—5E 55
Mountain St. OL5—2E 81
Mountain St. SK1—1A 132
Mount Av. OL12—5C 8
Mount Av. OL15—2E 9
Mountbatten Av. SK16—6D 92
Mountbatten Ct. BL3—5F 43
Mountbatten St. M18—2E 103
Mt. Carmel Ct. M5—6A 86
  (off Mt. Carmel Cres.)
Mt. Carmel Cres. M5—6A 86 & 3A 164
Mount Clo. OL7—4G 91
Mount Dri. M31—5H 97
Mount Dri. SK6—6D 134
Mountfield. M25—5F 59
Mountfield Ind. Pk. M25—2F 73
Mountfield Rd. SK3—4E 131
Mountfield Rd. SK7—2G 153
Mountfield Wlk. BL1—4A 24
  (in two parts)
Mountfield Wlk. M11—4B 88
  (off Hopedale Clo.)
Mountford Av. M8—1B 74
Mount Gro. SK8—5D 128

Mount La. OL3—6G 51
Mount Pl. OL12—3G 19
Mt. Pleasant. BL3—2E 39
Mt. Pleasant. M24—1E 61
  (in two parts)
Mt. Pleasant. M25—1A 60
Mt. Pleasant. SK3—3G 41
Mt. Pleasant. SK2—5G 133
Mt. Pleasant. SK6—6F 123
  (Compstall)
Mt. Pleasant SK6—4H 121
  (Woodley)
Mt. Pleasant. SK7—2D 144
Mt. Pleasant. SK9—6F 151
Mt. Pleasant Rd. BL4—1B 54
Mt. Pleasant Rd. M34—5F 105
Mt. Pleasant St. M34—6F 91
  (in two parts)
Mt. Pleasant St. OL4—2F 65
Mt. Pleasant St. OL6—1A 92
  (in two parts)
Mt. Pleasant Wlk. M26—3G 41
  (in two parts)
Mount Rd. M18 & M19—3E 103
Mount Rd. M24—2H 61
Mount Rd. M25—2F 59
Mount Rd. SK4—1E 131
Mount St. SK14—3E 123
Mountroyal Clo. SK14—2E 107
Mount St Joseph's Rd. BL3—2F 37
Mountside Clo. OL12—1H 19
Mountside Cres. M25—5D 58
Mt. Sion Rd. M26—5E 41
Mt. Skip La. M28—5C 54
Mount St. BL0—2D 4
Mount St. BL1—4A 24
Mount St. M2—5D 86 & 1H 165
  (in two parts)
Mount St. M3—2B 86 & 2D 160
Mount St. M7—5H 73
Mount St. M27—4F 71
Mount St. M30—5E 83
Mount St. M34—6H 105
Mount St. OL2—4C 46
  (Royton)
Mount St. OL2—6D 34
  (Shaw)
Mount St. OL10—4F 31
Mount St. OL11—4C 32
Mount St. OL12—3G 19
Mount St. SK14—5C 106
Mount St. SK15—3E 93
Mount Ter. BL9—2D 42
Mount Ter. M35—2G 89
Mount Ter. WA14—1F 137
  (off Central Way)
Mount, The. M7—3G 73
Mount, The. OL6—2B 92
Mount, The. SK5—5B 120
Mount, The. WA14—6F 125
Mount, The. WA15—5C 138
Mt. View. OL3—1E 53
Mount View Rd. OL2—1G 49
Mt. Zion Rd. BL9—2D 42
Mousell St. M8—1E 87
Mouselow Clo. SK14—4H 109
Mowbray Av. M25—1G 73
Mowbray Av. M33—6C 114
Mowbray St. BL1—4F 23
Mowbray St. OL1—3D 64
Mowbray St. OL7—3G 91
Mowbray St. OL11—2B 32
Mowbray St. SK1—3H 131
Mowbray Wlk. M24—5G 45
Mow Halls La. OL3—6A 52
Moxley Rd. M8—2A 74
Moyse Av. BL8—6H 13
Mozart Clo. M4—3G 87 & 3F 163
Mudhurst La. SK12—6H 157
Muirfield Av. M26—5G 121
Muirfield Clo. M10—3C 76
Muirfield Clo. M25—4F 59
Muirfield Clo. OL10—4F 31
Muirfield Clo. SK9—1G 159
Muirhead Ct. M6—6E 73
Mulberry Av. OL10—6B 30
Mulberry Clo. OL10—6B 30
Mulberry Clo. OL11—6G 19

Mulberry Clo. SK8—6G 141
Mulberry Clo. M6—2G 85
Mulberry M. SK4—1G 131
Mulberry Mt. St. SK3—3G 131
Mulberry Rd. M6—2G 85
Mulberry St. M2—4D 86 & 6G 161
Mulberry St. OL6—2A 92
Mulberry Wlk. M33—3F 113
Mulberry Wlk. M35—5G 89
Mulberry Way. OL10—6B 30
Mule St. BL2—5C 24
Mulgrave Rd. M28—3A 70
Mulgrave St. BL3—5G 37
Mulgrave St. M27—2D 70
Mulgrove Wlk. M9—6G 61
  (off Haverfield Rd.)
Mullacre Rd. M22—5B 128
Mull Av. M12—2B 102
Mulliner St. BL1—4B 24
Mullineux St. M28—1F 69
Mullion Dri. WA15—4G 125
Mullion Wlk. M8—5D 74
Mulmount Clo. OL8—4B 64
Mumps. OL1—2E 65
Munday St. M4—4H 87 & 5G 163
Munford Wlk. M10—6G 75
  (off Lodge St.)
Municipal Clo. OL10—3F 31
  (off Longford St.)
Munn Rd. M9—4D 60
Munro Av. M22—3D 140
Munslow Wlk. M9—5H 61
Munster St. M4—2E 87 &
                    2A 162
Muriel St. M7—6H 73
Muriel St. OL10—3G 31
Muriel St. OL16—6B 20
Murieston Rd. M15—3G 137
Murrayfield. OL11—5A 18
Murray Rd. BL9—3D 28
Murray St. M4—3F 87 & 4D 162
Murray St. M7—5H 73
Murrow Wlk. M9—3F 75
Murton Ter. BL1—1B 24
  (off Holly St.)
Musbury Av. M20—3A 130
Muscari Wlk. M12—6G 87 &
                    3E 167
Musden Wlk. SK4—2F 119
Museum St. M2—5D 86 & 1G 165
Musgrave Gdns. BL1—5G 23
Musgrave Rd. BL1—5F 23
Musgrave Rd. M22—2B 140
Muslin St. M5—4A 86 & 6B 160
Muter Av. M22—3D 140
Mutual St. OL10—2G 31
Myford Wlk. M8—6A 74
Myrescroft Clo. M10—2E 77
Myrrh St. BL1—2A 24
Myrrh Wlk. BL1—2A 24
  (off Myrrh St.)
Myrtle Bank. M25—2E 73
Myrtle Clo. OL8—4C 64
Myrtle Gdns. BL9—3F 29
Myrtle Gro. M25—1F 73
  (Prestwich)
Myrtle Gro. M25—5B 42
  (Whitefield)
Myrtle Gro. M34—4H 103
Myrtle Gro. M35—3C 90
Myrtleleaf Gro. M5—3D 84
Myrtle Pl. M7—1A 86
Myrtle Rd. M24—5C 46
Myrtle Rd. M31—6B 110
Myrtle St. BL1—5H 23
Myrtle St. BL9—3F 29
Myrtle St. M11—5A 88
Myrtle St. M16—3A 100
Myrtle St. OL10—4G 31
Myrtle St. SK3—3D 130
Myrtle St. S. BL9—3F 29
My St. M5—4E 85
Mytham Gdns. BL3—5B 40
Mytham Rd. BL3—4B 40
Mytholme Av. M30—6A 110
Mythorn Wlk. M10—6A 76
  (off Harmer Clo.)
Mytton Rd. BL1—1F 23

Nabbs Fold. BL8—6B 4
Nabbs Way. BL8—2A 14
Naburn Clo. SK5—3C 120
Naburn St. M13—3H 101
Nada Lodge. M8—2B 74
Nada Rd. M8—2B 74
Naden Wlk. M25—1E 59
Nadine St. M6—2E 85
Nadin St. OL8—6C 64
Nailsworth Wlk. M13—2G 101
  (off Plymouth Gro.)
Nairn Wlk. M10—2A 88
Nall St. M19—2D 118
Nall St. OL16—5E 21
Nameplate Clo. M30—3D 82
Nancy St. M15—1B 100 & 5C 164
Nandywell. BL3—4B 40
Nangreave Rd. SK2—5A 132
Nangreave St. M5—4A 86 &
                    6B 160
Nan Nook Rd. M23—2F 127
Nansen Av. M30—2E 83
Nansen Clo. M32—3E 99
Nansen Rd. SK8—1E 141
Nansen St. M6—3E 85
Nansen St. M11—5A 88
Nansen St. M32—4D 98
Nansmoss La. SK9—6B 150
Nantes Ct. BL1—3H 23
Nantwich Av. OL12—6F 7
Nantwich Clo. SK8—6C 130
Nantwich Rd. M14—6E 101
Nantwich Wlk. BL3—3A 38
Nantwich Way. SK9—2A 152
Napier Ct. M15—1A 100 &
                    6B 164
Napier Ct. SK4—5D 118
Napier Ct. SK14—6C 106
Napier Grn. M5—6H 85
Napier Rd. M21—1H 115
Napier Rd. M30—2D 82
Napier Rd. SK4—6D 118
Napier St. M15—1B 100 & 6C 164
Napier St. M27—4D 70
Napier St. OL2—5F 35
Napier St. SK7—2D 144
Napier St. SK14—6C 106
Napier St. E. OL8—4B 64
Napier St. W. OL8—4A 64
Naples Rd. SK3—5D 130
Naples St. M4—2E 87 & 2B 162
Narbonne Gdns. M30—2A 84
Narborough Wlk. M10—5E 75
Narbuth Dri. M8—4F 73
Narcissus Wlk. M28—6B 54
Narrow La. SK10—6G 155
Narrows, The. WA14—2E 137
Narrow Wlk. WA14—3E 137
Naseby Av. M9—5H 61
Naseby Pl. M25—6G 59
Naseby Rd. SK5—1G 119
Naseby Wlk. M25—1G 59
Nash Rd. M17—5G 83
Nasmyth Av. M34—3G 105
Nasmyth Rd. M30—5E 83
Nasmyth St. M8—5E 75
Nathan Dri. M3—3C 86 & 3E 161
Nathans Rd. M22—1A 140
Naunton Rd. M24—2B 62
Naunton Wlk. M9—3G 75
Naval St. M4—3G 87 & 3E 163
Navenby Av. M16—3A 100
Navigation Rd. WA14—4F 125
Naylor Ct. M10—2G 87 & 1F 163
Naylor St. M10—2G 87 & 1G 163
Naylor St. OL1—2C 64
Nazeby Wlk. OL9—4A 64
Naze Wlk. SK5—3C 120
Neal Av. OL6—2B 92
Neal Av. SK8—5E 141
Neale Av. OL3—4G 53
Neale Rd. M21—2G 115
Near Birches Pde. OL4—5A 66
Nearbrook Rd. M22—1A 140
Nearcroft Rd. M23—4G 127
Near Hey Clo. M26—4E 41
Nearmaker Av. M22—1A 140
Nearmaker Rd. M22—1A 140

Neasden Gro. BL3—2G 37
Neath Av. M22—4B 128
Neath Clo. M25—2G 59
Neath Clo. SK12—2D 154
Neath Fold. BL3—4H 37
Neath St. BL3—3H 37
Nebo St. BL3—3H 37
Nebraska St. BL1—4A 24
Neden Clo. M11—5D 88
Needham Av. M21—1H 115
Needham Ct. M25—2D 58
Needwood Clo. M10—6F 75
Needwood Rd. SK6—4H 121
Needwood St. M10—5F 75
Neenton Sq. M12—6C 88
Neill St. M7—1C 86
Neilson Clo. M24—2C 62
Neilston Av. M10—4B 76
Nellie St. OL10—3D 30
Nell La. M21 & M20—2A 116
Nell St. BL1—1A 24
Nelson Av. M30—2F 83
Nelson Av. SK12—4G 155
Nelson Clo. M15—3C 100
Nelson Clo. SK12—4G 155
Nelson Ct. M10—1H 87
Nelson Dri. M30—3C 110
Nelson Dri. M35—3F 89
Nelson Fold. M27—2C 21
Nelson Pl. M14—4G 101
Nelson Rd. M9—4F 61
Nelson Sq. BL1—6B 24
Nelson St. BL3—2C 38
(Bolton)
Nelson St. BL3—4B 40
(Little Lever)
Nelson St. BL4—1G 55
Nelson St. BL9—5D 28
(in two parts)
Nelson St. M4—2E 87 & 2B 162
Nelson St. M5—4E 85
Nelson St. M7—6H 73
Nelson St. M10—1H 87
Nelson St. M13—2F 101
Nelson St. M24—2C 62
Nelson St. M30—3F 83
Nelson St. M32—6D 98
Nelson St. M34—1F 105
(Audenshaw)
Nelson St. M34—3F 105
(Denton, in two parts)
Nelson St. OL4—4A 66
Nelson St. OL6—3A 92
Nelson St. OL10—4F 31
Nelson St. OL15—4F 9
Nelson St. OL16—4H 19
Nelson St. SK7—1F 145
Nelson St. SK14—5C 106
Nelson Way. OL9—5H 63
Nelstrop Cres. SK4—3F 119
Nelstrop Rd. SK4—3F 119
Nelstrop Rd. N. SK4—2E 119
Nelstrop Wlk. SK4—3E 119
Nepaul Rd. M9—2G 75
Nesbit St. BL2—2D 24
Nesfield Rd. M23—1F 127
Neston Av. BL1—6D 10
Neston Av. M20—3E 117
Neston Av. M33—1E 127
Neston Clo. OL2—6H 35
Neston Gro. SK3—6F 131
Neston Rd. BL8—1F 27
Neston Rd. OL16—1A 34
Neston St. M11—6H 89
Neston Way. SK9—4H 151
Neswick Wlk. M23—1E 127
Netherbury Clo. M18—4E 103
Nethercott Ct. WA14—6E 125
Nethercroft Rd. WA15—6C 126
Netherfield Rd. BL3—5H 37
Netherfields. SK9—6G 159
Netherhey La. OL2—5A 48
Nether Hey St. OL8—4F 65
(in two parts)
Nether Ho. Rd. OL2—6E 35
Netherlees. OL4—4H 65
Netherlow Ct. SK14—5C 106
Nether St. M12—5G 87 & 2E 167

Nether St. SK14—1D 122
Netherton Gro. BL4—5D 38
Netherton Rd. M14—6E 101
Nethervale Dri. M8—6G 61
Netherwood Rd. M22—4A 128
Netley Av. OL12—6F 7
Netley Gdns. M26—3E 41
Netley Gro. OL8—5G 65
Netley Rd. M23—1G 139
Nettlebarn Rd. M22—6A 128
Nettleford Rd. M16 & M21—1C 116
Nettleton Gro. M9—2H 75
Nevada St. BL1—4A 24
Nevendon Dri. M23—1F 139
Nevile Ct. M7—3F 73
Nevile Rd. M7—3F 73
Neville Cardus Wlk. M14—5G 101
Neville Clo. BL1—5A 24
Neville Dri. M30—3E 95
Neville St. OL2—6F 35
Neville St. OL9—2A 64
Neville St. SK7—2D 144
Nevill Rd. SK7—3G 143
Nevin Av. SK8—4A 142
Nevin Clo. OL8—1H 77
Nevin Clo. SK7—5A 144
Nevin Rd. M10—2D 76
Nevis Gro. BL1—6B 10
Nevis St. OL11—3G 33
New Allen St. M10—2G 87 & 1E 163
Newall Rd. M23—2F 139
Newall St. OL15—3F 9
Newark Av. M14—4F 101
Newark Av. M26—2C 40
Newark Pk. Way. OL2—6A 34
Newark Rd. M27—1H 71
Newark Rd. OL12—6F 7
Newark Rd. SK5—4G 119
Newark Sq. OL12—6F 7
New Bailey St. M3—4C 86 & 5E 161
New Bank St. M12—1A 102
New Bank St. SK14—2H 109
Newbank Tower. M3—2C 86 & 1E 161
New Barn Clo. OL2—6E 35
New Barn La. OL11—6G 19
New Barn Rd. OL8—1E 79
New Barn St. BL1—4F 23
Newbarn St. OL2—6E 35
New Barn St. OL16—6A 20
New Barton St. M6—6A 72
Newbeck St. M4—3E 87
New Beech Rd. SK4—1A 130
(in two parts)
Newbold Clo. M15—1D 100 & 5H 165
Newbold Moss. OL16—3B 20
Newbold St. BL8—3A 28
Newbold St. OL16—3C 20
Newboult Rd. SK8—5A 130
Newbourne Clo. SK7—2D 144
Newbreak Clo. OL4—1H 65
Newbreak St. OL4—1H 65
Newbridge Gdns. BL2—1G 25
New Bri. La. SK1—1A 132
New Bridge St. M3—2D 86 & 2H 161
(in two parts)
Newbrook Av. M21—5B 116
New Buildings Pl. OL16—3H 19
Newburn Av. M9—5H 61
Newbury Av. M33—5E 113
Newbury Clo. SK8—1C 152
Newbury Dri. M30—2D 82
Newbury Dri. M31—2E 97
Newbury Gro. OL10—5E 31
Newbury Pl. M7—4H 73
Newbury Rd. BL3—4H 39
Newbury Rd. SK8—6G 141
Newbury Wlk. BL1—4A 24
Newbury Wlk. M9—4F 75
(off Ravelston Dri.)
Newby Dri. M24—4H 45
Newby Dri. M33—6D 114
Newby Dri. SK8—6E 129
Newby Dri. WA14—5F 125
Newby Rd. BL2—4G 25
Newby Rd. SK4—1E 131
Newby Rd. SK7—2C 144
Newby Rd. Ind. Est. SK7—3C 144

Newcastle St. M15—6D 86 & 4H 165
(in two parts)
Newcastle Wlk. M34—6G 105
New Cateaton St. BL9—2D 28
Newchurch. OL8—3E 79
New Church Ct. M26—4H 41
New Church Rd. BL1—3D 22
Newchurch St. M11—5B 88
New Church St. M26—4G 41
Newchurch St. OL11—4C 32
New Church Wlk. M26—4H 41
New City Rd. M28—3C 68
Newcliffe Rd. M9—5H 61
Newcombe Clo. M11—4B 88
Newcombe Ct. M33—5H 113
Newcombe Dri. M28—3B 54
Newcombe Rd. BL2—2A 14
Newcombe St. M3—2D 86 & 1H 161
New Ct. Dri. BL7—1B 10
Newcroft Cres. M31—6H 97
Newcroft Dri. M31—6A 98
Newcroft Dri. SK3—5F 131
Newcroft Rd. M31—6H 97
New Cross. M4—3F 87
New Cross St. M5—3C 84
New Cross St. M26—4H 41
New Cross St. M27—4G 71
Newdale Rd. M12—5D 102
Newearth Rd. M28—3D 68
New Earth St. OL4—4G 65
New Earth St. OL5—1F 81
New Elizabeth St. M8—6C 74
Newell Ter. OL12—2G 19
New Elm Rd. M3—5B 86 & 2D 164
Newfield Clo. M26—4E 41
Newfield Clo. OL16—3C 20
Newfield Head La. OL16—6H 21
Newfield View. OL16—5G 21
(in three parts)
New Forest Rd. M23—3C 126
Newgate. OL16—4G 19
Newgate. SK9—2A 158
Newgate Dri. M28—3B 54
Newgate Rd. OL7—6C 90
Newgate St. M4—3E 87 & 3B 162
New George St. BL8—2A 28
New George St. M4—3E 87 & 3B 162
Newhall Av. BL2—1B 40
New Hall Av. M7—3H 73
New Hall Av. M30—6C 82
New Hall Av. SK8—6F 141
New Hall Dri. M23—1G 127
New Hall La. BL1—4E 23
Newhall Pl. BL1—5E 23
New Hall Rd. BL9—1A 30
New Hall Rd. M7—3H 73
New Hall Rd. M33—5F 115
Newhall Rd. SK5—5A 104
Newham Av. M11—3D 88
Newhaven Av. M11—6H 89
Newhaven Clo. BL8—4C 14
Newhaven Wlk. BL2—4D 24
New Herbert St. M6—6A 72
Newhey Av. M22—6B 128
New Hey Ct. M33—4B 114
Newhey Rd. M22—1B 140
Newhey Rd. OL16—6G 21
(in two parts)
Newhey Rd. SK8—5A 130
New Heys Way. BL2—5H 11
New Holder St. BL1—6A 24
Newholme Gdns. M28—5E 55
Newholme Rd. M20—4D 116
Newhouse Clo. OL12—3A 8
Newhouse Cres. OL11—3A 18
Newhouse Rd. OL10—5F 31
Newhouse St. OL12—3A 8
Newick Wlk. M9—6G 61
(off Levedale Rd.)
Newington. OL11—1F 33
Newington Av. M8—6B 60
Newington Ct. WA14—2D 136
Newington Dri. BL1—4B 24
Newington Dri. BL1—4B 24
Newington Wlk. BL1—4B 24
(in two parts)
New Inn Yd. OL12—5C 8
New Islington. M4—3G 87 & 4F 163

Newlands. M35—1G 89
Newlands Av. BL2—4H 25
Newlands Av. M25—6C 42
Newlands Av. M30—5B 82
(Eccles)
Newlands Av. M30—5D 94
(Irlam)
Newlands Av. SK7—5H 143
Newlands Av. SK8—6C 142
Newlands Clo. OL12—6F 7
Newlands Clo. SK8—6C 142
Newlands Dri. M20—3G 129
Newlands Dri. M25—4E 59
Newlands Dri. M27—5A 72
Newlands Dri. SK9—4B 158
Newlands Dri. SK14—3H 109
Newlands Rd. M23—3E 127
Newlands Rd. SK8—5H 129
Newland St. M8—2D 74
Newlands Wlk. M24—4G 45
(in two parts)
New La. BL2—4F 25
New La. M24—6A 46
New La. M30—4D 82
New La. OL2—3B 48
New Lawns. SK5—6A 104
New Lees St. OL6—6H 79
(in two parts)
Newlyn Av. SK15—2H 93
Newlyn Clo. SK7—4D 144
Newlyn Dri. M33—1C 126
Newlyn Dri. SK6—5G 121
Newlyn St. M14—5F 101
Newman St. OL6—2G 91
Newman St. OL16—6A 8
Newman St. SK14—4C 106
New Market. M2—4D 86 & 5H 161
Newmarket Clo. M33—1D 124
Newmarket Gro. OL7—6C 78
Newmarket Rd. M4—4E 87 & 5A 162
Newmarket M. M7—5H 73
Newmarket Rd. BL3—5A 40
Newmarket Rd. OL7—6C 78
New Meadow. BL6—6A 22
Newmill. OL16—1C 20
New Mill St. OL15—4E 9
Newmill Wlk. M8—5C 74
(off Alderford Pde.)
New Moor La. SK7—2D 144
New Moss Rd. M30—3B 110
New Mount St. M4—2E 87 & 2B 162
Newnham St. BL1—1A 24
New Park Rd. M5—6H 85
Newpark Wlk. M8—5C 74
(off Wellside Wlk.)
Newport Av. SK5—2G 119
Newport M. BL4—2F 55
Newport Rd. BL3—4C 38
Newport Rd. M21—6G 99
Newport Rd. M34—1H 121
Newport St. BL1—6B 24
Newport St. BL4—2F 55
Newport St. BL8—6A 14
Newport St. M6—3E 85
Newport St. M14—4F 101
Newport St. M24—6C 46
Newport St. OL8—4B 64
Newquay Av. BL2—4D 26
Newquay Av. SK5—2G 119
Newquay Dri. SK7—6H 143
New Quay St. M3—4B 86 & 5E 161
New Radcliff St. OL1—2C 64
New Ridd Rise. SK14—1B 122
New Riven Ct. BL3—4A 40
New Rd. M26—5H 41
New Rd. BL8—5C 64
New Rd. OL12—1B 6
New Rd. OL15—5C 8
New Rd. SK14—1H 109
New Royd Av. OL4—1B 66
New Royd Rd. OL4—1A 66
Newry Rd. M30—5G 83
Newry St. BL1—2H 23
Newry Wlk. M9—6D 60
Newsham Clo. BL3—2H 37
Newsham Wlk. M12—4D 102
Newshaw La. SK14—4H 109

Newsholme St. M8—4B 74
New Springs. BL1—1F 23
Newstead. OL12—3G 19
(off Spotland Rd.)
Newstead Av. M20—4H 117
Newstead Av. OL6—4G 79
Newstead Clo. SK12—2D 154
Newstead Gro. SK6—6E 121
Newstead M. M31—4G 97
Newstead Ter. WA15—4H 125
New St. BL1—1A 38
New St. BL8—5H 13
New St. M10—1A 88
New St. M26—5H 41
New St. M27—2G 71
New St. M30—4E 83
New St. M35—5A 90
New St. OL3—1F 53
New St. OL4—3A 66
New St. OL12—1G 19
New St. OL15—5D 8
New St. OL16—6G 21
New St. SK9—4B 158
New St. SK15—5E 93
New St. WA14—1E 137
New Tempest Rd. BL6—3A 36
New Ter. SK9—1E 159
New Thomas St. M6—1G 85
Newton Av. M12—3B 102
Newton Av. M20—3E 117
Newton Cres. M24—5F 45
Newtondale Av. OL2—3A 48
Newton Dri. BL8—2A 14
New Tong Field. BL7—4D 10
Newton Hall Ct. M4—2A 106
Newton Hall Rd. SK14—2A 106
Newton Moor Ind. Est. SK14
—2C 106
Newtonmore Wlk. M11—4D 88
Newton Rd. M24—2D 60
Newton Rd. M31—5E 97
Newton Rd. M35—6E 77
Newton Rd. SK9—6E 151
Newton Rd. WA14—4G 125
Newton St. BL1—3A 24
Newton St. BL9—5F 15
Newton St. M1—4F 87 & 5C 162
Newton St. M32—6D 98
Newton St. M35—2C 90
(Droylesden)
Newton St. M35—5C 76
(Failsworth)
Newton St. OL6—2A 92
Newton St. OL16—6A 20
Newton St. SK3—3G 131
Newton St. SK14—3B 106
Newton St. SK15—3D 92
Newton Ter. BL1—3A 24
Newton Ter. SK16—4H 91
Newton Wlk. BL1—3A 24
Newton Wood Rd. SK16—1H 105
Newtown Av. M34—5F 105
Newtown Clo. M11—5D 88
Newtown Clo. M27—1F 71
Newtown Ct. M25—5G 59
Newtown St. M25—5G 59
Newtown St. OL2—1F 49
New Union St. M4—3G 87 & 4E 163
New Vernon St. BL9—1D 28
New Viaduct St. M11 & M10—3A 88
Newville Dri. M20—4H 117
New Wakefield St. M1—6E 87 & 3A 166
New Way. OL12—4G 7
New York St. OL10—3D 30
New Zealand Rd. SK1—2A 132
Ney St. OL7—5D 78
Niagara St. SK2—5A 132
Nicholas Croft. M4—3E 87 & 4A 162
Nicholas Rd. OL8—5C 64
Nicholas St. BL2—5C 24
Nicholas St. M1—4E 87
Nicholls St. M6—2H 85
Nicholls St. M12—6H 87 & 4G 167
Nicholson Av. SK14—2A 106
Nicholson Sq. SK16—5H 91
Nicholson St. OL4—3A 66
Nicholson St. OL11—6H 19

Nicholson St. SK4—1G 131
Nicker Brow. OL3—5A 52
(in two parts)
Nickleby Rd. SK12—4D 154
Nick Rd. La. OL12—2F 7
Nico Ditch. M19—5E 103
Nicolas Rd. M21—6F 99
Nicola St. BL7—3C 10
Nield Rd. M34—4F 105
Nields Brow. WA14—3E 137
Nield St. OL5—1D 80
Nield St. OL8—5C 64
Nigel Rd. M9—4H 75
Nigher Moss Av. OL16—4C 20
Nightingale Clo. SK9—6F 151
Nightingale Dri. M34—3C 90
Nightingale Wlk. BL3—4B 38
Nile St. BL3—2B 38
Nile St. OL1—1C 64
Nile St. OL7—5F 91
Nile St. OL16—3A 20
Nile Ter. M7—6H 73
Nimble Nook. OL9—4G 63
Nina Dri. M10—6C 62
Nine Acre Ct. M5—6H 85
Nine Acres Dri. M5—6H 85
Ninehouse La. BL3—3B 38
Ninfield Rd. M23—1H 139
Ninian Ct. M24—6H 45
Ninian Gdns. M28—6F 55
Ninth Av. OL8—2B 78
Ninth St. M17—1C 98
Nipper La. M25—5C 42
Nisbet Av. M22—2C 140
Niven St. M12—6G 87 & 3E 167
Nixon Rd. BL3—4G 37
Nixon Rd. S. BL3—4G 37
Nixon St. M35—4E 77
Nixon St. OL11—2B 32
Nixon St. SK3—3G 131
Nobel St. M10—5C 76
Noble Meadow. OL12—4B 8
Noble St. BL3—2A 38
Noble St. OL8—5D 64
Noel Dri. M33—5D 114
Nolan St. M9—3G 75
Nole St. BL1—6A 24
Nona St. M6—3E 85
Nook Cotts. OL4—1C 66
Nook Farm Av. OL12—6F 7
Nook Fields. BL2—2G 25
Nook La. OL6—5H 79
Nook Side. OL12—6F 7
Nook Ter. OL12—6F 7
Nook, The. BL9—4H 29
Nook, The. M28—3H 69
Nook, The. M30—1C 82
Noon Sun Clo. OL3—5E 53
Noon Sun St. OL12—2H 19
Norah St. OL9—1H 77
Norbet Wlk. M9—4G 75
Norbreck Av. M21—2H 115
Norbreck Av. SK8—5C 130
Norbreck Gdns. BL2—5E 25
Norbreck Pl. BL2—5E 25
Norbreck St. BL2—5E 25
Norburn Rd. M13—5B 102
Norbury Av. M6—6B 72
Norbury Av. M33—5H 113
Norbury Av. OL4—3E 67
Norbury Av. SK6—5C 134
Norbury Av. SK14—5B 106
Norbury Cres. SK7—3D 144
Norbury Dri. SK6—5C 134
Norbury Gro. BL1—1C 24
Norbury Gro. M27—2F 71
Norbury Gro. SK7—3D 144
Norbury Hollow Rd. SK7—5H 145
Norbury Ho. OL4—4F 65
Norbury La. OL8—6H 65
Norbury M. SK6—5C 134
Norbury Sq. M10—1A 88
Norbury St. M7—5A 74
Norbury St. OL16—1H 33
Norbury St. SK2—2H 131
Norbury Way. SK9—2A 152
Norcliffe Wlk. M18—3D 102
Norcot Wlk. M15—1B 100 & 5D 164

Norcross Clo. SK2—6D 132
Nordale Pk. OL12—1A 18
Nordek Clo. OL2—2B 48
Nordek Dri. OL2—2B 48
Norden Av. M20—3E 117
Norden Clo. OL11—1G 17
Norden Ct. BL3—3A 38
Norden Rd. OL11—6H 17
Nordens Dri. OL9—6F 47
Nordens Rd. OL9—1F 63
Nordens St. OL9—1G 63
Norden Way. OL11—1G 17
Noreen Av. M25—4F 59
Norfield Clo. SK16—5A 92
Norfolk Av. M18—3E 103
Norfolk Av. M25—1E 59
Norfolk Av. M34—4H 103
Norfolk Av. OL10—3C 30
Norfolk Clo. SK4—3E 119
Norfolk Clo. BL3—3B 40
Norfolk Clo. M30—4A 110
Norfolk Clo. OL2—6D 34
Norfolk Clo. OL15—6G 9
Norfolk Cres. M35—5E 77
Norfolk Gdns. M31—4H 95
Norfolk Ho. M7—2A 74
Norfolk Ho. M33—5C 114
Norfolk Rd. M18—3E 103
Norfolk St. M2—4D 86 & 5H 161
Norfolk St. M6—6E 73
Norfolk St. M28—3F 55
Norfolk St. OL9—5H 63
(in two parts)
Norfolk St. OL11—5G 19
Norfolk St. SK14—5B 106
Norfolk Way. OL2—5B 48
Norford Way. OL11—3A 18
Norgate St. M20—6F 117
Norlan Av. M34—6E 91
Norland Wlk. M10—6H 75
Norleigh Rd. M22—3B 128
Norley Av. M32—4F 99
Norley Clo. SK11—5H 47
Norley Dri. M19—5E 103
Norley Rd. M33—5E 115
Norman Av. M7—2C 144
Normanby Chase. WA14—1D 136
Normanby Gro. M27—2E 71
Normanby Rd. M28—2E 69
Normanby St. BL3—5F 37
Normanby St. M14—3E 101
Normanby St. M27—2E 71
Norman Clo. M24—6C 46
Normandale Av. BL1—4E 23
Normandy Cres. M26—4F 41
Norman Gro. M12—3C 102
Norman Gro. SK5—2G 119
Norman Rd. M7—4A 74
Norman Rd. M14—5G 101
Norman Rd. M33—5B 114
Norman Rd. OL6—5G 79
Norman Rd. OL11—5F 19
Norman Rd. SK4—6D 118
Norman Rd. SK15—3D 92
Norman Rd. WA14—5E 125
Norman Rd. W. M9—4H 75
Norman's Pl. WA14—1F 137
Norman St. BL9—1F 29
Norman St. M12—2D 102
Norman St. M24—2B 62
Norman St. M35—2G 77
Norman St. OL1—1B 64
Norman St. SK14—5C 106
Normanton Av. M6—2C 84
Normanton Dri. M9—6G 61
Normanton Rd. SK3—4C 130
Norman Weall Ct. M24—5A 46
Normington St. OL4—2G 65
Norreys Av. M31—4A 96
Norreys St. OL16—3A 20
Norris Av. SK4—2E 131
Norris Bank Ter. SK4—2E 131
Norris Hill Dri. SK4—1E 131
Norris Rd. M33—1B 126
Norris St. BL3—2A 38
(Bolton)

Norris St. BL3—4A 40
(Little Green)
Norris St. BL4—2E 55
Norris St. M3—3B 86 & 3C 160
Norris Towers. SK4—1G 131
(off Wilkinson Rd.)
Northallerton Rd. M7—5E 73
Northampton Rd. M10—5G 75
Northampton Wlk. M34—6G 105
North Av. BL4—1C 54
North Av. BL8—2H 13
North Av. BL9—3F 43
North Av. M19—2B 118
North Av. M31—6G 83
North Av. OL3—4F 53
North Av. SK15—2E 93
Northavon Clo. M30—4A 84
(off Kearton Dri.)
Northbank Gdns. M19—3A 118
Northbank Ind. Est. M30—3C 110
Northbank Wlk. M33—6B 116
N. Blackfield La. M7—3G 73
Northbourne St. M6—3E 85
Northbrook Av. M8—5B 60
N. Brook Rd. SK14—3G 109
N. Broughton St. M3—3C 86 & 4E 161
North Circ. M25—3E 59
N. Clifden La. M7—5A 74
Northcliffe Rd. SK2—3C 132
North Clo. SK14—1H 109
Northcombe Rd. SK3—6G 131
Northcote Rd. SK7—6H 143
Northcote St. M26—5E 41
North Cres. M11—2F 89
N. Croft. OL8—6E 65
Northdale Rd. M9—4D 60
N. Dean St. M27—2G 71
Northdene Dri. OL11—5B 18
Northdown Av. M15—1B 100 & 5C 164
Northdown Av. SK6—4A 122
N. Downs Rd. OL2—5D 34
N. Downs Rd. SK8—2B 142
North Dri. M8—6B 60
North Dri. M27—4H 71
North Dri. M34—4C 90
Northenden Pde. M22—2B 128
Northenden Rd. M33—4B 114
Northenden Rd. SK8—5E 129
Northenden View. M20—1F 129
(off South Rd.)
N. End Rd. SK15—3F 93
Northen Gro. M20—5D 116
Northerley Cres. M10—6D 62
Northern Av. M27—6A 58
Northern Gro. BL1—4G 23
Northfield Av. M10—1F 77
Northfield Dri. SK9—1G 159
Northfield Rd. BL9—5F 15
Northfield Rd. M10—1F 77
Northfield St. BL3—2G 37
Northfleet Rd. M30—4B 82
North Ga. OL8—1C 78
Northgate. OL12—2C 6
Northgate La. OL1—3A 50
Northgate Rd. SK3—3F 131
N. George St. M3—2B 86 & 2C 160
Northgraves Dri. M7—5A 74
North Gro. M13—2H 101
North Gro. M28—6E 55
North Gro. M31—6E 97
N. Harvey St. SK1—2H 131
N. Hill St. M3—2B 86 & 2D 160
Northland Rd. BL1—5D 10
Northland Rd. M9—6A 62
Northlands. M26—2E 41
North La. OL12—3H 19
Northleach Clo. BL8—2G 27
Northleigh Dri. M25—6H 59
Northleigh Rd. M16—4H 99
N. Lonsdale St. M32—4E 99
N. Meade. M21—2H 115
Northmoor M. OL1—1C 64
Northmoor Rd. M12—3C 102
N. Nook. OL4—1C 66
Northolme Gdns. M19—4A 118
Northolt Ct. M11—3F 89
Northolt Dri. BL3—3B 38
Northolt Rd. M23—2F 127

North Pde. M3—4D 86 & 5G 161
North Pde. M33—1D 126
North Pde. OL16—1G 35
N. Park Rd. SK7—3F 143
N. Phoebe St. M5—5H 85
North Pl. SK1—2H 131
Northridge Rd. M9—3F 61
North Rise. OL3—4F 53
North Rd. M11—3D 88
North Rd. M17—2C 98
North Rd. M22—1A 150
North Rd. M25—4D 58
North Rd. M32—3A 98
North Rd. M34—4C 90
North Rd. SK15—3F 93
North Rd. WA15—5A 138
Northside Av. M31—6B 96
Northstead Av. M34—5H 105
North St. M8—6C 74
North St. M24—5A 46
North St. M26—3A 42
North St. OL2—3B 48
(in two parts)
North St. OL6—3G 91
North St. OL10—3D 30
North St. OL12—4G 7
North St. OL16—3A 20
Northumberland Av. OL7—1H 91
Northumberland Clo. M16—2A 100
Northumberland Rd. M16—3A 100
  & 6B 164
Northumberland Rd. SK5—2B 120
Northumberland St. M7—4H 73
Northumbria St. BL3—2G 37
N. Vale Rd. WA15—4H 137
North View. BL9—1B 14
North View. M25—5C 42
North View. OL5—2G 81
North View. OL12—4H 7
Northward Rd. SK9—3C 158
North Way. BL1—1D 24
Northway. M10—1F 77
Northway. M30—3H 83
Northway. M35—5A 90
North Way. SK5—3C 120
Northway. WA14—5G 125
N. Western St. M12—5G 87 & 2F 167
N. Western St. M19—1C 118
Northwold Dri. BL1—5C 22
Northwold Dri. M9—6B 62
Northwood. BL2—1F 25
Northwood Cres. BL3—2G 37
Northwood Gro. M33—5B 114
N. Woodley. M26—1A 58
Norton Av. M12—4D 102
Norton Av. M31—3F 97
Norton Av. M33—3F 113
Norton Av. M34—4A 104
Norton Ga. M25—6H 59
Norton Rd. SK4—2D 130
Norton Rd. M28—4A 68
Norton Rd. OL12—6F 7
Norton St. BL1—2B 24
Norton St. M1—4G 87 & 6F 163
Norton St. M3—3D 86 & 3G 161
Norton St. M7—4A 74
Norton St. M10—1A 88
Norton St. M16—3A 100
Norview Dri. M20—4F 129
Norville Av. M10—6D 62
Norway Gro. SK5—5H 119
Norway St. BL1—3H 23
Norway St. M6—3E 85
Norway St. M11—5A 88
Norway St. M32—4E 99
Norweb Way. OL9—1G 63
Norwell Rd. M22—6C 128
Norwich Av. M34—6F 105
Norwich Av. OL9—6G 47
Norwich Av. OL11—4C 18
Norwich Clo. OL6—4H 79
Norwich Clo. SK16—6E 93
Norwich Dri. BL2—2H 75
Norwich Rd. M32—4H 97
Norwich St. OL11—6A 20
Norwick Clo. BL3—3C 36
Norwood. M25—1F 73
Norwood Av. M7- 3G 73

Norwood Av. M20—5H 117
Norwood Av. SK6—6B 146
Norwood Av. SK7—2E 153
Norwood Av. SK8—2C 142
Norwood Clo. M28—3G 69
Norwood Clo. OL2—5E 35
Norwood Cres. OL2—5C 48
Norwood Dri. M27—4C 70
Norwood Dri. WA15—6D 126
Norwood Gro. BL1—5G 23
Norwood Gro. OL2—5C 48
Norwood Rd. M32—6E 99
Norwood Rd. M33—1B 144
Norwood Rd. SK8—5F 129
Nottingham Av. SK5—3C 120
Nottingham Dri. BL1—4A 24
Nottingham Dri. M35—6G 77
Nottingham Dri. OL6—4F 79
Nottingham Ter. SK5—3C 120
Nottingham Way. M34—6G 105
Nova Scotia St. M35—3F 77
Nowell Clo. M24—4A 46
Nowell Ho. M24—5A 46
Nowell Rd. M24—4A 46
Nudger Clo. OL3—5H 51
Nudger Grn. OL3—5H 51
Nuffield Rd. M22—1C 140
Nuffield Ho. BL1—4F 23
Nugent Rd. BL3—4A 38
Nugget St. OL4—3F 65
Nuneaton Dri. M10—2H 87 & 1G 163
Nuneham Av. M20—2G 117
Nunfield Clo. M10—1B 76
Nunnery Rd. BL3—3F 37
Nunthorpe Dri. M8—3E 75
Nursery Av. WA15—5G 137
Nursery Brow. M26—6A 42
Nursery Clo. M33—5D 114
Nursery La. SK3—4C 130
Nursery La. SK9—3C 158
Nursery Rd. M25—3E 59
Nursery Rd. M31—3C 96
Nursery Rd. M35—4G 77
Nursery Rd. SK4—6E 119
Nursery Rd. SK8—4B 142
Nursery St. SK14—4A 106
Nursery St. M6—1F 85
Nursery St. M16—4D 100
Nuthurst Rd. M10—2C 76
Nut La. M25—1A 60
Nutsford Vale. M18—3C 102
Nut St. BL1—3H 23
Nuttall Av. BL3—4C 40
Nuttall Av. M25—1D 58
Nuttall Clo. BL0—4E 5
Nuttall Hall Rd. BL0—3F 5
Nuttall La. BL0—4D 4
Nuttall Rd. BL0—5E 5
Nuttall Sq. BL9—2D 42
Nuttall St. BL4—5D 56
Nuttall St. BL9—4E 29
Nuttall St. M11—6C 88
Nuttall St. M16—2A 100
Nuttall St. M30—3C 110
Nuttall St. OL8—5F 65

Oadby Clo. M12—2C 102
Oak Av. BL0—1A 14
Oak Av. BL3—4B 40
Oak Av. M21—1H 115
Oak Av. M24—2A 62
Oak Av. M25—2D 58
Oak Av. M30—4B 110
Oak Av. OL2—1B 48
Oak Av. SK4—1D 130
Oak Av. SK6—1A 134
Oak Av. SK8—3C 142
Oak Av. SK9—4C 158
Oak Bank. M25—2D 72
Oak Bank Av. M9—2H 75
Oakbank Av. OL9—1E 63
Oak Bank Clo. M25—1F 59
Oakbank Dri. BL1—5B 10
Oakcliffe Rd. OL12—5A 8
Oak Clo. OL12—1H 7

Oak Clo. SK9—3C 158
Oak Clo. SK14—3C 108
Oak Cotts. SK8—3D 150
Oak Ct. SK6—5G 121
Oakcroft Clo. SK15—5H 93
Oakdale. BL2—1F 25
Oakdale Clo. M25—1B 58
Oakdale Ct. OL3—4G 51
Oakdale Ct. WA14—6E 125
Oakdale Dri. M20—2G 129
Oakdale Dri. SK8—3F 141
Oakdean Ct. SK9—6F 151
Oakdene. M27—5B 70
Oakdene Av. SK4—4F 119
Oakdene Av. SK8—6F 141
Oakdene Cres. SK6—4D 134
Oakdene Gdns. SK6—4D 134
Oakdene Rd. M24—1C 62
Oakdene Rd. SK8—4D 134
Oakdene Rd. WA15—3B 126
Oakdene St. M9—3H 75
Oak Dri. M14—6H 101
Oak Dri. M34—3A 104
Oak Dri. SK6—5B 134
Oak Dri. SK7—6E 143
Oaken Bank Rd. OL10 & M24—2H 45
Oakenbottom Rd. BL2—6F 25
Oaken Bridge. SK5—6G 119
Oakenclough. OL7—5D 78
Oaken Clough. OL7—5D 78
Oakenclough Clo. SK9—5H 151
Oakenclough Dri. BL1—3D 22
Oakenholme Wlk. M18—2E 103
  (off Beyer Clo.)
Oakenrod Hill. OL11—4E 19
Oakenshaw Av. OL12—3C 6
Oaken St. OL7—5E 79
Oaker Av. M20—5C 116
Oakes St. BL4—2H 55
Oakfield. M25—6H 59
Oakfield. M33—4A 114
Oakfield Av. M16—4G 99
  (Old Trafford)
Oakfield Av. M16—4B 100
  (Whalley Range)
Oakfield Av. M35—4H 89
Oakfield Av. SK8—5A 150
Oakfield Clo. SK9—6E 159
Oakfield Ct. WA15—5G 125
Oakfield Dri. M28—4A 54
Oakfield Gro. BL4—3E 55
Oakfield Gro. M18—3F 103
Oakfield M. M33—3A 114
Oakfield M. SK3—6H 131
Oakfield Rd. M20—6E 117
Oakfield Rd. SK3—6H 131
Oakfield Rd. SK9—6E 159
Oakfield Rd. SK12—3E 155
Oakfield Rd. SK14—4G 109
  (Hadfield)
Oakfield Rd. SK14—2C 106
  (Hyde)
Oakfield Rd. WA15—6G 125
Oakfield St. M8—5C 74
Oakfield St. WA15—6G 125
Oakfield Ter. OL11—3E 19
Oakfold Av. OL6—5H 79
Oakford Av. M10—2G 87 & 1F 163
Oakford Wlk. BL3—3G 37
Oak Gates. BL7—2C 10
Oak Gro. M30—4D 82
Oak Gro. M31—5G 97
Oak Gro. OL6—5H 79
Oak Gro. SK8—6A 130
Oak Gro. SK12—3D 154
Oakham Clo. BL8—6D 14
Oakham M. M7—2G 73
Oakham Rd. M34—6G 105
Oak Hill. OL15—4D 8
Oakhill Clo. BL2—6A 26
Oakhill Trading Est. M28—3E 55
Oakhill Way. M8—4B 74
Oakhouse Dri. M21—2H 115
Oakhurst Chase. SK9—4G 159
Oakhurst Dri. SK3—6D 130
Oakington Av. M14—4F 101
Oakland Av. M6—1A 84
Oakland Av. M16—3G 99

Oakland Av. M19—5A 118
Oakland Av. SK2—5C 132
Oakland Cotts. M7—3F 73
Oakland Ct. SK12—3D 154
Oakland Gro. BL1—3E 23
Oakland Ho. M16—2G 99
Oaklands. BL1—6D 22
Oaklands. BL6—5A 22
Oaklands. SK9—2G 159
Oaklands Av. SK6—3G 135
Oaklands Av. SK8—3C 142
Oaklands Clo. SK9—6A 152
Oaklands Dri. M25—5F 59
Oaklands Dri. M33—4A 114
Oaklands Dri. SK7—4E 145
Oaklands Dri. SK14—5E 107
Oaklands Pk. OL4—4H 67
Oaklands Rd. BL0—3A 4
Oaklands Rd. M7—4E 73
Oaklands Rd. M27—5D 70
Oaklands Rd. OL2—5C 48
Oaklands Rd. OL3 & OL4—4H 67
Oakland Ter. OL11—4C 32
Oak La. M25—1F 59
Oak La. SK9—3C 158
Oak Lea Av. SK9—4D 158
Oaklea Rd. M33—3G 113
Oakleigh. SK3—1H 143
Oakleigh Av. BL3—5C 38
Oakleigh Av. M19—2B 118
Oakleigh Av. WA15—4A 126
Oakley Clo. M26—1G 57
Oakley Clo. M9—5D 84
Oakley Pk. BL1—6D 22
Oakley St. M5—3D 84
Oakley St. OL15—5C 8
Oakley Vs. SK4—6D 118
Oak Lodge. SK7—6H 143
Oakmere Av. M30—1E 83
Oakmere Clo. M22—1B 140
Oakmere Rd. SK8—1B 142
Oakmere Rd. SK9—2H 151
Oak M. SK9—6G 151
Oakmoor Dri. M7—3E 73
Oakmoor Rd. M23—5G 127
Oakridge Wlk. M9—4F 75
Oak Rd. M7—5G 73
Oak Rd. M20—4F 117
Oak Rd. M31—6B 110
Oak Rd. M33—5D 114
Oak Rd. M35—5F 77
Oak Rd. OL8—1A 78
Oak Rd. SK8—5A 130
Oak Rd. WA15—2G 137
Oaks Av. BL2—1E 25
Oaksey Wlk. M7—4F 73
Oakside Clo. SK8—5H 129
Oaks La. BL2—6F 13
Oaks, The. SK8—3E 141
Oak St. BL0—4D 4
Oak St. M4—3E 87 & 4B 162
  (in two parts)
Oak St. M24—2D 62
Oak St. M26—6A 42
Oak St. M27—2G 71
Oak St. M30—4F 83
Oak St. M34—1F 105
Oak St. OL2—6G 35
Oak St. OL10—2D 30
Oak St. OL12—1H 7
Oak St. OL15—4G 9
  (Littleborough)
Oak St. OL15—6D 8
  (Smithy Bridge)
Oak St. OL16—1F 35
  (Newhey)
Oak St. OL16—4H 19
  (Rochdale)
Oak St. SK3—3D 130
Oak St. SK7—2D 144
Oak St. SK14—3C 106
Oak Ter. OL15—5H 9
Oak Tree Clo. SK2—3D 132
Oak Tree Ct. SK8—6H 129
Oak Tree Cres. SK15—5E 93
Oak Tree Dri. SK16—6D 92
Oak View Rd. OL3—4F 53
Oakville Dri. M6—1A 84

Oakville Ter. M10—2H 75
Oakway. M20—3G 129
Oakwell Dri. BL9—4F 43
Oakwell Dri. M8—2A 74
Oakwood. OL9—2E 63
Oakwood Av. M10—2D 64
Oakwood Av. M27—5E 57
Oakwood Av. M28—1H 69
Oakwood Av. M34—6E 91
Oakwood Av. SK8—6E 129
Oakwood Av. SK9—3B 158
Oakwood Clo. BL8—2H 27
Oakwood Dri. BL1—5D 22
Oakwood Dri. M6—6H 71
Oakwood Dri. M28—1H 69
Oakwood Ho. M21—1A 116
Oakwood La. WA14—5D 136
Oakwood Rd. SK6—1A 134
Oakwood Rd. SK12—1H 157
Oakworth Croft. OL4—3B 50
Oakworth St. M9—1E 75
Oatlands. SK9—6H 159
Oatlands Rd. M22—3A 140
Oat St. SK1—4A 132
Oats Wlk. M13—3G 101
Oban Av. M10—1D 88
Oban Av. OL1—6F 49
Oban Cres. SK3—1F 143
Oban Dri. M33—6E 115
Oban Gro. BL1—6C 10
Oban St. BL1—2H 23
Oberlin St. M14—2H 65
Oberlin St. OL11—6F 19
Oberon Clo. M30—3F 83
Occleston Clo. M33—2E 127
Occupation Rd. M17—6H 83
Ocean St. WA14—5D 124
Ocean Wlk. M15—2D 100
Ockenden Dri. M9—3F 75
Ocshell Ho. M6—2F 85
Octagon Ct. BL1—1B 38
Octavia Dri. M10—1E 89
*Octavia Ho. M6—2F 85
  (off Sutton Dwellings)*
Oddies Yd. OL12—1A 20
Odell St. M11—6D 88
Odessa Av. M6—6H 71
Odette St. M18—2E 103
Off Duke St. OL5—2G 81
Offerton Fold. SK2—4C 132
Offerton Grn. SK2—5F 133
Offerton La. SK2—3B 132
Offerton Rd. SK7 & SK2—2G 145
Offerton St. SK1—1B 132
Off Green St. M24—6A 46
Off Grove Rd. SK15—1H 93
*Off Kershaw St. OL2—6F 35
  (off Kershaw St., in two parts)
Off Lees St. OL2—6F 35
  (off Lees St.)*
Off Ridge Hill La. SK15—3D 92
Off Stamford St. SK15—1H 93
*Ogbourne Wlk. M13—1G 101
  (off Lauderdale Cres.)*
Ogden Clo. M25—6E 43
Ogden Clo. OL10—3C 30
Ogden Ct. SK14—5C 106
Ogden Gdns. SK16—5C 92
Ogden Gro. SK8—1D 140
Ogden La. M11—6F 89
Ogden Rd. M35—5F 77
Ogden Rd. SK7—2E 153
Ogden's Bldgs. SK15—3G 93
Ogden Sq. SK16—5H 91
Ogden St. M15—1A 100 &
                         5B 164
Ogden St. M20—6F 117
Ogden St. M24—1A 62
Ogden St. M25—5G 59
Ogden St. M27—4F 71
Ogden St. OL4—3H 65
Ogden St. OL6—6H 79
Ogden St. OL9—1A 64
Ogden St. OL11—3C 32
Ogden Wlk. M25—1E 59
Ogmore Wlk. M10—1C 76

Ogwen Dri. M25—4F 59
Ohio Av. M5—5F 85
Oil Works Rd. M14—4F 125
O'Kane Ho. M30—4F 83
Okehampton Clo. M26—2C 40
Okehampton Cres. M33—4F 113
Okeover Rd. M7—3H 73
Olaf St. BL2—4D 24
Old Bank St. M4—4D 86 & 5H 161
Old Barn Pl. BL7—3E 11
Old Barton Rd. M31—1E 97
Old Broadway. M20—4F 117
Old Brook Clo. OL2—5H 35
Old Brow. OL5—2E 81
  (in two parts)
Old Brow. OL16—6A 8
Oldbury Clo. M10—2H 87 & 2G 163
Oldbury Clo. OL10—6F 31
Oldcastle Av. M20—1E 117
Old Chapel St. SK3—4E 131
Old Church St. M10—5B 76
Old Chu. St. OL1—2D 64
Old Clough La. M28—3H 69
  (in two parts)
Old Cottage Clo. M28—6B 68
Old Crofts Bank. M31—3E 97
Old Cross St. OL6—2A 92
Old Delph Rd. OL11—2A 18
Old Doctors St. BL8—4H 13
Old Eagley M. BL1—5D 10
Old Edge La. OL2 & OL1—5C 48
Old Elm St. M13—1G 101 & 5F 167
Old Engine La. BL0—3F 5
Oldershaw Dri. M9—5F 75
Old Farm Cres. M35—5H 89
Old Farm Rd. SK2—5F 133
Oldfield Dri. WA15—5H 125
Oldfield La. WA14—1A 136
Oldfield M. WA14—6E 125
Oldfield Rd. M5—5A 86 & 2A 164
Oldfield Rd. M25—2G 59
Oldfield Rd. M33—4C 114
Oldfield Rd. WA14—6C 124
Oldfield St. M11—4D 88
Old Fold. M30—1E 83
Old Fold. SK7—2D 144
Old Gdns. St. SK1—3H 131
Oldgate Wlk. M15—1B 100 & 6D 164
Oldgreave Wlk. M15—1C 100 & 5E 165
Old Green. BL8—2H 13
Old Ground St. BL0—3E 5
Old Hall Clough. BL6—6A 22
Old Hall Ct. M33—5E 115
Old Hall Dri. M18—3F 103
Old Hall Dri. SK2—2H 145
Old Hall La. BL6—4A 22
Old Hall La. M14, M13 or M19
                         —6H 101
Old Hall La. M25 & M24—2A 60
  (Prestwich)
Old Hall La. M25—3A 58
  (Whitefield)
Old Hall La. SK6—6F 135
Old Hall La. SK7—6F 153
Old Hall La. SK14—2C 108
Old Hall Rd. M7—2H 73
Old Hall Rd. M10—4B 76
Old Hall Rd. M25—2A 58
Old Hall Rd. M32—3H 97
Old Hall Rd. M33—5E 115
Old Hall Rd. SK8—5E 129
Old Hall Sq. SK14—2H 109
Old Hall St. BL4—2G 55
Old Hall St. N. BL1—6B 24
Oldhall St. M24—1H 61
  (in two parts)
Old Hall St. SK16—6G 91
Old Hall St. N. BL1—6B 24
Oldham Av. SK1—2B 132
Oldham Central Trading Pk. OL1
                         —1E 65
Oldham Ct. M10—2G 87 & 2F 163
Oldham Dri. SK6—5G 121
Oldham Ho. OL2—2F 49
Oldham Rd. M4 & M10—3F 87 &
                         3C 162
Oldham Rd. M24—1A 62

Oldham Rd. OL2—3C 48
  (Royton)
Oldham Rd. OL2—3F 49
  (Shaw)
Oldham Rd. OL3—1C 50
Oldham Rd. OL4 & OL3—1E 67
  (Scouthead & Dobcross)
Oldham Rd. OL4 & OL3—3B 66
  (Springhead & Uppermill)
Oldham Rd. OL7—4E 79
Oldham Rd. OL7 & OL6—6E 79
Oldham Rd. OL11—4H 33
Oldhams Ter. BL1—6B 10
  (in three parts)
Oldham St. BL3—1H 37
Oldham St. M1 & M4—4E 87 & 5B 162
Oldham St. M5—4B 86 & 6C 160
Oldham St. M34—5C 104
Oldham St. M35—3B 90
Oldham St. OL8—1A 78
Oldham St. SK5—2G 119
Oldham St. SK14—5B 106
Oldham Way. OL9, OL8, OL1 & OL4
                         —1B 64
Oldheyes Rd. WA15—3B 126
Old Ho. Ter. OL6—6A 80
Old Kiln La. BL1—3A 22
Oldknow Rd. SK6—5E 135
Old La. BL0—3A 4
Old La. BL9—3F 15
Old La. M11—5F 89
Old La. M28—3B 54
Old La. OL3—5B 52
  (Dobcross)
Old La. OL3—6D 52
  (Pobgreen)
Old La. OL4—1B 66
  (Austerlands)
Old La. OL4—3G 67
  (Grasscroft)
Old La. OL9—5H 63
Old Lansdowne Rd. M20—5D 116
Old Lees St. OL6—6H 79
Old Market Pl. WA14—6F 125
Old Market St. M9—1E 75
Old Meadow Dri. M34—2F 105
Old Meadow La. WA15—2B 138
Old Medlock St. M3—5B 86 & 1D 164
Old Mill Clo. M27—3H 71
Old Mill Ho. OL4—4C 66
Old Mill La. OL4—4C 66
Old Mill La. SK7—5G 145
Old Mills Hill. M24—6D 46
Old Mill St. M4—4G 87 & 5E 163
Oldmill St. OL12—3H 19
Old Moat La. M20—2E 117
Oldmoor Rd. SK6—4E 121
Old Mount St. M4—2E 87 &
                         2C 162
Old Nans La. BL2—3H 25
Old Oake Clo. M28—1G 69
Old Oak St. M20—6F 117
Old Parrin La. M30—2D 82
Old Quarry La. BL7—2D 10
Old Rectory Gdns. SK8—6H 129
Old Rd. BL1—1A 24
Old Rd. M35—4E 77
Old Rd. OL6—6B 80
Old Rd. OL16—5C 8
Old Rd. SK4—6G 119
Old Rd. SK8—5B 130
Old Rd. SK9—4H 151
  (Handforth)
Old Rd. SK9—1E 159
  (Wilmslow)
Old Rd. SK14—2B 106
  (Hyde)
Old Rd. SK14—1B 108
  (Mottram)
Old Rd. SK15—5G 93
Old Rd. SK16—4A 92
  (in two parts)
Old Sq. OL6—2A 92
Oldstead Gro. BL3—3D 36
*Oldstead Wlk. M9—5F 75
  (off Parkstead Dri.)*
Old St. OL4—4H 65
Old St. OL6—3G 91
Old St. SK15—3E 93

Old Swan Clo. BL7—1C 10
Old Swan Cotts. BL7—1C 10
Old Thorn La. OL3—3H 53
Old Vicarage Gdns. M28—6F 55
Oldway Wlk. M10—6B 76
Old Wellington Rd. M30—3F 83
Old Wells Clo. M34—3C 54
Old Well Wlk. M33—1E 125
Old Wood La. BL2—5A 26
Oldwood Rd. M23—2G 139
Old Wool La. SK8—1B 142
Olerton Dri. M35—5F 77
Olga St. BL1—3H 23
Olivant St. BL9—5C 28
Olive Bank. BL8—1H 27
Olive Rd. WA15—3A 126
Oliver Clo. OL15—4D 8
Olive Rd. WA15—3A 126
Oliver St. OL1—3D 64
Oliver St. SK3—3G 131
Olive St. BL3—3H 37
Olive St. BL8—3B 28
Olive St. M35—3E 77
Olive St. OL8—3B 64
Olive St. OL10—3G 31
Olive St. OL11—4D 32
Olive Wlk. M33—3E 113
Olivia Gro. M14—4H 101
Ollerbarrow Rd. WA15—3G 137
*Ollerbrook Ct. BL1—3B 24
Ollerton. OL12—3G 19
  (off Spotland Rd.)*
Ollerton Av. M16—4A 100
Ollerton Av. M33—3F 113
Ollerton Clo. M22—2C 128
Ollerton Rd. SK9—2H 151
Ollerton St. BL1—5D 10
*Ollerton Ter. BL1—5D 10
  (off Ollerton St.)*
Ollier Av. M12—5C 102
Olney. OL11—5G 19
Olney Av. M22—5B 128
Olney St. M13—3H 101
Olwen Av. M12—3C 102
Olwen Cres. SK5—1H 119
Olympia Trading Est. M15—6C 86 &
                         3F 165
Olympic Ct. M5—5F 85
Omer Av. M13—5B 102
Omer Dri. M19—2A 118
Onchan Av. OL4—3F 65
One Ash Clo. OL12—1H 19
Oneoak Ct. SK7—3F 143
One Oak La. SK9—2H 159
Ongar Way. M9—6D 60
Onslow Av. M10—2E 77
Onslow Clo. OL1—1C 64
Onslow Rd. SK3—3E 131
Onslow St. OL11—1C 32
Onward St. SK14—5B 106
Oozewood Rd. OL2—2G 47
Opal St. M19—1D 118
Openshaw Fold Rd. BL9—6B 28
Openshaw La. M30—3C 110
Openshaw Pl. BL4—1D 54
Openshaw St. BL9—4E 29
Openshaw Wlk. M11—5E 89
Oracle Ct. M28—1E 69
Orama Av. M6—1A 84
Oram St. BL9—1E 29
Orange Hill Rd. M25—4G 59
Orange St. M6—2G 85
Orange St. OL6—2H 91
Orchard Av. BL1—2B 24
Orchard Av. M28—4D 68
Orchard Av. M31—5D 110
Orchard Clo. SK8—6E 143
Orchard Clo. SK9—4C 158
Orchard Clo. SK12—4E 155
Orchard Dri. SK9—5A 152
Orchard Dri. WA15—2A 138
Orchard Gdns. BL2—2H 25
Orchard Grn. SK9—5H 159
Orchard Gro. M20—4D 116
Orchard Gro. OL2—6E 35
Orchard Inst. Est. M6—6E 73
Orchard Pl. M33—4B 114
Orchard Pl. WA15—4B 126
Orchard Rd. M35—4F 77

Palatine St. M34—2E 105
Palatine St. OL16—4C 20
Palatine Ter. OL11—3C 18
Paley Bl. BL1—6B 24
Palfrey Pl. M12—6G 87 & 4F 167
Palgrave Av. M10—6F 75
Palin Wood Rd. OL3—2H 51
Pall Mall. M2—4D 86 & 5H 161
(in two parts)
Palm Clo. M33—4E 113
Palmer Av. SK8—5B 130
Palmer Clo. M8—1D 74
Palmerston Av. M16—5B 100
Palmerston Clo. BL0—5D 4
Palmerston Clo. M34—4B 104
Palmerston Rd. M34—4B 104
Palmerston Rd. SK2—2A 144
Palmerston St. M12—5H 87 & 1G 167
Palmer St. M7—6G 73
Palmer St. M33—5A 114
Palmer St. SK16—4H 91
Palm Gro. OL9—1H 63
Palm St. BL1—2A 24
Palm St. M13—4B 102
Palm St. M35—3F 89
Palm St. OL4—1G 65
Pandora St. M20—4E 117
Panfield Rd. M22—1A 140
Pangbourne Av. M31—4G 97
Pankhurst Wlk. M14—4F 101
Panmure St. OL8—5D 64
Pansy Rd. BL4—1C 54
Paper Mill Rd. BL7—4E 11
Parade Rd. M22—6A 140
Parade, The. M27—3F 71
Parade, The. SK6—2G 133
Paradise St. BL0—3E 5
Paradise St. M34—6F 91
Paradise St. SK14—2H 109
Paradise Wharf. M1—4F 87 & 6D 162
Parbold Av. M20—2E 117
Parbrook Clo. M10—6F 75
Parcel St. M11—3B 88
Pardoner's Ct. M5—3B 84
Pares Land Wlk. OL16—5B 20
Paris Av. M5—6H 85
Parisian Way. M15—2D 100
(off Moss Side Shopping Cen.)
Paris St. BL3—3F 37
Park Av. BL0—3F 5
Park Av. BL1—1A 24
Park Av. M8—3B 74
Park Av. M16—2A 100
Park Av. M19—6C 102
Park Av. M25—5F 59
(Prestwich)
Park Av. M25—3B 58
(Whitefield)
Park Av. M26—3B 42
Park Av. M27—4G 71
Park Av. M31—5E 97
Park Av. M35—3D 76
Park Av. OL9—6H 47
Park Av. SK3—4B 130
Park Av. SK6—6A 122
Park Av. SK7—2E 153
Park Av. SK8—4B 142
Park Av. SK9—1F 159
Park Av. SK12—3E 155
Park Av. SK14—3B 106
Park Av. WA14—3G 125
Park Av. WA15—4H 137
Park Bank. M3—3D 84
Parkbridge Wlk. M13—1F 101 & 5D 166
Parkbrook Rd. M23—4H 127
Park Brow Clo. M21—1A 116
Park Bungalows. SK6—6D 134
Park Clo. M25—3D 58
Park Clo. OL9—6H 47
Park Clo. SK15—2D 92
Park Clo. WA14—3H 125
Park Cotts. BL1—2G 23
Park Cotts. OL3—3E 81
Park Cotts. OL3—4G 67
Park Ct. M22—2B 140
Park Ct. M33—4A 114
Park Ct. OL11—5G 19
Park Ct. M. SK8—1A 142

Park Cres. M14—4G 101
Park Cres. OL6—3C 92
Park Cres. OL9—6F 47
Park Cres. SK9—6F 151
Parkdale. OL6—3C 92
Parkdale Av. M18—2E 103
Parkdale Av. M34—6D 90
Parkdale Rd. BL2—4E 25
Parkdene Clo. BL2—1F 25
Park Dri. M16—5A 100
Park Dri. M30—1F 83
Park Dri. SK4—1D 130
Park Dri. SK14—3B 106
Park Dri. WA15—4A 126
(Altrincham)
Park Dri. WA15—3H 137
(Hale)
Parkend Rd. M23—6G 127
Parker Arc. M1—4E 87
(off Piccadilly Plaza)
Parker St. BL9—3E 29
Parker St. M1—4E 87 & 6B 162
Parkfield. M5—3D 84
Parkfield. M24—6H 45
Parkfield. M30—3G 95
Parkfield. OL9—6G 47
Parkfield Av. BL4—2D 54
Parkfield Av. M14—4F 101
Parkfield Av. M25—6H 59
Parkfield Av. M31—6D 96
Parkfield Av. OL8—1H 77
Parkfield Av. SK6—5D 134
Parkfield Ct. WA14—1E 137
Parkfield Dri. M24—1G 61
Parkfield Est. M27—5G 71
Parkfield Ind. Est. M24—1G 61
Parkfield Rd. BL3—4B 38
Park Field Rd. OL4—3G 67
Parkfield Rd. SK8—4B 142
Parkfield Rd. WA14—1E 137
Parkfield Rd. N. M10—1E 77
Parkfield Rd. S. M20—5E 117
Parkfields. SK15—2H 93
Parkfield St. M14—4F 101
Parkfield St. OL16—1H 33
Parkgate. BL8—6G 13
Parkgate. OL9—6H 47
Park Ga. Av. M20—3F 117
Parkgate Dri. BL1—6D 10
Parkgate Dri. M27—4G 71
Parkgate Dri. SK2—1B 144
Park Gates Av. SK8—4E 143
Park Gates Rd. SK8—4E 143
Parkgate Way. OL2—6H 35
Parkgate Way. SK9—3H 151
Park Gro. M15—1A 100
Park Gro. M19—5C 102
Park Gro. M26—3F 41
Park Gro. M28—3F 69
Park Gro. SK4—5D 118
Park Hill. OL12—2H 19
Parkhill Av. M8—1D 74
Parkhill Dri. M25—1C 58
Park Hill Rd. WA15—4A 138
Parkhills Rd. BL9—5C 28
Park Hill St. BL1—5H 23
Parkhill Ter. SK15—2H 93
Park Ho. Bri. Rd. M6—5C 72
Parkhouse St. M11—5D 88
Parkhouse St. Ind. Est. M11
—5D 88
Parkhurst Av. M10—2E 77
Parkin Clo. SK16—5A 92
Parkinson St. BL3—2G 37
Parkinson St. BL9—6F 15
Parkin St. M12—4C 102
Park Lake Av. M7—3A 74
Parklands. M25—1C 58
Parklands. OL2—6A 34
(Royton)
Parklands. OL2—5H 35
(Shaw)
Parklands. SK9—2F 159
Parklands. SK12—3E 155
Parklands Cres. OL10—5C 30
Parklands Dri. M33—1F 125
Parklands Ho. OL2—1A 48
Parklands Rd. M23—3F 127
Parklands, The. SK4—5G 119

Parklands Way. OL10—5C 30
Parklands Way. SK12—3E 155
Park La. M25—2B 58
Park La. M27—4B 72
Park La. M28—4A 68
Park La. OL2—2B 48
(in four parts)
Park La. OL3—4G 53
Park La. OL8—1D 78
Park La. OL16—3H 19
Park La. SK1—3B 132
Park La. SK12—1E 157
(Disley)
Park La. SK12—3E 155
(Poynton)
Park La. WA15—4A 138
Park La. Ct. M7—3H 73
Park La. Ct. M25—2B 58
Park La. W. M27—4B 72
Park Lea Ct. M7—2A 74
Park Lodge. M7—3H 73
Park Lodge. M19—6C 102
Park Lodge Clo. SK8—1A 142
Park M. M16—5A 100
Park Mt. SK8—6E 129
Parkmount Rd. M9—2G 75
Park Pde. OL2—4G 35
Park Pde. OL7 & OL6—3G 91
Park Pl. M4—2E 87 & 1A 162
Park Pl. M6—2A 84
Park Pl. M25—4G 59
Park Pl. SK4—1B 130
Park Range. M14—4H 101
Park Rise. SK6—6A 122
Park Rise. SK15—2D 92
Park Rd. BL1—6G 23
Park Rd. BL3—3H 39
Park Rd. BL5—6A 36
Park Rd. BL9—1C 28
Park Rd. M24—1H 61
Park Rd. M25 & M8—6H 59
Park Rd. M28—2E 69
Park Rd. M30—1F 83
Park Rd. M30 & M6—1A 84
Park Rd. M31—6E 111
Park Rd. M32—3C 98
Park Rd. M33—3A 114
Park Rd. M34—5D 90
(Audenshaw)
Park Rd. M34—4E 105
(Denton)
Park Rd. OL8 & OL4—3D 64
Park Rd. OL12—1A 20
Park Rd. OL15—3F 9
Park Rd. SK6—5A 122
Park Rd. SK8—5A 130
(Cheadle)
Park Rd. SK8—4E 143
(Cheadle Hulme)
Park Rd. SK8—5D 128
(Gatley)
Park Rd. SK9—2D 158
Park Rd. SK12—1D 156
Park Rd. SK14—3B 106
Park Rd. SK16—4A 92
Park Rd. WA14 & WA15
—3G 125
(Altrincham)
Park Rd. WA14—2C 136
(Bowdon)
Park Rd. WA15—4G 137
Park Rd. N. M31—4E 97
Park Rd. S. M31—5E 97
Park Row. BL1—5D 10
Park Row. SK4—1A 130
Park Seventeen. M25—6E 43
Parkside. M24—3G 61
Parkside. OL12—3H 7
Parkside Av. M7—3A 74
Parkside Av. M28—2F 69
Parkside Av. M30—4E 83
Parkside Av. M35—6E 77
Park Side Av. OL5—5G 35
Parkside Clo. M26—3B 42
Parkside Clo. SK6—5B 146

Parkside Ho. OL2—3C 48
Parkside Ind. Est. OL2—3C 48
Parkside La. SK6—5G 135
Parkside Rd. M14—5D 100
Parkside Rd. M33—6D 114
Parkside St. BL2—4E 25
Parkside St. M12—6G 87
Parkside Wlk. BL9—4D 28
Parkside Wlk. SK7—2G 143
(in two parts)
Parks Nook. BL2—2E 55
Park Sq. M16—5G 99
Park Sq. OL6—1C 92
Parkstead Dri. M9—5F 75
Parkstone Av. M18—1H 103
Parkstone Av. M25—3B 58
Parkstone Dri. M27—5H 71
Parkstone La. M28—6H 69
Parkstone Rd. M30—4E 95
Park St. BL1—5H 23
Park St. BL4—6F 39
Park St. BL9—2D 28
Park St. M3—2D 86 & 1H 161
(Manchester)
Park St. M3—3B 86 & 4C 160
(Salford)
Park St. M7—3G 73
Park St. M25—5G 59
Park St. M26—3A 42
Park St. M27—4G 71
Park St. M34—4D 104
Park St. M35—3C 90
(Droylsden)
Park St. OL2—3C 48
(Royton)
Park St. OL2—6F 35
(Shaw)
Park St. OL5—3E 81
Park St. OL7—4G 91
(in two parts)
Park St. OL8—4C 64
(in two parts)
Park St. OL10—5G 31
Park St. OL16—5H 19
Park St. SK1—1H 131
Park St. SK6—6F 121
Park St. SK15—4F 93
Parkway. M9—4D 60
Parkway. M25—1G 73
Parkway. M27—5A 72
Parks Yd. BL9—3C 28
Park Ter. BL1—5D 10
Park Ter. M25—2B 58
Park Ter. OL5—3E 81
Park Ter. OL7—2F 31
Park, The. OL3—6G 53
Park, The. OL4—3F 67
Park View. BL1—5D 10
(in two parts)
Park View. BL4—6F 39
(Farnworth)
Park View. BL4—2H 55
(Kearsley)
Park View. M5—6H 85
Park View. M9—5E 75
Park View. M14—2A 118
Park View. OL2—5D 34
Park View. OL9—6G 47
Park View. SK3—4B 130
Park View. SK6—6C 120
Park View. SK7—5H 145
Park View. SK8—5E 129
Park View Clo. M25—6E 59
Park View Ct. M21—6F 99
Parkview Ct. M32—6F 99
Park View Rd. BL3—3G 37
Park View Rd. M25—6F 59
Parkville Rd. M20—4G 117
Parkville Rd. M25—2G 59
Park Way. M28—5A 54
(in two parts)
Park Way. M31, M32 & M17
—3H 97
Parkway. OL9—6G 47
Parkway. OL11—3D 18
Parkway. SK3—4B 130
Parkway. SK7—3G 143
Parkway. SK9—3E 159
Parkway Bus. Cen. M14—5D 100

Penhale M. SK7—6H 143
Penhall Wlk. M10—6A 76
(off Limerston Dri.)
Pen Ho. Clo. SK7—5G 143
Penistone Av. M6—2C 84
Penistone Av. M9—6A 62
Penistone Av. OL16—5C 20
Penketh Av. M18—3C 102
Penmere Gro. M33—2G 125
Penmore Chase. SK7—4B 144
Penmore Clo. OL2—6G 35
Pennant Dri. M25—4E 59
Pennant St. OL1—1F 65
Pennell St. M11—4F 89
Penn Grn. BL4—4D 142
Pennie Ct. SK2—5E 133
Pennie Rd. SK6—4A 122
Pennine Av. OL9—4G 63
Pennine Clo. BL8—1G 27
Pennine Clo. M9—5H 61
Pennine Clo. OL2—6G 35
Pennine Ct. M27—2G 71
Pennine Dri. OL4—3E 65
Pennine Dri. OL12—3A 8
Pennine Dri. OL16—4G 21
Pennine Dri. WA14—6D 124
Pennine Gro. OL6—5A 80
Pennine Rd. SK6—4A 122
Pennine Rd. SK7—4B 144
Pennine Ter. SK14—4A 92
(off Astley St.)
Pennine Vale. OL2—5G 35
Pennine View. M34—2E 105
Pennine View. OL2—3C 48
Pennine View. OL5—2F 81
Pennine View. OL15—5H 9
Pennine View. SK15—1G 93
Pennington Clo. M28—5A 54
Pennington Rd. BL3—4B 38
Pennington St. BL8—1E 27
Pennington St. M12—5C 102
Pennington St. M28—1G 69
Pennington St. OL9—6H 63
Pennistone Clo. M30—4F 95
Penn St. BL4—1E 55
Penn St. M10—3H 75
Penn St. OL8—4B 64
Penn St. OL10—4F 31
Penn St. OL16—3H 19
Penny Bri. La. M31—6C 96
Penny Brook Fold. SK7
—2E 145
Penny La. SK5—1H 131
(in two parts)
Penny Meadow. OL6—2A 92
(in two parts)
Pennymoor Dri. WA14—5D 124
Penrhos Av. SK8—6D 128
Penrhyn Av. M24—2A 62
Penrhyn Av. SK8—4A 142
Penrhyn Cres. SK7—5C 144
Penrhyn Dri. M25—5F 59
Penrhyn Rd. SK3—3D 130
Penrice Clo. M26—2D 40
Penrice Fold. M28—4D 68
Penrith Av. BL1—4E 23
Penrith Av. M11—2D 88
Penrith Av. M25—2F 59
Penrith Av. M28—1H 69
Penrith Av. M33—1C 126
Penrith Av. OL7—6D 78
Penrith Av. OL8—5A 64
Penrith Av. SK5—6H 103
Penrith Clo. M31—5C 110
Penrith St. OL11—6H 19
Penrod Pl. M6—1H 85
Penrose St. BL2—6E 25
Penroy Av. M20—6B 116
Penroyson Clo. M12—1B 102
Penruddock Wlk. M13—3B 102
(off St John's Rd.)
Penry Av. M30—3C 110
Penryn Av. M33—2C 126
Penryn Av. OL2—4D 48
Penryn Ct. M7—2H 73
Pensarn Av. M14—1A 118
Pensarn Gro. SK5—5H 119
Pensby Clo. M27—4A 72
Pensby Wlk. M10—6F 75

Pensford Ct. BL2—5A 12
Pensford Rd. M23—2F 139
Penshurst Rd. SK5—3B 120
Penshurst Wlk. M34—6G 105
Penthorpe Dri. OL2—4D 48
Pentland. BL1—4A 24
Pentland Av. M10—1C 76
Pentland Clo. SK7—4A 144
Pentlands Av. M7—5H 73
Penton Wlk. M16—4D 100
Pentrich Wlk. M15—1C 100 & 5E 165
Pentwyn Gro. M23—4H 127
Penwortham St. M10—1B 88
Penzance St. M10—2A 88
Peover Av. M33—5E 115
Peover Rd. SK9—2A 152
Peover Wlk. SK8—6C 130
Pepler Av. M23—1H 127
Peploe Wlk. M23—2D 126
Pepper Ct. SK9—3D 158
Pepperhill Wlk. M16—3D 100
Pepper Rd. SK7—3B 144
Perch Wlk. M4—3G 87
(off Kirby Wlk.)
Percival Wlk. OL2—4C 48
Percy Dri. M5—6H 85
Percy Rd. M34—5E 105
Percy St. BL0—4D 4
Percy St. BL1—3B 24
Percy St. BL4—2G 55
Percy St. BL9—2E 29
Percy St. M15—1B 100 & 6D 164
Percy St. OL4—2G 65
Percy St. OL5—2E 81
Percy St. OL16—6B 20
Percy St. SK1—1H 131
Percy St. SK15—3F 93
Peregrine Cres. M35—2C 90
Peregrine Dri. M30—3E 95
Peregrine Rd. SK2—1F 145
Periton Wlk. M9—6G 61
(off Levedale Rd.)
Perivale Dri. OL8—5F 65
Perkins Av. M7—6H 73
Pernham St. OL4—2G 65
Perrin St. SK14—5B 106
Perry Av. SK14—3E 107
Perrygate Av. M20—3E 117
Perryman Clo. M15—1D 100
& 5H 165
(in two parts)
Perrymead. M25—3G 59
Perrymead Clo. M15—2D 100
Perry Rd. WA15—5B 126
Pershore Dri. OL12—3G 19
(off Spotland Rd.)
Pershore Rd. M24—4A 46
Persian Clo. M26—2E 101
Perth. M30—3G 83
(off St Andrews Ct.)
Perth Av. OL9—5G 63
Perth Clo. SK7—2G 153
Perth Rd. OL11—3H 33
Perth St. BL3—4F 37
(in two parts)
Perth St. M27—4D 70
Perth St. OL2—3E 49
Peru St. M3—3B 86 & 3C 160
Peterborough Clo. OL6—5F 79
Peterborough Dri. BL1—4B 24
Peterborough St. M18—1H 103
Peterborough Wlk. BL1—4B 24
(off Charnock Dri.)
Peterchurch Wlk. M11—5E 89
Peterhead Clo. BL1—4H 23
Peterhead Wlk. M5—4G 85
Peterhouse Gdns. SK6—5A 122
Peterloo Ter. M24—5A 46
Peter Moss Way. M19—6E 103
Petersburg Rd. SK3—5E 131
Petersfield Dri. M23—4D 126
Petersfield Wlk. BL1—4A 24
Peterson St. M11—6C 88
Peter St. BL9—2D 28
Peter St. M2—5D 86 & 1G 165
Peter St. M24—2E 61
Peter St. M30—4F 83
Peter St. M34—4G 105

Peter St. OL1—2D 64
(in two parts)
Peter St. SK1—1A 132
(in two parts)
Peter St. SK7—2D 144
Peter St. SK14—1H 109
Peter St. WA14—2F 137
Peterswood Dri. M22—2H 139
Petheridge Dri. M22—4H 139
Petrel Av. SK12—3B 154
Petrel Clo. M35—2C 90
Petrel Clo. OL11—4B 18
Petrie Ct. M6—1H 85
Petrie St. OL12—3H 19
Petrock Wlk. M10—6C 76
Petts Cres. OL15—3E 9
Petunia Wlk. M28—6B 54
(off Madam Wood Rd.)
Petworth Rd. OL9—3H 63
Pevensey Ct. M9—1A 76
Pevensey Rd. M6—5C 72
Pevensey Wlk. OL9—3H 63
Peveril Clo. M25—2G 59
Peveril Cres. M21—5G 99
Peveril Dri. SK7—5F 145
Peveril Rd. M5—3D 84
Peveril Rd. OL1—6G 49
Peveril Rd. WA14—4E 125
Peveril St. BL3—4F 37
Peveril Ter. SK14—1D 122
Pewsey Rd. M22—2D 140
Pexwood. OL1—6E 47
Pheasant Clo. M28—5D 68
Pheasant Dri. M21—2B 116
Pheasant Rise. WA14—4F 137
Phelan Clo. M10—6E 75
Phethean St. BL2—6C 24
Phethean St. BL4—6E 39
Philip Av. M34—2D 104
Philip Dri. M33—1B 126
Philips Av. BL4—2F 55
Philips Dri. M25—3B 58
Philips Pk. Rd. M11—3A 88
Philip's Rd. M18—3F 103
Philip St. BL3—2H 37
Philip St. M30—4F 83
Philip St. OL4—1G 65
Philip St. OL11—6H 19
Phillimore St. OL4—4A 66
Phillips Pk. Rd. M25—4A 58
(in two parts)
Phillip Way. SK14—6A 108
Phipps St. M28—5E 55
Phoebe Clo. BL3—3G 37
Phoebe St. M5—5G 85
Phoenix Clo. OL10—4H 31
Phoenix Pk. Ind. Est. OL10
—4H 31
Phoenix Pl. OL4—2B 66
Phoenix St. BL1—5C 24
Phoenix St. BL4—2F 55
Phoenix St. BL9—3G 28
Phoenix St. M2—4E 87 & 5A 162
Phoenix St. OL1—3D 64
Phoenix St. OL4—2B 66
Phoenix St. OL12—2E 19
Phoenix St. OL15—3F 9
Phoenix Way. M26—5G 41
Phyliss St. M24—2C 62
Phyllis St. OL12—2D 18
Piccadilly. M1—4E 87 & 5B 162
(in two parts)
Piccadilly. SK1—2H 131
Piccadilly Pl. M1—4E 87 & 4B 162
Piccadilly Plaza. M1—4E 87 & 6B 162
Piccadilly Trading Est. M1—5G 87
& 1F 167
Piccadilly Village. M1—4G 87 & 6E 163
Pickering Clo. BL8—6B 14
Pickering Clo. M26—1A 56
Pickering Clo. M31—5D 96
Pickering Clo. WA15—4A 126
Pickford Av. BL3—4C 40
Pickford Clo. M15—2C 100
Pickford La. SK14—5A 92
Pickford M. SK16—5A 92
Pickford's Brow. SK1—2H 131
(off High Bankside)
Pickford St. M4—3F 87 & 4D 162

Pickford St. OL16—4A 20
Pickford Wlk. OL2—4C 48
Picklehill La. OL1—1F 53
Picklehill M. OL3—1F 53
Pickmere Av. M20—1F 117
Pickmere Clo. M33—1F 127
Pickmere Clo. M35—4B 90
Pickmere Clo. SK3—5E 131
Pickmere Ct. SK9—2H 151
Pickmere Gdns. SK8—6B 130
Pickmere Rd. SK9—2H 151
Pickmere Ter. SK16—4H 91
Pickmere Way. SK9—2H 151
Pickwick Pl. BL0—2E 5
Pickwick Rd. SK12—4D 154
Picton Clo. M3—3C 86 & 3E 161
Picton Dri. SK9—6A 152
Picton Sq. OL4—3E 65
Picton St. M7—2B 86 & 1D 160
Picton St. OL7—5E 79
Pierce St. OL1—6G 49
Piercy Av. M7—1B 86
Piercy St. M4—4H 87 & 4G 163
Piercy St. M35—4E 77
Piethorne Clo. OL16—1G 35
Pigeon St. M1—4E 87 & 5D 162
Piggott St. BL4—2E 55
Pike Av. M35—5A 78
Pike Fold La. M9—1E 75
Pike Mill Est. BL3—3A 38
Pike Rd. BL3—3H 37
Pike St. OL11—6H 19
Pike View Clo. OL4—4F 65
Pilgrim Dri. M11—4B 88
Pilkington Dri. M25—5F 43
Pilkington Rd. BL4—3H 55
Pilkington Rd. M9—1A 76
Pilkington Rd. M26—2F 41
Pilkington St. BL0—4D 4
Pilkington St. BL3—2A 38
Pilkington St. M24—6B 46
Pilkington Way. M26—4G 41
Pilling Field. BL7—2C 10
Pilling St. BL8—2A 28
Pilling St. M10—6H 75
Pilling St. M34—4F 105
Pilling St. OL12—3F 19
Pilling Wlk. OL9—3G 63
Pilning St. BL3—2D 38
Pilot St. BL9—4E 29
Pilsworth Rd. BL9—1E 43
Pilsworth Rd. OL10—6B 30
Pimblett St. M3—2D 86 & 1H 161
Pimhole Fold. BL9—4E 29
Pimhole Rd. BL9—3E 29
Pimlico Clo. M7—5H 73
Pimlott Gro. M25—1C 72
Pimlott Gro. SK14—2B 106
Pimlott Rd. BL1—2D 24
Pimmcroft Way. M33—6F 115
Pincher Wlk. M11—4E 89
Pinder Wlk. M15—1D 100 & 6H 165
Pineapple St. SK7—3E 145
Pine Av. M25—2D 58
Pine Clo. M34—1E 105
Pine Clo. SK6—1C 146
Pine Ct. M20—5E 117
Pine Ct. SK7—3F 143
Pine Gro. BL4—1D 54
Pine Gro. M14—3A 102
Pine Gro. M25—3E 59
Pine Gro. M27—4D 70
Pine Gro. M28—3G 69
Pine Gro. M30—1F 83
Pine Gro. M33—3F 113
Pine Gro. M34—4G 105
Pine Gro. OL2—1B 48
Pine Gro. SK16—5D 92
Pinehurst Rd. M10—6G 75
Pine Lodge. SK7—6H 143
Pine Rd. M20—5E 117
Pine Rd. SK7—5H 143
Pine Rd. SK12—4F 155
Pine Rd. SK15—5C 92
Pine St. BL1—3B 24
Pine St. M1—4E 87 & 6A 162
Pine St. M3—2B 86 & 2C 160
Pine St. M24—2C 62
Pine St. M26—3H 41

Pine St. OL6—1H 91
Pine St. OL9—1G 63
Pine St. OL10—3F 31
Pine St. OL15—3F 9
Pine St. OL16—2F 35
(Milnrow)
Pine St. OL16—4B 20
(Rochdale)
Pine St. SK6—4H 121
Pine St. SK4—2B 106
Pine St. N. BL9—3F 29
(in two parts)
Pine St. S. BL9—3F 29
Pinetop Clo. M21—2B 116
Pine Tree Rd. OL8—2B 78
Pine Trees. WA16—6A 148
Pinetree St. M18—2E 103
Pine Wlk. M31—6C 110
Pineway. OL4—3B 66
Pinewood. M33—5F 113
Pinewood. OL9—2E 63
Pinewood. WA14—3C 136
Pinewood Clo. BL1—3A 24
Pinewood Clo. SK4—6C 118
Pinewood Clo. SK16—4A 92
Pinewood Ct. M33—4D 114
Pinewood Ct. WA14—4G 137
Pinewood Cres. BL0—1B 14
Pinewood Rd. M21—2G 115
Pinewood Rd. SK9—6A 152
Pinfold. OL11—5G 19
Pinfold La. M25—3G 109
Pinfold Av. M9—1A 76
Pinfold Clo. WA15—6D 138
Pinfold Dri. SK8—4C 142
Pinfold La. SK6—5B 122
Pinfold La. WA15—1F 149
Pinfold Rd. M28—2E 69
Pingate Dri. SK8—1C 152
Pingate La. SK8—1C 152
Pingate La. S. SK8—1C 152
Pingle La. OL3—2G 51
Pingot. OL2—4H 35
Pingot Av. M23—1H 127
Pingot La. SK14—6D 108
Pingot, The. M30—4F 95
Pink Bank La. M12—3C 102
(in two parts)
Pin Mill Brow. M12—5H 87 & 2G 167
Pinnacle Dri. BL7—1B 10
Pinner Pl. M19—3C 118
Pinnington La. M32—6D 98
Pinnington Rd. M18—1F 103
Pioneer Rd. M27—1B 72
Pioneers St. OL4—4E 65
Pioneers St. OL11—5A 20
Pioneer St. M11—2D 88
Pioneer St. M24—2C 46
Pioneer St. OL15—4F 9
Pioneers Yd. OL16—5F 21
Piperhill Av. M22—2B 128
Pipit Clo. M34—3C 90
Pirie Wlk. M10—5C 76
Pitcairn Ho. M30—4F 83
Pitchcombe Rd. M22—3H 139
Pitfield Gdns. M23—4F 127
Pitfield La. BL2—1H 25
Pitfield St. BL2—6D 24
Pithouse La. OL12—1A 18
Pit La. OL2—5A 34
(in two parts)
Pitman Clo. M11—5C 88
Pitmore Wlk. M10—1D 76
Pitney Wlk. M16—4C 100
Pitsford Rd. M10—6G 75
Pitshouse. OL12—1A 18
Pit St. M34—1F 105
(Audenshaw)
Pit St. OL9—5H 63
Pittbrook St. M12—6H 87 & 3H 167
Pitts Farm Av. OL11—4E 19
Pitt St. M26—4E 41
Pitt St. M34—4F 105
(Denton)
Pitt St. OL4—3E 65
Pitt St. OL10—3E 31
Pitt St. OL12—3H 19

Pitt St. SK3—3F 131
Pitt St. SK14—4B 106
Pitt St. E. OL4—4F 65
Pixmore Av. BL1—1D 24
Place Rd. WA14—5E 125
Plain Pit St. SK14—2A 106
(in two parts)
Plainsfield Clo. M16—3D 100
Plane Ct. M6—3G 85
Plane Rd. M35—6F 77
Plane St. OL4—2G 65
Plane Tree Clo. SK6—6B 134
Plane Tree Rd. M31—6B 110
Planetree Rd. WA15—3A 138
Planet Way. M34—2E 105
Plantagenet Wlk. M10—1F 89
Plantation Av. M28—5E 55
Plantation St. M18—2G 103
Plantation St. OL6—3B 92
Plantation View. BL9—6E 5
Plant Clo. M33—4A 114
Plant Hill Rd. M9—4E 61
Plantree Wlk. M23—3C 126
Plant St. M1—4F 87 & 6C 162
Plate St. OL1—2D 64
Plato St. OL9—2B 64
Platt Av. OL6—5G 79
Plattbrook Clo. M14—6F 101
Platt Hill Av. BL3—3E 37
Platting Gro. OL7—6D 78
Platting La. OL11—1G 33
Platting Rd. OL4—1E 67
Platt La. M14—6D 100
Platt La. OL3—5H 51
Platts Dri. M30—5E 95
Platt St. OL4—3B 66
Platt St. SK8—5A 130
Platt St. SK16—6G 91
Platt Wlk. M34—6E 105
Plattwood Wlk. M15—1B 100 & 5D 164
Playfair Clo. OL16—6G 31
Play Fair St. BL1—5D 10
Playfair St. M14—3F 101
Pleachway. SK4—1B 130
Pleasant Gdns. BL1—5A 24
Pleasant Rd. M30—4G 83
Pleasant St. BL8—1F 27
Pleasant St. M9—4F 75
Pleasant St. OL10—1E 31
Pleasant St. OL11—3C 32
Pleasant Ter. SK16—4A 92
(off Astley St.)
Pleasant View. BL3—2F 39
Pleasant View. M9—5D 60
Pleasant View. M26—1H 57
Pleasant View. OL2—1H 49
Pleasant View. OL4—2B 66
Pleasant View. OL10—2D 30
Pleasant View. SK6—6F 123
Pleasant Way. SK8—1E 153
Pleasington Dri. BL8—3E 27
Pleasington Dri. M10—1C 76
Plevna St. BL2—6C 24
Plodder La. BL4—1B 54
Plodder La. BL5 & BL4—6E 37
Ploughbank Dri. M21—2B 116
Plough Clo. M31—5G 95
Plough St. SK16—5B 92
Plover Clo. OL11—4B 18
Plover Dri. BL9—1F 29
Plover Dri. M30—3E 95
Plover Dri. WA14—3D 124
Plover St. BL3—3B 38
Plover Ter. M21—2B 116
Plover Way. M35—2C 90
Plowden Clo. BL3—4G 37
Plowden Rd. M22—3H 139
Plowley Clo. M20—1F 129
Plucksbridge Rd. SK6—1C 102
Plumbley Dri. M16—4A 100
Plumbley St. M11—6G 89
Plumley Clo. M33—6F 115
Plumley Clo. SK3—6H 131
Plumley Rd. SK9—2H 151
Plummer Av. M21—3H 115
Plumpton Clo. OL2—5C 48
Plumpton Dri. BL9—5E 15
Plumpton Rd. OL11—5H 33

Plumpton Wlk. M13—3B 102
(off St John's Rd.)
Plum St. OL8—4B 64
Plum Tree Ct. M6—3G 85
Plunge Rd. BL0—2B 4
Plymouth Av. M13—2A 102
Plymouth Clo. OL6—4F 79
Plymouth Dri. BL4—1B 54
Plymouth Dri. SK7—6H 143
Plymouth Gro. M13—1G 101 & 6E 167
Plymouth Gro. M26—2D 40
Plymouth Gro. SK3—4D 130
Plymouth Gro. W. M13—2H 101
Plymouth Rd. M33—4F 113
Plymouth St. OL8—5D 64
Plymouth View. M13—1G 101 & 6E 167
Plymtree Clo. M8—1A 74
Pobgreen La. OL3—6D 52
Pochard Dri. SK12—3A 154
Pochard Dri. WA14—4D 124
Pochin St. M10—1A 88
Pocket Nook Rd. BL6—4A 36
Pocket Workshops, The. BL3—1G 37
Pocklington Dri. M23—4F 127
Podsmead Rd. M22—3H 139
Poise Brook Dri. SK2—6F 133
Poise Brook Rd. SK2—6F 133
Poise Clo. SK7—2G 145
Poland St. M4—3G 87 & 3E 163
Poland St. M34—5E 91
(in two parts)
Poland St. Ind. Est. M4—3G 87 &
3E 163
Polden Wlk. M9—2H 75
Poleacre La. SK6—3A 122
Pole Ct. BL9—4G 43
Polefield App. M25—3F 59
Polefield Circ. M25—3F 59
Polefield Gdns. M25—3F 59
Polefield Ga. M25—3F 59
Polefield Gro. M25—3F 59
Polefield Hall Rd. M25—3F 59
(in two parts)
Polefield Rd. M9—1F 75
Polefield Rd. M25—2F 59
Pole La. BL9—4G 43
Pole La. M35—3F 77
Pole St. BL2—4D 24
Pole St. OL7—1H 91
Polesworth Clo. M12—1C 102
Police St. M2—4D 86 & 5G 161
Police St. M30—3E 83
Police St. WA14—6F 125
Politt Av. OL6—6G 79
Pollard Ct. OL1—1C 64
Pollard Ho. BL3—5F 37
Pollard's La. BL9—1C 14
Pollard Sq. M31—6E 111
Pollard St. M4—4G 87 & 6F 163
Pollard St. E. M10—3H 87 & 4H 163
Pollen Clo. M33—1D 126
Pollen Rd. WA14—5E 125
Pollets Av. SK5—3C 120
Pollit St. OL8—5A 64
Pollitt Clo. M12—1B 102
Pollitt Croft. SK6—2F 133
Pollitts Clo. M30—3D 82
Pollitt St. M26—4A 42
Polperro Clo. OL2—3E 49
Polperro Wlk. SK14—4H 107
Polruan Rd. M21—5G 99
Polruan Wlk. SK14—5A 108
Polygon Av. M13—1G 101 & 5F 167
Polygon Rd. M8—2B 74
Polygon St. M13—6G 87 & 4F 167
Polygon, The. M7—5G 73
Polygon, The. M30—2A 84
Pomfret St. M6—6A 72
Pomfret St. M12—1C 102
Pomona Cres. M5—6H 85
Pomona Docks. M15—1A 100 & 5A 164
Pomona St. OL11—6H 19
Ponds Clo. M21—6H 99
Pondwood Wlk. M16—4C 100
Ponsford Av. M9—6A 62
Ponsonby Rd. M32—6D 98
Pool Bank St. M24—2D 60
(in three parts)

Poolcroft. M33—6F 115
Poole Clo. SK7—4E 143
Pooley Clo. M24—6D 44
Pool Field Clo. M26—4D 40
Pool Ho. Rd. SK12—2A 156
Pool La. SK1—6H 119
Pool Pl. BL1—3E 23
(off Church Rd.)
Poolscroft Dri. M33—6F 115
Pool St. BL1—5A 24
(in two parts)
Pool St. OL8—5D 64
Pool Ter. BL1—3E 23
Poolton Rd. M9—5D 60
Poorfield St. OL8—4C 64
Poot Hall. OL12—6F 7
Pope Way. M34—1G 121
Poplar Av. BL1—1B 24
Poplar Av. BL2—5G 11
Poplar Av. BL9—2F 29
Poplar Av. M19—1D 118
Poplar Av. OL4—5E 67
Poplar Av. OL8—1B 78
Poplar Av. OL12—2E 19
Poplar Av. SK9—4C 158
Poplar Av. WA14—5G 125
Poplar Clo. SK8—6F 129
Poplar Ct. M6—2G 85
Poplar Ct. M34—1F 105
Poplar Dri. M25—1E 73
Poplar Gro. BL0—2F 5
Poplar Gro. M18—3F 103
Poplar Gro. M30—3B 110
Poplar Gro. M31—5G 97
Poplar Gro. M33—6B 114
Poplar Gro. OL6—6G 79
Poplar Gro. SK2—1C 144
Poplar Rd. M19—6H 117
Poplar Rd. M27—4D 70
Poplar Rd. M28—1G 69
Poplar Rd. M30—1G 83
Poplar Rd. M32—1C 114
Poplar Rd. SK16—6D 92
Poplars Rd. SK15—2H 93
Poplars, The. OL5—2G 81
Poplars, The. WA14—1F 137
Poplar St. M11—5A 88
Poplar St. M24—2D 62
Poplar St. M34—1F 105
Poplar St. M35—5D 76
Poplar St. SK4—1A 130
Poplar Wlk. M31—6B 110
Poplar Wlk. OL9—1H 63
Poplar Way. SK6—6E 147
Poppy Clo. OL9—2E 63
Poppythorn La. M25—4E 59
(in two parts)
Porchester Dri. M26—2C 40
Porchfield Sq. M3—5C 86 & 1F 165
Porlock Av. M34—5C 90
Porlock Av. SK14—5G 107
Porlock Clo. SK1—3C 132
Porlock Rd. M23—5H 127
Porlock Rd. M31—1C 112
Porlock Wlk. SK14—5G 107
Porritt St. BL9—1E 29
(in two parts)
Porritt Way. BL0—2E 5
Portal Ct. M24—1C 62
Portal Gro. M34—6H 105
Portal Wlk. M9—3F 75
(off Alderside Rd.)
Porter St. BL9—1D 28
Porter St. OL9—4A 64
Portfield Wlk. M10—5A 76
(off Harmer Clo.)
Porthleven Dri. M23—5E 127
Porthtowen Wlk. SK14—4A 108
Porth Wlk. M10—6G 75
Portinscale Clo. BL8—2H 27
Portland Arc. M1—4E 87
(off Piccadilly Plaza)
Portland Clo. SK7—4B 144
Portland Ct. M20—4F 117
Portland Cres. M13—2H 101
Portland Dri. SK4—5D 118
Portland Ho. M6—2A 84
Portland Ho. OL6—3G 91

Portland Pl. OL7—3G 91
Portland Pl. OL16—1G 33
(off Oldham Rd.)
Portland Rd. SK15—3F 93
Portland Rd. M13—4B 102
Portland Rd. M27—4G 71
Portland Rd. M28—4E 55
Portland Rd. M32—3E 99
Portland Rd. M30—2H 83
Portland Rd. WA14—2E 137
Portland St. BL1—3A 24
Portland St. BL4—5F 39
Portland St. BL9—1E 29
Portland St. M1—5E 87 & 1A 166
Portland St. M35—4E 77
Portland St. OL16—3H 19
Portland St. N. OL6—2G 91
Portland St. S. OL6 & OL7—3G 91
(in two parts)
Portland Ter. OL6—3G 91
Portloe Rd. SK8—6F 141
Portman Clo. M16—4C 100
Portman St. OL5—2E 81
Porton Wlk. M22—4H 139
Portrea Clo. SK3—6G 131
Portree Clo. M30—3D 82
Portree Ct. OL10—4C 30
Portrush Rd. M22—3C 140
Portside Clo. M28—5D 68
Portslade Wlk. M23—6F 127
Portsmouth Clo. M7—6H 73
Portsmouth St. M13—1F 101 & 6D 166
(in two parts)
Port Soderick Av. M5—4G 85
Portsone Clo. M16—3C 100
Port St. M1—4F 87 & 5C 162
Port St. OL8—5D 64
Port St. SK1—1G 131
Portugal Rd. M25—1F 73
Portugal St. BL2—6D 24
Portugal St. M4—3G 87 & 3E 163
(in two parts)
Portugal St. OL7—4F 91
Portugal St. E. M1—5G 87 & 1E 167
Portville Rd. M19—5C 102
Portway. M22—3H 139
Portwood Ind. Est. SK1—1A 132
Portwood Pl. SK1—1H 131
Portwood Wlk. M9—4F 75
Posnett St. SK3—3E 131
Postal St. M1—4F 87 & 5C 162
Postbridge Clo. M13—1G 101 & 6F 167
Post Office St. WA14—6F 125
Potato Wharf. M3—5B 86 & 2D 164
Pot Hill. OL6—1A 92
Pot Hill Sq. OL6—1A 92
Pot Ho. La. OL12—4F 7
Pot St. WA14—1F 137
Potter Ho. OL8—4D 64
Potter's La. M9—4G 75
Potter St. BL9—2E 29
Potter St. M26—3B 42
Pottery La. M11 & M12—6C 88
Pottery Row. M11—3A 88
Pottery Wlk. M10—1D 76
Pottinger St. OL7—4F 91
Pott St. M10—6D 76
Poulton Av. BL2—6G 25
Poulton St. M11—6G 89
Poundswick La. M22—2A 140
Powell Av. SK14—4C 106
Powell St. BL1—5A 24
Powell St. BL8—4H 27
Powell St. M11—3F 89
Powell St. M16—3A 100
Power Dri. OL9—1G 63
Powicke Dri. SK6—2F 133
Powis Rd. M31—6G 95
Pownall Av. M20—1E 117
Pownall Av. SK7—6H 143
Pownall Ct. SK9—1B 158
Pownall Rd. SK8—4C 142
Pownall Rd. WA14—2F 137
Pownall St. SK7—2D 144
Poynings Dri. M22—4A 140
Poynt Chase. M28—5D 68
Poynter St. M10—2C 76

Poynter Wlk. OL1—3H 49
Poynton Clo. BL9—4E 29
Poynton Clo. M15—1D 100 & 5H 165
Praed Rd. M17—1C 98
Prark Ct. OL16—5H 19
Pratt Wlk. M11—4B 88
(off Turnpike Wlk.)
Precinct Cen. M13—1E 101 & 5B 166
Precinct, The. SK2—5D 132
Precinct, The. SK3—4F 131
Precinct, The. SK8—3D 142
Preece Clo. SK14—3E 107
Preesall Av. SK8—5F 141
Preesall Clo. BL8—5F 27
Premier Rd. M8—1D 86
Premier St. M16—3B 100
Prentice Wlk. M11—4C 88
Prenton St. M11—5G 89
Prenton Way. BL8—6H 13
Presall St. BL2—5E 25
Prescot Clo. BL9—4E 29
Prescot Rd. M9—4F 75
Prescot Rd. WA15—3H 137
Prescot St. SK9—6F 151
Prescott St. BL3—3G 37
Prescott St. M28—6D 54
Prescott St. OL16—1B 20
Prescott Wlk. M34—6H 105
Press St. M11—6F 89
Prestage St. M12—5D 102
Prestage St. M16—2A 100
Prestbury. OL11—1F 33
Prestbury Av. M14—6D 100
Prestbury Av. WA15—5G 125
Prestbury Clo. BL9—4E 29
Prestbury Clo. SK2—1D 144
Prestbury Dri. OL1—6B 48
Prestbury Dri. SK6—5E 121
Prestbury Rd. BL1—6E 11
Prestbury Rd. SK9—4H 159
Prestbury St. SK2—1D 144
Prestfield Rd. M25—2E 59
Presto Gdns. BL3—3F 37
Prestolee Rd. BL3—6A 40
Prestolee Rd. M26—6A 40
Preston Av. M30—2A 84
(Eccles)
Preston Av. M30—2D 110
(Irlam)
Preston Clo. M30—2A 84
Preston Rd. M19—1C 108
Preston St. BL3—3D 38
(Bolton)
Preston St. BL3—3F 37
(Willows)
Preston St. M18—1E 103
Preston St. M24—1A 62
Preston St. OL4—3E 65
Preston St. OL12—2E 19
Presto St. BL4—6G 39
Prestwich Clo. SK2—4B 132
Prestwich Hills. M25—6E 59
Prestwich Pk. Rd. S. M25—6E 59
Prestwich St. M34—3E 105
Prestwood Clo. BL1—4H 23
Prestwood Dri. BL1—4H 23
Prestwood Rd. BL4—6C 38
Prestwood Rd. M6—1C 84
Preswick Wlk. M10—1C 76
Pretoria Rd. BL2—6G 25
Pretoria Rd. OL8—6A 64
Pretoria St. OL12—2E 19
Price St. BL4—6F 39
Price St. BL9—4E 29
Price St. M4—4H 87 & 5H 163
Price St. SK16—5A 92
Prichard St. M32—5D 98
Prickshaw La. OL12—3A 6
Pridmouth Rd. M20—3G 117
Priest Av. SK8—1E 141
Priest Hill St. OL1—2C 64
Priestley Rd. M28—3C 70
Priestley Way. OL2—6H 35
Priestnall St. SK4—6C 118
(off Priestnall Rd.)
Priestnall Rd. SK4—6B 118
Priest St. SK1—4H 131
Priestwood Dri. OL4—3B 50

Primley Wlk. M9—3G 75
(off Edward St.)
Primrose Av. BL4—6C 38
Primrose Av. M28—1D 68
Primrose Av. M31—5F 97
Primrose Av. OL3—6C 52
Primrose Av. SK6—5C 134
Primrose Av. SK14—2B 122
Primrose Bank. BL8—4G 13
Primrose Bank. M28—1D 68
Primrose Bank. OL3—4F 53
Primrose Bank. OL8—4C 64
Primrose Bank. WA14—4E 137
Primrose Clo. BL2—1A 26
Primrose Clo. M5—3F 85
Primrose Cotts. WA14—4E 137
Primrose Cres. SK14—1B 122
Primrose Dri. BL9—1H 29
Primrose Dri. M35—2C 90
Primrose Hill Cotts. OL10—1A 32
Primrose St. BL1—1B 24
Primrose St. BL4—2G 55
Primrose St. SK15—2F 93
Primrose St. M4—3F 87 & 3D 162
Primrose St. OL8—4C 64 ⁿ
Primrose St. OL12—3F 19
Primrose Ter. M31—1E 97
Primrose Ter. SK15—3F 93
Primrose Wlk. OL8—4C 64
Primrose Wlk. SK6—5C 134
Primula St. BL1—1B 24
Prince Albert Av. M19—5C 102
Prince Charlie St. OL1—1F 65
Princedom St. M9—3G 75
Prince Edward Av. M34—5F 105
Prince Edward Av. OL4—2G 65
Prince George St. OL1—6G 49
Prince Rd. SK12—2A 156
Prince's Av. BL3—3B 40
Princes Av. M20—5G 117
Princes Av. M30—4G 95
Princes Av. SK6—6G 121
Prince's Bri. M3—5B 86 & 1D 164
Princes Ct. SK8—2F 83
Princes Dri. M33—6D 114
Princes Dri. SK6—4C 134
Prince's Incline. SK12—3E 155
Princes Rd. M33—6C 114
Princes Rd. SK4—5C 118
Princes Rd. SK6—6G 121
Princes Rd. WA14—5F 125
Princess Av. BL4—3H 55
Princess Av. M25—1G 73
Princess Av. M34—4E 105
Princess Av. OL12—5A 8
Princess Av. SK8—2C 142
Princess Clo. OL5—3G 81
Princess Clo. OL10—4F 31
Princess Clo. SK16—5B 92
Princess Ct. M15—1B 100 & 5C 164
Princess Dri. M24—1G 61
Princess Gro. BL4—1F 55
(in two parts)
Princess Pde. BL9—3D 28
Princess Pde. M14—6D 100
Princess Parkway. M23—4A 128
Princess Rd. M15 & M14—6D 86 &
4G 165
Princess Rd. M23, M21 & M20—6B 116
Princess Rd. M25—5G 59
Princess Rd. M31—4D 96
Princess Rd. OL2—1E 49
Princess Rd. OL9—6E 63
Princess Rd. OL16—4D 20
Princess Rd. SK9—4C 158
Princess St. BL1—6B 24
Princess St. M2 & M1—4D 86 & 6H 161
Princess St. M6—1G 85
Princess St. M10—1A 88
Princess St. M11—3C 88
Princess St. M15—1A 100 & 5B 164
Princess St. M26—4E 41
Princess St. M27—4G 71
Princess St. M30—3E 83
Princess St. M35—4E 77
Princess St. OL4—3A 66
Princess St. OL6—1B 92
Princess St. OL9—4G 63

Princess St. OL12—1C 6
(off Albert St.)
Princess St. OL12—3H 19
(Rochdale, in two parts)
Princess St. SK4—5C 106
Princess St. WA14—3E 125
Prince's St. SK1—2G 131
Prince St. BL1—5A 24
Prince St. OL1—2E 65
Prince St. OL10—3F 31
Prince St. OL16—6A 20
Princes Wlk. SK7—6H 143
Princethorpe Clo. BL6—1B 36
Prince Way. OL2—1A 48
Pringle St. OL16—4A 20
Prinknash Rd. M22—3B 140
Printers Fold. SK14—2F 109
Printer St. M11—5F 89
Printer St. OL1—3D 64
Printon Av. M9—5D 60
Print Works La. M19—6E 103
Printworks Rd. SK15—2F 93
Prior St. OL8—4F 65
Priory Av. M7—5G 73
Priory Av. M21—1H 115
Priory Clo. M33—3D 114
Priory Clo. OL8—6B 64
Priory Clo. SK16—1B 106
Priory Ct. M30—3G 83
Priory Ct. SK5—1G 119
Priory Ct. WA14—4E 137
Priory Gdns. M20—5F 117
Priory Gro. M7—5G 73
Priory Gro. OL9—5G 63
Priory Pl. BL2—3E 25
Priory Pl. M7—5G 73
Priory Rd. M27—2E 71
Priory Rd. M33—4C 114
Priory Rd. SK8—6C 130
Priory Rd. SK9—1B 158
Priory Rd. WA14—5D 136
Priory St. SK5—1G 119
Priory St. WA14—5E 137
Priory, The. M7—5G 73
Pritchard St. M1—5E 87 & 2B 166
Privet St. OL4—6H 49
Proctor St. BL8—4A 28
Proctor Way. M30—6B 82
Proffitt St. BL3—1H 37
Progress Av. M34—1F 105
Progress St. BL1—4B 24
Progress St. OL6—2G 91
Progress St. OL11—4C 32
Promenade St. OL10—3F 31
Props Hall Dri. M35—5D 76
Prospect Av. BL2—2H 25
Prospect Av. BL4—2E 55
Prospect Av. M30—3C 110
Prospect Dri. M35—6F 77
Prospect Dri. WA15—6D 138
Prospect Pl. BL4—2E 55
Prospect Pl. BL9—2E 43
Prospect Pl. M27—4G 71
Prospect Pl. OL6—6H 79
Prospect Pl. OL10—2F 31
Prospect Pl. SK6—6E 123
Prospect Rd. M30—3C 110
Prospect Rd. OL6—6A 80
Prospect Rd. OL9—2A 64
Prospect Rd. SK16—4B 92
Prospect St. BL1—4B 24
Prospect St. OL10—4G 31
Prospect St. OL11—1E 33
Prospect St. OL15—3F 9
Prospect Ter. BL8—1B 28
Prospect Vale. SK8—4F 141
Prospect View. M27—4G 71
Prospect Vs. M9—2H 75
Prout St. M12—4C 102
Providence St. BL3—2B 38
Providence St. M4—4H 87 & 5G 163
Providence St. M34—6F 91
Providence St. OL6—1B 92
Provident Av. M19—6E 103
Provident St. OL2—6F 35
Provident Way. WA15—5A 126

Provis Rd. M21—2H 115
Prubella Av. M34—2E 105
Pryce St. BL1—4H 23
Pryme St. M15—6C 86 & 3E 165
Pudding La. SK14—4G 107
(in two parts)
Puffin Av. SK12—3B 154
Pugin Wlk. M9—5F 75
(off Parkstead Dri.)
Pulborough Clo. BL8—4B 14
Pulford Av. M21—5B 116
Pulford Rd. M33—1C 126
Pullman Clo. M19—1D 118
Pullman St. OL11—6H 19
Pump St. M10—3A 88
Pump St. OL9—1H 77
Punch La. BL3—5B 36
(in three parts)
Punch St. BL3—1H 37
Purbeck Dri. BL8—5C 14
Purcell Clo. BL1—4H 23
Purcell St. M12—4C 102
Purdon St. BL9—5F 15
Purdy Ho. OL8—4D 64
Puritan Wlk. M10—6E 75
(off Elcot Clo.)
Purley Av. M23—2H 127
Purley Dri. M30—4A 110
Purslow Clo. M12—4A 88
Purton Wlk. M9—4G 75
(off Norbet Wlk.)
Putt St. M27—1F 71
Pyegreave Clo. M15—6C 86 & 4F 165
Pymgate Dri. SK8—3E 141
Pymgate La. SK8—3E 141
Pym St. M10—3H 75
Pym St. M30—3F 83
Pym St. OL10—4F 31
Pyramid Ct. M7—5H 73
Pyrus Clo. M30—5B 82
Pytha Fold Rd. M20—4G 11*

Quadrant, The. M9—6A 62
Quadrant, The. M35—4H 89
Quadrant, The. SK1—2B 132
Quadrant, The. OL16—1G 133
Quail Dri. M30—4E 95
Quail St. OL4—3G 65
Quakers Field. BL8—3H 13
Quantock Clo. M16—3C 100
Quantock Clo. SK4—1G 131
Quarlton Dri. BL8—1D 12
Quarmby Rd. M18—3H 103
Quarry Bank Rd. SK9—4D 150
Quarry Clough. SK15—5G 93
Quarry Hill. OL12—6E 7
Quarry Pond Rd. M28—6B 54
Quarry Rise. SK15—5D 92
Quarry Rd. BL4—2A 56
Quarry St. SK6—1H 133
Quarry St. BL0—3F 5
(in three parts)
Quarry St. M26—4H 41
Quarry St. OL12—2G 19
Quarry St. SK6—4H 121
Quarry St. SK15—4D 92
Quarry View. OL12—6E 7
Quarry Wlk. M11—4B 88
(off Pilgrim Dri.)
Quayside Clo. M28—6D 68
Quays, The. M5—6E 85
Quay St. M3—4C 86 & 6E 161
(Manchester)
Quay St. M3—3C 86 & 4F 161
(Salford)
Quay St. SK15—4D 92
Quebec Pl. BL3—2G 37
Quebec St. BL3—2H 37
Quebec St. M34—3E 105
Quebec St. OL9—1A 64
Queen Alexandra Clo. M5—5A 86 &
2A 164
Queen Ann Dri. M28—4D 68
Queenhill Dri. SK14—2E 107
Queenhill Rd. M22—2C 128
Queen's Av. BL3—3A 40
Queen's Av. BL7—4E 11
Queens Av. OL12—5A 8

Queens Av. SK6—6G 121
Queensbrook. BL1—6A 24
Queensbury. OL11—1E 33
Queensbury Ct. M10—2H 87 & 2H 163
Queensbury Pde. M10—2A 88
Queens Clo. M28—4B 68
(Mosley Common)
Queen's Clo. M28—5F 55
(Walkden)
Queens Clo. SK4—1C 130
Queen's Ct. M20—5E 117
Queen's Ct. SK4—1C 130
Queens Ct. SK6—5E 135
Queens Ct. SK9—3D 158
Queen's Dri. M25—1G 73
Queens Dri. OL11—2E 33
Queens Dri. SK4—1C 130
Queens Dri. SK8—3C 142
Queens Dri. SK14—2D 122
Queensferry St. M10—5C 76
Queens Gdns. SK8—5A 130
Queensgate. BL1—5G 23
Queensgate. SK7—2G 153
Queensgate Dri. OL2—1A 48
Queen's Gro. M12—3C 102
Queensland Rd. M18—2D 102
Queen's Pk. Rd. OL10—1F 31
Queens Pk. St. BL1—5H 23
Queens Pl. BL9—1C 14
Queen Sq. SK1—1A 132
Queen's Rd. BL3—3F 37
Queen's Rd. M8, M9 & M10
—6C 74
Queen's Rd. M31—6F 97
Queens Rd. M33—4H 113
Queens Rd. OL6—6H 79
Queens Rd. OL8—4E 65
Queens Rd. OL9—2G 63
Queens Rd. OL15—4F 9
Queens Rd. SK6—6G 121
Queen's Rd. SK7—2E 145
Queens Rd. SK8—1B 142
Queens Rd. SK9—3D 158
Queen's Rd. WA15—2G 137
Queen's Rd. Ter. OL15—4F 9
(off Queen's Rd.)
Queens Ter. SK9—3H 151
Queens Ter. SK16—4H 91
Queenston Rd. M20—5E 117
Queen St. BL0—3D 4
Queen St. BL1—6A 24
Queen St. BL4—1F 55
Queen St. BL9—3E 29
Queen St. M2—4D 86 & 6G 161
Queen St. M3—3C 86 & 3F 161
Queen St. M6—6B 72
Queen St. M24—6C 46
Queen St. M26—5A 42
Queen St. M28—6D 54
Queen St. M30—4H 83
Queen St. M34—1F 105
(Audenshaw)
Queen St. M34—3E 105
(Denton, in two parts)
Queen St. M35—4E 77
Queen St. OL1—2D 64
Queen St. OL2—3B 48
(Royton)
Queen St. OL2—1F 49
(Shaw)
Queen St. OL4—3B 66
Queen St. OL5—2E 81
Queen St. OL6—2A 92
Queen St. OL10—2F 31
Queen St. OL12—3H 19
Queen St. OL15—4D 64
Queen St. SK1—1A 132
(in two parts)
Queen St. SK6—5E 135
Queen St. SK8—5B 130
Queen St. SK14—3H 109
(Hadfield)
Queen St. SK14—5C 106
(Hyde)
Queen St. SK15—3E 93
Queen St. SK16—4H 91
Queen St. W. M20—2F 117
Queen's Wlk. M35—4A 90

Queensway. BL4—4H 55
Queensway. M19—1H 129
Queensway. M27—1G 71
Queensway. M28—3D 68
Queensway. M30—5D 94
Queensway. M31—3G 97
Queensway. OL3—3F 53
Queensway. OL5—3F 81
Queensway. OL11—3C 32
Queensway. SK8—5F 141
Queensway. SK12—4D 154
Queensway. SK16—6D 92
Queen Victoria St. M30—3E 83
Queen Victoria St. OL11—1G 33
Quenby St. M15—6B 86 & 4D 164
Quendon Av. M7—1C 86
Quick Edge La. OL4—5D 66
Quickedge Rd. OL5—1E 81
Quick Rd. OL5—5F 67
Quick View. OL5—6G 67
Quilter Gro. M9—1E 75
Quinney Cres. M16—3C 100
Quinn St. M11—4C 88
Quinton. OL2—3G 19
(off Spotland Rd.)
Quinton Wlk. M13—1F 101
&5D 166
Quixall St. M11—3C 88

Rabbit La. SK14—1C 108
Raby St. M16—3C 100
Raby St. M14—3D 100
Racecourse Pk. SK9—3C 158
Racecourse Rd. SK9—2B 158
Racecourse Wlk. M26—3F 41
Racefield Hamlet. OL1—3H 47
Racefield Rd. WA14—1E 137
Race, The. SK9—5H 151
Rachel Rosing Wlk. M8—3B 74
Rachel St. M12—5G 87 & 2F 167
Rackhouse Rd. M23—2H 127
Radbourne Clo. M12—1C 102
Radcliffe Moor Rd. BL2 & M26
—1B 40
Radcliffe New Rd. M25—5A 42
Radcliffe Pk. Cres. M6—6A 72
Radcliffe Pk. Rd. M6—6H 71
Radcliffe Rd. BL2 & BL3—6C 24
Radcliffe Rd. BL9—6B 28
Radcliffe Rd. OL4—5H 49
Radcliffe St. OL1—1D 64
Radcliffe St. OL2—3B 48
Radcliffe St. OL4—3C 66
Radcliffe View. M5—6H 85
(off Ordsall Dri.)
Radclyffe St. M24—5A 46
Radclyffe St. OL9—1H 63
Radclyffe Ter. M24—5A 46
Radelan Gro. M26—3D 40
Radford Clo. SK2—4D 132
Radford Dri. M9—3G 75
Radford St. M30—4E 95
Radford St. M7—3G 73
Radium St. M4—3G 87 & 3E 163
Radlet Dri. WA15—3A 126
Radlett Wlk. M13—2G 101
(off Plymouth Gro.)
Radley Clo. BL1—4E 23
Radley Wlk. M16—4D 100
(off Quinney Cres.)
Radnor Av. M34—4B 104
Radnormere Dri. SK8—1B 142
Radnor St. M15—2D 100
Radnor St. M18—3E 103
Radnor St. M32—5D 98
Radnor St. OL9—4A 64
Radstock Clo. BL1—4C 10
Radstock Clo. M14—6F 101
Radstock Rd. M32—5C 98
Raeburn Dri. SK6—3F 135
Rae St. SK3—3E 131
Raglan Av. M25—2F 59
Raglan Av. M27—1H 71
Raglan Clo. M11—4B 88
Raglan Dri. WA14—3G 125
Raglan Rd. M32—4B 98
Raglan Rd. M33—6H 113
Raglan St. BL1—3H 23

Raglan St. OL11—4C 32
Raglan St. SK14—5A 106
Raglan Wlk. M15—1D 100
&6H 165
Ragley Clo. SK12—3F 155
Raikes La. BL3—3D 38
(in two parts)
Raikes Rd. BL3—2F 39
Railton Av. M16—4B 100
Railton Ter. M9—4H 75
Railway App. M26—4H 41
Railway App. OL11—3C 32
Railway Brow. OL11—4C 32
Railway Rd. M31—5F 97
Railway Rd. M32—2E 99
Railway Rd. OL9—1G 77
(Chadderton)
Railway Rd. OL9—3B 64
(Oldham)
Railway Rd. SK1—3G 131
Railway Rd. SK6—5B 134
Railway St. BL0—3E 5
Railway St. BL4—6G 39
Railway St. BL9—1C 14
Railway St. M18—1E 103
Railway St. M26—4G 41
Railway St. OL10—4G 31
Railway St. OL15—4F 9
Railway St. OL16—1F 35
(Newhey)
Railway St. OL16—5A 20
(Rochdale)
Railway St. SK4—1G 131
Railway St. SK14—5B 106
Railway St. SK16—4H 91
Railway St. W. BL9—1B 14
Railway Ter. BL9—1C 14
(off Miller St.)
Railway Ter. M21—5H 99
Railway Ter. OL10—4F 31
Railway Ter. SK12—1H 157
Railway View. OL5—5G 103
Railway View. SK14—6A 106
Railway View. SK16—1A 106
Raimond St. BL1—2G 23
Rainbow Clo. M21—2H 115
Rainbow Way. SK9—6H 151
Raincliff Av. M13—5B 102
Raines Crest. OL16—5F 21
Rainford. OL11—1E 33
Rainford Av. M20—1E 117
Rainford Av. WA15—5A 126
Rainford Ho. BL1—5B 24
(off Beta St.)
Rainford La. BL0—3G 5
Rainford St. BL2—5G 11
Rainforth St. M13—4B 102
Rainham Dri. BL1—4A 24
Rainham Dri. M8—4C 74
Rainham Gro. BL1—4A 24
(off Rainham Dri.)
Rainham Way. OL9—4H 63
Rainham Way. SK5—3B 120
Rainhill Wlk. M10—6D 76
Rainow Av. M35—4G 89
Rainow Rd. SK3—6E 131
Rainsdale Flats. OL10—3E 31
(off Meadow Clo.)
Rainshaw St. BL1—1B 24
Rainshaw St. OL2—3B 48
Rainshaw St. OL4—1H 65
Rainsough Av. M25—2E 73
Rainsough Brow. M25—2D 72
Rainsough Clo. M25—2E 73
Rainton Wlk. M10—1D 76
Rainwood. OL9—1E 63
Raja Clo. M8—4D 74
Rake. OL11—4H 17
Rakehead Wlk. M15—2E 101
(off Botham Clo.)
Rake La. M27—6G 57
Rake St. BL9—1D 28
Rake Ter. OL15—3G 9
Rake Top. OL12—2E 19
Rakewood Dri. OL4—3A 50
Rakewood Rd. OL15—1H 21
Raleigh Clo. OL1—1D 64

Regency Clo. OL8—5B 64
Regent Av. M14—5E 101
Regent Av. M28—5E 55
Regent Bank. SK9—4C 158
Regent Clo. SK7—3F 153
Regent Clo. SK8—1E 143
Regent Clo. SK9—4C 158
Regent Ct. M7—2H 73
Regent Ct. SK4—4E 119
Regent Cres. M35—5E 77
Regent Cres. OL2—5B 48
Regent Dri. BL6—6A 22
Regent Dri. M34—6D 104
Regent Dri. OL5—3F 81
Regent Ho. M14—4H 101
Regent Pl. M14—3G 101
Regent Rd. BL6—1A 36
Regent Rd. M5 & M3—4H 85 & 1A 164
Regent Rd. SK2—5A 132
Regent Rd. M14—1E 137
Regent Rd. Ind. Area. M5—5B 86 &
                              2C 164
Regents Pl. M5—4H 85
Regent Sq. M5—5H 85
Regent St. BL0—5C 4
Regent St. BL9—1D 28
Regent St. M10—6D 76
Regent St. M24—5H 45
Regent St. M30—3H 83
Regent St. OL1—2E 65
Regent St. OL2—6F 35
Regent St. OL10—4D 30
Regent St. OL12—2H 19
Regent St. OL15—4F 9
Regent Wlk. BL4—1F 55
Regina Av. SK15—3E 93
Regina Ct. M6—2A 84
Reginald Latham Ct. M10—2H 87 &
                              1H 163
Reginald St. BL3—5E 37
Reginald St. M11—6H 89
Reginald St. M27—2D 70
Reginald St. M30—5C 82
Reid Clo. M34—1G 121
Reigate Clo. BL8—4H 27
Reigate Rd. M31—1A 112
Reins Lea Av. OL8—1E 79
Reins Lee Rd. OL7—5E 79
Reliance St. M10—5C 76
Rembrandt Wlk. OL1—3G 49
Rena Clo. SK4—6F 119
Rennell St. OL16—4A 20
Renshaw Av. M30—4F 83
Renshaw Dri. BL9—2G 29
Renshaw Av. M30—4E 83
Renshaw St. M12—1C 102
Renshaw St. M30—4F 83
Renshaw St. WA14—6G 125
Renton Rd. M22—1B 140
Renton Rd. M32—5E 99
Renwick Gro. BL3—4G 37
Repton Av. M10—2E 77
Repton Av. M31—5H 95
Repton Av. M34—4A 104
Repton Av. M35—2F 89
Repton Av. OL8—6B 64
Repton Av. SK4—4C 106
Reservoir Rd. SK3—4F 131
Reservoir St. M3—2C 86 & 2F 161
Reservoir St. M6—3F 85
Reservoir St. OL16—3C 20
Retford Av. OL16—1H 33
Retford Clo. BL8—6D 14
Retford St. OL4—4F 65
Retiro St. OL1—2D 64
Retreat, The. SK6—2A 134
Reuben St. SK4—5G 119
Revers St. BL8—2B 28
Reveton Grn. SK7—3A 144
Rex Bldgs. SK9—3E 159
Rex Ct. OL4—3D 66
Reynard Av. M21—2H 115
Reynard St. SK14—4B 106
Reynell Rd. M13—5B 102
Reyner Sq. OL6—3C 92
Reyner Stephens Way. OL6—
                              2H 91
Reyner St. M1—5E 87 & 1A 166
Reynolds Dri. M18—1F 103

Reynolds Dri. SK6—3F 135
Reynolds M. SK9—1H 159
Reynolds Rd. M16—3A 100
Reynold St. SK14—5B 106
Rhine Clo. BL8—4H 13
Rhiwlas Dri. BL9—5D 28
Rhodehouses. SK6—2D 146
Rhodes Av. OL3—6C 52
Rhodes Av. OL4—4B 66
Rhodes Bank. OL1—3D 64
Rhodes Cres. OL11—2F 33
Rhodes Dri. BL9—5E 43
Rhodes Hill. OL4—4B 66
Rhodes St. M10—1A 88
Rhodes St. OL1—2E 65
Rhodes St. OL2—4E 49
Rhodes St. OL4—2B 66
Rhodes St. OL12—6H 7
Rhodes St. SK14—4A 106
Rhodes St. N. SK14—4A 106
Rhode St. BL8—5H 13
Rhos Av. M14—1A 118
Rhos Av. M24—2A 62
Rhos Av. SK8—4A 142
Rhos Dri. SK7—4D 144
Rhosleigh Av. BL1—1H 23
Rhyl St. M11—5C 88
Rialto Gdns. M7—5A 74
Rial Wlk. M15—1E 101 & 6A 166
Ribble Av. BL2—6G 25
Ribble Av. OL9—6F 47
Ribble Av. OL15—3D 8
Ribble Dri. BL4—4A 56
Ribble Dri. BL9—3F 15
Ribble Dri. M25—6E 43
Ribble Dri. M28—5B 68
Ribble Gro. OL10—2C 30
Ribble Rd. OL8—6A 64
Ribblesdale Dri. M10—6E 75
Ribblesdale Rd. BL3—3H 37
Ribble St. OL11—1D 32
Ribbleton Clo. BL8—4F 27
Ribble Wlk. M35—5A 90
Ribchester Dri. BL9—6B 28
Ribchester Gro. BL2—4G 25
Ribchester Wlk. M15—1D 100 &
                              5G 165
Riber Bank. SK13—6G 109
*Riber Clo. SK13—6G 109
  (off Riber Bank)
*Riber Fold. SK13—6G 109
  (off Riber Bank)
*Riber Grn. SK13—6G 109
  (off Riber Bank)
Rice St. M3—5C 86 & 1E 165
Richard Burch St. BL9—2D 28
Richardson Clo. M25—5D 42
Richardson Rd. M30—3G 83
Richardson St. SK1—4A 132
Richard St. M26—4F 41
Richard St. OL2—2E 49
Richard St. OL11—5H 19
Richard St. SK1—1H 131
  (in two parts)
Richbell Clo. M30—2C 110
Richborough Clo. M7—6A 74
Richelieu St. BL3—3C 38
Richmond Av. M25—2G 73
Richmond Av. M31—5G 97
Richmond Av. OL2—3B 48
Richmond Av. OL9—5G 63
Richmond Av. SK9—2H 151
Richmond Clo. BL8—5H 13
Richmond Clo. M25—2B 58
Richmond Clo. M33—6F 115
Richmond Clo. OL2—2F 49
Richmond Clo. SK15—3G 81
  (Mossley)
Richmond Clo. SK15—4E 93
  (Stalybridge)
Richmond Clo. SK16—1B 106
*Richmond Ct. M9—4C 60
  (off Deanswood Dri.)
Richmond Ct. SK8—6G 129
Richmond Ct. WA14—3D 136
Richmond Cres. SK15—3G 81
Richmond Dri. M28—3C 70
Richmond Gdns. BL3—4D 38
Richmond Gro. BL4—6C 38

Richmond Gro. M12—2A 102
Richmond Gro. M13—3H 101
Richmond Gro. M30—2G 83
Richmond Gro. SK8—3B 142
Richmond Hill. SK14—6D 106
  (in two parts)
Richmond Hill. WA14—3D 136
Richmond Hill Rd. SK8—6G 129
Richmond Ho. SK15—4E 93
Richmond Rd. M14—1H 117
Richmond Rd. M17—6A 84
Richmond Rd. M28—4A 68
Richmond Rd. M34—4A 104
Richmond Rd. M35—3G 77
Richmond Rd. SK4—1B 130
Richmond Rd. SK6—6A 122
Richmond Rd. SK16—1A 106
Richmond Rd. WA14—6F 125
  (Altrincham)
Richmond Rd. WA14—3D 136
  (Bowdon)
Richmond St. BL9—5C 28
Richmond St. M1—5E 87 & 1B 166
Richmond St. M3—2C 86 & 2E 161
Richmond St. M34—1E 105
Richmond St. M35—3C 90
Richmond St. OL7 & OL6—1F 91
Richmond St. SK14—5C 106
Richmond St. SK15—3F 93
Richmond Ter. SK6—5F 147
Richmond Ter. SK9—5G 159
Richmond Wlk. M26—1F 41
Richmond Wlk. OL9—3B 64
Ricroft Rd. SK6—6F 123
Ridd Cotts. OL11—3F 17
Riddell Ct. M5—3C 84
Ridding Av. M22—2C 140
Ridding Clo. SK2—5D 132
Riddings St. WA15—3H 125
Riddings Rd. WA15—3H 125
  (Altrincham)
Riddings Rd. WA15—4H 137
  (Hale)
Riders Ga. BL9—1B 30
Ridge Av. SK6—1E 147
Ridge Av. WA15—1D 148
Ridge Clo. SK6—1C 134
Ridge Clo. SK14—3G 109
Ridge Cres. M25—1F 59
Ridge Cres. SK6—2D 146
Ridgedale Cen. SK6—5D 134
Ridgefield. M2—4D 86 & 6G 161
Ridgefield St. M35—4D 76
  (in two parts)
Ridge Gro. M25—1F 59
Ridge Hill La. SK15—3D 92
  (in two parts)
Ridge La. OL3—2D 52
Ridgemont Av. SK4—6D 118
Ridgemont Dri. M28—5B 68
Ridgemont Wlk. M23—1F 127
Ridge Pk. SK7—1F 153
Ridge Rd. SK6—1E 147
Ridge Wlk. M9—6F 61
Ridgeway. M27—1H 71
Ridgeway Gates. BL1—6B 24
Ridgeway Rd. WA15—6C 126
Ridgeway, The. SK6—2G 133
Ridgeway, The. SK12—1G 157
Ridgewood. OL9—1E 63
Ridgewood Av. M10—6F 75
Ridgmont Rd. SK7—2G 153
Ridgway St. M10—3H 87 & 3G 163
Ridgway St. E. M4—3H 87 & 4G 163
Ridingfold La. M28—6A 70
Riding Ga. BL2—5A 12
Riding Ga. M. BL2—5A 12
Riding Head La. BL0—1H 5
Ridings Rd. SK14—2H 109
Ridings St. M10—6H 75
Riding St. M3—3C 86 & 4E 161
Ridley Dri. WA14—2G 125
Ridley Gro. M33—6F 115
Ridley St. OL4—3E 65
Ridley Wlk. M15—2E 101
Ridling La. SK14—5C 106
Ridsdale Av. M20—3E 117
Ridsdale Wlk. M6—6E 73
Ridyard St. M28—5D 54

Rifle Rd. M33—4F 115
Rifle St. OL1—1D 64
Riga Rd. M14—6G 101
Riga Av. M26—2A 42
Rigby Av. M26—2A 42
Rigby Ct. BL3—3B 38
  (in two parts)
Rigby Ct. OL12—2A 18
Rigby Gro. M28—5A 54
Rigby La. BL2—5G 11
Rigby St. BL3—3B 38
Rigby St. M7—4H 73
  (in two parts)
Rigby St. WA14—2F 137
Rigby Wlk. M7—5A 74
Rigel Pl. M7—2A 86 & 1B 160
Rigel St. M4—2G 87 & 2F 163
Rigi Mt. OL2—1B 48
Rigton Clo. M12—2C 102
Riley Clo. M33—2D 124
Riley Ct. BL1—4B 24
Riley Wood Clo. SK6—2F 133
Rimmington Clo. M9—1A 76
Rimsdale Clo. SK8—2E 141
Rimsdale Wlk. BL3—2C 36
Rimworth Dri. M10—1G 87
Ringcroft Gdns. M10—2B 76
Ringfield Clo. M16—3C 100
  (in two parts)
Ringford Wlk. M10—6G 75
Ringley Chase. M25—1C 58
Ringley Dri. M25—2B 58
Ringley Gro. BL1—6C 10
Ringley Hey. M25—1B 58
Ringley Meadows. M26—2C 56
Ringley Old Brow. M26—2C 56
Ringley Pk. M25—1B 58
Ringley Rd. M26—1B 56
  (in three parts)
Ringley Rd. W. M26—1E 57
Ringley St. M9—3F 75
Ringlow Av. M27—4C 70
Ringlow Pk. Rd. M27—5C 70
Ring Lows La. OL12—5F 7
Ringmer Dri. M22—4A 140
Ringmere Ct. OL1—1C 64
Ringmore Rd. SK7—3A 144
Ring-O-Bells La. SK6—1H 157
Rings Clo. M35—5F 77
Ringstead Dri. M10—1G 87
Ringstone Clo. M25—6E 59
Ringway Gro. M33—1E 127
Ringway Rd. M22—5A 140
Ringway Rd. W. M22—5A 140
Ringway Trading Est. M22—5C 140
Ringwood Av. BL0—5C 4
Ringwood Av. M12—5D 102
Ringwood Av. M26—6H 41
Ringwood Av. M34—4C 90
Ringwood Av. SK7—4B 144
Ringwood Way. OL9—1A 64
Rink St. M14—4H 117
Ripley Av. SK2—1B 144
Ripley Av. SK8—2D 152
Ripley Clo. M4—5H 87 & 1G 167
Ripley Clo. M5—3H 85
Ripley Clo. SK7—5E 145
Ripley Cres. M31—2B 96
Ripley St. BL2—1D 24
Ripley Way. M34—1F 121
Ripon Av. M15—5D 22
Ripon Av. M25—5D 42
Ripon Clo. BL3—4H 39
Ripon Clo. M25—5D 42
Ripon Clo. M26—2B 42
Ripon Clo. OL9—3H 63
Ripon Clo. SK1—3H 131
Ripon Clo. WA15—4C 138
Ripon Cres. M32—4H 97
Ripon Dri. BL1—4D 22
Ripon Gro. M33—3H 113
Ripon Hall Av. BL0—5D 4
Ripon Rd. M32—4H 97
Ripon St. M15—2E 101
Ripon St. OL1—1B 64
Ripon St. OL6—2A 92
Ripon Wlk. SK6—2G 133
Rippenden Av. M21—5G 99

Rippingham Rd. M20—2F 11/
Rippleton Rd. M22—1C 140
Ripponden Rd. OL1 & OL4—1G 65
Ripponden St. OL1—6G 49
*Ripton Wlk. M9—5D 60
  (off Selston Rd.)
Risbury Wlk. M10—5C 76
Rises, The. SK14—2H 109
Rise, The. OL4—2B 66
Rishton Av. BL3—5B 38
Rishton Av. M10—6G 75
Rishton La. BL3—3B 38
Rishworth Clo. SK2—6D 132
Rishworth Dri. M10—3E 77
Rishworth Rise. OL2—4D 34
Rising La. OL8—1C 78
Rising La. Clo. OL8—1C 78
Risley Av. M9—3F 75
Risley St. OL1—1D 64
Risque St. SK4—6F 119
Rita Av. M14—4F 101
Ritson Clo. M18—1D 102
Riva Rd. M19—1H 129
Riverbank Dri. BL8—1B 28
Riverbank Lawns. M3—2C 86 & 1E 161
Riverbank Tower. M3—2C 86
                      & 2E 161
Riverbank Wlk. M20—5B 116
Riverdale Ct. M9—6D 60
Riverdale Rd. M9—6C 60
River La. M31—5D 110
River La. M34—4H 105
Rivermead Av. WA15—1C 148
Rivermead Clo. M34—2G 121
Rivermead Rd. M34—1G 121
Riverpark Rd. M10—2C 88
River Pl. M15—6C 86 & 3F 165
River Pl. OL16—5F 21
Riversdale Ct. M25—5E 59
Riversdale Dri. OL8—2E 79
Riversdale Rd. SK8—5G 129
Riversdale View. SK6—3G 12?
Rivershill. M33—3A 114
Rivershill Dri. OL10—4D 30
Rivers Hill Gdns. WA15—1D 148
Riverside. OL1—6E 47
Riverside. M7—2A 86 & 2B 160
Riverside. OL1—6E 47
River Side. SK16—3A 92
Riverside Av. M21—5B 116
Riverside Av. M30—6F 95
Riverside Ct. M20—6D 116
Riverside Ct. OL12—1H 7
Riverside Dri M31—1D 112
Riverside Dri. BL9—1B 14
Riverside Dri. M26—1B 56
Riverside Rd. M26—3B 42
Riverside Works. SK9—1E 159
Rivers La. M31—2D 96
Riversleigh Clo. BL1—2D 22
Riversmeade. BL7—4G 11
Riverstone Dri. M23—4D 126
River St. BL2—6C 24
River St. M12—5G 87 & 2F 167
River St. M15—6D 86 & 4G 165
River St. M26—4H 41
River St. OL10—1F 31
River St. OL16—4H 19
River St. SK1—6B 120
River St. SK9—1E 159
Riverton Rd. M20—3F 129
River View. SK5—2A 120
River View Clo. M25—1D 72
River View Ct. M7—3G 73
Riviera Ct. OL11—1G 17
Rivington. M6—1C 84
Rivington Av. M27—3A 72
Rivington Cres. M27—3A 72
Rivington Dri. BL8—4G 27
Rivington Dri. OL2—6H 35
Rivington Gro. M30—3B 110
Rivington Gro. M34—5C 90
Rivington Rd. M6—1C 84
Rivington Rd. OL4—2C 66
Rivington Rd. WA15—3H 137
Rivington St. OL1—6D 48
Rivington St. OL12—2H 19
Rivington Wlk. M12—2B 102
Rixson St. OL4—5H 49
Rix St. BL1 -3A 24

Rixton St. M5—1H 99
Roach Bank Rd. BL9—6F 29
Roaches Way. OL5—6H 63
Rochill Clo. WA14—6D 124
Roach Pl. OL16—3A 20
Roach St. BL9—3D 42
  (Bury)
Roach St. BL9—3G 29
  (Heap Bridge)
Roachwood Clo. OL9—2E 63
Roading Brook Rd. BL2—2B 26
Road La. OL12—5D 6
Roads Ford Av. OL16—4F 21
Roaring Ga. La. WA15—2E 139
Robert Adam Cres. M15—1C 100 &
                              6E 165
Robert Hall St. M5— -5H 85
                       & 2A 164
Robert Malcolm Clo. M10—6F 75
Robert Owens Gdns. M22—3B 128
Robert Owen St. M35—3C 90
Roberts Av. M14—3F 101
*Robert Saville St. OL11—5D 18
  (off Half Acre M.)
Robertscroft Clo. M22—1A 140
Robertshaw Av. M21—3H 115
Robertson Clo. M18—2E 103
Robertson St. M26—3G 41
Roberts Pas. OL15—5H 9
Roberts Pl. OL15—6D 8
Roberts St. M30—3F 83
Robert St. BL1—5C 24
Robert St. BL2—6A 12
Robert St. BL4—1G 55
Robert St. BL8—2A 28
Robert St. M3—2D 86 & 1H 161
Robert St. M10—6H 75
Robert St. M25—4G 59
Robert St. M26—3G 41
Robert St. M33—5E 115
Robert St. M35—2G 77
Robert St. OL8—6H 63
Robert St. OL10—5G 31
Robert St. OL16—3A 20
Robert St. SK14—4A 106
Robert St. SK16—5H 91
Robe Wlk. M11—1F 103
Robina Clo. M30—5B 82
Robin Clo. BL4—2B 54
Robin Croft. SK6—6D 120
Robin Dri. M30—4E 95
Robin Hood St. M8—3B 74
Robin La. M25—2D 58
  (in two parts)
Robin Rd. BL9—6D 4
Robinsbay Rd. M22—5C 140
Robins Clo. M35—2C 90
Robins Clo. SK7—6G 143
Robins Hill. SK7—6F 143
Robins La. SK7—6F 143
Robinson La. OL7—2F 91
Robinsons Fold. OL2—2D 66
Robinson St. OL1—3D 64
Robinson St. OL6—1H 91
Robinson St. OL8—6D 64
Robinson St. OL9—3H 63
Robinson St. OL16—4A 20
Robinson St. SK3—4F 131
Robinson St. SK14—4D 106
Robinson St. SK15—5C 92
Robin St. OL1—1C 64
Robinsway. WA14—4E 137
Robinswood Rd. M22—3B 140
Robson Av. M31—6G 83
Roby Rd. M30—5E 83
Roby St. M1—4F 87 & 6C 162
Roch Av. OL10—3C 30
Rochbury Clo. OL11—5B 18
Roch Clo. M25—6F 43
Roch Cres. M25—5F 43
Rochdale Ind. Cen. OL11—5F 19
Rochdale La. OL2—2B 48
Rochdale La. OL10—3F 31
Rochdale Old Rd. BL9—2G 29
Rochdale Rd. BL0—2B 4
  (Edenfield)
Rochdale Rd. BL9—3D 28
Rochdale Rd. M4, M10 & M9—2F 87
                             & 3C 162

Rochdale Rd. M24—5A 46
Rochdale Rd. OL1 & OL9—6C 48
Rochdale Rd. OL2—6A 34
  (Royton)
Rochdale Rd. OL2—4C 34
  (Shaw)
Rochdale Rd. OL10—3F 31
Rochdale Rd. OL16—4D 20
Rochdale Rd. E. OL10—3G 31
Roche Gdns. SK8—1D 152
Roche Rd. OL3—2G 51
Rochester Av. BL2—4C 38
Rochester Av. M25—1G 73
Rochester Av. M28—2E 69
Rochester Clo. OL6—4G 79
Rochester Clo. SK16—6E 93
Rochester Gro. SK7—2E 145
Rochester Rd. M31—3F 97
Rochester Way. OL9—3H 63
Rochford Av. M22—5B 140
Rochford Clo. M25—2B 58
Rochford Clo. M25—2B 58
Rochford Rd. M30—5B 82
Roch Mills Cres. OL11—6E 19
Roch Mills Gdns. OL11—6E 19
Roch St. OL16—2B 20
Roch Valley Way. OL11—5E 19
Roch Wlk. M25—6F 43
Roch Way. M25—6F 43
Rockall Wlk. M11—4B 88
Rock Av. BL1—3G 23
Rock Bank. OL5—2E 81
Rockdove Av. M15—6D 86 & 4G 165
Rockfield Dri. M9—3G 75
Rock Fold. BL7—2D 10
Rockhampton St. M18—2F 103
Rockhouse Clo. M30—5E 83
Rockingham Clo. OL2—5C 34
Rockland Wlk. M10—1C 76
Rockley Gdns. M6—1H 85
Rocklyn Av. M10—1C 76
Rocklynes. SK6—1H 143
Rockmead Dri. M9—6G 61
Rock Rd. M31—4F 97
Rock St. M7—5H 73
Rock St. M11—5G 89
Rock St. OL1—2D 64
  (in two parts)
Rock St. OL7—6E 79
Rock St. OL10—4G 31
Rock St. SK14—2C 122
Rock Ter. BL7—2D 10
Rock Ter. OL5—5E 81
Rock, The. BL9—3D 28
  (in three parts)
Rocky La. M30—6D 70
Roda St. M9—4H 75
Rodborough Gdns. M23—2F 139
Rodborough Rd. M23—2F 139
Rodeheath Clo. SK9—2G 159
Roden Ct. M25—5G 59
Rodenhurst Dri. M10—4A 76
Rodepool Clo. SK9—5H 151
Rodford Wlk. M7—5B 74
Rodmell Av. M10—5F 75
Rodmell Clo. BL7—4D 10
Rodmill Dri. SK8—2E 141
Rodney Ct. M4—2G 87 & 2F 163
Rodney Dri. SK6—4G 121
Rodney St. M3—4B 86 & 5D 160
Rodney St. M4—3G 87 & 3F 163
Rodney St. OL5—1E 81
Rodney St. OL6—1B 92
Rodney St. OL11—3B 32
Rodway Wlk. M7—5B 74
Roeacre St. OL10—3E 31
Roebuck Gdns. M33—5A 114
Roebuck La. M33—5A 114
Roebuck La. OL4—4C 50
Roebuck Low. OL4—4C 50
Roebuck M. M33—5B 114
Roeburn Wlk. M25—1G 59
Roe Cross Grn. SK14—2B 108
Roe Cross Rd. SK14—1B 108
Roedean Gdns. M31—5G 95
Roefield Ter. OL12—3E 19
Roe Grn. M28—3H 69

Roe Grn Av. M28—3A 70
Roe La. OL4—4H 65
Roe St. OL12—2E 19
Rogate Dri. M23—6G 127
Roger Byrne Clo. M10—6B 76
Roger Clo. SK6—2F 133
Rogerstead. BL3—1G 37
Roger St. M4—2E 87 & 1B 162
Rokeby Av. M32—6D 98
Roker Av. M13—5B 102
Roker Pk. Av. M34—6D 90
Roland Rd. BL3—3G 37
Roland Rd. SK5—2H 119
Role Row. M25—2F 73
Rolla St. M3—3C 86 & 3F 161
Rollesby Clo. BL8—6D 14
Rolleston Av. M10—3H 87 & 3G 163
Rollins La. SK6—6E 121
Rolls Cres. M15—1C 100 & 5E 165
Rollswood Dri. M10—5A 76
Roman Ct. M7—6H 73
Roman Rd. M25—2E 73
Roman Rd. M35 & OL8—3G 77
Roman Rd. OL2—4B 48
Roman Rd. SK4—1G 131
Romans, The. OL5—2F 81
Roman St. M4—3E 87 & 4B 162
Roman St. M26—4E 41
Roman St. OL5—6F 67
Romer Av. M10—2E 77
Romer St. BL2—6E 25
Romford Av. M34—3G 105
Romford Clo. OL8—4C 64
Romford Rd. M33—3G 113
Romford Wlk. M9—6C 60
Romiley Cres. BL2—5F 25
Romiley Dri. BL2—5F 25
  (Breightmet)
Romiley Dri. BL2—6C 24
  (Mill Hill)
Romiley St. M6—6B 72
Romiley St. SK1—6B 120
Romley Precinct. SK6—1A 134
Romley Rd. M31—3F 97
Romney Av. OL11—3F 33
Romney Rd. BL1—3C 22
Romney St. M6—6F 73
Romney St. M10—3A 76
Romney St. OL6—2A 92
Romney Wlk. OL9—3H 63
Romney Way. SK5—3B 120
*Romsey. OL12—3G 19
  (off Spotland Rd.)
Romsey Av. M24—4H 45
Romsey Dri. SK8—1E 153
Romsey Gdns. M23—5F 127
Romsley Dri. M12—1C 102
Romsley Dri. BL3—4G 37
Ronaldsay Gdns. M5—4E 85
Ronald St. M11—4F 89
Ronald St. OL4—2G 65
Ronald St. OL11—4C 32
Rona Wlk. M12—2A 102
Rondin Clo. M12—5A 88
Ronnis Mt. OL7—4E 79
Ronton Wlk. M8—3E 75
Roocroft St. BL1—4H 23
Roods La. OL11—2G 17
Rookery Av. M18—1H 103
Rookery Clo. SK15—6H 93
Rookerypool Clo. SK9—5H 151
Rooke St. M30—5C 82
Rookfield. M33—4C 114
Rookfield Av. M33—4C 114
Rookley Wlk. M14—4G 101
Rook Nook. OL15—6H 9
Rook St. BL0—2E 5
Rook St. BL9—1D 28
Rook St. OL4—4G 65
Rookswood Dri. OL11—2B 32
Rookway. M24—2H 61
Rookwood. OL1—6E 47
Rookwood Av. M23—4F 127
Rookwood Hill. SK7—4G 143
Rooley Moor Rd. OL12—2A 6
Rooley St. OL12—2E 19
Rooley Ter. OL12—3E 19
Roosevelt Rd. BL4—2H 55
Rooth St. SK4—1F 131

Rope St. OL12—3H 19
Ropley Wlk. M9—2H 75
(off Oak Bank Av.)
Rosa Gro. M7—5H 73
Rosalind Ct. M5—5A 86 & 2B 164
Rosamond Dri. M3—3B 86 & 3D 160
Rosamond St. BL3—3G 37
Rosamond St. W. M15—1E 101 &
5A 166
Rosary Clo. OL8—2D 78
Rosary Rd. OL8—2E 79
Roscoe Pk. Est. WA14—3G 125
Roscoe Rd. M30—6C 94
Roscoe St. OL1—3D 64
(in two parts)
Roscoe St. SK3—3F 131
Roscow Av. BL2—5G 25
Roscow Rd. BL4—2A 56
Rose Acre. M28—4D 68
Roseacre Clo. BL2—5E 25
Roseacre Dri. SK8—4G 141
Rose Av. BL4—6E 39
Rose Av. M30—6D 94
Rose Av. OL11—1H 17
Rose Av. OL15—6D 8
Rose Bank. BL6—6A 22
Rose Bank. M31—1E 97
Rosebank Clo. BL2—4C 26
Rose Bank Clo. SK14—2F 109
Rose Bank Rd. M10—1D 88
Rosebank Rd. M30—5A 110
Roseberry Av. OL1—6F 49
Roseberry Clo. BL0—6E 5
Roseberry St. OL8—3B 64
Roseberry St. M14—4D 100
Rosebery St. SK2—1D 144
Rose Cottage Rd. M14—
1F 117
Rose Cotts. M14—1H 117
(off Ladybarn La.)
Rose Cres. M30—6D 94
Rosecroft Clo. SK3—1G 143
Rosedale Av. BL1—6C 10
Rosedale Clo. OL1—6F 49
Rosedale Rd. M14—5E 101
Rosedale Rd. SK4—4F 119
Rosefield Cres. OL16—4C 20
Rosegarth Av. M20—5B 116
Rosegate Clo. M16—4D 100
Rose Gro. BL4—2H 55
Rosehay Av. M34—5F 105
Rose Hey La. M35—1G 89
Rose Hill. BL2—2C 38
Rose Hill. M34—4D 104
Rose Hill. M35—2G 77
Rose Hill. OL3—4H 51
Rose Hill. SK15—5E 93
Rose Hill Av. M40—1D 88
Rose Hill Clo. BL7—4E 11
Rosehill Clo. M5—3F 85
Rose Hill Ct. M6—3F 85
Rose Hill Ct. OL4—6A 50
Rose Hill Cres. OL6—6B 80
Rose Hill Dri. BL7—4E 11
Rosehill M. M27—1F 71
Rosehill Rd. M27—1F 71
Rose Hill Rd. OL6—6B 80
Rose Hill St. OL10—3D 30
Roseland Av. M20—5F 117
Roseland Dri. M25—3G 59
Roselands Av. M33—1H 125
Rose La. SK6—5C 134
Rose Lea. BL2—1G 25
Roseleigh Av. M19—2B 118
Rosemary Dri. SK14—2B 122
Rosemary Gro. M7—6G 73
Rosemary La. SK1—2A 132
Rosemary Wlk. M31—6D 110
Rosemead Ct. SK5—3H 119
Rosemount. M24—5H 45
Rosemount. SK14—2B 106
Rosemount Cres. SK14—2A 106
Roseneath Av. M19—6E 103
Roseneath Gro. BL3—5H 37
Roseneath Rd. BL3—4H 37
Rosen Sq. OL9—2H 63

Rose Rd. M31—4E 97
Rose St. M24—1C 62
Rose St. OL9—6G 63
Rose St. SK5—6H 119
Rose Ter. SK15—4E 93
Rosette Wlk. M27—4F 71
Rose Vale. SK8—4F 141
Rosevale Av. M19—3A 118
Rose Wlk. M31—6C 110
Rose Wlk. SK6—5C 134
Roseway. SK7—3H 143
Rosewell Clo. M10—1H 87
Rosewood. M34—4D 104
Rosewood. OL11—2A 18
Rosewood Av. M35—2C 90
Rosewood Av. SK4—2C 130
Rosewood Clo. SK16—1B 106
Rosewood Cres. OL9—6H 47
Rosewood Gdns. M33—6F 115
(off Marefield)
Rosewood Wlk. M23—3C 126
Rosford Av. M14—5F 101
Rosgill Clo. SK4—1A 130
Rosgill Wlk. M18—2E 103
Rosina St. M11—6H 89
Roslin Gdns. BL1—2G 23
Roslin St. M11—3F 89
Roslyn Av. M31—1A 112
Roslyn Rd. SK3—6G 131
Rossall Av. M26—6A 42
Rossall Av. M32—4C 98
Rossall Clo. BL2—5E 25
Rossall Ct. SK7—1G 153
Rossall Dri. SK7—1G 153
Rossall Rd. BL2—5E 25
(in two parts)
Rossall Rd. OL12—1A 20
Rossall St. BL2—5E 25
Rossall Way. M6—2G 85
Ross Av. M19—6B 102
Ross Av. M25—3D 58
Ross Av. OL9—6F 63
Ross Av. SK3—6G 131
Ross Dri. M27—5E 57
Rossenclough Clo. SK9—6H 151
Rossendale Av. M9—2H 75
Rossendale Clo. OL2—6H 35
Rossendale Rd. SK8—5G 141
Rossendale Way. OL2—5F 35
Rossett Av. M22—5B 140
Rossett Av. WA15—3A 126
Rossett Dri. M31—3B 96
Rossetti Wlk. M34—2G 121
Ross Gro. M31—5E 97
Rosshill Wlk. M15—1B 100
& 5D 164
Rossington St. M10—6D 76
Rossini St. BL1—2H 23
Rosslane Wlk. SK5—2C 120
Rosslare Rd. M22—3C 140
Ross Lave La. M34—1B 120
Rosslyn Gro. WA15—5A 126
Rosslyn Rd. M10—2A 76
Rosslyn Rd. M16—5G 99
Rosslyn Rd. SK8—4H 141
Rossmere Av. OL11—5E 19
Rossmill La. WA15—1B 148
Ross St. BL1—4A 24
Ross St. OL8—4B 64
Rostherne. SK9—5D 158
Rostherne Av. M14—6E 101
Rostherne Av. M16—4A 100
Rostherne Av. SK6—5C 146
Rostherne Gdns. BL3—3F 37
Rostherne Rd. M33—6F 115
Rostherne Rd. SK3—6G 131
Rostherne Rd. SK9—4C 158
Rostherne St. M6—3E 85
Rostherne St. WA14—2F 137
(in two parts)
Rosthernmere Rd. SK8—1B 142
Rosthwaite Clo. M24—6E 45
Roston Ct. M7—3A 74
Roston Rd. M7—3A 74
Rostrevor Rd. SK3—6G 131
Rostron Brow. SK1—2H 131
(off Churchgate)
Rostron Clo. M12—1A 102
Rostron Rd. BL0—3D 4

Rostron St. M19—6D 102
Rostron St. M26—3G 41
Rothay Clo. BL2—4F 27
Rothay Dri. M24—4G 45
Rothay Dri. SK5—1H 119
Rothbury Av. OL7—1E 91
Rothbury Clo. BL8—3F 27
Rothbury Ct. BL3—4F 37
Rotherby Rd. M22—1C 140
Rotherdale Av. WA15—6D 126
Rothermere Wlk. M23—4E 127
Rotherwood Av. M32—4E 99
Rotherwood Rd. SK9—3A 158
Rothesay Av. SK16—6A 92
Rothesay Cres. M33—1E 125
Rothesay Rd. BL3—4F 37
Rothesay Rd. M8—1A 74
Rothesay Rd. M27—4A 72
Rothesay Rd. OL1—6G 49
Rothesay Ter. OL16—1A 34
Rothiemay Rd. M31—6A 96
Rothley Av. M22—6B 128
Rothman Clo. M10—5C 76
Rothwell Cres. M28—3A 54
Rothwell St. BL0—3D 4
Rothwell St. BL3—2A 38
Rothwell St. M10—5C 76
Rothwell St. M28—6H 55
Rothwell St. M35—4F 77
Rothwell St. OL2—4A 48
Rothwell St. OL12—2A 20
Rottingdene Dri. M22—4A 140
Rough Bank. OL12—4C 6
Roughey Gdns. M22—1A 140
Rough Hey Wlk. OL16—5B 20
Rough Hill La. BL9—1H 29
Roughlee Av. M40—2D 70
Roughtown Rd. OL5—1F 81
Roundcroft. SK6—6C 122
Roundham Wlk. M9—3G 75
Round Hey. OL5—3E 81
Roundhey. SK8—5F 141
Round Hill Clo. M14—4H 109
Roundhill Way. OL4—6A 50
Roundthorn Ct. M23—4B 132
Roundthorn Ind. Est. M23—
4E 127
Roundthorn Rd. M23—5F 127
Roundthorn Rd. M24—2B 62
Roundthorn Rd. OL4—3F 65
Roundway. SK7—1F 153
Roundwood Rd. M22—4B 128
Rousden Clo. M10—6F 75
Rouse St. OL11—1C 32
Routledge Wlk. M9—3G 75
Rowan Av. M16—4B 100
Rowan Av. M31—4F 97
Rowan Av. M33—1C 126
Rowan Clo. M6—3G 85
Rowan Clo. M35—5F 77
Rowan Clo. OL12—6A 6
Rowan Cres. SK16—6D 92
Rowan Dri. SK8—5E 143
Rowan Pl. M25—6F 59
Rowanside Dri. SK9—1H 159
Rowans St. BL8—1A 28
Rowans, The. BL1—6C 22
Rowans, The. M28—4A 68
Rowan St. SK14—6D 106
Rowan Tree Dri. M33—2B 126
Rowan Tree Rd. BL8—2B 78
Rowan Wlk. M31—6C 110
Rowan Wlk. SK14—3H 109
Rowanwood. OL9—2E 63
Rowany Clo. M25—1E 73
Rowarth Av. M34—1G 121
Rowarth Av. SK13—5F 109
(off Eyam La.)
Rowarth Bank. SK13—5F 109
(off Grassmoor Cres.)
Rowarth Clo. SK13—5F 109
(off Grassmoor Cres.)
Rowarth Fold. SK13—5F 109
(off Eyam La.)
Rowarth Rd. M23—3F 139
Rowarth Way. SK13—5F 109
(off Eyam La.)
Rowbotham St. SK14—1C 122

Rowbottom Wlk. OL8—4C 64
Rowcon Clo. M34—2E 105
Rowdell Wlk. M23—1H 127
Rowden Rd. OL4—5A 66
Rowe Grn. M34—4F 105
Rowell Sq. M3—3B 86 & 4D 160
Rowell St. M3—3B 86 & 4C 160
Rowena St. BL3—5E 39
Rowendale St. M1—5C 86 & 2G 165
Rowfield Dri. M23—2F 139
Rowland Av. M31—4G 97
Rowland Ct. OL16—5B 20
Rowland Ho. OL2—3D 48
Rowlands Rd. BL9—1C 14
Rowland St. M5—5G 85
Rowland St. OL16—5B 20
Rowlands Way. M22—3B 140
Rowland Way. OL4—2A 66
Rowley Dri. SK7—5E 145
Rowley St. OL6—5H 79
Rowlsey Clo. SK13—5G 109
(off Melandra Castle Rd.)
Rowood Av. M8—5D 74
Rowood Av. SK5—5H 103
Rowrah Cres. M24—6D 44
Rowsley Av. BL1—4E 23
Rowsley Av. M20—5C 116
Rowsley Grn. SK13—5G 109
(off Melandra Castle Rd.)
Rowsley Gro. SK5—2G 119
Rowsley Gro. SK13—5G 109
Rowsley M. SK13—5G 109
Rowsley Rd. M30—5E 83
Rowsley Rd. M32—4A 98
Rowsley St. M6—6F 73
Rowsley St. M11—3A 88
Rowsley Wlk. SK13—5G 109
(off Melandra Castle Rd.)
Rowson Ct. M33—5D 114
Rowson Dri. M30—3B 110
Rowton St. BL2—2D 24
Roxalina St. BL3—3A 38
Roxburgh St. M18—2F 103
Roxbury Av. OL4—4H 65
Roxby Clo. M28—6D 54
Roxby Wlk. M10—1D 76
Roxholme Wlk. M22—5A 140
Roxton Rd. SK4—3E 119
Roxwell Wlk. M9—3F 75
(off Alderside Rd.)
Royal Av. BL9—6F 15
Royal Av. M21—1G 115
Royal Av. M31—5F 97
Royal Av. M35—3B 90
Royal Av. OL10—4F 31
Royal Carr Flats. SK6—6G 121
(off Wild St.)
Royal Exchange. M2—3D 86
Royal Exchange Arc. M2—4D 86
Royal George Cotts. OL3—4G 67
(off Church Rd.)
Royal George St. SK3—3G 131
Royal Oak Rd. M23—4F 127
(in two parts)
Royal Oak Yd. SK1—2H 131
Royal Rd. SK12—2H 157
Royal St. OL16—6A 8
Royalthorn Av. M22—5B 128
Royalthorn Dri. M22—5A 128
Royalthorn Rd. M22—5A 128
Royce Av. WA15—6G 125
Royce Ind. Est. M17—6H 83
Royce Rd. M15—1B 100 & 5D 164
Roydale St. M10—2A 88
Royden Av. M9—4F 61
Roydes St. M24—5B 46
Roydon Av. M30—1D 104
Royds Clo. M13—2H 101
Royds Pl. OL16—6A 20
Royds St. BL8—4H 13
Royds St. OL15—4G 9
Royds St. OL16—6G 21
(Milnrow)
Royds St. OL16—6B 20
(Rochdale)
Royds St. BL8—4H 13
Royds St. W. OL16—6A 20
Royd St. OL8—5A 64
Roy Grainger Ct. M16—4C 100

Royland Av. BL3—4C 38
Royle Barn Rd. OL11—3C 32
Royle Clo. SK2—6B 132
Royle Grn. Rd. M22—2C 128
Royle-Higginson St. M31—6E 97
Roylelands Bungalows. OL11
—2C 32
Royle Pennine Trading Est. OL11
—2D 32
Royle Rd. OL11—2C 32
Royles Cottages. M33—6B 114
Royle St. M6—4F 85
Royle St. M14—2H 117
Royle St. M28—1F 69
Royle St. M34—2F 105
Royle St. SK1—4H 131
Royley. OL2—4A 48
Royley Cres. OL2—4A 48
Royley Rd. OL8—5C 64
Royley Way. OL2—4A 48
Royon Dri. SK3—4D 130
Royston Av. BL2—5D 24
Royston Av. M16—4B 100
Royston Av. M34—4A 104
Royston Clo. BL8—2H 13
Royston Rd. M16—4H 99
Royston Rd. M31—4G 97
Roy St. BL3—3F 37
Roy St. M35—3G 77
Roy St. OL2—3B 48
Royton Av. M33—1E 127
Royton Hall Wlk. OL2—3C 48
Royton Ho. OL2—2F 49
Rozel Sq. M3—5C 86 & 1F 165
Ruabon Rd. M20—1G 129
Ruby St. BL1—2B 24
Ruby St. BL9—6E 5
Ruby St. M34—5E 105
Ruby St. Pas. OL11—5G 19
Rudcroft Clo. M13—1F 101 & 5D 166
Rudding St. OL2—5E 49
Ruddpark Rd. M22—4B 140
Rudd St. M10—4A 76
Rudford Av. M11—5G 89
Rudford Gdns. BL3—3B 38
Rudgwick Dri. BL8—4C 14
Rudheath Av. M20—2E 117
Rudkin St. M11—5C 88
Rudman Dri. M5—5A 86 & 2A 164
Rudman St. OL12—1G 19
Rudolph St. BL3—4B 38
Rudston Av. M10—1B 76
Rudyard Av. M24—4C 46
Rudyard Gro. M33—1G 125
Rudyard Gro. OL11—3F 33
Rudyard Gro. SK4—3F 119
Rudyard Rd. M6—6A 72
Rudyard St. M7—5H 73
Ruebens Clo. SK6—3F 135
Rufford Av. OL3—1D 32
Rufford Av. SK14—5D 106
Rufford Clo. M25—5E 43
Rufford Clo. OL2—6D 34
Rufford Clo. OL6—5G 79
Rufford Dri. BL3—5H 37
Rufford Dri. M25—5C 42
Rufford Gro. BL3—5H 37
Rufford Pl. M18—3H 103
Rufford Rd. M16—4B 100
Rufus St. M14—2A 118
Rugby Dri. M33—1A 126
Rugby Rd. M6—2A 84
Rugby Rd. OL12—2A 20
Rugby Rd. Ind. Est. OL12—2A 20
Rugby St. M7—1C 86
Rugeley St. M6—6F 73
Ruins La. BL2—1G 25
Ruislip Clo. OL8—5F 65
Rumbles La. OL3—3H 51
Rumbold St. M18—1G 103
Rumbold St. OL11—6H 19
Rumford St. M13—1F 101 & 6D 166
(in two parts)
Rumworth Rd. BL6—1A 36
Rumworth St. BL3—3H 37
Runcorn St. M15—6A 86 & 4B 164
Runger La. WA15—6F 139
Runhall Clo. M12—1C 102

Runimead Ct. OL2—3C 48
Running Hill Ga. OL3—6D 52
Running Hill La. OL3—5D 52
Runnymeade. M27 & M6—5G 71
Runnymede Clo. SK3—4E 131
Runnymede Ct. BL3—2H 37
Runnymede Ct. SK3—5E 131
Rupert St. BL3—3A 38
Rupert St. M10—1G 89
Rupert St. M26—6G 41
Rupert St. OL12—2E 19
Rupert St. SK5—2G 119
(in two parts)
Rupert Ter. SK5—2G 119
Rush Acre Clo. M26—4E 41
Rushall Wlk. M23—3F 139
Rush Bank. OL2—5D 34
Rushbrooke Av. M11—2E 89
Rushcroft Ct. M9—1A 76
Rushcroft Rd. OL2—5D 34
Rushden Rd. M19—5D 102
Rushen St. M11—4E 89
Rushes, The. SK14—3H 109
Rushey Av. M22—5A 128
Rushey Clo. WA15—6D 138
Rushey Field. BL7—3D 10
Rushey Fold La. BL1—3H 23
Rushey Rd. M22—6A 128
Rushfield Rd. SK8—6B 142
Rushford Av. M19—5C 102
Rushford Gro. BL1—1B 24
Rushford St. M12—3C 102
Rush Hill. OL3—2F 53
Rush Hill Rd. OL3—2F 53
Rush Hill Ter. OL3—2F 53
Rushlake Dri. BL1—4A 24
Rushley Av. M7—5F 73
Rushmere. OL6—5A 80
Rushmere Av. M19—6D 102
Rushmere Dri. BL8—6C 14
Rushmere Wlk. M16—2B 100
Rushmoor Clo. M30—5E 95
Rush Mt. OL2—5D 34
Rusholme Dri. M14—4G 101
Rusholme Gro. W. M14—4G 101
Rusholme Pl. M14—3G 101
Rushside Rd. SK8—1B 152
Rush St. SK16—5D 92
Rushton Clo. SK6—6E 135
Rushton Dri. SK6—6D 134
(Marple)
Rushton Dri. SK6—6A 122
(Romiley)
Rushton Dri. SK7—2F 143
Rushton Gdns. SK7—2F 143
Rushton Gro. M11—6G 89
Rushton Gro. OL4—4A 50
Rushton Rd. BL1—4F 23
Rushton Rd. SK3—4D 130
Rushton St. SK8—1C 152
Rushton St. M20—1F 129
Rushton St. M28—1F 69
Rushwick Av. M10—5G 75
Rushworth Ct. SK4—4E 119
Rushworth St. M10—2H 87 & 2G 163
Rushyfield Cres. SK6—6B 122
Rushy Hill View. OL12—2E 19
Ruskin Av. BL4—2H 55
Ruskin Av. M14—3F 101
Ruskin Av. M34—6C 90
(Audenshaw)
Ruskin Av. OL9—6F 63
(Denton)
Ruskin Av. M34—6D 104
Ruskin Cres. M25—6D 58
Ruskin Gdns. SK6—6G 121
Ruskin Gro. SK6—6G 121
Ruskington Dri. M9—4F 75
Ruskin Rd. BL3—3B 40
Ruskin Rd. M16—4A 100
Ruskin Rd. M25—6C 58
Ruskin Rd. M35—3A 90
Ruskin Rd. OL11—3F 33
Ruskin Rd. SK5—6G 103
Ruskin St. M26—3A 42
Ruskin St. OL1—1B 64
Rusland Ct. M9—6A 62
Rusland Ct. M33—4A 114

Rusland Dri. BL2—3G 25
Rusland Wlk. M22—3A 140
Ruslip Av. M10—6G 75
Russell Av. M16—5B 100
Russell Av. M33—4D 114
Russell Av. SK6—6C 146
Russell Clo. BL1—5G 23
Russell Ct. BL4—1G 55
Russell Ct. M28—6E 55
Russell Dri. M30—5E 95
Russell Gdns. SK4—2D 130
Russell Rd. M6—6H 71
Russell Rd. M16—4B 100
Russell Rd. BL11—5B 33
Russell St. BL1—5H 23
Russell St. BL9—1D 28
Russell St. M8—1C 86
Russell St. M16—4D 100
Russell St. M25—5F 59
Russell St. M28—6E 55
Russell St. M30—3H 83
Russell St. M34—4F 105
Russell St. OL5—2E 81
Russell St. OL6—1B 92
Russell St. OL9—2H 63
Russell St. OL10—3G 31
Russell St. OL11—6G 19
(off Grove St.)
Russell St. SK2—5A 132
Russell St. SK6—6F 123
Russell St. SK14—4B 106
Russell St. SK16—5A 92
Russet Rd. M9—2F 75
Rustons Wlk. M10—2E 77
Ruth Av. M10—2E 77
Ruthen La. M16—3H 99
Rutherford Av. M14—4F 101
Rutherglade Clo. M10—5E 75
Rutherglen Dri. BL3—1D 36
Rutherglen Wlk. M10—6G 75
Ruthin Av. M9—4E 61
Ruthin Av. M24—2A 62
Ruthin Av. SK8—3A 142
Ruthin Clo. M6—3G 85
Ruthin Clo. OL8—1H 77
Ruthin Ct. M6—3G 85
Ruth St. BL0—3A 4
Ruth St. BL1—5A 24
Ruth St. M18—4F 103
Ruth St. OL1—1D 64
Ruth St. OL12—4G 7
Rutland. OL11—5G 19
Rutland Av. M16—4G 99
Rutland Av. M20—3E 117
Rutland Av. M27—1F 71
Rutland Av. M31—5G 97
Rutland Av. M34—5G 105
Rutland Clo. BL3—3B 40
Rutland Clo. OL6—3B 92
Rutland Clo. SK8—5F 129
Rutland Ct. M20—6F 117
Rutland Ct. SK2—6A 132
Rutland Cres. SK5—4D 120
Rutland Dri. BL9—5E 29
Rutland Dri. M7—2G 73
Rutland Gro. BL1—4G 23
Rutland Gro. BL4—2E 55
Rutland La. M33—5F 115
(in two parts)
Rutland Rd. M28—2E 69
Rutland Rd. M30—4B 110
(Cadishead)
Rutland Rd. M30—1H 83
(Eccles)
Rutland Rd. M35—2G 89
Rutland Rd. M43—1C 105
Rutland Rd. WA14—5F 125
Rutland St. BL3—3H 37
Rutland St. M18—1G 103
Rutland St. M27—2E 71
Rutland St. M35—5B 90
(Droylsden)
Rutland St. M35—3F 77
(Failsworth)
Rutland St. OL6—3B 92
Rutland St. OL9—4A 64
Rutland St. OL10—2F 31

Rutland St. SK14—2B 106
Rutter's La. SK7—3C 144
Rutter St. BL4—3A 56
Ryall Av. M5—5H 85
Ryall Av. S. M5—5H 85
Ryan St. M11—6G 89
Ryburn Flats. OL10—3E 31
(off Meadow Clo.)
Ryburn Sq. OL11—5A 18
Rydal Av. M24—3H 61
Rydal Av. M30—1D 82
Rydal Av. M31—1C 112
Rydal Av. M33—4H 113
Rydal Av. M35—4G 89
Rydal Av. OL2—5A 34
Rydal Av. OL9—6E 47
Rydal Av. SK6—5C 146
Rydal Av. SK7—2C 144
Rydal Av. SK14—2A 106
Rydal Clo. BL9—6C 28
Rydal Clo. M34—5B 104
Rydal Clo. SK8—2F 141
Rydal Cres. M27—5F 71
Rydal Cres. M28—2G 69
Rydal Dri. WA15—5D 138
Rydal Gro. B—2B 54
Rydal Gro. M25—1E 59
Rydal Gro. OL7—1F 91
Rydal Gro. OL10—5F 31
Rydal Mt. SK5—5H 103
Rydal Mt. SK9—6B 158
Rydal Rd. BL1—4E 23
Rydal Rd. BL3—4A 40
Rydal Rd. M32—4D 98
Rydal Rd. OL4—2G 65
Rydal Wlk. OL4—2H 65
Rydal Wlk. SK15—2E 93
Ryde Av. M34—1H 121
Ryde Av. SK4—1D 130
Ryder Av. WA14—4G 125
Ryder Brow. M18—3F 103
Ryder St. BL1—3G 23
Ryder St. M10—1B 87
Ryder St. M26—4B 42
Ryder St. OL10—3F 31
Ryde St. BL3—3E 37
Rydings La. OL12—3G 7
Rydings Rd. OL12—5H 7
Rydley St. BL2—1D 38
Ryebank Gro. OL6—6H 79
Ryebank M. M21—6F 99
Rye Bank Rd. M16—5G 99
Ryebank Rd. M21—6F 99
Ryeburn Av. M22—2B 140
Ryeburne St. OL4—2G 65
Ryeburn Wlk. M31—3B 96
Rye Croft. M25—2A 58
Ryecroft Av. BL8—5H 13
Ryecroft Av. M6—2C 84
Ryecroft Clo. OL10—3G 31
Ryecroft Clo. OL9—6F 63
Ryecroft Gro. M23—4G 127
Ryecroft La. M28—1B 82
Ryecroft Rd. M34—6E 91
Ryecroft Rd. M32—6C 98
Ryecroft St. OL7—4F 91
Ryecroft View. M34—5C 90
Ryedale Av. M10—6F 75
Ryedale Clo. SK4—6D 118
Ryefield. M6—5B 72
Ryefield. OL7—4F 91
Ryefield Clo. WA15—6C 126
Ryefield Rd. M33—1E 125
Ryefields. OL12—5B 8
Ryefield St. BL1—4C 24
Ryelands Clo. OL16—1H 33
Rye St. OL10—2G 31
Rye Wlk. M13—2G 101
Rye Wlk. M9—3G 63
Rygate Wlk. M8—5B 74
Ryhope Wlk. M7—6A 74
Rylance St. M11—4A 88
Ryland Clo. SK5—6H 103
Rylands Ct. M15—1B 100 & 6C 164
Rylane Wlk. M10—6F 75
(off Ridgewood Av.)

Rylatt Ct. M33—4A 114
Ryley Av. BL3—2F 37
Ryleys La. SK9—5F 159
Ryley St. BL3—1G 37
Rylstone Av. M21—6B 116
Ryther Gro. M9—4D 60
Ryton Av. M18—4E 103

Sabden Clo. BL9—4F 15
Sabden Clo. M10—2A 88
Sabden Clo. OL10—3C 30
Sabden Rd. BL1—3C 22
Sabrina St. M8—6A 74
Sack St. SK14—2B 106
Sackville Clo. OL2—4E 35
Sackville St. BL2—6E 25
Sackville St. BL9—2E 29
Sackville St. M1—5E 87 & 1B 166
(in three parts)
Sackville St. M33—3C 86 & 4E 161
Sackville St. OL6—2H 91
Sackville St. OL11—4C 32
Saddleback Clo. M28—5D 68
Saddlecote. M28—1C 82
Saddle Gro. M35—2D 90
Saddle St. BL2—3D 24
Saddlewood Av. M19—1H 129
Sadie Av. M32—3A 98
Sadler Clo. M14—4E 101
Sadler St. BL3—3C 38
Sadler St. M24—6H 45
Saffron Dri. OL4—5H 49
Saffron Wlk. M22—4B 140
Saffron St. M31—6D 110
Sagars Rd. SK9—3F 151
Sagar St. M8—1D 86
Sahal Ct. M7—1B 86
St Agnes Rd. M13—5B 102
St Agnes St. SK5—4H 103
St Aidans Clo. M26—6G 41
St Aidan's Clo. OL11—6E 19
St Aidan's Gro. M7—5F 73
St Albans Av. M10—6B 76
St Albans Av. OL6—4F 79
St Alban's Av. SK4—4E 119
St Alban's Cres. WA14—3E 125
St Albans Ho. OL16—5G 19
(off St Albans St.)
St Albans St. OL16—5G 19
St Alban's Ter. M8—6A 74
St Alban's Ter. OL11—5G 19
St Aldates. SK6—1F 133
St Aldwyn's Rd. M20—4F 117
St Ambrose Gdns. M6—3F 85
St Ambrose Rd. OL1—6G 49
St Andrews Av. M30—4G 83
St Andrew's Av. M35—4G 89
St Andrew's Av. WA15—4G 125
St Andrews Clo. BL0—4E 5
St Andrews Clo. M33—2E 125
St Andrews Clo. SK4—5D 118
St Andrew's Clo. SK6—2H 133
St Andrew's Ct. BL1—6B 24
(off Chancery La.)
St Andrews Ct. WA15—2H 137
St Andrew's Dri. OL10—5F 31
St Andrew's Rd. M26—1F 41
St Andrews Rd. M32—5B 98
St Andrews Rd. SK4—5D 118
St Andrew's Rd. SK8—4D 141
St Andrew's Sq. M1—5G 87 & 1F 167
St Andrew's St. M1—5G 87
& 1F 167
St Andrew's St. M26—1F 41
St Andrews View. M26—1F 41
St Anne's Av. M6—2E 85
St Anne's Av. OL2—4C 48
St Annes Ct. M6—1F 85
St Annes Ct. M33—5C 114
St Anne's Cres. OL4—4E 67
St Anne's Dri. M34—3G 105
St Annes Gdns. OL10—3H 31
St Annes Rd. M21—2H 115
St Anne's Rd. M34—2F 105
(Denton)
St Annes Sq. OL3—3H 51
St Annes Rd. M34—1F 105
(Audenshaw)

St Anne's St. BL9—1D 28
St Anne's St. M10—6H 75
St Anne St. M12—1C 102
(off Hyde Rd.)
St Ann's All. M2—4D 86
(off St Ann's Pl.)
St Ann's Arc. M2—4D 86
(off St Ann's Sq.)
St Ann's Chyd. M2—4D 86
(off St Ann St.)
St Anns Clo. M28—6E 59
St Ann's Pl. M2—4D 86 & 5H 161
St Ann's Rd. OL16—3C 20
St Anns Rd. SK7—4C 144
St Ann's Rd. N. SK8—4G 141
St Ann's Rd. S. SK8—5G 141
St Ann's Sq. M2—4D 86 & 5H 161
St Ann's Sq. SK8—5G 141
St Ann's St. M27—3E 71
St Ann's St. M33—6F 115
St Ann St. BL1—4A 24
St Ann St. M2—4D 86 & 5H 161
St Asaph's Dri. M8—3B 74
St Asaph's Dri. OL6—5F 79
St Aubin's Rd. BL2—1D 38
St Augustine's Rd. SK3—3D 130
St Augustine St. BL1—3H 23
St Augustine St. M10—4D 74
St Austell Dri. BL8—1H 13
St Austell Dri. SK8—5F 141
St Austell Rd. M16—6C 100
St Austells Dri. M25—4F 59
St Austell's Dri. M27—4A 72
St Barnabas Pl. OL15—3E 9
St Barnabas Sq. M11—5D 88
St Bartholomew's Dri. M5—5A 86 &
2A 164
St Bartholomew St. BL3—3C 38
St Bedes Av. BL3—5F 37
St Bees Clo. M14—3E 101
St Bees Clo. SK8—2F 141
St Bees Rd. BL2—3E 25
St Bees Wlk. M24—5G 45
St Bernards Clo. M6—6G 73
St Bernards St. M6—6G 73
St Boniface Rd. M7—6G 73
St Brannock's Rd. M21—6A 100
St Brannocks Rd. SK8—6D 142
St Brelades Dri. M8—3B 74
St Brendan's Rd. M20—2F 117
St Brendan's Rd. N. M20—2F 117
St Bride St. M16—2B 100
St Brides Way. M16—2B 100
St Catherine's Rd. M20—2F 117
St Chads Av. SK6—1A 134
St Chad's Clo. OL16—4H 19
St Chads Cres. OL3—1G 53
St Chads Cres. OL8—2B 78
St Chads Gro. SK6—1A 134
St Chads Rd. M20—2H 117
St Chads St. M8—1E 87
St Charles Clo. SK14—2H 109
St Christopher's Av. OL6—5A 80
St Christopher's Dri. SK6
—1G 133
St Christopher's Rd. OL6—5H 79
St Clair Rd. BL8—6B 4
St Clement's Ct. M25—5G 59
St Clements Clo. M30—4F 95
St Clements Ct. OL8—4D 64
St Clement's Dri. M5—6H 85
St Clement's Rd. M21—1G 115
St Davids Av. SK6—1H 133
St David's Clo. OL6—4H 79
St Davids Rd. SK7—4C 144
St David's Rd. SK8—6B 130
St David's Wlk. M32—5A 98
St Domingo St. OL9—2C 64
St Dominic's M. BL3—4G 37
St Dominics Way. M24—2A 62
St Dunstan Wlk. M10—5A 76
(off Rollswood Dri.)
St Edmund's Rd. M10—5G 75
St Edmund St. BL1—6A 24
St Edmund's Wlk. M28—5D 54
St Elizabeth's Way. SK5—1G 119
St Elmo Av. SK4—2D 131
St Elmo Pk. SK12—3A 156
St Ethelbert's Av. BL3—2F 37

St Gabriels Clo. OL11—4D 32
St Gabriel's Ct. OL11—3C 32
(off Atkinson St.)
St George's Av. M15—6B 86 & 4C 164
St George's Av. WA15—4A 126
St Georges Cen. M6—1H 85
St George's Ct. BL1—5A 24
St Georges Ct. BL9—3G 43
St Georges Ct. M30—4H 83
St George's Ct. M32—6C 98
St George's Ct. WA14—4D 124
St George's Cres. M6—2A 84
St George's Cres. M28—1F 69
St George's Cres. WA15—3A 126
St Georges Dri. M10—4B 76
St Georges Dri. SK14—5B 106
St George's Gdns. M34—6G 105
St Georges Pl. M6—6E 73
St George's Rd. BL1—5A 24
St George's Rd. BL9—3G 43
St George's Rd. M14—2A 118
St George's Rd. M31—3H 111
St Georges Rd. M32—5C 98
St George's Rd. M35—2H 89
St George's Rd. OL11—3B 18
St Georges Sq. BL1—5A 24
(off All Saints St.)
St George's Sq. OL9—6E 63
St George's St. BL1—5B 24
St George's St. SK15—2D 92
St George St. M4—2G 87 & 2E 163
St Georges Way. M6—6E 73
(in two parts)
St Germain St. BL1—1E 55
St Giles Dri. SK14—5D 106
St Helena Rd. BL1—6A 24
(in two parts)
St Helens Clo. WA3—6A 110
St Helens Rd. BL3—6E 37
St Helier's Dri. M8—3B 74
St Helier St. BL3—3H 37
St Herberts Ct. OL9—2H 63
St Hilda's Clo. M22—2C 128
St Hilda's Dri. OL1—1B 64
St Hilda's Rd. M16—2A 100
St Hilda's Rd. M22—2B 128
St Hilda's Rd. M34—1F 105
St Hilda's View. M34—2E 105
St Hughe's Clo. WA14—3G 125
St Ignatius Wlk. M5—5H 85
St Ives Av. SK8—5B 130
St Ives Cres. M33—2A 126
St Ives Rd. M14—5F 101
St James Av. BL8—1H 27
St James Clo. M6—2B 84
St James Clo. OL16—5A 34
St James Ct. M20—3F 129
St James Ct. OL4—1G 65
St James Dri. SK9—3D 158
St James Gro. OL10—3E 31
St James Ho. SK4—6F 119
St James Rd. SK4—4D 118
St James's Av. BL2—5G 25
St James's Gro. WA14—2H 125
St James's Rd. M7—5A 74
St James's Sq. M2—4D 86
& 5H 161
St James Rd. BL4—2D 54
St James St. M1—5E 87 & 1A 166
St James St. M5—1G 99
St James St. M30—3G 83
St James St. OL1—2F 65
St James's Av. SK4—1E 131
St James St. OL2—6F 35
St James St. OL6—3B 92
St James St. OL10—3E 31
St James St. OL16—5F 21
St James Ter. OL10—3E 31
St James Way. SK8—5B 130
St Johns Av. M35—3B 90
St Johns Clo. SK6—1H 133
St Johns Clo. SK16—5C 92
St John's Ct. M7—5G 73
St John's Ct. M26—5H 41
St Johns Ct. OL4—2B 66
St John's Ct. OL16—5B 20
St Johns Dri. OL16—5B 20
St Johns Dri. SK14—4D 106
St John's Gdns. OL5—1F 81

St John's Ind. Est. OL4—3A 66
St John's Pas. M3—4C 86 & 1F 165
St John's Pl. SK4—1A 130
St John's Rd. M13—3B 102
St John's Rd. M16—3A 100
St John's Rd. M28—4A 68
St John's Rd. M34—2F 105
St John's Rd. SK4—1A 130
St Johns Rd. SK7—4B 144
St John's Rd. SK9—6B 158
St John's Rd. WA14—2E 137
St John's St. BL4—1G 55
St John's St. M7—4H 73
St John's St. M26—5H 41
St John's St. OL9—4A 64
St John St. M3—5C 86 & 1F 165
St John St. M27—5B 72
St John St. M28—5E 55
St John St. M30—4F 83
(Eccles)
St John St. M30—5E 95
(Irlam)
St John St. M35—5H 89
St John St. OL4—3A 66
St John St. SK16—5C 92
(in two parts)
St John's Wlk. OL9—3A 64
St Johns Wlk. SK3—3D 130
(off Oak St.)
St Johns Wood. SK15—5C 92
St Joseph's Av. M25—2G 59
St Joseph's Dri. M5—5H 85
St Joseph St. BL1—3H 23
St Kilda Av. BL4—3H 55
St Kilda's Av. M35—2H 89
St Kilda's Dri. M8—3B 74
St Lawrence Ct. M34—5F 105
St Lawrence Rd. M34—4F 105
St Leonard's Ct. M33—5H 113
St Leonards Rd. WA15—5H 125
St Leonards Rd. SK4—4F 119
St Leonards St. M24—6A 46
St Leonard St. M13—1G 101 & 6E 167
St Lesmo Ct. SK3—4E 131
St Lesmo Rd. SK3—3D 130
St Lukes Ct. BL1—5G 23
St Lukes Ct. OL11—6H 19
St Lukes Cres. SK16—5A 92
St Luke's Rd. M6—3D 84
St Lukes St. OL11—6H 19
St Lukes Wlk. M10—5A 76
St Margaret's Rd. M25—3G 59
St Margaret's Av. M19—3B 118
St Margarets Clo. BL1—5F 23
St Margarets Clo. WA14—1E 137
St Margaret's Rd. BL1—5F 23
St Margaret's Rd. M10—6D 62
St Margaret's Rd. SK8—5C 102
St Margaret's Rd. WA14—2E 137
St Marks Av. OL2—3E 49
St Marks Clo. OL2—3E 49
St Mark's Ct. OL9—1H 63
St Mark's La. M8—4B 74
St Mark's St. BL9—1D 28
St Mark's St. BL3—2B 38
St Mark's St. M19—5E 103
St Mark's St. SK6—5G 121
St Mark's View. SK16—4H 91
St Mark's View. BL3—3B 38
St Mark's Wlk. BL3—3A 38
St Martin's Av. SK4—1E 131
St Martin's Clo. M35—2H 89
St Martin's Clo. SK14—5D 106
St Martin's Dri. M8—3B 74
St Martins Rd. M33—3F 113
St Martin's Rd. OL16—1E 79
St Martin's Rd. SK6—5E 135
St Martins St. OL11—4D 32
St Marys'. SK1—2A 132
St Mary's Av. BL3—2F 37
St Mary's Av. M34—1G 121
St Mary's Clo. SK1—2A 132
St Mary's Ct. M8—2B 74
St Mary's Ct. M10—3B 76
St Mary's Crest. OL3—6G 53
St Mary's Dri. OL3—4G 53
St Mary's Dri. SK5—3H 119
St Mary's Dri. SK8—5B 130

St Mary's Ga. M1—3D 86 & 4H 161
St Marys Ga. OL2—6F 35
St Mary's Ga. OL3—1F 53
St Mary's Ga. OL16—4G 19
St Marys Ga. SK1—2H 131
St Mary's Hall Rd. M8—2B 74
St Mary's Parsonage. M3—4C 86 &
5F 161
St Mary's Pl. BL9—3C 28
St Mary's Rd. M10—4B 76
St Mary's Rd. M25—5E 59
St Mary's Rd. M28—4E 55
St Marys Rd. M30—3H 83
St Mary's Rd. M33—4H 113
St Mary's Rd. SK12—2H 157
St Mary's Rd. SK14—2C 106
St Mary's Rd. WA14—3D 136
(in two parts)
St Mary's St. M3—4D 86 & 5G 161
(Manchester)
St Mary's St. M15—2C 100
St Mary's St. M27—3G 71
St Mary's St. OL1—1D 64
St Mary St. M3—3B 86 & 4D 160
(Salford)
St Marys Way. OL1—2C 64
St Marys Way. SK1—1A 132
St Matthews Dri. OL1—5G 47
St Matthew's Rd. SK3—3F 131
St Matthews Ter. BL1—4A 24
(off St Matthews Wlk.)
St Matthews Ter. SK3—3F 131
St Matthews Wlk. BL1—4A 24
(in two parts)
St Michael's Av. BL3—5D 38
St Michael's Av. SK7—6G 143
St Michael's Clo. BL8—5G 27
St Michael's Ct. M30—5C 82
St Michaels Ct. M33—3G 113
St Michaels Rd. SK14—5D 106
St Michael's Sq. M4—2E 87
& 2B 162
St Michael's Sq. OL6—2A 92
St Modwin Rd. M32—2H 97
St Osmund's Dri. BL2—6G 25
St Osmund's Gro. BL2—6G 25
St Oswalds Rd. M19—5D 102
St Pauls Clo. M26—6G 41
St Paul's Clo. SK15—2G 93
St Paul's Ct. M7—2G 73
St Paul's Ct. M28—1F 69
St Pauls Ct. OL8—5D 64
St Paul's Hill Rd. SK14—5D 106
St Paul's Pl. BL1—2G 23
St Paul's Rd. M7—2G 73
St Paul's Rd. M20—3G 117
St Paul's Rd. M28—1G 69
St Paul's Rd. SK4—5D 118
St Paul's St. BL9—2E 29
St Paul's St. SK1—6A 120
St Pauls St. SK14—4C 106
St Paul's St. SK15—3G 93
St Paul's Vs. BL9—2E 29
St Peter Quay. M5—6G 85
St Peter's Av. BL1—3E 23
St Peter's Dri. SK14—5D 106
St Petersgate. SK1—2G 131
St Peter's Rd. BL9—6C 28
St Peter's Rd. M27—4E 71
St Peter's Sq. M2—5D 86
St Peter's Sq. SK1—2G 131
St Peters St. OL6—3G 91
St Peter's St. OL16—5B 20
St Peter's Ter. BL2—2F 55
St Peter's Way. BL1, BL2 & BL3
—4B 24
St Philip's Av. BL3—3H 37
St Philip's Pl. M3—3B 86 & 4C 160
St Phillip's Dri. OL2—6C 48
St Quen Precinct. M28—6F 55
St Saviour's Rd. SK2—6C 132
Saintsbridge Rd. M22—3A 140
St Simons Clo. SK2—3C 132
St Simon St. M3—2B 86 & 1D 160
St Stephen's Av. M34—5E 91
St Stephen's Clo. BL2—2E 39
St Stephens Gdns. BL4—3A 56
St Stephen's Gdns. M24—5A 46
St Stephen's St. BL4—3A 56

St Stephen St. M3—3B 86 & 4D 160
St Stephen St. OL1—1E 65
St Teresa's Rd. M16—4G 99
St Thomas Circ. OL8—4B 64
St Thomas Ct. BL8—6B 24
St Thomas's Pl. M8—1E 87
St Thomas's Pl. SK1—3H 131
St Thomas's Rd. BL1—3H 23
St Thomas St. N. OL8—4B 64
St Thomas St. S. OL8—4B 64
St Vincent St. M4—3G 87 & 4F 163
St Vincent St. WA15—1G 137
St Westburgh's Rd. M21—6A 100
St William's Av. BL3—4A 38
St Winifred's Pl. SK15—3D 92
Salcombe Av. BL2—4D 26
Salcombe Clo. M33—4G 113
Salcombe Gro. BL2—1A 40
Salcombe Rd. M11—5F 89
Salcombe Rd. SK2—3C 132
Salcot Wlk. M10—2G 87 & 1F 163
Sale Eastern & Northenden By-Pass.
M33, M23 & M22—2C 114
Sale Heys Rd. M33—6H 113
Sale La. M29—3A 68
Salem Gro. OL4—3H 65
Sale Rd. M23—1G 127
Sales's La. BL9—1H 15
Sale St. OL15—3F 9
Salford App. M3—3D 86 & 3G 161
Salford St. BL9—1E 29
Salford St. OL4—4G 65
Salisbury Av. OL10—5E 31
Salisbury Cres. OL6—4H 79
Salisbury Dri. M25—1G 73
Salisbury Dri. SK16—6E 93
Salisbury Rd. M21—6H 99
Salisbury Rd. M25—1D 58
Salisbury Rd. M26—2E 41
Salisbury Rd. M27—4E 71
Salisbury Rd. M30—1H 83
Salisbury Rd. M31—3F 97
Salisbury Rd. OL4—3F 65
Salisbury Rd. WA14—4F 125
Salisbury St. BL3—1H 37
Salisbury St. M14—3E 101
Salisbury St. M24—6B 46
Salisbury St. OL2—5D 34
Salisbury St. SK5—1H 119
Salisbury Ter. BL3—4B 40
Salix Ct. M6—2G 85
Salkeld St. OL11—6H 19
Salley St. OL15—5G 9
Salmesbury Clo. BLO—5D 4
Salmon Fields. OL2—4D 48
Salmon St. M4—3E 87 & 4B 162
Salop St. BL2—1C 38
Salop St. M6—1G 85
Saltash Clo. M22—4B 140
Saltburn Wlk. M9—3G 75
(off Naunton Wlk.)
Saltdene Rd. M22—4A 140
Saltergate M. M5—3G 85
Saltersbrook Gro. SK9—6A 152
Saltersgate Clo. BL3—3C 36
Salter Sq. M15—1D 100 & 5G 165
Salterton Wlk. M10—4A 76
Salteye Rd. M30—4C 82
Saltford Av. M4—3G 87 & 4F 163
Saltford Ct. M4—3H 87 & 4G 163
Salthill Av. OL10—6G 31
Salthill Dri. M22—3C 140
Salthouse Clo. BL8—5C 14
Saltire Gdns. M7—3A 74
Saltney Av. M20—2D 116
Saltram Clo. M26—2C 40
Saltrush Rd. M22—3B 140
Salts Dri. OL15—3E 9
Salts St. OL2—6E 35
Saltwood Gro. BL1—4B 24
Salvin Wlk. M9—6G 61
Sam Cowan Ct. M14—4E 101
Sam Fritton Way. OL1—2D 64
Samian Gdns. M6—6G 73
Samlesbury Clo. OL2—6D 34
Sammy Cookson Clo. M14—4E 101
(in two parts)
Samouth Clo. M10—2H 87 & 2G 163
Sampson Sq. M14—3E 101

Sam Reid Wlk. M16—3C 100
Sam Rd. OL3—2C 52
Samson St. OL16—3C 20
Samuel Ogden St. M1—5E 87 & 2B 166
Samuel La. OL2—5C 34
Samuel St. BL3—3A 40
Samuel St. BL9—2E 29
Samuel St. M19—1D 118
Samuel St. M24—5A 46
Samuel St. M35—3F 77
Samuel St. OL10—3E 31
Samuel St. OL11—3C 32
Samuel St. SK4—7F 119
Samuel St. SK14—3E 109
Sanby Av. M18—3E 103
Sanby Dri. SK6—3F 135
Sanby Rd. M18—3E 103
Sandacre Rd. M23—4H 127
Sandal Ct. M10—2A 88
Sandal St. M10—2A 88
Sandbach Av. M14—1D 116
Sandbach Rd. M33—6F 115
Sandbach Rd. SK5—5G 103
Sandbach Wlk. SK8—1C 142
Sandbank Gdns. OL12—3G 7
Sand Banks. BL1—5D 10
Sandbed La. OL3—2A 52
Sandbed La. OL5—1E 81
Sandbrook Way. M34—2F 105
Sanderling Rd. SK2—6G 133
Sanderson Av. M10—6G 75
Sanderson Clo. M28—4A 70
Sanderson Rd. M10—6G 75
Sanderson St. BL9—2E 29
Sanderson St. M10—6G 75
Sanderstead Dri. M9—6G 61
Sandfield Dri. BL6—1A 36
Sandfield Rd. OL16—6B 20
Sandfold La. M19—5E 103
Sandfold La. SK5—5F 103
(in two parts)
Sandford Av. M18—1F 103
Sandford Clo. BL2—1G 25
Sandford Rd. M33—6F 115
Sandford St. M3—2C 86
Sandgate Av. M11—3F 89
Sandgate Dri. M31—3E 97
Sandgate Rd. M25—2F 59
Sandgate Rd. OL9—3H 63
Sandham St. BL3—3B 38
Sandham Wlk. BL3—3B 38
Sandheys. M34—2F 105
Sandheys Gro. M18—3G 103
Sandhill Clo. BL3—3B 38
Sandhill St. SK14—3D 106
Sandhill Wlk. M22—3H 139
Sand Hole La. OL11—6A 18
(Kenyon Fold)
Sand Hole La. OL11—4F 33
(Kirkholt)
Sand Hole Rd. BL4—3A 56
Sandhurst Av. M20—3E 117
Sandhurst Ct. BL2—1G 39
Sandhurst Dri. BL2—1G 39
Sandhurst Rd. BL8—2H 27
Sandhurst Rd. M20—1F 129
(in two parts)
Sandhurst Rd. SK2—6B 132
Sandhurst St. OL8—5G 65
Sandhutton St. M9—2F 75
Sandilands Rd. M23—3D 126
Sandileigh Av. M20—4F 117
Sandileigh Av. SK8—5C 130
Sandileigh Av. WA15—2H 137
Sandileigh Dri. WA15—2H 137
Sandiway. M5—6A 86
(off Ordsall Dri.)
Sandiway. M30—5E 95
Sandiway. OL10—3G 31
Sandiway. SK6—6F 121
Sandiway. SK7—3G 143
Sandiway Clo. SK6—3D 134
Sandiway Dri. M20—6E 117
Sandiway Pl. WA14—4F 125
Sandiway Rd. M33—5H 113
Sandiway Rd. SK9—2H 151

Sandiway Rd. WA14—5F 125
Sandmere Wlk. M9—6G 61
Sandon St. BL3—3H 37
Sandown Av. M6—3E 85
Sandown Clo. OL1—6E 49
Sandown Clo. SK9—1G 159
Sandown Cres. BL3—5A 40
Sandown Cres. M18—4F 103
Sandown Dri. M33—6G 113
Sandown Dri. M34—1H 121
Sandown Dri. WA15—1D 148
Sandown Gdns. M31—5C 96
Sandown Rd. BL2—2G 25
Sandown Rd. BL9—4E 43
Sandown Rd. SK3—3D 130
Sandown Rd. SK7—3F 145
Sandown St. M18—1G 103
Sandpiper Clo. OL11—4B 18
Sandpiper Clo. SK16—6C 92
Sandpits. OL10—5H 31
Sandray Clo. BL3—2D 36
Sandray Gro. M5—4E 85
Sandridge. OL11—1E 33
Sandridge Wlk. M12—1A 102
Sandringham Av. M34—1D 104
(Audenshaw)
Sandringham Av. M34—4A 104
(Denton)
Sandringham Av. SK15—2E 93
Sandringham Ct. M9—4C 60
(off Deanswood Dri.)
Sandringham Ct. M33—3C 126
Sandringham Ct. SK9—3D 158
Sandringham Dri. BL8—2A 14
Sandringham Dri. OL16—5G 21
Sandringham Dri. SK4—2C 130
Sandringham Dri. SK12—4D 154
Sandringham Dri. SK16—6D 92
Sandringham Grange. M25—6A 60
Sandringham Rd. M28—5C 68
Sandringham Rd. SK6—6C 120
Sandringham Rd. SK7—3F 145
Sandringham Rd. SK8—2C 142
Sandringham Rd. SK14—2C 122
Sandringham St. M18—3E 103
Sandringham Way. OL2—1A 48
Sandringham Way. SK9—3D 158
Sands Av. OL9—6D 46
Sands Clo. SK14—6H 107
Sandsend Clo. M8—6A 74
Sandsend Rd. M31—4E 97
Sandstone Rd. OL16—4F 21
Sandstone Way. M21—2B 116
Sand St. M10—1G 87
Sand St. SK15—5D 92
Sands Wlk. SK14—6H 107
Sandwich Cres. BL3—2H 37
Sandwich Rd. M30—2H 83
Sandwich St. M28—1F 69
Sandwood Av. BL3—1C 36
Sandy Bank. OL2—5D 34
Sandy Bank Av. SK14—6H 107
Sandybank Clo. SK14—3G 109
Sandy Bank Ct. SK14—6H 107
Sandy Bank Rd. M8—3B 74
Sandy Bank Wlk. SK14—6H 107
Sandybrook Clo. BL8—5H 13
Sandy Brow. M9—1F 75
Sandy Clo. BL9—3D 42
Sandy Ga. Clo. M27—4E 71
Sandy Gro. M6—1E 85
Sandy Gro. M27—3F 71
Sandy Gro. SK16—4B 92
Sandy Haven Clo. SK14—6H 107
Sandy Haven Wlk. SK14—6H 107
Sandyhill Ct. M9—6C 60
Sandyhill Rd. M9—6C 60
Sandylands Dri. M25—2E 73
Sandy La. M6—2E 85
Sandy La. M21—1H 115
Sandy La. M23—4D 126
Sandy La. M24—1C 62
Sandy La. M25—6D 58
Sandy La. M30—4E 95
Sandy La. M32—6B 98
Sandy La. M35—2C 90
Sandy La. OL2—3B 48
Sandy La. OL3—5A 52
Sandy La. OL11—4E 19

Sandy La. SK5—6G 119
Sandy La. SK6—1A 134
Sandy La. SK9—1A 158
Sandy Meade. M26—6D 58
Sandyshot Wlk. M22—2D 140
Sandy Vale. SK16—4C 92
Sandy Wlk. OL2—3B 48
Sandy Way. M25—6E 59
Sandywell Clo. M11—6F 89
Sandywell St. M3—2C 86 & 2F 161
Sandywell St. M11—5F 89
Sangster Ct. M5—5G 85
Sankey Gro. M9—6D 60
Sankey St. BL9—3B 28
Santiago St. M14—4F 101
Santley St. M12—4C 102
Santon Av. M14—1A 118
Sapling Gro. M33—1F 125
Sapling Rd. BL3—5F 37
Sapling Rd. M27—6D 70
Sarah Ann St. M11—4B 88
Sarah Butterworth Ct. OL16—4B 20
Sarah Butterworth St. OL16—5B 20
Sarah Jane St. OL16—5F 21
Sarah St. BL0—2B 4
Sarah St. M11—5B 88
Sarah St. M24—1H 61
Sarah St. M30—4D 82
Sarah St. OL2—2E 49
Sarah St. OL11—5A 20
Sargent Dri. M16—3C 100
Sargent Rd. SK6—1D 132
Sark Rd. M21—5G 99
Sarn Av. M22—1B 140
Sarnesfield Clo. M12—3C 102
Sarnia Ct. M7—4H 73
Saunton Av. BL2—2H 25
Saunton Rd. M11—5F 89
Sautridge Clo. OL11—6D 32
Savernake Rd. SK6—4A 122
Savick Av. BL2—6G 25
Saville Rd. M26—6F 27
Saville Rd. SK8—5F 129
Saville St. BL2—6C 24
Saville St. M24—2D 62
Saviours Ter. BL3—2G 37
Savio Way. M24—2A 62
Savoy St. M25—5C 42
Savoy St. OL2—5B 48
Savoy St. M12—1C 102
Savoy St. OL4—4F 65
Savoy St. OL11—3E 19
Sawley Av. M25—5D 42
Sawley Av. OL4—5H 65
Sawley Av. OL15—2E 9
Sawley Dri. SK8—1E 153
Sawley Rd. M10—1H 87
Sawston Wlk. M10—6C 62
Sawyer Brow. SK14—3D 106
Sawyer St. BL8—1H 27
Sawyer St. OL12—2H 19
Saxbrook Wlk. M22—2D 140
Saxby St. M6—6A 72
Saxelby Dri. M8—4D 74
Saxfield Dri. M23—5A 128
Saxholme Wlk. M22—3A 140
Saxon Av. M8—1C 74
Saxon Av. SK16—5A 92
Saxon Clo. BL8—3H 27
Saxon Dri. M34—6E 91
Saxon Dri. OL9—1E 63
Saxonholme Rd. OL11—6C 32
Saxon Ho. OL15—4G 9
Saxonside. M24—5G 45
Saxon St. M10—2A 88
Saxon St. M24—1B 62
Saxon St. M26—4F 41
Saxon St. M34—4F 105
Saxon St. M35—3B 90
Saxon St. OL4—2G 65
Saxon St. OL5—6F 67
Saxthorpe Clo. M33—4F 113
Saxthorpe Wlk. M12—2A 102
Saxwood Av. M9—2F 75
Saxwood Clo. OL12—2B 18

Scafell Av. OL7—1F 91
Scafell Clo. OL1—6D 48
(in two parts)
Scafell Clo. SK6—5C 146
Scalby Wlk. M22—4B 140
Scale St. M5—4G 85
Scarborough St. M10—3A 76
Scarcroft Rd. M12—2C 102
Scaresdale Av. BL1—4E 23
Scarfield Dri. OL11—2A 18
Scargill Clo. M14—1G 117
Scargill Rd. BL3—3E 37
Scarisbrick Rd. M19—1B 118
Scarisbrook Av. M20—6H 117
Scarr Av. M26—5A 42
Scarr Dri. OL12—6F 7
Scarr La. OL12—6G 35
Scarr Ter. OL12—3H 7
Scarr Wheel. M7—4G 73
Scarsdale Rd. M14—3A 102
Scarsdale St. M6—2H 85
Scarth Wlk. M15—1D 100 & 6G 165
Scarthwood Clo. BL2—6A 12
Scawfell Av. BL2—3D 24
Scawton Wlk. M9—4D 60
Sceptre St. M10—6C 76
Schofield Av. M31—6H 97
Schofield Pl. OL15—5H 9
Schofield Rd. M30—4C 82
Schofield Rd. M35—4B 90
Schofield St. M3—3B 86 & 4D 160
Schofield St. M11—4E 89
Schofield St. M35—3F 77
Schofield St. OL2—2B 48
Schofield St. OL8—6C 64
Schofield St. OL10—3F 31
Schofield St. OL11—1G 33
Schofield St. OL15—5H 9
(Calderbrook)
Schofield St. OL15—3G 9
(Littleborough)
Schofield St. OL16—6G 21
Schofield St. SK14—2E 107
Scholar's Way. M24—6H 45
Scholes Clo. M8—3B 74
Scholes Dri. M10—1E 77
Scholes La. M25—6F 59
Scholes St. BL8—2A 28
Scholes St. M27—3F 71
Scholes St. OL9—5G 63
Scholes St. OL11—4C 32
Scholes Wlk. M25—6F 59
Scholes Walker St. BL9—1D 28
Scholey St. BL2—2C 38
School Av. M32—4F 99
School Av. OL6—5H 79
School Brow. BL9—3D 28
School Brow. M28—5H 69
School Brow. SK6—1G 133
School Clo. SK12—3F 155
School Gro. M20—3G 117
School Gro. M25—1E 73
School Gro. W. M20—3G 117
School Hill. BL1—5A 24
School Ho. Flats. OL8—1A 78
School La. BL9—3E 15
School La. M20—6F 117
School La. M30—4B 110
(Cadishead)
School La. M30—5D 94
(Irlam)
School La. M31—3A 112
School La. OL11—3G 17
School La. OL16—4H 19
School La. SK4—4E 119
School La. SK6—6F 123
School La. SK8—5B 142
School La. SK12—3F 155
(in two parts)
School La. SK14—2C 122
School La. SK15—4G 81
School La. WA14—4A 124
School Rd. M30—5E 83
School Rd. M32—5C 98
School Rd. M33—4B 114
(in two parts)

School Rd. M35—4F 77
School Rd. OL8—1H 77
School Rd. SK9—3H 151
School Rd. WA15—2H 137
Schools Hill. SK8—2H 141
Schoolside La. M24—2D 60
Schools Rd. M18—2G 103
School St. BL0—4D 4
School St. BL3—4B 40
School St. BL7—4D 10
School St. BL9—4F 29
School St. M4—2E 87 & 2B 162
School St. M7—1C 86
School St. M26—4F 41
School St. M30—2D 82
School St. OL1—2E 65
School St. OL3—1F 53
School St. OL4—3C 66
School St. OL8—4B 64
School St. OL10—3E 31
School St. OL12—3H 19
School St. OL15—4C 8
School St. SK7—3E 145
School Wlk. M15—2B 100
School Yd. SK4—2A 130
Schwabe St. M24—1E 61
Scobell St. BL8—6H 13
Scope o' th' La. BL2—1E 25
Scopton St. BL1—5G 23
Score St. M11—4C 88
Scorton Av. BL2—6H 25
Scorton Wlk. M10—1D 76
Scotforth Clo. M15—6C 86 & 4E 165
Scotland. M4—2E 87 & 2A 162
Scotland Hall Rd. M10—6B 76
Scotland St. M10—6C 76
Scotland St. OL6—2A 92
Scotta Rd. M30—5D 82
Scott Av. BL9—1D 42
Scott Av. M21—5H 99
Scott Av. M30—2E 83
Scott Clo. SK8—3D 142
Scott Dri. SK6—3F 135
Scottfield. OL8—4C 64
Scottfield Rd. OL8—4D 64
Scott Ga. M34—6E 91
Scott Rd. SK6—6D 58
Scott Rd. M34—6E 105
Scott St. M6—1A 86
Scott St. M26—2D 56
Scott St. M34—6F 91
Scott St. OL8—4D 64
Scott St. OL16—1D 34
Scout Dri. M23—1F 139
Scout View. BL8—5A 14
Scovell St. M7—5H 73
Scowcroft La. OL2—2E 49
Scowcroft St. BL2—4D 24
Scowcroft St. BL4—2F 55
Scroggins La. M31—5C 110
Scropton St. M10—5F 75
Seabright Wlk. M11—4B 88
Seabrook Cres. M31—3E 97
Seabrook Rd. M10—1E 89
Seacombe Av. M14—6E 101
Seacombe Gro. SK3—3D 130
Seaford Rd. BL2—5H 11
Seaford Rd. M6—6F 73
Seaford Wlk. OL9—3H 63
Seaford Way. M9—6E 61
Seaforth Rd. BL1—6C 10
Seaham Dri. BL8—6C 14
Seaham Wlk. M14—4F 101
Sealand Clo. M33—1E 127
Sealand Dri. M30—5C 82
Sealand Rd. M23—1F 127
Sealand Way. SK9—3H 151
Seale Av. M34—6D 90
Sealey Wlk. M10—1A 88
(off Filby Wlk.)
Seal Rd. SK7—5H 143
Seamons Dri. WA14—6D 124
Seamons Rd. WA14—5C 124
Seamons Wlk. WA14—6D 124
Searby Rd. M18—3D 102
Searness Rd. M24—5E 45
Seascale Av. M11—2D 88

Seascale Wlk. M24—5G 45
Seathwaite Wlk. M18—2E 103
Seatoller Ct. OL2—3C 48
(off Shaw St.)
Seatoller Dri. M24—6E 45
Seaton Clo. SK7—4D 144
Seaton M. OL7—1E 91
Seaton R. BL1—3G 23
Seaton Way. M14—3E 101
Sebastopol Wlk. M4—3G 87 & 4E 163
Second Av. BL1—6F 23
Second Av. BL3—3H 39
Second Av. BL9—1H 29
Second Av. M11—2E 89
Second Av. M17—2D 98
Second Av. M27—6D 70
Second Av. OL8—1A 78
Second Av. SK10—6D 154
Second Av. SK16—5G 81
Second St. BL1—1D 22
Sedan Clo. M5—4G 85
Sedbury Clo. M23—2E 127
(in two parts)
Seddon Av. M18—1F 103
Seddon Av. M26—2B 42
Seddon Gdns. M26—1A 56
Seddon La. M26—1A 56
Seddon Rd. WA14—3F 137
Seddons Av. BL8—5G 27
Seddon St. BL3—4B 40
Seddon St. M12—5D 102
Seddon St. M26—4G 41
Seddon St. M28—4B 54
Sedgeborough Rd. M16—3C 100
Sedge Clo. SK5—1A 120
Sedgefield Clo. M5—3G 85
Sedgefield Dri. BL1—2F 23
Sedgefield Pk. OL4—3H 65
Sedgefield Rd. M26—6F 41
Sedgefield Wlk. M23—1F 127
Sedgeford Rd. M10—6F 75
Sedgemoor Clo. SK8—3D 142
Sedgemoor Vale. BL2—3H 25
Sedgemoor Way. OL1—2C 64
Sedgley Av. M25—1G 73
Sedgley Av. OL16—1H 33
Sedgley Clo. M24—2C 62
Sedgley Ct. M24—2C 62
Sedgley Pk. Rd. M25—1G 73
Sedgley Rd. M8—3C 74
Sedgley St. M24—2C 62
Sedon St. M11—3B 88
Seedfield Rd. BL9—6F 15
Seedley Av. M28—5D 54
Seedley Pk. Rd. M6—3E 85
Seedley Rd. M6—2E 85
Seedley St. M14—4F 101
Seedley Ter. M6—2E 85
Seedley View Rd. M6—2E 85
Seed St. BL1—6G 23
Seel St. OL5—2D 80
Sefton Clo. M13—1F 101 & 5D 166
Sefton Clo. M24—1G 61
Sefton Cres. M33—3B 114
Sefton Dri. BL9—5G 15
Sefton Dri. M27—5D 70
Sefton Dri. M28—6A 70
Sefton Dri. SK9—5G 151
Sefton Ho. BL1—5A 24
(off School Hill)
Sefton Rd. BL1—3F 23
Sefton Rd. M21—1H 115
Sefton Rd. M24—1G 61
Sefton Rd. M26—6E 27
Sefton Rd. M27—2E 71
Sefton Rd. M33—4B 114
Sefton St. BL9—5F 15
Sefton St. M8—3C 74
Sefton St. M25—2D 58
Sefton St. M26—6A 42
Sefton St. OL9—1H 77
Sefton St. OL10—4G 31
Sefton St. OL11—6H 19
Selborne Rd. M21—6H 99
Selborne Clo. SK5—5G 103
Selbourne St. OL8—2D 78
Selby Av. M25—5D 42
Selby Av. OL9—6F 47

Selby Clo. M26—2B 42
Selby Clo. M32—4A 98
Selby Clo. OL16—5E 21
Selby Clo. SK12—2D 154
Selby Dri. M6—2B 84
Selby Dri. M31—2B 96
Selby Gdns. SK8—1E 153
Selby Rd. M24—4H 45
Selby Rd. M32—4A 98
Selby St. M11—5C 88
Selby St. OL16—3B 20
Selby St. SK4—5F 119
Selden St. OL8—4B 64
Selham Wlk. M13—6G 87 & 4E 167
Selhurst Av. M11—3E 89
Selkirk Av. OL8—5B 64
Selkirk Dri. M9—6H 61
Selkirk Pl. OL10—4C 30
Selkirk Rd. BL1—6B 10
Selkirk Rd. OL9—5F 63
Sellars Sq. M35—5A 90
Sellers Way. OL9—6G 63
Selsby Av. M30—3D 82
Selsey Av. M33—6H 113
Selsey Av. SK3—4B 130
Selsey Dri. M20—3G 129
Selside Wlk. M14—1G 117
Selstead Rd. M22—4A 140
Selston Rd. M9—5D 60
Selwood Wlk. M9—4F 75
(off Carisbrook St.)
Selworth Av. M33—5E 115
Selworth Clo. WA15—5G 125
Selworthy Rd. M16—3C 100
Selwyn Av. M9—3F 75
Selwyn Clo. OL8—4C 64
Selwyn Dri. SK8—6E 143
Selwyn St. BL2—1C 38
Selwyn St. OL8—4C 64
Senior Av. M14—2A 118
Senior Rd. M30—5C 82
Senoir St. M3—2C 86 & 2F 161
Sepal Clo. SK5—6A 104
Sequoia St. M9—3H 75
Sergeants La. M25—2A 58
Serin Clo. SK2—6D 133
Service St. SK3—3D 130
Set St. SK15—4D 92
Settle Clo. BL8—3F 27
Settle St. BL3—4H 37
  (Bolton)
Settle St. BL3—4C 40
  (Little Lever)
Settle Wlk. M15—1D 100 & 6G 165
Settstones La. OL3—6D 52
Sevenacres. OL3—2H 51
Seven Acres La. OL12—1A 18
Sevenoaks Av. M31—3F 97
Sevenoaks Av. SK4—5C 118
Sevenoaks Dri. M27—5G 71
Sevenoaks Rd. SK8—5F 129
Sevenoaks Wlk. M13—2G 101
(off Lauderdale Cres.)
Seven Stiles Dri. SK6—4C 134
Seventh Av. OL8—2A 78
Severn Clo. BL9—4F 15
Severn Clo. WA14—5E 125
Severn Clo. M16—5G 21
Severn Dri. SK7—1E 153
Severn Dri. OL8—2H 77
Severn Rd. OL9—1F 63
Severn Rd. OL10—2C 30
Severnside Trading Est. M17
  —2B 98
Severn Way. BL4—3B 96
Severn Way. SK5—4H 119
Sevilles Bldgs. OL5—1E 81
Seville St. OL2—5C 48
  (Royton)
Seville St. OL2—2E 49
  (Shaw)
Sewerby Clo. M16—3D 100
Sexa St. M11—5F 89
Sexton St. OL10—3E 31
Seymour Av. M11—3F 89
Seymour Clo. M16—2A 100
Seymour Ct. M7—3B 74

Seymour Ct. M26—4H 41
Seymour Ct. SK4—1A 130
Seymour Dri. BL2—5G 11
Seymour Gro. BL4—6C 38
Seymour Gro. M16—2H 99
Seymour Gro. M33—5B 114
Seymour Gro. OL16—2H 33
Seymour Gro. SK6—5C 134
Seymour Gro. WA15—6A 126
Seymour Pl. M16—2H 99
Seymour Rd. BL1—2A 24
Seymour Rd. M8—2B 74
Seymour Rd. SK2—6B 132
Seymour Rd. SK8—5C 142
Seymour Rd. S. M11—3F 89
Seymour St. BL2—5G 11
Seymour St. M18—1F 103
Seymour St. M26—4H 41
  (in two parts)
Seymour St. M34—4D 104
  (in two parts)
Seymour St. OL10—4E 31
  (in two parts)
Shackliffe Rd. M10—1B 76
Shackleton Ct. M10—1E 89
Shackleton Gro. BL1—3C 22
Shackleton St. M30—2E 83
  (in two parts)
Shaddock Av. OL12—2B 18
Shade St. SK7—3E 145
Shade Ter. SK6—6D 146
Shadow Moss Rd. M22—6C 140
Shadows La. OL5—5G 67
Shadwell St. E. OL10—2F 31
Shadwell St. W. OL10—2F 31
Shadworth La. OL3—6H 67
Shady La. BL7—5F 11
Shady La. M23—4D 126
  (in two parts)
Shady Oak Rd. SK2—5F 133
Shaftesbury Av. M30—5E 83
Shaftesbury Av. OL15—6D 8
Shaftesbury Av. SK8—4E 143
Shaftesbury Av. WA15—6B 126
Shaftesbury Clo. BL1—4A 24
Shaftesbury Dri. OL10—5E 31
Shaftesbury Dri. OL12—3B 8
Shaftesbury Gdns. M31—5H 95
Shaftesbury Ho. M6—2F 85
Shaftesbury Rd. M8—4C 74
Shaftesbury Rd. M27—4F 71
Shaftesbury Rd. SK3—5C 130
Shafton Wlk. M10—1D 76
Shakespeare Av. BL9—1D 42
Shakespeare Av. M26—3E 41
Shakespeare Av. M34—1F 121
Shakespeare Av. SK15—1H 93
Shakespeare Clo. OL15—6G 9
Shakespeare Cres. M30—3F 83
Shakespeare Cres. M35—3A 90
Shakespeare Dri. SK8—5B 130
  (in two parts)
Shakespeare Rd. M25—6D 58
Shakespeare Rd. M27—3D 70
Shakespeare Rd. M35—3A 90
Shakespeare Rd. OL1—5F 49
Shakespeare Rd. SK6—6E 121
Shakespeare Wlk. M13—1G 101 &
  6F 167
Shakleton Av. M9—6A 62
Shalbourne Rd. M28—6E 55
Shaldon Dri. M10—1G 89
Shalfleet Clo. BL2—6A 12
Shalford Dri. M22—5B 140
Shambles Sq. M3—3D 86 & 4H 161
Shamrock Ct. M28—6D 54
Shandon Av. M22—2A 128
Shanklin Clo. M21—6G 99
Shanklin Clo. M34—1H 121
Shanklin Wlk. BL3—2E 39
Shanklyn Av. M31—5E 97
Shannon Clo. OL10—2C 30
Shannon Rd. M22—1C 140
Shap Av. WA15—6D 126
Shap Cres. M28—2H 69
Shap Dri. M28—1H 69
Shapwick Clo. M9—3F 75
Sharcott Wlk. M16—3D 100

Shardlow Clo. M10—1H 87
Sharman St. BL3—2D 38
Sharnbrook Wlk. BL2—4D 24
Sharnbrook Wlk. M8—1A 74
Sharnford Clo. BL2—1D 38
Sharnford Sq. M12—1C 102
Sharon Av. OL4—4G 67
Sharon Clo. OL7—4E 91
Sharples Av. BL1—5C 10
Sharples Dri. BL8—1F 27
Sharples Hall. BL1—5D 10
Sharples Hall Dri. BL1—5D 10
Sharples Hall Fold. BL1—6D 10
Sharples Hall M. BL1—5D 10
Sharples Hill. OL4—6H 49
Sharples Pk. BL1—1H 23
Sharples St. SK4—6G 119
Sharples Vale. BL1—2A 24
Sharples Vale Cotts. BL1—2A 24
Sharp St. M4—2F 87 & 2C 162
Sharp St. M24—1A 62
Sharp St. M25—5E 59
Sharp St. M28—6G 55
Sharrington Dri. M23—5E 127
Sharrow Wlk. M9—4F 75
(off Ockendon Dri.)
Sharston By-Pass. M22 & SK8—4A 128
Sharston Grn. M22—5C 128
Sharston Ind. Area. M22—4C 128
Sharston Rd. M22—5B 128
Shaving La. M28—2F 69
Shaw Av. SK14—1D 122
Shawbrook Av. M28—3D 68
Shawbrook Rd. M19—3B 118
Shawbury Clo. M24—2C 62
Shawbury Gro. M33—1H 125
Shawbury Rd. M23—1H 139
Shawclough Clo. OL12—6D 6
Shawclough Dri. OL12—6D 6
Shawclough Rd. OL12—5C 6
Shawclough Way. OL12—6C 6
Shawcroft Clo. OL2—2E 49
Shawcross La. M22—6C 140
Shawcross St. M6—4F 85
Shawcross St. SK1—3H 131
Shawcross St. SK14—1D 122
Shawdene Rd. M22—3A 128
Shawe Hall Av. M31—1C 112
Shawe Hall Cres. M31—1C 112
Shawe Rd. M31—5C 96
Shawe View. M31—5C 96
Shawfield La. M14—1E 117
Shawfield Ct. SK2—6D 132
Shawfield La. OL12—1B 18
Shawfield Rd. SK14—4H 109
Shawfields. SK15—2H 93
Shawfold. OL2—6F 35
Shawford Cres. M10—1C 76
Shawford Rd. M10—1C 76
Shaw Ga. OL3—3F 53
Shawgreen Clo. M15—1B 100 & 5D 164
Shaw Hall Av. SK14—2F 107
Shaw Hall Bank Rd. OL3—4H 67
Shaw Hall Clo. OL3—4H 67
Shawhead Dri. M35—5F 77
Shaw Heath. SK3 & SK2—3G 131
Shawheath Clo. M15—1B 100 & 5D 164
Shawhill Wlk. M10—3A 88
Shaw Ho. OL2—2F 49
Shaw La. OL16—2G 21
Shaw La. SK13—5G 109
Shawlea Av. M19—3A 118
Shaw Lee. OL3—3D 52
Shaw Moor Av. SK15—4G 93
Shaw Rd. OL1—6E 49
Shaw Rd. OL2—4C 48
Shaw Rd. OL16—2F 35
  (Newhey)
Shaw Rd. OL16—4H 33
  (Rochdale)
Shaw Rd. SK4—4D 118
Shaw Rd. Est. OL1—6D 48
Shaw Rd. S. SK3—5G 131
  (in two parts)
Shaws Fold. OL4—2D 66
Shaws Fold. SK9—4D 150
Shaws La. OL3—1F 53
Shaw's Rd. WA14—1F 137

Shaw St. BL3—2A 38
Shaw St. BL3—5E 39
Shaw St. BL9—2F 29
Shaw St. M3—2D 86 & 1H 161
Shaw St. OL1—1D 64
Shaw St. OL3—4C 48
Shaw St. OL3—3F 53
Shaw St. OL4—3C 66
Shaw St. OL6—2B 92
Shaw St. OL12—1B 20
Shaw St. SK14—3C 108
Shaw Ter. SK16—4A 92
Shay Av. WA15—4E 139
Shayfield Av. M22—6B 128
Shayfield Dri. M22—6B 128
Shayfield Rd. M22—6B 128
Sheader Dri. M5—3C 84
Sheaf Field Wlk. M26—3G 41
Sheard Av. OL6—5H 79
Sheardhall Av. SK12—2H 157
Shearing Av. OL12—2B 18
Shearsby Clo. M15—2C 100
Shearwater Dri. M28—6E 55
Shearwater Gdns. M30—5C 82
Shearwater Rd. SK2—5F 133
Sheddings, The. BL3—3C 38
Shed St. BL3—2B 38
Shed St. OL12—4H 7
Sheepfoot La. M25—6H 59
Sheepfoot La. OL1—6B 48
Sheep Gap. OL12—2D 18
Sheepgate Dri. BL8—6G 13
Sheep La. M28—3B 68
Sheerness St. M18—2F 103
Sheffield Rd. SK14—3D 106
  (in two parts)
Sheffield St. M1—5F 87 & 1D 166
Sheffield St. SK4—6G 119
Shefford Clo. M11—5B 88
Sheiling Ct. WA14—1E 137
Shelbourne Av. BL1—4F 23
Shelden Clo. SK13—6F 109
Shelden Fold. SK13—6F 109
(off Brassington Cres.)
Shelden M. SK13—6F 109
Shelden Pl. SK13—6F 109
(off Brassington Cres.)
Shelderton Clo. M10—4A 76
Sheldon Av. M31—5D 96
Sheldon Clo. BL4—5D 38
Sheldon Clo. M31—6D 110
Sheldon Ct. OL7—6F 79
Sheldon Rd. SK7—6E 145
Sheldon St. M11—3D 88
Sheldrake Clo. SK16—6C 92
Sheldrake Rd. WA14—3D 124
Shelfield. OL11—2B 18
Shelfield Clo. OL11—3B 18
Shelfield La. OL11—2A 18
Shelford Av. M18—3D 102
Shellbrook Gro. SK9—6H 151
Shelley Av. M24—5B 46
Shelley Ct. SK8—4C 142
Shelley Gro. M35—3A 90
Shelley Gro. SK14—2B 106
Shelley Gro. SK15—1H 93
Shelley Rise. SK16—6F 93
Shelley Rd. M25—6D 58
Shelley Rd. M27—3D 70
Shelley Rd. M28—4C 54
Shelley Rd. OL1—6G 49
Shelley Rd. OL9—6F 63
Shelley Rd. SK5—6F 103
Shelley St. M10—3C 76
Shelley Way. BL1—4H 23
Shelley Way. M34—1F 121
Shelmerdine Gdns. M6—1C 84
Shelton Av. M33—5F 113
Shenfield Wlk. M10—2H 87 & 1G 163
Shentonfield Rd. M22—5C 128
Shenton Pk. Av. M33—1E 125
Shenton St. SK14—3A 106
Shepherd Ct. OL16—4B 20
Shepherd Cross St. BL1—4G 23
Shepherds Brow. WA14—2C 136
Shepherds Clo. BL8—2H 13

Singleton Av. BL2—6G 25
Singleton Clo. M7—2G 73
Singleton Lodge. M7—2H 73
Singleton Rd. M7—2G 73
Singleton Rd. SK4—5D 118
Singleton St. M26—3D 40
Sion St. M26—5F 41
(in two parts)
Sirdar St. M11—5H 89
Sirius Pl. M7—1C 160
Sir Robert Thomas Ct. M9—3F 75
(off Conninsby Dri.)
Siskin Rd. SK2—6F 133
Sisson St. M35—4F 77
Sisters St. M35—5A 90
Sixth Av. BL1—6F 23
Sixth Av. BL3—3H 39
Sixth Av. BL9—1H 29
Sixth Av. OL8—2A 78
Sixth St. M17—2D 98
Size St. OL12—4H 7
Skagen Cir. BL1—4A 24
(in two parts)
Skaife Rd. M33—5E 115
Skarratt Clo. M12—1B 102
Skegness Clo. BL8—6D 14
Skelton Gro. BL2—5H 55
Skelton Gro. M13—5B 102
Skelton Rd. M32—4D 98
Skelton Rd. WA14—4G 125
Skelwith Av. BL3—5B 38
Skelwith Clo. M31—3C 96
Skerry Clo. M13—6F 87 & 4D 166
Skerton Rd. M16—2H 99
Skilgate Wlk. M10—5C 76
Skip Pl. M3—2E 87 & 1A 162
Skipton Av. M10—2D 76
Skipton Av. OL9—6F 47
Skipton Clo. BL8—3F 27
Skipton Clo. SK7—5C 144
Skipton Dri. M31—2B 96
Skipton St. BL2—5E 25
Skipton St. OL8—5F 65
Skipton Wlk. BL2—6E 25
Skrigge Clo. M8—3B 74
Skye Rd. M31—2F 97
Slackey Brow. BL4—4C 56
Slack Fold La. BL4—6G 37
Slack Ga. OL12—1E 7
Slack La. BL2—4H 11
Slack La. M27—2G 71
Slack La. OL3—1E 51
Slack Rd. M9—2F 75
Slack St. OL16—4H 19
Slack St. SK14—3D 106
Slade Gro. M13—4B 102
Slade Hall Rd. M12—5C 102
Slade La. M19 & M13—1B 118
Sladen St. OL12—2H 19
Sladen Ter. OL15—1H 9
Slade St. BL3—4A 40
Slades View Clo. OL3—2C 52
Slaidburn Av. BL2—1H 39
Slaidburn Clo. M22—3G 139
Slaidburn Clo. OL16—6F 21
Slaidburn Dri. BL8—2E 27
Slaithwaite Dri. M11—3E 89
Slateacre Rd. SK14—2D 122
Slate Av. M4—3G 87 & 4F 163
(in three parts)
Slate La. OL7—4E 91
Slaterfield. BL3—2A 38
Slater La. BL1—5C 24
Slater St. BL1—4B 24
Slater St. BL4—1F 55
Slater St. M30—3D 82
Slater St. M35—2F 77
Slater St. OL9—3C 64
Slattocks Link Rd. M24—2D 46
Slaunt Bank. OL12—1H 17
Slawson Way. OL10—2H 31
Sleaford Clo. BL8—6D 14
Sleaford Clo. M10—2H 87 & 1G 163
Sleddale Clo. SK2—6D 132
Sledmere Clo. BL1—3B 24
Sledmere Clo. M11—4C 88

Sledmoor Rd. M23—2F 127
Sligo St. BL1—5C 24
Slimbridge Clo. BL2—4A 26
Sloane Av. OL4—1B 66
Sloane St. BL3—4F 37
Sloane St. M11—3C 88
Sloane St. OL6—2A 92
Slough Ind. Est. M5—5A 86
Smallbrook. OL2—5G 35
Small Brook Rd. OL2—3G 35
Smalldale Av. M16—4D 100
Smalley St. OL11—3C 32
Smallfield Dri. M9—3F 75
Small La. WA16—6A 148
Smallridge Clo. M10—2H 87 & 2G 163
Smallshaw Fold. OL6—6F 79
Smallshaw La. OL6—6F 79
Smallshaw Rd. OL12—5A 6
Smallshaw Sq. OL6—6F 79
Smallwood St. M10—5C 74
Smart St. M12—4C 102
Smeaton St. M8—5E 75
Smedley Av. BL3—4C 38
Smedley Av. M8—5D 74
Smedley La. M8—5D 74
Smedley Rd. M8—5D 74
Smedley St. M8—5C 74
Smethurst St. BL3—5F 37
(off Smethurst La.)
Smethurst Hall Rd. M9—1A 30
Smethurst La. BL3 & BL5—5F 37
Smethurst St. BL2—5D 24
Smethurst St. BL8—1H 27
Smethurst St. M9—2F 75
Smethurst St. M24—2D 62
Smethurst St. OL10—3D 30
Smithfold La. M28—5C 54
Smith Hill. OL16—5F 21
Smithies Av. M24—5A 46
Smithies St. OL10—3G 31
Smithills Croft Rd. BL1—2E 23
Smithills Dean Rd. BL1—1E 23
Smithills Dri. BL1—3D 22
Smithills Hall Clo. BL0—4E 5
Smith La. BL7—3D 10
Smiths Lawn. SK9—4D 158
Smith's Rd. BL3—4F 39
Smith St. BL0—4D 4
Smith St. BL9—1E 29
Smith St. M5—6G 85
Smith St. M16—1A 100 & 5A 164
Smith St. M28—6F 55
Smith St. M34—5F 105
Smith St. OL4—1A 66
Smith St. OL5—1D 80
Smith St. OL7—4F 91
Smith St. OL10—3F 31
Smith St. OL15—4F 9
Smith St. OL16—4H 19
Smith St. SK8—5B 130
Smith St. SK14—2B 106
Smith St. SK16—5G 92
Smithy Bri. Rd. OL16 & OL15—5C 8
Smithy Croft. BL7—3D 10
Smithy Field. OL15—3E 9
Smithy Fold. OL12—2E 19
Smithy Fold Rd. SK14—6C 106
Smithy Grn. SK6—4H 121
Smithy Grn. SK8—5C 142
Smithy Gro. OL6—1A 92
Smithy Hill. BL3—3E 37
Smithy La. M3—4D 86 & 5G 161
Smithy La. M31—6D 110
Smithy La. OL3—1F 53
Smithy La. SK14—6C 106
Smithy La. WA14—2A 136
Smithy Moor. OL15—6G 9
Smithy St. SK7—2D 144
Smyrna St. M5—4E 85
Smyrna St. M26—3F 41
Smyrna St. OL4—3G 65
Smyrna St. OL10—4E 31
Snapebrook Gro. SK9—6A 152
Snape St. M26—1F 41
(in two parts)
Snell St. M4—4H 87 & 6G 163
Snipe Av. OL11—4B 18
Snipe Clo. SK12—3A 154

Snipe Rd. OL8—1F 79
Snipe St. BL3—2B 38
(in two parts)
Snowden Wlk. M31—6C 110
Snowden Av. M31—1D 112
Snowden St. BL1—5A 24
Snowden St. OL8—5D 64
Snowden St. OL10—5G 31
Snowden Wlk. M10—1C 76
Snowdon Rd. M30—2A 84
Snowdon Clo. OL11—3G 33
Snowdrop Wlk. M7—5H 73
Snow Hill Rd. BL3—2F 39
Snow Hill Ter. M25—5G 59
Snydale Way. BL3—6A 36
Soap St. M4—3E 87 & 4B 162
Society St. OL2—6F 35
Sofa St. BL1—4F 23
Soho St. BL3—1B 38
Soho St. OL4—2F 65
Solden Wlk. M8—6A 74
Solent Av. M8—1C 74
Solent Dri. BL3—2E 39
Solness St. BL9—5F 15
Solway Clo. BL3—4H 37
Solway Clo. M27—5E 57
Solway Clo. OL8—4C 64
Solway Rd. M22—1C 140
Somerby Dri. M22—4A 140
Somerfield Rd. M9—2F 75
Somerford Av. M20—1E 117
Somerford Rd. SK5—5H 103
Somerford Way. SK9—2H 151
Somerhill Ct. SK8—6F 129
Somersby Ct. SK7—4G 143
Somersby Wlk. BL3—2B 38
(off Hallington Clo.)
Somersdale Av. BL1—5E 23
Somerset Av. OL2—6D 34
Somerset Av. OL4—6D 34
Somerset Clo. M30—3B 110
Somerset Clo. SK5—5D 28
Somerset Dri. BL9—5D 28
Somerset Gro. OL11—3C 18
Somerset Pl. M33—3B 114
Somerset Rd. BL1—5F 23
Somerset Rd. M30—1A 84
Somerset Rd. M35—2H 89
(Droylsden)
Somerset Rd. M35—5E 77
(Failsworth)
Somerset Rd. WA14—5F 125
Somerset St. M3—4C 86 & 5F 161
Somerset St. OL4—3G 65
Somers Rd. SK5—6H 103
Somers Wlk. M9—6D 60
Somerton Av. M22—2A 140
Somerton Av. M33—6C 114
Somerton Ct. M9—6A 62
Somerton Rd. BL2—1H 39
Somerville Sq. BL1—2G 23
Somerville St. BL1—2G 23
Somerwood Wlk. M12—1B 102
Sommerseat Clo. OL4—2C 66
Sommerville Ct. M7—3H 73
Sonning Wlk. M8—5D 74
Sopwith Dri. M14—6E 101
Sorbus Clo. M6—3H 85
Sorby Rd. M30—2E 111
Sorrel Bank. M6—1F 85
Sorrel Bank. SK5—6A 104
Sorrel Dri. OL15—3D 8
Sorton St. M1—6E 87 & 3B 166
Soudan Rd. SK2—5A 132
Soudan St. M24—6C 46
Sour Acre Fold. SK15—2F 93
Southacre Dri. SK9—4H 151
Southall St. M3—2D 86
Southampton Clo. M7—6H 73
Southam St. M8—4B 74
Southam St. M15—6C 86 & 3E 165
South Av. BL4—3H 55
South Av. M19—2B 118
South Av. M25—5C 42
South Av. M27—6D 70
South Av. M31—1G 97
South Av. OL3—3F 53
South Av. OL10—3D 30
S. Bank Clo. SK9—4H 159

S. Bank Rd. BL9—4C 28
Southbank Rd. M19—4H 117
Southbourne Av. M31—5H 97
Southbourne St. M6—3E 85
Southbrook Av. M8—6B 60
Southbrook Clo. M34—3G 109
Southbrook Gro. BL3—4B 38
S. Charles St. M1—6E 87 & 3A 166
Southchurch Pde. M10—1G 87
Southcliffe Rd. SK5—3H 119
S. Cliffe St. M11—6H 89
South Clo. BL9—4E 43
South Clo. SK9—3C 158
South Clo. SK14—1H 109
Southcombe Wlk. M15—2D 100
South Ct. OL16—3A 20
South Cres. M11—3F 89
S. Croft. OL8—6F 65
Southcross Rd. M18—4F 103
S. Cross St. BL9—3D 28
Southdene Av. M20—5C 116
Southdown Clo. OL11—6E 19
Southdown Clo. SK4—1F 131
Southdown Cres. M9—1A 76
Southdown Cres. SK8—5B 142
Southdown Dri. M28—5B 68
S. Downs Clo. OL2—5D 34
S. Downs Dri. WA14—5F 137
S. Downs Rd. WA14—4E 137
South Dri. BL2—2G 25
South Dri. M21—2H 115
South Dri. M31—2B 96
South Dri. SK8—1E 141
South Dri. SK8—3E 159
South Dri. WA15—4A 126
Southend Av. M15—1B 100 & 5C 164
Southend St. BL3—4G 37
Southerley Cres. M10—6D 62
Southern App. M27—1A 72
Southernby Clo. M13—3B 102
Southern Clo. M34—1F 121
Southern Clo. SK7—4H 143
Southern St. M3—5C 86 & 2F 164
Southern St. M6—3E 85
Southern St. M28—4F 55
Southey Clo. OL15—6D 8
Southey Ct. M34—1G 121
Southey Wlk. M34—2G 121
Southfield Av. BL9—5F 15
Southfield Clo. SK9—4G 151
Southfield Rd. BL0—1A 14
Southfields. WA14—3F 137
Southfields Av. M11—3E 89
Southfields Dri. WA15—4B 126
Southfield St. BL3—3C 38
Southgarth Rd. M6—2F 85
Southgate. M3—4D 86 & 5G 161
Southgate. M21—2H 115
Southgate. M31—1D 112
Southgate. OL3—5A 52
Southgate. OL12—2B 6
Southgate. SK4—4E 119
Southgate. M10—1C 88
Southgate Ho. OL1—3D 64
(off Southgate St.)
Southgate M. SK4—4E 119
Southgate Rd. BL9—4D 42
Southgate Rd. OL9—6E 63
Southgate St. OL1—3D 64
Southgate Way. OL7—4G 91
South Gro. BL3—2H 101
South Gro. M28—1E 69
South Gro. M33—6B 114
South Gro. SK9—5G 159
Southgrove Av. BL3—5C 10
S. Hall St. M5—5A 86 & 2B 164
South Hill. OL4—4B 66
S. Hill St. OL4—3E 65
S. King St. M2—4D 86 & 5G 161
S. King St. M30—3D 82
Southlands. BL2—5G 25
South Langworthy Rd. M5—5E 85
Southlands Av. M30—5B 82
S. Langworthy Rd. M5—5E 85
Southlea Rd M20 & M19—4H 117

Southleigh Dri. BL2—1A 40
Southlink Bus. Pk. OL4—3E 65
S. Lonsdale St. M32—4E 99
S. Mead. SK12—2B 154
S. Meade. M21—2H 115
S. Meade. M25—1H 73
S. Meade. M27—5E 71
S. Meade. WA15—4A 126
Southmere Clo. M10—6C 62
Southmill St. M2—5D 86 & 1G 165
(in two parts)
Southmoor Rd. M23—4E 127
Southmoor Wlk. BL3—2A 38
(off Parrot St.)
S. Oak La. SK9—3C 158
Southolme Gdns. M19—5A 118
S. Parade. OL16—4H 19
South Pde. SK3—3H 143
S. Park Dri. SK12—3E 155
S. Park Rd. SK8—5F 129
South Pl. OL16—3A 20
Southpool Clo. SK7—3A 144
S. Pump St. M1—5F 87 & 1C 166
S. Radford St. M7—4E 73
South Ridge. M34—2F 105
South Rd. M17—3C 98
South Rd. M20—1F 129
South Rd. M27—1B 72
South Rd. M32—3A 98
South Rd. WA14—3E 137
(Bowdon, in two parts)
South Rd. WA14—5F 137
(Hale)
South Row. M25—2D 72
Southsea St. M11—6F 89
Southside. SK6—3E 121
South St. BL0—3F 5
South St. BL3—4A 38
South St. M11—5D 88
(in two parts)
South St. M12—2A 102
South St. OL7—5E 91
South St. OL8—1H 77
South St. OL10—3D 30
South St. OL16—3A 20
South St. SK9—5G 159
South Ter. BL9—6B 28
South Ter. SK9—5G 159
S. Terrace Ct. OL16—6A 20
S. Vale Cres. WA15—6H 125
S. View. OL11—5A 18
South View. SK5—4H 103
South View. SK6—3A 122
South View. SK15—5H 81
Southview Rd. OL16—5C 8
S. View St. BL2—6E 25
S. View Ter. OL16—5C 8
Southview Wlk. OL4—6H 49
South Wlk. SK15—4E 93
Southwark Dri. SK16—1B 106
Southway. M10—1F 77
Southway. M30—3H 83
Southway. M35—5A 90
Southway. OL7—5F 79
South Way. OL8—1C 78
Southway. WA14—5G 125
Southwell Clo. BL1—5H 23
Southwell Clo. SK6—2G 133
Southwell Gdns. OL6—4F 79
Southwell St. M9—4G 75
Southwick Rd. M23—1G 127
Southwold Clo. M19—6E 103
Southwood Clo. BL3—4B 38
Southwood Dri. M9—4C 60
Southwood Rd. SK2—1B 144
Sovereign Enterprise Pk. M5
—5G 85
Sovereign Ho. SK8—5B 130
Sovereign St. M6—1G 85
Sowerby Wlk. M9—5D 60
(off Chapel La.)
Spa Clo. SK15—1G 119
Spa Cres. M28—3B 54
Spa Gro. M28—3C 54
Spa La. M28—3C 54
Spa La. OL4—4H 65

Spalding Dri. M23—3G 139
Sparkford Av. M23—2D 126
Sparkle St. M1—4F 87 & 6D 162
Spark Rd. M23—4F 127
Spa Rd. BL1—1H 37
Sparrow Clo. SK5—5G 103
Sparrow Hill. OL16—4G 19
Sparrow St. OL2—5C 48
Sparta Av. M28—1E 69
Sparta Wlk. M11—5C 88
Sparth Bottoms Rd. OL11 -5F 19
Sparth Ct. SK4—6F 119
Sparthfield Av. OL11—6G 19
Sparthfield Rd. SK4—6F 119
Sparth La. SK4—6F 119
Spa St. M15—2F 101
Spathfield Ct. SK4—6F 119
Spath Holme. M20—6E 117
Spath La. SK8—2B 152
Spath La. SK9—2H 151
Spath La. E. SK8—2D 152
Spath Rd. M20—5D 116
Spath Wlk. SK8—2D 152
Spaw St. M3—4C 86 & 4E 161
(in two parts)
Spean Wlk. M11—4E 89
Spear St. M1—4E 87 & 5B 162
Spectator St. M4—3H 87 & 4H 163
Specton Wlk. M12—4D 102
Speedwell. SK14—1H 109
Speke Wlk. M34—6E 105
Spencer Av. BL3—4C 40
Spencer Av. M16—5A 100
Spencer Av. M25—5C 42
Spencer Av. SK14—2B 106
Spencer La. OL11—6A 18
Spencer St. BL0—4D 4
Spencer St. BL8—2A 28
Spencer St. M26—3A 42
Spencer St. M30—4E 83
Spencer St. OL1—2E 65
Spencer St. OL5—2D 80
Spencer St. OL9—5H 63
Spencer St. OL15—3G 9
Spencer St. SK5—1H 119
Spencer St. SK16—5A 92
Spender Av. M8—5C 74
Spen Fold. BL8—5G 27
Spenlow Clo. SK12—6E 155
Spennithorne Rd. M31—5D 96
Spenser Av. M26—3E 41
Spenser Av. M34—1G 121
Spenwood Rd. OL15—4D 8
Spey Clo. WA14—5E 125
Spindle Av. SK15—2G 93
Spindle Croft. BL4—1F 55
Spindles Shopping Cen , The. OL1
—3C 64
Spinks St. OL4—4F 65
Spinners Gdns. OL12—5A 8
Spinners Grn. OL12—1H 19
Spinney Clo. SK9—4G 151
Spinney Dri. BL9—5E 15
Spinney Dri. M33—6F 113
Spinney Gro. M34—2F 105
Spinney Nook. BL2—3F 25
Spinney Rd. M23—4H 127
Spinney, The. BL1—6F 23
Spinney, The. BL7—1G 11
Spinney, The. M25—2A 58
Spinney, The. M31—5C 96
Spinney, The. OL4—1C 66
Spinney, The. SK8—2A 142
Spinningfields. BL1—5H 23
Spinningield Way. OL10—6F 31
Spinning Jenny Wlk. M4—3G 87
(off Slate Av.)
Spinning Meadows. BL1—5H 23
Spire Wlk. M12—5A 88
Spirewood Gdns. SK6—2G 133
Spodden Cotts. OL12—3H 7
Spodden St. OL12—3F 19
Spodden Wlk. M25—6G 43
Spod Rd. OL12—2E 19
Spooner Rd. M30—4E 83
Sportside Av. M28—6G 55
Sportside Clo. M28—6F 55

Sportside Gro. M28—5F 55
Sportsmans Dri. OL8—6E 65
Spotland Rd. OL12—3F 19
Spotland Tops. OL12—2D 18
Spout Brook. SK15—6D 80
Spreadbury St. M10—4A 76
Spring Av. M25—5C 42
Spring Av. SK14—1D 122
Spring Bank. M6—2E 85
Springbank. OL3—1F 53
Springbank. OL9—2G 63
Springbank. OL12—5D 6
(Rochdale)
Spring Bank. OL12—4H 7
(Whitworth)
Spring Bank. SK15—5F 93
Spring Bank Av. M34—6C 90
Spring Bank Av. OL6—6F 79
Springbank Clo. SK6—3A 122
Springbank Ct. M8—2B 74
Spring Bank La. OL11—4A 18
(in two parts)
Spring Bank La. SK15—6E 81
Springbank Pl. SK1—3G 131
Spring Bank Rd. SK6—3A 122
Spring Bank St. OL8—5A 64
Spring Bank St. SK15—4F 93
Spring Bank Ter. M34—6C 90
Spring Bri. Rd. M16—5D 100
Spring Clo. BL0—3D 4
Spring Clo. BL8—5G 13
Spring Clo. OL4—4H 65
Spring Clough. M27—6B 70
Spring Clough Av. M28—1H 69
Spring Clough Dri. M28—1H 69
Spring Ct. OL12—2H 19
Springdale Gdns. M20—6E 117
Springfield. BL2—1C 38
Springfield. M26—3C 56
Springfield Av. OL15—2E 9
Springfield Av. SK5—2G 119
Springfield Av. SK6—5D 134
Springfield Av. SK7—2D 144
Springfield Clo. M35—3E 77
Springfield Clo. OL10—4G 31
Springfield Clo. SK14—3G 109
Springfield Dri. SK9—4A 158
Springfield Gdns. BL4—3A 56
Springfield La. M3—2C 86 & 1F 161
Springfield La. M30—5D 94
Springfield La. OL2—6A 34
Springfield La. OL16—6B 8
Springfield Rd. BL4—3G 55
(Kearsley)
Springfield Rd. M24—6H 45
Springfield Rd. M33—5B 114
Springfield Rd. M35—2H 89
Springfield Rd. SK8—1F 141
Springfield Rd. WA14—6F 125
Springfield St. BL3—3C 38
Springfield St. M34—1F 105
Springfield St. OL6—6A 80
Springfield St. OL10—3C 30
Springfield Trading Est. M17
—1D 98
Spring Gdns. BL2—1G 25
Spring Gdns. M2—4E 87 & 5A 162
Spring Gdns. M6—2F 85
Spring Gdns. M24—5A 46
Spring Gdns. OL15—4F 9
(off Church St.)
Spring Gdns. OL16—4G 19
Spring Gdns. SK1—2A 132
Spring Gdns. SK7—2D 144
Spring Gdns. SK14—2H 109
(Hadfield)
Spring Gdns. SK14—3B 106
(Hyde)
Spring Gdns. WA15—6C 126
Spring Garden St. OL2—3B 48
(in two parts)
Spring Gro. M25—5C 42

Spring Hall Rise. OL4—3B 50
Springhead Av. M20—2E 117
Springhead Av. OL4—4B 66
Springhill. OL2—3B 48
Spring Hill. OL16—2H 33
Spring Hill Ct. OL4—1H 65
Spring La. M26—4G 41
Spring La. OL4—4A 66
Spring Lees Ct. OL4—3B 66
Spring Meadow La. OL3—1G 53
Spring Mill Clo. BL3—3A 38
Spring Mill Wlk. OL16—6A 8
Spring Pl. OL12—3H 7
Spring Rise. OL2—4E 35
Spring Rise. SK15—2D 92
(in two parts)
Spring Rd. SK12—5F 155
Spring Rd. WA14—3F 137
Springs. OL11—4A 18
Spring Side. OL12—1H 7
Springside. SK4—2F 119
Springside Av. M28—6G 55
Springside Clo. M28—6G 55
Springside Gro. M28—6G 55
Springside Rd. BL9—3D 14
(in two parts)
Springside View. M28—6G 55
Springside Wlk. M15—1B 100 & 6D 164
Springs La. SK15—1D 92
(in four parts)
Springs Rd. M24—3E 63
Springs, The. WA14—3D 136
(in two parts)
Spring St. BL0—3D 4
(Ramsbottom)
Spring St. BL0—2F 5
(Shuttleworth)
Spring St. BL3—2B 38
(Bolton)
Spring St. BL3—4B 40
(Little Lever)
Spring St. BL4—6F 39
Spring St. BL8—6G 13
(Tottington)
Spring St. BL8—1F 27
(Walshaw)
Spring St. BL9—3D 28
Spring St. M12—5C 102
Spring St. OL3—1F 53
Spring St. OL4—1G 65
(Oldham)
Spring St. OL4—3C 66
(Springhead)
Spring St. OL5—1E 81
Spring St. SK9—2D 158
Spring St. SK14—2E 109
Spring St. SK15—3E 93
Spring Ter. OL9—2G 63
Spring Ter. OL11—3C 18
Spring Ter. OL16—2F 55
Spring Vale. M24—1A 62
Spring Vale. M25—1E 73
Spring Vale. SK7—3E 145
Springvale Clo. OL7—6D 78
Spring Vale Ct. M24—1B 62
Springvale Dri. BL8—6G 13
Spring Vale St. BL8—5G 13
Spring Vale Ter. OL15—4F 9
(off Victoria St.)
Spring View. BL3—4B 40
Springville Av. M9—4H 75
Springwater Av. BL0—6C 4
Springwater Clo. BL2—2G 25
Springwater La. M25—5C 42
Springwell Clo. M6—3E 85
Springwell Gdns. SK14—6A 108
Springwell Way. SK14—6A 108
Springwood. OL3—2G 51
Springwood Av. M27—5H 71
Springwood Av. OL9—6E 47
Springwood Cres. SK6—1C 134
Springwood Hall Rd. OL8—1E 79
Springwood La. SK6—1D 134
Springwood Way. OL7—5E 79
Spruce Av. BL9—3F 29
Spruce Ct. M6—3H 85

Spruce Lodge. SK8—5H 129
Spruce St. BL0—4C 4
Spruce St. OL16—4B 20
Spruce Wlk. M33—3E 113
Spurn La. OL3—4B 52
Spurslow M. SK8—5E 143
Spur, The. OL8—6E 65
Spur Wlk. M8—4B 74
Square Fold. M35—3B 90
Square St. BL0—3E 5
Square, The. BL3—4D 36
Square, The. BL9—3D 28
Square, The. M25—1C 58
Square, The. M27—6E 71
Square, The. OL3—5A 52
(Dobcross)
Square, The. OL3—1F 53
(Uppermill)
Square, The. SK1—2G 131
Square, The. SK4—6E 119
Square, The. SK14—5B 106
Square, The. WA15—5C 138
Squire Rd. M8—4B 74
Squire's Ct. M5—3A 84
Squirrels Jump. SK9—5H 159
Stable Fold. M28—6A 70
Stablefold. OL5—3E 81
Stableford Av. M30—1E 83
Stable M. M25—6G 59
Stables, The. M35—2D 90
Stable St. M3—3C 86 & 4F 161
Stable St. OL1—1F 65
Stable St. OL9—1G 77
Stablings, The. SK9—4D 158
Staffin Ct. OL10—4B 30
Stafford Rd. M27—3F 71
Stafford Rd. M28—2E 69
Stafford Rd. M30—2G 83
Stafford Rd. M35—6G 77
Stafford St. BL8—1B 28
Stafford St. OL9—5A 64
Stafford View. M5—6H 85
Stafford Wlk. M34—6G 105
Stag Ind. Est. WA14—5D 124
Stag Pasture Rd. OL8—2B 78
Stainburne Rd. SK2—5C 132
Staindale. OL4—3H 65
Stainer St. M12—4C 102
Stainforth Clo. BL8—2F 27
Stainforth St. M11—5B 88
Stainmoor Ct. SK2—5D 132
Stainsbury St. BL3—3G 37
Stainton Av. M18—3G 103
Stainton Clo. M26—2F 41
Stainton Dri. M24—4F 45
Stainton Rd. M26—2E 41
Staithes Rd. M22—5B 140
Stakeford Dri. M8—3E 75
Stakehill Ind. Est. M24—3D 46
Stakehill La. M24—1D 46
Staley Clo. SK15—3G 93
Staley Dri. SK15—3G 93
Staley Hall Rd. SK15—2G 93
Staley St. OL4—3F 65
(Oldham)
Staley St. OL4—3B 66
(Springhead)
Staley Ter. SK15—2H 93
Stalham Clo. M10—2H 87 & 1H 163
Stalham Wlk. M10—2H 87 & 1G 163
Stalmine Av. SK8—5F 141
Stalybridge Dri. BL1—1B 24
Stambourne Dri. BL1—1B 24
Stamford Arc. OL6—2A 92
Stamford Av. SK15—3C 92
Stamford Av. WA14—6C 124
Stamford Clo. SK15—3C 92
Stamford Ct. OL6—3B 92
Stamford Dri. M35—5H 77
Stamford Dri. SK15—3C 92
Stamford Gro. SK15—2D 92
Stamford New Rd. WA14—1F 137
Stamford Pk. Rd. WA15—2G 137
Stamford Pl. M33—5C 114
Stamford Pl. SK9—2E 159
Stamford Rd. M7—5F 73
Stamford Rd. M13—4A 102

Stamford Rd. M31—3H 111
(Carrington)
Stamford Rd. M31—5D 96
(Urmston)
Stamford Rd. M34—6D 90
Stamford Rd. OL4—1B 66
Stamford Rd. OL5—1E 81
Stamford Rd. SK9—5H 159
(Alderley Edge)
Stamford Rd. SK9—6E 151
(Wilmslow)
Stamford Rd. WA14—3E 137
Stamford Sq. OL6—3C 92
Stamford St. M16—2A 100
(in two parts)
Stamford St. M27—2G 71
Stamford St. M33—3A 114
Stamford St. OL4—3A 66
Stamford St. OL5—3D 80
Stamford St. OL6—2A 92
(in two parts)
Stamford St. OL10—4G 31
Stamford St. OL16—5B 20
Stamford St. SK3—3H 131
Stamford St. SK15—1H 93
(Millbrook)
Stamford St. SK15—3C 92
(Stalybridge, in two parts)
Stamford St. WA14—6F 125
Stamford St. Central. OL6—3H 91
Stamford St. W. OL6—3G 91
Stamford Way. WA14—6F 125
Stampstone St. OL1—1F 65
Stanage Av. M9—5H 61
Stanbank St. SK4—5G 119
Stanbrook St. M19—6E 103
Stanbury Wlk. M10—2H 87
(off Berkshire Rd.)
Stancliffe Rd. M22—6C 128
Stancross Rd. M23—2C 126
Standall Wlk. M9—2G 75
Stand Av. M25—6C 42
Stand Clo. M25—1A 58
Standedge Clo. BL0—5E 5
Standedge Dri. OL3—4B 52
Standedge St. M11—5F 89
Standedge Wlk. SK15—5G 81
(off Crowswood Dri.)
Standfield Dri. M28—4C 68
Standford Hall Clo. BL0—5D 4
Standish Rd. M14—1H 117
Standish Wlk. M34—6E 105
Standmoor Ct. M25—2B 58
Standmoor Rd. M25—2B 58
Standon Wlk. M10—1D 76
Standring Av. BL8—5G 27
Stand Rise. M26—1H 57
Stangate Wlk. M11—5B 88
Stanhope Av. M25—4E 59
Stanhope Av. M34—1E 105
Stanhope Clo. SK9—1G 159
Stanhope Ct. M25—4E 59
Stanhope Rd. M6—6C 72
Stanhope St. M19—6D 102
Stanhope St. M34—2E 105
Stanhope St. OL5—3E 81
Stanhope St. OL6—1B 92
Stanhope St. OL11—6H 19
Stanhope St. SK5—2G 119
Stanhope Way. M35—3E 77
Stanhorne Av. M8—1C 74
Stanhurst. M30—2G 83
Stanier Av. M30—2F 83
Stanier St. M9—3G 75
Stanion Gro. SK16—5B 92
Stan Jolly Wlk. M11—5E 89
Stanley Av. M14—4G 101
Stanley Av. SK6—4B 134
Stanley Av. SK7—2D 144
Stanley Av. S. SK14—3C 106
Stanley Av. N. M25—3E 59
Stanley Av. S. M25—3E 59
Stanley Clo. M16—2H 99
Stanley Clo. M25—6D 42
Stanley Ct. BL9—2D 28
Stanley Dri. M25—3D 58
Stanley Dri. SK9—1H 151

Stanley Dri. WA15—6A 126
Stanley Grn. Trading Est. SK8
—3A 152
Stanley Gro. M12—3B 102
Stanley Gro. M12 & M18—3C 102
Stanley Gro. M21—1G 115
Stanley Gro. M31—5F 97
Stanley Gro. SK4—5D 118
Stanley Hall La. SK12—1G 157
Stanley Mt. M33—6A 114
Stanley Pk. Wlk. BL2—6E 25
Stanley Pl. OL12—3G 19
Stanley Rd. BL1—4F 23
Stanley Rd. BL4—1A 54
Stanley Rd. M7—3A 74
Stanley Rd. M16—2H 99
(Old Trafford)
Stanley Rd. M16—5C 100
(Whalley Range)
Stanley Rd. M25—6C 42
Stanley Rd. M26—1E 41
Stanley Rd. M28—1F 69
Stanley Rd. M30—4E 83
Stanley Rd. M34—3B 104
Stanley Rd. OL9—5H 63
Stanley Rd. SK4—5D 118
Stanley Rd. SK8—1H 151
Stanley Sq. SK15—4D 92
Stanley St. BL0—4D 4
Stanley St. M3—4C 86 & 5E 161
Stanley St. M8—1E 87
Stanley St. M10—6H 75
Stanley St. M11—6G 89
Stanley St. M25—5G 59
(Prestwich)
Stanley St. M25—6D 42
(Whitefield)
Stanley St. M35—5G 89
Stanley St. OL4—4A 66
(Lees)
Stanley St. OL4—3C 66
(Springhead)
Stanley St. OL9—2H 63
Stanley St. OL10—4F 31
Stanley St. OL12—2G 19
Stanley St. SK1—1A 132
Stanley St. SK15—4D 92
Stanley St. S. BL3—1A 38
Stanmore Av. M32—5B 98
Stanmore Av. OL6—4G 79
Stanmore Dri. BL3—2G 37
Stannard Rd. M30—4B 82
Stanneybrook Clo. OL16—3B 20
Stanneylands Clo. SK9—5G 151
Stanneylands Dri. SK9—5F 151
Stanneylands Rd. SK9—3F 151
Stanney Rd. OL16—3B 20
Stannybrook Rd. M35—4B 78
Stanrose Clo. BL7—2C 10
Stansbury Pl. SK2—5E 133
Stansfield Dri. OL11—4A 18
Stansfield Hall. OL15—6G 9
Stansfield Rd. M35—3G 77
Stansfield St. SK14—3C 106
Stansfield St. M10—1F 89
Stansfield St. OL1—1C 64
Stansfield St. OL9—4H 63
Stansted Wlk. M23—2D 126
Stanthorne Av. M20—1E 117
Stanton Av. M7—4F 73
Stanton Av. M20—5C 116
Stanton Gdns. SK4—2D 130
Stanton St. M11—3E 89
Stanton St. M32—3D 98
Stanton St. OL9—6H 63
Stanton St. Flats. M32—3D 98
Stanway Av. BL3—1H 37
Stanway Clo. BL3—1H 37
Stanway Clo. M24—3B 62
Stanway Dri. WA15—2H 137
Stanway Rd. M25—1F 59
Stanway St. M32—4D 98
Stanwell Rd. M10—2C 76
Stanwell Rd. M27—4E 71
Stanwick Av. M9—5C 60
Stanworth Av. BL2—6G 25
Stanworth Clo. M16—4C 100
Stanyard Ct. M5—5G 85

Stanycliffe La. M24—4B 46
Stanyforth St. SK14—3H 109
Stapenhill Dri. M8—6A 74
Stapleford Clo. M23—1F 139
Stapleford Clo. M33—4E 115
Stapleford Wlk. M34—6E 105
Staplehurst Rd. M10—1C 88
Staplers Wlk. M14—4G 101
Stapleton Av. BL1—4C 22
Stapleton St. M6—6A 72
Starcliffe St. BL3—5F 39
Starcross Wlk. M10—5B 76
Starfield Av. OL15—1F 21
Star Ind. Est. OL8—4D 64
Starkey St. OL10—2F 31
(in two parts)
Starkie Rd. BL2—6D 24
(Tonge Fold)
Starkie Rd. BL2—4D 24
(Tonge Moor)
Starkies. BL9—6C 28
Starkie St. M28—3A 70
Starling Dri. BL4—2B 54
Starling Rd. M26 & BL8—5E 27
Starmoor Wlk. M8—5C 74
Starr Gro. M7—5A 74
Starring Gro. OL15—4D 8
(off Starring Rd.)
Starring La. OL15—4C 8
Starring Rd. OL12—4C 8
Starring Rd. OL15—4C 8
Starring Way. OL15—4D 8
Starry Wlk. M7—1A 86 & 1B 160
Stash Gro. M23—4H 127
State Mill Cen. OL16—6B 20
Statham Clo. M34—4G 105
Statham Fold. SK14—3E 107
Statham St. M6—2H 85
Statham Wlk. M13—6F 87 &
3D 166
Station App. M1—4F 87 & 6C 162
Station App. WA15—6G 125
Station Bri. M31—5F 97
Station Brow. M26—5G 41
Station Cotts. M31—5E 111
Station Cotts. OL3—2D 52
(off Station Rd.)
Station Cotts. WA14—3F 125
Station La. OL4—4E 53
Station La. OL4—4C 66
Station Rd. BL4—2H 55
Station Rd. BL8—2H 13
Station Rd. M8—2C 74
Station Rd. M27—3F 71
Station Rd. M30—4E 83
(Eccles)
Station Rd. M30—2C 110
(Irlam)
Station Rd. M31—5F 97
Station Rd. M32—4C 98
Station Rd. OL1—5E 49
Station Rd. OL3—2D 52
(Diggle)
Station Rd. OL3—1F 53
(Uppermill)
Station Rd. OL4—4C 66
Station Rd. OL5—2F 81
Station Rd. OL11—5H 19
(in two parts)
Station Rd. OL12—4B 6
(Broadley)
Station Rd. OL12—2H 7
(Whitworth)
Station Rd. OL15—4F 9
Station Rd. OL16—6F 21
Station Rd. SK3—2G 131
(in two parts)
Station Rd. SK4—2A 130
Station Rd. SK5—5G 103
Station Rd. SK6—5D 134
(Marple)
Station Rd. SK6—4H 121
(Woodley)
Station Rd. SK8—3C 142
Station Rd. SK9—4H 151
(Handforth)
Station Rd. SK9—4E 151
(Styal)

Station Rd. SK9—2E 159
(Wilmslow)
Station Rd. SK12—4G 147
Station Rd. SK14—2H 109
(Hadfield)
Station Rd. SK14—5E 107
(Hyde)
Station St. BL3—1B 38
Station St. OL4—3B 66
Station St. SK7—3D 144
Station St. SK16—4H 91
Station View. M19—6C 102
Staton Av. BL2—5E 25
Staton St. M11—5E 89
Statter St. BL9—3E 43
Staveleigh Way. OL6—2H 91
Staveley Av. BL1—5C 10
Staveley Av. SK15—2E 93
Staveley Clo. M24—5G 45
Staveley Clo. OL2—1H 49
Staveley Wlk. OL2—3C 48
(off Shaw St.)
Staverton Clo. M13—6G 87 & 4E 167
Staveton Clo. SK7—2A 144
Stavordale. OL12—3G 19
(off Spotland Rd.)
Staycott Clo. M16—3D 100
Stayley Rd. OL5—3F 81
Steadway. OL3—4G 53
Stedman Clo. M11—4A 88
Steele Gdns. BL2—2G 39
Steeles Av. SK14—4C 106
Steeple Dri. M5—4G 85
Stelfox Av. WA15—3C 126
Stelfox La. M34—6E 91
Stelfox St. M30—5D 82
Stella St. M9—5D 60
Stelling St. M18—2F 103
Stenbury Clo. M14—4G 101
Stenner La. M20—1E 129
Stenson Sq. M11—6F 89
Stephen Clo. BL8—3A 28
Stephen Lowry Wlk. M10—4A 76
Stephenson Av. M35—4A 90
Stephenson St. M35—2G 77
Stephens Rd. M20—4G 117
Stephens St. SK15—1D 92
Stephens St. BL2—6F 25
Stephens Ter. M20—6F 117
Stephen St. BL8—3A 28
Stephen St. M3—1D 86
Stephen St. M31—5G 97
Stephen St. OL4—1H 65
Stephen St. SK1—3B 132
Stephen St. BL8—4A 28
Stephen Wlk. SK1—5B 132
Steps Meadow. OL12—5A 8
Sterndale Av. M28—5B 68
Sterndale Rd. SK3—6G 131
Sterndale Rd. SK6—2H 133
Sterratt St. BL1—6H 23
Stetchworth Dri. M28—4D 68
Stevenson Dri. OL1—3A 50
Stevenson Rd. M27—3E 71
Stevenson Sq. M1—2C 54
Stevenson Sq. M1—4F 87 & 5C 162
Stevenson Sq. OL12—6A 8
Stevenson St. M3—4B 86 & 5C 160
Stevenson St. M28—6D 54
Stevens St. SK9—5G 159
Stewart Av. BL4—2D 54
Stewart St. BL1—3A 24
Stewart St. BL8—2H 27
(in two parts)
Stewart St. OL7—3F 91
Stewart St. OL9—5F 63
Stewart St. OL16—2F 35
Stile Clo. M31—5G 95
Stiles Av. SK6—4C 134
Stiles Clo. SK14—2G 109
Stilton Dri. M11—5C 88
Stirling. M30—3H 83
(off St Andrews Ct.)
Stirling Av. M20—1D 116
Stirling Av. SK6—6D 134
Stirling Av. SK7—4D 144
Stirling Clo. SK3—5E 131
Stirling Ct. SK4—4E 119

Stirling Dri. SK15—2E 93
Stirling Gro. M25—1E 59
Stirling Pl. OL10—4B 30
Stirling Rd. BL1—6C 10
Stirling Rd. OL9—5F 63
Stirling St. OL9—2A 64
Stirrup Brook Gro. M28—6B 68
Stirrup Ga. M28—6A 70
Stitch La. SK4—6F 119
Stitch Mi La. BL2—3G 25
Stiups La. OL16—1H 33
Stobart Av. M25—1F 73
Stockbury Gro. BL1—4B 24
(off Lindfield Dri.)
Stockdale Av. SK3—6H 131
Stockdale Gro. BL2—4H 25
Stockdale Rd. M9—5G 61
Stockfield Mt. OL9—3H 63
Stockfield Rd. OL2—3G 25
Stock Gro. OL16—4F 21
Stockholm Rd. SK3—4D 130
Stockholm St. M11—3D 88
Stockland Clo. M13—6F 87 & 3C 166
Stock La. OL9—2H 63
Stockley Av. BL2—3G 25
Stockley Wlk. M15—1B 100 & 6D 164
Stockport Rd. M12, M13 & M19
—1G 101 & 5F 167
Stockport Rd. M34—4F 105
Stockport Rd. OL5 & OL4—1E 81
Stockport Rd. OL7—5F 91
Stockport Rd. SK6—5H 133
(Marple)
Stockport Rd. SK6—1H 133
(Romiley)
Stockport Rd. SK8 & SK3—5H 129
(Hattersley)
Stockport Rd. SK14—6A 108
(Hattersley)
Stockport Rd. SK14—6C 106
(Hyde)
Stockport Rd. SK14—2B 122
(Marple)
Stockport Rd. WA15—6G 125
Stockport Rd. E. SK6—5F 121
Stockport Rd. W. SK6—6C 120
Stockport Trading Est. SK3
—2D 130
Stockport Trading Est. SK4
—2E 131
Stockport Village. SK2—1G 131
Stock Rd. OL12—1A 20
Stocksfield Dri. M9—6G 61
Stocksfield Dri. M28—4B 54
Stocks Gdns. SK15—4G 93
Stocks La. SK15—4F 93
Stocks St. M8—2E 87
Stocks St. OL11—3B 32
Stocks St. E. M8—1E 87
Stock St. BL8—6D 15
Stockton Av. SK3—3D 130
Stockton Dri. BL8—6B 14
Stockton Pk. OL4—3H 65
Stockton Rd. M21—1G 115
Stockton Rd. SK9—5C 158
Stockton St. BL4—5E 39
Stockton St. M16—3C 100
Stockton St. M27—3E 71
Stockton St. OL15—4E 9
Stockwood Wlk. M9—4F 75
Stoke Abbot Clo. SK7—6G 143
Stoke Abbot Lodge. SK7—6G 143
Stokesay Clo. BL9—2D 42
Stokesay Dri. SK7—4C 144
Stokesay Rd. M33—4G 113
Stokesley Wlk. BL3—3A 38
(in two parts)
Stokes St. M11—3F 89
Stoke St. OL16—5B 20
Stokoe Av. WA14—6C 124
Stolford Wlk. M8—5B 74
(off Ermington Dri.)
Stonall Av. M15—1B 100 & 5D 164
Stoneacre Ct. M27—3F 71
Stoneacre Rd. M22—3A 140
Stonebeck Ct. BL5—6D 36
Stonebeck Rd. M23—6F 127
Stone Breaks. OL4—2C 66
Stone Breaks Rd. OL4—3C 66

Stonebridge Clo. BL6—1A 36
Stonechat Clo. M28—3D 68
Stonechat Clo. M35—2C 90
Stonecliffe Av. SK15—3E 93
Stonecliffe Ter. SK15—2E 93
Stone Clo. BL0—5C 4
Stoneclough Rd. BL4 & M26—2H 55
Stonecroft. OL1—2C 64
Stonedale Clo. OL2—2C 48
Stonedelph Clo. BL2—4D 26
Stonefield Dri. M8—6A 74
Stonefield St. OL16—6F 21
Stoneflat Ct. OL12—3F 19
Stonehead St. M9—4H 75
Stonehewer St. M26—5H 41
Stonehill Cres. OL12—6A 6
Stonehill Dri. OL12—6A 6
Stone Hill La. OL12—1C 18
Stone Hill Rd. BL4—3F 55
Stonehill Rd. OL12—6A 6
Stonehouse Wlk. M23—4E 127
(off Sandy La.)
Stonehurst Clo. M12—1C 102
Stoneleigh Av. M33—4F 113
Stoneleigh Dri. M26—2B 56
Stoneleigh Rd. OL4—2C 66
Stoneleigh St. OL1—6F 49
Stonelow Clo. M15—1D 100 & 5H 165
Stone Mead Av. WA15—6C 138
Stonemead Clo. BL3—3B 38
Stonemill Ter. SK5—6H 119
Stonepail Clo. SK8—6D 128
Stonepail Rd. SK8—6E 129
Stone Pits. BL0—2B 4
Stoneridge. SK14—2H 109
Stone Row SK6—5E 135
(in two parts)
Stonesby Clo. M16—3B 100
Stonesteads Dri. BL7—3E 11
Stonesteads Way. BL7—3E 11
Stone St. BL2—4D 24
Stone St. M3—5C 86 & 2E 165
Stone St. OL16—6F 21
Stoneswood Rd. OL3—4G 51
Stoneway. M5—6H 85
(off W. Park St.)
Stoneyboyd. OL12—4H 7
Stoneyfield. SK15—1E 93
Stoneyfield Clo. M16—5D 100
Stoneygate Wlk. M11—6F 89
Stoney Knoll. M7—5H 73
Stoney La. SK9—4C 158
Stoneyside Av. M28—5G 55
Stoneyside Gro. M28—5G 55
Stonie Heyes Av. OL12—1B 20
Stonyford Rd. M33—5D 114
Stonyhurst Av. BL1—6C 10
Stonyhurst Clo. M15—1D 100 & 6G 165
Stopes Rd. BL3 & M26—4C 40
Stopford Av. OL15—5C 8
Stopford St. M11—5C 89
Stopford St. SK3—3F 131
Stopford Wlk. M34—4F 105
Stopley Wlk. M11—5C 88
Stores Cotts. OL4—3G 67
Stores St. M25—5G 59
Store St. M1—5F 87 & 1D 166
Store St. M11—6D 88
Store St. OL2—5G 35
Store St. OL7—5E 79
Store St. OL11—2A 18
Store St. SK2—1C 144
Storey Pas. OL15—4D 8
Stortford Dri. M23—1H 127
Stothard Rd. M32—6B 98
Stott Bri. M31—6H 95
Stottfield. OL2—4H 47
Stott Ho. OL8—4C 64
Stott La. BL2—4D 24
Stott La. M6—2B 84
Stott La. M24—2H 45
Stott Milne St. OL9—4H 63
Stott Rd. M27—5D 70
Stott Rd. OL9—6E 63
Stott's La. M10—5D 76
Stott St. M11—3B 88
Stott St. M35—5D 76

Stott St. OL12—2H 19
Stott St. OL16—6B 8
Stourbridge Av. M28—3C 54
Stour Clo. WA14—5E 125
Stourport St. OL1—6E 49
Stovell Av. M12—5C 102
Stovell Rd. M10—3A 76
Stow Clo. BL8—6D 14
Stowell St. BL1—4A 24
Stowell St. M5—4E 85
Stowfield Clo. M9—5D 60
Stow Gdns. M20—3E 117
Stracey St. M10—2A 88
Stradbroke Clo. M18—2D 102
Strain Av. M9—5F 61
Strand Ct. M32—1C 114
Strand La. M26—6A 42
Strand, The. OL11—3F 33
Strand Way. OL2—5B 48
Strangford St. M26—3D 40
Stranton Dri. M28—3C 70
Stratfield Av. M23—2D 126
Stratford Av. BL1—4E 23
Stratford Av. BL9—3E 15
Stratford Av. M20—4D 116
Stratford Av. M30—5E 82
Stratford Av. OL8—6C 64
Stratford Av. OL11—6G 19
Stratford Clo. BL4—6B 38
Stratford Gdns. SK6—6F 121
Stratford Rd. M24—4B 62
Stratford Sq. SK8—6G 141
Strathaven Pl. OL10—4B 30
Strathblane Clo. M20—2F 117
Strathfield Dri. M11—3E 89
Strathmere Av. M16—5H 99
Strathmere Av. M32—4D 98
Strathmore Av. M34—5H 105
Strathmore Clo. BL0—5E 5
Strathmore Rd. BL2—6G 25
Stratton Rd. M16—5H 99
Stratton Rd. M27—2F 71
Stratton Rd. SK2—3C 132
Strawberry Bank. M6—2H 85
Strawberry Dri. WA14—4D 124
Strawberry Hill. M6—2H 85
Strawberry Hill Rd. BL2—2D 38
Strawberry La. OL5—5E 67
Strawberry La. SK9—3B 158
Strawberry Rd. M6—2G 85
Stray, The. BL1—1D 24
Stream Ter. SK1—2B 132
Street Bri. Rd. OL1—5G 47
Streetgate. M28—4B 54
Streethouse La. OL3—6H 51
Street La. M26—5E 27
Stretford By-Pass. M28 & M30
—6H 69
Stretford-Eccles By-Pass. M31
—4H 97
Stretford Motorway Est. M32—2A 98
Stretford Pl. OL12—6E 7
Stretford Rd. M16 & M15—2A 100 & 6C 164
Stretford Rd. M31—6F 97
Stretton Av. M20—6G 117
Stretton Av. M32—4A 98
Stretton Av. M33—5G 113
Stretton Clo. M10—6F 75
Stretton Rd. BL0 & BL8—1A 14
Stretton Rd. BL3—3F 37
Stretton Way. SK9—2H 151
Striding Edge Wlk. OL1—6E 49
Strines Ct. SK14—3C 106
Strines Rd. SK6—5E 135
Strines Rd. SK6 & SK12—3F 147
Stringer Av. SK14—5B 108
Stringer Clo. SK14—5B 108
Stringer St. SK1—1A 132
Stringston Wlk. M16—4C 100
(off Westerling Wlk.)
Stroma Gdns. M31—2E 97
Stromness Gro. OL10—4B 30
Strong St. M7—1C 86
Strontian Wlk. M11—4E 89
Stroud Av. M30—2D 82
Stroud Clo. M24—4A 62
Struan Ct. WA14—6E 125

Stuart Av. M30—5D 94
Stuart Av. SK6—4B 134
Stuart Rd. M32—4D 98
Stuart Rd. SK6—3D 120
Stuart St. M11—3B 88
(in two parts)
Stuart St. M24—1C 62
Stuart St. OL8—4C 64
Stuart St. OL16—5A 20
(in two parts)
Stuart Wlk. M24—2H 61
Stubbins Clo. M23—2E 127
Stubbins La. BL0—2E 5
Stubbins La. BL0—1E 5
Stubbins Vale Rd. BL0—1E 5
Stubbins Vale Ter. BL0—1D 4
Stubley La. OL15—4D 8
Stubley Mill Fold. OL15—5D 8
Stubley Mill Rd. OL15—5C 8
Studforth Wlk. M15—2E 101
(off Botham Clo.)
Studland Rd. M22—1D 140
Studley Clo. OL2—3E 49
Styal Av. M32—4A 98
Styal Av. SK5—3H 119
Styal Gro. SK8—2E 141
Styal Rd. M22 & SK8—1D 150
Styal Rd. SK9—4E 151
Styhead Dri. M24—4F 45
Style St. M4—2E 87 & 2B 162
Style View. SK9—5F 151
Sudbury Clo. M16—2A 100
Sudbury Dri. BL6—1A 36
Sudbury Dri. SK8—5H 141
Sudbury Rd. SK7—5E 145
Sudden St. OL11—1C 32
Sudell St. M4 & M10—2F 87 & 2D 162
Sudley Rd. OL11—6E 19
Sudlow St. OL16—1B 20
Sudren St. BL8—2F 27
Sue Patterson Wlk. M10—6F 75
Suffield St. M24—1H 61
Suffield Wlk. M22—4B 140
Suffolk Av. M35—2A 90
Suffolk Clo. BL3—2B 40
Suffolk Dri. SK5—3C 120
Suffolk Dri. SK9—6G 151
Suffolk Rd. WA14—1D 136
Suffolk St. M6—6E 73
Suffolk St. OL9—5H 63
Suffolk St. OL11—5H 19
Sugar La. OL3—5A 52
Sugden St. OL6—2B 92
Sulby Av. M32—5E 99
Sulby St. M40—3A 76
Sulby St. M26—1B 56
Sulgrave Av. SK12—3F 155
Sullivan St. M12—4C 102
Sultan St. BL9—5C 28
Sulway Clo. M27—4G 71
Sumac St. M11—3F 89
Sumbland Ho. M27—1H 71
Summer Av. M31—5G 97
Summer Castle. OL16—4H 19
Summercroft. OL9—6H 63
Summerdale Dri. BL0—1B 14
Summerfield Av. M35—2G 89
Summerfield Dri. M24—5C 46
Summerfield Dri. M25—2E 73
Summerfield Pl. SK9—3D 158
Summerfield Rd. BL3—3D 38
Summerfield Rd. M22—3A 140
Summerfield Rd. M28—4A 70
Summerlea. SK8—5D 142
Summer Pl. M14—5G 101
Summers Av. SK15—3G 93
Summerseat Clo. M5—5G 85
Summerseat La. BL0—6C 4
Summersgill Clo. OL10—4G 31
Summershades La. OL4—3F 67
Summers St. OL9—2A 64
Summers St. SK15—5C 92
Summer St. OL16—4A 20
Summerville Av. M9—4H 75
Summerville Rd. M6—6C 72
Summit Clo. BL9—1B 30
Summit St. OL10—3B 30
Sumner Av. BL2—4D 26
Sumner Rd. M6—6B 72

Sumner St. BL3—5F 37
Sumner St. OL2—2F 49
Sunbank Clo. OL12—1F 19
Sunbank La. WA15—2D 148
Sunbeam Wlk. M11—4B 88
(off Hopedale Clo.)
Sunbury Clo. SK16—5D 92
Sunbury Dri. M10—1F 89
Sundance Ct. M5—5E 85
Sunderland Av. OL6—1A 92
Sundew Pl. M24—2D 62
Sundial Clo. SK14—4H 107
Sundial Rd. SK2—4D 132
Sundial Wlk. SK14—4H 107
Sunfield. SK6—6H 121
Sunfield Av. OL4—4A 50
Sunfield Cres. OL4—4C 48
Sunfield Dri. OL2—4D 48
Sunfield Est. OL3—3C 52
Sunfield La. OL3—3C 52
Sunfield Rd. OL1—1D 64
Sunfield Way. OL4—2A 66
Sun Ga. OL15—2F 21
Sunk La. M24—2A 62
(in two parts)
Sunlight Rd. BL1—6G 23
Sunningdale Av. M11—3D 88
Sunningdale Av. M25—2A 58
Sunningdale Av. M26—2D 40
Sunningdale Av. M33—6E 115
Sunningdale Clo. BL8—5C 27
Sunningdale Clo. SK16—5D 92
Sunningdale Ct. M34—3B 104
Sunningdale Dri. M6—6G 71
Sunningdale Dri. M25—4E 59
Sunningdale Dri. M30—4D 94
Sunningdale Ho. OL10—5F 31
Sunningdale Dri. SK7—6H 143
Sunningdale Ho. M33—6E 115
Sunningdale Rd. M31—6D 96
Sunningdale Rd. M34—6G 105
Sunningdale Rd. SK8—6C 142
Sunningdale Wlk. BL3—2H 37
Sunninghill St. BL3—3H 37
Sunny Av. BL9—6F 15
Sunny Bank. M26—1A 56
Sunny Bank. OL4—4A 66
Sunnybank. SK9—3D 158
Sunnybank Av. M30—2H 83
Sunny Bank Av. M35—4H 89
Sunny Bank Av. SK4—5B 118
Sunnybank Dri. SK9—3A 158
Sunnybank Rd. BL1—3G 23
Sunny Bank Rd. BL9—4D 42
Sunny Bank Rd. M13—4A 102
Sunny Bank Rd. M35—4H 89
Sunny Bank Rd. WA14—4F 65
Sunny Bower St. BL8—5G 13
Sunny Brow Rd. M18—2E 103
Sunny Brow Rd. M24—1G 61
Sunny Dri. M25—5D 58
Sunnyfield Rd. M25—2G 59
Sunnyfield Rd. SK4—6B 118
Sunnylea Av. M19—4A 118
Sunny Lea M. SK9—3D 158
Sunnymead Av. BL1—1B 24
Sunnymede Vale. BL0—6C 4
Sunny Side. M18—3G 103
Sunnyside. M35—2H 89
Sunnyside. OL7—6D 78
Sunny Side Cotts. OL12—1F 17
Sunnyside Ct. M5—6H 85 & 3A 164
Sunnyside Gro. OL6—3B 92
Sunnyside Cres. OL6—3B 92
Sunnyside La. M35—1H 89
Sunnyside Rd. BL1—3G 23
Sunnyside Rd. M35—2H 89
Sunnywood Dri. BL8—5A 14
Sunnywood La. BL8—5A 14
Sunrise View. OL15—6H 9
Sunset Av. M22—1B 128
Sun St. BL0—2D 4
Sun St. OL5—2E 81
Sunwell Ter. SK6—2D 146
Surbiton Rd. M10—1D 88
Surrey Av. M35—2H 89
Surrey Av. OL2—6D 34
Surrey Clo. BL3—3B 40

Surrey Dri. BL9—5D 28
Surrey Pk. Clo. OL2—5F 35
Surrey Rd. M9—1F 75
Surrey St. M9—1E 75
Surrey St. OL6—6H 79
Surrey St. OL9—4A 64
Surrey Way. SK5—4C 120
Surtees Rd. M23—1G 127
Sussex Av. BL9—4A 30
Sussex Av. M20—5F 117
Sussex Clo. M27—1F 71
Sussex Clo. SK9—3H 63
Sussex Dri. BL9—5D 28
Sussex Dri. M35—2A 90
Sussex Pl. SK14—2D 106
Sussex Rd. M30—3A 110
Sussex Rd. SK3—3D 130
Sussex St. M2—4D 86 & 5H 161
Sussex St. M7—2B 86
Sussex St. OL16—5H 19
Sutcliffe Av. M12—5D 102
Sutcliffe St. BL1—3A 24
Sutcliffe St. M24—1C 62
Sutcliffe St. OL2—4E 49
(Heyside)
Sutcliffe St. OL2—2E 49
(Shaw Side)
Sutcliffe St. OL7—4F 91
Sutcliffe St. OL8—4C 64
Sutcliffe St. OL15—3F 9
Sutherland Clo. OL8—2D 78
Sutherland Flats. OL10—3E 31
(off Meadow Clo.)
Sutherland Gro. BL4—1E 55
Sutherland Rd. BL1—4E 23
Sutherland Rd. M16—4G 99
Sutherland Rd. OL10—4A 30
Sutherland St. BL4—1E 55
Sutherland St. M27—2E 71
Sutherland St. M30—2D 82
Sutherland St. OL6—2C 92
Suthers St. M26—6A 42
Suthers St. M33—2A 64
Sutton Dri. M35—2G 89
Sutton Dwellings. M6—2F 85
Sutton Ho. M6—2F 85
(off Sutton Dwellings)
Sutton Rd. BL3—3D 36
Sutton Rd. M18—4E 103
Sutton Rd. SK4—4E 119
Sutton Rd. SK9—4F 159
Sutton Rd. SK12—5F 155
Suttons La. SK6—6E 135
Sutton St. M12—1C 102
Sutton Way. M6—2G 85
Sutton Way. SK9—2A 152
Swailes St. OL4—3F 65
Swaine St. SK3—2G 131
Swainsthorpe Dri. M9—3G 75
Swain St. OL12—2G 19
Swalecliff Av. M23—2D 126
Swaledale Clo. OL2—2C 48
Swale Dri. WA14—5E 125
Swallow Bank Dri. OL11—2B 32
Swallow Clo. SK15—4H 81
Swallow Dri. BL9—1F 29
Swallow Dri. M30—4E 95
Swallow Dri. OL11—4B 18
Swallow La. SK15—4H 81
Swallow St. M12—5C 102
Swallow St. OL8—1B 78
Swallow St. SK1—4H 131
Swanage Av. M23—3D 126
Swanage Av. SK2—5D 132
Swanage Clo. BL8—5C 14
Swanage Rd. M30—2D 82
Swanbourne Gdns. SK3—5E 131
Swan Clo. SK12—3B 154
Swan Ct. OL12—1F 49
Swanhill Clo. M18—1H 103
Swan La. SK3—3H 37
Swanley Av. M10—6G 75
Swann St. SK8—4D 142
Swann Gro. SK8—4D 142
Swann La. SK8—4C 142
Swann St. OL6—2A 92
Swan Rd. BL8—1H 13
Swan Rd. WA15—2A 126
Swansea St. OL8—5F 65

Swan St. M4—3E 87 & 3B 162
Swan St. M26—5H 41
Swan St. SK9—2E 159
Swan Ter. M30—5E 83
Swanton Wlk. M8—5B 74
(off Kenford Wlk.)
Swarbrick Rd. M25—1D 72
Swarthdale Ho. M6—2F 85
(off Sutton Dwellings)
Swayfield Av. M13—4B 102
Swaylands Dri. M33—2B 126
Sweet Briar Clo. OL12—1G 19
Sweet Briar La. OL12—1G 19
Sweetlove's Gro. BL1—6C 10
Sweetlove's La. BL1—6C 10
Sweetnam Dri. M11—3D 88
Swettenham Rd. SK9—2H 151
Swift Clo. SK6—4A 122
Swift Rd. OL1—3A 50
Swift Rd. OL11—4B 18
Swift St. OL6—6H 79
Swift Wlk. M10—5C 76
Swinbourne Gro. M20—2G 117
Swinburne Av. M35—2A 90
Swinburne Grn. SK5—6F 103
Swinburne Way. M34—2G 121
Swinburn St. M9—2H 75
Swindell's St. M11—6G 89
Swindells St. SK14—2C 106
Swindon Clo. M18—2F 103
Swinfield Av. M21—1F 115
Swinford Gro. OL2—2C 48
Swinford Wlk. M9—6G 61
Swinley Chase. SK9—6B 152
Swinside Clo. M24—5E 45
Swinside Rd. BL2—5H 25
Swinstead Av. M10—6G 75
Swinton Cres. BL9—6E 43
Swinton Gro. M13—2G 101
Swinton Hall Rd. M27—2F 71
Swinton Pk. M6—6H 71
Swinton St. BL2—6G 25
Swinton St. OL4—4G 65
Swiss Hill. SK9—5H 159
Swithin Rd. M22—5C 140
Swythamley Clo. SK3—3C 130
Sybil St. OL15—3E 9
Sycamore Av. M25—3D 58
(off Beech Av.)
Sycamore Av. M26—1F 57
Sycamore Av. M34—5F 105
Sycamore Av. OL4—1H 65
Sycamore Av. OL9—6F 63
Sycamore Av. OL10—5G 31
Sycamore Av. OL16—2E 35
Sycamore Av. WA14—6C 124
Sycamore Clo. OL15—4D 8
Sycamore Clo. SK9—6F 151
Sycamore Clo. SK16—5D 92
Sycamore Ct. M6—2G 85
Sycamore Ct. M10—2A 88
Sycamore Cres. OL6—6G 79
Sycamore Dri. M35—3C 90
Sycamore Gro. M35—4H 77
Sycamore Lodge. SK7—6H 143
Sycamore Pl. M25—3D 58
Sycamore Rd. BL8—6H 13
Sycamore Rd. M30—1C 82
Sycamore Rd. M31—6C 110
Sycamore Rd. SK6—5G 121
Sycamores, The. M33—6C 114
Sycamores, The. OL4—1A 66
Sycamores, The. OL5—2G 81
Sycamores, The. SK14—4H 109
Sycamores, The. SK15—5F 93
Sycamore St. M33—5C 11
Sycamore St. SK3—3D 130
Sycamore St. SK15—4D 92
Sycamore Wlk. SK8—5H 129
Syddall Clo. SK7—2F 153
Syddall Cres. SK7—3F 153
Syddal Grn. SK7—2F 153
Syddall Av. SK8—5H 141
Syddall St. SK14—6B 106
Syddal Rd. SK7—2F 153
Sydenham St. OL1—6E 49
(in two parts)
Sydenham Ter. OL12—6D 6
Sydney Av. M30—3F 83

Sydney Gdns. OL15—6G 9
Sydney Rd. SK7—2H 153
Sydney St. M6—3E 85
Sydney St. M27—4D 70
Sydney St. M32—5D 98
Sydney St. M35—4E 77
Sydney St. OL5—3F 81
Sydney St. SK2—4C 132
Syke Croft. SK6—6B 122
Syke La. OL12—5F 7
Syke Rd. OL12—5F 7
Syke Rd. OL15—1H 21
Sykes Av. BL9—3F 43
Sykes Clo. OL3—4F 53
Sykes Ct. OL16—5B 20
Sykes Meadow. SK3—5F 131
Sykes St. BL9—2E 29
Sykes St. OL16—1E 35
   (Milnrow)
Sykes St. OL16—5B 20
   (Rochdale)
Sykes St. SK5—1H 119
Sykes St. SK14—6D 106
Sykes Wlk. SK5—1H 119
   (off Sykes St.)
Sylvan Av. M16—4B 100
Sylvan Av. M31—4F 97
Sylvan Av. M33—6C 114
Sylvan Av. M35—6E 77
Sylvan Av. SK9—4C 158
Sylvan Av. WA15—3H 125
Sylvandale Av. M19—6C 102
Sylvan Gro. WA14—6F 125
Sylvan St. OL9—2A 64
Sylvester Av. SK2—5B 132
Sylvester Clo. SK14—5A 108
Sylvester St. BL1—5A 24
Sylvester Way. M34—2G 121
Sylvester Way. SK14—5A 108
Sylvia Gro. SK5—2G 119
Symms St. M6—1H 85
Symond Rd. M9—4G 61
Symons Rd. M33—4B 114
Symons St. M7—4A 74
Syndall Av. M12—1H 101 & 5G 167
Syndall St. M12—1H 101 & 5G 167

Tabley Av. M14—5F 101
Tabley Gdns. M35—4B 90
Tabley Gdns. SK6—1E 147
Tabley Gro. M13—5B 102
Tabley Gro. SK5—2G 119
Tabley Gro. WA15—2H 125
Tableymere Gdns. SK8—2B 142
Tabley Rd. BL3—3F 37
Tabley Rd. M33—1F 127
Tabley Rd. SK9—2H 151
Tabley St. M6—6F 73
Tabley St. OL5—3F 81
Tabley St. SK16—5C 92
Tabor St. M24—5H 45
Tackler Clo. M27—4F 71
Tadcaster Wlk. OL1—2D 64
Taddington Bank. SK13—6G 109
   (off Castleton Cres.)
Taddington Clo. SK13—6G 109
   (off Castleton Cres.)
Taddington Pde. SK13—6G 109
   (off Castleton Cres.)
Taddington Pl. SK13—6G 109
   (off Castleton Cres.)
Tadlow Wlk. M10—2G 87
Tadman Gro. WA14—5C 124
Tadmor Clo. M28—5B 54
Tagge La. M27—5C 72
Tagore Clo. M13—3A 102
Tahir Clo. M8—4D 74
Tait M. SK4—1B 130
Talavera St. M7—6H 73
Talbot Av. BL3—3A 40
Talbot Clo. OL4—1G 65
Talbot Ct. BL1—1B 24
Talbot Gro. BL9—5G 15
Talbot Pl. M16—2H 99
Talbot Rd. M14—2A 118
Talbot Rd. M32 & M16—4E 99
Talbot Rd. M33—5E 115
Talbot Rd. SK9—5H 159

Talbot Rd. SK14—2C 106
Talbot Rd. WA14—3D 136
   (in two parts)
Talbot St. M24—5H 45
Talbot St. M30—4G 83
Talbot St. OL6—2G 91
Talbot St. OL11—5H 19
Talbot St. SK7—1D 144
Talford Gro. M20—4E 117
Talgarth Rd. M14—1G 87
Talkin Dri. M24—4G 45
Talland Wlk. M13—2H 101
Tallarn Clo. M20—2G 117
Tallis St. M12—4C 102
Tall Trees. M7—2H 73
Tall Trees Pl. SK2—5C 132
Talmine Av. M10—6G 75
Tamar Clo. BL4—4B 56
Tamar Ct. M15—1B 100 & 6C 164
Tamar Dri. M23—1G 139
Tamarin Clo. M27—2C 70
Tamar Way. OL10—2C 30
Tame Barn Clo. OL16—5G 21
Tame Clo. SK15—2G 93
Tame Ct. SK15—3F 93
Tamerton Dri. M8—5C 74
Tame St. M4—4H 87 & 6G 163
Tame St. M34—6F 91
   (Audenshaw)
Tame St. M34—2E 105
   (Denton)
Tame St. OL3—1F 53
Tame St. OL5—6G 67
Tame St. SK15—4C 92
Tame View. OL5—1E 81
Tame Wlk. SK9—5A 152
Tamewater Vs. OL3—5H 51
   (off Brook La.)
Tamworth Av. M5—5H 85
Tamworth Av. M25—2E 59
Tamworth Av. W. M5—5G 85
Tamworth Clo. M15—2C 100
Tamworth Clo. SK7—5C 144
Tamworth Ct. M15—2C 100
Tamworth Ct. OL9—4A 64
Tamworth Dri. BL8—6C 14
Tamworth Grn. SK1—1B 132
Tamworth St. OL9—4A 64
Tamworth St. SK1—1B 132
Tamworth Wlk. M5—5H 85
Tandis Ct. M6—1A 84
Tandle Hill Rd. OL2—1H 47
Tandlewood M. M10—6C 76
Tandlewood Pk. OL2—1H 47
Tanfield Rd. M20—4F 129
Tangmere Clo. M10—6C 62
Tangshutts La. SK6—1B 134
Tang, The. SK6—1H 133
Tanhill La. OL8—1E 79
Tanhouse Rd. M31—4H 95
Tanner Brook Clo. BL3—3A 38
Tannersfield Lodge. M35—5E 77
Tanners Fold. OL8—1E 79
Tanners Grn. M6—2F 85
Tanners St. BL0—3D 4
Tanners St. M18—2G 103
Tanner St. SK14—4B 106
Tannock Ct. SK7—4F 145
Tannock Rd. SK7—4F 145
Tan Pit Cotts. OL10—1F 31
Tanpits Rd. BL9—2C 28
Tanpit Wlk. M22—3A 140
Tansey Gro. M8—4H 73
Tansley Pl. M8—1D 74
Tanthill Clo. SK2—5E 133
Tanworth Wlk. BL1—3A 24
Tan Yd. Brow. M18—3G 103
Tanyard Dri. WA14—1C 148
Tanyard La. WA15—2A 148
Taper St. BL0—3D 4
Tape St. BL0—3D 4
Tapley Av. SK12—5E 155
Taplow Gro. SK8—3B 142
Taplow Wlk. M14—4A 102
Tarbet Dri. BL2—6H 25
Tarbet Rd. SK16—6A 92
Tarbet Wlk. M8—5B 74
Tarbolton Cres. WA15—2C 138
Tariff St. M1—4F 87 & 5C 162

Tarland Wlk. M11—4E 89
Tarleton Clo. BL8—4F 27
Tarleton Ho. M6—1C 84
Tarleton Pl. BL3—4E 37
Tarleton Wlk. M13—1H 101 & 6G 167
Tarnbrook Clo. M25—1G 58
Tarnbrook Wlk. M15—2E 101
   (off Wellhead Clo.)
Tarn Dri. BL9—1C 42
Tarn Gro. M28—2H 69
Tarnside Clo. SK2—5F 133
Tarns, The. SK8—2F 141
Tarporley Av. M14—1E 117
Tarporley Clo. SK3—6F 131
Tarporley Wlk. SK9—5A 152
Tarran Grn. M34—6H 105
Tarran Gro. M34—6H 105
Tarran Pl. WA14—5G 125
Tarrington Clo. M12—2C 102
Tartan St. M11—3D 88
Tarves Wlk. M11—4D 88
Tarvin Av. M20—2E 117
Tarvin Av. SK4—2F 119
Tarvin Dri. SK6—5E 121
Tarvington Clo. M10—5E 75
Tarvin Rd. SK8—6C 130
Tarvin Wlk. BL1—3A 24
Tarvin Way. SK9—2H 151
Tasle Av. M2—4D 86 & 6H 161
Tatchbury Rd. M35—4G 77
Tate St. OL8—5F 65
Tatham St. OL16—4A 20
Tatland Dri. M22—2D 140
Tattenhall Wlk. M14—1H 117
Tattersall Av. BL1—3C 22
Tattersall St. OL3—4E 37
Tatton Clo. SK7—1F 145
Tatton Clo. SK8—1C 142
Tatton Ct. M14—1H 117
Tatton Ct. SK4—5E 119
Tatton Ct. SK9—2A 152
Tatton Gdns. SK6—4A 122
Tatton Gro. M20—3F 117
Tatton Mere Dri. M35—4B 90
Tattonmere Gdns. SK8—1C 142
Tatton Pl. M33—4B 114
Tatton Rd. M33—4B 114
Tatton Rd. M34—6G 105
Tatton Rd. SK9—2A 152
Tatton Rd. N. SK4—4E 119
Tatton Rd. S. SK4—5E 119
Tatton St. M5—5H 85
Tatton St. M15—1B 100 & 5C 164
Tatton St. SK1—2H 131
Tatton St. SK14—2C 122
Tatton St. SK15—3F 93
   (in two parts)
Tatton Ter. SK16—4H 91
Tatton View. M20—3F 117
Taunton Av. M30—2D 82
Taunton Av. M31—1D 112
Taunton Av. OL7—1G 91
Taunton Av. SK5—4C 120
Taunton Clo. BL1—4G 23
Taunton Dri. BL4—6B 38
Taunton Grn. OL7—6D 78
Taunton Gro. M25—3E 59
Taunton Hall Clo. OL7—6D 78
Taunton Pl. OL7—6D 78
Taunton Rd. M33—5F 113
Taunton Rd. OL7—1G 91
Taunton Rd. OL9—5G 47
Taunton St. M4—4H 87 & 5H 163
Taunton Wlk. M34—6G 105
Taurus St. OL4—1G 65
Tavern Ct. M35—4H 77
Tavern Ct. Av. M35—4H 77
Tavery Clo. M4—3H 87 & 4G 163
Tavistock Clo. SK14—5A 108
Tavistock Dri. OL9—6F 47
Tavistock Rd. BL1—1H 37
Tavistock Rd. M33—4F 113
Tavistock Rd. OL11—2F 33
Tavistock Sq. M9—4F 75
   (off Grangewood Dri.)
Tawton Av. SK14—4A 108
Tay Clo. OL8—4C 64

Tayfield Rd. M22—3A 140
Taylor Av. OL11—3B 18
Taylor Grn. Way. OL4—2B 66
Taylor Bldgs. BL4—3B 56
Taylor La. M34—3D 104
Taylor Rd. M31—6G 83
Taylor Rd. WA14—6C 124
Taylor's La. BL2—6A 26
Taylor's La. M10—6C 76
Taylorson St. M5—1H 99
   (in two parts)
Taylorson St. S. M5—1G 99
Taylor's Pl. OL4—3E 65
Taylor's Pl. OL12—2H 19
Taylor's Rd. M32—3D 98
Taylor St. BL9—1E 29
Taylor St. M18—1E 103
Taylor St. M24—1A 62
Taylor St. M25—5F 59
Taylor St. M26—4G 41
Taylor St. M34—3F 105
Taylor St. M35—4H 89
Taylor St. OL1—1G 65
Taylor St. OL2—2B 48
Taylor St. OL4—3A 66
Taylor St. OL9—2G 63
Taylor St. OL10—3E 31
Taylor St. OL12—2H 19
   (Rochdale)
Taylor St. OL12—1D 6
   (Whitworth)
Taylor St. SK14—2F 109
   (Hollingworth)
Taylor St. SK14—4D 106
   (Hyde)
Taylor St. SK15—4F 93
Taylor Ter. OL15—4G 9
   (off Ealees Rd.)
Taylor Ter. SK16—4H 91
   (off Astley St.)
Taywood Rd. BL3—5B 36
Teak Dri. BL4—5D 56
Teak St. BL9—3F 29
Teal Av. SK12—3A 154
Tealby Av. M16—3A 100
Tealby Ct. M21—1A 116
Tealby Rd. M18—3D 102
Teal Clo. SK2—6F 133
Teal Clo. WA14—3D 124
Teal Ct. OL11—4B 18
Teal St. BL3—3B 38
Teasdale Clo. OL9—6E 63
Tebbutt St. M4—2F 87 & 1D 162
Tedburn Wlk. M10—1D 76
Tedder Clo. BL9—5F 43
Tedder Dri. M22—6D 140
Teddington Rd. M10—2C 76
Ted Jackson Wlk. M11—5B 88
Teesdale Av. M31—3C 96
Teesdale Clo. SK2—5E 133
Teesdale Wlk. M9—6G 61
Tees St. OL16—5B 20
Tees Wlk. OL4—6C 64
Teignmouth Av. M10—1G 87
Telegraphic Ho. M5—6G 85
Telegraph Rd. M17—1A 98
Telfer Av. M13—5A 102
Telfer Rd. M13—5A 102
Telford Clo. M34—6E 91
Telford Rd. SK6—1E 147
Telford St. M8—6E 75
Telford Wlk. M16—3B 100
Telford Way. OL11—3G 33
Telham Wlk. M23—6G 127
Tellson Clo. M6—5B 72
Tellson Cres. M6—5B 72
Tell St. OL12—4F 19
Telryn Wlk. M8—3E 75
   (off Stakeford Dri.)
Temperance Sq. SK14—3C 108
Temperance St. M12—5G 87 & 2E 167
Temperance Ter. SK6—5D 134
Tempest Rd. BL6—4A 36
Tempest Rd. SK9—5H 159
Tempest St. BL3—3F 37
Temple Clo. OL4—1A 66
Templecombe Dri. BL1—5B 10
Temple Dri. BL1—2G 23
Temple Dri. M27—4H 71

Temple La. OL15—6G 9
Temple Rd. BL1—2G 23
Temple Rd. M33—5D 114
Temple Sq. M8—5D 74
Temple St. M24—6B 46
Temple St. OL1—2F 65
Templeton Dri. WA14—5D 124
Temsbury Wlk. M6—6G 75
Ten Acre La. M28 58
Ten Acres La. M10—6A 76
Tenax Rd. M17—6B 84
Tenby Av. BL1—4E 23
Tenby Av. M20—3F 117
Tenby Av. M32—3E 99
Tenby Ct. M15—1A 100 & 6B 164
Tenby Dri. M6—6B 72
Tenby Dri. SK8—4D 142
Tenby Gro. OL12—2E 19
Tenby Rd. OL8—1H 77
Tenby Rd. SK3—4D 130
Tenby St. OL12—2E 19
Tenement La. SK7—2E 143
Teneriffe St. M7—6H 73
Tenham Way. M9—6G 61
(off Ravenswood Dri.)
Tennis St. BL1—2H 23
Tennis St. M16—3H 99
Tennyson Av. BL9—1D 42
Tennyson Av. M26—3E 41
Tennyson Av. M34—2G 121
Tennyson Av. SK16—6E 93
Tennyson Gdns. M25—6D 58
Tennyson Rd. BL4—3D 54
Tennyson Rd. M24—5B 46
Tennyson Rd. M27—3D 70
Tennyson Rd. M35—3A 90
Tennyson Rd. SK5—6F 103
Tennyson Rd. SK8—5B 130
Tennyson St. BL1—4H 23
Tennyson St. M6—1A 86
Tennyson St. OL1—6G 49
Tennyson St. OL11—6A 20
Tennyson Wlk. BL1—3A 24
Tensing Av. OL7—6F 79
Tensing St. OL8—3E 79
Tenter Brow. SK15—3D 92
Tentercroft. OL1—2C 64
Tentercroft. OL12—4G 19
Tenterden St. BL9—3B 28
(in two parts)
Tenterden Wlk. M22—2A 140
Tenterhill La. OL12—1H 17
Tenters St. BL9—3B 28
Tenth St. M17—1C 98
Terence St. M10—6D 76
Terling Way. M10—6G 75
(off Lodge St.)
Terminal Rd. E. M22—6A 140
Terminal Rd. N. M22—6H 139
Terminal Rd. S. M22—6H 139
Tern Av. BL4—1B 54
Tern Clo. OL11—4B 18
Tern Clo. SK16—6C 92
Tern Clo. WA14—3D 124
Tern Dri. SK12—3B 154
Ternhill Ct. BL4—1F 55
Terrace St. OL4—2F 65
Terrace, The. M25—6F 59
Terrington Clo. M21—2C 116
Tetbury Dri. BL2—4H 25
Tetbury Rd. M22—4H 139
Tetlow Gro. M30—4E 83
Tetlow La. M7 & M8—3A 74
Tetlow St. M10—6C 76
Tetlow St. M24—1A 62
Tetlow St. OL8—3B 64
Tetlow St. SK14—2C 106
Tetlows Yd. OL15—5H 9
Tetsworth Wlk. M10—1D 76
Teviot St. M13—2A 102
Tewkesbury Av. M24—4H 45
Tewkesbury Av. M31—3F 97
Tewkesbury Av. M35—2A 90
Tewkesbury Av. OL6—4G 79
Tewkesbury Av. OL9—5G 47
Tewkesbury Av. WA15—2C 138
Tewkesbury Clo. SK8—1D 152
Tewkesbury Clo. SK12—2D 154

Tewkesbury Dri. M25—1G 73
Tewkesbury Rd. M10—2H 87 & 2H 163
Tewkesbury Rd. SK3—5D 130
Texas St. OL6—3A 92
Textile St. M12—6C 88
Textilose Rd. M17—2B 98
Teynham Wlk. M22—4A 140
Thackeray Clo. M8—5C 74
Thackeray Gro. M35—3A 90
Thackeray Rd. OL1—6G 49
Thames Clo. BL9—3F 15
Thames Clo. M11—5D 88
Thames Ct. M15—1B 100 & 6C 164
Thames Rd. OL16—5H 21
Thames St. OL1—1E 65
Thames St. OL16—5B 20
Thanet Clo. M7—6A 74
Thankerton Av. M34—4D 90
Thatcher St. OL8—5E 65
Thatch Leach. OL9—4F 63
Thatch Leach La. M25—2E 59
Thaxmead Dri. M10—1F 89
Thaxted Dri. SK2—6G 133
Thaxted Pl. BL1—5G 23
Thaxted Wlk. M22—5C 140
Theatre St. OL1—2D 64
Thekla St. BL0—3D 4
Thelma St. BL0—1B 64
Thelwall Av. BL2—5F 25
Thelwall Av. M14—1D 116
Thelwall Rd. M33—6E 115
Thelwall Clo. WA15—5G 125
Theobald Rd. WA15—4F 137
Theodore Wlk. M12—1H 101 & 5H 167
Theta Clo. M11—3D 88
Thetford. OL12—3G 19
(off Spotland Rd.)
Thetford Clo. BL8—6D 14
Thetford Dri. M8—4C 74
Thicketford Brow. BL2—4F 25
Thicketford Clo. BL2—3E 25
Thicketford Rd. BL2—4D 24
Thimble Clo. OL12—5B 8
Thimbles, The. OL12—5B 8
Third Av. BL1—6F 23
Third Av. BL3—3H 39
Third Av. BL9—1H 29
Third Av. M11—2E 89
Third Av. M17—2D 98
Third Av. M27—6E 71
Third Av. OL8—1A 78
Third Av. SK10—6D 164
Third Av. SK15—5G 81
Third St. BL1—1D 22
Thirkhill Pl. M30—3H 83
Thirlby Dri. M22—4B 140
Thirlestone Av. OL4—3B 50
Thirlmere Av. M27—4G 71
Thirlmere Av. M32—4C 98
Thirlmere Av. OL7—1F 91
Thirlmere Clo. SK9—5F 159
Thirlmere Clo. SK15—1E 93
Thirlmere Dri. BL9—6C 28
Thirlmere Dri. M24—5G 45
Thirlmere Dri. M28—4C 54
Thirlmere Gro. BL4—1A 54
Thirlmere Gro. OL2—1B 48
Thirlmere Rd. M31—5C 110
(Partington)
Thirlmere Rd. M31—4A 96
(Urmston)
Thirlmere Rd. SK1—4B 132
Thirlspot Clo. BL1—5C 10
Thirsfield Dri. M11—3E 89
Thirsk Av. M33—6E 113
Thirsk Av. OL9—6F 47
Thirsk Clo. BL8—5B 14
Thirsk M. M7—5H 73
Thirsk Rd. BL3—4A 40
Thirsk St. M12—6G 87 & 3E 167
Thistle Clo. SK15—6H 93
Thistle Sq. M31—6C 110
Thistleton Rd. BL3—4D 36
Thistle Wlk. M31—6C 110
Thistlewood Dri. SK9—2G 159
Thistleyfield. OL16—4E 21
Thistley Fields. SK14—1A 122
Thomas Clo. M34—3G 105

Thomas Dri. BL3—2H 37
Thomas Greenwood Clo. M11—5A 88
Thomas Henshaw Ct. OL11—1C 32
Thomas Holden St. BL1—5H 23
Thomas Ho. OL2—3C 48
(off Royton Hall Wlk.)
Thomason Sq. OL15—4E 9
Thomas Regan Ct. M18—1F 103
Thomasson Clo. BL1—4A 24
Thomas St. BL3—2H 37
Thomas St. BL4—1G 55
(Farnworth)
Thomas St. BL4—2G 55
(Kearsley)
Thomas St. M4—3E 87 & 4B 162
Thomas St. M8—3B 74
Thomas St. M26—4H 41
Thomas St. M32—3D 98
Thomas St. M35—3G 77
Thomas St. OL2—4D 48
(Royton)
Thomas St. OL2—1G 49
(Shaw)
Thomas St. OL4—4A 66
Thomas St. OL12—3H 7
Thomas St. OL15—5C 8
Thomas St. OL16—3A 20
Thomas St. SK1—4H 131
Thomas St. SK6—6F 121
(Bredbury)
Thomas St. SK6—1F 135
(Compstall)
Thomas St. SK14—5C 106
Thomas St. WA15—1G 137
Thomas St. W. SK1—4H 131
Thomas Telford Basin. M1—4G 87 & 6E 163
Thompson Av. BL2—4D 26
Thompson Av. M25—2E 59
Thompson Clo. M34—4B 104
Thompson Dri. BL9—2G 29
Thompson La. OL9—5G 63
Thompson Rd. BL1—4F 23
Thompson Rd. M17—5G 83
Thompson Rd. M34—4B 104
Thompson St. BL3—2B 38
Thompson St. M3—1G 161
Thompson St. M4—2F 87 & 2C 162
Thompson St. M10—6H 75
Thompson St. OL9—2B 64
Thomson Rd. M18—3E 103
Thomson St. M13—1G 101 & 6F 167
Thomson St. SK3—3G 131
Thoralby Clo. M12—2C 102
Thorburn Dri. OL12—2B 6
Thoresby Clo. M26—2C 40
Thoresway Rd. M13—4A 102
Thoresway Rd. SK9—4C 158
Thorgill Wlk. M10—4A 76
Thor Gro. M5—5A 86 & 2B 164
Thorley Clo. OL9—1F 77
Thorley Dri. M31—5F 97
Thorley Dri. WA15—6B 126
Thorley La. WA15—2B 138
Thorley La. WA15 & M22—4F 139
(Ringway)
Thorley La. WA15—2B 138
(Timperley)
Thorley M. SK7—6H 143
Thorley St. M35—3F 77
Thornaby Wlk. M9—5F 75
(off Kirklington Dri.)
Thornage Dri. M10—1G 87
Thornam New Rd. OL11—5D 32
Thorn Av. M35—5E 77
Thornbank. M30—2G 83
Thornbank Clo. OL10—6G 31
Thornbank E. BL3—2G 37
(off Deane Rd.)
Thornbank Est. BL3—1G 37
Thornbeck Dri. BL1—4D 22
Thornbeck Rd. BL1—4D 22
Thornbridge Av. M21—1H 115
Thornbury. OL11—5G 19
Thornbury Av. SK14—5A 108
Thornbury Rd. M32—3E 99
Thornbury Way. M18—2E 103
Thornbush Way. OL16—3C 20
Thornby Wlk. M23—6G 127

Thorncliff Av. OL8—6C 64
Thorncliffe Av. OL2—1A 48
Thorncliffe Av. SK16—6A 92
Thorncliffe Gro. M19—6E 103
Thorncliffe Ho. M15—2F 101
Thorncliffe Pk. OL2—6A 34
Thorncliffe Rd. BL1—6C 10
Thorncliffe Rd. SK14—3H 109
Thorn Clo. OL10—2D 30
Thorncombe Clo. M16—4C 100
Thorn Ct. M6—3H 85
Thorncross Clo. M15—6A 86 & 4B 164
Thorndale Ct. WA15—6A 126
Thorndale Gro. WA15—6A 126
Thornden Rd. M10—1H 87
Thorn Dri. M22—5E 141
Thorndyke Av. BL1—6C 10
Thorndyke Wlk. M25—6F 59
Thorne Av. M31—4C 96
Thorneside. M34—2F 105
(in two parts)
Thorne St. BL4—6E 39
Thorneycroft Av. M21—4H 115
Thorneycroft Clo. WA15—6B 126
Thorneycroft Rd. WA15—6B 126
Thorney Dri. SK7—1E 153
Thorney Hill Clo. OL4—3E 65
Thorneyholme Clo. BL6—1A 36
Thorneylea. OL12—4H 7
Thornfield. BL2—5G 25
Thornfield Cres. M28—4B 54
Thornfield Dri. M27—4E 71
Thornfield Gro. M28—4B 54
Thornfield Gro. OL6—2C 92
Thornfield Gro. SK8—3C 142
Thornfield Hey. SK9—1H 159
Thornfield Rd. BL8—4F 13
Thornfield Rd. M19—4A 118
Thornfield Rd. SK4—6C 118
Thornfield St. M5—4D 84
Thornfield Ter. OL6—3A 92
Thornford Wlk. M10—1D 76
Thorn Gro. M14—1H 117
Thorn Gro. M33—5B 114
Thorn Gro. SK8—1C 152
Thorn Gro. WA15—2G 137
Thorngrove Av. M23—4D 126
Thorngrove Dri. SK9—3F 159
Thorngrove Hill. SK9—3F 159
Thorngrove Ho. M23—4D 126
Thorngrove Rd. SK9—3F 159
Thornham Clo. BL8—5C 14
Thornham Dri. BL1—5E 11
Thornham La. M24—1D 46
Thornham La. OL2—5A 34
Thornham Old Rd. OL2—6G 33
Thornham Rd. M33—1G 125
Thornham Rd. OL2—6B 34
Thornhill. OL11—1E 33
Thornhill Clo. BL1—2G 23
Thornhill Clo. M34—5A 104
Thornhill Dri. M28—3G 69
Thornhill Rd. BL0—2A 14
Thornhill Rd. M35—3B 90
Thornhill Rd. SK4—1B 130
Thornholme Clo. M18—4D 102
Thornholme Rd. SK6—1D 146
Thornileby Brow. M4—3E 87 & 3A 162
Thorn Lea. BL2—1F 25
Thornlea Av. M27—5D 70
Thornlea Av. OL8—2A 78
Thorn Lea Clo. BL1—6D 22
Thornlee Ct. OL4—4D 66
Thornleigh Rd. M14—6E 101
Thornley Av. BL1—5C 10
Thornley Clo. OL4—4C 66
Thornley Cres. OL4—4C 66
Thornley Cres. SK6—5G 121
Thornley La. OL4—4C 66
Thornley La. N. SK5—4H 103
Thornley La. S. SK5 & M34—5H 103
Thornley Pk. Rd. OL4—4C 66
Thornley Rd. M25—2G 59
Thornley Rd. M34—3G 105
Thornley St. M24—6B 46
Thornley St. M26—5H 41
Thornley St. SK14—6C 106
Thornmere Clo. M27—1C 70

Thorn Pl. M6—3H 85
Thorn Rd. M27—5E 71
Thorn Rd. OL8—6G 65
Thorn Rd. SK7—2F 153
Thorns Av. BL1—1A 24
Thorns Clo. BL1—2H 23
Thornsett Clo. M9—3G 75
Thornsgreen Rd. M22—5B 140
Thorns Rd. BL1—2H 23
Thorns, The. M21—2H 115
Thorn St. BL1—3B 24
Thorn St. BL9—6E 5
Thornton Av. BL1—4D 22
Thornton Av. M31—5C 96
Thornton Av. M34—5C 90
Thornton Clo. BL3—4C 40
Thornton Clo. BL4—2D 54
Thornton Clo. M28—4A 68
Thornton Dri. SK9—4H 151
Thornton Ga. SK8—5E 129
Thornton Pl. SK4—5D 118
Thornton Rd. M14—5E 101
Thornton Rd. M28—4A 68
Thornton Rd. SK8—4G 141
Thornton St. BL2—6C 24
Thornton St. M10—1G 87
Thornton St. M11—5C 88
Thornton St. OL4—4D 64
Thornton St. OL11—6H 19
Thornton St. N. M10—6E 75
Thorntree Clo. M9—4G 75
Thorntree Pl. OL12—3F 19
Thorn View. BL9—2G 29
Thorn Wlk. M31—6C 110
Thornway. M28—3C 68
Thornway. SK6—6D 146
Thornway. SK7—5E 143
Thornwood Av. M18—3G 103
Thorold Gro. M33—5E 115
Thorpe Av. M26—2B 42
Thorpe Av. M27—2E 71
Thorpebrook Rd. M10—5A 76
Thorpe Clo. M34—3F 105
Thorpe Clo. OL4—1C 66
Thorpe Gro. SK4—3F 119
Thorpe Hall Rd. SK14—1D 106
Thorpe Hill. OL1—2C 64
Thorpe La. M34—2F 105
Thorpe La. OL4—1B 66
Thorpeness Sq. M18—1F 103
Thorpe St. BL0—4D 4
Thorpe St. BL1—3H 23
Thorpe St. M16—3A 100
Thorpe St. M24—2E 61
Thorpe St. M28—5F 55
Thorpe View. M5—6A 86
(off Ordsall Dri.)
Thorp Rd. M10—5A 76
Thorp Rd. OL2—3B 48
Thorp St. M25—5C 42
Thorp St. M30—5D 82
Thorp View. OL2—1A 48
Thorsby Av. SK14—5D 106
Thorsby Clo. M18—2G 103
Thorsby Rd. WA15—6G 125
Thorsby Way. M34—6G 105
Thorverton Sq. M10—3B 76
Thrapston Av. M34—4D 90
Threaphurst La. SK7—4A 146
Threapwood Rd. M22—4C 140
Three Acre Av. OL2—3E 49
Three Pits. M24—2C 46
Threlkeld Rd. BL1—4B 10
Threlkeld Rd. M24—6E 45
Thresher Clo. M33—6F 115
Threshfield Clo. BL9—4F 15
Threshfield Dri. WA15—4B 126
Throstle Bank St. SK14—3A 106
Throstle Ct. OL2—3B 48
Throstle Gro. BL8—6C 14
Throstle Gro. SK6—6B 134
Throstle Hall Ct. M24—6H 45
Throstle Nest La. M17 & M16
(in two parts)   —2G 99
Throstles Clo. M35—2C 90
Thrum Hall La. OL12—6D 6
(in three parts)
Thrush Av. BL4—1B 54

Thrush Dri. BL9—1F 29
Thrush St. OL12—2E 19
Thruxton Clo. M16—4C 100
Thurland Rd. OL4—3G 65
Thurland St. OL9—1E 63
Thurlby Av. M9—4G 61
Thurlby St. M13—3H 101
Thurleigh Rd. M20—5F 117
Thurleston Dri. SK7—2A 144
Thurlestone Av. BL2—4D 26
Thurlestone Dri. M31—4F 97
Thurlestone Rd. WA14—6D 124
Thurloe St. M14—4G 101
Thurlow St. M5—5F 85
Thurlston Cres. M8—4C 74
Thurlwood Av. M20—2E 117
Thurnham St. BL3—4G 37
Thurnley Wlk. M8—6B 74
Thursby Av. M20—3E 117
Thursby Wlk. M24—5E 45
Thursfield St. M6—6E 73
Thurstane St. BL1—3G 23
Thurston Clo. BL9—5E 43
Thurston Clough Rd. OL4 & OL3
                              —6E 51
Thyme Clo. M21—5B 116
Thynne St. BL3—1B 38
Thynne St. BL4—6E 39
Tiber Av. OL8—2A 78
Tib La. M2—4D 86 & 6H 161
Tib St. M4—4E 87 & 5B 162
Tib St. M34—5F 105
Tichfield Rd. OL8—5G 65
Tidebrook Wlk. M10—6F 75
(off Sedgeford Rd.)
Tideswell Av. M10—2H 87 & 1G 163
Tideswell Bank. SK13—6G 109
Tideswell Clo. SK8—6H 141
Tideswell Rd. M35—2G 89
Tideswell Rd. SK7—5E 145
Tideswell Wlk. SK13—6G 109
(off Riber Bank)
Tideswell Way. M34—1G 121
Tidworth Av. M4—3H 87 & 4G 163
Tiefield Wlk. M21—2C 116
Tiflis St. OL12—3G 19
Tig Fold Rd. BL4—1A 54
Tilbury St. OL1—1C 64
Tilbury Wlk. M10—1H 87
Tilby Clo. M31—5A 96
Tildsley St. BL3—3A 38
Tilehurst Ct. M7—4F 73
Tile St. BL9—2D 28
Tilgate Wlk. M9—6G 61
(off Haverfield Rd.)
Tillard Av. SK3—3D 130
Tillhey Rd. M22—3B 140
Tillington Clo. BL1—2A 24
Tilney Av. M32—6D 98
Tilshead Wlk. M13—1G 101
(off Dilston Clo.)
Tilson Rd. M23—6E 127
Tilstock Wlk. M23—3D 126
Tilston Wlk. SK9—5A 152
Tilton St. OL1—5G 49
Timberbottom. BL2—1E 25
Timbercliffe. OL15—6H 9
Timberhurst. BL9—3H 29
Timbersbrook Gro. SK9—5H 151
Times St. M24—1B 62
Timothy Clo. M6—2B 84
Timperley Clo. OL8—1F 79
Timperley Fold. OL6—5G 79
Timperley Rd. OL6—5G 79
Timperley St. M11—5E 89
Timperley St. OL9—2C 64
Timpson Rd. M23—4E 127
Timsbury Clo. BL2—2H 39
Timson St. M35—4F 77
Tim's Ter. OL16—5F 21
Timwood Wlk. M16—3C 100
Tindall St. M30—5D 82
Tindall St. SK5—4H 103
Tindle St. M28—6H 55
Tinker's Pas. SK14—5C 106
Tinker St. SK14—4B 106
Tinline St. BL9—3E 29
Tinningham Clo. M11—6G 89
Tinsdale Wlk. M24—6E 45

Tinshill Clo. M12—2C 102
Tinsley Clo. M10—2A 88
Tinsley Gro. BL2—5D 24
Tin St. BL3—2A 38
Tin St. OL9—1B 64
Tintagel Clo. SK15—3D 92
Tintagel Cres. M26—2C 40
Tintagel Wlk. SK14—4A 108
Tintern Av. BL2—3D 24
Tintern Av. M20—4D 116
Tintern Av. M25—5D 42
Tintern Av. M31—1C 112
Tintern Av. OL10—1E 31
Tintern Av. OL12—6E 7
Tintern Av. OL15—2E 9
Tintern Clo. SK12—2D 154
Tintern Dri. WA3—3C 138
Tintern Gro. SK1—2B 132
Tintern Pl. OL10—1E 31
Tintern Rd. M24—4H 45
Tintern Rd. SK8—1D 152
Tintern St. M14—5F 101
Tintern Wlk. OL8—5G 65
Tipperary St. SK15—6G 81
Tippinge's Rd. BL1—2B 24
Tipping St. M12—6F 87 & 3D 106
Tipping St. WA14—2F 137
Tipton Clo. M26—2D 40
Tipton Clo. SK8—1D 142
Tipton Dri. M23—1H 127
Tiptree Wlk. M9—3G 75
Tiree Clo. SK7—4F 145
Tirza Av. M19—1B 118
Tissington Bank. SK13—6F 109
(off Youlgreave Cres.)
Tissington Grn. SK13—6F 109
(off Youlgreave Cres.)
Tissington Ter. SK13—6F 109
(off Youlgreave Cres.)
Tissington Wlk. M15—1C 100
(off Ipstone Clo.)
Titan Rise. OL1—3H 49
Tithe Barn Clo. OL12—5B 8
Tithe Barn Cres. BL1—1D 24
Tithe Barn Rd. SK4—5B 118
Tithebarn St. BL9—3D 28
Tithebarn St. M26—3B 42
Tithebarn St. WA15—5C 138
Titterington Av. M21—5H 99
Tiverton Av. M33—6H 113
Tiverton Clo. M26—2C 40
Tiverton Dri. M33—6H 113
Tiverton Pl. OL7—6E 79
Tiverton Rd. M31—3G 97
Tiverton Wlk. BL1—4G 23
Tiviot Dale. SK1—1H 131
Tiviot Way. SK5—6G 119
Tixall Wlk. M8—1A 74
Toad La. OL12 & OL16—3H 19
(in two parts)
Tobermory Rd. SK8—4G 141
Toddbrook Clo. M15—6C 86 & 4F 165
Todd's Pl. M8—2E 75
Todd St. BL9—1C 28
Todd St. M3—3E 87 & 3A 162
Todd St. M7—5H 73
Todd St. OL10—3C 30
Todd St. OL16—4A 20
Todmorden Rd. OL15—5H 9
(Calderbrook)
Todmorden Rd. OL15—3F 9
(Littleborough)
Toft Way. SK9—3A 152
Toftwood Wlk. M10—6F 75
Toledo St. M11—4F 89
Tolland La. WA15—5H 137
Tollard Av. M10—6F 75
Tollard Clo. SK8—1D 152
Toll Bar St. M12—1A 102
Tollbar St. SK1—3H 131
Tollemache Clo. SK14—2C 108
Tollemache Rd. SK14—2C 108
Tollesbury Clo. M10—1H 87
Toll Ga. Clo. M13—3A 102
Tollgate Way. OL16—3C 20
Toll St. M26—2D 40
Tolworth Dri. M8—4D 74
Tomcroft La. M34—5D 104
Tom La. WA14—6A 136

Tomlinson Clo. OL8—4C 64
Tomlinson St. M10—6C 62
Tomlinson St. OL11—1C 32
Tomlin Sq. BL2—5E 25
Tom Lomas Wlk. M11—3D 88
Tommy Browell Clo. M14—4E 101
Tommy Johnson Wlk. M14—4E 101
Tommy La. BL2—4C 26
Tommy Taylor Clo. M10—6C 76
Tom Shepley St. SK14—5C 106
Tonacliffe Rd. OL12—4C 6
Tonacliffe Ter. OL12—3C 6
Tonacliffe Way. OL12—3C 6
Tonbridge Clo. BL8—4C 14
Tonbridge Pl. BL2—4D 24
Tonbridge Rd. M19—1D 118
Tonbridge Rd. SK5—1H 119
Tong Clough. BL7—3D 10
(in two parts)
Tonge Bri. Way. BL2—6D 24
Tonge Bri. Way Ind. Est. BL2
(off Tonge Bri. Way)   —6D 24
Tonge Clo. M25—6F 43
Tonge Ct. M24—1B 62
Tonge Fold Rd. BL2—6D 24
Tonge Hall Clo. M24—1B 62
Tonge Moor Rd. BL2—4D 24
Tong End. OL12—3G 7
Tonge Old Rd. BL2—6E 25
Tonge Pk. Av. BL2—4E 25
Tonge Roughs. M24—1D 62
Tonge St. M12—6H 87 & 3H 167
Tonge St. M24—3E 63
Tonge St. OL3—3F 31
Tonge St. OL16—5A 20
Tongfields. BL7—3D 10
Tong Head Av. BL1—1D 24
Tong La. OL12—4G 7
Tongley Wlk. M10—1D 76
Tong Rd. BL3—3A 40
Tong St. BL4—4B 56
Tonman St. SK5—3C 86 & 1F 165
Tontin St. M5—3H 85
Tooley Ho. M30—5F 83
Toon Cres. BL8—5C 14
Tootal Dri. M6 & M5—2C 84
Tootal Gro. M6—3C 84
Tootal Rd. M5—3C 84
Topaz St. M11—3B 88
Topcroft Clo. M22—3C 128
Topfield Rd. M22—2A 140
Topham St. BL9—5E 29
(in two parts)
Topley St. M10—5F 75
Top of Heap. OL10—3B 30
Top o'th' Fields. M25—2D 58
(in two parts)
Top o' th' Gorses. BL2—2E 39
Top o' th' Grn. OL9—5A 64
Top o' th' Meadow La. OL4—6C 50
Topphome Ct. BL4—2G 55
Topping Fold Rd. BL9—2G 29
Toppings Grn. BL7—4E 11
Toppings, The. SK6—6G 121
Topping St. BL1—4A 24
Topping St. BL9—2D 28
Topp St. BL4—2G 55
Topp Way. BL1—5A 24
Top Schwabe St. M24—1E 61
Topsham Wlk. M10—6D 76
Top St. M24—6H 45
Top St. OL4—1H 65
Torah St. M8—1E 87
Tor Av. BL8—2H 13
Torax Clo. M6—5H 71
Torbay Clo. BL3—1G 37
Torbay Dri. SK2—4B 132
Torbay Rd. M21—1A 116
Torbay Rd. M31—6G 97
Torcross Rd. M9—3D 60
Tor Hey M. BL8—1H 13
Torkington Av. M27—2F 71
Torkington La. SK7 & SK6—2B 146
Torkington Rd. SK7—3E 145
Torkington Rd. SK8—6F 129
Torkington Rd. SK9—3F 159
Torkington St. SK3—3F 131
Torksey Wlk. M9—4D 60

Turner La. SK6—2F 121
Turner La. SK14—3D 106
Turner Rd. SK6—5D 134
Turners Pl. OL12—6E 7
Turner St. BL1—5C 24
Turner St. BL4—3A 54
Turner St. M4—3E 87 & 4B 162
Turner St. M7—4A 74
Turner St. M11—4E 89
Turner St. M16—1A 100 & 5A 164
Turner St. M18—2F 103
Turner St. M25—2D 58
Turner St. M34—2E 105
Turner St. OL4—1A 66
Turner St. OL6—1H 91
Turner St. OL12—2G 19
Turner St. SK1—1H 131
Turner St. SK16—5G 91
Turnfield Rd. SK8—2G 141
Turnhill Rd. OL16—2H 33
Turnough Rd. OL16—4F 21
Turnpike Grn. M6—1F 85
(off Nursery St.)
Turnpike, The. SK6—4B 134
Turnpike Wlk. M11—4B 88
Turnstone Rd. SK2—6G 133
Turton Av. BL3—3A 40
Turton Clo. BL8—5G 27
Turton Clo. OL3—3C 30
Turton Ho. BL1—5B 24
Turton Rd. BL2—5F 11
Turton Rd. BL8—1C 12
Turton St. BL1—5B 24
Turton St. M11—6F 89
Turves Rd. SK8—4A 142
Tuscan Rd. M20—3F 129
Tutbury St. M4—4H 87
                      & 6G 163
Tuxford Wlk. M10—6F 75
(off Monsall St.)
Tweedale Av. M9—4E 61
Tweedale St. OL11—5G 19
Tweed Clo. OL8—4C 64
Tweed Clo. WA14—5E 125
Tweedle Hill Rd. M9—5D 60
Tweedsdale Clo. M25—6F 43
Tweenbrook Av. M23—2G 139
Twelfth St. M17—1D 98
Twelve Yards Rd. M30—2D 94
Twentypits Clo. M16—3D 100
Twigworth Rd. M22—3A 140
Twining Brook Rd. SK8
                      —2D 142
Twining Rd. M17—5G 83
Twinnies Ct. SK9—6F 151
Twinnies Rd. SK9—6F 151
Twin St. OL10—4G 31
Twirl Hill Rd. OL6—2A 80
Twisse Rd. BL2—6H 25
Twoacre Av. M22—6A 128
Two Acre Dri. OL4—5D 34
Two Acre La. OL4—5C 50
Two Bridges Rd. OL16—2F 35
Two Brooks La. BL8—1D 12
Two Trees La. M34—5F 105
Tybyrne Clo. M28—4B 68
Tydden St. OL8—6D 64
Tydeman Wlk. OL16—6F 21
Tyersall Clo. M30—1G 83
Tyldesley Ho. M6—2F 85
(off Sutton Dwellings)
Tyldesley St. M14—4E 101
Tyler St. SK9—5G 159
Tymm St. M10—3C 76
Tyndall Av. M10—2A 76
Tyndall St. OL4—3G 65
Tyne Ct. M28—6E 55
Tynedale Clo. SK5—4H 119
Tynesbank. M28—1E 69
Tyne St. OL4—2G 65
Tynwald St. OL4—2G 65
Tynwell Wlk. M10—6E 75
Tyrol Wlk. M11—5B 88
Tyrone Clo. M23—3D 126
Tyrone Dri. OL11—6A 18
Tyro St. OL8—6D 64
Tyrrell Rd. SK5—6H 103
Tysoe Gdns. M3—3B 86 & 3D 160
Tyson St. M8—3B 74

Tywald Mt. OL2—4C 48

Uganda St. BL3—5G 37
Ukraine Rd. M7—5F 73
Uldale Dri. M24—6G 45
Ullesthorpe. OL12—3G 19
(off Spotland Rd.)
Ulleswater Clo. BL3—4H 39
Ulleswater St. BL1—3B 24
Ullock Wlk. M24—5F 45
Ullswater Av. OL2—1B 48
Ullswater Av. OL7—1G 91
Ullswater Av. OL12—2E 19
Ullswater Dri. BL4—2A 54
Ullswater Dri. BL9—6C 28
Ullswater Dri. M24—4H 45
Ullswater Gro. OL10—5F 31
Ullswater Rd. M31—3A 96
Ullswater Rd. SK1—4B 132
Ullswater Rd. SK9—3G 151
Ullswater Ter. SK15—1E 93
Ullswater Wlk. M9—6G 61
(off Rockmead Dri.)
Ulster Av. OL11—6G 19
Ulundi St. M26—4G 41
Ulverston. OL11—1E 33
Ulverston Av. M20—2D 116
Ulverston Av. OL9—3G 63
Umehurst Av. M20—1D 116
Una Rd. OL5—6G 67
Uncouth Rd. OL16—4E 21
Underhill. SK6—1H 133
Underhill Wlk. M10—1D 88
Under La. OL9—6H 63
Under St. OL9—6H 63
Underwood. OL12—4G 19
Underwood Clo. M18—1H 103
Underwood Ct. SK14—5H 107
Underwood Rd. SK9—5H 159
Underwood Rd. SK14—5G 107
Underwood St. SK16—5H 91
Underwood Wlk. SK14—5H 107
Underwood Way. OL2—5H 35
Undsworth Ct. OL10—3F 31
Unicorn St. M26—4E 41
Unicorn St. M30—5D 82
Union Arc. BL9—3D 28
Union Pl. BL9—3D 28
Union Rd. BL2—3C 24
Union Rd. OL6—1A 92
Union Rd. OL12—5C 8
Union Rd. SK6—5D 134
Union St. BL9—3E 5
Union St. BL1—5B 24
(in two parts)
Union St. BL7—1B 10
Union St. BL9—3D 28
Union St. M4—3E 87 & 4B 162
Union St. M6—1G 85
Union St. M12—6G 87 & 3F 167
Union St. M14—4F 101
Union St. M18—1G 103
Union St. M24—6A 46
Union St. M27—3G 71
(Pendlebury)
Union St. M27—3E 71
(Swinton)
Union St. OL1—3C 64
Union St. OL2—3B 48
Union St. OL4—3A 66
Union St. OL6—1H 91
Union St. OL9—5H 63
Union St. OL12 & OL16—3H 19
(Rochdale, in two parts)
Union St. OL12—1C 6
(Whitworth)
Union St. SK1—3H 131
Union St. SK14—5B 106
Union St. W. OL8 & OL1—3C 64
(in two parts)
Union Yd. OL4—2F 65
Unity Clo. OL10—4D 30
Unity Cres. OL10—4D 30
Unity St. OL10—4D 30
Unity Way. SK1—3H 131
University Rd. M6—2H 85
University Rd. W. M5—3H 85
Unsworth St. M26—3F 41

Unsworth Way. OL1—1C 64
Unwin Av. M18—3F 103
Upavon Ct. M8—5B 74
Upavon Rd. M22—2D 140
Upcast La. SK9—6A 158
Upland Dri. M28—3B 68
Upland Rd. OL8—5C 64
Uplands. M24—2A 62
Uplands Av. M26—5A 42
Uplands Rd. M31—1A 112
Uplands Rd. SK14—3E 123
Uplands, The. OL5—2F 81
Up. Brook St. M13—6F 87 & 4C 166
Up. Brook St. SK1—2H 131
Up. Camp St. M7—6H 73
Up. Chorlton Rd. M16—5A 100
Up. Cliff Hill. OL2—4G 35
Up. Conran St. M9—3G 75
Up. Cyrus St. M11—4C 88
Up. Dover St. M11—4C 88
Up. Downs. WA14—2E 137
Up. George St. OL12—2H 19
Up. Gloucester St. M6—2G 85
Up. Hayes Clo. OL16—3C 20
Up. Helena St. M10—3A 88
Up. Hibbert La. SK6—1D 146
Up. Kent Rd. M14—4H 101
Up. Kirby St. M4—4G 87 & 5F 163
Up. Lloyd St. M14—4E 101
Up. Mead. BL7—2D 10
Uppermill Dri. M19—6H 117
Up. Monsall St. M10—5G 75
Up. Park Rd. M7—2H 73
Up. Park Rd. M14—3G 101
Up. Passmonds Gro. OL11—3D 18
Upperstone Dri. OL16—5D 20
Up. West Gro. M13—2H 101
Up. Wharf St. M5—4A 86 & 5B 160
Up. Wilton St. M25—5G 59
Uppingham Dri. BL0—2D 4
Upton. OL11—5G 19
Upton Av. SK4—5A 118
Upton Av. SK8—5C 142
Upton Clo. M24—4A 62
Upton Dri. WA14—3G 125
Upton St. M1—4F 87 & 6C 162
Upton Wlk. OL7—4G 91
Upton Way. BL8—6H 13
Upton Way. SK9—2H 151
Upwood Wlk. M9—6G 61
Urban Av. WA15—1G 137
Urban Dri. WA15—1G 137
Urban Rd. M33—5A 114
Urban Rd. WA15—1G 137
Urmson St. OL8—6D 64
Urmston La. M32—6A 98
Urmston Pk. M31—5G 97
Urwick Rd. SK6—1H 133
Usk Clo. M25—2G 59
Utley Field View. WA15—2G 137
Uttley St. BL1—3H 23
Uttley St. OL11—1C 32
Uvedale Ho. M30—4F 83
(off Adelaide St.)
Uxbridge Av. M11—3E 89
Uxbridge St. OL6—2G 91

Vaal St. OL8—6A 64
Valance Clo. M12—1C 102
Valdene Clo. BL4—2F 55
Valdene Dri. BL4—2F 55
Valdene Dri. M28—2F 67
Vale Av. BL9—6B 28
Vale Av. M26—2C 56
Vale Av. M27—2G 71
Vale Av. M31—6A 96
Vale Av. SK14—4E 107
Vale Clo. M33—4E 115
Vale Clo. SK4—1B 130
Vale Clo. SK6—1D 134
Vale Clo. SK7—1E 145
Vale Coppice. BL9—6E 5
Vale Cotts. OL16—1E 9
Vale Ct. SK4—1B 130
Vale Ct. WA14—4D 136
Vale Cres. SK8—3B 142
Vale Dri. M25—1E 73
Vale Dri. OL9—3B 64

Vale Edge. M26—2G 41
Vale Head. SK9—5A 152
Vale La. M35—1A 90
Valencia Rd. M7—5F 73
Valentina St. M35—4E 77
Valentine St. OL4—3G 65
Valerie Wlk. M15—6D 86
(off Loxford St.)
Vale Rd. M35—2B 90
Vale Rd. OL2—1H 49
Vale Rd. SK4—2B 130
Vale Rd. SK6—2H 133
Vale Rd. SK9—1C 158
Vale Rd. SK15—5B 81
Vale Rd. WA14—4D 136
Vale Rd. WA15—5B 126
Vale Side. OL5—3E 81
Vale St. BL2—6A 26
Vale St. M11—3E 89
Vale St. M24—6A 46
Vale St. OL7—5E 79
Vale St. OL10—3G 31
(in two parts)
Vale, The. OL5—3E 81
Vale Top Av. M9—4H 75
Valetta Clo. M14—1F 117
Valewood Av. SK4—2C 130
Valiant Wlk. M10—2E 77
Valletts La. BL1—4G 23
Valley Av. BL8—6B 14
Valley Clo. OL5—1D 80
Valley Clo. SK8—2A 142
Valley Cotts. OL5—1F 81
Valley Ct. SK4—2D 130
Valley Dri. SK9—4G 151
Valleyfield. OL11—1E 33
Valley Gdns. SK14—6A 108
Valley Gro. M34—5H 105
Valley New Rd. OL2—4C 48
Valley Rise. OL2—4E 35
Valley Rd. M23—5B 46
Valley Rd. M31—3H 95
Valley Rd. OL2—4C 48
Valley Rd. OL11—1E 33
Valley Rd. SK4—2B 130
Valley Rd. SK6—5D 120
Valley Rd. SK7—4H 143
Valley Rd. SK8—1A 142
Valley Rd. SK14—6A 108
Valley Rd. S. M31—5G 95
Valley View. BL7—4E 11
Valley View. OL12—1H 7
Valley View. SK14—3E 107
Valley Way. SK15—4G 93
Valpy Av. BL2—2D 24
Vancouver Quay. M5—6F 85
Vandyke Av. M6—1B 84
Vandyke St. OL12—2B 18
Vane St. M30—3F 83
(in two parts)
Vanguard Clo. M30—6B 82
Vantomme St. BL1—1A 24
Vant St. OL8—5G 65
Varden Gro. SK3—6F 131
Varden Rd. SK12—4E 155
Vardon Dri. SK9—3G 159
Varey St. M18—2F 103
Varley Rd. BL3—3E 37
Varley St. M10—1H 87 & 1H 163
Varna St. M11—6F 89
Vauban Dri. M6—2B 84
Vaudrey Dri. SK7—3E 145
Vaudrey Dri. SK8—2C 142
Vaudrey Dri. WA15—3A 126
Vaudrey La. M34—5G 105
Vaudrey Rd. SK6—4G 121
Vaughan Av. M10—3A 76
Vaughan Gro. OL4—3B 66
Vaughan Rd. M21—1B 116
Vaughan Rd. SK4—6F 119
Vaughan St. M12—6B 88
Vaughan St. M30—2D 82
Vaughan St. OL2—4C 48
Vauxhall St. M10—1F 87
Vavasour Ct. OL16—5B 20
Vavasour St. OL16—5B 20
(in two parts)

Wade Wlk. M11—5C 88
Wadham Gdns. SK6—6A 122
Wadham Way. WA15—4H 137
Wadhurst Wlk. M13—2G 101
Wadsley St. BL1—5A 24
Wagg Fold. OL15—3D 8
Waggon Rd. BL2—2F 25
Waggon Rd. OL5—3E 81
Wagner St. BL1—2H 23
Wagstaff Dri. M35—4F 77
Wagstaffe St. M24—6A 46
Wagstaff St. SK15—4C 92
Waincliffe Av. M21—5B 116
Wain Clo. M30—3D 82
Waingap Cres. OL12—1D 6
Waingap Rise. OL12—5E 7
Wainman St. M6—6F 73
Wain Stones Grn. SK2—6E 133
Wainwright Clo. OL4—2C 66
Wainwright Rd. WA14—6D 124
Wainwright St. OL8—4C 64
Wainwright St. SK16—4B 92
Waithlands Rd. OL16—5B 20
Wakefield Cres. SK6—2G 133
Wakefield Dri. M27—4D 56
Wakefield Dri. OL1—6A 48
Wakefield Rd. SK15—3E 93
Wakefield St. M1—5E 87 & 2A 162
Wakefield St. OL1—6A 48
Wakefield Wlk. M34—6G 105
Wakeling Rd. M34—1E 121
Walcott Clo. M13—2A 102
Wald Av. M14—2A 118
Waldeck St. BL1—5G 23
Waldeck Wlk. M9—6G 61
(off Ravenswood Dri.)
Walden Av. OL4—5H 49
Walden Clo. M14—1E 117
Walden Cres. SK7—2C 144
Walden Flats. OL10—3E 31
(off Fox St.)
Walderton Av. M10—4A 76
Waldon Av. SK8—6H 129
Waldon Clo. BL3—3G 37
Waldorf Sq. M12—1A 102
Wales St. OL1—6G 49
Walford Clo. M16—3C 100
Walkdene Dri. M28—6D 54
Walkden Rd. M28—1F 69
Walkden St. OL12—2H 19
Walker Av. BL3—4B 38
Walker Av. M25—3E 59
Walker Av. M35—5H 77
Walker Av. SK15—3G 93
Walker Clo. BL4—3A 56
Walker Clo. SK14—5D 106
Walker Fold Rd. BL1—2A 22
Walker Grn. M30—6B 70
Walker Ho. M30—4F 83
Walker La. SK14—5C 106
Walker Rd. M9—5G 61
Walker Rd. M30—1C 82
(Eccles)
Walker Rd. M30—6D 94
(Irlam)
Walker Rd. OL9—1F 77
Walkers Bldgs. M1—4F 87 & 5D 162
Walkers Clo. OL3—1F 53
Walkers Ct. BL4—1F 55
Walkers Ct. OL4—3C 66
Walker's Croft. M3—3D 86 & 3H 161
Walker's La. OL4—3C 66
Walker's Rd. OL8—1A 78
Walker St. BL1—1H 37
Walker St. BL9—5C 28
Walker St. M3—2A 86 & 2B 160
Walker St. M9—3G 75
Walker St. M24—2D 60
(in two parts)
Walker St. M26—6A 42
Walker St. M34—3E 105
Walker St. OL8—3B 64
Walker St. OL10—4E 31
Walker St. OL16—4A 20
Walker St. SK14—2H 109
Walkers View. OL4—2C 66
Walkerwood Dri. SK15—2H 93
Walk Mill Clo. OL12—5B 8

Walk St. SK1—2G 131
Walk, The. OL16—4H 19
Walkway, The. BL3—2D 36
(in two parts)
Wallace Av. M14—4H 101
Wallace St. OL8—5D 64
Wallacre Clo. M15—1C 100 & 5E 165
Wallasey Av. M14—6E 101
Wallbank Dri. OL12—2B 6
Wallbank Rd. SK7—4A 144
Wallbank St. BL8—4H 13
Wallbrook Cres. M28—3C 54
Wallbrook Gro. BL4—5D 38
Waller Av. M14—1G 117
Walley St. BL1—2A 24
Wall Hill Rd. OL3—6G 51
Wallingford Rd. M31—4G 97
Wallingford Rd. SK9—2G 151
Wallis St. M10—6C 76
Wallis St. OL9—5G 63
Wallness La. M6—1H 85 & 1A 160
Wallshaw Pl. OL1—2E 65
Wallshaw St. OL1—2E 65
(in two parts)
Wall St. M6—3F 85
Wall St. OL8—4D 64
Wallwork Clo. OL11—2A 18
Wallwork St. M11—5G 89
Wallwork St. M26—3G 41
Wallwork St. SK5—5H 103
Wallworth Av. M18—2F 103
Wallworth Ter. SK9—1B 158
Wally Sq. M7—5A 74
Walmer Dri. SK7—4H 143
Walmersley Ct. SK6—5D 134
Walmersley Old Rd. BL9—3F 15
Walmersley Rd. BL9—1E 15
Walmersley Rd. M10—1E 77
Walmer St. M14—4F 101
Walmer St. M18—1G 103
Walmer St. E. M14—4G 101
Walmley Gro. BL3—4G 37
Walmsley Av. OL15—6D 8
Walmsley Gro. M31—5F 97
Walmsley St. BL8—1H 27
Walmsley St. SK5—6H 119
Walmsley St. SK15—5E 93
Walney Rd. M22—1B 140
Walnut Av. BL9—2F 29
Walnut Av. OL4—1H 65
Walnut Clo. M27—5D 56
Walnut Rd. M30—1C 82
Walnut Rd. M31—6B 110
Walnut St. BL1—2B 24
Walnut St. M18—1F 103
Walnut Tree Rd. SK3—3C 130
Walnut Wlk. M32—1C 114
Walpole St. OL16—4A 20
Walsall St. M6—6E 73
Walsden St. M11—3E 89
Walsh Av. M9—1E 75
Walshaw Brook Clo. BL8—1F 27
Walshaw La. BL8—1F 27
Walshaw Rd. BL8—1F 27
Walshaw Wlk. BL8—6H 13
Walshaw Way. BL8—6H 13
Walshe St. BL9—3B 28
Walsh St. OL9—3H 63
Walsingham Av. M20—5D 116
Walter Greenwood Ct. M6—2G 85
(off Meyrick St.)
Walter La. BL9—6E 43
Walter Scott St. OL1—1F 65
Walter St. BL4—5D 38
Walter St. M16—3A 100
Walter St. M18—1G 103
Walter St. M25—5D 58
Walter St. M26—6F 27
Walter St. M28—1F 69
Walter St. OL1—3D 64
Waltham Dri. SK8—1D 152
Waltham Gdns. M26—3E 41
Waltham Rd. M16—6C 100
Waltham St. OL4—5G 65
Walton Clo. M24—6E 45
Walton Clo. OL10—5F 31
(in two parts)
Walton Ct. BL3—3B 38
Walton Dri. BL9—3E 15

Walton Dri. SK6—4B 134
Walton Ho. M4—4H 87
(off Harrison St.)
Walton Ho. M35—3F 77
Walton Pl. BL4—2G 55
Walton Rd. M9—4F 61
Walton Rd. M33—2H 125
Walton Rd. WA14—6D 124
Walton St. M24—5A 46
Walton St. OL7—6E 79
Walton St. SK1—4H 131
Walton Way. M34—6H 105
Walworth St. BL3—3G 37
Walwyn Clo. M32—6E 99
Wandsworth Av. M11—3F 89
Wanley Wlk. M9—6G 61
Wansbeck Clo. M32—6E 99
Wansfell Wlk. M4—3H 87 & 4H 163
Wansford St. M14—4E 101
Wanstead Av. M9—6B 62
Wapping St. BL1—3H 23
Warbeck Clo. SK5—5A 104
Warbeck Rd. M10—1D 76
Warbreck Gro. M33—6D 114
Warburton Clo. SK6—2F 133
Warburton Clo. WA15—1D 148
Warburton Dri. WA15—1D 148
Warburton La. M31—6C 110
Warburton Rd. SK9—3H 151
Warburton St. BL1—3B 24
Warburton St. M5—1H 99
Warburton St. M8—5C 74
Warburton St. M20—6F 117
Warburton St. M30—4G 83
Warcock Rd. OL4—2G 65
Wardale Ct. M33—5C 114
Ward Ct. OL3—3C 52
(off Ward La.)
Wardend Clo. M28—3C 54
Warden La. M10—5B 76
Warden St. M10—5B 76
Ward La. OL3—3C 52
Wardle Brook Av. SK14—4G 107
Wardle Brook Wlk. SK14—4H 107
Wardle Clo. M26—2E 41
Wardle Clo. M32—5E 99
Wardle Edge. OL12—6H 7
Wardle Fold. OL12—2A 8
Wardle Rd. M33—6B 114
Wardle Rd. OL12—6A 8
Wardle St. BL2—2D 38
Wardle St. M10—2H 87
Wardle St. OL4—3F 65
Wardle St. OL15—3E 9
Wardley Av. M16—6C 100
Wardley Av. M28—6D 54
Wardley Hall La. M28—3A 70
(in two parts)
Wardley Hall Rd. M28 & M27—2B 70
Wardley Ind. Est. M28—2B 70
Wardley St. M27—3F 71
Wardlow Av. SK13—6F 109
(off Wardlow M.)
Wardlow Fold. SK13—6F 109
(off Wardlow M.)
Wardlow Gdns. SK13—6F 109
(off Wardlow M.)
Wardlow Gro. SK13—6F 109
(off Wardlow M.)
Wardlow M. SK13—6F 109
Wardlow St. BL3—3F 37
Wardlow Wlk. SK13—6F 109
(off Wardlow M.)
Ward Rd. M35—4B 90
Wardsend Wlk. M15—1B 100 & 5D 164
Ward St. M3—2D 86 & 1G 161
Ward St. M9—1E 75
Ward St. M10—3H 75
Ward St. M20—6F 117
Ward St. M35—3E 77
Ward St. OL1—1B 64
Ward St. OL4—2E 64
Ward St. SK1—4A 132
Ward St. SK6—6F 121
Ward St. SK14—5C 106
Wareham Gro. M30—2E 83
Wareham St. M8—2D 74
Wareham St. SK9—2E 159

Wareing Way. BL3—1A 38
Warfield Wlk. M9—6G 61
Warford Av. SK12—5G 155
Warford St. M4—1F 87 & 1C 162
Warhurst Fold. SK14—2H 109
Warke, The. M28—5H 69
Warley Clo. SK3 5A 130
Warley Gro. SK16—5A 92
Warley Rd. M16—4G 99
Warley St. OL15—3F 9
Warlingham Clo. BL8—4H 27
Warlow Crest. OL3—5E 53
Warlow Dri. OL3—5E 53
(in two parts)
Warmbley Gdns. OL8—2B 78
Warmley Rd. M23—3D 126
Warmton View. OL5—6G 67
Warne Av. M35—3C 90
Warner Wlk. M11—4B 88
(off Hopedale Clo.)
Warnford Clo. M10—1F 89
War Office Rd. OL11—5A 18
Warp Wlk. M4—4G 87
(off Cardroom Rd.)
Warren Av. SK8—6H 129
Warren Bank. M9—6F 61
Warren Clo. M34—5D 104
Warren Clo. SK7—3F 143
Warren Clo. SK12—3B 154
(off Distaff Rd.)
Warren Clo. SK12—2E 155
(off Warren Lea)
Warren Dri. M27—6D 70
Warren Dri. M25—6D 138
Warrener St. M33—5G 114
Warren Hey. SK9—1H 159
Warren La. OL8—5F 65
Warren Lea. SK6—1F 135
Warren Rd. M17—1B 98
Warren Rd. M28—6G 55
Warren Rd. SK3—5G 131
Warren Rd. SK8—3D 142
Warren St. BL8—4H 27
Warren St. M8—3B 74
Warren St. M9—1E 75
Warren St. SK1—1H 131
Warre St. OL6—2H 91
Warrington Rd. M9—5E 61
Warrington St. OL4—4A 66
Warrington St. OL6—2H 91
Warrington St. SK15—4F 93
Warsall Rd. M22—5C 128
Warslow Dri. M33—2E 127
Warsop Av. M22—6C 128
Warstead Wlk. M13—2G 101
(off Plymouth Gro.)
Warth Cotts. OL3—3C 52
(off Huddersfield Rd.)
Warth Fold Rd. M26—1A 42
Warth Rd. BL9—6B 28
Warton Clo. BL8—4F 27
Warton Clo. SK7—6A 144
Warton Dri. M23—6G 127
Warwick Av. M20—5D 116
Warwick Av. M25—2F 59
Warwick Av. M27—1D 70
Warwick Av. M34—6F 105
Warwick Clo. BL8—1H 27
(Bury)
Warwick Clo. BL8—2A 14
(Greenmount)
Warwick Clo. M24—3A 62
Warwick Clo. M25—2E 59
Warwick Clo. OL2—6D 34
Warwick Clo. SK4—5F 119
Warwick Clo. SK8—1C 142
Warwick Ct. M16—4G 99
Warwick Dri. M31—3D 96
Warwick Dri. M33—5D 114
Warwick Dri. SK7—4D 144
Warwick Dri. WA15—4G 137
Warwick Gdns. BL3—5F 37
Warwick Gro. M34—5C 90
Warwick Ho. M19—5C 102
Warwick Ho. M33—5D 114
Warwick Mall. SK8—5H 129
Warwick Pl. M17—2F 99
Warwick Pl. M17—2F 99

Warwick Rd. M21—6H 99
Warwick Rd. M24—3B 62
Warwick Rd. M26—1F 41
Warwick Rd. M28—2E 69
Warwick Rd. M30—4B 110
Warwick Rd. M35—6F 77
Warwick Rd. OL6—6G 79
Warwick Rd. SK4—6E 119
Warwick Rd. SK6—1G 133
Warwick Rd. WA15—4G 137
Warwick Rd. N. M16—2F 99
Warwick Rd. N. M16—4G 99
Warwick St. BL1—1A 24
Warwick St. M1—3F 87 & 4C 162
Warwick St. M3—2D 100 & 6G 165
Warwick St. M25—5E 59
(in two parts)
Warwick St. M27—2F 71
Warwick St. OL9—5A 64
(in two parts)
Warwick St. OL12—1B 20
Warwick Ter. SK16—4H 91
(off Astley St.)
Wasdale Av. BL2—4H 25
Wasdale Av. M31—4D 96
Wasdale Dri. M24—5G 45
Wasdale St. SK8—2F 141
Wasdale Ter. SK15—1E 93
Wasdale Wlk. OL1—1E 65
Wash Brook. OL9—5H 63
Washbrook Av. M28—2D 68
Washbrook Ct. OL9—5H 63
Washbrook Dri. M32—5B 98
Washbrook Ho. M6—2F 85
(off Sutton Dwellings)
Wash Brow. BL8—6B 14
Wash Fold. BL8—6B 14
Washford Dri. M23—3D 126
Washington Ct. BL9—2D 28
Washington St. BL3—1G 37
Washington St. OL9—2A 64
Wash La. BL9—2E 29
Wash Ter. BL8—6B 14
Washway Rd. M33—2G 125
Washwood Clo. M28—3D 54
Wasnidge Wlk. M15—2D 100
Wasp Av. OL11—2G 33
Wastdale Av. BL9—4E 43
Wastdale Rd. M23—1F 139
Wast Water St. OL1—6E 49
Watch Hall St. OL16—1C 20
Waterbridge. M28—6H 69
Watercroft. OL11—2H 17
Waterdale Clo. M28—5D 68
Waterfield Clo. BL9—4F 15
Waterfoot Cotts. SK14—3C 108
Waterford Av. M20—6B 116
Waterford Av. SK6—1C 134
Waterford Dri. BL9—5E 29
Waterfront Quay. M5—6F 85
Watergate. M34—5C 90
(in two parts)
Water Ga. OL3—1F 53
Water Ga. La. BL3—6G 37
Watergate Milne Ct. OL4—1H 65
Watergrove Rd. SK16—6D 92
Waterhead. OL4—1A 66
Waterhouse Clo. OL12—4A 8
Waterhouse Rd. M18—3G 103
Waterhouse St. OL12—3H 19
Water La. BL0—3A 4
Water La. BL4—2G 55
Water La. M26—3F 41
Water La. M35—4G 89
(in two parts)
Water La. OL16—6G 21
Water La. SK9—2D 158
Water La. SK14—2F 109
Water La. S. M26—4F 41
(in two parts)
Waterloo Ct. BL9—5C 28
Waterloo La. BL9—4G 29
Waterloo Pde. M10—1D 86
Waterloo Pk. SK1—2A 132
Waterloo Pl. SK1—2H 131
(off Watson Sq.)
Waterloo Rd. M8—1D 86
Waterloo Rd. OL6—6F 79

Waterloo Rd. SK1—2H 131
Waterloo Rd. SK6—1C 134
Waterloo Rd. SK7—4H 143
Waterloo Rd. SK12—5G 155
Waterloo Rd. SK15—3E 93
Waterloo St. BL1—4B 24
Waterloo St. BL8—3B 28
Waterloo St. M1—5E 87 & 1A 166
Waterloo St. M8 & M9—3E 75
Waterloo St. M34—3B 104
Waterloo St. OL1 & OL4—2D 64
Waterloo St. OL6—6H 79
Watermead Clo. SK3—1G 143
Watermeetings La. SK6—1C 134
Watermill Clo. OL16—5D 20
Watermill Ct. OL7—6E 79
Watermillock Gdns. BL1—1B 24
Waterpark Rd. M7—3A 74
Water Rd. SK15—3D 92
Waters Edge. BL4—5C 38
Watersedge. M28—1H 69
Watersedge Clo. SK8—2D 142
Watersfield Clo. SK8—5B 142
Watersheddings St. OL4—6H 49
Waterside. BL3—2E 39
Waterside. SK6—1D 146
Waterside. SK14—1H 109
(Hadfield)
Waterside. SK14—5H 107
(Hyde)
Waterside Av. SK6—6D 134
Waterside Clo. M21—5B 116
Waterside Clo. M26—3B 42
Waterside Clo. SK14—5H 107
Waterside Ct. M31—5H 95
Waterside Dri. SK4—2B 130
Waterside La. OL16—3B 20
Waterside Rd. BL9—1B 14
Waterside Wlk. SK14—5G 107
Watersmead Clo. BL1—3B 24
Waterson Av. M10—4A 76
Waters Reach. SK6—6C 146
Waters Reach. SK12—2F 155
Water St. BL0—4O 4
Water St. BL1—6B 24
Water St. BL7—1B 10
Water St. M3—5B 86 & 2C 164
(Manchester)
Water St. M3—3D 86 & 4G 161
(Salford)
Water St. M9—3F 75
Water St. M24—6H 45
(in two parts)
Water St. M26—4F 41
Water St. M34—6F 91
(Audenshaw)
Water St. M34—3C 104
(Denton)
Water St. OL1—2C 64
Water St. OL2—3E 49
Water St. OL6—2H 91
Water St. OL12—1C 6
Water St. OL16—5F 21
(Milnrow)
Water St. OL16—4H 19
(Rochdale)
Water St. SK1—1H 131
Water St. SK14—4B 106
Water St. SK15—3E 93
(in two parts)
Waterton Av. OL5—1D 80
Waterton La. OL5—1D 80
Waterway Enterprise Pk. M17—1F 99
Waterworks Rd. OL4—6A 50
Watfield Wlk. M9—4F 75
(off Foleshill Av.)
Watford Av. M14—5F 101
Watford Clo. BL1—3A 24
(off Sham Av.)
Watford Rd. M19—3C 118
Watkin Clo. M13—1G 101 & 6E 167
Watkins Dri. M25—6A 60
Watkin St. M3—2B 86 & 1D 160
Watkin St. OL16—1G 33
Watkin St. SK14—2E 107
Watling St. BL8—1B 12
(Affetside)
Watling St. BL8—4F 27
(Bury)

Watson Gdns. OL12—1F 19
Watson Rd. BL4—1B 54
Watson Sq. SK1—2H 131
Watson St. M3 & M2—5D 86 & 2G 165
Watson St. M26—3G 41
Watson St. M27—2F 71
Watson St. M30—3E 83
Watson St. M34—4H 105
Watson St. OL1—1G 65
Watts St. M19—1D 118
Watts St. OL8—1B 78
Watts St. OL9—2H 63
Watts St. OL12—3A 20
Waudrey Clo. SK15—4E 93
Waugh Av. M35—5F 77
Wavell Dri. BL9—6E 43
Wavell Rd. M22—2B 140
Waveney Flats. OL10—3E 31
(off Fox St.)
Waveney Rd. M22—1C 140
Waveney Rd. OL2—5E 35
Waverley Av. BL4—3H 55
Waverley Av. M32—4E 99
Waverley Ct. M9—4C 60
Waverley Cres. M35—2A 90
Waverley Dri. SK8—1D 152
Waverley Pl. M26—4G 41
Waverley Rd. BL1—2A 24
Waverley Rd. M9—4H 75
Waverley Rd. M24—4A 46
Waverley Rd. M28—2D 68
Waverley Rd. M33—3C 114
Waverley Rd. SK3—4E 131
Waverley Rd. SK14—1B 122
Waverley Rd. W. M9—4H 75
Waverley Sq. BL4—3E 55
Waverley St. OL1—1F 65
Waverley St. OL11—4C 32
Waverton Av. SK4—2F 119
Waverton Rd. M14—6E 101
Wavertree Ho. BL1—5A 24
(off Prince St.)
Wavertree Rd. M9—5E 61
Wayford Wlk. M9—4E 75
(off Hendham Vale)
Wayland Rd. M18—3F 103
Wayland Rd. S. M18—4F 103
Wayne Clo. M35—1C 90
Wayne St. M11—5G 89
Wayside Dri. SK12—3C 154
Wayside Gro. M28—5G 55
Wayverley. OL12—3G 19
(off Spotland Rd.)
Weald Clo. M13—1G 101 & 5E 167
Wealdstone Gro. BL2—3D 24
Weardale Rd. M9—4D 60
Wearhead Row. M5—4F 85
Weaste Av. M28—5D 54
Weaste Dri. M5—2D 84
Weaste La. M6 & M5—2C 84
(in three parts)
Weaste Rd. M5—3D 84
Weaste Trading Est. M5—3D 84
Weatherall St. N. M8—4B 74
(in two parts)
Weatherley Dri. SK6—5B 134
Weaver Av. M28—1C 68
Weaver Ct. M15—1B 100 & 6C 164
Weaver Dri. BL9—3F 15
Weaverham Clo. M13—4B 102
Weaverham Wlk. M33—6E 115
Weaverham Way. SK9—3A 152
Weavers Ct. M24—6H 45
Weavers Grn. BL4—1F 55
Weavers Rd. M24—6H 45
Weaver Wlk. M11—6F 89
Webb Gro. SK14—6A 108
Webb La. SK1 & SK6—2A 132
Webb St. BL8—2B 28
Webdale Dri. M10—4A 76
Weber Dri. BL3—2H 37
Webster Arc. OL1—2D 64
Webster Gro. M25—1D 72
Webster St. BL3—2D 38
Webster St. M15—2E 101
Webster St. OL5—1E 81
Webster St. OL8—4D 64
Webster St. OL12—2G 19

Wedgewood Rd. M27—1A 72
Wedgewood St. M10—1B 88
Wedhurst St. OL4—2G 65
Wedneshough. SK14—2E 109
Weedall Av. M5—1G 99
Weedon St. OL16—3B 20
Weeton Av. BL2—6H 25
Weft Wlk. M4—4G 87 & 5F 163
Weir Rd. OL16—4E 21
Weir St. M35—4E 77
Weir St. OL16—4H 19
Welbeck Av. M31—4G 97
Welbeck Av. OL9—6D 62
Welbeck Av. OL15—2E 9
Welbeck Clo. M25—5D 42
Welbeck Clo. OL16—5E 21
Welbeck Gro. M7—4A 74
Welbeck Ho. OL6—3G 91
Welbeck Rd. BL1—5E 23
Welbeck Rd. M28—5B 70
Welbeck Rd. M30—1G 83
Welbeck Rd. OL16—1H 33
Welbeck Rd. SK5—6H 103
Welbeck Rd. SK14—5D 106
Welbeck St. M18—1F 103
Welbeck St. N. OL6—3G 91
Welbeck St. S. OL6 & OL7—3G 91
(in two parts)
Welbeck Ter. OL6—3G 91
Welburn Av. M22—2C 140
Welburn St. OL11—6H 19
Welbury Rd. M23—2F 127
Welby St. M13—3H 101
Welch Rd. SK14—3D 106
Welcomb Clo. SK6—5F 121
Welcomb St. M11—6D 88
Welcomb Wlk. M25—2D 58
Welcome Pde. OL8—6G 65
Welcroft St. SK1—3H 131
Weldon Av. BL3—5E 37
Weldon Cres. SK3—1G 143
Weldon Dri. M9—4F 61
Weldon Rd. WA14—5E 125
Weld Rd. M20—2H 117
Welfold Ho. OL4—4F 65
Welford Clo. SK9—1H 159
Welford Rd. M6—1H 85
Welford Rd. M8—5B 60
Welkin Rd. SK5—6C 120
Wellacre Av. M31—5H 95
Welland Av. OL10—2C 30
Welland Clo. M15—1B 100 & 6C 164
Welland Rd. OL2—5E 35
Welland St. M11—5F 89
Welland St. SK5—6H 103
Wellbank. SK15—5G 93
Wellbank Av. OL6—5A 80
Wellbank St. BL8—5H 13
Wellbank View. OL12—2B 18
Wellbridge Rd. SK16—1H 105
Well Brow Ter. OL12—1F 19
Wellbrow Wlk. M9—6G 61
Wellcroft. SK8—6E 129
Wellens Way. M24—2E 61
Weller Av. M21—2B 116
Weller Av. SK12—5D 154
Weller Clo. SK12—5D 154
Weller Gdns. M21—2B 116
Wellesbourne Dri. M23—4F 127
Wellesley Av. M18—1F 103
Wellfield. SK6—5A 122
Wellfield Clo. BL9—1C 42
Wellfield Gdns. WA15—2C 138
Wellfield La. WA15—1C 138
Wellfield Pl. OL11—6A 20
Wellfield Rd. BL3—2G 37
Wellfield Rd. M8—3C 74
Wellfield Rd. M23—4G 127
Wellfield Rd. SK2—5C 132
Wellfield St. OL11—6A 20
Wellgate Av. M19—1D 118
Wellgreen Clo. WA15—2C 138
Well Gro. M25—4C 42
Wellhead Clo. M15—2E 101
Wellhouse Dri. M10—6C 62
Well-i-Hole Rd. OL5—5G 67
Welling Rd. M10—3E 77
Welling St. BL2—4D 24
Wellington Av. M16—5B 100

Wellington Bldgs. OL1—3D 64
Wellington Clo. M33—3C 114
Wellington Clough. OL7—5E 79
Wellington Ct. BL8—4H 27
Wellington Ct. OL8—5B 64
Wellington Cres. M16—4A 100
Wellington Gdns. BL8—3H 27
Wellington Gro. M15—1B 100 & 6D 164
Wellington Gro. SK2—4H 131
Wellington Ho. BL8—4H 27
(off Haig Rd.)
Wellington Lodge. OL15—3F 9
(off Lodge St.)
Wellington Pde. SK16—4H 91
(off Astley St.)
Wellington Pl. M3—5C 86 & 1E 165
Wellington Pl. OL16—3A 20
Wellington Pl. WA14—1F 137
Wellington Rd. BL9—5C 28
Wellington Rd. M8—3D 74
Wellington Rd. M16—5C 100
Wellington Rd. M20 & M14—2G 117
Wellington Rd. M27—3F 71
Wellington Rd. M30—3G 83
Wellington Rd. OL3—3E 53
Wellington Rd. OL6—2G 91
Wellington Rd. OL8—5A 64
(in two parts)
Wellington Rd. SK7—5H 145
Wellington Rd. WA15—5G 125
Wellington Rd. N. SK4—2D 118
Wellington Rd. S. SK4, SK1 & SK2
—2G 131
Wellington Sq. BL8—4H 27
Wellington St. BL3—1H 37
Wellington St. BL4—1F 55
Wellington St. BL8—4A 28
Wellington St. M3—3B 86 & 3D 160
Wellington St. M18—2F 103
Wellington St. M26—3A 42
(in two parts)
Wellington St. M32—6C 98
Wellington St. M34—1F 105
Wellington St. M35—2G 77
Wellington St. OL4 & OL1—3D 64
Wellington St. OL6—3H 91
Wellington St. OL9—1H 63
Wellington St. OL12—2H 19
Wellington St. OL15—4F 9
Wellington St. OL16—5G 21
Wellington St. SK1—2G 131
Wellington St. SK7—2F 145
Wellington St. SK14—4A 106
Wellington St. E. M7—4H 73
Wellington St. W. M7—5H 73
Wellington Ter. M5—3D 84
Wellington Ter. SK16—4H 91
(off Astley St.)
Wellington Wlk. BL3—1H 37
Wellington Wlk. BL8—4H 27
Well i' th' La. OL11—6A 20
Well La. M25—5D 42
Well Mead. SK6—6E 121
Wellmead Clo. M8—6B 74
Well Meadow. SK14—3B 106
Well Meadow La. OL3—1G 53
Wellock St. M10—5H 75
Wellpark Wlk. M10—6C 76
Well Row. SK14—2F 107
Wells Av. M25—1G 73
Wells Av. OL6—6G 47
Wells Clo. M24—1E 61
Wells Clo. M35—5H 89
Wells Clo. SK8—6G 141
Wells Dri. SK4—1H 129
Wells Dri. SK16—1A 106
Wellside Wlk. M8—5C 74
Wellsprings. BL1—6B 24
(off Victoria Sq.)
Wells Rd. OL1—3A 50
Wells St. BL9—4C 28
Well St. BL1—6C 24
Well St. BL2—4C 26
Well St. M4—3E 87 & 4A 162
Well St. OL10—4G 31
Well St. OL11—6A 20
Well St. N. BL0—3A 4
Well St. W. BL0—4D 4
Wellwood Dri. M10—4A 76

Wellyhole St. OL4—3H 65
Welney Rd. M16—4H 99
Welsby Sq. BL4—3B 56
Welshpool Clo. M23—1H 127
Welshpool Way. M34—6G 105
Welton Av. M20—1G 129
Welton Clo. SK9—5C 158
Welton Dri. SK9—5B 158
Welton Gro. SK9—5B 158
Welwyn Clo. M31—2D 96
Welwyn Dri. M6—6G 71
Welwyn Wlk. M10—3H 87 & 3H 163
Wembley Gro. M14—1G 117
Wembley Rd. M18—4E 103
Wembury St. M9—3G 75
Wembury St. N. M9—3G 75
Wemsley Gro. BL2—4D 24
Wem St. OL9—5G 63
Wemyss Av. SK5—6H 103
Wenderholme Lodge. BL1—5C 22
Wendlebury Grn. OL2—2E 49
Wendon Rd. M23—6H 127
Wendover Dri. BL3—2C 36
Wendover Ho. M5—4G 85
Wendover Rd. M23—2D 126
Wendover Rd. M31—5E 97
Wenfield Dri. M9—6B 62
Wenlock Av. OL6—6F 79
Wenlock Clo. SK2—5F 133
Wenlock Rd. M33—1A 126
Wenlock St. M27—3D 70
Wenlock Way. M12—1B 102
Wenning Clo. M25—6G 43
Wensley Ct. M7—2E 73
Wensleydale Av. SK8—5G 129
Wensleydale Clo. BL9—4E 43
Wensleydale Clo. OL2—2A 48
Wensley Dri. M20—4F 117
Wensley Dri. SK7—5D 144
Wensley Rd. M7—3E 73
Wensley Rd. SK5—5H 119
Wensley Rd. SK8—5G 129
Wensley Way. OL16—5B 20
Wentbridge Rd. BL1—5H 23
Wentworth Av. BL4—2E 55
Wentworth Av. BL8—1H 27
Wentworth Av. M6—2C 84
Wentworth Av. M18—1G 103
Wentworth Av. M25—2B 58
Wentworth Av. M30—4E 95
Wentworth Av. M31—6D 96
Wentworth Av. OL10—5F 31
Wentworth Av. WA15—5A 126
Wentworth Clo. M24—6G 45
Wentworth Clo. M26—3D 40
Wentworth Clo. SK6—3D 134
Wentworth Dri. M33—4H 113
Wentworth Dri. SK7—4A 144
Wentworth Rd. M27—4D 70
Wentworth Rd. M30—1H 83
Wentworth Rd. SK5—6H 103
Wentworth View. SK14—2D 106
Werneth Av. M14—5F 101
Werneth Av. SK14—1D 122
Werneth Clo. M34—5F 105
Werneth Ct. SK7—1E 145
Werneth Ct. SK14—6C 106
Werneth Cres. OL8—5A 64
Werneth Hall Rd. OL8—4B 64
Werneth Hollow. SK6—3H 121
Werneth Low Rd. SK6 & SK14—5B 122
Werneth Rise. SK14—2D 122
Werneth Rd. SK6—4A 122
Werneth Rd. SK14—5D 106
Werneth St. M34—2F 105
Werneth St. SK1—1B 132
Werneth View. SK7—5A 146
Werneth Wlk. M34—5F 105
Wesley Clo. OL12—6H 7
Wesley Ct. BL8—4G 13
Wesley Ct. M28—5E 55
Wesley Ct. SK4—1B 130
Wesley Dri. M28—3H 69
Wesley Dri. OL6—5H 79
Wesley Grn. M5—5H 85
Wesley M. BL2—6C 24
Wesley Mt. SK4—1G 131
(off Dodge Hill)

Wesley Sq. M31—5C 96
Wesley St. BL3—2A 38
Wesley St. BL4—2G 55
Wesley St. BL7—3E 11
Wesley St. BL8—4G 13
Wesley St. M11—5C 88
Wesley St. M27—3E 71
Wesley St. M30—3E 83
Wesley St. M32—3E 99
Wesley St. M35—2G 77
(in two parts)
Wesley St. OL2—4C 48
Wesley St. OL10—3E 31
Wesley St. OL16—5E 21
Wesley St. SK1—2H 131
Wesley St. SK7—2E 145
Wesley St. SK14—2H 109
Wessenden Bank E. SK2—6D 132
Wessenden Bank W. SK2—6D 132
Wessex Pk. Clo. OL2—5E 35
Wessington Bank. SK13—5G 109
(off Wessington M.)
Wessington Fold. SK13—5G 109
(off Langsett La.)
Wessington Grn. SK13—5G 109
(off Wessington M.)
Wessington M. SK13—5G 109
W. Ashton St. M5—4F 85
West Av. BL4—1D 54
West Av. M10—3D 76
West Av. M18—2G 103
West Av. M19—2B 118
West Av. M25—5C 42
West Av. M28—6E 55
West Av. OL12—6A 8
West Av. SK8—4G 141
West Av. SK15—3E 93
West Av. WA14—6C 124
West Bank. M11—6A 90
West Bank. OL3—4H 67
West Bank. SK9—6H 159
Westbank Rd. BL6—1B 36
Westbank Rd. M20—4H 117
W. Bank St. M5—5A 86 & 1A 164
Westbourne Av. BL3—4C 38
Westbourne Av. M25—6B 42
Westbourne Av. M27—4D 56
Westbourne Dri. OL7—1G 91
Westbourne Gro. M9—3F 75
Westbourne Gro. M20—3E 117
Westbourne Gro. M33—5A 114
Westbourne Gro. SK5—1H 119
Westbourne Pk. M31—4F 97
Westbourne Range. M18—3H 103
Westbourne Rd. M14—1H 117
Westbourne Rd. M30—1D 82
Westbourne Rd. M31—5F 97
Westbourne Rd. M34—5E 105
Westbridge Pl. M7—4F 73
Westbrook Ho. M17—6C 84
Westbrook Rd. M27—4E 71
Westbrook Sq. M12—1D 102
Westbrook St. BL2—1C 38
Westbrook Wlk. M20—5E 117
Westbury Av. M33—2E 125
Westbury Clo. BL8—4G 27
Westbury Dri. SK6—5C 134
Westbury Rd. M8—2C 74
Westbury St. OL6—2A 92
Westbury St. SK14—2A 106
Westby Clo. SK7—5A 144
Westby Gro. BL2—5E 25
W. Central Dri. M27—4H 71
W. Charles St. M5—4H 85
W. Church St. OL10—3E 31
Westcliffe Ho. OL12—5B 8
Westcliffe Rd. BL1—5D 10
Westcombe Dri. BL8—1A 28
West Cotts. OL3—4H 67
Westcott Av. M20—3E 117
Westcott Clo. BL2—6A 12
Westcott Gro. OL2—2E 49
Westcourt Rd. BL3—4H 37
Westcourt Rd. M33—3H 113
West Craig Av. M10—6C 62
W. Craven St. M5—5H 85
West Cres. M24—2H 61

W. Croft Ind. Est. M24—2E 61
Westcroft Rd. M20—5H 117
Westdale Gdns. M19—4C 118
Westdean Cres. M19—3B 118
W. Dean St. M5—4A 86 & 6B 160
Westdene. M8—5B 74
(off Kilmington Dri.)
W. Downs Rd. SK8—2B 142
West Dri. BL9—6E 15
(in two parts)
West Dri. M6—5C 72
West Dri. M27—4H 71
West Dri. M35—4H 89
West Dri. SK8—1E 141
West Dri. SK14—1G 109
W. Duke St. M5—4B 86 & 6C 160
W. Egerton St. M5—4H 85
West End Av. SK8—5E 129
Westend St. BL4—6D 38
W. End St. OL9—1B 64
Westerdale. OL4—3G 65
(in two parts)
Westerdale Dri. BL3—2E 37
Westerdale Dri. OL2—2A 48
Westerham Av. M5—4G 85
Westerham Clo. BL8—4C 14
Wester Hill Rd. OL8—2E 79
Westerling Wlk. M16—4C 100
Western Access Trading Est. M17
—5A 84
Western Av. M27—1B 72
Western Circ. M19—3B 118
Western Rd. M31—6A 96
Western St. M6—2E 85
Western St. M18—1G 103
Westerton Ct. BL3—2H 37
Westfield. M6—1E 85
Westfield. WA14—2E 137
Westfield Av. M24—1A 62
Westfield Clo. OL11—2B 18
Westfield Dri. SK6—4A 122
Westfield Gro. M34—2E 105
Westfield Lodge. WA14—3G 125
(off Park Rd.)
Westfield Rd. BL3—5F 37
Westfield Rd. M21—6H 99
Westfield Rd. M35—3G 89
Westfield Rd. SK8—5B 142
Westfields. WA15—5H 137
Westfield St. M7—2H 73
Westfield St. OL9—1A 64
W. Fleet St. M5—5A 86 & 1B 164
Westgate. M31—6D 96
Westgate. M33—5A 114
Westgate. OL12—2B 6
Westgate. SK9—4D 158
Westgate. WA15—3G 137
Westgate Av. BL0—1A 14
Westgate Av. BL1—6G 23
Westgate Av. BL9—4C 28
Westgate Av. M9—1E 75
Westgate Clo. OL12—2B 6
Westgate Dri. M27—5F 71
Westgate Gdns. M33—4E 89
Westgate Rd. M6—6H 71
Westgate St. OL7—4G 91
West Grn. M24—2D 60
West Gro. M13—2H 101
West Gro. M33—6B 114
West Gro. OL5—2E 81
Westgrove Av. BL1—5C 10
Westhide Wlk. M9—2H 75
West Hill. OL11—5G 19
Westhill Clo. SK15—3D 92
Westholme Rd. M20—4F 117
Westholme Rd. M25—2G 59
W. Hope St. M5—4H 85
Westhorne Fold. M8—1A 74
Westhulme Av. OL1—6B 48
Westhulme St. OL1—6B 48
Westinghouse Rd. M17—1B 98
Westland Av. BL1—4E 23
Westland Av. BL4—3E 55
Westland Av. SK1—2B 132
Westland Dri. M9—5F 61

Westlands. M25—3D 58
Westlands, The. M27—5H 71
West Lea. M34—4G 105
Westlea Dri. M18—4F 103
Westleigh. BL6—5A 22
Westleigh Dri. M25—6H 59
Westleigh St. M9—2G 75
Westman Wlk. M16—3C 100
Westmarsh Clo. BL1—4A 24
W. Marwood St. M7—5A 74
Westmead Dri. M8—6A 74
Westmead Dri. WA15—4B 126
W. Meade. BL3—5H 37
W. Meade. M21—2G 115
W. Meade. M25—1H 73
W. Meade. M27—5E 71
Westmeade Rd. M28—4E 55
W. Meadow. SK5—6A 104
Westmere Dri. M9—5E 75
West M. BL2—6H 11
Westminster Av. BL4—1E 55
Westminster Av. M16—5A 100
Westminster Av. M25—1D 58
Westminster Av. M26—3D 40
Westminster Av. OL2—1A 48
Westminster Av. OL6—4H 79
Westminster Av. SK5—2G 119
Westminster Clo. OL2—5F 35
Westminster Clo. SK6—4B 134
Westminster Dri. SK8—1D 152
Westminster Dri. SK9—5D 158
Westminster Rd. BL1—6C 10
Westminster Rd. M28—1F 69
Westminster Rd. M30—2G 83
Westminster Rd. M31—3F 97
Westminster Rd. M35—3H 77
Westminster Rd. WA15—2A 138
Westminster St. BL4—1E 55
Westminster St. BL9—4C 28
Westminster St. M15—6A 86 & 4B 164
Westminster St. M19—6D 102
Westminster St. M27—2D 70
Westminster St. OL1—1F 65
Westminster St. OL11—6F 19
Westminster Wlk. BL4—1E 55
Westminster Way. SK16—1A 106
Westmoor Gables. SK4—5C 118
Westmorland Av. OL7—1H 91
Westmorland Av. SK16—5C 92
Westmorland Clo. BL9—1C 42
Westmorland Clo. SK5—3C 120
Westmorland Dri. OL12—3B 8
Westmorland Dri. SK5—3B 120
Westmorland Rd. M20—1E 129
Westmorland Rd. M30—6G 71
Westmorland Rd. M31—2G 97
Westmorland Rd. M33—1C 126
Westmorland Wlk. OL2—3C 48
W. Mosley St. M2—5D 86 & 1H 165
(in two parts)
Westmount Clo. M10—5E 75
W. Oak Pl. SK8—4B 142
Weston Av. M10—2E 77
Weston Av. M27—5E 57
Weston Av. M31—6D 96
Weston Av. OL16—1H 33
Weston Dri. M34—4G 105
Weston Dri. SK8—1F 143
Weston Gro. M22—3C 128
Weston Gro. SK4—3E 119
Weston Rd. M26—6E 27
Weston Rd. M30—5F 95
Weston Rd. SK9—3G 159
Weston St. BL3—3B 38
Weston St. OL6—5G 65
Weston St. OL16—5E 21
(in two parts)
Weston St. SK5—5G 119
W. Over. SK6—3G 133
Westover Rd. M31—4E 97
Westover St. M27—2E 71
West Pde. M33—6E 113
West Pk. SK14—2B 122
West Pk. Av. M34—5H 105
West Pk. Est. OL7—4G 91
W. Park Av. SK12—3A 154
W. Park Rd. SK1—1B 132
W. Park Rd. SK7—3F 143
W. Park Rd. M5—6H 85 & 3A 164

West Pl. M19—2B 118
W. Point Enterprise Pk. M17—6H 83
West Point Ind. Est. OL9—3A 64
Westray Cres. M5—4E 85
Westray Rd. M13—5A 102
West Rd. M25—4D 58
West Rd. M31—6G 83
West Rd. M32—3A 98
West Row. WA14—3E 137
West Row. M25—2D 72
W. Starkey St. OL10—2E 31
W. Stockport Rd. SK6—5E 121
West St. BL0—4D 4
West St. BL1—6G 23
West St. BL4—6G 39
West St. M9—6C 60
West St. M11—3D 88
West St. M24—5A 46
West St. M26—4G 41
West St. M34—4C 104
West St. M35—3F 89
(Droylsden)
West St. M35—4F 77
(Failsworth)
West St. OL1—2C 64
West St. OL4—4A 66
West St. OL6—2H 91
West St. OL9—3B 64
(off Featherstall Rd. S.)
West St. OL10—3F 31
West St. OL15—4G 9
West St. OL16—4D 20
(Firgrove)
West St. OL16—3A 20
(Rochdale)
West St. SK3—2F 131
West St. SK9—5G 159
West St. SK14—1H 109
(Hadfield)
West St. SK14—2B 106
(Hyde)
West St. SK15—3D 92
West St. SK16—4H 91
W. Towers St. M6—4F 85
W. Vale. M26—2G 41
W. Vale Rd. WA15—5H 125
West View. M34—6E 91
West View. OL15—4G 9
Westview Gro. M25—6B 42
W. View Rd. M22—3C 128
Westville Gdns. M19—4A 118
West Wlk. BL7—1B 10
Westward Ho. OL16—5F 21
Westward Rd. SK9—3C 158
West Way. BL1—2D 24
Westway. M9—2D 60
West Way. M28—4C 54
Westway. M35—5A 90
Westway. OL2—1F 49
Westway. OL4—4A 66
Westwell Gdns. BL1—4A 24
(off Halliwell Rd.)
W. Whitehill St. SK4 & SK5—5G 119
Westwick Ter. BL1—3A 24
Westwood Av. M7—3A 74
Westwood Av. M10—2E 77
Westwood Av. M28—6C 54
Westwood Av. M31—6H 97
Westwood Av. WA15—4H 125
Westwood Bus. Cen. OL9—3B 64
Westwood Clo. BL4—1F 55
Westwood Cres. M30—1C 82
Westwood Dri. M27—5A 72
Westwood Dri. M33—1B 126
Westwood Dri. OL9—2B 64
Westwood Ind. Est. OL9—2A 64
Westwood Rd. BL1—5G 23
Westwood Rd. M32—5B 98
Westwood Rd. SK2—1B 144
Westwood Rd. SK8—5F 141
Westwood St. M14—3D 100
W. Works Rd. M17—3C 98
Westworth Clo. BL1—5H 23
Wetheral Dri. BL3—4A 38
Wetherall St. M19—6D 102
Wetherby Dri. OL2—2A 48
Wetherby St. SK7—3G 145
Wetherby St. M11—6G 89
Wexford Wlk. M22—3C 140

Weybourne Av. M9—1A 76
Weybourne Dri. SK6—5F 121
Weybourne Gro. BL2—1D 24
Weybridge Clo. BL1—4B 24
Weybridge Rd. M4—3G 87 & 4F 163
Weybrook Dri. SK4—2D 118
Weycroft Clo. BL2—1A 40
Wey Gates Dri. WA15—6C 138
Weyhill Rd. M23—6G 127
Weylands Gro. M6—6H 71
Weymouth Rd. M30—2D 82
Weymouth Rd. OL6—5A 80
Weymouth St. BL1—3A 24
Weythorne Dri. BL1—1B 24
Weythorne Dri. BL9—6D 16
Whalley Av. BL1—2D 22
Whalley Av. M16—4B 100
Whalley Av. M19—5D 102
Whalley Av. M21—1A 116
Whalley Av. M31—4G 97
Whalley Av. M33—4C 114
Whalley Av. OL15—3E 9
Whalley Clo. M25—6D 42
Whalley Clo. WA15—3H 125
Whalley Dri. BL8—3F 27
Whalley Gdns. OL12—2D 18
Whalley Gro. M16—5B 100
Whalley Gro. OL6—3G 79
Whalley Rd. BL0—3A 4
(Edenfield)
Whalley Rd. M16—4A 100
Whalley Rd. M24—4H 45
Whalley Rd. M25—6D 42
Whalley Rd. OL10—3C 30
Whalley Rd. OL12—2D 18
Whalley Rd. SK2—4C 132
Whalley Rd. WA15—3A 138
Whalley St. OL1—2D 64
Whally Clo. OL16—5E 21
Wham Bar Dri. OL10—3D 30
Wham Bottom La. OL12—5D 6
Wham St. OL10—3D 30
Wharf Clo. WA14—4F 125
Wharfedale Av. M20—2A 76
Wharfedale Rd. SK5—1G 119
Wharf Rd. M33—4C 114
Wharf Rd. WA14—4F 125
Wharf St. OL9—6H 63
Wharf St. M4—6G 119
Wharf St. SK14—4A 106
Wharf St. SK16—4H 91
Wharmton Rise. OL4—3F 67
Wharmton View. OL3—3E 53
Wharton Av. M21—2B 116
Wharton La. M28—4A 54
Wharton Lodge. M22—6D 83
Wheat Clo. M13—2G 101
Wheat Croft. SK3—6H 131
Wheatcroft. SK14—3G 109
Wheater's Cres. M7—1A 86
Wheater's Ter. M7—1B 86
Wheatfield. SK15—6H 93
Wheatfield Clo. BL9—4F 15
Wheatfield Clo. SK6—5G 121
Wheatfield Cres. OL2—4A 48
Wheatfield St. BL2—2D 38
Wheathill St. OL16—1G 33
Wheatley Rd. M27—1D 70
Wheatley Wlk. M12—1B 102
Wheatsheaf Cen., The. OL1—5F 55
Wheatsheaf Ind. Est. M27—2H 71
Wheeldale. OL4—3H 65
Wheeldale Clo. BL1—3A 24
Wheeldale St. M14—4E 101
Wheelock Clo. SK9—6H 151
Wheelton Clo. BL8—4G 27
Wheelwright Clo. OL11—1B 32
Wheelwright Clo. SK6—3D 134
Whelan Av. BL9—6C 28
Whelan Clo. BL9—6C 28
Wheler St. M11—5F 89
Whelmar Est. SK8—2D 142
Whernside Av. OL6—4G 79
Whernside Av. M10—2A 76
Whernside Clo. SK4—6G 119
Whetstone Hill Clo. OL1—5F 49
Whetstone Hill La. OL1—6G 49
Whetstone Hill Rd. OL1—5F 49

Whewell Av. M26—2B 42
Whiley St. M13—3B 102
Whimbrel Rd. SK2—1G 145
Whinberry Rd. WA14—4D 124
Whinberry Way. OL4—3A 50
Whinchat Clo. SK2—1G 145
Whinfell Dri. M24—6D 44
Whingroves Wlk. M10—4A 76
Whinmoor Wlk. M10—4B 76
Whins Av. BL4—1A 54
Whins Crest. BL6—6A 22
Whinslee Dri. BL6—6A 22
Whinstone Way. OL1—6E 47
Whipney La. BL8—1F 13
Whirley Clo. SK4—4F 119
Whiston Dri. BL2—1E 39
Whiston Rd. M8—2D 74
Whitaker St. M24—1H 61
Whitbrook Way. M24—2D 46
Whitburn Av. M13—5A 102
Whitburn Clo. BL3—3C 36
Whitburn Dri. BL8—6C 14
Whitburn Rd. M23—1G 139
Whitby Av. M6—2C 84
Whitby Av. M14—1A 118
Whitby Av. M16—4B 100
Whitby Av. M31—5G 97
Whitby Av. OL10—2E 31
Whitby Clo. BL8—3F 27
Whitby Clo. SK8—5G 129
Whitby Clo. SK12—3C 154
Whitby Rd. M14—1H 117
Whitby Rd. OL8—6G 65
Whitby St. M24—6C 46
Whitby St. OL11—6A 20
Whitchurch Dri. M16—2B 100
Whitchurch Gdns. BL1—3A 24
(off Gladstone St.)
Whitchurch Rd. M20—2D 116
Whitchurch St. M3—2C 86 & 1F 161
Whiteacres. M27—4C 70
Whiteacres Rd. OL6—2A 92
Whiteacre Wlk. M15—2C 100
(off Shearsby Clo.)
Whitebank Av. SK5—5C 120
White Bank Rd. OL8—1B 78
Whitebeam Clo. OL16—2E 35
Whitebeam Ct. M6—2G 85
Whitebeam Wlk. M33—4F 113
Whitebeck Ct. M9—5A 62
White Birk Clo. BL8—1H 13
White Bri. SK16—1A 106
White Brook La. OL3—3H 53
(Greenfield)
White Brook La. OL3—1G 53
(Uppermill)
Whitebrook Rd. M14—6F 101
White Brow. BL9—2D 42
Whitecar Av. M10—2E 77
Whitechapel Clo. BL2—6G 25
Whitechapel St. M20—6F 117
White City Way. M16—2G 99
Whitecliff Clo. M14—4G 101
Whitecroft Av. OL2—6H 35
Whitecroft Gdns. M19—5A 118
Whitecroft Rd. BL1—4D 22
Whitecroft Rd. SK12—4G 147
Whitecroft St. OL1—6G 49
Whitefield. M6—5B 72
Whitefield Av. M6—4E 119
Whitefield Bottoms. OL16—2F 35
Whitefield Cen. OL1—1F 59
Whitefield Cres. OL16—2F 35
Whitefield Rd. BL9—6B 28
(in two parts)
Whitefield Rd. M33—4H 113
Whitefield Rd. SK6—5E 121
White Friar Ct. M3—2C 86 & 2E 161
Whitefriars Wlk. M22—5B 140
Whitegate. BL3—5A 36
Whitegate. OL15—5C 8
Whitegate Av. OL9—5F 63
Whitegate Dri. BL1—6D 10
Whitegate Dri. M5—2D 84
Whitegate Dri. M27—1H 71

Whitegate La. OL9—5F 63
(in two parts)
Whitegate Pk. M31—5A 96
Whitegate Rd. OL9—6D 62
Whitegates Av. M24—3C 46
Whitegates Clo. WA15—6B 126
Whitegates Rd. SK8—6H 129
Whitehall. OL4—3B 50
Whitehall Clo. SK9—4D 158
(in two parts)
Whitehall La. OL4—3B 50
Whitehall Rd. M20—6G 117
Whitehall Rd. M33—1B 126
Whitehall St. OL1—1D 64
Whitehall St. OL12 & OL16—2H 19
(in two parts)
White Hart Meadow M24—5A 46
White Hart St. SK14—3B 106
Whitehaven Gdns. M20—1E 129
Whitehaven Pl. SK14—2A 106
Whitehaven Rd. SK7—2E 153
Whitehead Cres. BL8—5C 14
Whitehead Cres. M26—2C 56
Whitehead Pl. OL4—2B 66
Whitehead Rd. M21—1F 115
Whitehead Rd. M27—1H 71
Whitehead St. M24—6C 46
Whitehead St. M28—5F 55
Whitehead St. M34—6E 91
Whitehead St. OL2—5D 34
Whitehead St. OL16—4E 21
(Milnrow, in two parts)
Whitehead St. OL16—1H 35
(Newhey)
Whitehill Clo. OL12—5D 6
Whitehill Cotts. BL1—5B 10
Whitehill Dri. M10—4A 76
Whitehill Ind. Est. SK4—4G 119
Whitehill La. BL1—5B 10
Whitehill St. SK4—5F 119
Whiteholme Av. M21—5B 116
White Horse Gdns. M27—5C 70
White Ho. M8—6A 60
Whitehouse Av. OL4—3G 65
Whitehouse Clo. OL10—6F 31
Whitehouse Dri. M23—6G 127
Whitehouse Dri. WA15—5B 138
Whitehouse La. M31—4A 124
White Houses. BL1—4D 22
Whitehouse Ter. M9—2H 75
Whitehurst Rd. SK4—5B 118
Whitekirk Clo. M13—1F 101 & 5D 166
White Lady Clo. M28—6B 54
Whitelake Av. M31—5B 96
Whitelake View. M31—4B 96
Whiteland Av. BL3—2G 37
Whitelands. OL6—3A 92
Whitelands Rd. OL6—3A 92
Whitelands Ter. OL6—3A 92
Whitelea Dri. SK3—6F 131
Whitelees Rd. OL15—4E 9
Whitelegge St. BL8—1H 27
Whiteley Dri. M24—2C 62
Whiteley Pl. WA14—5F 125
Whiteleys Pl. OL12—3G 19
Whiteley St. M11—3D 88
Whiteley St. OL9—5H 63
White Lion Brow. BL1—6A 24
Whitelow Rd. BL9—3G 5
Whitelow Rd. M21—1G 115
Whitelow Rd. SK4—6C 118
White Meadows. M27—4F 71
White Moss Av. M21—1A 116
White Moss Gdns. M9—1A 76
White Moss Rd. M9—6G 61
Whiteoak Clo. SK6—4C 134
Whiteoak Rd. M14—1G 117
Whites Croft. M27—3F 71
Whitesheadstop SK12—2H 157
Whitestone Clo. BL6—1B 36
Whitestone Wlk. M13—2H 101
White St. BL8—4A 28
White St. M6—4E 85
White Swallows Rd. M27—5G 71
Whitethorn Av. M16—4B 100
Whitethorn Av. M19—2B 118
Whitethorn Clo. SK6—4C 134
Whiteway St. M9—4G 75
Whitewell Clo. OL16—3C 20

Whitfield Av. OL11—3B 18
Whitfield Brow. OL15—2G 9
Whitfield Rise. OL2—4E 35
Whitfield St. M3—2E 87
Whitford Wlk. M10—2H 87 & 1G 163
Whiting Gro. BL3—1C 36
Whitland Dri. OL8—1H 77
Whit La. M6—5D 72
(in two parts)
Whitley Gdns. WA15—3B 126
Whitley Pl. WA15—4B 126
Whitley Rd. M10—1G 87
Whitley Rd. SK4—6D 118
Whitley St. BL3—5F 39
Whitlow Av. WA14—3D 124
Whitman St. M9—3H 75
Whitmore Rd. M14—6F 101
Whitnall Clo. M16—3C 100
Whitnall St. SK14—2B 106
Whitsbury Av. M18—4F 103
Whitstable Clo. OL9—3H 63
Whitstable Rd. M10—2C 76
Whitswood Clo. M16—4C 100
Whittaker Clo. M25—5G 59
Whittaker Dri. OL15—1F 21
Whittaker La. M25—5G 59
Whittaker La. OL11—2H 17
Whittaker St. M10—3H 75
Whittaker St. M12—5H 87 & 2H 167
Whittaker St. M26—3H 41
Whittaker St. OL2—3B 48
Whittaker St. OL6—6H 79
Whittaker St. OL11—2A 18
Whittingham Dri. BL0—5E 5
Whittingham Gro. OL1—1B 64
Whittington St. OL7—4G 91
Whittlebrook Gro. OL10—6G 31
Whittle Dri. M28—4E 55
Whittle Dri. OL2—5H 35
Whittle Gro. BL1—1F 23
(in two parts)
Whittle Gro. M28—6G 55
Whittle Hill. BL7—1C 10
Whittle La. OL10—2C 44
Whittles Av. M34—4G 105
Whittle's Croft. M1—4F 87 & 6D 162
Whittles St. OL12—1H 7
Whittles Ter. OL16—1F 35
Whittle St. BL8—2A 28
Whittle St. M4—3F 87
Whittle St. M27—4E 71
Whittle St. M28—6F 55
Whittle St. OL15—4D 8
Whittles Wlk. M34—5G 105
Whitwell Bank. SK13—5F 109
(off Eyam La.)
Whitwell Clo. BL9—6B 28
Whitwell Clo. SK13—5F 109
Whitwell Fold. SK13—5G 109
(off Melandra Castle Rd.)
Whitwell Grn. SK13—5G 109
(off Hathersage Cres.)
Whitwell Lea. SK13—5F 109
(off Melandra Castle Rd.)
Whitwell Wlk. M13—3A 102
Whitwell Way. M18—2E 103
Whitworth Clo. OL6—1A 92
Whitworth La. M14—6H 101
Whitworth Pk. Mans. M14—3E 101
Whitworth Rake. OL12—1D 6
Whitworth Rd. OL12—5D 6
Whitworth Rd. OL16—5F 21
Whitworth Sq. OL12—1D 6
Whitworth St. M1—5E 87 & 2A 162
Whitworth St. M11—6C 88
(in two parts)
Whitworth St. OL16—1C 20
Whitworth St. W. M1—5C 86 & 2F 165
Whoolden St. BL4—6E 39
Whowell Fold. BL1—2G 23
Whowell St. BL3—1A 38
Wibbersley Pk. M31—5B 96
Wichbrook Rd. M28—6B 54
Wicheaves Cres. M28—6B 54
Wicheries, The. M28—6B 54
Wicken Bank. OL10—6G 31
Wickenby Dri. M33—5A 114
Wicken St. SK2—4C 132
Wickentree La. M35—2F 77

Wicker La. WA15—5B 138
Wickham Clo. M14—4F 101
Wickliffe Pl. OL11—5H 19
Wickliffe St. BL1—5A 24
Wicklow Av. SK3—4D 130
Wicklow Dri. M22—3C 140
Widcombe Dri. BL2—2H 39
Widdow St. OL9—2B 64
Widecombe Clo. M31—3D 96
Widgeon Clo. M14—1F 117
Widgeon Clo. SK3—5B 154
Widgeon Rd. WA14—3D 124
Wigan Rd. BL3—5B 36
Wiggins Teape Rd. BL9—1F 43
Wiggins Wlk. M14—4G 101
Wighurst Wlk. M22—4B 140
Wigley St. M12—6A 88
Wigmore Rd. M8—4D 74
Wigmore St. OL6—1B 92
Wigsby Av. M10—1C 76
Wigston Wlk. M8—6A 74
(off Fairy La.)
Wigwam Clo. SK12—3C 154
Wike St. BL8—2B 28
Wilberforce Clo. M15—2D 100
Wilbraham Rd. M21, M16 & M14
                              —6G 99
Wilbraham Rd. M28—6F 55
Wilburn St. M5—5B 86 & 1C 164
(in two parts)
Wilby Av. BL3—2A 40
Wilby Clo. BL8—6D 14
Wilby St. M8—5D 74
Wilcock Clo. M16—3C 100
Wilcott Dri. M33—4G 113
Wilcott Dri. SK9—5C 158
Wilcott Rd. SK8—6E 129
Wildbank Chase. SK15—1A 108
Wildbrook Clo. M28—6A 54
Wildbrook Cres. OL8—6E 65
Wildbrook Gro. M28—6A 54
Wildbrook Rd. M28—5A 54
Wildcroft Av. M10—2A 76
Wilderswood Rd. M20—4G 117
Wilde St. M30—1H 91
Wild Ho. BL8—4D 64
Wildhouse Ct. OL16—3F 21
Wild Ho. La. OL16—3F 21
Wildman La. BL4—1B 54
Wildmoor Av. OL4—5A 66
Wilds Bldgs. OL16—4D 20
Wilds Pas. OL15—5H 9
(Calderbrook)
Wild's Pas. OL15—5C 8
(Rochdale)
Wild St. M26—3B 42
Wild St. M34—4F 105
Wild St. OL1—2E 65
Wild St. OL2—1G 49
Wild St. OL4—3A 66
Wild St. SK2—5A 132
Wild St. SK6—1F 133
Wild St. SK7—3D 144
Wild St. SK16—5B 92
Wildwood Clo. BL0—5C 4
Wileman Ct. M5—3D 84
Wilford Av. M33—1A 126
Wilfred Dri. BL9—1E 29
Wilfred Rd. M28—1F 69
Wilfred Rd. M30—5C 82
Wilfred St. BL7—4E 11
Wilfred St. M3—1C 86
Wilfred St. M10—3A 76
Wilfred St. M35—5B 90
Wilfrid St. M27—3F 71
Wilham Av. M30—4F 83
Wilkes St. OL1—3H 49
Wilkin Croft. SK8—4A 142
Wilkins La. SK9—2C 150
Wilkinson Av. BL3—2A 40
Wilkinson Rd. BL1—6B 10
Wilkinson Rd. SK4—1G 131
Wilkinson St. M24—6H 45
Wilkinson St. M33—5D 114
Wilkinson St. OL4—2F 65
Wilkinson St. OL6—3G 91
Wilks Av. M22—3D 140

Willand Clo. BL2—1A 40
Willand Dri. BL2—2A 40
Willan Ind. Est. M5—4F 85
Willan Rd. M9—4E 61
Willan Rd. M30—3G 83
Willard St. SK7—2D 144
Willaston Clo. M21—2G 115
Willaston Way. SK9—2H 151
Willbutts La. OL11—3E 19
Willdale Clo. M11—3C 88
Willdor Gro. SK3—5D 130
Willenhall Rd. M23—1A 128
Willerby Rd. M7—6A 74
Willert St. M10—6F 75
Willesden Av. M13—4A 102
Will Griffiths Wlk. M11—5A 88
William Chadwick Clo. M10—2F 87
                              & 1F 163
William Coates Ct. M16—4B 100
William Henry St. OL11—1G 33
William Jessop Ct. M1—4G 87 & 6E 163
William Kay Clo. M16—3C 100
William Kent Cres. M15—1C 100 &
                              6E 165
William Lister Clo. M10—1F 89
William Murray Ct. M4—3G 87
(off Jackroom Dri.)
Williams Cres. OL9—6F 63
Williamson Av. M26—1F 41
Williamson Av. SK6—5G 121
Williamson La. M35—5B 90
Williamson St. M4—2F 87 & 1C 162
Williamson St. OL6—2H 91
Williamson St. SK5—2H 119
Williamson's Yd. OL12—1F 65
Williams Pas. OL15—6H 9
Williams Rd. M10—4B 76
Williams Rd. M18—2E 103
Williams St. BL3—4B 40
Williams St. M18—2E 103
William St. BL0—1E 5
William St. M1—6D 86 & 3A 166
William St. M3—3C 86 & 4E 161
William St. M12—5H 87 & 2G 167
William St. M20—6F 117
William St. M24—1B 62
William St. M26—3H 41
William St. M31—5E 97
William St. M34—3G 105
William St. M35—2G 77
William St. OL7—3F 91
William St. OL11—5H 19
(in two parts)
William St. OL12—4G 7
William St. OL15—4E 9
William St. OL16—5B 8
William St. SK1—4B 132
William Wlk. WA14—2F 137
Willingdon Clo. BL8—4C 14
Willingdon Dri. M25—4F 59
Willis Rd. OL8—3E 79
Willis Rd. SK3—5G 131
Willis St. BL3—3G 37
Williton Wlk. M22—2D 140
Willock St. M7—5A 74
Willoughby Av. M20—5G 117
Willoughby Clo. M33—4A 114
Willow Av. M24—2C 62
Willow Av. M31—5G 97
Willow Av. SK5—5H 119
Willow Av. SK8—3B 142
Willow Bank. M9—3G 75
(off Church La.)
Willow Bank. M14—1G 117
Willowbank. M26—1F 57
Willowbank. M27—1G 71
Willow Bank. OL4—1A 66
(in two parts)
Willow Bank. SK8—1C 152
Willow Bank. WA15—5A 126
Willowbank Av. BL2—1D 38
Willow Bank Ct. M20—3F 129
Willowbrook Av. M10—4A 76
Willow Clo. BL3—3F 37
Willow Clo. SK12—4E 155
Willow Ct. M14—1G 117
Willow Ct. M33—4E 115
Willowdale Av. SK8—3F 141
Willowdene Clo. BL7—7D 10

Willowdene Clo. M10—6E 75
Willow Dri. M33—1G 125
Willow Dri. SK9—4H 151
Willowfield Rd. OL4—5H 49
Willow Fold. M35—5B 90
Willow Gro. M18—3G 103
Willow Gro. M34—4E 105
Willow Gro. OL9—1H 63
Willow Gro. SK6—6D 134
Willow Hey. BL7—4G 11
Willow Hill Rd. M8—1C 74
Willow Lawn. SK8—2C 142
Willowmead Ct. SK4—5D 118
Willowmoss Clo. M28—2G 69
Willow Pk. M14—1G 117
Willow Rise. OL15—6D 8
Willow Rd. M25—3E 59
Willow Rd. M31—6C 110
Willow Rd. OL3—2G 53
Willow Rd. SK6—6D 146
Willows Dri. M35—6F 77
Willows La. BL3—3F 37
Willows La. OL16—5D 20
Willows Rd. M5—3D 84
Willows, The. M21—2G 115
Willows, The. M31—6D 110
Willows, The. OL4—4B 66
Willows, The. OL5—2G 81
Willows, The. OL12—4C 6
  (off Tonacliffe Rd.)
Willow St. BL9—3F 29
  (in two parts)
Willow St. M7—1C 86
Willow St. M11—4C 88
Willow St. M27—6D 70
Willow St. M28—4C 70
Willow St. M35—4D 76
Willow St. OL1—2E 65
Willow St. OL10—3F 31
Willow Tree Ct. M33—6B 114
Willowtree Rd. WA14—2F 137
Willow Wlk. M35—3C 90
Willow Way. M20—6G 117
Willow Way. SK7—6E 143
Wilma Av. M9—5E 61
Wilmcote Clo. BL6—1B 36
Wilmcote Gdns. SK6—6F 121
Wilmcote Rd. M10—1H 87
Wilmers. OL15—5H 9
Wilmington Rd. M32—5B 98
Wilmot St. BL1—2G 23
Wilmott St. M15—6D 86 & 4H 165
  (in two parts)
Wilmslow Av. BL1—6C 10
Wilmslow Old Rd. WA15—1F 149
Wilmslow Pk. Rd. SK9—2F 159
Wilmslow Rd. M14—3G 101
Wilmslow Rd. SK8—5H 129
Wilmslow Rd. SK8 & SK9—3H 141
Wilmslow Rd. SG9—4G 159
Wilmslow Rd. WA15 & SK9—1F 149
Wilmur Av. M7—5A 74
Wilmur Av. M25—2E 59
Wilna Ter. M5—4H 85
Wilpshire Av. M12—4D 102
Wilshaw Gro. OL7—5E 79
Wilshaw La. OL7—6E 79
Wilshaw Pl. OL7—5E 79
Wilson Av. M27—1H 71
Wilson Av. OL10—3C 30
Wilson Clo. SK16—6D 92
Wilson Gro. OL6—1C 92
Wilson Rd. M9—2F 75
Wilson Rd. SK4—5D 118
Wilsons Brow. BL4—6H 39
Wilson St. BL4—1G 55
Wilson St. BL9—4E 29
Wilson St. M10—6G 75
Wilson St. M11—5C 88
Wilson St. M13—1G 101 & 6F 167
Wilson St. M18—2F 103
Wilson St. M26—3F 41
Wilson St. M32—3E 99
Wilson St. M33—4B 114
Wilson St. OL3—4E 53
Wilson St. OL8—5C 64
Wilson St. OL12—3H 19
Wilson St. SK14—5C 106

Wilson Way. OL1—1D 64
Wilsthorpe Clo. M19—3E 119
Wilton Av. M16—4G 99
Wilton Av. M25—1H 73
Wilton Av. M27—4A 72
Wilton Av. SK8—6G 141
Wilton Ct. M9—6C 60
Wilton Ct. M34—3A 104
Wilton Cres. SK9—4F 159
Wilton Dri. BL9—2E 43
Wilton Dri. WA15—5C 138
Wilton Gdns. M26—2A 42
Wilton Gro. M34—3A 104
Wilton Gro. OL10—4F 31
Wilton Paddock. M34—3A 104
Wilton Pl. M7—3B 86 & 4C 160
Wilton Polygon. M8—2B 74
Wilton Rd. BL1—6C 10
Wilton Rd. M8—1B 84
Wilton Rd. M8—1B 74
Wilton Rd. M21—1H 115
Wilton St. BL1—2B 24
Wilton St. BL9—2E 43
Wilton St. M5—4G 85
Wilton St. M24—2D 60
Wilton St. M25—5G 59
  (Prestwich)
Wilton St. M25—2D 58
  (Whitefield)
Wilton St. M34—3E 105
Wilton St. OL9—6H 63
Wilton St. OL10—3D 30
Wilton St. SK5—5H 103
Wilton Ter. OL12—3G 19
Wiltshire Av. SK5—5C 120
Wiltshire Clo. BL9—5E 29
Wiltshire Rd. M31—6C 110
Wiltshire Rd. M35—5G 77
Wiltshire Rd. OL9—4H 63
Wiltshire St. M7—5A 74
Wimbledon Dri. SK3—4E 131
Wimbledon Rd. M35—3G 77
Wimbledon Ter. M10—1D 88
Wimborne Av. M31—3F 97
Wimborne Av. OL9—6G 47
Wimborne Clo. SK8—1E 143
Wimborne Wlk. M5—3G 85
Wimbourne St. M10—1B 88
Wimpenny Ho. OL8—4C 64
Wimpole St. OL1—6E 49
Wimpole St. OL6—2A 92
  (in three parts)
Wimpory St. M11—6F 89
Winbolt St. SK2—1C 144
Wincanton Av. M23—3D 126
Wincanton Dri. BL1—4B 10
Wincanton Pk. OL4—3H 65
Wincebrook. M24—1A 62
Wince Clo. M24—3C 62
Wincham Clo. M15—1B 100 & 6D 164
Wincham Rd. M33—1G 125
Winchester Av. M25—1G 73
Winchester Av. M34—6F 105
Winchester Av. OL6—3H 79
Winchester Av. OL9—6F 47
Winchester Av. OL10—5E 31
Winchester Clo. BL8—4C 14
Winchester Clo. OL11—4C 18
Winchester Clo. SK9—4B 158
Winchester Cres. SK16—6E 93
Winchester Dri. M33—5F 113
Winchester Dri. SK4—1D 130
Winchester Pk. M20—5D 116
Winchester Rd. M6—1C 84
Winchester Rd. M26—2D 40
Winchester Rd. M30—6G 71
Winchester Rd. M31 & M32—4F 97
Winchester Rd. SK16—6E 93
Winchester Rd. WA15—4C 138
Winchester Way. BL2—4F 25
Wincle Av. SK12—5F 155
Wincombe St. M14—5F 101
Windale. M28—6D 54
Windcroft Clo. M11—5B 88
Winder Dri. M4—3G 87 & 4F 163
Windermere. BL4—1A 54
Windermere Av. BL3—3A 40
Windermere Av. M27—4G 71
Windermere Av. M33—1D 126

Windermere Av. M34—5A 104
Windermere Clo. M11—5C 88
Windermere Cres. OL7—1F 91
Windermere Dri. BL0—2E 5
Windermere Dri. BL9—6C 28
Windermere Dri. SK9—5F 159
Windermere Rd. M24—5D 44
Windermere Rd. M31—6E 97
Windermere Rd. OL2—6B 34
Windermere Rd. SK1—4B 132
Windermere Rd. SK6—5C 146
Windermere Rd. SK9—3G 151
Windermere Rd. SK14—2A 106
Windermere Rd. SK15—2E 93
Windermere St. BL1—2B 24
Windermere St. OL12—1H 19
Windermere Wlk. OL1—1G 65
Winders Way. M6—1H 85
Windfields Clo. SK8—2C 142
Windham St. OL16—6A 8
Windle Av. M8—6B 60
Windle Ct. SK2—6E 133
Windlehurst St. SK6—6B 146
Windlehurst Dri. M28—4D 68
Windlehurst Old Rd. SK6—3D 146
Windlehurst Rd. SK6—5B 146
Windley St. BL2—5C 24
Windley St. Caravan Site. BL1—5C 24
  (off Windley St.)
Windmill Av. M5—6H 85
Windmill Clo. M28—4E 55
Windmill Clo. M34—5B 104
Windmill Ct. OL16—5B 20
Windmill Field. M5—6H 85
  (off W. Park St.)
Windmill La. SK5 & M34—6H 103
Windmill La. Ind. Est. M34—4C 104
Windmill Rd. M28—4E 55
Windmill Rd. M33—6F 115
Windmill St. M2—5D 86 & 1G 165
Windmill St. OL16—5B 20
Windover St. BL3—3E 37
Windrush Av. BL0—1A 14
Windrush Dri. M9—4F 75
Windrush, The. OL12—5C 6
Windsor Av. BL3—4A 40
Windsor Av. M25—2E 59
Windsor Av. M27—1H 71
Windsor Av. M28—4D 54
Windsor Av. M30—4F 95
Windsor Av. M31—5B 96
Windsor Av. M33—3B 114
Windsor Av. M35—3H 77
Windsor Av. OL9—5G 63
Windsor Av. OL10—3D 30
Windsor Av. SK4—6C 118
Windsor Av. SK8—6D 128
Windsor Av. SK9—2C 158
Windsor Clo. BL8—2A 14
Windsor Clo. SK12—3D 154
Windsor Ct. M9—4B 60
Windsor Ct. M33—4H 113
Windsor Cres. M25—6A 60
Windsor Dri. BL8—5H 27
Windsor Dri. M34—4D 90
Windsor Dri. OL7—1F 91
Windsor Dri. SK6—6C 120
  (Bredbury)
Windsor Dri. SK6—6C 134
  (Marple)
Windsor Dri. SK15—2E 93
Windsor Dri. SK16—6D 92
Windsor Dri. WA14—3F 125
Windsor Gdns. WA15—6E 127
Windsor Gro. BL1—4G 23
Windsor Gro. M26—2B 56
Windsor Gro. OL6—4G 79
Windsor Gro. SK6—1C 134
Windsor Gro. SK8—5B 142
Windsor Rd. BL7—4E 11
Windsor Rd. M9—4G 75
Windsor Rd. M10—1G 89
Windsor Rd. M19—6B 102
Windsor Rd. M25—1A 74
  (in two parts)
Windsor Rd. M34—3A 104
Windsor Rd. M35—3F 89
Windsor Rd. OL8—4B 64
Windsor Rd. SK7—3F 145

Windsor Rd. SK14—2B 122
Windsor Rd. WA15—1G 137
Windsor St. M5—4H 85
Windsor St. M10—1G 89
Windsor St. M18—3E 103
Windsor St. M35—3G 77
Windsor St. OL1—6E 49
Windsor St. OL11—6A 20
Windsor St. SK2—5H 131
Windsor Ter. OL16—5E 21
  (Milnrow)
Windsor Ter. OL16—4C 20
  (Rochdale)
Windsor Ter. SK2—5A 132
  (off Russell St.)
Windsor Wlk. SK2—5H 131
  (off Windsor St.)
Windybank. M9—4E 61
Windycroft. BL7—3F 11
Windy Harbour La. BL7—3F 11
Winfell Dri. M10—2H 87 & 2H 163
Winfield Av. M20—3H 117
Winfield Dri. M18—1F 103
Winfield Gro. SK6—2F 135
Winfield St. SK14—5D 106
Winford Rd. M24—3C 62
Winford St. M9—3G 75
Wingate Av. BL8—3H 27
Wingate Dri. M20—1G 129
Wingate Dri. M25—6C 42
Wingate Rd. WA15—6A 126
Wingate Rd. M28—5D 54
Wingate Rd. SK4—5E 119
Wingate St. OL11—2A 18
Wingfield Av. SK9—3B 158
Wingfield Dri. M27—5G 71
Wingfield Dri. SK9—3B 158
Wingfield St. M32—3D 98
Wingfield Vs. OL15—2G 9
Wingham St. M7—1C 86
Wingrave Ho. M5—3F 85
Wings Gro. OL6—6F 31
Winifred Av. BL9—1A 30
Winifred Rd. BL4—6C 38
Winifred Rd. M10—4B 76
Winifred Rd. M20—6F 117
Winifred Rd. M31—5F 97
Winifred Rd. SK2—4G 133
Winifred St. BL0—4D 4
Winifred St. M30—4D 82
Winifred St. OL12—2D 18
Winifred St. SK14—2C 122
Winmarith Dri. WA15—6D 138
Winmarleigh Clo. BL8—4F 27
Winnall Wlk. M10—5C 76
Winnie St. M10—3A 76
Winnington Grn. SK2—5D 132
Winnington Rd. SK6—3D 134
Winnipeg Quay. M5—6F 85
Winnows, The. M34—4D 104
Winscombe Dri. M10—1G 87
Winser St. M1—5E 87 & 2A 166
Winsfield Rd. SK7—5D 144
Winsford Gro. OL11—6B 18
Winsford Gro. BL3—2D 36
Winsford Rd. M14—6E 101
Winsford Wlk. M33—6E 115
Winskill Rd. M30—1E 111
Winslade Clo. SK7—3A 144
Winsley Rd. M23—1F 127
Winslow Av. SK14—5B 108
Winslow Pl. M19—3B 118
Winslow Rd. BL3—4A 36
Winslow St. M11—5C 88
Winson Clo. BL3—3A 38
Winstanley Clo. M6—6B 72
Winstanley Rd. M10—2H 87 & 1G 163
Winstanley Rd. M33—4C 114
Winster Av. M7—5F 73
Winster Av. M20—5C 116
Winster Av. M32—4A 98
Winster Clo. BL2—4H 25
Winster Dri. M25—1F 59
Winster Dri. BL2—4G 25
Winster Dri. M24—5G 45
Winster Grn. M30—5D 82
Winster Gro. SK2—4A 132
Winster M. SK13—5G 109
  (off Melandra Castle Rd.)

Winster Rd. M30—5D 82
Winston Av. BL3—4C 40
Winston Av. OL11—5A 18
Winston Clo. M26—2E 41
Winston Clo. M33—4H 113
Winston Clo. SK6—4B 134
Winston Rd. M9—2H 75
Winswell Clo. M11—3D 88
Winterbottom Gro. SK14—5B 108
Winterbottom St. BL3—2A 38
Winterbottom St. OL9—2B 64
Winterbottom Wlk. SK14—5B 108
Winterburn Av. M21—5A 116
Winterburn Grn. SK2—6E 133
Winterdyne St. M9—4G 75
Winterford Av. M13—2H 101
Winterford La. OL5—1F 81
Winterford Rd. M8—4B 74
Winterford Rd. OL5—1F 81
Wintergreen Wlk. M31—6D 110
Wintermans Rd. M21—2B 116
Winterslow Av. M23—2D 126
Winter St. BL1—2H 23
Winterton Rd. SK5—6A 104
Winthorp Av. M10—6F 75
Winton Av. M10—2D 76
Winton Av. M34—6D 90
Winton Clo. SK7—4E 143
Winton Ct. WA14—3E 137
Winton Gro. BL3—3C 36
Winton Rd. M6—5B 72
Winton Rd. WA14—3E 137
Winton St. OL6—2H 91
Winton St. OL15—6F 9
Winton St. SK15—4F 93
Winward St. BL3—3A 38
Winwood Rd. M20—3G 129
Wireworks St. M10—3C 76
Wirral Clo. M27—1G 71
Wirral Cres. SK3—3C 130
Wisbech Dri. M23—2F 127
Wisbeck Rd. BL2—5A 26
Wiseley St. M11—5A 88
Wiseman Ter. M25—5G 59
Wishaw Sq. M21—2C 116
Wisley Clo. SK5—1H 119
Wistaria Rd. M18—2F 103
Witham Av. M22—6C 128
Witham Clo. OL10—2C 30
Witham St. OL6—1C 92
Withenfield Rd. M23—3F 127
Withens Grn. SK2—5E 133
Withern Flats. OL10—3E 31
(off Fox St.)
Withies, The. M30—3D 82
Withington Grn. M24—3A 46
Withington Rd. M16—3B 100
Withington Rd. M21 & M16—1B 116
Withington St. M6—2H 85
Withington St. OL10—5G 31
Withins Av. M26—2A 42
Withins Clo. BL2—5G 25
Withins Dri. BL2—5G 25
Withins Gro. BL2—5G 25
Withins La. BL2—5G 25
Withins La. M26—2A 42
Withins Rd. OL8—1H 77
Withins St. M26—3A 42
Withnell Dri. BL8—4G 27
Withnell Rd. M19—6H 117
Withycombe Pl. M6—6E 73
Withy Gro. M4—3E 87 & 4A 162
Withypool Dri. SK2—6B 132
Withytree Gro. M34—5G 105
Witley Dri. M33—3F 113
Witley Rd. OL16—4B 20
Witney Clo. BL1—3A 24
Wittenbury Rd. SK4—1D 130
Witterage Clo. M12—1B 102
Witton Wlk. M8—5B 74
Woburn Av. BL2—2E 25
Woburn Clo. M16—4D 100
Woburn Clo. OL16—5E 21
Woburn Dri. BL9—2D 42
Woburn Dri. WA15—3B 138
Woburn Rd. M16—4G 99
Woden's Av. M5—5A 86 & 2A 164
Woden St. M5—6A 86 & 3B 164
Woking Gdns. BL1—4A 24

Woking Rd. SK8—1B 152
Woking Ter. BL1—4A 24
(off Bk. Woking Gdns.)
Wolfenden St. BL1—3A 24
Wolfenden Ter. BL1—3A 24
Wolfreton Cres. M27—6C 57
Wollaton Wlk. M34—6E 105
Wolseley Ho. M33—3C 114
Wolseley Pl. M20—4F 117
Wolseley St. M33—3B 114
Wolseley St. OL16—1F 35
Wolsely St. BL8—4H 27
Wolsey Clo. M26—4G 41
Wolsey St. M26—4G 41
Wolsey St. OL10—4E 31
Wolstenholme Av. BL9—5F 15
Wolstenholme Coalpit La. OL11
—1F 17
Wolstenholme La. OL12 & OL11
—1G 17
Wolstenvale Clo. M24—6B 46
Wolver Clo. M28—3D 54
Wolverton Av. OL8—6B 64
Wolverton St. M11—6B 88
Wolvesey. OL11—5C 18
Woodacres Ct. SK9—3C 158
Woodall Clo. M33—5D 114
Woodbank. BL2—3F 25
Woodbank Av. SK1—3C 132
Woodbank Av. SK6—6E 121
Woodbank Ct. M31—4D 96
Woodbank Dri. BL8—1A 28
Woodbank Pk. SK1—2B 132
Woodbank Rd. OL15—6F 9
Woodbank Ter. OL5—1F 81
Woodbine Av. M30—5B 110
Woodbine Cres. SK2—4H 131
Woodbine Pas. OL15—4E 9
(off William St.)
Woodbine Rd. BL3—4G 37
(in two parts)
Woodbine St. M14—3E 101
Woodbine St. OL16—6A 20
(in two parts)
Woodbine St. E. OL16—6B 20
Woodbine Ter. M30—5F 95
Woodbourne Rd. M33—1A 126
Woodbourne Rd. SK4—3E 119
Woodbray Av. M19—4A 118
Woodbridge Av. M34—6D 90
Woodbridge Dri. BL2—4D 24
Woodbridge Gdns. OL12—1E 19
Woodbridge Gro. M23—2G 127
Woodbridge Rd. M31—4H 95
Woodbrook Av. OL4—2C 66
Woodbrooke Av. SK14—5D 106
Wood Brook La. OL4—2D 66
Wood Brook Rd. OL4—2C 66
Woodbrook Rd. SK9—5H 159
Woodburn Dri. BL1—2F 23
Woodburn Rd. M22—3B 128
Woodbury Rd. SK3—4D 130
Woodchurch Clo. BL1—4A 24
Woodchurch Wlk. M33—6F 115
Woodchurch Wlk. OL9—3H 63
Woodcock Clo. M35—2C 90
Woodcock Clo. OL11—4B 18
Woodcock Sq. M15—1D 100 & 5H 165
Woodcote Av. SK7—3E 143
Woodcote Rd. WA14—2F 125
(off Manchester Rd.)
Woodcote Rd. WA14 & M31—2C 124
(off Sinderland Rd.)
Woodcote Wlk. M8—3E 75
(off Crescent Rd.)
Wood Cottage Clo. M28—6B 54
Woodcott Gro. SK9—6A 152
Wood Cres. OL4—6A 66
Woodcroft. SK2—5D 132
Woodcroft Av. M19—5A 118
Woodeaton Clo. OL2—3E 49
Wooded Clo. BL9—6F 15
Wood End. SK7—3F 143
Woodend Ct. SK14—6B 106
Woodend La. OL12—3B 8
Woodend La. SK14—6A 106
Wood End La. SK15—6H 93
Woodend Rd. M22—1B 140

Woodend Rd. SK3—1H 143
Woodend St. OL1—6C 48
Woodend St. OL4—4B 66
Woodend View. OL5—1F 81
Woodfield. M22—2B 140
Woodfield Av. OL12—1G 19
Woodfield Av. SK6—5G 121
Woodfield Av. SK14—1B 122
Woodfield Clo. OL8—5A 64
Woodfield Clo. SK14—3H 109
Woodfield Ct. SK2—1A 144
Woodfield Cres. SK6—1F 133
Woodfield Dri. M28—5D 68
Woodfield Gro. BL4—3E 55
Woodfield Gro. M33—3A 114
Woodfield M. SK14—1B 122
Woodfield Rd. M6—1D 84
Woodfield Rd. M8—2C 74
Woodfield Rd. M23—3G 61
Woodfield Rd. SK8—6D 142
Woodfield Rd. WA14—5E 125
Woodfields Ter. BL9—2D 28
Woodfield St. BL3—4C 38
Woodfield Ter. OL10—2G 31
Wood Fold. BL7—5G 11
Woodfold Av. M19—5C 102
Woodford Av. M30—2D 82
Woodford Av. M34—3G 105
Woodford Av. OL2—6H 35
Woodford Dri. M27—1E 71
Woodford Gdns. M20—1E 129
Woodford Gro. BL3—3G 37
Woodford Rd. M35—3G 77
Woodford Rd. SK7—2G 153
Woodford Rd. SK14—3A 154
Wood Gdns. SK9—4H 159
Woodgarth Av. M10—5D 76
Woodgarth Dri. M27—5E 71
Woodgarth La. M28—6H 69
Woodgate Av. BL9—1H 29
Woodgate Av. OL11—5C 18
Woodgate Clo. SK6—6F 121
Woodgate Dri. M25—5G 59
Woodgate Hill Rd. BL9—2G 29
(Bury)
Woodgate Hill Rd. BL9—1H 29
(Woodgate Hill)
Woodgate Rd. M16—6C 100
Woodgate St. BL3—4C 38
Woodgrange Clo. M6—3E 85
Woodgreen Dri. M26—1G 57
Wood Gro. M25—4C 42
Wood Gro. M34—3F 105
Wood Gro. SK6—4G 121
Woodhall Av. M20—2E 117
Woodhall Av. M25—3B 58
Woodhall Clo. BL2—2E 25
Woodhall Clo. BL8—6D 14
Woodhall Clo. SK7—4G 153
Woodhall Cres. SK5—5A 120
Woodhall Rd. SK5—5H 119
Woodhall St. M35—3F 77
Woodhalt Rd. M8—5C 74
Woodham Rd. M23—2F 127
Woodham Wlk. BL3—2H 37
Woodhead Clo. BL0—5E 5
Woodhead Clo. M16—3C 100
Woodhead Dri. WA15—4H 137
Woodhead Rd. WA15—4H 137
Wood Hey Clo. M26—4D 40
Wood Hey Gro. M34—5G 105
Wood Hey Gro. OL12—5E 7
Woodhey Rd. BL0—6C 4
Woodheys. SK4—6B 118
Woodheys Dri. M33—2F 125
Woodheys Rd. OL15—1G 21
Woodheys St. M6—4F 85
Wood Hill. M24—5H 45
Wood Hill Rd. M12—3D 102
Woodhill Clo. M24—5H 45
Woodhill Dri. M25—1F 73
Woodhill Fold. BL8—2B 28
Woodhill Gro. M25—6F 59
Woodhill Ho. M6—2F 85
Woodhill Rd. BL8—2B 28
Woodhill St. BL8—1B 28
Woodhouse Ct. M31—3C 96
Woodhouse Farm Cotts. OL12—1H 17

Woodhouse Knowle. OL3—3G 51
Woodhouse La. M22—1B 140
Woodhouse La. M33—1D 124
(in three parts)
Woodhouse La. OL12—1H 17
Woodhouse La. WA14—1A 136
Woodhouse La. WA15—2A 126
Woodhouse La. N. M22—5B 140
Woodhouse La. S. M22—6B 140
Woodhouse Rd. M22—5B 140
Woodhouse Rd. M33—3B 96
Woodhouse St. M10—6H 75
Woodhouse St. M18—2G 103
Woodhouse St. OL8—4D 64
Wooding Clo. M31—5E 111
Woodlake Av. M21—5A 116
Woodland Av. BL3—5D 38
Woodland Av. M18—3G 103
Woodland Cres. M25—1F 73
Woodland Grn. BL7—1B 10
Woodland Pk. OL2—1H 47
Woodland Rd. M18—3G 103
Woodland Rd. M19—1C 118
Woodland Rd. OL10—2G 31
Woodland Rd. OL12—1E 19
Woodlands. M31—4E 97
Woodlands. M35—1G 89
Woodlands. OL16—6A 8
Woodlands Av. M25—6C 42
Woodlands Av. M27—5C 70
Woodlands Av. M30—5C 82
(Eccles)
Woodlands Av. M30—4E 95
(Irlam)
Woodlands Av. M32—5D 98
Woodlands Av. OL11—5C 18
Woodlands Av. SK6—4G 121
Woodlands Av. SK7—4D 144
Woodlands Av. SK8—3C 142
Woodlands Clo. M28—4G 69
Woodlands Clo. SK14—6B 108
(Broadbottom)
Woodlands Clo. SK14—1H 109
(Tintwistle)
Woodlands Clo. SK15—6H 93
Woodlands Ct. WA15—6H 125
Woodlands Dri. M33—2C 126
Woodlands Dri. SK2—3C 132
Woodlands Dri. SK6—4G 121
Woodlands Gro. BL8—2H 27
Woodlands Gro. SK14—6B 108
Woodlands La. WA15—6G 125
Woodlands Pk. Rd. SK2—3D 132
Woodlands Parkway. WA15—6G 125
Woodlands Rd. BL0—3A 4
Woodlands Rd. M8—3C 74
Woodlands Rd. M16—6C 100
Woodlands Rd. M28—4G 69
Woodlands Rd. M33—4C 114
Woodlands Rd. OL16—6E 21
Woodlands Rd. SK4—1H 129
Woodlands Rd. SK9—4A 152
(Handforth)
Woodlands Rd. SK9—6D 150
(Wilmslow)
Woodlands Rd. SK12—1E 157
Woodlands Rd. SK15—6G 93
Woodlands Rd. WA14 & WA15
—6F 125
Woodlands St. M8—3C 74
Woodlands, The. BL6—5A 22
Woodlands, The. BL8—6D 14
Woodlands, The. M35—2G 89
Woodland St. M7—6A 74
Woodland St. M12—2D 102
Woodland St. OL10—3F 31
Woodland St. OL12—1A 20
Woodland Ter. M31—6C 110
Woodland View. BL7—3F 11
Woodland Way. M24—3H 61
Wood La. M24—2B 62
Wood La. M31—6B 110
Wood La. OL6—6F 79
Wood La. SK6—6B 134
Wood La. WA15—4A 126
Wood La. WA16—6A 148
Woodlawn Ct. M16—4A 100

Woodlea. M28—3G 69
Woodlea. M30—1E 83
Woodlea. OL9—2D 62
Woodlea Av. M19—3A 118
Woodleigh. WA14—6C 124
Woodleigh Ct. SK9—4G 159
Woodleigh Dri. M35—1C 90
Woodleigh St. M9—2H 75
Woodley Av. M26—6H 41
Woodley Clo. SK2—4D 132
Woodley Precinct. SK6—4G 121
Woodley St. BL9—5D 28
Woodliffe St. M16—2A 100
Woodlinn Wlk. M9—4F 75
Woodman Dri. BL9—5E 15
Woodman St. SK1—1G 131
Woodmeadow Ct. OL5—1E 81
Woodmere Dri. M9—6G 61
Wood Mt. WA15—6B 126
Woodmount Clo. SK6—1C 134
Wood Newton Clo. M18—3E 103
Woodpark Clo. OL8—6E 65
Woodridings. WA14—2D 136
Wood Rd. M16—4A 100
Wood Rd. WA15 & M33—2B 126
  (in two parts)
Wood Rd. La. BL8 & BL9—3B 14
Wood Rd. N. M16—4A 100
Woodrow Wlk. M12—1B 102
Woodrow Way. M30—2D 110
Woodroyd Clo. SK7—4F 143
Woodroyd Dri. BL9—2G 29
Woodruffe Gdns. SK6—3G 133
Woodruff Wlk. M31—6D 110
Woodsend Circ. M31—4H 95
  (in two parts)
Woodsend Cres. M31—5H 95
Woodsend Grn. M31—4H 95
Woodsend Rd. M31—3H 95
Woodsend Rd. S. M31—5A 96
  (in two parts)
Woods Gro. SK8—6D 142
Woodshaw Gro. M28—3E 69
Woodside. OL2—5H 35
Woodside. SK4—2B 130
Woodside Av. M19—4B 118
Woodside Av. M28—1H 69
Woodside Dri. BL0—4C 4
Woodside Dri. M6—2C 84
Woodside Dri. SK6—6C 146
Woodside Dri. SK14—6C 106
Woodside Gdns. M31—5D 110
Woodside Pl. BL2—2E 39
Woodside Rd. M16—5H 99
Woodside St. SK15—5G 81
Woods La. OL3—6A 52
Woods La. SK8—6D 142
Woods Lea. BL1—6D 22
Woodsley Rd. BL1—3D 22
Woods Moor La. SK3 & SK2—2H 143
Woodsmoor Rd. M27—4D 70
Woods Pas. OL15—4D 8
Wood Sq. M35—5A 90
Wood Sq. OL3—3F 53
Woods Rd. M30—1D 110
Woods, The. OL4—3D 66
Woods, The. OL11—2C 32
Woods, The. WA14—5G 125
Woodstock Av. SK5—4H 119
Woodstock Av. SK8—6C 142
Woodstock Clo. OL10—3G 31
Woodstock Cres. SK6—4G 121
Woodstock Dri. BL1—4E 23
Woodstock Dri. BL8—4F 13
Woodstock Dri. M27—5G 71
Woodstock Dri. M28—6A 70
Woodstock Grn. SK5—3A 120
Woodstock Rd. M10—2C 76
Woodstock Rd. M16—4H 99
Woodstock Rd. SK6—4G 121
Woodstock Rd. WA14—3E 125
Woodstock St. OL4—4D 64
Woodstock St. OL12—2E 19
Wood St. BL0—4D 4
Wood St. BL1—6B 24
Wood St. BL4—5F 39
Wood St. BL8—2A 28

Wood St. M3—4C 86 & 5F 161
  (Manchester)
Wood St. M3—3C 86 & 4F 161
  (Salford)
Wood St. M11—5D 88
Wood St. M24—5F 45
Wood St. M26—1E 57
Wood St. M30—4H 83
Wood St. M34—3F 105
Wood St. OL1—1F 65
Wood St. OL2—5C 34
Wood St. OL6—3H 91
Wood St. OL10—3F 31
Wood St. OL15—4F 9
Wood St. OL16—1G 35
  (Newhey)
Wood St. OL16—4A 20
  (Rochdale)
Wood St. SK3—3F 131
Wood St. SK8—5H 129
Wood St. SK14—2F 109
  (Hollingworth)
Wood St. SK14—5C 106
  (Hyde)
Wood St. SK15—3E 93
Wood St. SK16—1A 106
Wood St. WA14—1F 137
Wood Ter. BL2—4D 26
Woodthorpe Dri. SK8—2C 142
Wood Top Av. OL11—6B 18
Woodvale. M24—3A 46
Woodvale Av. BL3—5H 37
Woodvale Dri. BL3—5H 37
Woodvale Gdns. BL3—5H 37
Woodvale Gro. BL3—5H 37
Woodvale Wlk. M11—4B 88
  (off Limetree Wlk.)
Wood View. M22—2B 128
Wood View. OL10—1E 31
Woodview Av. M19—4B 118
Woodville Dri. M33—4A 114
Woodville Dri. SK6—6B 134
Woodville Dri. SK15—2H 93
Woodville Gro. SK5—3H 119
Woodville Rd. M33—4A 114
Woodville Rd. WA14—1E 137
Woodville Ter. M10—2H 75
Woodward Clo. BL9—6F 15
Woodward Ct. M4—3H 87 & 3G 163
Woodward Pl. M4—3C 87 & 4F 163
Woodward Rd. M25—1D 72
Woodward St. M4—3G 87 & 4F 163
Woodwise La. M23—2E 127
Wood Yd. OL16—4B 34
Woolden Rd. M30—1A 110
Woolden St. M27—1E 71
Woolden St. M30—2D 82
Wooley Clo. SK14—3F 109
Wooley Ter. SK16—4H 91
Woolfall Clo. M12—1B 102
Woollacot St. OL1—2D 64
Woollam Pl. M3—5B 86 & 1D 164
Woolley Av. SK12—5D 154
Woolley Bri. Rd. SK14—3G 109
Woolley La. SK14—1F 109
  (Hollingworth)
Woolley La. SK14—3E 109
  (Woolley Bridge)
Woolley Mill La. SK14—1G 109
Woolley St. M8—1D 86
Woolley St. OL6—5A 80
Woolpack Grn. M6—1F 85
Wool Rd. OL3—6B 52
Woolston Ho. M6—1C 84
Woolton Clo. M10—1C 76
Wootton St. SK14—3B 106
  (in two parts)
Worcester Av. M34—6G 105
Worcester Av. SK5—4C 120
Worcester Clo. M6—1C 84
Worcester Clo. OL6—3H 79
Worcester Clo. SK6—2G 133
Worcester Rd. BL3—4H 39
Worcester Rd. M6—1C 84
Worcester Rd. M24—3H 61
Worcester Rd. M27—1D 70
Worcester Rd. M33—6F 113
Worcester Rd. SK8—1C 142
Worcester St. BL1—4A 24

Worcester St. BL8—1B 28
Worcester St. OL9—4H 63
Worcester St. OL11—6G 19
Wordsworth Av. BL4—2D 54
Wordsworth Av. M8—5C 74
Wordsworth Av. M26—3E 41
Wordsworth Av. M35—3A 90
Wordsworth Clo. SK16—6E 93
Wordsworth Cres. OL7—6C 78
Wordsworth Cres. OL15—1F 21
Wordsworth Gdns. M25—6D 58
Wordsworth Rd. M16—4H 99
Wordsworth Rd. M24—5B 46
Wordsworth Rd. M27—2D 70
Wordsworth Rd. M28—4D 54
Wordsworth Rd. M34—2G 121
Wordsworth Rd. OL1—6F 49
Wordsworth Rd. SK5—6F 103
Wordsworth St. BL1—4H 23
Wordsworth St. M6—1A 86
Wordsworth Way. OL11—5A 18
Workesleigh St. M10—6C 76
Worrall St. M5—6A 86 & 3A 164
Worrall St. M10—5A 76
Worrall St. SK3—4G 131
Worral St. OL12—1F 19
Worrell Clo. M26—3F 41
Worsefold St. M10—3A 76
Worsel St. BL3—3G 37
Worsley Av. M10—2H 75
Worsley Av. M28—6C 54
Worsley Brow. M28—5H 69
Worsley Cres. SK2—4B 132
Worsley Gro. M19—6C 102
Worsley Gro. M28—1C 68
Worsley Pl. OL2—1E 49
Worsley Pl. OL16—4B 20
Worsley Rd. BL3—3E 37
Worsley Rd. BL4—3F 55
Worsley Rd. M28 & M27—6H 69
Worsley Rd. M30—1C 82
Worsley Rd. N. M28—4F 55
Worsley St. BL8—4G 13
Worsley St. M3—5C 86 & 2F 165
  (Manchester)
Worsley St. M3—3C 86 & 4F 161
  (Salford)
Worsley St. M15—6B 86 & 3D 164
Worsley St. M27—4G 71
  (Pendlebury)
Worsley St. M27—1F 71
  (Swinton)
Worsley St. OL8—4F 65
Worsley St. OL16—4B 20
Worston Av. BL1—2D 22
Worthenbury Wlk. M13—4A 102
Worthing Clo. SK2—5D 132
Worthing St. M14—5F 101
Worthington Av. M31—6D 110
Worthington Av. OL10—6G 31
Worthington Clo. OL7—6E 79
Worthington Clo. SK14—5A 108
Worthington Ct. M33—5E 115
Worthington Dri. M7—2H 73
Worthington Rd. M33—5E 115
Worthington Rd. M34—5H 105
Worthington St. BL3—4G 37
Worthington St. M16—3A 100
Worthington St. OL7—6E 79
Worthington St. OL8—3B 64
Worthington St. SK15—4D 92
Worth's La. M34—2G 121
Wortley Av. M6—2C 84
Wortley Gro. M10—1B 76
Wragby Clo. BL8—6D 14
Wray Pl. OL16—5C 20
Wraysbury Wlk. M10—4A 76
  (off Hugo St.)
Wrayton Lodge. M33—1B 126
Wrekin Av. M23—2G 139
Wren Av. M27—6H 57
Wrenbury Av. M20—2D 116
Wrenbury Cres. SK3—5E 131
Wrenbury Dri. BL1—5D 10
Wrenbury Dri. SK8—5A 130
Wrenbury Wlk. M33—6E 115
Wren Clo. BL4—1B 54
Wren Clo. M34—4C 90

Wren Clo. SK2—6F 133
Wren Dri. BL9—1F 29
Wren Grn. OL16—5B 20
Wrens Nest Av. OL2—5G 35
Wren St. OL4—6G 65
Wren St. OL9—1H 63
Wrexham Clo. OL8—1H 77
Wrigglesworth Clo. BL8—2F 27
Wright Robinson Clo. M11—5A 88
Wrights Bank N. SK2—6D 132
Wrights Bank S. SK2—6E 133
Wright St. M16—1A 100 & 6A 164
Wright St. M26—4F 41
Wright St. M34—5E 91
Wright St. M35—3F 77
Wright St. OL6—1B 92
Wright St. OL9—4H 63
Wright St. WA14—4E 125
Wright Tree Vs. M30—4B 110
Wrigley Cres. M35—4F 77
Wrigley Head. M35—3F 77
Wrigley Head Cres. M35—3F 77
Wrigley Pl. OL15—6D 8
Wrigley's Pl. OL8—6C 64
Wrigley Sq. OL4—3B 66
Wrigley's Sq. OL12—3H 19
  (Lees)
Wrigley St. OL4—2F 65
  (Oldham)
Wrigley St. OL4—1D 66
  (Scouthead)
Wrigley St. OL6—1H 91
Wrigley St. OL16—5B 92
Wroe St. M3—4B 86 & 5C 160
Wroe St. M27—6F 57
Wroe St. OL4—3B 66
Wrotham Clo. M5—4G 85
Wroxeter Wlk. M12—1B 102
  (off Wenlock Way)
Wroxham Av. M34—4D 96
Wroxham Av. M34—4A 104
Wroxham Clo. BL8—6D 14
Wroxham Rd. M9—6D 60
Wuerdle Clo. OL16—5C 8
Wuerdle Pl. OL16—5C 8
Wuerdle St. OL16—5C 8
Wyatt Av. M5—6H 85 & 3A 164
Wyatt St. SK4—1F 131
Wyatt St. SK16—5A 92
Wybersley Rd. SK6—5E 147
Wychbury St. M5—3E 85
Wychelm Rd. M31—6D 110
Wycherley Rd. OL12—1D 18
Wych Fold. SK14—2C 122
  (in two parts)
Wych Clo. SK6—3H 91
Wychwood. WA14—4D 136
Wychwood Clo. M24—2B 62
Wycliffe Av. SK9—2D 158
Wycliffe Ct. M31—5E 97
Wycliffe Rd. M31—5E 97
Wycliffe St. M30—3E 83
Wycliffe St. SK4—1F 131
Wycliffe Wlk. M12—1A 102
Wycombe Av. M18—1G 103
Wycombe Clo. M31—2E 97
Wye Av. M35—4F 77
Wyecroft Clo. SK6—4H 121
Wye St. OL8—4B 64
Wykeham Gro. OL12—2D 18
Wykeham M. BL1—5E 23
Wykeham St. M14—4E 101
Wyke Pk. OL4—3H 65
Wylam Wlk. M12—4D 102
Wylde, The. BL9—3C 28
Wynchgate Rd. SK7—2G 145
Wyndale Dri. M35—6F 77
Wyndale Rd. OL8—6D 64
Wyndcliff Dri. M31—6A 96
Wyndham Av. BL3—5E 37
Wyndham Av. M27—6F 57
Wyndham Clo. SK7—6H 143
Wyndham St. BL9—4D 28
Wyne Clo. SK7—2G 145
Wynfield Av. M22—6D 140
Wynford Sq. M5—4F 85
Wyngate Rd. SK8—4B 142

Wyngate Rd. WA15—5H 137
Wynne Av. M27—6F 57
Wynne Clo. M11—5B 88
Wynne Clo. M34—6F 105
Wynne Gro. M34—6E 105
Wynne St. BL1—3A 24
Wynne St. M6—1H 85
Wynne St. M28—5C 54
Wynnstay Gro. M14—1G 117
Wynnstay Rd. M33—4B 114
Wynn St. M10—2E 77
Wynt, The. M31—5D 110
Wynyard Clo. M33—1D 126
Wynyard Rd. M22—2A 140
Wyre Clo. M25—6F 43
Wyre Dri. M28—4D 68
Wyresdale Rd. BL1—5G 23
Wyresdale Wlk. M15—1C 100
(off Ipstone Clo.)
Wyre St. M1—5F 87 & 2D 166
Wyre St. OL5—2D 80
Wythall Av. M28—3D 54
Wythburn Av. BL1—4E 23
Wythburn Av. M8—5E 75
Wythburn Av. M31—4D 96
Wythburn Rd. M24—4G 45
Wythburn Rd. SK1—4B 132
Wythburn St. M5—3E 85
Wythenshawe Rd. M23—3E 127
Wythenshawe Rd. M33—5E 115
Wythens Rd. SK8—5F 141
Wythop Gdns. M5—4G 85
Wyvern Av. SK5—4G 119
Wyverne Rd. M21—6B 100
Wyville Av. M27—5E 71
Wyville Clo. SK7—2G 145
Wyville Dri. M6—2F 85
Wyville Dri. M9—3D 60

Yarburgh St. M16—4C 100
Yardley. OL11—1E 33
Yardley Av. M32—5A 98
Yardley Clo. M32—5A 98
Yarmouth Dri. M23—2H 127
Yarnton Clo. OL2—2E 49
Yarn Wlk. M4—4G 87
(off Kirby Wlk.)
Yarrow Clo. OL11—6H 19
Yarrow Pl. BL1—4H 23
Yarrow Wlk. M25—6G 43

Yarwell. OL12—3G 19
(off Spotland Rd.)
Yarwood Av. M23—4F 127
Yarwood Clo. OL10—2G 31
Yarwoodheath La. WA14—5A 136
Yarwood St. BL9—3E 29
Yarwood St. WA14—2F 137
Yates St. BL2—4C 24
Yates St. M24—2E 61
Yates St. OL1—1E 65
Yates St. SK1—6B 120
Yates Ter. BL8—6E 15
Yattendon Av. M23—3D 126
Yeadon Rd. M18—4F 103
Yealand Av. SK4—6F 119
Yealand Clo. OL11—5D 18
Yeardsley Clo. SK7—2G 143
Yelverton Wlk. M13—1G 101
(off Lowndes Wlk.)
Yeoford Dri. WA14—5D 124
Yeoman Clo. SK7—2D 144
Yeoman's Clo. OL16—4F 21
Yeoman Wlk. M11—4B 88
Yeovil Wlk. M16—4D 100
Yewbarrow Rd. OL1—1E 65
Yew Clo. BL3—3F 37
Yew Ct. OL12—1B 20
Yew Cres. OL4—1H 65
Yewdale. M27—1H 71
Yewdale Av. BL2—3H 25
Yewdale Dri. M24—6G 45
Yewdale Gdns. BL2—3H 25
Yewdale Gdns. OL11—1B 32
Yewdale Rd. SK1—4B 132
Yewlands Av. M9—4F 61
Yew St. BL9—2G 29
Yew St. M7—5G 73
Yew St. M34—1F 105
Yew St. OL10—3D 30
Yew St. SK4—2E 131
Yew Tree Av. M14—5E 101
Yew Tree Av. M19—6C 102
Yew Tree Av. M22—2B 128
Yew Tree Av. SK7—4F 145
Yew Tree Clo. OL7—5E 79
Yew Tree Clo. SK6—6C 134
Yew Tree Cotts. OL3—1C 52
Yew Tree Cres. M14—6F 101
Yew Tree Dri. BL6—6A 22
Yew Tree Dri. M22—2B 128
Yew Tree Dri. M25—5F 59

Yew Tree Dri. M31—3B 96
Yew Tree Dri. M33—5E 115
Yew Tree Dri. OL9—2D 62
Yew Tree Dri. SK6—6D 120
Yewtree Gro. SK8—2E 141
Yew Tree La. BL1—6E 11
Yew Tree La. M23 & M22—1H 127
Yewtree La. SK12—5E 155
Yewtree La. SK16—6C 92
Yewtree La. WA15—6F 139
Yew Tree Pk. Rd. SK8—1D 152
Yew Tree Rd. M14—4F 101
Yew Tree Rd. M34—6E 105
Yew Tree Rd. SK3—2H 143
Yew Tree Rd. SK10—6H 155
Yew Wlk. M31—6C 110
York Arc. M1—4E 87
(off Piccadilly Plaza)
York Av. BL3—4A 40
York Av. M16—5A 100
York Av. M25—1H 73
York Av. M27—1D 70
York Av. M31—4G 97
York Av. M33—4B 114
York Av. OL8—5B 64
York Av. OL11—5C 18
York Clo. M34—3F 105
York Clo. SK8—6C 130
York Cres. SK9—1F 159
Yorkdale Rd. OL4—2H 65
York Dri. BL0—5C 4
York Dri. SK7—3F 145
York Dri. WA14—4F 137
York Dri. WA15—6F 139
York Ho. M33—4B 114
York Pl. OL6—3G 91
York Rd. M21—1H 115
York Rd. M30—4B 110
York Rd. M33—4A 114
York Rd. M34—3E 105
York Rd. M35—2H 89
York Rd. OL9—1F 63
York Rd. SK4—4D 118
York Rd. SK14—1C 122
York Rd. WA14—4E 137
York Rd. E. M24—4C 62
York Rd. W. M24—4C 62
Yorkshire St. M3—3C 86 & 4F 161
Yorkshire St. OL1—2D 64
Yorkshire St. OL6—1H 91
  (in two parts)

Yorkshire St. OL16 & OL12—4H 19
  (in three parts)
York Sq. OL2—3B 48
York St. BL4—1G 55
York St. BL9—3E 29
York St. M1—5E 87 & 2A 166
  (in two parts)
York St. M2 & M1—4E 87 & 5A 162
York St. M9—3G 75
  (in two parts)
York St. M15—6C 86 & 4E 165
York St. M19—1C 118
York St. M20—6F 117
York St. M25—1D 58
York St. M26—2B 42
York St. M34—5E 91
York St. M35—3G 77
York St. OL9—3C 64
York St. OL10—3F 31
York St. OL16—5B 20
York St. SK3—3G 131
York St. WA15—2F 137
York Ter. BL1—3A 24
York Ter. M33—3A 114
Youlgreave Cres. SK13—6F 109
Young St. BL0—3D 4
Young St. BL4—2G 55
Young St. M3—4C 86 & 6E 161
Young St. M26—2F 41
Yulan Dri. M33—5E 113
Yule St. SK3—3F 131

Zama St. BL0—5C 4
Zealand St. OL4—6G 49
Zebra St. M8—4B 74
Zedburgh. OL12—3G 19
(off Spotland Rd.)
Zennor. OL11—1E 33
Zeta St. M9—4H 75
Zetland Av. BL3—5F 37
Zetland Av. N. BL3—5F 37
Zetland Pl. OL16—3B 20
Zetland Rd. M21—1H 115
Zetland St. SK16—4A 92
Zinnia Dri. M30—1C 110
Zion Cres. M15—1C 100 & 6F 165
Zion Ter. OL12—2A 18
Zurich Gdns. SK7—2G 143
Zyburn Ct. M6—2A 84

Every possible care has been taken to ensure that the information given in this publication
is accurate and whilst the publishers would be grateful to learn of any errors, they regret
they cannot accept any responsibility for loss thereby caused.

The representation on the maps of a road, track or footpath is no evidence of the existence
of a right of way.

The grid on these maps is the National Grid taken from the Ordnance Survey Maps with the
permission of the Controller of Her Majesty's Stationery Office.

Copyright of Geographers' A-Z Map Co. Ltd.

No reproduction by any method whatsoever of any part of this publication
is permitted without the prior consent of the copyright owners.